W9-BQC-254

JOHN LE CARRÉ

BY THE SAME AUTHOR

A. J. P. Taylor: A Biography
Boswell's Presumptuous Task
The Friendship: Wordsworth and Coleridge
Hugh Trevor-Roper: The Biography
One Hundred Letters from Hugh Trevor-Roper
(with Richard Davenport-Hines)

JOHN LE CARRÉ

The Biography

Adam Sisman

HARPER
An Imprint of HarperCollins*Publishers*

JOHN LE CARRÉ. Copyright © 2015 by Adam Sisman. All rights reserved. Printed in the United States of America. No part of this book may be used or reproduced in any manner whatsoever without written permission except in the case of brief quotations embodied in critical articles and reviews. For information, address HarperCollins Publishers, 195 Broadway, New York, NY 10007.

HarperCollins books may be purchased for educational, business, or sales promotional use. For information, please e-mail the Special Markets Department at SPsales@harpercollins.com.

First published in the United Kingdom in 2015 by Bloomsbury.

FIRST U.S. EDITION

Original personal archives, photographs, documents, letters and other materials © David Cornwell 2015

Photographs are from private sources except where credited otherwise.

The acknowledgements on p. xi constitute an extension of this copyright page.

Library of Congress Cataloging-in-Publication Data has been applied for.

ISBN: 978-0-06-210627-8

15 16 17 18 19 OFF/RRD 10 9 8 7 6 5 4 3 2 1

For PD

Writers aren't people exactly. Or, if they're any good, they're a whole lot of people trying so hard to be one person.

F. Scott Fitzgerald, *The Love of the Last Tycoon*

Contents

Acknowledgements

In working on a long book like this one a writer relies on the help of many people.

My first debt is to my subject, David Cornwell. I express my gratitude to him in my Introduction, but it is right that I should record it here too. I also want to give special thanks to Jane Cornwell, who has made me welcome, and generously helped me in innumerable ways throughout a long and sometimes difficult process.

I am especially grateful to those who kindly read the whole book in typescript and gave me valuable comments and suggestions: Bob Gottlieb, Bruce Hunter, Toby Manning, Roland Philipps, Nicholas Shakespeare and Henry Woudhuysen. I must state, however, that I have not taken every piece of advice which I have been given, and that responsibility for any mistakes is mine alone.

I am also grateful to those who read portions of the text and offered me their comments and suggestions: Richard Barrett, Robin and Charlotte Cooke, Charlotte Cornwell, David Greenway, Robert Harris, Tim Hely Hutchinson, Derek Johns, Sir John and Lady Margetson, Sir Tom Stoppard, Michael Truscott, Susan Vereker (Susie Kennaway) and Michela Wrong.

Apart from those already mentioned, I wish to thank those who gave up their time to talk to me, and in several cases allowed me to see letters and other documents in their possession: Rupert Allason, Erica von Almen, Al and Anne Alvarez, Neal Ascherson, Michael Attenborough,

Anthony Barnett, Elizabeth Bennett, Buzz and Janet Berger, Charlotte Bingham, François Bizot, Margaret Body, Tom Bower, The Reverend Tim Bravington, Susan Brigden, Siv Bublitz, Richard and Anne Bull, Lady Bullard, Susie Burgin, David Burnett, John Burgess, Sir Bryan Cartledge, Willy Cave, Alexander Chancellor, Jane Clark, Jean Cornwell, Rupert Cornwell, Simon Cornwell, Stephen and Clarissa Cornwell, Tim and Alice Cornwell (Alice Greenway), Tony and Nettie Cornwell, Prue Downing, Sarah Edmonds, Erhard Eppler, Margaret Foster-Moore, Timothy Garton Ash, the late Newton Garver, Ronnie Geary, Jonny Geller, John J. Geoghegan, Sir William Gladstone, John Goldsmith, Jo Goldsworthy, Livia Gollancz, Nan Graham, Richard Greene, Miriam Gross, Valerie Grove, Nick Harkaway (Nicholas Cornwell) and Clare Algar, Graham Hayman, Bryan Haynes, Henry Hemming, Andreas Heumann, the late Denys Hodson, Michael Horniman, Carla Hornstein, Sabine Ibach, John Irvin, Sir Jeremy Isaacs, John E. Jackson, Michael Jago, Alan Judd, Phillip Knightley, Haug von Kuenheim, Zachary Leader, Richard Leggett, Joe Lelyveld, Andrew Lownie, Mikhail Lyubimov, Robert McCrum, David Machin, the late Angela (Winkie) McPherson, Bryan Magee, Loring Mandel, Geoffrey Marsland, Roger Martin, the late Stanley Mitchell, Ferdinand Mount, Holly Nowell, Michael Overton-Fox, Gerald Peacocke, Hayden Peake, Hugh Peppiatt, Ed Perkins, Martin Pick, Jonathan Powell, Anna Rankin, Brian Rees, Roland Reinäcker, Tristram Riley-Smith, the late Christopher Robbins, John C. Q. Roberts, the late Hilary Rubinstein, Edward Russell, William Scolar, Sir Kenneth Scott, Jean Seaton, Michael Selby, John Shakespeare, William Shawcross, Xan Smiley, Godfrey Smith, Strobe Talbott, Hugh Thomas (Lord Thomas), the late Ion Trewin, Glenda Voakes, Petronilla Weschke (Petronilla Silver), Francis Wheen and Alex Williams. I apologise to anybody whose name I may have inadvertently omitted.

I particularly want to thank Buzz and Janet Berger, Sir John and Lady Margetson (Miranda Margetson) and Stanley and Susan Vereker for their hospitality. I also wish to thank the staff at Tregiffian for their help and kindness, particularly Vicki Philipps, Brenda Bolitho and Wendy Le Grice.

I wish to extend special thanks to Gina Thomas for her help in finding me German reviews of John le Carré's books.

I have been helped by various professional archivists and those in charge of archives, and I wish to thank them all: Katie Heaton, Local History Librarian at the Poole Museum; the staff of the National Archives, Kew; David Livingstone, Headmaster of St Andrew's School; Rachel Hassall, Archivist at Sherborne School; Andrew Mussell, former Archivist at Lincoln College, Oxford, and his successor, Lindsay McCormack; Roger Parsons, Archivist at Edgarley; Michael Meredith, Archivist at Eton College; Caradoc King, for access to the A. P. Watt archives; Malcolm Edwards, for access to the Gollancz archives; Jean Rose, for access to the Heinemann papers in the Random House archives; Sally Harrower, for access to the Kennaway papers in the National Library of Scotland; the staff of the Bodleian Library, for access to the le Carré archive, particularly Richard Ovenden and Oliver House; Jeff Cowton of the BBC Written Archives at Caversham; Jonny Davies of the British Film Institute Archive; Ian Johnston of the University of Salford Library, for access to the Arthur Hopcraft archive; the staff of the Harry Ransom Humanities Research Center, particularly Natalie Zelt, in the University of Texas at Austin; and the staff of the British Library, especially Arnold Hunt.

I am grateful to Stephen Fry, and to the estate of the late Sir Alec Guinness, for permission to publish extracts from letters to David Cornwell. I am also grateful to all those who supplied photographs for the book.

I am indebted to the excellent staff at Bloomsbury, particularly my publisher Michael Fishwick and Anna Simpson, senior editor.

Peter James has not worked on any of my books before this one. I had assumed that his very high reputation as a copy editor must be exaggerated; now I am embarrassed to find that it is not. I am very grateful to him, for correcting many slips, for pointing out infelicities, and overall for doing such a splendid job of editing. My book is much better for his attention. I am also grateful to Catherine Best for her meticulous work on the proofs and to Christopher Phipps for compiling an excellent index.

I wish to thank my agent Andrew Wylie, for his wise counsel, and for always being there when I needed him.

Lastly I must thank Penelope Dening, who has helped me in more ways than I can adequately describe. I am hugely grateful, and this book is for her.

Introduction

'People who have had very unhappy childhoods', John le Carré once wrote, 'are pretty good at inventing themselves.' He is exceptionally good at this himself. As a boy he learned to invent, making up stories to entertain, to fantasise, escaping from reality, and to dissemble, adopting one persona to conceal another. As a man he put these skills to professional use, first as a spy, and then as a writer. 'I'm a liar,' he explains. 'Born to lying, bred to it, trained to it by an industry that lies for a living, practised in it as a novelist.'

Who is John le Carré? Readers are always curious about the lives of writers whom they admire, but this is particularly so of le Carré's readers. For more than half a century he has been a bestselling novelist. From the start of his success, there has been speculation about the extent to which he has drawn on his own experiences in his books. And le Carré has encouraged this speculation, by drip-feeding stories about his past over the years.

Of course, 'John le Carré' does not exist. The name is a mask, for somebody called David Cornwell. To use an espionage expression, it is a cover name. And even though his cover was blown long ago, it has helped him to keep the public at a distance. It is one of several means he has used to conceal his tracks and confuse those on his trail. His decision to adopt a pseudonym, given that he was doing secret work when he began writing, was understandable; but his choice of the name John le Carré remains mysterious. Over the years he has provided several explanations for it, but has subsequently admitted that none of them is true.

So what sort of person is David Cornwell? It is clear that he is a man of manifold talents, who could have made a good career as an artist or an actor had he not become one of the world's most successful authors. His editor at Knopf, Bob Gottlieb (who in a long and distinguished career in book and magazine publishing has known a few clever people), describes him as the cleverest person he has ever met. In private Cornwell is courteous, sophisticated and amusing. It can be surmised that beneath the surface lie strong and perhaps passionate feelings. But the real man has yet to be investigated. While his books may appear revealing, they are fiction.

Though famous, le Carré remains unknown. He has perfected the art of hiding in full view – or, as Americans say, in plain sight. As his career has progressed, details of his history have accumulated, though these are not always consistent. For years he denied to interviewers that he had ever been a spy, albeit for understandable reasons. In the narrative of his life fact and fiction have become intertwined. One suspects that le Carré enjoys teasing his readers, like a fan dancer, offering tantalising glimpses, but never a clear view of the figure beneath.

To write the life of a writer who is still alive and writing is a sensitive task. Readers have a right to know what they are reading, and readers of a biography of a living person are bound to be curious about the conditions under which it has been written. It seems appropriate therefore to provide a brief history of this book. After finishing my biography of Hugh Trevor-Roper in 2010, I had lunch with Robert Harris, who had been commissioned almost twenty years before to write le Carré's life. He told me that he no longer intended to write a full biography, and encouraged me to undertake the book myself. I wrote to David Cornwell with this suggestion. 'There are huge hindrances,' he replied: 'my own messy private life, the demise of so many people I worked with or otherwise knew, and my habitual reluctance to discuss my very limited & unspectacular career in intelligence.' We subsequently met at his house in Hampstead. By this time he had read my Trevor-Roper and had decided that I was an appropriate person to write his biography. He made it clear that he wished me to write 'without restraints', which indeed was the only basis on which I was willing to proceed. This seemed to me a wise decision, though of course this was easier for me to abide by than it was for him. I estimated that it would take me four years to write, as has proved to be the case. We came to an agreement, by which David (as he quickly became to me) granted me access to his archives, a list of introductions to people he has known (friends and enemies) and long interviews. I was to have a free hand to write what I wanted, provided that I showed 'due respect to the sensitivities of living third parties'. I also agreed that he should have the opportunity to read the typescript before anyone else saw it. This seemed to me the best possible arrangement to produce a biography in the lifetime of the subject.

In the intervening years I have conducted several long interviews with David, amounting to perhaps fifty hours in total – far more time, so he tells me, than he has given to anyone previously. Most of these sessions have lasted all day. The usual pattern has been for me to arrive at his house in Hampstead around 11.00 in the morning, to talk for a couple of hours, and then head off for lunch, usually in his local pub. Afterwards we have gone back to his house, and continued into the early evening, with a fortifying drink in the late afternoon. I have enjoyed his company, and it may be that my account of his life has been influenced by feelings of liking, gratitude and respect – for his wife Jane and other members of his family, as well as for David. Though I acknowledge these warm feelings, I have endeavoured to preserve the splinter of ice in my heart that every writer needs, according to Graham Greene. Readers will have to judge whether the splinter has remained frozen.

While I am aware that it has been a privilege to interview my subject in such depth, I am conscious too of the need to be wary of relying on his testimony. I remember in particular a conversation over lunch, in which David described to me how he came to teach at Eton; I rather baldly informed him that his account did not correspond with the documents I had seen in the archives. I am quite sure that David had not told me this knowing it to be untrue; he was obviously disconcerted that his recall had played him false. All memory is fallible, and should be treated with caution by the biographer.

In the spring of 2011 I made my first visit to Tregiffian, David's house in Cornwall. Jane showed me where David's papers were kept, in a converted garage at right angles to the main house. The weather was gloriously mild, and I kept the door open to enjoy the warm sunshine. At one point a shadow over my shoulder caused me to look up, and there was David in the doorway. 'It's very strange to have you here, poking about in my mind,' he said with a grin.

It would be disingenuous to suggest that there have not been difficulties between us while I have been writing the book over the past four years. 'I think our continuing relationship is an achievement in itself,' David wrote to me in 2014. I can only imagine how hard it has been for him to have a comparative stranger explore every room of his life, from attic to basement, to expose his mistakes and quarrels, and to probe his sore spots. I wish to pay tribute to him for his generosity, his tolerance and his continuing sense of humour. There have been some tense moments during the last four years, but there have also been a lot of laughs. 'I know it's supposed to be warts and all,' he said to me at one point; 'but so far as I can gather it's going to be all warts and no all.'

It was obvious to me from the outset that David has thought deeply about biography. One of my difficulties has been to keep up with him; all too often he has anticipated my question and formulated his reply before it has even occurred to me. I have sometimes felt like a whaler in my skiff, being towed by a leviathan.

On the other hand, David has been reluctant to talk to me in detail about his time serving in the intelligence services. On this subject he has largely maintained the silence which he adopted when it was first revealed that he had done secret work. David refers to the promises he made to his old German contacts, as well as to the Official Secrets Act. 'I am bound, legally and morally, not to reveal the nature of my work in SIS,' he wrote to me recently. My account of this period of his life is therefore derived principally from other sources. Readers may share my frustration that he has not been more open in this regard, when the enemy against which the Cold War was fought has ceased to exist. Even if one respects his loyalty to his former services, one does not have to be excessively cynical to see that it has served his purpose to keep this aspect of his life hidden.

David is known to be an excellent raconteur, and, as is normal, his anecdotes have improved as they have been retold over the years. I have sometimes reflected that my unintended role has been to spoil a fund of good stories. He has of course explored his past in the innumerable interviews he has given since his first success. Reading these, one cannot help noticing how often the answers he gives do not tally. One can see why it has sometimes been necessary for him to obfuscate, but at other times this seems to arise from no more than a cultivated air of mystery. Everything he says, therefore, needs to be examined sceptically. For example, he has talked repeatedly about his refusal to meet 'Kim' Philby when the opportunity arose on a visit to Moscow in 1987. By 2010, when he gave an interview to Olga Craig of the *Telegraph*, this decision had become elevated to one of the highest principle. 'I couldn't possibly have shook his hand,' he told Ms Craig. 'It was drenched in blood. It would have been repulsive.' But the diary of his travelling companion records David as saying at the time that one day he would 'dearly love' to meet Philby – 'purely for zoological purposes, of course!'[1]

This is not necessarily a paradox. Confronted with the opportunity to meet Philby, David recoiled from an encounter that he had been willing to contemplate in principle. Such discrepancies, if they are discrepancies, are not, in my opinion, examples of bad faith, but merely evidence that David, like all of us, edits his past as he revisits it, which he does more than most people. He has reimagined incidents in his past for his fiction, and what he remembers afterwards tends to be the fictional reimagining rather than what actually occurred. In my narrative I have occasionally drawn attention to what seem to me examples of false memory on David's part, and I hope that readers will find these interesting rather than a distraction.

In case there should be any doubt on the matter, I wish to state unequivocally that this book is my responsibility, and mine alone. David has helped me by drawing my attention to inaccuracies or distortions, but I know that there remain passages in it which he dislikes, or even disputes, while recognising the fallibility of human memory, and his own in particular. I can only say that I have tried to tell the truth as it appears to me.

As this book shows, David is still active in his eighty-fourth year – perhaps as active as he has ever been. This book is therefore a work-in-progress. I hope to publish a revised and updated version of this biography in the fullness of time, and I should like to take this opportunity to encourage anybody who feels that he or she may have something to contribute to David's story, especially letters from him, to write to me, care of my publishers.

Even now, after twenty-three novels over a period of more than fifty years, John le Carré's reputation remains curiously ambiguous. He has received very high praise from some: being compared to Graham Greene and Joseph Conrad, and having been described by Blake Morrison as 'the laureate of Britain's post-imperial sleepwalk', and as a keeper of the country's conscience, analysing the national psyche. Writers ranging from William Boyd to Carlos Ruiz Zafón have written admiringly about his work.[2] However, there has always been, in some quarters, a prejudice against him, as a writer of 'mere' spy stories. 'Mr le Carré's talents cry out to be employed in the creation of a real novel,' wrote Anthony Burgess in 1986, reviewing *A Perfect Spy* – the book described by Philip Roth as 'the best English novel since the war'.

The condescending attitude taken by some towards le Carré is explained in part by the idea that 'genre' novels are innately inferior. But that raises the question of whether, as is sometimes said, his writing transcends the genre. 'I think he has easily burst out of being a genre writer and will be remembered as perhaps the most significant novelist of the second half of the 20th century in Britain,' Ian McEwan wrote in 2013. 'Most writers I know think le Carré is no longer a spy writer. He should have won the Booker Prize a long time ago. It's time he won it and it's time he accepted it. He's in the first rank.'[3]

In a *New York Times* series entitled 'Writers on Writing', David Mamet stood this argument on its head, arguing that 'for the past 30 years the greatest novelists writing in English have been genre writers: John le Carré, George Higgins and Patrick O'Brian'.[4]

To me, the argument about whether a genre novelist can ever be 'literary' is a circular one. The very distinction is meaningless. Is Jane Austen a genre novelist? Is *Nineteen Eighty-Four* a genre novel? or *A Tale of Two Cities*? or *Wolf Hall*? or *The Quiet American*? All that one can usefully say is that there are good novelists and bad novelists.

I confess that I stand among le Carré's admirers. I first encountered le Carré as a teenager, and have been reading him ever since. Like all readers of all writers, I like some of his books more than others; but then I have always subscribed to the view that one should judge a writer by his best books, and his best books have given me pleasure even on the fourth or fifth reading. I am among those who believe that he is one of the most important English writers of the post-war period; when future generations look back to the end of Empire, the Cold War and the collapse of

Communism, they will turn to his books to understand how these momentous events appeared to the people living through them. But it is the writing itself which provides the most satisfaction: what William Boyd has described as 'the sheer aesthetic pleasure' of reading le Carré. He is a writer of silky skill, with a finely tuned ear for the nuances of speech, a craftsman capable of evoking a character in a snatch of dialogue.

I suspect that his enormous success has prejudiced some critics against le Carré. If a writer is so popular, he must have lowered himself to the level of the masses. Quite apart from being manifestly untrue, this is no more than snobbery. We should delight in the fact that such a sophisticated and subtle writer has so many readers. A further problem for le Carré is that his books are often tense, exciting and even thrilling – qualities not often present in literary fiction, and ones that perhaps disqualify him from entering the pantheon.

I see an analogy with Alfred Hitchcock, a filmmaker whose artistry was often overlooked in his lifetime because he made the mistake of being popular. The novels of le Carré blend art and entertainment, a mix to be relished by those who have the taste to enjoy it.

Adam Sisman
June 2015

1

Millionaire paupers

It is a Saturday afternoon in the late 1920s, in Parkstone, a suburb of Poole on the Dorset coast, a Free Church stronghold. A team representing the Parkstone Tabernacle has just won a football tournament; the successful players line up beside the pitch for the presentation ceremony. The cup is being presented by a local dignitary, the former chairman of Poole Football Club and Liberal candidate for East Dorset, Alec Ewart Glassey, whose middle name is taken from that of the Grand Old Man himself, Mr Gladstone of blessed memory – and why not, since he came into the world while the GOM was highest in the land? Now in early middle age, Alec Glassey is an imposing figure, six feet four inches tall, his head held upright by a stiff collar, his hair scraped back from his forehead, his massive lower jaw suggesting firmness. Glassey is a prominent person in the Congregational Church, who in time will become chairman of the Congregational Union of England and Wales. As a lay preacher, he is renowned locally for his oratorical skill and his beautiful diction; as a politician, he is known for passionate sincerity.

The Glasseys have been 'chapel' for generations: narrow in their beliefs, strict in their observance, and of course teetotal. Alec Glassey's late father was a respected Congregational minister, who died of pneumonia in his forties after conducting a funeral on a cold night, leaving his widow penniless – but providentially Alec married the daughter of a rich Barnsley coal merchant, so that he no longer needs to earn his living by giving lessons in elocution, as he did in the bad old days after the Reverend Mr Glassey's death. (For her part, the coal merchant's daughter has gained a presentable husband, three years her junior, in the process shedding her maiden name of Longbottom, which has always been a torment to her.) In 1929, Alec Glassey will be elected to parliament, one of fifty-nine Liberal MPs, no fewer than thirty-two of them nonconformists. There he will win admiration for his deep, strong, melodious voice, free of any taint of accent, though his pulpiteering manner and sermonising style will be less welcome.[1]

For all their advantages, the Glasseys are a miserable pair. They live at The Homestead, a substantial half-timbered house in Lower Parkstone, more sought after than Upper Parkstone because it is nearer the shoreline. Accordingly it is in Lower Parkstone that one finds most of the larger residences, while Upper Parkstone has more modest artisan dwellings, and even a gypsy settlement. The Homestead is a large, sprawling property in the Arts and Crafts style, with many gloomy rooms, surrounded by grounds extensive enough to host church parties, with a monkey-puzzle tree, an old orchard and several grass tennis courts.

As Mr Glassey moves along the line of players shaking hands, his sister Olive trails after him, pinning a rosette on the chest of each member of the victorious football team. Thin and bony like her brother, she is a shy young woman eighteen years his junior, effectively an orphan from childhood, as her mother, the Reverend Mr Glassey's widow, a resident in a nursing home since she was a little girl, is now no more. Olive was despatched to a boarding school for the children of dissenting ministers, and parcelled out from place to place in the holidays; and since leaving school has lived at The Homestead, where she is treated as if she were still a child, though she is in her early twenties, with a modest inheritance. Her sister-in-law, a small, managing woman, never tires of scolding her, unless she is telling her how lucky she is. Olive is kept away from visitors to the house, especially the former leader of the Party, that old goat David Lloyd George, with whom the Glasseys are on surprisingly good terms. She is rarely allowed out, except under escort. But she will not be a dependant much longer, because they have found her a suitable partner in life, a Bournemouth solicitor, to whom she is engaged to be married.

First in line is the captain Ronald Cornwell, who plays centre forward, a young man of Olive's age. Though shorter than average – he is only five foot seven – Ronnie has a presence which demands attention. Olive has met him before, at a meeting of the Young Liberals, for whom he acts as treasurer. He is too cheeky for Glassey, who gazes down on him unsmiling. Though young Cornwell's father is a town councillor and managing director of a local firm of motor engineers, he began his rise as a tiler and bricklayer; he still wears the lace-up boots of a manual labourer, and speaks in a West Country accent which betrays his humble origins. Nor is his wife any better, being Irish; it is believed that she came to England in service. Moreover the Cornwells are Baptists, which in the narrow world of Dorset dissent is a step down. Doctrinally Parkstone Congregationalists and Baptists are similar, but socially they are distinct. The Baptists are concentrated on the wrong side of the Ashley Road, in Upper Parkstone. (The Cornwells' house is on the correct side, but only just.)

As Olive fixes the clasp of the rosette, Ronnie emits a playful cry of pain and sinks to one knee. He clutches his breast, declaring that she has pierced him to the heart. Her brother frowns his disapproval, but Olive laughs aloud, a gesture of independence, almost of rebellion. Thawing a little, Glassey accedes to Ronnie's request to be allowed to visit The Homestead on Sunday afternoons, ostensibly to pay his respects to a housemaid with whom he has struck up an acquaintance. It will emerge later that this is no more than a blind for courting Olive. She breaks off her engagement to the solicitor, much to the annoyance of the Glasseys. Worse still, she becomes pregnant by the upstart Cornwell, and gives birth to a child out of wedlock, a boy named Anthony, only three months after her brother is elected to parliament.

Or so the story goes. But is it true? In fact the boy was born ten months after Ronnie and Olive married in October 1928, a discrepancy which casts doubt on the rest of the narrative. There may have been no football team, no line-up and no presentation. It is possible that they met at a cricket match, because Ronnie was joint honorary secretary of the Poole Park Cricket Club from the age of eighteen; or at one of the successful dances which he organised for the Club. More likely is that they met at a tennis tournament which he directed at The Homestead in the summer of 1924, as part of a social event for the East Dorset Liberals hosted by their newly chosen candidate; or perhaps a few months later, at a garden fête held in the grounds of The Homestead to raise funds for the Upper Parkstone

Baptist Church, which had included a sale of work by the Sewing Guild, tennis and croquet tournaments, and a concert after tea. Though they had thrown open their grounds Mr and Mrs Glassey were unfortunately unable to be present for the occasion, and in their absence Olive had received their guests alone. But perhaps not, because Ronnie was recovering from an accident, after he had collided with a coach while riding his motorcycle towards Penn Hill Avenue, the road on which The Homestead stands.[2]

The story of the football match first appeared in print in 2002, more than seventy years later, in a piece published in the *New Yorker*, written by Ronnie and Olive's younger son David: the events it tells of had taken place before he was born. He gave as a source a conversation with his mother in the early 1950s. Half a century later, she was long dead, and unable to confirm or deny the story. Perhaps she embellished it; perhaps he did; perhaps she never told it to him in the first place. He has a powerful imagination, capable of inventing such a story and realising it so fully that it becomes impossible to say whether it really happened, even for him.

To be fair to David, the story was family lore, not his own fabrication. He had already alluded to it in his autobiographical novel *A Perfect Spy*, published in 1985, some seventeen years before the *New Yorker* article. In the novel, the affronted MP pays a substantial sum to the seducer to leave the area, taking his fallen sister away, so that he should not be shamed by her continued presence.

In our family histories, the frontier between fact and fiction is vague, especially in the record of events that took place before we were born, or when we were too young to record them accurately; there are few maps to these remote regions, and only the occasional sign to guide the explorer. It is possible that Olive never pinned a rosette on Ronnie's chest. But perhaps the anecdote is symbolically true, even if not literally so. Olive felt herself to be a prisoner in her brother's house; she loathed what she later termed the 'Bible-punching hypocrisy' of her background; she longed to escape, and Ronnie came to her rescue, winning her affection with a characteristically flamboyant gesture, and carrying her off – though not out of the area, as he does in the novel. They were married locally, at the Richmond Hill Congregational Church in Bournemouth, and Olive's brother gave her away, no doubt holding his nose as he did so. Far from taking flight to another part of the country, the newlyweds had a house built less than a mile from The Homestead, on a plot of land that Ronnie had purchased only a few months before they married, in an area of Parkstone then being developed, known as Lilliput. On an adjacent plot they erected a tennis court. This was an enviable home for a young couple in their early twenties. There was 'help', which was just as well, because Olive confessed to being clueless about the practical aspects of domesticity. She was naïve and gullible, ill equipped for adult life. Ronnie called his young bride 'Wiggly' and treated her like a princess, showering her with presents. For her, at first, 'everything was marvellous'. Ronnie was the most exciting person she had ever met – 'a ball of fire', she said of him later. Only gradually did she come to perceive that he had been unfaithful to her from the beginning. In their new house, which they called Ambleside and which Ronnie promptly mortgaged, their second child was born, on 19 October 1931: a boy whom they named David John Moore (a family name), who in adulthood would become famous as the writer John le Carré.

In later life Ronnie would boast that he had never read a book. He had left school at the age of fifteen, and worked two years for an insurance broker in Bournemouth before entering into a partnership with his father as F. Cornwell & Son, Insurance Brokers and Claims Assessors. The management of the business was left almost entirely to Ronnie, and at first it was considered highly successful, generating profits of between £1,500 and £2,000 annually, of which each partner received a half share. For Ronnie's father Frank, this was a logical development of his existing motor-engineering works. There was a synergy between the two concerns: one made and repaired coaches and charabancs, the other insured them. Frank Cornwell was a self-made man, who had built a thriving business, using the profits to buy cheap houses, which then provided rental income. Among David's early memories was the weekly round of rent collecting in the Morris 8 with one or other of his aunts: 'there was always a Mrs Somebody who pretended she wasn't in'.

Much later, long after Frank Cornwell was dead, Olive would intimate to her sons that her father-in-law had been just as crooked as her husband.[3] He had been a black-marketeer during the First World War, she said. And there is a fragment of evidence to support Olive's claim: at a dinner party, decades later, Ronnie's daughter would be told by a fellow guest (on unknown authority) that her grandfather had been no better than her father.

If this was true – and after so much time has passed it is difficult to tell – it was not apparent to the citizens of Poole. Outwardly, Frank was a beacon of respectability: a pillar of the Baptist Church, a successful businessman, a founding member of the local Chamber of Commerce and a freemason, Master of two local lodges. In 1922 he had been elected to Poole town council, where he served successively as councillor, sheriff, mayor, deputy mayor and alderman.[4] There may have been some connection between these affiliations, hinted at by a dissident speaker during the Council meeting at which Frank Cornwell was chosen mayor. The speaker 'had referred to the borough maces as clubs', and stated that 'he also knew of another kind of club, a secret place where things were done that should be done in the Council Chamber' – referring to meetings of the local masonic lodge. Several of those present expressed their vehement approval of the speaker's interjection.

Frank Cornwell was a small man, with a drooping moustache that matched his heavy eyebrows. On Remembrance Day he would take part in the wreath-laying ceremony in Poole Park, looking very grand in his alderman's robes. He was an active Baptist, superintendent of the York Road Mission and Sunday School (a small tin chapel) and an enthusiastic lay pastor at the Baptist church in nearby Swanage. The daughter of family friends remembered him driving them to Swanage, his arms outstretched to clutch the wheel; he would suddenly start singing a hymn, his favourites being 'We're Marching to Zion' and 'Standing on the Promises of God'. The car was always beautifully kept, Bible-black and shiny, swooping into the drive of the Cornwells' house in Mount Road and scattering the gravel.[5] Later Frank became secretary of the much more substantial Parkstone Tabernacle, where after his death his widow would pay for a handsome wooden screen to be erected in his memory, still there to be admired today. In 1936 he would be elected president of the Southern Baptists, an association which embraced around eighty churches across the south of England.

The Cornwells were strict nonconformists. Their religion preached steadfastness and self-denial in this world, in the comfort and consolation of eternal life in the hereafter. Every Sunday they sang hymns at home, as one of their three daughters thumped away at the harmonium. No newspapers were allowed in their house on the Sabbath. 'God is watching you,' the boys were warned. Frank's wife Elizabeth, generally known as Bessie, was a kindly woman who still spoke with the Irish lilt of her girlhood. She presided at midweek mothers' meetings of the York Road Mission. The congregation consisted mainly of very poor women, laden with shopping baskets, hoping for better things to come. After Sunday school there would be charabanc outings to the outlying villages of Lytchett Matravers or Corfe Mullen, or 'magic lantern' slide shows and tea parties if it rained. One of the children who attended regularly later recalled Mr Cornwell summoning them outside, carrying a big jar: he would scoop out a handful of boiled sweets and hurl them down the hill, where they would scramble to pick them up.[6]

In the narrow nonconformist community of the south coast, religion, commerce and local politics were intertwined. The highest standards were expected in each of these three branches of life. The slightest hint of impropriety in business was taken very seriously – much more seriously than any sexual transgression. Anyone guilty of improper commercial activity faced the threat of being ostracised. In his acceptance speech as mayor of Poole, Frank Cornwell declared his intent to rely on 'the Supreme Ruler of all Councils' for the necessary wisdom and strength to carry out his duties. 'It has been said', he added, 'that when standing on a high position it is wise to look upward for safety.' To general applause, Frank paid tribute to his wife, who was such a great help to him in his public, social and religious duties. He was proud to see her present that morning, and also his son. A week later Ronnie organised an event with a nautical theme, to celebrate his father's role as mayor of a borough intimately connected with the sea. The speaker who proposed a vote of thanks afterwards expressed his hope that the mayor's son might 'follow in his father's footsteps to the Mayoralty'.[7]

Later it would be said that Ronnie had been given too much too early. He was the only son of the family, and everybody's favourite. His mother doted on him, as did his three sisters. They took a lenient attitude towards his scrapes. Ronnie learned early to expect women to love him and to give him whatever he wanted. His gingery hair was kept immaculately combed with sweet-smelling hair-oil. In later life women were always telling him what lovely hands he had; he was forever grooming them with nail-clippers, which he kept in his jacket pocket. He was equally proud of his large head, which he was said to have mortgaged for fifty pounds, cash in advance, the goods not to be delivered until his death. As a boy David fantasised about killing his father by chopping it off, and studied Ronnie's broad neck, speculating about the best point to aim his axe.[8] There was a story, perhaps apocryphal, that when Ronnie was born the doctor had commented on his remarkably large cranium. 'This boy', the doctor is supposed to have said, 'will be either a master criminal or a very successful businessman' – innocently assuming a distinction between the two. For Ronnie there was no such boundary; in fact there were no boundaries at all. By his own reckoning he was a moral man, yet his behaviour was unscrupulous. He would stop at nothing to satisfy his greedy appetites, even groping his own children. As well as taking advantage of institutions such as friendly societies and benevolent funds, he persuaded a succession of trusting widows, pensioners and other vulnerable people to invest their savings with him; few would ever see their money again. Ronnie's apparent sincerity, indeed his air of injured sanctity, was one of his strengths.[9] To deceive others he had first to deceive himself. Even as he swindled his friends and relations, he remained confident that he was doing them a favour. There was an element of theatre in all his performances. As his son Tony (who himself would become one of Ronnie's victims) wrote many years later, 'He could put a hand on your shoulder and the other in your pocket and both gestures would be equally sincere. He could rob you and love you at the same time.'[10]

If his shenanigans were exposed, Ronnie would show no shame. He would not dwell on his past misdeeds; on the contrary, he lived in a state of permanent amnesia about them.

In later life, at least in his kinder moods, David would come to think of his father as a version of P. G. Wodehouse's Stanley Featherstonehaugh Ukridge, a man who will do anything for money – except work. A creative opportunist, Ukridge ensures that no kindness shown to him, however small, goes unexploited for financial gain. He always has a scheme to make his fortune, lacking only the capital to carry it out; in repeatedly sponging on his friends and family he exhorts them to have 'vision'.

A man of extraordinary energy, warmth and vitality, Ronnie exuded optimism. From an early age he lived far beyond his means, confident that something would turn up to avert disaster. He smoked large cigars, drank brandy and whisky by the quart, ate at the best restaurants, stayed at the finest hotels, entertained generously and dispensed extravagant presents. He seldom settled an account unless pressed to do so, and often not even then. All debts, he considered, were negotiable. Towards women he radiated an unstinting and inexhaustible virility, with unfailing results.[11] Yet menace lurked beneath the charm. There was a glint of violence in his eye. His hugs were a demonstration of ownership as much as of affection. When he came home sozzled Ronnie would sometimes climb on to David's bed, pawing and fondling him, while David feigned sleep.*

He believed himself to be a good father. 'Son,' he would say, 'there's Somebody up there looking down on us, and when it comes to my turn to be judged – as judged we all must be – He's going to judge me on how I treated you boys.' Indeed he tended to suggest that his misdeeds had been committed for their sake. Like everybody else, David found Ronnie hard to resist. Again and again Ronnie would ask the question, 'Love your old man?' – and whatever he may have felt in his heart, David would never be strong enough to say no. Ronnie was histrionic, able to cry at will if it served his purposes. 'He would weep until he got you weeping too,' David would write later, 'while you hugged him and forgot whatever it was you were trying to confront him with.'

He was immensely proud of his sons, though he dominated them as he did everyone else, to the extent that it would become necessary to escape. 'How I got out from under Ronnie, if I ever did,' David would write many years later, 'is the story of my life.'[12]

Ronnie's dynamism made him the centre of any gathering. He was a natural leader, who soon attracted a following: a former schoolmaster, a part-time chauffeur, a speculative builder, a crooked lawyer and a dodgy accountant. These were his loyal footsoldiers, ever ready to meet his summons, to support his schemes and to help implement them, to enjoy

* Many years later David raised this subject with his half-sister Charlotte, who had been suffering from depression. 'Did he touch you up?' he asked her – before adding, 'It's all right, Sis, he did it to me too.'

his hospitality, to laugh at his jokes and, if necessary, to take the rap for him. David's private term for them was 'the Court'. Ronnie demanded faith from his subjects, as he did from his creditors; doubters, if there were any, were forced to recant. To express doubt was to be a cynic, and cynics were among the worst creatures in Ronnie's bestiary, alongside flunkies (civil servants), airy-fairies (intellectuals) and twerps (unbelievers).[13]

Ronnie inherited from his father an oratorical style and an evangelical vocabulary, both of which he adapted for commercial purposes. He was a fluent and entertaining speaker, able to make an audience laugh and to move them with his apparent conviction. As the years passed, he shed the West Country accent of his boyhood, becoming 'well spoken', though he would lapse into a Dorset burr when angered. Conscious that he lacked polish, he was receptive to guidance on etiquette from his young bride. She taught him the correct way to use a knife and fork, for example. He was always sensitive to a slight, Olive said, especially at times of stress. David came to believe that his mother dwelt on Ronnie's social inferiority as a figleaf of dignity to cover her own helpless subservience to him. 'Olive never forgave Ronnie for marrying above himself . . . By keeping open the wounds that Ronnie's low breeding had inflicted on her, by deriding his vulgarities of speech and lapses of delicacy, she was able to blame him for everything and herself for nothing, except her stupid acquiescence.'[14]

Ronnie would strive to ensure that his boys were free of the social shortcomings which he believed had impeded his own progress, by sending them to expensive private schools. Each of them should become the gentleman that he never quite succeeded in becoming himself. This set up a social distance between father and sons; the nearer they approached the objective that he had set for them, the further they left him behind.

Outwardly Ronnie was a success. He always dressed smartly. 'Son,' he would tell David, 'all you really need in life is a clean shirt and a good suit.' Ronnie favoured double-breasted pinstripes, a neatly folded silk handkerchief projecting from his breast pocket. Looking the part was half the battle in getting people to do what he wanted. He was impatient with the pettifogging restrictions imposed by small-minded bureaucrats or bank managers. ('Who says no? Who did you speak to? Get him on the blower. Let me speak to him.')[15]

When he married Olive at the age of twenty-two Ronnie was already a member of the local Chamber of Commerce, and active in the Poole Rotary Club. A month after their wedding, he had organised the local Rotary Club's annual 'Ladies' Evening' in the splendid new ballroom of the Haven Hotel. As mayor of Poole, Frank Cornwell gave a short address, and the new 'Mrs Ronald Cornwell' responded to the toast to 'The Ladies' in a lively spirit, providing a riposte to every crack made at their expense.[16]

In 1929 Ronnie would be elected the first president of the newly formed Poole Round Table. The Round Table movement was a fast-growing network of local clubs in which younger businessmen could exchange ideas, learn from the experiences of their colleagues and together contribute to civic life. It had been founded only a couple of years before, drawing its inspiration from a speech that the Prince of Wales had made in 1927 to the British Industries Fair. Records show that 'Tabler Cornwell' played an extremely active part in Round Table affairs during his year of office. He attended the first National Conference of Round Tables, where he proposed the adoption of a set of rules and a constitution for the movement.[17] At a joint meeting of the Poole Rotary Club and Round Table, Ronnie expressed the junior body's debt to the Club, which had 'in a large measure started it upon its journey'. Responding to the main speaker's talk on 'Personality', he argued that 'expressive personality was particularly needed in these present days of keen competition. It had been said the business was 10% knowledge and 90% bluff, but was not that 90% really personality?'[18]

Like his father, Ronnie was a freemason. In the future, whenever Ronnie moved to a new area, he would always seek out the local masonic temple. And though he would hardly ever attend a religious service of any kind, he would invariably contact the Baptist minister, which his mother found reassuring.

Ronnie was active too in the Liberal Party. In the summer of 1930, for example, he spoke in support of his brother-in-law at a fund-raising garden party in a Bournemouth suburb. He attacked the town's Conservative MP, Sir Henry Page Croft, mocking his equivocal stance towards the Empire Free Trade 'Crusade', launched by the Beaverbrook press as a new political party. 'He reminds me of the young man who endeavoured to keep two young ladies on the go,' Ronnie joked: 'he sent his best wishes to one, and his love to the other.'[19] Such humour was perhaps a little risqué for such an audience, but Ronnie could carry it off. His political views were unsophisticated. Like most of his fellow countrymen at the time, he took British superiority to be self-evident. Did not the King of England rule over the largest empire ever known, 'the empire on which the sun never sets'? The ubiquitous maps on school walls, showing one-quarter of the globe's surface in pale red, reinforced such complacency. Ronnie liked to quote from the great imperial writer Rudyard Kipling, especially his best-known poem 'If' which articulated his own philosophy of life: 'If you can meet with triumph and disaster . . .'

Early in 1931 he was adopted as the prospective Liberal candidate for South Dorset, a constituency won by the Liberals in the 1906 landslide, but held by the Conservatives at subsequent elections. Still only in his mid-twenties, Ronnie seemed to have a future in politics – but his political debut would be curtailed by dramatic events at Westminster. Later that summer the Labour Prime Minister James Ramsay MacDonald, facing a rebellion within his own Cabinet, invited 'men of all parties' to join him in a National Government. A coalition of MPs drawn from all three major parties was formed, with only the rump of the Labour Party and a few Liberals in opposition. The new National Government sought a mandate from the people by calling a general election. This parliamentary realignment permeated down to a local level. In the run-up to the election Frank Cornwell wrote an open letter to Alec Glassey, published in the *Poole and East Dorset Herald*. Though a Conservative, he declared his 'whole-hearted support' for Glassey, as one of those men 'who have proved themselves to have put the nation before party politics'. Whether Glassey was grateful for this endorsement is not recorded.

Only a week before the vote, in a dramatic speech to a crowded meeting at the Grand Theatre, Swanage, Ronnie announced that he was standing down to allow the sitting Conservative MP, Lord Cranborne, a clear run against the socialist candidate. 'Adversity makes strange bedfellows,' declared Ronnie, 'but when the existence of the country is at stake I stand shoulder to shoulder with the National Government.' He ended with a fine peroration: 'I do not love my party less, but I love my country more.'[20]

'God in Heaven, Wiggly, why can't you get a move on for once?' In his imaginary reconstruction of his own birth, as his mother struggled to bring him into the world, David depicted Ronnie as impatient for the process to be finished – as well he may have been, because his Swanage speech was delivered that same evening.

Olive soon found that she had exchanged a life of dependency and dullness for one of exhilarating insecurity. Ronnie spent other people's money with generous freedom, leaving behind him a trail of bounced cheques, unpaid bills and broken promises. His great hero, according to Olive, was Clarence Hatry, the flamboyant financier who had built a swimming pool on the roof of his Mayfair mansion, and once owned the largest yacht in British waters. Hatry had begun as an insurance clerk. He made his first fortune by profiteering during the First World War, and in the 1920s he built a business empire, always emerging richer despite three successive bankruptcies. The collapse of the Hatry Group in September 1929 is said to have triggered the Wall Street Crash. Hatry himself was imprisoned for forgery and fraud.

Soon after they were married Olive began to sense that Ronnie was in financial trouble. She was flummoxed when tradesmen turned up at the house demanding to be paid; this was something quite outside her experience. In fact Ronnie had ventured into very deep water. Some years earlier he had diversified into property dealing, following the successful example of his father. He began to buy houses, generally providing about 10 per cent of the purchase price from his own funds and raising the remainder by mortgages. Quite quickly he accumulated a stock of about thirty-five properties. But this was during the Great Depression, a period when rental values slumped, and soon the income from the rents was insufficient to meet the outgoings. Mortgagees began to foreclose. By 1932 he estimated his losses from property speculation at £5,000. Moreover he had suffered an even larger loss from the failure of another venture. Ronnie had believed that the regulation of local coach services, introduced by the Labour Minister of Transport Herbert Morrison as part of the Road Traffic Act 1930, provided a golden opportunity. Until then coach services in Britain had operated in a kind of free-for-all; now local licences were being introduced, which would grant their holders the exclusive right to run services in that area. Ronnie speculated that these licences would be very valuable, and that they were likely to be awarded to those companies which already controlled most or all of the existing coach services. For some years he had been buying up local coach companies, with the aim of amalgamating them and eventually selling them on at a profit to a larger concern. He was well placed to do so, because the local proprietors were all existing clients of F. Cornwell & Son for insurance purposes. To raise the necessary cash he borrowed money from friends. Unfortunately most of the coaches had been obtained on hire purchase, and Ronnie found himself short of capital to make the repayments. Eventually the vehicles were reclaimed, and the business collapsed, with losses estimated at £6,000.[21]

By May 1932, Ronnie was so seriously in debt that his father felt obliged to come to his aid. An agreement was reached by which Frank and one of his associates took charge of all Ronnie's assets, including Ambleside, the house in which David had been born. Ronnie relinquished his interest in F. Cornwell & Son and bound himself not to enter into further transactions without consulting Frank. This caused, in Ronnie's words, 'a tremendous amount of friction' between father and son, and Ronnie decided to leave the area, unwilling to accept any further curb on his activities.

According to Olive, however, the rift was simulated. She told her own sons many years afterwards that Ronnie had been forced to quit the Poole area because he was suspected of setting fire to the Hamworthy garage where the coaches were kept in order to collect the insurance pay-out. She alleged that Ronnie's father had been part of the swindle, indeed that he had put his son up to it, and had kept his head down afterwards. But no one was charged, and no evidence has emerged of any fire, started deliberately or otherwise, so maybe there is no basis to Olive's story.

Whatever the impetus, the young family now left Poole and moved to Exeter. It would prove the start of a nomadic life for the children, never staying anywhere long enough to make friends or put down roots. Ronnie again set up as an insurance broker, and also started a parallel business, much more profitable, as an assessor specialising in accident claims. He was 'ambulance chasing', rushing to the scene of an accident, and thence to the hospital bed, where he would encourage the injured person to pursue a claim against the perpetrator, and offer to invest the pay-out on favourable terms. Perhaps because he was always in such a hurry, he incurred numerous speeding fines.

This was an anxious time for Ronnie. Moneylenders back in Bournemouth were pressing him hard. In desperation, he forged a cheque for £215 4s. The police came to the house and took him away. On 17 February 1934 he was sentenced at the Winchester Assizes to six months' imprisonment for fraud.

Ronnie's trial and subsequent sentence shocked his family. The shame was intense, though the accused himself seemed oblivious to it. He conducted his own appeal against the conviction, arguing that it was based on a succession of mistakes and misunderstandings. His sisters remembered watching him shave on the morning when the verdict was due to be announced, apparently certain that he would be exonerated.

His appeal was rejected by the court. The judge refused to reduce the sentence, commenting that it was, in his opinion, a lenient one. But there was worse to come. While on bail awaiting trial, Ronnie had moved his family to Farnham Common in Buckinghamshire, a village between Maidenhead and Slough. On a visit to London he had opened an account with the Clydesdale Bank, depositing a cheque that turned out to be worthless; and over the days that followed he had presented a succession of Clydesdale Bank cheques to shopkeepers and garage proprietors in neighbouring villages, for small amounts up to £10. None had been honoured, because there was no money in the account. In July Ronnie was brought from Winchester Prison to answer charges of obtaining money by deception at the Buckinghamshire Quarter Sessions. In his defence, he claimed that at the time the cheques were presented he had been expecting to receive £50 promised by a friend; and further claimed that he had hoped to deposit a life policy for £1,000, which he had given to another friend in exchange for a loan of £10. Finally he argued that he was owed £50 by a garage proprietor in Exeter. The court rejected his claims, and found him guilty on seven charges of obtaining money and goods on false pretences. The judge sentenced him to a further nine months' imprisonment with hard labour, to run concurrently.

Again Ronnie appealed, and this time the case was heard before the Court of Criminal Appeal, where he was represented by the young Edward Ryder Richardson, later a recorder and Queen's Counsel; and prosecuted by Norman Birkett KC, later Lord Birkett, a former Methodist preacher and Liberal MP who would serve as a judge at the Nuremberg trials. This appeal too was dismissed.

Olive had been 'horrified' when the police arrived to arrest Ronnie, she told her eldest son many years afterwards. She had never shown much interest in her husband's business activities, beyond feeling a vague unease about them. Now tradesmen were queuing in the garden while the house was emptied of furniture. Alec Glassey arrived to collect his sister and his two nephews, then aged four and two, who were too young to understand what was happening. Going back to The Homestead was a form of imprisonment for Olive, but she felt that she had nowhere else to go. Returned to the house from which she had escaped, she reverted to being an obedient child again, unable to shield her sons from their uncle, who beat them at any sign that they might have strayed into 'vice'. The memory of these beatings, and those he received subsequently at school, could stir David to fury even in old age.

Neither Tony nor David had any idea where Ronnie had gone, and nobody enlightened them. When questioned, adults became evasive. Like their mother, the boys too were forced to live out a gloomy penance, keeping quiet and out of sight, banned from the main reception rooms in The Homestead and confined to the orchard when they played outside. For month after month they suffered a purgatory of 'dripping laurels . . . with red windswept beaches always out of season and creaking swings and sodden sandpits that were closed to enjoyment on the Sabbath'.[22] On Sundays they were smuggled into church, amid much whispering, and endured Uncle Alec's sermons, which seemed to David appallingly long. The 'Other House' where their Cornwell grandparents lived was a forbidden subject, never to be mentioned in the presence of the Glasseys: that was where the wickedness had been spawned.

It was characteristic of Ronnie's breezy attitude that while serving his sentence he ingratiated himself with the prison governor, as if they were golfing chums. He told Olive that when her letters arrived he would show them to the governor, and together they would agree that he was lucky to have such a wonderful wife.

Ronnie was much impressed by the way that Birkett had conducted the prosecution, and sportingly wrote from prison to congratulate him, rather as a loser might congratulate the victor on winning a fair fight. No doubt surprised, Birkett replied, and a correspondence ensued. This was the beginning of an unlikely connection, which strengthened after

Ronnie's release. Birkett accepted Ronnie's hospitality, and his introductions to obliging young ladies; like so many others, he would be corrupted by Ronnie. In his letters to Birkett from prison, Ronnie pledged to study law after he had served his sentence; on his release he would indeed enrol as a student at Gray's Inn, purchasing a wig and gown that would accompany him on his journey through life – though this ceremonial purchase marked both the beginning and the end of his legal studies. He would subsequently resolve that his sons should practise law in his place, Tony (for his solidity) as a solicitor and David (for his glibness) as a barrister. Ryder Richardson, who would become a regular guest at Ronnie's table in the 1940s and 1950s, always said that Ronnie had a fine legal mind; had he been on the right side of the law, he might have risen to the heights of the legal profession.

Though hinted at from time to time, it was not made explicit to the boys that their father had served a prison sentence until they were grown up. Searching his memory David recalled a scene from his boyhood: standing in the road outside Exeter Prison, clutching his mother's hand and waving up at his father behind a barred window, yelling 'Daddy, Daddy!' Excited by this long-forgotten image, David asked Ronnie whether he too recalled this moving moment. 'Sheer invention from start to finish, son.' Ronnie conceded that he had done a bit of time in Exeter, but mostly he had been in Winchester Prison and Wormwood Scrubs. (Apparently Winchester was the roughest, 'because of the gypsies'.) Besides, he explained, it was impossible to see or be seen from within the walls. 'Anyone who knows Exeter Prison knows that.' David decided that the scene outside Exeter Prison must have been a false memory, one that had never existed except in his imagination. And yet, in some way, it remained true to him. 'We should find another name for the way we see past events that are still alive in us,' he wrote. 'I *saw* him at that window but I also *see* him there now, grasping the bars, his bull's chest encased in a convict's uniform, with arrows printed on it, as worn in all the best school comics.'[23]

After a miserable year, Olive left The Homestead and took the boys to their Cornwell grandparents' house in Mount Road – known as Bay View, because it stood on high ground, offering a panorama across Poole Harbour to Brownsea Island and the Purbeck Hills beyond. This was a comparatively cheerful place. The boys were treated kindly by their grandparents, while their three unmarried aunts, all still living at home, would fuss over them and feed them sweets. Their great-grandfather lived in a cottage at the back, with a collection of Toby jugs displayed on his mantelpiece at which the boys gazed with fascination. The only thing lacking, apart from their father, was pocket money. It seemed somehow generally accepted that Ronnie's boys could not be trusted with cash.

Olive and her two boys were soon on the move again. Frank Cornwell bundled his daughter-in-law and grandsons into the car and took them for a long drive, further from Parkstone than they had ever been before. Presumably he had decided that his son should make a new start, far enough away that nobody would be familiar with his record. In St Albans, on the far side of London, he showed them around a newly built house, named Ambleside after their house in Lilliput. It was fully furnished, to the extent of teddy bears on the beds for the boys. 'He has provided it for you,' Olive whispered to them: the boys made appropriate expressions of thanks to their grandfather. In preparation for Ronnie's release, she went up to London with her sister-in-law Ella, and together they found a smart apartment in Baker Street from which he could begin again in business. Tony and David started at a local nursery school, run by a Mrs Hitchcock. The day came when Ronnie reappeared, the Court reassembled with some new courtiers, and life was fun again.

'I have paid the price for what I did,' Ronnie told Olive, 'but I can never have a receipt for it.' To her, he seemed unchanged by his recent confinement, except that he had lost weight, which in her view was a good thing. She seemed never to consider that he might have suffered, physically or psychologically, and perhaps Ronnie concealed this from her. In retrospect, David thinks that prison may have accentuated Ronnie's propensity for violence. Occasionally he would thrash the boys, bizarrely enough with his braces, which had metal fasteners and heavy leather ends that really hurt.

In business, Ronnie took up where he had left off. Using £50 borrowed from a friend he formed Courage & Company insurance brokers, and was soon handling large sums of money – though somehow earnings fell short of expenses. Then he formed another company, Artistic Dwellings and Estates Limited, to acquire and develop property in various parts of the country. In June 1935 an advertisement appeared in the *Bath Weekly Chronicle and Herald*, addressed 'To Builders and those interested in Estate Development'; it proclaimed that 'R. Cornwell & Co., of 7–9 Baker Street, London W.1', had 'unlimited funds immediately available for all types of building finance and every type of mortgage'.

On 10 August 1935 a damaging article about Ronnie's development business appeared in *John Bull* (a patriotic weekly periodical once owned by the demagogue Horatio Bottomley, coincidentally one of Ronnie's heroes). Providing details of his convictions, it was illustrated with a photograph of one of the prisons in which he had served his sentence. Ronnie threatened legal action, but facts were facts. According to Ronnie, the article was 'disastrous' for the business, which went into voluntary liquidation soon afterwards; 'it entirely knocked the bottom out of things'. His insurance business ceased trading also. The boys noticed that he began to park the car in the woods behind the house, where it could not easily be spotted. Ronnie kept afloat by borrowing £300 from Olive and £600 from a friend, but this only postponed the inevitable. On 31 March 1936 he was adjudged bankrupt, with liabilities amounting to £20,064 0s 6d, against assets of £795 4s 5d.* Olive too found herself temporarily bankrupt, though the order against her was discharged five weeks later.

The Cornwell household endured serious domestic shortages as the family's credit dried up. Once again tradesmen lined up in the garden as the house was emptied. In the London Bankruptcy Court, Ronnie was cross-examined at length by the Official Receiver. The court ruled that he should be forbidden from taking part in the management of any company while he remained an undischarged bankrupt.

The case was reported in full in the local Dorset press, causing further embarrassment to the Cornwell family. One piquant detail of the cross-examination concerned a transaction with an unnamed young woman, who had answered an advertisement for a clerical position. During her interview Ronnie had offered to put her in touch with a solicitor looking for someone prepared to advance a loan of £250 in exchange for a position

* The average annual wage at the time was £200, and one could buy a three-bedroom house for a few hundred pounds.

in his office. She agreed to these conditions, and subsequently advanced a further £100. Asked by the Official Receiver whether he thought this a safe investment, Ronnie answered, 'At the time I had no qualms at all.' He admitted that he had received a 'nice fee' for introducing the young woman to the solicitor.

Frank Cornwell again came to his aid. On his daughter Ruby's twenty-first birthday in 1936, he apologised that he was not going to be able to give her so much as he had hoped, explaining that he had felt obliged to assist his son. In fact he asked the girls to raid their Post Office savings accounts to help their brother. Through nominees, Ronnie formed a new company, Moreland Developments Limited, engaged in what has become known as 'buy to let': the company purchased houses with the aid of mortgages provided by building societies, servicing the interest payments out of the rent roll. As an undischarged bankrupt, Ronnie was forbidden by law from purchasing property or playing a formal role in any company, but he circumvented such snags by using trusted nominees, who were compensated accordingly, and was engaged by Moreland Developments as its 'financial consultant'. His usual practice was to buy the property himself in the first place, and then sell it on to the company at a profit.

Once on his feet again, Ronnie took Hazel Cottage, a large 'Tudorbethan' house in Rickmansworth, built on what had until recently been farmland. For the boys, the relocation to Rickmansworth was the first of a bewildering succession of moves within the Metroland on the edge of north-west London, where old villages had become islands in stockbroker-belt suburbia, and green fields had been replaced by golf courses. David came to loathe its bogus rusticity; his character Aldo Cassidy would sneer at its cautious commuters as 'Gerrards Crossers'.

In the mock-raftered drawing room stood one of the earliest television sets, 'an upended mahogany coffin', as David remembers it, 'with a tiny screen that shows fast-moving spots and just occasionally the misted features of a man in a dinner jacket'.[24] Looking back on his boyhood, David would write that he and his brother had lived 'in the style of millionaires or paupers'. When Moreland Developments went into compulsory liquidation three years after its formation, the company supposedly owed Ronnie £80,000. This colossal sum (the equivalent of £11 million today) gives some indication of the kind of accounting that enabled Ronnie to support himself in such style. For the boys, these ups and downs were disturbing; even when times were good, they could not feel secure.

At Hazel Cottage the Cornwells employed a cook, a cleaning woman and a gardener. A very beautiful girl arrived to be the boys' nanny. This was Annaliese Lieschwitz, a German refugee in her late teens whom Ronnie had met through some American officers. In retrospect, David assumed that she was his father's mistress and associated her with 'a hazily remembered memory of carnal flurry', though he was never certain whether this was a real memory or an imagined one. Annaliese taught the boys snatches of German, a language which took hold of him and never let go. From her they learned to ask *Bitte, darf ich den Tisch verlassen?* when they wanted to get down from the table after a meal. If we can trust the fictionalised version given in *A Perfect Spy*, David loved her in a way that he never loved his own mother. But then she too was gone, and though he searched for her over the years, he would never find her.*

Once again everything was 'marvellous'. The boys' bedroom cupboards were stuffed with new toys – though, like the houses they had inhabited before, it was empty of books. Weekends were one long adult party. The boys kicked footballs around the garden with riotous 'uncles'; at night they went to sleep to the sound of music and raucous laughter from downstairs. Ronnie made a down payment on a stylish car, manufactured by a new British company called SS (which changed its name to Jaguar after the war). One memorable day he and the boys motored to Pendine Sands in South Wales, a seven-mile stretch of beach where several world land-speed record-breaking runs had been made. There they raced the car back and forth as fast as it would go.

Tony was growing into a tall, gangly youth, with curly brown hair, strong and confident. Ronnie would always cast him as the stolid, reliable one, against David's more erratic and unpredictable nature. The two boys were close; their shared experience of life on the move had isolated them from the conventional world and bound them together. Tony recalls his little brother as very charming, but also very vulnerable; he felt a duty to watch over him. 'Tony was my minder, protector and only friend,' David recalls. He looked towards his big brother as his guardian.

* After he joined MI6 he put through a trace for her, to no avail.

At Christmas Ronnie took the family off to St Moritz, accompanied as always by several members of the Court. Though St Moritz was going through a period of decline in the late 1930s, ski resorts remained the preserve of the privileged, inaccessible to most Britons. They stayed at the Kulm, a luxurious five-star, family-run hotel with a long tradition of providing for wealthy English visitors. Ronnie and Olive took a suite, with the two boys sharing a room. For Tony and David this was an adventure, the first time they had ever been abroad. They learned to ice skate, and Ronnie took up curling. As in England, but on a grander scale, he entertained lavishly, giving cocktail parties in the Grill and keeping open house in the Cornwell suite, where they received a stream of visitors. Olive became increasingly concerned about how they would pay for it all, but Ronnie told her not to worry. On the evening before their departure he marched into their suite and announced airily that he had bought the hotel.

As so often with Ronnie, this was fantasy masquerading as fact. Having learned that the Kulm was deep in debt, he had sought a private conversation with the general manager, a grandson of Johannes Badrutt, the hotel's founder. Ronnie had confided that he represented a consortium of investors who were considering the possibility of making an offer (perhaps not an unwelcome one) to buy the Kulm. He had brought his family here, he explained, to test whether it came up to the consortium's exacting standards; and was happy to inform Herr Badrutt that he would be making a favourable report to his colleagues when he returned to England. Presenting a newly printed business card, Ronnie asked him to be so kind as to forward the bill (should he wish to present one) to this address, where it would of course receive his prompt attention. The gratified general manager expressed his satisfaction that Herr Cornwell and his family had enjoyed his stay with them. In the circumstances he was happy to waive all charges.

Life was no longer marvellous for Olive. She had been mortified to be summoned before the bankruptcy court for cross-examination. In the past she had never questioned it when Ronnie had asked her to sign papers – 'Just witness this, will you, Wiggly?' He would ask her to cash cheques, which bounced. By now he had run through almost all her money: she had only the few pounds in her handbag remaining. The bankruptcy court had asked her to explain the large sums in her account – an account of which she apparently knew nothing. 'One just couldn't live like it,' she told her sons later. Moreover she found it hard to cope with her husband's philandering. He was now having an affair with her best friend, Mabel George; twice Mabel had become pregnant, and both times she had terminated the pregnancy. On at least one occasion he persuaded Olive to share a bed with the pair of them. Ronnie would often stay out late and come back reeking of drink. Olive still adored him, 'but he was quite incorrigible'.

A business associate of Ronnie's, a land agent called John Hill, came to stay with them for a few days. Seeing what was happening, he begged Olive to make a stand. When she refused Ronnie's next request to cash a cheque, there was 'one hell of a row'; for the first time in their marriage, Ronnie hit her. Afterwards he tried to make amends with chocolates and flowers, but Olive could take no more: she decided to elope with Hill, leaving her sons behind. One night when Ronnie was out, she hurriedly packed some clothes – in her honeymoon suitcase bought from Harrods, a reminder of better days, covered in luxurious white hide and lined in pink silk – then slipped out of the house, locking the door behind her. The two boys were sleeping upstairs. She lugged the suitcase along the dark streets to Rickmansworth Cricket Club, where Hill collected her in his car. 'I feel positively unclean,' she told him.

2

'We seek higher things'

Nobody told the boys that their mother had gone for good. Ronnie indicated that she was ill, implying that she would soon return. After a while he began to hint that she had fallen into immoral ways. ('Never judge, son. That's God's job, not ours.') It would be years before they realised that she was never coming back. Even then, they found it hard to accept that she had abandoned them. When they were sent away to boarding school Tony and David kept a biscuit tin of coins hidden in the hollow of a tree, saving up for bus fares so that one day, like Peter Pan's lost boys, they could go and find their mother. David sometimes wondered if she might be dead, especially when Ronnie hinted that her illness was worse than first thought. ('These medical boys, son, they just won't give it to a fellow straight.') When he tried to pursue the point, Ronnie seemed hurt and even insulted to be questioned. ('Isn't your old man good enough for you, then, son?')[1]

Oddly, Tony has no memories of his mother at home, though he must have been at least seven when she left. David was only five; he remembered only her scent and clutching a gloved hand. After she had gone he would approach each woman who came to the house, and ask her shyly if she was his mother.

'We were frozen children, & will always remain so,' David wrote in an impassioned letter to his brother almost a lifetime later. Denied maternal love, his response was to try and make everybody else love him. 'You chase after it, act it, imitate it, and eventually, if you're old & lucky, you believe in it,' he wrote to Tony, 'but it comes hard, it's flawed, & we fake it a lot, like religion, in the hope that one day we'll have it for real.'[2] Magnus Pym, the protagonist in *A Perfect Spy*, the most autobiographical of David's novels, is another motherless son, whose upbringing is almost identical to his own. He seduces everybody he meets, in a vain search for love. 'Love was all he cared about,' Magnus's old schoolmate Sefton Boyd says of him. 'Didn't know where to find it.'[3]

David has never been able to forgive his mother for deserting him. Though the wound healed over, he remained raw inside. He would develop a carapace of relaxed ease, but inwardly he was racked with rage and wretchedness. Looking back at his childhood, he has written of the 'sixteen hugless years' that followed his mother's departure. He was left ignorant of women, and mistrustful of them. Women were people who disappeared without explanation, not to be relied upon. 'He never loved a woman in his life,' Magnus's mistress tells his friend Jack Brotherhood. 'We were enemy, all of us.'[4]

The theme of abandonment recurs again and again in his books. It is there in the very first paragraph he wrote, in his first book, *Call for the Dead*, when Smiley's wife leaves him for the first time. Another of David's autobiographical characters, Aldo Cassidy, the central figure in his novel *The Naïve and Sentimental Lover*, has been abandoned by his mother as a small boy; when asked what effect this had on him, he replies: 'Well . . . it made me lonely I suppose . . . it sort of . . . robbed me of my childhood.' Pressed to explain what he means, Cassidy continues: 'Denied normal growth, I suppose . . . a sense of fun . . . I had no female reference, no one to make women human.'

David has admitted that he finds it difficult to write about women as a consequence. By comparison with the men, the woman in his work are often curiously blank. 'Whenever I start to write a female character, Olive always seems to get in the way.'

With John Hill, she settled in East Anglia, where they eventually started another family. Olive was still besotted with Ronnie, however, and after a while she began going up to London to see him. 'It was always a very happy time,' she told Tony many years later. They would have lunch, holding hands across the table, while Ronnie expanded on his latest schemes, ever more grandiose; and, as David pictured it, after the coffee and the brandy, Olive 'yielded to him in some safe house before he scurried off to run the world'.

She would later claim to have agreed with Ronnie that the boys should board during the term-time and that she should have them on alternate holidays; but if there was such an agreement, she seems to have made little attempt to enforce it. In old age, she recalled that as a boy David had visited her a couple of times, though he is adamant that this never happened. Tony remembers being taken to see her once, when he was about ten years old, and shouting at Hill in fury.

The boys were sent to board at a nearby preparatory school, St Martin's in Northwood. The school historian suggests that Ronnie may have met the headmaster at the local golf club.[5] Tony was then seven; David only five, by far the youngest child at the school. Even then he was conscious of being an outsider, from the wrong kind of background – a sense of not belonging that would dog him all his life. He remembers little else, beyond 'the harrowing daily routine of bed-making, clothes-changing, and bell-ringing, and the extraordinary kindness of my brother Tony, who appeared from nowhere to scoop me up, brush the grime off me, and set me back on my feet'.[6]

The period after Olive's departure was a confusing time. Soon afterwards they moved from Hazel Cottage to Greengates, a large detached house on the outskirts of Amersham. For a while Mabel George looked after the boys: the first, and David's favourite, of many substitute 'mothers', who came and went at regular intervals. The one constant in the boys' lives at this time was their grandparents' home in Parkstone, where they would often spend their holidays.[7] In those days children roamed free of adult supervision: the boys would play with cap guns among the pine trees on Constitution Hill, or wander down to the shore at Sandbanks or to the Victorian Boating Lake. David remembers being taken by his doting aunts to the Bournemouth Palace Court Theatre on successive nights, and seeing Emlyn Williams perform in his own play *Night Must Fall*. He was fascinated by Williams's portrayal of a psychopathic murderer who conceals his true nature beneath a polite, unassuming, cheerful exterior. 'I had an enormous appetite for narrative and fantasy, without knowing what was gnawing at me,' David would tell an interviewer many years later. Looking back on his childhood from the perspective of an adult, he expressed the frustration of growing up in households that were 'artless, bookless and cultureless'.[8] The first books that he can remember reading were *Treasure Island* and a volume of the Sherlock Holmes stories.

Before they left Hazel Cottage, Ronnie had thrown a party for the West Indies cricket team, then touring England. This was an unusual gesture: not many black faces were to be seen in Rickmansworth at the time. Ronnie reacted with indignation to any prejudice shown towards his friends.* The Cornwell boys were thrilled to play French cricket in the garden with the West Indies' star player, the Trinidadian Learie Constantine, dubbed 'the coloured catapult' because of his big-hitting batting, hostile fast bowling and athletic fielding. After the tour Constantine settled in England, and Ronnie would co-opt him on to the local cricket team. David remembered a jovial domestic ceremony in which, without the benefit of a clergyman, Constantine was formally inducted as his godfather. In fact this was a false memory, because Constantine's godson was not David but his brother.[9]

The West Indies tour of 1939 was cut short by the outbreak of war. David was staying with his grandparents in Parkstone when Neville Chamberlain broadcast to the nation at eleven o'clock in the morning of 3 September. Germany had invaded Poland two days before, in defiance of Britain's guarantee of Polish independence. Across the nation people gathered anxiously around their 'wireless' radio sets to hear the Prime Minister's mournful announcement that no reply had been received to the British ultimatum, 'and that consequently this country is at war with Germany'. The scene remained fixed in David's memory like a family portrait. 'Dear Lord, where will the battlefield be?' asked Bessie. 'Could be out there on the tennis court,' his grandfather replied grimly. Thereafter David shunned the tennis court – which was perhaps just as well, because later in the war a bomb fell on it.

Fear of enemy bombing caused many London schools to relocate to safer locations in the countryside. Pupils at St Martin's were evacuated from

* During the war Constantine took legal action, with Ronnie's active support, against a hotel which had refused him accommodation. The case came up before Norman Birkett, by now Mr Justice Birkett, who found in Constantine's favour. This has been regarded as a landmark case in the struggle against racial discrimination. Constantine was knighted in 1962, and was made a life peer in 1969, becoming the first black man to sit in the House of Lords.

Northwood to Chard in Somerset – but the Cornwells were not among them, because Ronnie had arranged for them to start at another preparatory school: St Andrew's, near Pangbourne in Berkshire.* As an economy measure Ronnie persuaded St Andrew's to take them as day-boys, rather than as boarders, and fixed it for them to live with Mabel George's sister Vi and her husband Frank at Flint Cottage, a lodge at the school gates. This double anomaly would set them apart, in a regime where conformity was all important, reinforcing their sense of difference.

Hours after the boys arrived at Flint Cottage the air-raid warning sounded. Frank led them into the woods to shelter until they heard the 'all clear'. He had been exempted from military service because of a heart condition, and ran the nearby Herons Farm. Sometimes he would take the boys with him as he did his milk rounds by horse-drawn cart.

Vi had a stiff leg and walked with a stick. Unlike her sister she did not treat the boys kindly. David was only seven when he arrived at St Andrew's, a sensitive, vulnerable child. Instead of sympathising with his distress when he wet the bed, she beat him – repeatedly, as David remembers it. Cruelly she made him wear a nappy to school. Every morning when he arrived, he would have to find a private place to take it off, to escape the ridicule of his peers; and then, at the end of the day, to put it back on again, because she would check and punish him if she found him not wearing it. He would continue wetting his bed into his middle teens, a constant humiliation because it was impossible to conceal.

St Andrew's had been founded only five years earlier, as a partnership between two men who had themselves met as schoolboys some thirty years before, Bill Ward-Clarke and Robert Robertson-Glasgow. These two, one a short and bespectacled Englishman and the other a tall and bald Scot, acted as joint headmasters, though Robertson-Glasgow tended to take the senior role.[10] They had adopted a school motto: *Altiora Petimus* ('We seek higher things'). Being so new, St Andrew's was still a small and growing school, with fewer than a hundred pupils. This meant that the atmosphere was more intimate and less impersonal than in a larger institution, for better or worse. Robertson-Glasgow made a practice of awarding

* Then boys only, but now co-educational. Among its more recent pupils are the Middleton sisters, Kate and Pippa.

humorous nicknames to the boys, such as 'Titus' or 'Beetle'. David was known as 'Maggot'.

Many of the younger masters were absent on war service. The shortfall was made up largely by older men called out of retirement, including one who had taught the headmasters themselves when they were schoolboys at Radley. Another of the older men, the mathematics master Colonel Airey, had lost a leg during the Boer War. The music mistress was a Frenchwoman stranded in England with her son at the outbreak of war; she was delighted when a young *maquisard* joined the staff after escaping from occupied France. For a short period David scratched away at a violin, until she made him stop and promise never to try again. By contrast, he showed an aptitude for art, especially for humorous cartoons. In this he was encouraged by the art master Peter Probyn,* a successful commercial artist who illustrated books and designed dust-jackets for publishers. Probyn was responsible for several Guinness advertisements and *Punch* cartoons, and drew a comic strip for the boys' magazine *Eagle* after the war.†

The English master was the headmaster's brother, Raymond Robertson-Glasgow, a celebrated Somerset cricketer in his time and afterwards a cricket correspondent. 'Crusoe' Robertson-Glasgow‡ was a big, kindly man, with a reverberating laugh and a powerful baritone singing voice which rang out in the dining hall; the boys were hugely impressed when he responded to their urging and punted a football right over the roof of the three-storey school building. He was known to the boys as 'RG 2', to differentiate him from his elder brother the headmaster, who was 'RG 1'. The Cornwell boys were of course known as 'Cornwell 1' and 'Cornwell 2'.

The main building of St Andrew's was a Victorian mansion in the Gothic style designed by Alfred Waterhouse for one of the Watney

* Christopher 'Kit' Probyn is one of the protagonists in le Carré's *A Delicate Truth* (2013).

† One of David's contemporaries, the artist Howard Hodgkin, has acknowledged the debt he feels to Probyn, though he was otherwise unhappy at St Andrew's and left prematurely.

‡ His nickname of 'Crusoe' came, according to Robertson-Glasgow himself, from a batsman whom he had bowled first ball. When his captain asked how he had been dismissed, he replied: 'I was bowled by an old —— I thought was dead two thousand years ago, called Robinson Crusoe.'

family of brewers, set in fifty-four acres of woods and playing fields, and reached by a mile-long drive from the school gates. Every morning the Cornwell boys would bicycle from Flint Cottage along this drive to school. Once David fell off his bike, and Tony stopped to wait for him. Seeing his little brother in tears, though not obviously hurt by his fall, Tony laid his bike on the ground and walked back to comfort him. 'Are you unhappy?' he enquired.

'Yes,' sobbed David.

Embracing him, Tony told him not to worry. 'I will look after you,' he promised. 'I will be your mother.'

Beyond the main school building was a stable yard, and then a track continued to an old chalk-pit, now grass covered, with tall hummocks on the northern side, a privileged lair for the biggest and strongest boys.* Each year group of St Andrew's pupils speculated about this pit: some said it had been an open-cast silver mine, others an ancient fort. Naïve newcomers were told that it was a bomb-crater, but initiates knew where bombs had dropped, and most had examined the resultant craters in person. Only two had fallen in the vicinity of the school: one in a field between Moulsford and Streatley, and the other between the railway and the river at Cleeve Lock.

Soon after arriving at St Andrew's David read *Oscar Danby V.C.*, a story by Rowland Walker about a brave boy scout who volunteers for espionage duty during the First World War. This patriotic tale filled him with a strong desire to die a hero's death before a German firing squad. David was conscious that the fathers of many of his schoolfellows were serving in the forces, so it was awkward that his own father was something of a spiv. For boys of David's generation, the participation or otherwise of their fathers in the national struggle was a matter of intense pride or shame, a test of manhood. David quietly let it be known that Ronnie had joined the secret service, was being trained for an important mission and would soon be parachuted into Germany. Unknown to him, his father was peddling similar stories to his cronies in London, even as he traded in black-market

* Thursgood's Academy in *Tinker, Tailor, Soldier, Spy* is modelled on St Andrew's; in the novel the chalk-pit is known as 'the Dip'.

goods such as petrol coupons, ration coupons and emergency ration cards.

The Robertson-Glasgows were high Anglicans, with a low opinion of nonconformists. This religious difference distanced the Cornwell brothers from family and home. Schoolboys at St Andrew's attended chapel services twice daily, and were expected to say prayers before bedtime. On Sundays there were extra services.

The school day began with lessons in the morning. Lunch during wartime was frugal, with meat (or occasionally fish) served only once a week. During the shooting season, the more privileged boys received pheasants from their fathers' estates, which they ate at a special table reserved for the offspring of landed families. David once sat as this table as a guest. He had never before tasted pheasant, and this one was high and undercooked, but he ate every morsel before vomiting in one of the doorless lavatories.[11] After lunch the boys would be sent to rest in their dorms, while masters relaxed in the common room, correcting the boys' work or reading the papers. Then classes resumed, following a tea of buns and milk. Each class did a 'working-party' once a week, undertaking chores such as shoe cleaning or picking fruit in the walled garden, and occasionally lifting potatoes at a nearby farm.

Sometimes, when there was a shoot on at a neighbouring estate, boys would be recruited as beaters. David has always been squeamish; he remembers his disgust at the line of dead animals nailed up by the gamekeeper afterwards, the birds' wings spread wide. Ward-Clarke was a keen shot, and when he bagged anything unusual like a barn owl, he would bring it back to the school and pin it on the noticeboard. This inspired the scene in *Tinker, Tailor, Soldier, Spy*, in which a master efficiently despatches an owl that has emerged dazed from a chimney into a classroom full of rapt boys. While staying with one of his father's landed girlfriends in the holidays David was made to hold chickens still while the farmhand cut their tongues so that they bled to death.

After David and Tony had been at Flint Cottage a year or so, Herons Farm went bust, and they moved into dormitories alongside the other boys. Boarders were given a prayer card before going to bed, which included prayers for the army one night, for the navy another and for the air force another. 'For love, at dead of night, we had one another's trembling little bodies, which stole from bed to bed like sticky frogs in search of a pool,' David wrote in a memoir of his schooldays. 'There at last we embraced like the infants we were not supposed to be, whispered fantastic lies to each other about our parents, and listened to the slow chug of airplanes, wondering whose they were . . .'[12]

On Sunday, there was compulsory chapel, and in the afternoon Mrs Robertson-Glasgow would read from the Bible. For the rest of the day the boys roamed free within the grounds, where gangs clashed frequently over territorial control. As at other schools, there were periodic crazes which preoccupied the boys for a while and then ended: marbles, conkers, roller skating, 'Battleships' during exams, and twirling tin lids on a loop of string against the brick wall of the gym, producing a shower of sparks.

The war loomed large in the imagination of the St Andrew's schoolboys, who soon learned to identify aircraft in the skies overhead. After dark they would gaze out of their dormitory windows and sweep the school grounds with their torches in search of enemy parachutists. At Herons Farm David and Tony peered through gaps in the doors at Spitfires stored inside an octagonal brick barn. In the winter of 1940, after term had started, a boy arrived at the school without a uniform, one of only thirteen survivors of the ninety children aboard the passenger ship *City of Benares*, which had been torpedoed by a German U-boat. Later in the war the boys would collect the strips of metal dropped by aircraft to confuse radar, called 'Window' by the British and *Düppel* by the Germans. Before D-Day the St Andrew's boys were taken to see tanks assembled in woods near by, and to watch Dakotas with gliders in tow practise take-off and landing.

As an adult David would write scathingly about all his schools, and claim that he was 'not educated at all'.[13] He depicted St Andrew's as a reactionary, philistine institution, riddled with snobbery and prejudice, in which pupils were terrorised into becoming loyal servants of a fast-fading empire. 'For History, we had "Our Empire Story", written by I forget whom;* for Literature, we had Percy Westerman,† Sapper and Henty; for Heroes, we had Biggles, Bulldog Drummond and, later, Dornford Yates's

* H. E. (Henrietta Elizabeth) Marshall (1908).

† Percy F. Westerman (1876–1959), prolific author of adventure books for boys, lived on a converted Thames barge on the River Frome at Wareham in Dorset.

Berry: the whole stable, you might say, of Empire-bloodstock novelists.' Colonel Airey blamed the world's troubles on 'niggers', and extolled the benefits of colonial rule in Kenya, Rhodesia, Malaya and Burma.

Yet a contemporary of David's rated the quality of teaching at St Andrew's as 'pretty good'. In particular, 'Crusoe' Robertson-Glasgow seems to have been an inspirational teacher, who more than anybody else was responsible for introducing David to the pleasures of literature. In class 'Crusoe' read aloud to the boys, from Jerome K. Jerome's *Three Men in a Boat*, or the Father Brown stories, or the stories of Sherlock Holmes; David has never forgotten his mellifluous reading of 'The Speckled Band'. 'I loved him because he knew he was crazy,' David has said.* 'Crusoe' had written several books himself, mostly about cricket; among them was a collection of fictitious autobiographies, *I was Himmler's Aunt* (1940). He had an extensive vocabulary, and loved new coinages. While he was playing cricket for Somerset his fellow team members would take a dictionary to dinner, so that they could challenge him whenever he used an unfamiliar word.[14]

According to Tony, his brother was 'noticeably bright' even as a small boy. At this stage, however, David does not seem to have been an exceptional student. It tended to be Tony who won the form prizes as he progressed up the school, rather than his younger brother: though at eleven David did win the IVth-form 'Good Work' prize, and at thirteen, just before he left, he would be awarded the Greig Character Cup. It was on the playing field that David excelled. At only ten years old, he joined boys two or three years his senior in the cricket 1st XI (captained by Tony), showing promise as both batsman and bowler. ('May become a leg-break exponent', speculated the coach.) By the time he reached eleven, he was a regular member of the football 1st XI, playing in goal, where he won a reputation for courage and 'a safe pair of hands'. David would also play hockey and rugby for St Andrew's, and be runner-up in the school lawn tennis singles competition.

From the outside David appeared well integrated into the life of the school. But inside he seethed with misery and resentment. His anger at

* Though described as being of 'incessant good humour', 'Crusoe' took his own life during a snowstorm in 1956.

the corporal punishment inflicted on him was palpable when he wrote about it half a lifetime later:

> . . . I see myself, sprawled inelegantly over the arm of the headmaster's chair, waiting for the pain, which was acute. I smell pipe smoke and leather, like the smell of a limousine.
>
> I always knew when he was going to beat me because he became dreadfully slow in his movements, like a man moving through water. He would stand up, put down his pipe and stare at me in dull confusion before waking to pronounce sentence. 'Cornwell,' he would say . . . 'there's only one thing for . . .' – followed by the definition of the crime: cheek, slackness, filth, lying; the menu was awesome.
>
> After the beating, we showed off our marks. When our bottoms bled, Matron dabbed iodine on them.

The headmaster used a riding whip to punish the boys. Other masters hit them with their hands; David bitterly attributed his later deafness in one ear to a Mr Fansworth, 'now eking out a well-earned retirement on the esplanades of Eastbourne'.[15]

St Andrew's boys referred to those who hadn't been to private school as 'oiks', and doubled up with mirth at the sound of lower-class accents. David was soon doing the same, 'while I hugged to myself the shameful secret that my aunts and uncles spoke that way themselves'. He became especially sensitive to social nuance, noticing details to which boys from more secure backgrounds might be oblivious.

To avoid being thought different, David pretended to share the attitudes and assumptions he found around him.[16] The unthinking propaganda with which they were force-fed led him to sympathise secretly with the Germans, 'since everyone hated them so much'.[17] His was a hidden life, of outward conformity and inner rebellion. In retrospect, he would feel that he had been schooled into becoming a spy, learning the enemy's language, wearing his clothes, aping his opinions and pretending to share his prejudices. Like Graham Greene, he learned to live a secret life, and would later liken his boyhood to living in occupied territory. 'The catastrophes in our family were so great and the disproportion between the domestic situation and the orthodoxy of my educated programme was so great that I seemed to go about in disguise.'[18]

Parents were not much in evidence at St Andrew's, as the shortage of petrol during wartime made travel difficult. Ronnie had his own ways of overcoming such difficulties, however; from time to time he would announce that he would be coming on a 'leave-out day'. His habit was to pick the boys up in the car from the end of the drive, presumably to avoid being accosted by the bursar, who might want to raise the awkward issue of overdue school fees. Then they would be carried off to a restaurant, or to the home of Ronnie's current lady friend. More than half a century afterwards David would provide an ironic description of these occasions: 'He would bring the latest candidate for Olive's job and a member of his Court for protection. Lunch would be a three-hour affair with a lot of brandy, which at that age we didn't drink. At some point before the treat ended, we knew he was going to take us aside and ask us what we thought of the candidate, and we were going to reply "not much".' The boys were invited to share Ronnie's disrespectful attitude towards women, as supplicants to be recruited and dismissed.

Often Ronnie would not turn up at all, which was too humiliating to admit. After waiting in vain for an hour or so, Tony and David would take themselves on a long walk, and on their return to school pretend that all had gone to plan. ('Had a good day, Cornwell?' 'Super, sir, thank you.' 'Parents OK?' 'Fine, sir, thank you.')[19]

In 1943 Tony left St Andrew's for Radley, about twenty-five miles away. Ronnie had originally intended for both boys to go on to Sherborne, and to this end he had been corresponding with one of the Sherborne housemasters for more than a year, after meeting him at a cricket match; but when Tony won a scholarship to Radley, this seemed an opportunity too good to be missed, though it meant sending the boys to separate schools. Tony was aware that his little brother would feel desolate without his comfort and protection. From Radley he wrote David long letters to cheer him up. Tony even managed to telephone him once, a considerable feat for a schoolboy in those days. At weekends and half-holidays, the brothers would cycle to a prearranged rendezvous in a wood or in a field, for a hug and a picnic.

Once Tony had gone, David retreated still further into fantasy. 'Much of my time was spent planning escapes across moonlit playing fields partly given over to wartime agriculture. In the romantic dreams that temporarily released me from those huge and lonely dormitories, I likened myself to those young pilots of the propaganda films that were our sole entertainment.'

Sickness provided another escape route. During this period of early adolescence David twice pretended to be seriously ill. On the first occasion he faked epilepsy convincingly enough to be admitted to hospital. Emboldened by this success, he simulated a hernia, so successfully that doctors operated on him. While he was recuperating in bed, one of his father's girlfriends read him *The Wind in the Willows*, and he liked it so much that he asked her to read it to him again, and again.

For Ronnie, the outbreak of war had presented new opportunities. In 1939, as the nation girded itself for the coming struggle, he had formed Moore Medicinal Products, to manufacture and market his own versions of proprietary medicines formerly imported from Germany. The boys spent one of their school vacations in the cellar of an Aberdeen boarding house, squeezing figs and prunes through a press and rolling the resulting sludge in glucose, to be sold as laxative pills. Why they were in Aberdeen is difficult to ascertain, except that Ronnie had influential connections among the masons in Scotland. Later they accompanied him on a tour of chemist shops in the Midlands, sitting bored in the car outside as their father tried to offload nasal inhalers on to sceptical shopkeepers.

In June 1940 there had been an irritating interruption to Ronnie's money-making operations. The proceedings to wind up Moreland Developments Limited had revealed that he had taken an active part in the management of the company, breaching the conditions of his 1936 bankruptcy. He was tried at the Central Criminal Court in London, sentenced to two days' imprisonment and ordered to pay a comparatively modest fine. Once again the boys were told nothing of this.

In school holidays the boys would be taken to stay with proxy 'mothers', usually landed or otherwise prosperous ladies with conveniently remote husbands whom Ronnie had somehow befriended. Among them David remembers 'Topsy' Holcroft of Shrewsbury, a Mrs Mole of Honeyback Hall, Kidderminster, a Mrs Grove of Abergavenny, and a Mrs Fowler who ran a boarding house in Dawlish, where he was reprimanded for shooting at fish in a local stream with an airgun. In intervals between such stays Ronnie would often dump his sons with their grandparents; and, as they grew older, they sometimes hitchhiked down to Parkstone of their own accord, weary of their neglected existence at home. Or they were sent to holiday schools, including one outside Bruton, in North Somerset, originally a field barracks, where they slept in tents recently occupied by soldiers, and the discipline was as harsh, and as apparently random, as in the army itself. On the night of 25 April 1942 the Germans launched a 'Baedeker' bombing raid on Bath,* only twenty-five miles to the north. The boys heard the distinctive roar of the bombers approaching and emerged from their tent to watch them passing overhead.

This was a rootless, itinerant existence. Like a soldier on the move, David learned techniques for making himself comfortable: picking out the best bed in the dormitory, fixing an eye on the most susceptible lady members of staff, getting to know the cook, and so on.

In the early summer of 1942 Ronnie volunteered his services as political agent to a young army officer (later a successful playwright), the Honourable William Douglas Home, standing in a by-election in Windsor. Recently the Cornwells had moved yet again, to a house in Stoke Poges, just outside the constituency. The seat had been made vacant by the death of the MP, a Conservative who had first been elected in 1922 and who had been returned unopposed in the last two elections. Though, in the candidate's own description, 'a Liberal of the old school', Ronnie showed no hesitation in pledging his support for Douglas Home, who was standing as an Independent Progressive. No Liberal candidate had come forward, under the terms of a pact made among the three major parties participating in the National Government, that for the duration of the war they would not contest by-elections against the incumbent party. As a result many wartime by-elections resulted in candidates being returned unopposed. But the pact did not prevent Independents and candidates from minor parties from standing.

* In 1942, incensed by an RAF attack on Lübeck, Hitler ordered that the Luftwaffe should launch retaliatory raids on historic British cities. It was said that these were selected according to their ratings in the Baedeker travel guides.

One curiosity of the election was that the Conservative candidate and his Independent challenger had been friends at Eton. Douglas Home was a younger brother of Lord Dunglass, Neville Chamberlain's parliamentary private secretary who had accompanied the Prime Minister to Munich to meet Hitler in 1938 (and who would eventually, as Alec Douglas-Home, become Prime Minister himself). Unlike his elder brother, William Douglas Home* was virtually a pacifist. He had been an idealistic appeaser before the war, and even now, in the middle of hostilities, he was still seeking an accommodation with Germany. Earlier in the year he had stood as an Independent candidate in a Glasgow by-election.

Ronnie organised a vigorous campaign, forming cells of supporters in each district, and ensuring that attendances at the meetings Douglas Home addressed grew to capacity as the campaign progressed, until it seemed possible that he might take the seat from the Conservatives. Against his better judgement, Douglas Home agreed to Ronnie's proposal that he accept offers of support from other Independent MPs, including the voluble member for Rugby, W. J. Brown. This proved an embarrassing mistake: Brown's vocal support for a 'Second Front'† contradicted everything that Douglas Home was standing for. In the Windsor poll he came a respectable second, losing by a margin of 2,000 votes.[20]

Douglas Home stood in several more by-elections during the war, each time unsuccessfully. In October 1944 he was court-martialled and cashiered for refusing to obey an order.‡ There was some speculation that he might stand in the general election of 1945: Ronnie, referred to as 'a close friend', would tell the *Sunday Express* that 'he will contest a seat as an independent, but I cannot say where'.[21]

* William omitted the hyphen from the family name.

† A section of British public opinion argued for a 'Second Front' in Europe to relieve the pressure on Russia as it fought the German invaders.

‡ Douglas Home was liaison officer with the German forces occupying the besieged town of Le Havre. The German commander's proposal to evacuate French civilians before the Allied bombardment began was rejected by his British counterpart. Douglas Home's refusal to obey an order sprang from his view that this decision was morally unacceptable. He told David that his commanding officer had threatened him at pistol-point.

Ronnie's renewed interest in politics may have been connected with his fear of imminent call-up. Intensive research on his behalf had revealed that political candidates could choose to be exempt from conscription. Though not strictly a reserved occupation, politics was considered 'work of national importance'. It is possible, therefore, that his involvement in the by-election was a dry run, in case he might want to take advantage of this loophole in the future. In August 1942, two months after the Windsor poll, he succeeded in deferring his call-up by pleading that he was essential to his business, only to be called up later in the year. He disposed of his half-share in Moore Medicinal Products for £1,500 and made ready to combat Hitler; in preparation for his coming ordeal, he took the unusual step of having a private's uniform made up in Savile Row. Fortunately he was required to serve only one day before being released to the reserve 'on compassionate grounds', following his plea that, as a single parent, he was needed at home.

For a while after that he traded under his own name, buying and selling 'general merchandise', much of it usually available only on the black market, including chocolate, Benzedrine inhalers, nylon stockings and ballpoint pens. When the school bursar, weary of the struggle to obtain settlement of the school fees, demanded payment up front, he received it in kind, in the form of dried fruit – figs, bananas and prunes – plus a case of gin.[22]

In April 1943 Ronnie was again summoned for military service, and this time was unable to defer it. After basic training, he transferred to the Royal Corps of Signals, but within a few months he had once more obtained his release on compassionate grounds. By this time he had moved yet again, to Carriden House, a substantial neo-Georgian property in Gerrards Cross. As Tony returned there one day he was greeted by a hail, and looked up to see his father leaning out of an upstairs window, alongside a smiling young woman. This was Jean Gronow (née Neal), a divorcee who worked for the BBC at Bush House as a studio manager on the European Service, broadcasting messages to resistance organisations in Europe. She shared a flat in Weymouth Mews with another young woman, where they entertained a string of male visitors, many of them foreigners exiled in London for the duration of the war. David was billeted there for a while, and took a strong dislike to one of these, the young Claus von Bülow.

Now in their early teens, the Cornwell boys were often left alone for days at a time, and ran a little wild as a result. David tells the worrying story of how they came across an abandoned goods wagon while exploring the untended common land beyond the large wooded garden at Carriden House. Parked near the rim of an old quarry, it was too tempting to resist. With a length of old iron, they levered it to the lip of the quarry and pushed it over the edge. As it crashed on to the quarry floor, a scream rang out. The boys fled in horror. They never knew who had screamed, and never asked.

For a while Ronnie and Jean shared Carriden House with Edward Ryder Richardson and his wife Glyn. Ryder Richardson, always known by Ronnie as Ryder, was the barrister who had unsuccessfully defended him in the mid-1930s; Ronnie took the boys to watch him plead in court, perhaps hoping that they might be inspired by what they saw. The Ryder Richardsons had two sons around the same age as David and Tony; the four boys would be 'allowed' to sleep in the garage, which in the eyes of the adults was a great romp. In fact the 'romping' seems to have taken place in the main house.

Jean and Ronnie were married on 21 December 1944, at Marylebone Town Hall. During the reception, held in a smart London hotel, two policemen arrived and took the groom outside. There was much whispering that Ronnie had been arrested, before he returned alone, beaming. Though Ronnie had yet again been called up, he served only a few weeks before requesting leave to contest the upcoming Chelmsford by-election as an Independent Progressive. The seat had become vacant as a result of the death of the sitting Conservative MP on active service. Under the terms of the wartime pact his successor benefited from the official backing of all three major parties participating in the coalition government, though each studied the by-election closely for clues about the mood of the electorate, aware that peace was not far off, when competitive politics would resume. The Conservative candidate was opposed by one standing on behalf of the new Common Wealth party, founded in 1942 by the former Liberal MP Sir Richard Acland and the left-wing maverick Tom Wintringham. Like the Conservative candidate, he was a young RAF officer.

Ronnie's participation threatened to turn a straight fight into a three-horse race. By standing for election, he ran the risk that his record might be exposed, though he seemed blind to this danger. The new candidate was 'a mystery' according to the Common Wealth spokeswoman Peggy Duff.[23] 'He has no real policy,'* she suggested to the local paper; 'his background is obscure, though he calls himself a "businessman".' This may have been a veiled threat.

Ronnie delayed his arrival in the constituency, pleading a severe attack of influenza, and then withdrew from the contest altogether five weeks before the poll, claiming he did not want to split the anti-Conservative vote – the very antithesis of the reason he had given for withdrawing in 1931. In the event, the Common Wealth candidate overcame a huge Conservative majority to win by 6,431 votes. This stunning result signalled the shift in public opinion away from the Conservatives and influenced the Labour Party to withdraw from the coalition government, precipitating a general election only ten weeks after the Chelmsford poll, in which Labour would win a landslide victory. Ronnie played a small part in this general election, acting as political agent for Edgar Granville, who stood successfully as a Liberal in the Eye Division of Suffolk, a seat he had represented as an Independent beforehand.

Ronnie was now free of military obligations. On his wedding certificate he had given his occupation as 'property & finance broker', and in his election literature he had defined his business as being 'connected with property and estate development'. Just as the war had presented opportunities, so would the peace.

Meanwhile David had discovered 'the fickleness of the fair sex' for himself. Towards the end of the war the boys were sent to another holiday school at Thorpeness, on the Suffolk coast. There he met a girl called Judy, who allowed him to row her around a boating lake in a small dinghy. Like David, Judy was twelve years old, though unlike him she was brazen. Back at school, he received from her through the post a cheque for a hundred kisses, 'payable on presentation'. David was appalled. He understood her

* Ronnie advocated a 'Three-Point Policy', as follows: '1. Full recognition of the part played by Russia in the defeat of Germany; 2. A vigorous agricultural policy to be in the forefront of our post-War plans; 3. Extensions of our social services, and provision of permanent homes at the earliest possible moment.'

motive only too well, for a Mr Lawry had told his pupils 'what girls are after' in a series of school lectures. She wanted to get pregnant by him during the next school holidays, so that he would have to marry her; then she would take all his money (two shillings a week), thereby holding him back from a fulfilling career. He hid the cheque, told nobody and awaited the holidays with dread. Back at Thorpeness he contrived to avoid Judy for the first week, until he met her coming out of church. To his eyes she looked about twenty.

'Did you get my cheque?' she asked. 'Well, don't try to cash it, or it'll bounce. Mickie got me first.'

David saw Mickie for the first time at the tennis courts the next day. He was short, foul-mouthed and spotty, and played a lousy game. Yet for years to come he would remain for David his archetypal supplanter. 'He was that robust Other Man who lacked all the delicate inhibitions which I had been taught to believe were synonymous with good breeding. He took what he wanted, as Judy did.'[24]

Encouraged by 'Crusoe' Robertson-Glasgow, David began filling exercise books with lurid short stories. In one of these, an heroic old racehorse expired after being ridden to victory by an unscrupulous jockey, who had loaded his whip with buckshot. 'I thought this the most moving tragedy I had ever read, let alone written,' David told an interviewer thirty years later. He persuaded the school secretary to type it out for him. Unfortunately she was discovered doing so. The headmaster returned the manuscript to its source, informing David that if he wanted to write 'trash' he should get it typed out at his own expense.

Summer term 1944 saw David elected to the school Literary Society. The Society's activities included readings (poetry from Keats, stories from *The Ingoldsby Legends* and Chesterton's 'Father Brown', Conan Doyle's 'The Speckled Band' and passages from Dickens), debates ('Town Life is preferable to Country Life'), picnic excursions on the river and dramatised play readings (Shaw's *Pygmalion* and Barrie's *The Admirable Crichton*). One of David's contemporaries remembers David's sophisticated vocabulary, which (so he subsequently surmised) had been acquired during these play-reading sessions. On the last day of term David was one of a quartet who recited 'The Walrus and the Carpenter' in front of the whole school. 'Alice would have known them anywhere,' commented the anonymous reviewer in the school magazine – presumably 'Crusoe'.

David was proving himself to be a skilful performer. That autumn, when bad weather kept the boys indoors, he gave an impromptu act in the gymnasium, taking the role of an American woman conducting a long-distance conversation with her husband, via a roller skate improvised as a telephone. According to the school magazine, this 'greatly entertained the house'. At the end of the Easter Term 1945 David played Captain Billy Bones in a production of *Treasure Island*. The school magazine described his performance as 'rollicking', while deploring his 'tendency to over-act'.

Another role he took was that of a police sergeant in a production of Erich Kästner's classic children's story *Emil and the Detectives*, anglicised to avoid any embarrassment over the use of German names and places. By now David, aged thirteen, had become a big fish within the small pond of St Andrew's: section leader of his house ('Blue'), a prefect and, in his final term, head of school, as Tony had been two years before.

In his penultimate term at St Andrew's, David, together with most of the other boys of his age-group, had been confirmed into the Church of England by the Bishop of Reading. Two years earlier Tony had undergone the same rite of passage. As a matter of course Robertson-Glasgow had asked their father beforehand whether the boys had been baptised. Ronnie had paused before replying. 'I think they were,' he said at last, 'but perhaps it wouldn't do any harm if you did it again.'

The celebrations marking the end of the war in Europe in early May 1945 took place just as St Andrew's was reassembling for the summer term. On VE Day itself a Thanksgiving service was held in the Chapel, though only fifty of the school's seventy-eight boys had arrived by then, and David was not among them; he was at a crammed party held in Ronnie's Conduit Street office, full of 'lovelies'. Somebody poured water from a window on the revellers in the street below, and a policeman came upstairs to remonstrate. Three days later a vast bonfire on the school lawn consumed an effigy of Adolf Hitler.

That month David sat the examination for a leaving scholarship from St Andrew's. Perhaps surprisingly, he did not perform well. Neither did he succeed in obtaining an entrance scholarship to Sherborne, though he was accepted there as an ordinary pupil, to start in September. In his testimonial

Robertson-Glasgow had assessed David's work as 'very steady – without brilliance!' He noted that David was 'weak at maths'. As for his character, the headmaster rated him 'good' for truthfulness, industry, obedience and general conduct. Concerning his leadership qualities, he wrote that 'he is beginning to be a most useful member of the school'. In a conclusion marked 'confidential', Robertson-Glasgow added, 'I don't like his father! The boy is a good lad, though, like his elder brother.'

David was more successful at cricket, topping the batting averages and captaining the 1st XI. On 21 July he captained the school for the last time in the Fathers' match. Tony appeared for the visitors, temporarily promoted to parental status; during his innings, according to the school magazine, he 'lashed out with controlled fury'. Despite this formidable onslaught, the 1st XI was victorious, by a margin of thirty runs. Ronnie, who had opened the batting for the Fathers, was out for a duck.

The housemaster at Sherborne sent a letter of welcome to David, who replied that he was 'very much looking forward' to going there. His letter was written in an informal, man-to-man style, though he was still only thirteen; reporting on the cricket season, for example, he referred to a match that his team had won easily, 'though after some absolutely frightful fielding!' His last sentence seemed less assured, however. 'Could you please tell me some of the routine and customs of your house, so that I shall be sufficiently prepared for next term?'[25]

3

God and Mammon

More than 1,300 years ago St Aldhelm became Bishop of Sherborne and founded a school where, according to legend, Alfred the Great was a pupil. For centuries this school was linked to the Benedictine abbey that still dominates the town. After the Dissolution of the Monasteries, it was refounded, like so many others across England, as a free grammar school for local boys. To this day Sherborne's anthem sings the praises of King Edward VI, who in 1550 graciously gave the school its charter ('Vivat Rex Edwardus Sextus! Vivat! Vivat! Vivat!'). By the mid-nineteenth century, dwindling student numbers and a dispirited staff prompted a transformation to a fee-paying boarding school. The public school that David attended from 1945 onwards is therefore comparatively modern. An historian of Sherborne refers to its establishment as 'an example of the rising educational expectations of the Victorian era, its high-mindedness mixed with a nose for business, the impact of the new railways, and, not least, the Victorian genius for creating new institutions and then pretending that they were, after all, very old'.[1]

The illusion is sustained by the fact that the school stands adjacent to the Norman abbey, on land that once belonged to the abbey's monastery. Its Victorian founders commandeered buildings associated with the abbey, and added new ones in a compatible architectural style. As it expanded, the school established boarding houses in the town, to accommodate the growing number of pupils: around 500 by the time David arrived in 1945, and still increasing. Under a forceful headmaster, Alexander Ross Wallace, Sherborne seemed in good health – though 'the Chief' feared for the future. Soon after David arrived, Wallace gave a solemn address to the boys. The newly elected Labour government, he announced with a choke in his thunderous voice, planned to abolish public schools. He spoke as if the world were about to end. The new Prime Minister, Clement Attlee, and many of his ministers were themselves public schoolboys, traitors to their class. You boys, he told them, should gird yourselves and wait bravely for the worst. You are the last of the Romans. The barbarians are at the gates.[2]

Sherborne celebrated values that seemed dated in democratic, post-war Britain. 'It is taken for granted that all boys will strictly observe the standards of behaviour of a gentleman,' read one of the school rules, published in January 1946.

'The Chief' was a big man, whose dynamism contrasted strongly with the lackadaisical approach of his predecessor. Indeed, in his very first term one housemaster had resigned after a minor row with the new headmaster; his body was subsequently washed up on the beach at Lyme Regis. Wallace characterised his own response to this tragedy as 'great agony of mind', but there was no doubt that his combative style antagonised some of his colleagues.[3] There was an inherent tension between the headmaster and the housemasters, who enjoyed considerable independence, collecting their own fees from the parents and running their houses as separate concerns. This separation between houses was intrinsic to the culture of the school. Members of different houses were not encouraged to mix; when David became friendly with a boy from another house, it was taken as a sign of incipient homosexuality.

Like the Robertson-Glasgows, Wallace was a high Anglican, whose religious belief was central to his life; in 1938 he had taken holy orders, and in 1942 he became a canon of Salisbury Cathedral. Striding across the Sherborne courts in clerical collar, mortarboard and gown, he resembled an active nineteenth-century don. Before the war he had established a link with a local community of Anglican Franciscans, based first at Batcombe and later at Cerne Abbas, where the occasional boy would be sent on retreat.

Unquestioning allegiance to the Empire was expected of all Shirburnians. 'The best life you can get is in the Colonial Service,' a careers adviser visiting the school told the boys. 'Of course, you've got to learn how to talk to the natives.' Under Canon Wallace's leadership the school continued to emphasise the public school ethos of duty, service (to the school, and by extension to the nation and to the Empire), fortitude, self-denial, fair play and physical courage. Pupils at Sherborne were being trained as leaders – in warfare above all. Military training with the junior division of the Officers' Training Corps (OTC) was compulsory, two afternoons a week, one in uniform and the other in plain clothes.

If 'games' were no longer, as they had been in the past, the only thing that mattered, it was still held that athletic competition was essential in developing 'character', which meant holding your ground without flinching, whether on the rugby field, in the boxing ring or on the field of combat.[4] 'We fought rugger wars almost literally to death,' David wrote thirty years afterwards. 'Boxing was obligatory and I was knocked out cold.' Around the end of his first year, David was summoned by his housemaster to explain why he wanted to give up boxing. 'People are saying that you're a funk,' the housemaster told him. David responded that he didn't mind what people said. 'I'm a pacifist,' he announced.

Like St Andrew's and every other school throughout Britain, Sherborne had been depleted by the war just ended. Almost one-third of the regular teaching staff had left to serve in the forces; many of these had not yet returned when David arrived. For obvious reasons it had been the younger and fitter masters who had left; those who had taken their place were often elderly, and not necessarily of the highest quality. To some extent the boys were able to exploit this. One of those brought back out of retirement to fill the gaps in the ranks was an elderly brigadier. 'Please, sir,' the boys would ask him, 'is it true that you were at the Battle of Ypres?'

'Well, yes, as a matter of fact I was,' the retired soldier confessed.

'Please, sir, what was it like?'

'I'll tell you exactly what happened,' started the brigadier, and continued for some time while the boys enjoyed a period of relaxation.

David's housemaster, R. S. (Stanley) Thompson, known to the boys as 'Thompers', was an awkward, balding man, another high Anglican, inflexible in his beliefs and inclined to be pompous in manner. In the mid-1930s, soon after Wallace had become headmaster, Thompson had arrived to take control of Westcott House, a much extended building several hundred yards from the main school site, the most distant of the boarding houses. By 1945 there were around sixty pupils at Westcott House, and as

Thompson seemed unable to turn anybody away the number grew every year, so that by the late 1940s it was becoming uncomfortably crowded. Thompson was forced to send some of his boys to board with families around the town; far from feeling exiled, they considered themselves privileged, delighted to escape from Westcott House's cold, noisy and smelly dormitories,* and the crushed scramble in the dining room at mealtimes. Worst was the tyranny of the prefects: whenever one of them yelled 'fag', the smaller boys near by scurried to his summons, and the last to arrive was punished with a chore: cleaning his shoes, tidying his study, cooking him toast on his gas range.[5]

It was Thompson whom Ronnie had met at a cricket match in Bruton early in the war, and with whom he had corresponded about sending both his sons to Sherborne. Thompson had been irritated when Ronnie had chosen to send Tony to Radley instead. This irritation developed into dislike, which increased with familiarity. David's school fees were always in arrears, a matter of personal concern to a housemaster, since the deficit came out of his pocket.† Ronnie innocently made matters worse by advising Thompson how he should run Westcott House as a more effective business. He may also have irritated Thompson by carelessly addressing his letters to 'Westgate House'.

David would provide a recognisable portrait of Thompson in *A Perfect Spy*. 'Mr Willow was a big homely man in tweeds and a cricket tie, and the Christian plainness of his home after Ascot filled Pym at once with an assurance of integrity.' Pym is David's imagined self, and Willow's loathing for Pym's corrupt father is immediately apparent, as is his determination to beat the bad out of the boys under his care.[6] But here the novel deviates from life, for David was never beaten by Thompson. He was not the sort of boy to be beaten by a housemaster: more likely to be invited to tea.

* There was no heating in the dormitories, and the upper windows were left open throughout the year. Each morning at the bell the boys were made to take a cold shower.

† Ronnie seems to have failed to pay the first term's school fees, and by 22 March 1947 the outstanding account stood at £71 12s 10d, against annual boarding fees of £165.

David's autobiographical fiction provides clues to the mysteries of his past, but such clues can be misleading. Even when describing real experience, he is doing so from a different perspective. The satirical, self-mocking attitude of the fifty-something-year-old John le Carré should be distinguished from the much less confident, less detached mental state of the fifteen-year-old David Cornwell.

In general it was the head of house (the most senior schoolboy) rather than the masters who beat the boys, having first obtained Thompson's permission. Punishment was administered in a silent ritual that accentuated the terror of the regime. In the early evening the younger boys would be seated in the day room, quietly doing their homework, when the door opened. A prefect would enter, identify the miscreant and march him off to a washroom, without a word being uttered. There the unhappy boy would be made to lower his head into a filthy hand-basin; clutching both taps with throbbing hands while his forelock hung limp, he would be flogged with a swishy bamboo in the shape of a walking-stick, until it was judged that he had expiated his crimes. This happened once to David, and even twenty-five years later he still burned for revenge.[7] According to him, the long list of beatable offences included untidiness, and failing to put the Bible on top of the pile of books you were carrying to school. Some of David's contemporaries say that this is an exaggeration; but one remembers that you could get a black mark for 'almost anything', and that three black marks meant being beaten. Others say that this too was an exaggeration, and that beatings resulted from a large accumulation of black marks.

Like Wallace, Thompson was a man of deep Christian faith. Some boys found his concern for their moral well-being intrusive. In the late evenings he would summon them individually to his study in their pyjamas and dressing gowns, to conduct embarrassing conversations about masturbation and the 'facts of life'. Usually the interview would conclude with a prayer. At moments of particular intensity, Thompson would put his arms around the boy and plant a fervent kiss on his forehead. David never forgot the texture of Thompson's thick tweed jacket as he was enfolded in such embraces.

Ronnie may have unwittingly encouraged Thompson's pastoral interest in his son. Towards the end of David's first year at Sherborne he wrote to the housemaster commenting on 'the very great improvement in David's outlook this term'. He was sure, he continued, that 'you must have given him a good talking to, with very profitable results'. In his first term Jean had written to Thompson expressing her conviction that 'your influence on David will be invaluable. Needless to say he wraps me around his little finger and I have to guard constantly against spoiling him!'[8]

Thompson's rigid and uncompromising beliefs left little scope for disagreement. He would not take contradiction, not even from his colleagues. According to his deputy, the house tutor Peter Currie, 'Thompers was the worst possible housemaster for David,' who was noticeably more independent than most of the boys, as well as being more sensitive. But the looming confrontation was not immediately apparent. Indeed, one might say that at the start David was one of Thompson's best prospects: intelligent, artistic and athletic. He was no longer the vulnerable little boy who needed protection from his elder brother; he was growing into a good-looking young man, with startlingly clear eyes and thick fair hair, parted at the side. By comparison with his peers David seemed mature both physically and psychologically, successful in his academic work and on the sports field (he was captain of the junior cricket team), witty and popular with his schoolmates, a charismatic individual apparently at ease with himself – though guarded about his family.

To Gerald Peacocke, who studied School Certificate (the equivalent of GCSEs) alongside David, he was almost unfairly gifted. It seemed that he could turn his hand to anything, and the only question was: which gift would he fulfil? Peacocke remembers David's cartoon displayed on the classroom wall, which depicted Hannibal's army, complete with elephants, crossing the Rhône and routing the Gauls drawn up on the far bank. Possibly this inspired the classics master's pithy report: 'Full of ideas, but many of them not Latin'.

Peacocke had come to England in 1945 from German-speaking Switzerland, where he had been marooned for the duration of the war, after being sent there in 1938 for the sake of his health. Cut off from his family, and under the remote care of the British Consul in Zurich, Peacocke had spent the war in St Moritz, where he had formed a lifelong friendship with one of the Badrutt sons, and become friendly too with a boy from Germany; these two played together happily while elsewhere their fathers and uncles were trying to kill one another. For David, Peacocke's story brought back memories of that glorious holiday in St Moritz before the war, the last with his mother. Perhaps he stored away the image of an isolated child, confined to a half-empty Swiss sanatorium, to fetch it out again half a lifetime later when he came to write the story of Karla's daughter Tatiana in his novel *Smiley's People*.

David was especially friendly with Robin Cooke, who had arrived at Westcott House late one night, and awoke the next morning to find himself in a dormitory, surrounded by strangers. Cooke's father, an Indian civil servant, had died suddenly, and his mother had sent him back to England, while choosing to remain in India herself. Perhaps his lack of parents was one of the reasons why he and David were drawn to each other. Whatever the reason, they became close friends, and Cooke would spend many of his holidays at David's house. An affectionate playfulness characterised their relations; David suggested that they should call each other 'Tig', a nickname that stuck. Cooke proved to be a fine actor, who 'walked away' with the school elocution prize and took leading parts in plays and play-readings. To Gerald Peacocke, he and David seemed very sophisticated, the *jeunesse dorée* of their generation at Sherborne.

Thompson's high hopes for David are obvious in his house reports. 'After a somewhat uncertain start he has settled down to a quiet and steady outlook,' he wrote at the end of David's first term at Sherborne. 'He is intelligent and very responsive and straightforward. If he keeps his head he should do very well here.' At the end of the second term Thompson assessed him as 'a lively and interesting person . . . apt to be a bit domineering and obstinate among his contemporaries'; and at the end of his first year he summarised David as 'a very cheerful and pleasant boy, whose main problem at the moment is how to control his rather nervous temperament'.

David's outward poise was a mask for his inner unrest. This was a motherless boy, uneasy about his father, searching for something worthwhile, something to believe in. He confessed his disquiet to Thompson, who steered him towards Father Algy Robertson of the Franciscans. Thus began a struggle for David's soul. In keeping with the teachings of their founder, the Franciscans emphasised poverty, simplicity and ascetism, not virtues that Ronnie celebrated. Father Algy was a powerful preacher, whose mission was to recruit public schoolboys and undergraduates into the monastic life – 'the Christian equivalent', as David later perceived, 'of the secret Communist recruiters who threw their net over the likes of Kim Philby in the thirties'. Prompted by Father Algy, David signed up for a series of three-day retreats. In farm buildings on a Dorset hillside he mouthed plainsong, breathed incense and tried to feel holy. The part he enjoyed most was looking after the white rabbits, until he discovered that they were being bred to make gloves. Denis Marsh, the Father Guardian, was his confessor. In response to David's anxious questioning about Ronnie, the Father Guardian rather unhelpfully advised him to endure his natural father as a sacrifice.[9]

By the middle of David's second year a note of caution entered Thompson's reports: 'I am all in favour of originality, but as a means to an end, not as an end in itself,' he commented. 'I do not think he has lost his sense of proportion yet, but he must guard against it.' No doubt Thompson was responding to the recent reports on David's work, several of which had used the word 'original' in assessing his performance. David's English master wrote that 'at present his work is largely experimental', a description that was clearly not intended as a commendation. 'When he settles down he will do very well,' the report continued. The same master used the term 'experimental' again in his report at the end of the summer term, adding, 'I can never be sure of results.'

David's verse, which appeared regularly in the *Shirburnian*, could hardly be styled experimental, showing as it did the influence of such diverse masters as Gray, Betjeman and A. A. Milne. His poems were generally comic, or at least mock-heroic, like his 'Ode to Gertrude', whom he addressed as 'thou withering rose of love, false vegetable of passion':

> For thou with reckless perfidy encouraged my elation,
> Since first the fates united us upon Victoria Station.
> And now with deadly sword I pierce my broken heart yet through;
> My loving-kindness sheds its oyster's tears anew,
> That e'er Victoria Station formed my only Waterloo.

In the Vth form, David was taught English by a younger master, recently demobbed, called Robin Atthill, who would publish a volume of his own poems in 1947. Atthill was more appreciative of David's talents than his predecessors. 'He is not afraid to experiment and the result has been some very promising work,' he reported at the end of his first term teaching David. 'He has a sensitive and original mind – a real artist with words,' he wrote at the end of the year.

Atthill encouraged play-reading, at which David was generally acknowledged to be outstanding. On the other hand, his performance as the soothsayer in a school production of *Julius Caesar*, though 'clearly played', was criticised by the reviewer in the *Shirburnian* as not conveying 'the quality of mystery and tension which Shakespeare surely intended that it should'.[10]

In 1948 David would be awarded a school prize for a long free-verse poem called 'The Dream of the Deserted Island' – an island deserted by the god Pan. He had longed for the prize 'more than anything else I had heard of, even girls'. In later life David would cringe to be reminded of this mannered, adolescent work, but according to the adjudicator Littleton Powys, 'it showed great imagination and was full of pleasing poetic imagery'. He praised it as 'a joy to read with its musical rhythm and mastery of vowel sounds'.[11]

Littleton Powys, a former headmaster of Sherborne preparatory school, was one of the Powys family, brother to the poet Llewelyn and the novelists John Cowper and Theodore Francis, all of whom had been pupils at Sherborne. He wrote David an encouraging letter, urging him to 'write your heart out', and invited him to tea. Powys showed David a letter from one of his brothers, to whom he had sent the poem.* 'The boy has IT,' the brother had written, underlining 'IT' three times.

Fortified by this support, David read 'The Dream of the Deserted Island' to his peers at the school's annual Commemoration. In middle age he pictured his adolescent self, 'convinced that the new Keats was making his mark on the Barbarians; while they, no doubt, thought how nice it would be to strangle me'.[12] The climax of the Commemoration came in a speech by Sir Norman Birkett KC, whose participation had been secured

* According to David's later account, the enthusiastic letter had been written by Llewelyn Powys, but this cannot be right, as he had died in 1939.

by his old friend Ronald Cornwell, the man whom he had prosecuted for fraud fourteen years earlier.

The award of the poetry prize to David for 'The Dream of the Deserted Island' had been opposed by some masters who believed that boys should be discouraged from writing poems that neither rhymed nor scanned; they changed the rules to exclude such work in the future. In response David, together with several of his fellow schoolboy poets, wrote a defiant letter of protest to the *Shirburnian*.

> We feel it is a tragedy that we should be censured for writing free verse for the prize poem competition, and that in future, without exception, only poems in the conventional forms of rhymes and metre ought to be entered. Poetry is an expression of thoughts that cannot always be contained by feet and regularity, and it is an injustice to a poet to force his hand, and demand that he write in a traditional style. The future poets of Sherborne* should be allowed and encouraged to express themselves in the form that their thoughts demand, and remain unfettered by the necessity of subjecting them to a style that is both incongruous with, and unsuited for, modern ideas.[13]

David's proficiency in German reflected his interest in, and feeling for, language in general; but it was spurred too by his developing interest in German literature and thought. He was influenced by his German master Frank King, who had taught him that 'the love we have for other languages intensifies and explains the love we have for our own'. To possess another language, King told the boys, is to possess another soul (a saying attributed to Charlemagne). He was always at pains to remind his pupils that, whatever the crimes of the Nazi period, 'there was another Germany, a decent one, far removed from the one we thought we knew about, and that was the Germany we would be able to explore once we understood its language'.[14] The message sank deep into David, and surfaces in book after

* Among the past poets of Sherborne was Cecil Day-Lewis, who had been a pupil at the school just after the First World War.

book. 'Nothing I have ever written in my life has been free of the German influences of my youth,' he wrote recently.[15]

There was also an element of contrariness in David's attraction to German culture, of course. While almost everybody around him was expressing bigoted dislike of all things German, David was instinctively drawn the other way.

David's aptitude for languages was obvious too in his French classes. One of his contemporaries remembers an occasion when the master was preparing them for the oral examination in School Certificate; he wrote on the blackboard a number of questions in French, of the kind that were liable to be asked, and then required each pupil to give his own answer in the same language. One such question was 'Qu'est-ce que c'est, le métier de votre père?' This boy listened intently for David's answer, because he had heard from his own father, a chartered surveyor who knew the commercial property market well, that Cornwell Senior had a reputation as 'a bit of a vagabond' – though he had given no details and warned his son not to mention this in the school. When his turn came, David said: 'Mon père s'employe aux occupations nombreuses: il est un petit peu homme d'affaires, un petit peu politicien, un petit peu voyageur . . .' His listener admired the adroitness, as well as the fluency, of this response.

The late 1940s were Ronnie's golden years, when he lived without restraint; when he rode in comfortable, chauffeur-driven limousines with personalised number plates, beginning with RC 1; when he owned a string of racehorses; when he was a regular at the Goat in Clifford Street and the Albany Club in Old Burlington Street, where showbiz met the underworld, and off-course bookmakers operated illegally but openly, despite the presence of off-duty police officers, while cheerful prostitutes offered their services in upstairs rooms; when he played snooker with music-hall stars, who would stop the show to greet him when he arrived late at the Victoria Palace theatre ('Why, it's Ronnie Cornwell. Hello, Ronnie'); when he held court to enthralled suburban neighbours and less respectable business associates; when he contrived to escape 'Austerity Britain' on exotic foreign holidays; and when he hosted lively parties for a startling array of guests, including senior officials and civil servants, permanent under-secretaries, members of parliament, peers of the realm, champion jockeys and snooker stars, bookies, film stars, radio stars, members of the Crazy Gang, whichever cricket teams happened to be touring, directors of Arsenal Football Club, judges, barristers, senior police officers and members of Scotland Yard's Flying Squad, and a hand-picked selection of 'lovelies', mainly dance hostesses from Churchill's and the Astor nightclubs.[16] Ronnie was everybody's fixer, 'seeing people right', finding attractive and compliant young women for his influential contacts, ensuring that those found drunk at the scene of a car accident were not prosecuted, or if they were, that evidence was produced clearing them of any liability.

In such society David learned that early sophistication which can pass for maturity. He could be relied upon to look after his elders, often staying up late into the night to serve the drinks, jumping to his feet when Ronnie tapped on his empty glass with his fingernail. 'Get your old man another glass of Drambuie, old son, there's a good fellow . . .'

Ronnie encouraged his guests to entertain the gathering with witty anecdotes and quickfire gags. ('What's a Grecian urn?' 'I don't know.' 'Forty bob a week.') Knowing David to possess a precocious talent for storytelling and especially for mimicry, his father would make him perform before the assembled company. ('Son, come over here. Tell these people that story you heard the other day.') The professional funny men present did not always appreciate being upstaged by this young amateur. After one of David's comic turns, the comedian Jack Train, famous as 'Colonel Chinstrap' in the 1940s comedy *ITMA*, muttered *sotto voce*, 'I could tell that story and make it funny.'

By his own admission, David was a show-off. Half a lifetime later, in an attempt to explain why he felt the need to make people laugh, he quoted Frankie Howerd: 'All my life I've been terrified of ridicule.' It might seem odd for someone who felt this way to want to perform, but he provided an explanation. 'If you're growing up in a chaotic world without reason, your instinct is to become a performer and control the circumstances around you. You lead from weakness into strength, you have an undefended back.'[17]

Though he had never progressed beyond the rank of private during his short army career, Ronnie allowed himself to be known as 'Colonel Cornwell' (or Cornhill) in the shadier parts of the West End in the years after the war. With characteristic cheek he affected to be embarrassed by this title. 'Colonel?' he would say. 'What's all this about *Colonel*? Don't be so damn foolish. We're all civilians now.'[18]

After the war Ronnie had resumed trading as R. Cornwell & Co., operating from an office at 91 Regent Street, W1. Later, as his business empire expanded, he would move into 51 Mount Street, in the heart of Mayfair, taking over more and more of the building until eventually he occupied it all, from attic to basement. His practice was essentially the same as it had been in the 1930s, but on a larger scale. He began with a spectacular coup: he bought a property company for £90,000 and sold it again for £105,000. There was no need for him to raise the purchase price, as both the purchase and the sale took place on the same day. Ronnie had only to produce the deposit of £1,000 to make an instant profit of £15,000. This provided him with the capital to start buying property to rent, usually in blocks ranging from three or four houses to as many as a hundred at a time. Having bought a block of houses, his usual practice would be to create leases and then sell them on at a profit to one of his companies, while retaining the freeholds and selling these separately. The company would then mortgage the property, raising capital that could then be used to fund further purchases. Following the principle of his first big strike, he would try to set up these transactions in advance, so that they took place simultaneously. Between 1945 and 1950, he acquired approximately 4,000 houses, in more than 180 transactions. By October 1951, he had accumulated a personal fortune estimated at £191,000 – the equivalent of £13 million in today's money.

One problem was that the government, as part of its programme of austerity, had set a limit on borrowing of £50,000, beyond which any transaction required Treasury consent. To breach this limit without such permission was a criminal offence. In 1947 Ronnie was twice convicted (in seven cases) of exceeding these limits without consent, and fined accordingly. To overcome this obstacle he created an empire of separate companies with such names as Universal Trading Corporation Limited, supposedly independent of him, using a system of trusted nominees, just as he had done before the war. One of his confederates, Arthur Lowe, was later shown to be a director of no fewer than fifty companies forming part of the Cornwell group.

An underlying principle of the operation was that when the time was right the houses would be sold, either to the existing tenants or to new buyers for development once vacant possession had been obtained. This proved more difficult than anticipated, some tenants having to be 'persuaded' to move to other premises. Ronnie took the view that sooner or later there would be some increase in rent, and therefore some appreciation in the value. Things did not work out that way. Moreover, the rents often proved insufficient to meet the outgoings. Ronnie had personally guaranteed all the mortgages, the guarantees eventually totalling almost £1.5 million.

Whatever difficulties might lie ahead, Ronnie was determined to enjoy himself while he could. He ordered gin by the crate, and Trumper's hair-lotion in cartons of two dozen each. He opened an account at Harrods. A Bentley was delivered, after one of Ronnie's companies (Woodville Developments Limited) had paid a £500 deposit. In the late 1940s, he ran a small farm in Hampshire, and though it was soon disposed of, the concept of owning a farm would remain in his mind as an ideal, a haven when other forms of business became too difficult.

Soon after the end of the war Ronnie returned in triumph to St Moritz, then rapidly regaining the glamour of its 1920s heyday. An habitué of post-war St Moritz, the Earl of Kimberley, remembered it as 'a wonderful place to be: lush, smart, fashionable, full of beautiful people, a magnet for the rich and famous, a marvellous playground, the glossiest of social life. And, oh yes, a paradise for philanderers and affairs.'[19]

Ronnie brought with him a riotous group of jockeys and other sportsmen and women, members of the Court, their friends and their friends' friends. Once again, he was welcomed by Herr Badrutt, who had been persuaded to grant unlimited credit to his English guests. There would be no difficulty with currency restrictions, because Ronnie had contrived that the other members of his party could settle their bills with him in pounds, which he would then exchange for Swiss francs via a helpful contact at the Embassy in London.[20] Though illegal, such arrangements were common for wealthy Britons. As Kimberley explained, there were ways around currency difficulties 'if you knew the ropes – via head porters at top London hotels'.

As he had done before the war, Ronnie enjoyed himself in uninhibited style, donning a false wig and beard for a party in which all the men were required to wear at least a moustache. He was generous with the hotel's credit, even endowing a Cornwell Cup for Curling, which he presented with some ceremony.[21] And while Ronnie was sliding curling stones across the ice, David learned to ski.

Ronnie always kept a lookout for possible 'marks', and he soon got alongside the free-spending Kimberley, who was induced to cash several cheques for him. Predictably these bounced when the Earl later presented them to pay a currency fine. Back in London, Kimberley sought out Ronnie at his West End office, which he would later portray as having 'brass plaques right down to the jambs on each side of the main entrance, with Cayman Islands and other dodgy tax haven addresses'. He found Ronnie nursing a glass of brandy and smoking an enormous cigar, his feet up on his red-leather desk, playing centrepiece to a quartet of telephones, red, white, blue and green. 'You owe me five hundred quid,' Kimberley told Ronnie, threatening to have him beaten up if the money was not repaid. The Earl's posthumously published memoirs do not reveal the outcome.[22] Possibly Ronnie was induced to open the office safe, which often held surprisingly large amounts of cash.

Frank Cornwell had died suddenly in 1946, leaving a considerable sum, though much less than he might have done had he not been repeatedly required to bail out his son. Ronnie and his sister Ella were joint executors of their father's will. Ella struggled to resist pressure from her brother for access to funds from their father's estate: David's cousin can remember his mother collapsing in tears after one of their executors' meetings.

Earlier that year Jean had given birth to her first child, a son whom they named Rupert. In December, she and Ronnie sailed on the *Queen Mary* to New York, where they were photographed sitting alongside Sugar Ray Robinson in his Harlem nightclub. This was at a time when, because of currency restrictions, the average Englishman had about as much chance of going to America as he had of visiting the North Pole.[23] As so often with Ronnie, the trip was not purely for pleasure: he was developing a business connection, having set his sights on expansion into the New World. He aspired to be a tycoon, with interests spanning the globe, though in reality his business empire consisted of little more than short-term fixes and one-off deals, many of them shady in character. Some of his enterprises had an element of the absurd. At some stage, for example, he bought the patent in a device for peeling oranges, a strange-looking instrument shaped like a dagger. Another bizarre money-making scheme was to corner the market in Christmas crackers by buying up surplus stock in January, when the price was at its lowest. In those days crackers were sold from barrows in the street. Ronnie stored his stock in a cellar and waited until December, before placing an advertisement in a London evening paper. The next day the street outside his West End office was thronged by clamorous barrow boys, to the astonishment of the passers-by. David helped his father to complete the transactions on the doorstep.

As quickly as money came his way, Ronnie found ways to spend it – on racehorses, for example. Typically, he sought the advice of the greatest jockey of them all, Gordon Richards, in deciding which horses to buy, and hired another former jockey, Billy Griggs, as trainer. He named his first horse Prince Rupert, after his infant son: subsequent horses were named Dato, after his sons David and Tony; Rose Sang, after his redheaded daughter Charlotte, born in 1949; and Tummy Tunmers, after the house he moved to in the late 1940s. Ronnie had his own colours, chosen by Jean: red, with white chevrons and striped sleeves, and a red and white quartered cap. Gordon Richards rode for him on a number of occasions, as did the young Lester Piggott; David remembers coming across the apprentice jockey dressed in Ronnie's colours at Chester, reclining in the straw of a horsebox and reading the *Beano*.

Keeping racehorses was an expensive pursuit, but it had its compensations. Years later, Jean would list for her daughter some of the pleasures of being married to Ronnie: 'putting on my mink coat, while your father dressed in top hat and tails; climbing into the Bentley while the chauffeur held the door open for us; being driven to Ascot; admiring our horse in the ring and chatting to the jockeys; the excitement of watching our own horse race, and the glamour of the owners' enclosure . . .' From time to time Ronnie was able to defray some of his expenses by manipulating the odds. In 1947, for example, David was despatched to Newmarket, where Prince Rupert was running, with a briefcase containing several hundred pounds in cash. Before the race the horse was backed from 33–1 to 100–9, which suggested to informed observers that a great deal of money had been placed on him in the on-course market. After Prince Rupert had won the race by a neck, David collected his winnings and left the course with a briefcase stuffed with banknotes. On the train back to London he was accosted by a bookie. 'Are you Ronnie Cornwell's boy?' David admitted that he was. 'Well, watch it, son.' David handed over the briefcase to his father at the Mount Street office. Ronnie carefully counted the cash before locking it away.

Around this time Ronnie moved again, to Tunmers, a 1930s mansion set in nine acres of land adjoining a golf course in Chalfont St Peter, Buckinghamshire. Tony knew this as 'the beautiful house', as it seemed to have everything the heart could desire. Ronnie soon settled comfortably into the local community, becoming vice-president of the South Buckinghamshire Liberals and president of the Chalfont Cricket Club, for whom he recruited Learie Constantine as an occasional player. He cultivated business contacts in local golf clubs. Ronnie became a member of the committee of the Albany Club Sports Society, which in 1949 presented a cheque for £8,000 to His Royal Highness the Duke of Edinburgh, in his capacity as patron of the National Playing Fields Association. In Pathé News footage of the presentation ceremony, Ronnie can be seen in the background, apparently trying to elbow his way alongside the future Queen's husband.

One summer holiday Ronnie despatched his sons on a commercial mission to Paris. They were to call on the Panamanian Ambassador, to whom Ronnie had apparently been shipping bottles of unbranded Scotch whisky under diplomatic protection. The Ambassador, he explained, forwarded the bottles to his own country, again under diplomatic protection, now bearing whichever labels he considered most suitable, for sale at a fat profit. As the scheme had been running for some time, Ronnie indicated that there should be a substantial sum of money to be collected, of which the boys could help themselves to the first £50 to spend as they liked in Paris. And while they were there, he continued, they could collect his golf clubs, which he had left at the George V hotel.

Tony and David called on the Ambassador, a middle-aged playboy, who took them to dinner in a nightclub, where he and his glamorous wife sang Russian love songs; but no money was forthcoming. On the contrary, the Ambassador claimed to have paid Ronnie upfront for the whisky, and to be still waiting for the first consignment. The boys apologised and left. Next day they set out on their second errand. At the George V they discovered that Ronnie had left the golf clubs there as surety for an unpaid bill, a detail that he had failed to mention in his briefing: the manager refused to release the clubs until the account was settled. It was a bad moment for the boys, who feared for their own liberty. From a telephone box they called Ronnie's Mayfair office (now at 13a Old Burlington Street), only to hear him explain down the line that it was all a misunderstanding. Now almost penniless, the brothers eked out the remaining three days in Paris alongside the vagrants under a bridge over the Seine, subsisting on baguettes and cheap red wine.[24]

In May 1948 Ronnie threw a party at Tunmers for the touring Australian cricket team, known as 'the Invincibles' because they were seemingly unbeatable. Their arrival in England had been keenly anticipated, especially as their captain Don Bradman had made it known that this would be his farewell international tour. For English cricket enthusiasts this would be the last opportunity to watch the batsman widely acknowledged to be the greatest ever. 'Crusoe' Robertson-Glasgow expressed a widespread sentiment when he wrote in his newspaper column, 'We want him to do well. We feel we have a share in him. He is more than Australian. He is a world batsman.' As well as Bradman, there were plenty of other star players in the Australian team, including several outstanding batsmen, the vice-captain Lindsay Hassett, Arthur Morris, Sid Barnes and Neil Harvey, and the fiery fast bowling attack of Bill Johnston, Keith Miller and Ray Lindwall. The tour party docked at Tilbury in mid-April to a resounding welcome. On landing, Bradman announced a gift of 17,000 food parcels from the state of Victoria to the people of Britain, where rationing would continue until 1954. Despite their on-field dominance and a succession of one-sided victories, the touring team attracted record crowds and unprecedented media interest. Bradman received hundreds of personal letters every day, and one of his dinner speeches was broadcast live on radio, causing the BBC to postpone the news bulletin. Ronnie had 5,000 tulips planted in the garden at Tunmers in anticipation of the Australians' arrival.

The party was a riotous success. For Tony and David one highlight was witnessing the handshake between Don Bradman and Gordon

Richards, the greatest of all batsmen and the greatest of all jockeys. Frolics continued late into the night, with Hassett (who had taken a shine to Jean) performing an impromptu striptease on the kitchen table. Several of the Australians stayed overnight, and Ronnie took them off to play golf the next morning.

For the Cornwell boys, this had been an unmissable opportunity to meet the uncrowned champions of world cricket. Afterwards, when David casually mentioned at Sherborne that the entire Australian team had been guests at his house, the other boys were open-mouthed. In normal circumstances boarders were not allowed home in term-time, but David had obtained a special dispensation to come up to London at the weekend in order to attend the party. Ronnie wrote to Canon Wallace beforehand expressing his gratitude 'for the concession you make in this case', and promising that David would return to Sherborne by the four o'clock train on Sunday.[25]

It is possible that this dispensation annoyed Thompson, especially as Ronnie seems to have gone above his head in writing directly to the headmaster; and it followed recent friction between the two men over David's absence from school. There had been a skirmish between them when it seemed possible that David might not return by the start of the spring term. Boarders were required to begin each term on a Friday. A letter from Ronnie explained that David and his brother had been 'invited to stay with friends in Basel for a matter of ten days or a fortnight', and referred to the possibility that David might return to school a day late for the new term, that is on the Saturday. In fact these 'friends' were business contacts, the father a manufacturer of soaps and other chemical products whom Ronnie was cultivating. Thompson had replied by telegram, insisting that David return on time, and followed this up with what seems to have been a stiff reprimand. A second, apologetic letter from Ronnie three days later contained an assurance that David would return 'strictly in accordance with school requirements'. He wanted Thompson to know that the holiday had been arranged without consulting David or his brother, 'but simply with a desire that they should avail themselves of an invitation they received from friends in Switzerland'. Evidently Thompson wrote again to express his high hopes for the boy, because Ronnie wrote a third letter a few days later, affirming that he too hoped that David would 'justify all the potentialities that you feel'.[26]

Both Cornwell boys were good cricketers, Tony exceptionally so, good enough to play for Dorset in the Minor Counties Championship. Ronnie saw him as a future England fast bowler, and somehow arranged for the famous Bedser twins, Alec and Eric, to give him private coaching in the nets at the Oval. This was like arranging for Don Bradman to give him batting lessons. Indeed, Bradman credited Alec Bedser with bowling the finest ball ever to take his wicket in his long and illustrious career.

From time to time Ronnie would arrive at Radley or Sherborne to watch a match. In the summer of 1947, for example, he announced to Thompson his plans to come down to Sherborne with Jean and a carload of friends for the annual cricket match against Radley. Tony would be captaining the visitors, and Ronnie hinted that David might be picked as wicketkeeper for the home side. He grandly offered to entertain both teams to dinner in a restaurant after the match. Disappointingly it was cancelled, when a case of infantile paralysis (polio) caused the whole school to be placed in quarantine.

To David, Ronnie had become an embarrassment, simultaneously flamboyant and not quite the thing, arriving at school to collect him at the weekend in the Bentley and offering to take his schoolfellows out to lunch or dinner, while failing to pay the school fees on time. 'Is it true that your father keeps racehorses?' asked an exasperated Thompson.

In his housemaster's report at the end of the 1948 spring term Thompson wrote that David 'is going though an effervescent stage in his general outlook and he needs a calm and controlled mind if he is to solve his problems satisfactorily; and a sympathetic patience from others'. Thompson and his family often invited boys to join them at their holiday home in North Cornwall; he suggested that David might spend the Easter break with them there. A curt reply from Jean suggests that she thought this suggestion inappropriate. She thanked Thompson for his kind invitation, but explained that she had already made arrangements for David's holidays.[27] A letter from Ronnie to Thompson written during the Easter vacation refers to 'David's possible visit to America under the auspices of the English-Speaking Union'.[28] This suggestion may have antagonised Thompson further. Perhaps he felt his grip on David slipping. When the term resumed, he increased the pressure. During one of their intense, late-night conversations, David confessed to finding a disturbing contrast between home and school. He feared that if he stayed at Sherborne he might 'lose' his family.[29] Thompson told the boy that he must choose between God and Mammon. It was obvious to David that 'Mammon' meant Ronnie.*

One episode in particular was troubling David. It seems that Ronnie was going through a bad patch, his whole edifice tottering. During the holidays he had ordered his sons to reassure an elderly neighbour, Sir Eric Ansorge, who lived across the road from the Cornwells. He was a former colonial administrator from the Indian Civil Service who had retired to Chalfont St Peter after serving thirty-five years in Bengal, a lepidopterist who kept his collection of butterflies and other insects and spiders in glass-covered drawers. He and his wife were on friendly terms with the Cornwell children, particularly Tony, now doing National Service in the RAF before going up to Cambridge, where Sir Eric had been an undergraduate some forty years earlier. 'Get yourselves over to Sir Eric's house,' Ronnie had barked down the telephone, 'and tell him everything's all right.'

'How all right?' the boys had enquired.

'All right, for God's sake! Don't shilly-shally! Tell him if he kicks up a stink he'll spoil everything. It's going to be all right. The cheque's on its way.'

Reluctantly the boys had called on the Ansorges, and sipped their sherry, while Sir Eric and his wife explained their fears. They were anxious about the capital that they had entrusted to Ronnie. He had offered to invest this on their behalf, claiming to be able to obtain for them a much better rate of interest than they could find elsewhere. The sum that they had handed into his care represented most of their life-savings. Could

* In David's novel *The Naïve and Sentimental Lover* (p. 121), Aldo Cassidy, who has been a pupil at Sherborne, recalls how his housemaster had told him that his father was the devil, and that his father had said very much the same about his housemaster; and that he 'had found it very hard to know whom, if either, to believe'.

the boys assure them, from everything they knew of their father, that he could be trusted with their money? The elderly couple phrased their question politely, but they could not conceal their terror that they might have lost the savings on which they depended for their security.* Being faced with this frightened elderly couple had obliged the boys to confront the reality of Ronnie's business practices. He bullied them into making several more reassuring visits across the road before they told him that they couldn't go again.[30]

At the end of the 1948 summer term Thompson congratulated David on 'an excellent report'. Even so, he continued, 'I do not feel that he is happy and I wish I knew how to help him solve his fundamental problems.' The headmaster echoed Thompson in complimenting David on 'a very creditable and successful term'. He was sorry to hear that David was unhappy, 'and I wonder why for he has all the ingredients: good brains, poetic and artistic sense, good health, the high regard of the whole community. What is lacking, I wonder?'

David was struggling with what he would later term 'an unbearable moral conflict'. He was torn between loyalty towards his father on the one hand, and what the school told him was doing the right thing on the other. Sherborne instilled in its pupils ethics of honour, decency and duty, and never telling fibs. By contrast, Ronnie co-opted his sons as accomplices, so that they were covering up his deceits, making excuses for him, keeping creditors at bay. At school David was being trained to run an empire; at home he was helping to diddle widows out of their pensions. His attempt to reconcile the two, as he would later admit to Thompson, 'nearly drove me mad'.[31]

During the summer holidays David screwed up his courage to tell Ronnie that he was not going back to school for his final year. Instead he would go to Switzerland, and enrol at the University of Bern, a city he had visited only briefly, en route to St Moritz. He had no guarantee of a place, but was willing to chance his arm.

David's premature departure from Sherborne at the age of sixteen seems to have taken everyone by surprise. There is no hint of it in his summer-term

* Ronnie cannot have robbed them of all their savings, because Sir Eric would leave a bequest to the Amateur Entomologists' Society on his death in 1977.

report, nor did he sign the leavers' register at the end of term.* Whatever he may have written latterly, contemporary evidence suggests that his decision to leave was spontaneous and sudden. The fact that he left some of his possessions behind at Westcott House supports this interpretation.

Ronnie seems to have accepted his son's decision, though he made David write to his housemaster himself to explain that he would not be coming back. There remained the problem of the belongings he had left behind. Not wanting a confrontation with Thompson, David enlisted the help of the matron, Miss Berryman. At the beginning of the autumn term he returned to Sherborne and crept into Westcott House, planning to collect his things and steal away unseen. David was with Miss Berryman when her telephone rang. 'He knows you're here,' she said, clearly frightened. A moment later Thompson himself appeared. 'What on earth do you think you're doing?' he bellowed. 'You've no business to be in house. Get out.'

Thompson admitted later that he had handled the situation badly. After David had left he summoned Robin Cooke to his study and told him what had happened. Cooke was stunned to hear that his friend had decided not to come back to the school for his final year: it made no sense to him. 'Do you think that you could get David to change his mind?' asked Thompson.

Thompson spoke to Ronnie on the telephone, following up with a letter. He referred to David's 'mental and spiritual immaturity', and conjectured that his decision not to return had been impulsive. He told Ronnie that his son had 'a great future', which would be jeopardised if he left school prematurely. Thompson urged Ronnie to persuade the boy to return. Not to do so, he indicated, would be cowardly.

At first Ronnie seemed inclined to agree, suggesting that he should come down to Sherborne to discuss the matter in person, with or without David. But on further consideration he decided that such a discussion would be of no avail. 'I am satisfied from what he has told me that whatever would be in his power to give the school, over the next twelve months, and

* In a memoir of David, Vivian Green recalls shaking hands with him at the gathering to say farewell to those boys who were leaving Sherborne at the end of the 1948 summer term. Green was then chaplain and history master at the school. His account, written many years after the event, is inconsistent with evidence from the time, and I am inclined to regard it as an imagined memory.

whatever they might have to give him, it would be a desperately unhappy year for him,' he wrote. 'Knowing him as I do I must acquit him entirely of the allegation of cowardice . . .'

> I agree with you entirely that he has infinite possibilities and I admit that they may be for good or ill. So it is with many other boys, and having given this matter serious consideration and with a full sense of the heavy responsibility which must inevitably rest on my shoulders, I have decided, so far as the visit to Switzerland is concerned, to give the boy his head – as I believe in him completely . . .
>
> He will never be out of our thoughts, and if I may say so with great respect, my prayers. I shall have the additional knowledge that the grounding he has received at Sherborne, and perhaps more particularly at your hands, will stand him in good stead, and make him always conscious of the duty he has to his fellow-men, and to his God.[32]

Thompson discussed the matter with the headmaster and showed him Ronnie's letter. In response, Canon Wallace expressed his belief that 'the parent gives the whole story away when he talks, on top of page two, of giving the boy his head'.

> If that is what he has done, then it is one of the oldest of old stories, at any rate, from the schoolmaster's point of view, though of course fresh for every parent. I can remember literally dozens of similar cases, in which a headstrong boy, anxious to be free of the irksome discipline of bells and school routine etc., has persuaded his parent to let him leave prematurely for the continent. The parent, perhaps not unmindful of the saving to his pocket, has agreed, and in my recollection, in every single instance it has been disastrous, and both have bitterly regretted it. But of course we are powerless, the boy is under the parent's guardianship. The parent pays the fees, and if he decides to take the boy away and send him to Switzerland, there is no power on earth that can stop him. We can only tell him what is a fact, that he is making a big mistake, and will presently resent it bitterly.[33]

Thompson knew that the story was more complex than Wallace realised, but there was nothing that he could do. 'I regretted his leaving very much indeed and did my best to stop it, but unsuccessfully,' he wrote later. 'It was all the result of an unsatisfactory home background working unhappily on a very sensitive mind.'[34] In another letter he would write that 'it was a Faustus story in miniature'.[35] This was an extraordinary comparison to make. Faustus was a mature scholar who sold his soul to the devil in exchange for knowledge and earthly pleasures. David was a sixteen-year-old who had decided that he wanted to continue his studies elsewhere.

David himself has given various explanations for his decision to leave school prematurely, referring to it recently as 'a blind act of adolescent anger'.[36] In trying to justify his action, he has described his three years at Sherborne as the worst in his life, and referred to 'the indelible scars that a neo-fascist regime of corporal punishment and single-sex confinement inflicts upon its wards'.[37] In 1991, forty-three years later, David gave an interview in which he talked about his schooldays. 'What I remember most about my time at Sherborne was being beaten. In my mind, it was one long act of sadism, broken very rarely by spontaneous acts of kindness. Most of the time I cried alone.'[38]

When this interview was published in the *Mail on Sunday*, Thompson was reported to be 'in high dudge'. Several of David's contemporaries wrote letters of support to their former housemaster, criticising what David had said. 'Much of what he wrote just wasn't true,' wrote one. 'David always lived in his imagination,' wrote another. 'My belief is that for his first year or so he was actually *happier* than some . . . I think that as he found things awful at home . . . he probably did withdraw from time to time.'[39]

There are several legends to explain why David left Sherborne prematurely; at least one of them is ascribed to David himself, when up at Oxford some years later. He apparently told an undergraduate friend, an angry young Communist, that he had quit Sherborne after punching his housemaster, who had tried to kiss him. Thompson was certainly fond of David, perhaps over-fond, and perhaps his fondness could become oppressive. But those who knew him judge that such behaviour would have been out of character. And if David had lashed out at Thompson, it is difficult to understand why he should then have written him an apologetic letter following their sharp exchange in Miss Berryman's office, in which he volunteered to come back to the school, to say 'a slightly more conventional goodbye'.[40] Nor would it explain their comparatively cordial correspondence in later years. It is only fair to add that David has no memory of telling this story. If he did, it seems more likely that he invented the incident to impress on his rebellious undergraduate friend his own anti-establishment credentials.

On 1 April 1948, just before what would prove to be David's final term at Sherborne, a new system for the payment of school fees had been introduced: henceforth boarding and tuition fees would be paid directly to the bursar rather than to the housemaster. Because David's fees were always in arrears, one might deduce that this change had precipitated his departure. Indeed the general belief among David's contemporaries and others connected with the school is that David left Sherborne early because his father failed to pay the fees. But correspondence from the time leaves no doubt that this is a misconception. Thompson had told David not to worry about the money, saying that if necessary he could arrange a bursary. 'We don't want to lose you,' he had assured his prized pupil.

Of course, David was not just leaving Sherborne; he was leaving England. He was escaping from his father as much as from Thompson. As he would write many years later, 'It was time to move on, and it was definitely time to get away from Ronnie.'[41]

Almost four years after he had left the school David wrote revealingly to Thompson:

> I believe now, more than ever, that what I did was right, though I am sorry that it caused such pain. I have not – as you once suggested – chosen Mammon rather than God. I chose the natural rather than the unnatural; the free rather than the repressed, for the choice was mine, as I think you always knew.[42]

4

Wandering in the fog

Bern is a natural fortress. The old town, still largely medieval, clings to the slopes of a high peninsula circled by the fast-flowing River Aare, which sweeps around its base in a great horseshoe. For hundreds of years the only crossing point was the heavily fortified Nydegg Bridge. In the nineteenth century Bern expanded westwards beyond its city walls to create the suburb of Länggasse, where a university was founded in 1834; and north, south and east to new suburbs on the other side of the river, including the diplomatic quarters of Kirchenfeld and Elfenau after the city became capital of the Swiss federal state in 1848. But its core remained almost unchanged.

'Everything is forbidden in Bern.' The old saying still held true in the late 1940s. Bern was an ordered, sober city, puritan, conservative and suspicious of foreigners. Germans were especially unwelcome after the war, as were displaced persons from the East: as fast as they arrived, the Swiss police rounded them up and sent them back again. Britons, on the other hand, were tolerated.

David arrived in Bern in mid-October 1948, a few days before his seventeenth birthday. For once in funds, he took a taxi direct from the railway station to the best hotel in the city, the Bellevue Palace, where he booked a room for one night only, and admired the magnificent view of the Alps from its south-facing terrace. The next morning he walked the short distance to the Kantonalbank in the Bundesplatz. A kindly Herr Joss opened an account for the young Englishman and gave him directions to the University.

The University registrar sat David down and marvelled at his lack of qualifications. When David's schoolboy German failed him, they continued the conversation in English. David told the registrar that he wished to study German language and literature; the registrar suggested that he might find it easier to take an introductory course in philosophy instead, but David was adamant. With a droll smile the registrar wished the young man luck and shook his hand.[1]

By the end of that day David was the proud possessor of a student card, and had found himself a place to live, unfortunately in a French-speaking household.

A few weeks later Ronnie arrived in Bern. Together they went to the Kantonalbank and deposited a few hundred francs in David's account, with a promise of more to follow. Under the illusion that Swiss bank managers could be manipulated as easily as their English counterparts, Ronnie treated Herr Joss to a long lunch before departing for St Moritz.

The first few weeks at the University were difficult for David. He attended seminars at which he did not dare open his mouth, and lectures on literature that he could not have understood even if they had been in English. Both his professors were German-born: one was Fritz Strich, whose important book *Goethe und die Weltliteratur* had been published only two years earlier. Strich portrayed Goethe as an advocate of 'world literature', to counter the Nazis' appropriation of German cultural figures for narrow nationalist purposes. David's other professor was Jonas Fränkel, who was mainly interested in Keller and Spitteler,* two Swiss German writers unfamiliar to David. Furtively he noted down their names and later looked them up in the library. As a Jew, Fränkel had been resented by Swiss Nazis, who had successfully intrigued to have him ousted as editor of Keller's complete works (the canton of Zurich went so far as to deny him access to Keller's archives), and had made his work on Spitteler as difficult as possible.[2] Though the Swiss far right had been less prominent since the end of the war, neo-Nazi groups continued to agitate against 'over-foreignisation'.

After one of these seminars, at which David was obviously struggling, Professor Strich took him aside. 'Young man,' he asked, 'what are you doing here?'

* Gottfried Keller (1819–90), novelist and short-story writer; Carl Spitteler (1845–1924), poet, awarded the Nobel Prize for Literature in 1919.

'I'm an Englishman,' David replied, 'studying German culture.'

'You are welcome,' the Professor said gravely.*

Under Strich's tutelage, David embraced German literature and letters with the zeal of a convert. Suddenly, instead of Keats he had Hölderlin; instead of Byron, Heine; and for his narcissistic hours of introspection and impossible love, *The Sorrows of Young Werther*. He took to writing self-conscious poetry about lost horizons, and painting lurid skyscapes that seemed to him, at the time, every bit as good as the equivalent works by Nolde. Losing himself in the cobbled winter streets of Bern, many of them covered by vaulted arcades, he recited Hermann Hesse: 'strange to wander in the fog, everyone is alone, no tree knows the other, each is alone'.†

Not that he was alone all the time: he soon made friends, among them Kaspar von Almen, a fellow student at the University, with whom he engaged in intense conversations on poetry and the soul, and on the cultural differences between the English and the Swiss. Von Almen was a wealthy young man; his family owned hotels at Kleine Scheidegg in the Bernese Oberland and at Trümmelbach in the valley above Lauterbrunnen, below the Jungfrau. (Trümmelbach was a romantic situation: it was here that Byron had stayed in 1816 and been inspired to write his poem *Manfred*.) Perceiving that David was lonely and short of money, von Almen invited him to come skiing during the Christmas vacation.

In the Bern pension where von Almen lived during term-time was a young woman called Erica, who would eventually become his wife. When he invited her to accompany him to the cinema, her hopes were raised. Unknown to her, however, von Almen had lent his heart, albeit temporarily, to an English girl. Outside the cinema she found another young man waiting for them. 'I wait for somebody else, but here I present to you my friend David,' von Almen explained. She was disappointed at first, but when she examined David more closely, she began to change her mind. 'Not too bad,' she decided.

* So David recounted in a lecture given in Oxford in 2010. In another verison of this exchange, provided in a 2000 television interview, David said, 'I'm a refugee from England,' to which the Professor replied, 'You'd better stay.'

† Hesse lived in Bern before the First World War.

In Bern David made timid excursions into the field of love. He developed a romantic obsession with a girl named Ursula, daughter of a don at the University, who allowed him to walk with her along the river, always accompanied by a chaperone.

With tears in his eyes, Herr Joss informed David that there was no more money in his bank account. A cheque received from Herr Cornwell had not been honoured. David left the French-speaking household and found himself the cheapest possible place to live, a tiny attic room, one of several that opened on to a corridor under the eaves of a house on the Längstrasse. The others were occupied by poor people, mostly unemployed. The only source of water was a cold tap and a basin that served the whole corridor. The house stood next to the Tobler factory, so that the whole house smelt of chocolate. His landlady, a Frau Schreuers, who lived with her son Lothar on the third floor, fed David breakfasts of salami and mint tea to keep up his strength. Meanwhile David found part-time work as a waiter in the railway-station buffet, and, he says, mucked out cages and washed elephants for the Circus Knie. Cycling to work he was stopped by the police, who threatened him with repatriation to England for the crime of riding an unlicensed bicycle.*

On Saturday afternoons David would put on his best suit and buy a ticket to the *thé dansant* at the Bellevue Palace. On Sundays he would stroll with the Schreuers along the Aare, or in the Gurten, a high park overlooking the city, reached by a funicular railway.

It did not take David long to appreciate that Swiss German was not High German: going to Bern to study German literature, he would later say, was like going to New Orleans to learn classical French. He spent some of his last francs on language tuition provided by a Frau Karsten from Hamburg. Some Swiss students were kind enough to speak High German to him, but most wanted to practise their English, so he sought out German students instead. Only three years after the end of the war, they could tell of extraordinary experiences in the recent past, and hardship difficult for a young Englishman to imagine. One of these was the crippled Alexander Heussler, from Kemnitz on the Baltic coast, in

* So David said in his 2010 lecture. In his 2000 television interview he said that the police had come to his house while he was out, and had confiscated his bicycle.

the Russian zone. He was older than David, and already in possession of a doctorate. Another was Horst Nözholt, who like Heussler was a few years David's senior, old enough to have served in the army. He too came from the east, and would return there after completing his studies. Both would go into the blend from which emerged the figure of Axel in *A Perfect Spy*. 'Neither fits the final portrait,' David has subsequently written, 'because in the end you have to give people bits of yourself so that you can understand them.'[3] By contrast, Roland Reinäcker, who was introduced to David by Kaspar von Almen, was from Essen in the British zone, and his mother was Swiss. He was suspicious of Nözholt, whom he suspected of spying.

In *A Perfect Spy* Magnus Pym reflects that the German muse had no particular draw for him, then or later, 'for all his loud enthusiasm':

> The point was she supplied Pym with the means, for the first time, to regard himself intellectually as a gentleman . . . When he went down to the warehouse in Ostring where Herr Ollinger had obtained illegal night work for him at the hands of a fellow philanthropist, he neither walked nor took the tram but rode with Mozart in his coach to Prague. When he washed his elephants at night he endured the humiliations of Lenz's *Soldaten*. When he sat in the third-class buffet bestowing soulful looks on Elizabeth he imagined himself as Young Werther, planning his wardrobe before committing suicide. And when he considered his hopes and failures together, he was able to compare his *Werdegang** with Wilhelm Meister's years of apprenticeship, and planned even then a great autobiographical novel that would show the world what a noble sensitive fellow he was compared to Rick.

This interpretation is laden with self-mockery. David's intellectual engagement with the German muse was profound. References to German literature abound in his work, even if few English-speaking readers notice them.[4]

Perhaps identifying with Young Werther, David underwent a crisis while in Bern, as he would confess two years afterwards in a letter to a

* Development.

girlfriend, written at four o'clock one morning. 'I shall tell you of things I shall never tell anyone else,' he told her, 'and have certainly never yet told anyone.' He detailed his feelings of alienation. 'Everywhere I went, people seemed to be trampling on all that I loved,' he wrote. 'It seemed to me that God had played a huge joke on me, and the thing I held most important was the mirror of all the evil of mankind. I learned to mistrust love completely . . .' David's meaning is obscure, but it is obvious from the context that he is unburdening himself of something important.

> I made a decision, rightly or wrongly I shall never know, to cut myself always from all the towering problems that seemed to be everywhere, and create a world of my own entirely. Already at school in England I had written 'escapist' poems for my own pleasure, and it was the memory of these that kindled the idea. On pretence of going on a ski-ing expedition I took a small room away from Bern and lived in it for several weeks – nearly three, I think – just writing and thinking, living in my own world – creating my own characters – or rather, principal character. Most of what I wrote was sheer nonsense, raving mad.

He told how he had created an imaginary girlfriend called 'Judy', to whom he addressed love poems – possibly a version of the girl in Thorpeness. But then Kaspar von Almen had invited him skiing, and physical activity had turned him outward again.[5]

On the slopes he was accosted by a dauntingly thin, gimlet-eyed Englishwoman. This was the formidable Ros Hepworth, secretary of the Downhill Only Club,* home of British skiing at Wengen since 1925. She was scouting for recruits to the Club's new racing team, intended to develop British skiers capable of competing at international events. In commanding cadences that he would later hear employed by Britain's first female Prime Minister, she insisted that he join. It was his patriotic duty, she instructed him. When he showed reluctance, she told him

* So called because, uniquely in the Alps, Wengen had a cog railway right to the centre of the ski slopes, from Lauterbrunnen to Kleine Scheidegg. Skiers in Wengen could enjoy the downhill run without having to walk up or climb the mountains first.

not to be ridiculous. 'It will do you good and you'll be serving your country.'[6]

David was summoned by Frau Schreuers to the telephone to take a call from Ronnie: 'Son, I've got a job for you.' He was to go to St Moritz, where the account for last winter's visit was still outstanding. David's task was a familiar one: to explain that the obstacles to passing on the money had proved more challenging than anticipated, but the matter was now in hand and would soon be dealt with. 'And while you're there,' Ronnie added, 'have yourself a steak on your old man.'

David made his way to St Moritz, and stammered out his lines to Herr Badrutt, a big, tender man, red-faced and anxious, who seemed just as embarrassed by the interview as his young visitor.* The manager was too courteous to do more than thank the young emissary for his good offices and tell him the time of the next train back to Bern, innocent of the fact that David lacked the money for the fare and intended to hitchhike.[7]

So David tells the story, though he was unaware of evidence that Ronnie did try to pay the hotel bill, albeit illegally. In 1954 he would be convicted of an offence dating from this period, of borrowing Swiss francs from an unauthorised dealer – perhaps his contact at the Swiss Embassy in London. Maybe the Badrutts, despairing of ever being paid, had alerted the authorities to the proposed method of payment.

David's wanderings took him to the English church in Kirchenfeld, more from a desire to hear English voices again than out of any need to commune with his maker. There, on Christmas Day, he made the acquaintance of a county lady in tweeds and sensible shoes who introduced herself as 'Wendy Gillbanks', and her handsome, chummy, amusing friend 'Sandy', both of the Consular Section of the British Embassy. They invited him back for a glass of sherry and a spot of lunch the next day, and gently probed him on his attitudes and beliefs. When the subject of service to one's country came up in the conversation, David was keen to prove himself a patriot,

* David claimed that Ronnie's failure to settle his account had 'brought the hotel to its knees', but this seems hard to believe.

conscious that his father had contributed not very much to the struggle against Hitler. When presented with a legal document pledging him to secrecy – perhaps a version of the Official Secrets Act – at the British Embassy, he had no hesitation in signing.

In 1948 it was not hard to make the case that Britain faced a threat from the East. As Nazi Germany collapsed, the Red Army had occupied Eastern and much of Central Europe. One by one, democratic governments in the countries occupied by Soviet forces were being replaced by Communist regimes owing their allegiance to Moscow. Earlier in the year a Communist coup had overthrown the Czech government of President Beneš, an event with particular resonance in Britain, because of the lingering shame felt at the betrayal of the Czechs at Munich. Even in countries not occupied by the Red Army, fragile democracies were threatened by Communist takeover. It seemed conceivable that all Europe might fall into Stalin's dominion, that the Red Army might soon be encamped on the Channel coast. In June 1948 the Russians had begun blockading the Western zones of Berlin, the only territory behind the Iron Curtain outside their control. In response the Western Allies were flying in supplies to keep the Berliners from starving.

So when Sandy asked David to attend meetings of left-wing student groups, and report the names of any other British citizens he spotted there, or of any Czechs or Hungarians who might happen to be present, he was happy to do so, even if they did take place late at night and even if he did find some of the debate hard to comprehend. And when they asked him to pop down to Geneva for a day, and sit on a park bench with a volume of Goethe's poems open on his lap, until a passing stranger asked whether he had seen his lost dog, he was happy to do that too.

Before David's year in Bern came to an end, he attended a lecture given by Thomas Mann at the baroque concert hall of the Casino, to commemorate the bicentenary of Goethe's birth. It was an appropriate subject for Mann, now in his seventies, who had been awarded the Goethe Prize that year. After the First World War he had written an important essay on the role of the artist in society, based on a comparative study of Goethe and Tolstoy. And in 1939 he had brought out *Lotte in Weimar*, a novel about Goethe, in which the poet is reunited in old age with the woman whom he had loved forty years earlier, the woman who had inspired him to write *The Sorrows of Young Werther*. Mann's fictional Goethe had reflected on the immoderate character of the German people, in particular their susceptibility to 'any mad scoundrel who appeals to their lowest instincts, who confirms them in their vices and teaches them to conceive nationalism as isolation and brutality'. No one reading *Lotte in Weimar* in the post-war years could fail to make the connection with the mad scoundrel who had so recently led the German people into the abyss. Indeed, this passage from Mann's novel had been quoted in his summing-up by the chief British prosecutor at the Nuremberg trials, Hartley Shawcross, in the mistaken belief that these were the authentic words of Goethe himself.

To David's indignation, Mann's lecture had been picketed by neo-Nazis, who complained that the novelist had become Anglicised during his exile in America.

Full of enthusiasm for what he had heard, David made his way to the distinguished speaker's dressing room. His first impression of the man who opened the door was that he looked like the film actor Clifton Webb. The Great Man asked David what he wanted. 'I want to shake your hand,' David replied. 'Here it is,' said Thomas Mann, offering his hand.

After a year in Bern David had learned to speak fluent German. But Frau Karsten told him, in her severe way, that in order to know the real Germany, he must go there, 'even in these bitter times'. So, at the end of the 1949 summer term, David crossed into Germany, or rather into the Federal Republic (West Germany), which had only just come into being, following the *de facto* partition of Germany between the zones occupied by the Western Allies and the Russians. The Berlin blockade had failed, but West Berlin remained an island surrounded by a sea of Communist-controlled territory. With Roland Reinäcker as his guide, David travelled to Essen, where Reinäcker's parents lived, and toured the industrial Ruhr district, pulverised by Allied bombers during the war and still largely in ruins. In Lower Saxony, he walked the empty alleys of Bergen-Belsen concentration camp, where the foul stench of dying humanity still lingered, and struggled to reconcile what he was witnessing with the high cultural abstractions he had been studying over the past year. David obtained a pass to visit West Berlin, where he gazed across the frontier into the Eastern sector of the city, capital of the new German Democratic Republic (GDR, or East Germany).

In Berlin, David suffered a painful swelling in his testicles. A British doctor diagnosed mumps and advised bed-rest, but refused to admit him to the main British military hospital on the grounds that David was a civilian, with a visa to West Germany stamped 'Visitor No Facilities'; instead he was put to bed in what had been an air-raid shelter, a former *U-bahn* station, listening to the often horrifying stories of his German fellow patients. When he had recovered enough to travel, he returned to England to recuperate further at Tunmers, lying in bed while Jean read to him.

Roland Reinäcker came to visit him and stayed a fortnight. To him, Chalfont St Peter seemed very civilised, by comparison with the wreckage of the Ruhr. Every morning at seven o'clock a maid brought him a cup of tea, and then he and David would go riding before breakfast.

Reinäcker, who was very much a ladies' man, found David's stepmother very attractive and sympathetic. She and Ronnie took the two young men to the Café Royal, where Marlene Dietrich was making a comeback. Reinäcker's godfather, a Swiss plastic surgeon living in London, who had been invited to join them, was momentarily disconcerted when Ronnie offered to obtain for him a cut-price Bentley. On another day Ronnie despatched his son and his guest to the Nottingham races, to put money on Prince Rupert. Following his instructions they placed a large each-way bet; the horse came in second, ensuring that they had some winnings to take back to Ronnie. Reinäcker remembers David proudly declaring that 'We are not punters, we are owners' when asked to pay the entrance fee. This announcement may have undermined the essentially covert nature of the operation.

Back at Tunmers, David showed his German visitor the manuscript of a short story he had written. Reinäcker was already familiar with David's skill as a cartoonist. After reading the story he offered his frank opinion. 'You should keep drawing, but stop writing,' he advised. 'My friend, promise me that you will *never* write a book.'

David was now in limbo, conscious that he was liable to be called up at any time once he reached the age of eighteen in October. National Service had been introduced the previous year, making it compulsory for all British men aged between eighteen and twenty-six to do eighteen months' military service, with a further four years in the reserves. As he awaited his call-up papers, David dated his first real girlfriend, Ann Taylor, daughter of Stanley Taylor, a golfing chum of Ronnie's and a partner in the firm of luxury grooming products for men, Taylor of Old Bond Street. Then someone else Ronnie knew, Roger Constant of the Constant Shipping Line, which operated a fleet of tramp steamers, suggested a passage aboard a boat carrying coal to North Africa. The boy was welcome to take a friend if he wanted, so David invited his schoolmate Robin Cooke, who happened to be staying as a guest at Tunmers, to accompany him. 'I'd love to, but I'm due to join the army in October,' Cooke explained. 'Don't worry about that,' interjected Ronnie. 'I'll phone up the War Office and get it postponed.' Cooke was astonished when Ronnie's intervention proved successful. The two boys embarked at Hull, and steamed first to Lisbon and then past Gibraltar to Oran, where the purser dispensed contraceptives to those going ashore. 'This is to stop you getting dust in your eye,' he said as he handed them to the puzzled boys, who had never seen a condom before.

Ronnie was busily cultivating another golfing pal, Sir James Barnes, the Permanent Under-Secretary of State for Air and a director of Arsenal Football Club. He introduced Sir James to a succession of attractive young women, in the hope that Barnes's influence would secure for him the concession to lay down the aggregate for the new air bases then being built across the south of England in response to the Soviet threat. Ronnie involved himself also in a new charitable scheme to provide winter sports for wounded or traumatised RAF pilots, run by the head of the RAF station at Abingdon, Group Captain Ray Collins. He generously undertook to find hotel accommodation in Switzerland, transport, skis and other equipment, all at the best possible prices. Through his contact with Barnes, Ronnie arranged a few months' work at the Air Ministry for David, helping with the practical arrangements for the new scheme. This job, which paid £4 a week, was David's first experience of bureaucracy. As time passed he began to sniff corruption. The suspicion grew in his mind that his father's motives for becoming involved in the RAF Winter Sports Scheme might not have been purely charitable.

Ronnie always tried to control his sons by monitoring their activities. David had learned to expect that his room would be searched, his post opened and his telephone calls listened in to on the extension. He now responded in kind by spying on his father, making stealthy sorties into Ronnie's dressing room, to delve into the pockets of his camel-hair coats and to leaf through his pocket diaries. He learned to move silently, noting Ronnie's surprising ability to do the same. From time to time he would attempt to spring the lock of a large green filing cabinet that his father kept at home rather than in the office. Ronnie had occasionally referred to its contents as the ultimate solution to all his problems. 'All the answers are in that cabinet, son. One day everybody will be seen right.'

Around Christmas David was summoned to St Moritz by his father, there to lend his essential weight to the RAF scheme. With barely credible cheek, Ronnie was staying at the Kulm, with the RAF Winter Sports Association billeted in the hotel annexe; somehow he had once again persuaded the trusting Badrutts to accept his credit.

Ronnie was not above using his good-looking son, now just eighteen, as bait to lure a profitable catch, in this instance to escort the daughter of a potential business associate. Though David complied, he did so reluctantly. The girl bored him, and when he took her skiing, he led her deliberately into a snowdrift.

In a café where a band was playing David found Group Captain Collins taking tea with his wife. Also at the table was a slight, pretty girl who looked younger than her real age of seventeen, her dark hair pinned up in plaits. A year later he would recall 'a little girl I met in St. Moritz . . . the image of an almost childlike face gazing into mine'.[8] This was Ann Sharp,* the elder of two daughters of an air vice-marshal recently posted to the Air Ministry. When David asked her to dance, she mutely accompanied him on to the dance-floor. Ronnie arrived and sat with her companions for a few minutes watching them, before he beckoned David back to the table.

Over the next few days David and Ann met several times. At the Chesa Veglia, a converted farmhouse attached to the Badrutt's Palace Hotel, they

* Her first name was Alison, but she was always known by her second name Ann to avoid confusion with her mother, also called Alison.

danced cheek to cheek. He boasted to her of imaginary sexual conquests. To her, he seemed sophisticated and glamorous, like a hero of the romantic fiction she had devoured in her mid-teens – if a little smug. She admired his skill on the slopes, and was impressed when he told her that he was likely to ski for England. But Ronnie kept him on a short rein. 'I have to slip out when my father doesn't need me,' he told her. On her last night in St Moritz she waited for him until it was so late that she had almost given him up. He arrived at her hotel shortly before midnight, apologising that this had been the earliest moment when he could escape from the family party, by pretending that he was retiring to bed. Together they walked along a path out of town, slipping in the compacted snow. Ann's feet became cold inside her soaking high-heeled shoes, and her long dress became wet and bedraggled; but suddenly he turned to face her, and kissed her full on the mouth. She responded, and the two of them kissed for hours in the darkness, as the snow fell softly around them. The next morning he came to the railway station to see her off, promising to write.

In Britain a general election was looming. Ronnie decided that the nation required his services, and suddenly departed, leaving his wife and son at the Kulm without the means to sustain themselves. For several days they were forced to steal bread from the hotel breakfast-table in order to have anything to eat at lunchtime. Eventually they crept out through a back entrance and made their way discreetly to the station.

Ronnie had been chosen to stand for the Liberals in the Yarmouth Division of Norfolk, embracing the coastal town of Great Yarmouth and the surrounding countryside. Doubtless his connection with Edgar Granville, who had represented the nearby Eye Division of Suffolk since 1929, mostly but not exclusively as a Liberal, played a part in his adoption. Granville's interests encompassed all his neighbouring constituencies, since one of his policies was to make East Anglia a self-supporting region.

For half a century control of the borough of Great Yarmouth had swung back and forth between Liberals and Conservatives, until 1945 when it had been seized by Labour. In 1950 the sitting Labour MP was facing a strong Conservative challenge. But the last-minute intervention of a Liberal candidate turned this into the first three-cornered contest in Yarmouth since 1929. Boundary changes had enlarged the constituency to take in many fenland villages, more than doubling the size of the electorate in the process. These changes made the 1950 election especially unpredictable. The campaign promised to be an active one, with all three candidates speaking at numerous public meetings.

Why did Ronnie want to become a member of parliament, now that he no longer faced the threat of being called up? It seems unlikely that political conviction supplied his primary motive; what seems more plausible is that he believed it would further his interests. For Ronnie, politics and business went hand in hand. Politicians played a part in the awarding of lucrative contracts and could receive valuable rewards from the grateful contractor, as he had reason to know. But there was another motive. Ronnie craved the status of an MP. What he longed for, perhaps more than anything else, was respect, and in his world MPs were respected very highly. As a member of parliament, he would be able to claim belated parity with Alec Glassey.

Thirty-six years later David would provide an entertaining fictionalised account of the election in *A Perfect Spy*. Just as in the novel, Ronnie rode into this sleepy Norfolk constituency in his Bentley, rousing the locals with his eloquence and warming them with his energy. In his wake trailed family and friends, including members of the Court, several of whom were concealing a criminal past which would have shocked the people of Yarmouth had they known of it. The Cornwell team set up its headquarters at a small temperance hotel in the centre of town, equipping it with a temporary bar. David obtained two weeks' deferment of his National Service call-up in order to campaign for his father, while Tony interrupted his studies at Pembroke College, Cambridge. William Douglas Home turned out for Ronnie, as did several other well-known personalities, bringing with them a whiff of glamour. But, despite all the razzmatazz, the campaign was doomed from the start. Thirty years later, in a *Sunday Times* article coinciding with the publication of *A Perfect Spy*, David represented Ronnie's decision to stand for parliament in 1950 as a perfect example of his inability 'to distinguish between the world as it existed and the world that he thought he could control'.

> Anyone in the street could have told him that, if you stand in an election, the details of your past life are likely to be subjected to unfriendly

> scrutiny. Yet Ronnie stood. A kind of hot air bubble of his own making conveyed him inexorably towards the hustings . . . First he talked his friends into it, then they talked him into it. Doubters, if there were any, were booed off the stage, as they always were . . . Never mind that he knew not the first thing about politics. Never mind that in any serious debate, matched against less generous minds and deprived of his rhetoric, he would have fallen as surely as one of his racehorses at the first fence. His *personality* – ever a buzzword among the faithful – would vanquish. His *incredible brain* – another buzzword – would absorb, rewrite and parrot everything an honest man needed to know in order to become an MP. To know more was to be a snob.[9]

Ronnie had waited until 20 January, just over a month before the poll, before announcing that he would stand. According to the *Eastern Daily Press*, he had been approached some time before and had agreed to contest the seat, but his name had been withheld at his own request.[10] During this period, the *Yarmouth Mercury* commented that by leaving it so late to come forward, 'the mystery candidate' faced 'an uphill task'. But the paper believed that there was still sufficient Liberal sentiment in the constituency to justify the Party's intervention.[11] There was a strong nonconformist tradition in the area, which the Liberals had drawn on in the past and might do so again. Ronnie flung himself into the campaign with gusto. 'Never was Liberalism more necessary, more vital to the recovery, well-being and future prosperity of this country than at the present day,' he asserted at the outset. The *Eastern Daily Press* quoted freely from Ronnie's election literature. In politics, it reported, he had been 'a lifelong Liberal' (omitting to mention his plans to stand as an Independent Progressive in the 1945 Chelmsford by-election). 'During the War, Mr Cornwell served with the Royal Corps of Signals until his release in 1945.' The *Eastern Daily Press* and the *Yarmouth Mercury* both repeated his claim that 'the property companies in which he was interested had provided some 1,000 homes for workers in the south of England'. The provision of adequate housing for all sections of the community, Ronnie told them, was 'a problem constantly engaging his attention'.

'To me, Liberalism is a way of life,' he declared at his adoption meeting. 'In my view it stands for justice and fair play for all.' He launched a strong attack on conscription, referring to the fact that he had two sons of National Service age, and spoke of young men occupied at work that was of no benefit to them or to their country. Anyone who was a father or who had anything to do with boys knew what a completely stupid thing conscription was, he said.[12]

Ronnie conceded that the Party's policy of world government was at the moment no more than an ideal. But ideals, he added, were like the stars – 'We might never reach them, but always profited by their presence.' Let them hitch their wagons to this star, he continued, in an unfortunate mangling of metaphors, and go along the road as far as they possibly could.[13]

The candidate's wife also addressed the adoption meeting: saying that, if her husband were returned, she would, as the mother of a young family, 'be able to acquaint him with the housewife's difficulties'. (This was at a time when the Cornwell family was spending at a rate of £7,000 per annum – about £500,000 in today's money.)

Two days later, at his first public meeting, Ronnie urged the voters to give the Liberals 'a fair crack of the whip'. He was supported by Bruce Belfrage, Liberal candidate for South Buckinghamshire, where Ronnie was vice-president of the local Party. Belfrage was a well-known actor and BBC radio presenter, especially famous for having continued to read the news while covered in plaster dust, after an enemy bomb had exploded in Broadcasting House.[14] His wife was one of Ronnie's longstanding mistresses. When Ronnie died, she laid a mauve boa on the doorstep of her house in tribute to her former lover.

In an open letter to the electors of Yarmouth, Ronnie rejected the fear that a Liberal vote was a wasted one. He asked the electors to forget the 'split vote bogey' and vote for what they believed in. Voting Tory was playing into the hands of the Communists. He believed that the world was moving leftwards, and that unless the people wanted a permanent socialist government, gradually turning to Communism, they should set up an effective, progressive opposition.[15]

The campaign continued apace. Driven by his chauffeur Mr Nutbeam, Ronnie sped around the fenland villages giving stirring speeches. On several successive bitterly cold nights in the week before the poll, he spoke at four different venues within the space of an hour. He presented himself as a teetotaller, like so many of those assembled, though the boot of the Bentley had been equipped with a special rack to hold bottles of comparatively odourless champagne, from which the candidate could safely refresh himself between speaking engagements, indeed sometimes offering a nip to his chauffeur – 'Have one on me, Nutty.' David's role was to persuade the voters of Yarmouth that Ronnie was a loving and abstemious father, with frugal Christian habits, who had done his bit for the country during the war and who was now ready to serve the folk of this remote East Anglian constituency. Bellowing through a loudspeaker mounted on the roof of a van, he cruised the streets of Yarmouth, urging its citizens to vote for his father, the Liberal candidate Ronald Cornwell.

On the Friday before the poll, a Liberal 'Brains Trust' was staged at the Yarmouth Town Hall assembly rooms, chaired by the candidate. The format derived from the hugely popular BBC radio series of the same name. Among those taking part were 'the candidate's eldest son, Mr Tony Cornwell', 'the well-known West Indian cricketer, Mr Learie Constantine'* and 'Mr Edward Ryder Richardson, the Recorder of Walsall'. At the finish Ryder Richardson congratulated the chairman on his 'brainwave' in organising the meeting to ease the tension of the election, and commended him to the voters of Yarmouth as a man of proven capacity, resource and steel.[16]

As the election approached, Ronnie intensified his efforts. Three days before the poll, he addressed a well-attended meeting at Yarmouth Town Hall, at which David also spoke. 'I know what it is to fight against fearful odds,' Ronnie declared. 'The greater the odds, the better you will find me.'[17]

When David returned to the Commercial Hotel after a day's canvassing, he noticed that everyone was looking very solemn. Ronnie turned to address him. 'Son, we've got to talk.' The Conservative candidate's agent had approached him, he explained in a sanctimonious tone. 'He's said that if I don't stand down, they're going to let it be known that many years ago I had certain difficulties.' He then touched briefly on his conviction and subsequent sentence. 'I was in the position of the office-boy who had taken a few stamps out of the box and was caught before he had a chance to put them back.'

* In the post-war years Constantine made regular appearances on BBC radio panel shows.

This was the first time that Ronnie had ever spoken openly to David about going to prison. 'The question is,' he concluded, 'do we fight or do we give in?'

There was only one answer that a loyal son could provide to such an appeal. 'We fight,' said David; and when told this, the assembled courtiers cheered. 'Told you he had it in him, Ronnie.'[18]

Thinking about it afterwards, David suspected that his uncle Alec Glassey had leaked the truth about his brother-in-law's criminal past, in a letter exhorting the local Tories not to reveal their source.

That evening, addressing a small audience at a local school, Ronnie prefaced his speech with a statement of masterly obfuscation:

> In the light of reports reaching me as to certain completely inaccurate statements being made concerning my personal character and reputation, I feel it might be appropriate if I had a word or two to say on that subject. I recognise, of course, that at the time of a General Election, it is inevitable that all kinds of rumours must be expected, and this one is no exception. It is, however, of paramount importance that when statements are made concerning the personal character of a candidate, due regard should be paid to the words we know so well, 'the truth, the whole truth and nothing but the truth'.*
>
> No candidate can have complaint if the requirements of these words are observed, but speaking for myself, I shall have no hesitation in taking legal proceedings against any person who participates in the circulation of any statement that does not conform to these requirements.

Ronnie went on to express his satisfaction that 'the electorate of this division will not be misled by such tactics'.[19]

After Ronnie had delivered his address, a woman at the back asked whether it was true that the candidate had served a prison sentence for fraud – just as Peggy Wentworth does in *A Perfect Spy*; and Ronnie dealt with the question just as his fictional equivalent Rick Pym did. He moved forward and looked into the faces of the thirty or so people gathered in

* A phrase with which Ronnie was of course familiar, from his frequent appearances in court.

the hall that evening. 'I see here mothers, fathers and grandparents. I ask each of you, if one of your sons or grandsons had made a mistake, and paid the price for it, and then he asked to be taken back, which one of you would slam the door in his face?' The response was tumultuous applause. There was a repeat performance at subsequent meetings in the run-up to the poll, to the extent that David began to suspect his father of having planted the question.

So David remembers, though if this is a true record of what happened it seems odd that no hint of the allegations against Ronnie appeared in the local press, which covered the election in considerable detail. Perhaps his threat of legal action explains why. In another version of this story, which David told in a television interview, the question from the woman in the audience was his first intimation that anything was wrong, and Ronnie explained himself only afterwards, in the car on the way back from the meeting.[20] This parallels the storyline of *A Perfect Spy*, which suggests that, in David's memory, fiction may have replaced reality.

In any case the bluff worked. On polling day, 23 February, 5,854 of the electors of Yarmouth voted for Ronnie, 13.6 per cent of the turnout – a respectable showing, about 2 per cent more than the average vote across the country for a Liberal candidate, ensuring that he saved his deposit. The sitting Labour MP was re-elected with a majority of only 1,162, which convinced many on the Tory team that the Liberal interloper had cost them victory, as they had feared he would.

After the election Ronnie spoke to a reporter from the local paper, and stated his ambition of winning the seat 'for Liberalism' at the next election. Far from drooping, the tails of the Liberals of Yarmouth 'were well up'. A fortnight after the poll, he spoke to a crowded meeting at the Central Liberal Club and pronounced 'the rebirth of Liberalism in Yarmouth'. But it was all bluster. Ronnie had shot his bolt.[21]

5

Serving your country

David had postponed his enlistment date to assist his father in the Yarmouth election, but once the poll was over there was no excuse for further delay. He enlisted in the 17th Training Regiment of the Royal Artillery, and soon afterwards presented himself at Park Hall Camp, Oswestry, to begin his Basic Training.

The first days passed in a whirlwind of Blanco and Brasso, Dos and Don'ts, instructions on how to lace boots and make a bed. David polished buttons and buckles, and rubbed the toecaps of his boots with spit and polish – and then was made to do it again after the sergeant had hurled the boots across the room, shouting that it had not been done properly. The day began with Reveille at 6.15 and ended with Lights Out at 22.30. It seemed that David had barely gone to sleep before he was woken by a screaming drill sergeant.

Basic Training was designed to teach recruits to obey orders without questioning them. For ten weeks, they were bullied by foul-mouthed NCOs, to break their spirit. 'Discipline is the foundation of the Army,' they were told repeatedly. David remembers being frightened all the time, though one gains a different impression from *A Perfect Spy*. 'He reaped the plentiful rewards of his upbringing,' David wrote of his fictional self. 'While Welsh miners and Glaswegian cut-throats wept unashamedly for their mothers, went absent without leave and were carted off to a place of punishment, Pym slept soundly and wept for no one . . . He neither took fright at being shouted at nor expected the logic of authority.'[1] It was often remarked that those young men who had been to boarding school found it easier to adapt to the harshness and the arbitrariness of the regime.[2]

In retrospect David would look back at his service in the army with wry detachment. Like many other former National Servicemen, he would find much of what he had been required to do meaningless and occasionally ludicrous. The experience would heighten his scepticism about the wisdom of authority. At the time, however, he was eager to conform. The moral clarity of the army was a relief from the murkiness of home.

During his training David was selected to lay a 25-pounder field gun during an exercise in the Welsh hills, chosen to do so because of his supposedly superior education. When ordered to open fire, David hesitated, as a flock of sheep had wandered into range. His non-committal gesture was interpreted as 'optically demonstrating resistance to an order', a breach of military discipline which might have earned him a court martial.

The recruits were granted two weeks' leave at the end of Basic Training; then David and those other recruits identified as 'potential officer material' were ordered to report to the War Office Selection Board (WOSB, known colloquially as 'Wosbee') at Barton Stacey in Hampshire for three days of interviews and tests of physical endurance and initiative. Selectors also observed the potential officers' table manners. The army favoured young men who had been to public school or grammar school – not least because most of these had received OTC training there.

Those that failed the Board faced the humiliation of being 'RTUd' (Returned to Unit). But David proceeded to the infantry's Officer Cadet School at Eaton Hall in Cheshire, a magnificent Gothic-revival mansion designed by Alfred Waterhouse in the late nineteenth century for the 1st Duke of Westminster. The building's sumptuous interiors were neo-medieval, with rich furnishings, marble mosaics, alabaster chimneypieces and Chinese silk wallpaper. Officer cadets slept four to a room in elegant staterooms, and washed in luxurious bathrooms, with outsize baths and marble hand-basins equipped with brass taps.

After a few weeks at Eaton Hall David received a note from the War Office, directing him towards the Intelligence Corps. He assumed that this was a consequence of his work for the SIS station in Bern. Once he received his commission he would wear the Corps' cypress-green beret and its badge, provoking the inevitable taunts about 'intelligence' from NCOs.

Officer training was divided into two phases: a primary phase, lasting six weeks, devoted to basic military subjects; and a secondary phase of ten weeks, concentrating on tactics, weapons and 'Tewts' (tactical exercises without troops). Asked in a Tewt how he would defend his position, David replied that he would dig a very big trench and fill it with poisonous snakes. This flippant response was not well received. Cadets also undertook two three-day Battle Camps, on Dartmoor and in the Brecon Beacons, which included live firing with .303 rifles and the use of thunder flashes to simulate grenades.

An underlying principle of officer training was (and remains) constant competition at every level, whether between individuals, platoons or companies. This encouraged a strong *esprit de corps*, as each unit was judged by the standard of its weakest member. David was part of 17 Platoon, 'C' Company. Because he was considered hopeless at 'Turnout', always scruffy and never ironing his battledress properly, the other members of his platoon took him in hand, helping to smarten him up before parade. One of them, Bryan Cartledge, would later join the Foreign Office, eventually becoming Ambassador to Moscow.

To his fellow cadets, most of whom had arrived direct from school, David seemed mature and sophisticated. His detached attitude to training impressed them even as it made them anxious that he might appear on parade with a button undone. And unlike most of them, he had a girlfriend. Though he had not written to Ann Sharp as he had promised when he saw her off from St Moritz, they had met again at an RAF dance ten months later, while he was on leave from Eaton Hall. She now looked much more womanly, the childlike plaits replaced by a glamorous bob. 'She's got a figure like a pocket Venus!' he told Robin Cooke excitedly when they next met. On that first evening she had ignored him, preferring to dance with a young RAF officer whom she had been seeing since returning from St Moritz, while David was left to dance with her mother; but they had spent the next weekend together at the house of Group Captain Collins, becoming close enough for him to address her as 'Ann darling' when he wrote to her subsequently from Eaton Hall. From this time on David would see her regularly whenever he had any leave. His letters became increasingly affectionate. 'I love you with all that I possess,' he wrote soon afterwards, adding, 'I promise that I have never said that to anybody else.'[3]

Ann was the elder of two daughters, clever, serious and bookish, dreaming inwardly of princes and princesses, described by her glamorous but empty-headed mother as a 'funny little thing'. At her boarding school she was regarded as defiant and argumentative; there she seems to have had some form of lesbian experience that (so David believed) later disgusted her. She was surrounded by women at home as well as at school, since she had no brothers and her mother was one of half a dozen sisters; her grandmother, who had disowned her grandfather, had taught her daughters that females were queens who should be served by the male bee (but only after marriage) and then left in peace. David would come to believe that from childhood he and Ann had been on different sides of the sex-war. While he had grown up in a household devoid of women, Ann had grown up in a household dominated by them.

Not surprisingly, Ann's father, Alfred 'Bobby' Sharp, was a rogue husband, who neglected his wife and daughters and chased after other women. He was an extravagant, aggressive personality, whose character and behaviour offended Ann as it did her mother. Though educated in England, Bobby Sharp had been born in Bangalore, to an Indian mother; according to Ann, who herself had been born in India,* he tried to conceal his Anglo-Indian origins by acting more English than the English.†

Training completed, David passed out with the rank of 2nd lieutenant on 21 October 1950. After a short parachute course at RAF Abingdon, in

* In Murree, the summer capital of the British Raj in the Punjab, part of Pakistan since partition in 1947.

† A career RAF officer, he was admired as a fearless pilot and commander, and had been awarded the DSO in recognition of his outstanding courage, skill and leadership in commanding a light bomber squadron during the early years of the war. Air Commodore Sharp (as he then was) had continued to fly sorties over Germany after he had been promoted out of the front line. While commanding officer of RAF Coningsby, he had flown with the legendary 617 Squadron, then led by Leonard Cheshire, who was always pleased to take 'passengers' under his wing. (As a schoolgirl, Ann had served bacon and eggs to the 617 bomber crews.) Following his appointment as Deputy Chief of Staff to the US 8th Air Force in February 1943, he had taken part as a volunteer in numerous B-17 bombing raids. On one of these, acting as gunner, he had driven off repeated attacks by enemy aircraft, displaying gallantry which earned him the Silver Star, an unusual award for a British officer. In fact he had continued to fly B-17 missions until an order came through prohibiting him from doing so any further. For a while he had served as air aide de camp to King George VI. The tradition of patriotric sevice in Ann's family contrasted with the lamentable record of the Cornwells.

which he jumped from a tethered balloon, he was posted to the Intelligence Corps Depot, at Maresfield Camp near Uckfield in East Sussex, to undergo further specialist training before being sent abroad. By this time he knew that his destination would be Austria, which like Germany was divided into zones controlled by the victorious Allies. Britain occupied the southern zone of the country, with garrisons at Graz, Villach and Klagenfurt, and an infantry battalion stationed in Vienna for ceremonial duties. This was a comparatively cushy posting, given that other National Servicemen were being sent to Malaya, where they faced Communist insurgents, or even to Korea, where British troops were fighting an all-out war under the auspices of the United Nations. The invasion of South Korea by the forces of the Communist North in June had come as a complete surprise. In its early stages there seemed a genuine prospect that the conflict in Korea might escalate into a third world war.[4] In response the government had extended the period of National Service from eighteen months to two years.

David found the months he spent at the Maresfield Camp shockingly directionless. To his fellow Shirburnian Gerald Peacocke, who was already there when David arrived, he seemed to glide effortlessly through the exercises. They were taught methods of interrogation by one Sergeant Kauffmann,* who horrified them with accounts of methods used in the field which seemed to David indistinguishable from torture. Among the practical tips David learned during the course was not to interview prisoners across a narrow, flimsy table, but always to use one too wide to reach across and too heavy to overturn. But most of the training exercises took place on paper, which was hardly exciting for restless young men. To relieve the boredom, David staged a play for the NCOs and other ranks at the Depot, *The Ghost of Jerry Bundler*, in which he took a leading part himself. This one-act play, first performed in 1899 and combining comedy with a supernatural frisson, was well received.

David's training was interrupted by an accident, after he had escorted Ann to another RAF dance. A staff car was driving them to the railway station late at night. The driver, perhaps distracted by the young couple's

* In *A Perfect Spy* Magnus Pym is driven to a rendezvous on the Czech frontier by a Corporal Kauffmann, a self-confessed coward.

passionate embraces visible in his rear-view mirror, took a bend too fast, skidded, lost control of the car, mounted the verge and crashed into a telegraph pole. The driver was left unconscious, slumped across the steering wheel. David was concussed, his nose broken; Ann suffered a cut across her eye which required stitches.

The accident seems to have brought the two of them closer together. Looking back on the incident afterwards David would refer to it as a 'God-sent car smash'.[5]

At Ronnie's insistence David saw a specialist, who advised that he should convalesce in a darkened room at home for several weeks, not reading or moving his head more than absolutely necessary. In a larky letter to Ann from Tunmers David pretended that the children's nanny was trying to seduce him. 'She *is* rather pretty,' he wrote mischievously, 'but has a strong Kentish accent.'[6] David's letters to Ann were characterised by youthful high spirits, and sometimes strayed into fantasy or plain invention. Repeatedly he apologised for being 'an ass', for feeling 'a bit light-headed', for writing 'nonsense'. The margins of his letters were illustrated with jokey cartoons. He sent her some poems, which he cheerfully admitted were no good. 'I have *no* poetic pretensions whatsoever!' he insisted. 'I write to amuse myself and no one else. I do it not as vanity but as a pastime, and I am the first to admit that it is quite hopeless.'[7]

In mid-December, by then fully recovered from his accident, David left for Switzerland to take part in the Downhill Only Club's training scheme, in preparation for the British Ski Championships in January. The War Office had granted him leave from his duties so that he could participate in the annual races held at the main ski resorts. Six young skiers gathered under the guidance of a Swiss professional to undertake an arduous and often frightening programme, racing at up to eighty miles per hour, learning to ski on one leg and to ski-jump.[8] Ronnie and Jean watched and cheered him on. David did well enough in the races to be awarded his DHO racing colours, but suffered the greatest disappointment of his skiing career when he was disqualified from taking part in the championships for an infringement. 'I broke down and cried like a child when I saw what had happened,' he admitted.

Ann was due to come out to Chamonix in her capacity as honorary secretary of the RAF Winter Sports Association. To fill the time before her arrival David found temporary work as a ski instructor. One day he paid a visit to a Frenchwoman in hospital who had broken both her legs in a skiing accident. He found her lying on her back, both legs in traction, 'a little scrap of a woman in her fifties with short peroxide hair and a fat lipstick mouth drawn over the thin one underneath'. She told him that she had been in the Resistance during the war: she had parachuted into France she forgot how many times, but had never broken anything until she went skiing. She had spent the last year of the war in a concentration camp where they had shaved her head, she explained, as if she had been talking of a few weeks on the Riviera. Though other people's hair had grown back again, hers for some reason had not, and she feared that it never would. The memory of this remarkable woman with her insouciant humour lodged in his mind, and would form the basis of the character Elsa Fennan in his first book.[9]

Once Ann had joined David in Chamonix their relations reached a new level of intensity. 'A dream came true,' he wrote to her after they had spent a night together, though stopping short of intercourse. 'Love was greater than shame, because it was more powerful . . . There was no law of custom to control, no power to restrain.'[10] What had happened between them filled David with wonder. 'There used to be something rather attractive in longing for the totally unattainable,' he mused; and continued by borrowing a favourite maxim of his father's: 'for ideals are supposed to be like stars: "we cannot reach them yet we prophet [sic] by their presence".* I am a little frightened at having reached the stars so soon.' He assured Ann that 'both Jeanie and Daddy . . . regard you as "a good influence"'. There had been some tension between their families, after Rosemary Collins, wife of the group captain, had painted 'a very black picture of our family to your mother'.[11] It seems that the RAF Winter Sports Scheme was at the root of this; though Collins was in on the racket, he would later tell David that Ronnie had gulled him into it.

* David's spelling was surprisingly poor for someone of his age (nineteen) and intelligence, one result perhaps of the premature end to his schooling. In other letters written around this time he spells 'weather' as 'wheather', 'bizarre' as 'bazaar' and 'vacuum' as 'vaccuum'.

By this time David had returned to Maresfield to complete his training. He confided to Ann that he had received 'an absolute rocket from Daddy for spending too much' in Switzerland.[12] This was a difficult time for Ronnie: the building societies were becoming restive, and increasingly he was having to borrow money to support his position. Moreover he was being harassed by bankruptcy petitions from builders and other suppliers. A receiving order was made against him, though this was rescinded a few days later.

As David's overseas posting approached, Ann's anxiety that he would stray while they were apart became manifest. Her fears were exacerbated by a morbid dread of venereal infection. David pledged himself to be faithful, but he would continue to tease her with stories of other women.[13]

He took some leave at the end of his Intelligence Corps training before going abroad. He stayed a few days with another member of the Downhill Only Club racing team, Michael Barnard-Hankey, at his family's Dorset manor house, Plush, a name which David would later borrow for Mary Pym's family home in *A Perfect Spy*. This was a feudal village; even the pub was named the Hankey Arms. David had never before stayed in a house where one was expected to dress for dinner. He found himself seated next to Betty Kenward, the notoriously snobbish 'Jennifer' whose social 'diary' then appeared regularly in the *Tatler*. Perhaps fortunately, the Cornwell family was beneath her notice.

David left England in the middle of March 1951. With Gerald Peacocke and another British officer, he took a 'Med Loc' (Mediterranean location) military train up the Rhine into southern Germany, and then across the eastern Alps into Austria. Much later David would rhapsodise about the sight of bare-breasted peasant women working in the fields, though it seems odd that Peacocke has no memory of these, and it was a little early in the year for such a display. David would later claim that these were the first breasts that he had ever seen, perhaps forgetting his girlfriend's.

They separated at Villach, near the Yugoslav border, then a very sensitive region; Peacocke continued to Trieste, while David was stationed at Graz, capital of Styria, the most easterly of the regions overseen by Western powers in Europe. Like so many soldiers, he had taken up smoking – cigarettes, cigars and a pipe. Graz was widely held to be an ideal posting, where the price of almost everything – especially alcohol and cigarettes – was about half the English equivalent. Only clothing cost more. In these circumstances, rackets proliferated, and plenty of military supplies went missing.

David was designated a field security officer, based in the Palais Meran, an elegant neo-classical villa on the outskirts of Graz. There telephone interceptions were written in shorthand, translated and transcribed, for later processing. In the evenings listeners could sometimes hear drunken Russian technicians singing on the line. David inherited from his predecessor a string of informants ('joes'), who regularly passed on low-grade information in return for sweeteners of various kinds.

From the balcony of a small hotel outside Villach David wrote to Ann. 'This is life!' he enthused. 'This great transformation from the grey indifference of England to the bewitching colour and the bright rebirth of Spring in Austria.' On his limited acquaintance he thought the Austrians 'wonderful people . . . kinder and happier than the Swiss or the French – or even the Germans'. A few days later he was aboard a sleeper, bound for Vienna, passing through the Russian zone. 'It's amusing to say to oneself, "out there are Russians",' he reflected. 'If I got off this train now I would be interrogated, tortured and shot.'[14] Perhaps this was an exaggeration, but it was certainly true that relations between British and Russian soldiers, congenial after the war, had deteriorated sharply by the early 1950s, especially along the Yugoslav border. While in Vienna he dressed in civilian clothes to attend a 'very interesting' Communist meeting.[15]

'Did you read in the paper about the Napier case?' he asked Ann in another letter. Captain Neville Napier, a transport officer married to an Austrian-born countess, had received a nine-year prison sentence from a British military court at Graz for supplying information to a Czech spy, on the flimsy pretext that he had been appointed 'military correspondent' for a Middle European press agency.* Perhaps this sensational spy trial came as a salutary warning to David; he seemed to hint as much. 'If I had not made the mistake of getting to know people too well, I should be

* In *The Spy who Came in from the Cold* an East German agent makes a similar offer to Alec Leamas.

very happy,' he wrote to Ann. 'As it is I shall change my routine and my company and, apart from my work, start again.'[16]

The Napier trial, itself relatively insignificant, was one of a succession of scandals that shook confidence in British security. In 1949 it had been revealed that the Russians had successfully tested an atomic bomb. The defection of the experimental physicist Bruno Pontecorvo, who had been working on the British nuclear energy project at Harwell, followed only six months after the confession of the British theoretical physicist Klaus Fuchs that he had passed atomic secrets to the Russians. Some years earlier Alan Nunn May, who like Fuchs had worked on the Manhattan Project, had confessed to passing samples of uranium isotopes to the Russians. Taken together, these revelations had led to a crisis in intelligence co-operation with the Americans, who doubted whether the British could be trusted with their secrets. The Americans deplored what they saw as lax British procedures, while the British were resistant to what seemed to them anti-Communist hysteria. Nevertheless, the British government took steps to tighten security after Fuchs's confession and subsequent conviction.[17]

A few weeks after the Napier trial, David was summoned by his commanding officer and shown two photographs. 'If you see either of these men you will report that information to a senior officer immediately, do you hear?' If he could not find a senior officer, he was ordered to arrest the pair himself. Their names, he learned a few days later, courtesy of the *Daily Express*, were Guy Burgess and Donald Maclean, members of the British Foreign Service suspected of spying for the Soviet Union.

One of David's principal tasks was to interrogate illegal frontier crossers (IFCs), being held in camps while their fate was decided. Hundreds of thousands of people were on the move, most trying to escape from countries under Communist control. In *A Perfect Spy* David would provide a vivid picture of this exodus:

> For five years the refugees of Eastern Europe had been pouring into Austria through every fast-closing gap in the barbed wire: crashing frontiers in stolen cars and lorries, across minefields, clinging to the underneath of trains, to be corralled and questioned and decided over in their thousands, while they played chess on wooden packing cases and showed each other photographs of people they would never see again. They came from Hungary and

> Romania and Poland and Czechoslovakia and Yugoslavia and sometimes Russia, and they hoped they were on their way to Canada and Australia and Palestine. They had travelled by devious routes and often for devious reasons. They were doctors and scientists and bricklayers. They were truck drivers, thieves, acrobats, publishers, rapists and architects.

David travelled in his jeep from camp to camp interrogating such people. In doing so, he had to ask himself several questions. Is this man who he says he is? Is he a security risk? Is he a criminal? Does he have any intelligence that we need? In fact most of those whom he interrogated were merely desperate refugees. Many of them were subsequently passed on to bodies such as the International Relief Organisation or the Jewish Resettlement Agency. In liaising with the Austrian authorities about the fate of such refugees, David was conscious that almost every official he dealt with had previously worked for the Nazi regime. This was a period of extraordinary reversals, when former foes became friends, and former friends foes. The Germans, against whom the British had poured out all their strength only a few years previously, had been co-opted into the Cold War against Communism; while the Russians, who had done so much to slay the Nazi monster, had become adversaries in a worldwide ideological struggle. This turnaround had occurred with shocking rapidity. The same pilots who had bombed Berlin in 1945 were running the Berlin airlift in 1948. This inversion of alliances led some to question what they were being told by their masters. George Orwell's *Nineteen Eighty-Four* (1949) imagined a world of perpetual warfare, in which the state cynically manipulates the patriotic fervour of the populace, a world in which an orator could change the identity of the hated enemy in mid-sentence, without pause or protest.

'At first his sensitivity was offended by so much misery and he had a hard time disguising his sympathy for everyone he spoke to,' David wrote of his fictional double Magnus Pym in *A Perfect Spy*. But he soon became hardened to it, and confessed to Ann that he was 'beginning to get frightened' by his own indifference towards other people's suffering. 'Sometimes I almost welcome the misfortunes of people around me, for when a man is sad he is weak.'[18] He would consult his own nature to assess when someone was lying to him, or at least not telling him the whole truth, making small talk while he watched and read the signals that came back to him. If the person he was interrogating seemed to be lying, he would take rapid back-bearings on likely versions of the truth with the aid of his own mental compass:

> Questions teemed in him and, budding lawyer that he was, he learned quickly to shape them into a pattern of accusation. 'Where do you come from? What troops did you see there? What colour shoulder boards did they wear? What did they drive around in, what weapons did they have? Which route did you take, what guards, obstructions, dogs, wire, mine-fields did you meet along the way? What shoes were you wearing? How did your mother manage, your grandmother, if the mountain pass was so steep? How did you cope with two suitcases and two small children when your wife was so heavily pregnant? Is it not more likely that your employers in the Hungarian secret police drove you to the border and wished you luck as they showed you where to cross? Are you a spy, and if so, would you not prefer to spy for us? Or are you merely a criminal, in which case you would surely like to take up spying, rather than be tossed back across the border by the Austrian police?'[19]

In the middle of his tour David returned to England on leave. It had been arranged that he would spend a weekend with Ann's family. After so many loving letters, Ann had been eagerly anticipating his arrival, so she was disappointed that their time together was repeatedly interrupted by telephone calls from Ronnie, and she was bemused when David left prematurely on the Sunday morning. He explained that his father had paid for his trip back to England and required his presence at home.

If David was surprisingly compliant to his father's wishes, he nevertheless resented Ronnie's attempts to dictate what he would do after he left the army. 'Daddy sent me a whole lot of nonsense about legal study and what have you,' he grumbled to Ann, and continued, 'I've written to Daddy demanding independence and a room in town when I get back.'[20] He was determined not to be bullied into submission, as he felt his brother had been. Tony had gone up to Cambridge on a classical scholarship, and had succumbed to paternal pressure to switch to law, though his heart was never in it; he had suffered the humiliation of being summoned to appear before the Master of his college when one of Ronnie's cheques had bounced. After two years at Cambridge Tony had left in 1951 without taking his degree, going on to Bowdoin College in Maine on a scholarship to study creative writing. Though afterwards he kept his promise to his father to return and complete his course, studying alongside Learie Constantine at Gray's Inn, Tony would leave England again, this time for Canada, the day after he was called to the Bar. He would never practise law.

'Our world means freedom from the sordid and beastly grind of the "dark satanic mills",' David insisted. 'I'm damned if I'll be hemmed in like a rat in a trap.' He emphatically did not want a conventional career. 'They can keep their stiff collars and paper cuffs, their quills and files, test-tubes and blue-prints . . .' In a frisky, sometimes incoherent letter to Ann, David tried to:

> make you dream of the things I dream of – independence, divorce from tiresome people, far away lands flowing with milk & honey. Pictures and poems. Vast and beautiful paintings – light and wonderful poetry. And then suddenly something happens: like a falling rafter, a crash of the inevitable practical resounds like an explosion among the rivers and banks of the Lethe:* parents, bar-exams, money. Then finally – revolt.
>
> I shall always end up as a revolutionary.[21]

Gerald Peacocke bumped into David again during a period of leave in Vienna in September. From David's demeanour he gained the impression that his old schoolmate was concerned with 'hush-hush' matters. In fact David's most vivid experience of a clandestine intelligence operation had been a fiasco, as he would later readily concede.

He had been recruited for a top-secret mission by the Air Intelligence Officer, or AIO, a man called Joe Kraemer, a mysterious, solitary figure

* One of the rivers of the Underworld in Greek mythology. All who drank from it forgot their past lives.

within the Graz headquarters about whom little definite was known, but who, so it was hinted, was a member of MI6, involved in agent-running. The mission required a trip to the frontier to meet a high-ranking officer in the Czech air force, apparently willing to supply precious intelligence in exchange for cash.

'Why me, Sir?' David had asked, as they took a quiet stroll along the river together.

'Because you've got what it takes,' the AIO replied tersely.

David persisted. 'How do you know I have, Sir?' he asked.

'Been watching you.'

For the operation David decided to wear a green loden coat, plus, for additional cover, a green Tyrolean hat, purchased at personal expense.

The AIO collected him in an unmarked Volkswagen Beetle with civilian number plates. On the back seat lay a brown briefcase containing, he told David, 10,000 US dollars. They drove across country as darkness fell. At first David could think of nothing but the heavy 9mm Browning automatic jammed down his waistband against his left hip, as instructed by the AIO, so that he could draw it easily across his body. Now and then he fingered the safety catch nervously.

The rendezvous was a bar in a frontier village just inside Austria. The AIO entered first, followed by David carrying the briefcase. In a single, low-ceilinged room, the inhabitants stared through the tobacco smoke at the two Englishmen in mute amazement. The AIO ordered two beers from the landlord, and then gestured towards a billiards table. 'Fancy a game?' he asked from the corner of his mouth. David muttered his assent. By this time he had become accustomed to the presence of the Browning automatic on his hip. As he stooped to play the ball, he was startled by the clang of metal on the tiled floor; by the time he realised what had happened and bent to retrieve his weapon, the inn had emptied. 'Abort,' ordered the AIO, pausing only to finish his beer.

Afterwards David reflected on what had happened. Had the Czech airman attempted to cross the frontier? Had there ever been a Czech airman? The AIO had vanished two days after the operation, so there was no one to ask. David concluded that the AIO might not have been an MI6 officer at all, but simply a forgotten soul, living in a secret bubble of his own, dreaming the Great Spy's Dream. 'He imagined himself at the Spies'

Big Table, playing the world's game. Gradually, the gap between the dream and the reality became too much for him to bear, and one day he decided to fill it. He needed a believer, so I got the job.'[22]

This is the story as it was published in the *New Yorker* in 2008. But the magazine's fact-checkers failed to notice a troubling detail: the Czech border was in the Soviet zone. It seems scarcely credible that two plain-clothed British officers, armed with at least one weapon and carrying a suitcase full of dollars, could have driven a hundred miles or more through the Soviet zone for a rendezvous with a Czech agent. Perhaps David misremembered the details; perhaps he and the AIO met the Czech airman on the Yugoslav border, indeed perhaps he was a Yugoslav airman. Or perhaps the whole story is imaginary.

Some time after this confusing episode, David received a visit from a uniformed officer, 'from Vienna', who introduced himself as 'Major Smith'. He represented the Secret Service, he said. 'We are thinking of you down the line,' the Major told him. But first, he made clear, David would need to obtain a degree.

Towards the end of 1951 David returned to Switzerland, to rejoin the Downhill Only Club's racing team at Wengen. He hoped to do well enough to gain selection for the British team for the 1952 winter Olympics. In a letter to Ann he confessed to 'a rather cheap little affair in Graz before I left, which made me feel rotten – and realise how much you really meant to me'.[23] By 'affair' he meant not a sexual relationship, but what would more usually be called a flirtation. There was an element of braggadocio in his letters to Ann.

After a few weeks' training with the team in Wengen, David went ahead to St Moritz, the location for their first race, to find accommodation for the others. This was not easy. St Moritz was so full over the New Year that, as one newspaper reported, 'Maharajahs were sleeping in bathrooms!' Somehow David was able to persuade the ever-helpful Herr Badrutt to find places for them. In his report on the 1951–2 season, the team captain congratulated David on doing 'an excellent job as Billeting Officer'.

In Wengen David had already shown himself to be one of the two fastest members of the team, and in St Moritz he raced faster and faster. On 6 January 1952 he was the quickest British entrant in a race organised by the local Skiclub Alpina, despite taking a bad fall and suffering severe concussion. To get up again and finish the race in these circumstances, and in such a quick time, was, in the words of the team captain, 'an amazing display of courage and determination'. The team then moved on to Klosters, where the British Championships were due to be held, leaving David to recover in the care of the St Moritz clinic – or so they thought, but he climbed out of a window and followed them, appearing in Klosters the next evening. By 12 January David was racing again – inadvisedly, because he took another fall, which was enough to bring on the concussion in an aggravated form, blinding him for thirty-six hours. 'His courage in insisting on continuing to race after his accident at St. Moritz should have been restrained,' commented the team captain in his annual report.[24]

'No cause whatever for worry – except that there is no earthly chance of going to the Olympics or anything else,' David wrote to assure Ann, who was once again in Chamonix with the RAF Winter Sports Association. A few days later he was back at Tunmers. 'I've got to take a month's complete rest, and so I don't think I shall go back to Austria at all,' he told her. This would be the end of his active service in the army, though like other National Servicemen he would remain a reservist, required to undertake two weeks' refresher training at Maresfield annually, for several successive summers. A week later David sent Ann another bulletin. 'As far as I can make out I shan't be able to race again, so I shall just have to ski prettily instead. How foul . . .' He passed the time by trying to paint, drawing caricatures of 'Wengen Faces' for the Downhill Only Club's journal, and writing 'bad poetry'.[25]

While David was recovering, a visitor came to stay at Tunmers. This was 'Mr Flynn', a dreadfully thin, wild-eyed, unshaven man of indeterminate middle age, who dressed as if just released from prison. At a family briefing, attended by a couple of his courtiers and by Flynn himself, Ronnie explained that Flynn was a hero. Years later David would paint the scene:

> We were to tell nobody what we were about to hear. During the war Flynn had served in the most secret of secret services: an unsung tiny band of intrepid men and women who were under Winston Churchill's personal command. None of us sitting in this room – except Flynn, of

> course – would ever know what contributions Flynn had made to the Allied victory. Yet without him we might not be sitting here at all, and wasn't that right, Flynn? And Flynn, who had a rich Irish accent, was very pleased, and said yes, it was quite right.

Ronnie went on to explain that the Prime Minister wished to reward Flynn for his services, but for obvious reasons couldn't do so publicly, and a medal was out of the question. So in two weeks' time, at a private ceremony in Buckingham Palace, to which Ronnie and a few other trusted friends were privileged to be invited, His Majesty the King *in person* was going to appoint Flynn to the very important and lucrative post of Consul-General in Lisbon, after which Flynn would put Ronnie in the way of all sorts of lucrative business.

For the following fortnight Flynn was billeted at Tunmers – in David's bedroom, in the spare bed next to his. Flynn would wander around the room in borrowed pyjamas like a prisoner pacing out his cell, whispering to himself in a rich, unintelligible Irish brogue. Some mornings Ronnie would take him up to London; there were debts to be paid off, because the poor chap had been down on his luck until dear old Winston had remembered him. There was a morning suit to be bought, not hired, because it would be needed in Lisbon; and a trousseau of suits, shirts and underclothes because, as Ronnie explained, Flynn was too proud to ask for an advance against his salary.

After a week of this David took his courage in his hands and told Ronnie that he thought Flynn was barking mad, only to be rebuked for his cynicism.

When the due day arrived, Messrs Cornwell and Flynn drove up to London in their morning coats, top hats on the back seat. Arriving at Ronnie's office in Mount Street, Flynn explained that he had some business to attend to before going to the Palace, and disappeared in a taxi, saying 'meet you there'.

A couple of hours later, Ronnie left his office, hailed a taxi and instructed the driver to take him to the Palace. On the way he confided in the cabbie, having first of course sworn him to secrecy. But as they entered the Mall, the driver pointed out that there was no flag flying from the Palace roof. Even then Ronnie did not lose faith. Since the investiture was private, the King was rightly keeping his presence quiet until the ceremony was over, he decided. The policeman at the Palace gates disillusioned him. His Majesty was at Sandringham and was expected to remain there for some time.[26]

The missing Flynn was arrested a few weeks later on a string of charges, including the theft of David's Burberry raincoat.

As David recovered from his skiing accident, Ronnie renewed the pressure on him. 'The ball of my "future career" has started to roll,' he wrote to Ann while she was still out in Chamonix:

> So much so that I am at present supposed to be
>
> 1. In the Army
> 2. At Oxford
> 3. At Cambridge
> 4. At Gibson & Weldon's, Law Tutors . . .
>
> One thing is beyond doubt – that by the time you come back I shall be studying somewhere with a view to doing something afterwards. I think that I should rather like to open a small pub in the East-end.
>
> I am pretty mobile now and will soon have to totter back to the army to get myself officially released. After that it's the oak table and the inky nose for yours truly . . .
>
> It's probably the bar for me. One way or the other.[27]*

A few days later he told her that he would 'probably' go up to Oxford in October – though the deadline for entries was past, so the only way he could obtain a place would be by special pleading. When Ann protested that he didn't seem to have any ideas of his own about his future, he insisted that he did, 'and believe me, those are the ones that are going to count!' He was relaxing with his father and stepmother 'among the monkey-puzzle trees and rhododendrons of Bournemouth – the place is full of dying aunts and

* He illustrated this comment with a cartoon showing himself in alternate poses: one leaning against a bar, on which rested a soda siphon; the other declaiming in wig and gown.

Baptist clergymen . . . Actually it's quite fun here and I do very little but play Daddy billiards for drinks . . .'[28] Possibly Ronnie was using his visit to extract money from his mother, because around this time she put £6,000 into one of his companies.

David often addressed his girlfriend as 'Mousey' or 'Ann Mouse' (he kept his St Andrew's nickname of 'Maggot'), and his letters were sometimes illustrated with cartoons depicting her as such. 'I spend all day drawing now,' he told her. He had established a studio in the attic at Tunmers. 'I draw from morning till night and am terribly happy.'[29]

Meanwhile Ronnie had sought the help of Sir James Barnes, who had prevailed upon Sir Folliott Sandford, an Air Ministry colleague who knew the Rector of Lincoln College,* to write to him on David's behalf. 'Barnes is very much interested in finding a possible vacancy at Oxford in October for the son of an old friend, who is anxious to read modern languages with a view to entering the Foreign Service.' The Rector, Keith Murray, had a word with the college chaplain and history tutor, the Reverend Vivian Green, who had taught at Sherborne before coming to Oxford; Green remembered David as 'very intelligent' and recommended that the college should find a place for him if possible. Murray warned Sandford that the prospects were not good at this late date, as the college already had its full quota of freshmen for the academic year beginning in October, by then only six months away; but there remained a faint possibility that someone might drop out, and he offered to consider young Cornwell for any vacancy which might arise if he were willing to take a college entrance examination. David duly submitted an application form. Under 'other interests' he listed 'writing' as well as 'painting and caricaturing'.

Ronnie believed that, like Tony, David planned to read law, and David, like Magnus Pym in *A Perfect Spy*, did not disabuse him. So David recalled several decades later: according to him, Ronnie discovered the truth that he was reading modern languages only after he had been up at Oxford for a while.[30] He has written of Ronnie's distress at the discovery and a subsequent confrontation with Vivian Green, by then the college senior tutor.

* The head of Lincoln College, Oxford, is known as its Rector. This post has no ecclesiastical status.

Such an encounter between two contrasting father figures is psychologically beguiling. But the story is difficult to reconcile with the letter from Sir James Barnes's colleague Sir Folliott Sandford, which mentions David's wish to read modern languages. If Sandford knew that he was not planning to read law, then so, presumably, did Barnes, and it would be strange if he had concealed this from his chum Ronnie. David told Ann of his plan to read modern languages, without asking her to keep this secret. Vivian Green's unpublished memoir, written many years later, provides a vivid description of a visit from Ronnie 'with his well-brushed brilliantined hair, smart blue suit and polished black shoes' to discuss his son's future; but, far from coming to confront him, Ronnie is portrayed as 'the acme of charm'. Moreover this account is apparently at odds with a letter from David to Green written in the autumn of 1954, which refers to his upcoming wedding as 'a chance for you to meet Papa', implying that they had not met before. (A further complication is that Ronnie was not invited to the wedding, though perhaps this had not been decided at the time.) Weighing the evidence, it seems possible that the confrontation is an example of false memory on David's part, perhaps a result of the imaginative effort required to recast his life in fictional form. Just possibly this imaginative reconstruction was so powerful that Green too absorbed it.

Having little else to do, and being now well enough to travel, David joined Ronnie and the family for a ten-day holiday in Monte Carlo. They stayed at the five-star Hôtel de Paris, only yards from the Casino. 'One seems either to be acquiring or sleeping off a hangover,' David wrote to Ann, though he did find time to paint and play tennis. 'Daddy plays in the Casino a good deal, but doesn't have much luck.'[31] One evening David watched Ronnie playing at the big table, a complimentary brandy and ginger in front of him. Also there was King Farouk's equerry, a polished, grey-haired man, with a white telephone at his elbow. This linked him directly to the Egyptian King, then in the last months of his reign, who had become notorious for gluttony, extravagance and gambling. From time to time the white telephone would ring, the equerry would raise the receiver and listen impassively to his master's instructions, and then transfer some of the chips from the diminishing pile in front of him on to the appropriate square. David imagined the King at the other end, surrounded by astrologers. To his alarm, he noticed Ronnie raising his bids. As his father splashed out the last of his chips and beckoned imperiously for more, David realised that he was not playing a hunch, or playing the house, or playing the numbers: he was playing the King. He watched with horror as more and more chips disappeared into the croupier's maw. At last, in the small hours of the morning, Ronnie was done. In the pre-dawn twilight father and son sauntered down the esplanade to the twenty-four-hour jewellers to pawn Ronnie's platinum cigarette case and gold wristwatch. As they parted in the foyer of the Hôtel de Paris, Ronnie boasted that he had shown 'that chap Farouk' a thing or two. The King's losses, he reckoned, had been two or three times his own. 'Win it all back tomorrow with interest, right, old son?'[32]

While in Monaco David witnessed a pigeon shoot, devised to allow disappointed punters to let off steam. On a lawn facing out to sea, half-cut guests reclined on day-beds, shotguns at the ready. Among them were Hector Caird, owner of the society magazine the *Queen*; and a crony of Ronnie's, Sir Bracewell Smith, a former Conservative MP and lord mayor of London. Pigeons emerged in front of them from underground tunnels, stumbling their way into the sunlight, only to be shot at by the recumbent guests. David was horrified by the pile of dead birds, some still fluttering in their death-agony. Those few that escaped homed naturally to the place where they had been bred, the Casino roof, and so were captured and put back into the tunnel, only to run the gauntlet again. This grotesque image left a lasting impression.* David identified with the pigeons, unable to escape and lacking the wit to fly away. In a letter to Ann he wrote that 'the sooner I get out of this utterly crazy place, the happier I shall be'.[33]

Ann and David were reunited after he returned to England towards the end of March 1952. By now she was longing to marry him. In her diary she confessed to being 'infernally jealous' when he told her that he had met a debutante in Wengen who wanted to do 'the season' with him. 'Are you in love with me?' she had demanded, 'or are you just pretending?' David replied that he didn't know, and asked her the same question. Ann paused,

* He contemplated using the title 'The Pigeon Tunnel' for several of his books: among them *The Naïve and Sentimental Lover*, *The Honourable Schoolboy* and *Smiley's People*.

and replied, 'I know I can't imagine being without you.' In her diary she confided her fears that he had grown away from her, and agonised about whether or not to spend a night with him, as she had done in Chamonix – 'probably better not', she eventually decided, 'or I'd have been virgin no longer'.

Ann cherished an ambition to be a writer. She encouraged David to pursue his artistic talent, imagining the two of them as a creative couple. When he telephoned to say that he was going up to Oxford for an interview, she felt disappointed in him. 'Oh he's weak really, I suppose – yet his paintings are really good,' she recorded in her diary. 'He needs to be poor, properly poor, and have to live by it.' No doubt one reason why she did not want him to go to university was that it meant continuing to be dependent on his father for the next three years.

David breezed through the interview with the Rector. According to Vivian Green, who was also present, he arrived in a smart pepper-and-salt suit and 'displayed the charismatic qualities which at later dates have enchanted his interviewers'. The next step was for him to take the entrance exam. Ann secretly hoped that he would fail. In fact he passed, achieving marks of α–?–* in German and of β+ in his general paper.

Meanwhile the college had sought an opinion from David's former housemaster. In due course a 'private and confidential' response arrived from Thompson. 'He is an extremely sensitive boy, artistic and a poet, and he has a good brain' wrote Thompson. 'Perhaps by now he has steadied down, at any rate I hope so, for he has it in him to do very well at anything to which he gives his mind with conviction. He strikes me as the sort who might become either Archbishop of Canterbury or a first-rate criminal!' Thompson was in favour of awarding a place to David, but not in 1952.

> I really do not think he ought to step in at the last minute where others have tried and failed, who have passed the necessary tests. The Cornwells tend to assume that what they want they get, at least that is the impression I have of his father. Mr Cornwell is an enigma – very charming and persuasive, but wholly without principle, I should say.[34]

* A nice donnish discrimination, somewhere between alpha minus and alpha double minus.

The college chose not to take Thompson's advice. In mid-May, after another candidate had dropped out, the Rector wrote to David offering him a place starting in October, which he gratefully accepted.

At a celebratory dinner David explained to Ann that he would need a few weeks' extra tuition in Oxford during the summer to bring him up to the required standard for a first-year undergraduate – especially to prepare for a Latin exam.[35] He promised her that he had not forgotten his ambition to become an artist, and spoke of going to art school in the university vacations, using drawing 'as a sideline' to begin with, and possibly graduating to it full time later on. Over the weeks that followed he tried to obtain private commissions to earn extra money. One evening he plucked up courage to go up to town alone, and succeeded in selling three caricatures at five guineas each to members of the Albany Club.[36]

Ann came to stay a weekend at Tunmers, which gave her an opportunity to observe her boyfriend's father at close hand. Ronnie was very much in control, she noticed, remaining slumped in his armchair in the sitting room with a large brandy and ginger by his side, while David (who was permitted only sherry) was called upon to run hither and thither. She was surprised by his docility, in contrast to the rebellious tone of his letters. Ronnie attempted to charm her, without success. Ann was suspicious of him from the outset. His entire way of life offended against her moral code. He was, she would say later, 'the only really evil person I ever met'.

She was now working for Odhams Publishers. Her job was mostly secretarial, but with some proof-reading and paste-up work. She had begun writing poetry again. 'If only it was any good!' she lamented in her diary. Some short stories she had submitted to the weekly literary magazine *John O'London's* were returned with a rejection slip.

Once again at a loose end and short of cash, David accepted an offer of temporary work from his father, who had acquired the *Cricketer*, a fortnightly publication founded in 1921 by the former England Test match player Sir Pelham 'Plum' Warner and still edited by him. After some weeks in Ronnie's Mount Street offices fruitlessly trying to promote the moribund journal, David agreed to undertake a tour of the north of England with Robin Cooke, selling copies to retailers. They would travel in Ronnie's Triumph two-seater, with Cooke taking the wheel, as David had not yet learned to drive; Ronnie undertook to pay them each £6 per week. He warned them not to fill up the car at the nearest garage, but they forgot; as they motored on to the forecourt, Cooke spotted the attendant rushing to the telephone, so he accelerated away without stopping. Although David wrote to Ann from Newport to say that they were 'doing quite well', the reality was rather different: they dumped hundreds of copies in a ditch by the side of the road rather than admit that no one would take them. After five weeks they reported back to Ronnie, expecting to collect £30 each. 'What shall I say?' he asked rhetorically. 'Fifteen pounds?' Cooke was particularly annoyed, as he had arranged to buy a dinner jacket on the strength of his promised earnings. After protests from the young men, Ronnie reluctantly stumped up the amount agreed, before taking the boys to an expensive lunch at Claridge's.

David went up Oxford to begin his extra tuition in August, and found lodgings in St John Street. A few days later he wrote that he was working very hard – 'harder than you would credit me with'. He had cancelled a holiday in Switzerland because of pressure of work.[37]

When Ann came to visit, he took her punting with Colin Simpson, a neighbour from Chalfont St Peter who was also coming up to Oxford in October. 'I have decided that in future I will let D touch my breasts, but nothing more,' she wrote in her diary afterwards. Meanwhile Tony, who had returned from America to resume his legal studies, came up to Oxford for the day, with a friend from Bowdoin College in tow. David complained to Ann that he could not understand them: 'We had Dollars at Balliol, Fraternities at Lincoln and Cookies at Univ.' He felt alienated from his brother, he told her. 'When I am away from him I admire him, when I am with him I find him incomprehensible.'[38]

Once his summer cramming was over David took a short working holiday in France, narrated in a series of postcards to Ann. 'A crazy, penniless, amusing week doing everything from serving as a barman to taking mass at Notre Dame,' he wrote to her in mid-September. Three days later he sent another postcard, boasting that he had 'walked repeat *walked* Paris–Orleans. Thence Orleans–Blois also on foot. Quel héro!'[39]*

* Eighty-four and thirty-nine miles respectively.

Towards the end of September Tony received a paternal summons to Ronnie's office in the West End, where he found David and his father with a stranger, a middle-aged woman who spoke in a strong Middle European accent. She was introduced as a baroness, the widow of a member of the Rothschild family murdered by the Nazis. Ronnie explained that the baroness had come to him in great secrecy for help. He asked her to repeat her story for the benefit of his sons. This she did, partly in German which David translated, and punctuated by tears. At the time of the *Anschluss* she and her late husband had entrusted a treasure chest to Roman Catholic priests, who had kept it hidden throughout the war. Its contents included American bullion, a Gutenberg Bible and rolled-up canvases of Old Master paintings.* She now planned to reclaim the chest by smuggling it across the Swiss border. All she needed was a little seed-capital to pay off the priests and bribe the customs officials as necessary. Once the chest was secured, she would be content to entrust its contents to Ronnie, asking only a few thousands to cover her expenses in locating the treasure. She was not interested in money for herself, she said, and seemed content to be guided by Ronnie in managing the capital; she required merely a modest annuity.

Tony saw his brother's eyebrows rise as the 'baroness' recounted her story. Once she had left, Ronnie asked their opinion of what they had heard. David said at once that the woman was a fraud and her story ludicrous. When he suggested that they should contact the Rothschild family to check her identity, Ronnie would hear nothing of it. The poor woman was living in hiding, under an assumed name. The whole family was after that treasure, and they might be after her blood too. He appealed to his sons to suppress their cynicism just for a few days, in order to accompany the baroness to Switzerland. It was touching, David later reflected, to note the chivalry with which his father rushed to the defence of a fellow artist.

As so often in the past, David surrendered to his father's wishes. 'Afraid I've got to go to Switzerland – possibly Austria,' he wrote to Ann. 'Hope to be back early next week. Sorry. Business calls!'[40] He asked her to write

* The details remembered by the two brothers differ. According to Tony, the treasure was all gold, and was to be smuggled across the border concealed in a hay cart.

to the Dolder Grand Hotel, Zurich. Thus David escorted the baroness to Switzerland, an adventure relived by Magnus Pym. The Dolder was a smart hotel overlooking the city, frequented by royalty and film stars. The Baroness did a lot of shopping, and charged everything to the room. She warned David that it was too risky for her to accompany him to the Austrian border, as she might be recognised. 'They' would stop at nothing. Now committed, David set out for the rendezvous with the Catholic priests alone. For two days he lurked around the railway station of an Alpine hamlet while rain fell unceasingly, waiting for a contact named 'Turi Amsler'. When he gave up and returned to the Dolder, he found that the baroness had vanished, with only a stack of unpaid bills to record that she had ever been there. Ronnie never spoke of her again. 'The most he could manage was a martyred frown and a pious lowering of the eyes, indicating that human decency forbade comment.'[41]

On the morning of 6 October 1952 David went up to Oxford to begin his undergraduate career. 'Henceforward I am a strictly intellectual beast with rapidly greying hair,' he informed Ann.[42]

6

'That little college in Turl'

In *A Perfect Spy*, David's alter ego Magnus Pym represents Oxford in the early 1950s as 'a conventional sort of place'. Just to appear in public in an open-necked shirt was a statement of rebellion. Undergraduates wore tweed jackets, club or regimental ties and flannel trousers; some clenched a pipe between their teeth to demonstrate their manliness. Most came from public schools, and spoke in accents that would nowadays seem laughably posh.

Undergraduates were still woken every morning by college servants ('Scouts'), who expected to be addressed by their first names. Discipline was imposed by dons known as 'Proctors' ('Progs'), whose bowler-hatted deputies ('Bulldogs') patrolled the streets of the city and punished undergraduates detected in misbehaviour. Bulldogs still toured the pubs of Oxford in the evenings and took the names of undergraduates they found there. For though students were known collectively as 'men' and addressed respectfully as 'Mr ——', they were treated much like schoolboys.

Such a regime was especially irksome to those who had served in the forces. Among the undergraduates there was a clear distinction between those who had already done National Service (and who used service jargon) and those who had chosen to defer it until they had taken their degree (many hoping that it would have been abolished by then). Of course, those who had done their National Service straight after leaving school were on average two years older than those who had not, with correspondingly more experience of life. Moreover the majority of them had served as officers, with authority over older men; accustomed to command, they were reluctant to accept the restrictions imposed on undergraduates.

There was a scattering of female undergraduates, of course, but these occupied their own colleges on the suburban periphery. Women appeared at lectures, dressed, like the men, in gowns, and could be seen bicycling through the streets of the town in bell skirts, but they were barred from the Union, and were permitted to visit men's colleges only at restricted times, and certainly not late in the evening.[1] They were anyway regarded with some derision as bluestockings. Girls from the local secretarial schools were generally reckoned more desirable.

Lincoln is one of the smaller Oxford colleges, and in the early 1950s it was smaller still. David was one of an intake of only fifty-five undergraduates in October 1952. This small size gave the college an intimate atmosphere. Among the intake were a handful of overseas students, including Chukwuemeka Odumegwu Ojukwu, who fifteen years on would become leader of the short-lived independent republic of Biafra. The evidence suggests that Ojukwu was a popular figure in the college, though he had to endure some heavy-handed ribbing about his colour of a kind that would nowadays be considered unacceptable.

Lincoln's relative poverty has preserved it from being spoiled by ugly development in modern times. Many of its buildings and their interiors have remained virtually unchanged since they were built. According to Pevsner, Lincoln preserves 'more of the character of a 15th century college than any other in Oxford'. Given that he had been accepted at the last moment, David had not planned to live in college, but a further late withdrawal by another undergraduate meant that Lincoln was able to offer him a room at the top of a staircase on Chapel Quad. He depicted it to Ann as 'a charming attic room with worm-eaten rafters and a rickety bed'.[2] Around the fireplace was an early seventeenth-century wall-painting.

Soon after he arrived, David found a note in his pigeonhole from Hugh Peppiatt, a friend from Beaconsfield, only a stone's throw from Tunmers. He was the son of Sir Kenneth Peppiatt, former Chief Cashier at the Bank of England, whose signature appeared on British banknotes. Peppiatt was now in his third year at Oxford, reading history at Trinity, generally regarded as one of the smartest colleges socially; he referred to Lincoln dismissively as 'that little college in Turl'. He was part of a coterie of public schoolboys who called 'our lot' Chaps and their social inferiors Charlies, and pronounced bad things Harry Awful and good things Fairly Decent. Peppiatt introduced David to the Gridiron in Carfax, a socially exclusive dining club of which he was an officer. According to David, 'The Grid' carried on much as it had done when Evelyn Waugh was up at Oxford in the 1920s: he remembers an evening when a member burst in bearing a police constable's helmet, and deposited it proudly on the table; as several policemen came crashing up the stairs in hot pursuit, David and his fellow diners dived for cover.

David seemed comfortable with Peppiatt's friends; he was well liked, and was appreciated as an excellent and witty raconteur. But he remained on the fringes of this set, at least partly because he had not enough money to keep up. And though he appeared socially at ease, he was vulnerable. He admitted to Ann that he had 'relations he'd be ashamed to be seen with, shop assistants etc.'.[3] Occasionally he would make jokey remarks to his smart friends about 'having to go and see his old man in the nick' – but, like Eliza Doolittle swearing at the races, these were understood to be a frightfully good joke. 'It was concealment by confession,' one of his Oxford friends recalled, 'like a bank-robber walking down the street shouting "I've got a million pounds in my bag." No one took it seriously.'[4]

Among Peppiatt's friends was John Shakespeare: they had been at the same school, had done National Service together in the Brigade of Guards, and both were now in their final year at Trinity. Like David, Shakespeare was studying modern languages and thought himself 'rather good' at German, having won prizes in the subject; but he readily conceded that David's German was 'vastly superior'. David told Ann that when he undertook an oral for a travelling scholarship, the invigilator asked him to speak English at the end, to prove that he wasn't German.[5]

Shakespeare invited David to a birthday party for his girlfriend Lalage, and introduced him to her father, the prolific author S. P. B. Mais, best known for his wartime radio broadcasts. David was always interested to meet writers and artists, not least because he hoped to find an alternative to a conventional career. As a young man during the First World War Mais had been an assistant master at Sherborne, until he had brought out a novel so obviously set at the school that he had been forced to resign.

By now David felt relaxed enough towards his old school for him to attend a Sherborne reunion dinner, perhaps influenced by Vivian Green, and perhaps too by Gerald Peacocke, who like David was in his first year at Oxford. The fact that Thompson had left Sherborne during the summer, to become headmaster of Bloxham, a small independent school in north Oxfordshire, may have encouraged David to return. Former Westcott House pupils had been solicited to contribute to their housemaster's retirement present; David had chosen not to do so.

In the Michaelmas term 1953,* David would be elected to the Goblins, a dining society, perhaps through the offices of the vice-president, an Old Shirburnian. Through Peppiatt and his friends, he was invited to join the Canning Club, whose members gathered at intervals to hear a paper presented by one of their number in his rooms. David began to wear the Club tie around Oxford; in his second year he would become Club secretary. As its name suggested, the original purpose of the Canning had been to promote and discuss Tory principles, and it retained its conservative character. At Club meetings a silver cup was circulated so that members could toast 'Church and Queen'. David joined in the toast, but perhaps not in the spirit of the Canning. 'Most of my friends' views are in total opposition to my own,' he confided to Ann.[6]

Only a fortnight into his first term, David returned home to Tunmers for a party to celebrate his twenty-first birthday. Parked in the driveway were several gleaming cars, with the number plates RC 1, RC 2 and RC 3. David made a speech to welcome his guests, a mixture of his own friends and older people invited by Ronnie. The revels continued until the last of them left, some time after four o'clock in the morning. Ann confessed that she had felt jealous when he danced cheek to cheek with a very pretty girl. 'Darling, you are a chump with a capital "C" to complain that I hardly spoke to you the whole weekend,' he wrote to her afterwards. 'On Saturday I had not one but 63 people to speak to, and on Sunday I was still "celebrating my birthday" and could not disappear with you the whole afternoon.'[7]

Ann's dreams of literary success were going nowhere. 'Will I ever be a writer?' she wrote in her diary: 'sometimes I doubt it.' A short story she

* The University calendar consists of three eight-week terms, called Michaelmas (autumn), Hilary (spring) and Trinity (summer).

had submitted to *Woman's Own* was rejected. She tried *Good Housekeeping*, without much hope: 'another rejection slip in the offing', she told herself. Meanwhile David sent her his lecture notes to type up, and once a short story of his own: 'not as good as mine, I think, and I can't help being glad, and yet in a way I would like him to be better than me in everything', she noted in her diary. She began writing a novel. At last there was some good news: the *Lady* accepted an article she had sent them, a travel piece about Chamonix. 'Oh, the wonderful joy of having something published,' she exclaimed. 'All at once the future stretches before me as something that will happen. I will get somewhere and do something.'

In his first term David began drawing cartoons for the undergraduate journal *Isis*. Pretty girls and besotted boys were among his favourite subjects; but some of his cartoons had a satirical edge, depicting 'cruel, ugly people' in positions of authority.[8] He was also contributing cartoons to the college magazine the *Imp*, and attending evening life classes at the Ruskin School of Drawing.

The Lincoln Junior Common Room was supposed to be a place for quiet relaxation. One Sunday night, however, it became the setting for a lively debate, in which three characters from history, one of them taken by David, were invited to plead their case. The other two undergraduates read from prepared scripts in a low-key presentation; but David donned a German uniform and false moustache to act the part of Adolf Hitler. He made a powerful case for the *Führer*, prompting much hilarity in his listeners. At one point in his address he referred to the pair of 'incubi', the two destructive forces in the modern world, 'and these are . . .' – he paused for rhetorical effect, at which point a heckler shouted 'Syphilis and gonorrhoea!' – '. . . Jews and Communism'.

Towards the end of his first term David put on a German play, Andreas Gryphius's one-act comedy *Absurda Comica, oder Herr Peter Squenz* (1663), based on the story of Pyramus and Thisbe as done by the mechanicals in *A Midsummer Night's Dream*. There would be only a single performance, attended by most of the lecturers in the subject, and broadcast on BBC radio. David intended to play the leading part, but realised that he had taken on too much. 'Panic, panic, panic – and hellishly little work into the bargain,' he wrote to Ann. 'To live as I would like, I require about a hundred thousand pounds, and ten days in every week.' Instead he offered the lead to Gerald Peacocke, whom he had seen in an Oxford production of Sartre's *Les Mouches*. Peacocke found David to be a shrewd and skilled director, who put the actors at their ease. David was able to report to Ann that the play 'came off very well, and proved a roaring success both socially and financially'.[9]

He made time too to help organise a production of Patrick Hamilton's play *Rope*, and took on the task of organising the Lincoln Ball: 'arranging for bands, dance floor, champagne, buffet, accommodation, and all the rest'.[10] So much extracurricular activity seems to have left him too little time for his academic work, as his reports in his first year were, if not poor, mediocre – 'Mr Cornwell has made a reasonable start,' being a typical comment. 'He is by no means lazy, or limited in mental power, but he seems to need something explosive behind him,' commented his German tutor, W. D. Williams; 'he should still try to put himself into his work more.' Perhaps it was not surprising that the college's Governing Body refused David's request to stage *Androcles and the Lion* during the Trinity term.

Ann felt alienated when she came up to Oxford for the occasional week-end. David had new friends, new interests and new activities, while she remained the same. Whereas he sparkled at sophisticated undergraduate parties, she was a shy and silent presence. By this time it was three years since they had met at St Moritz, and two years since they had become involved as a couple – long enough, so her parents felt, for him to decide if he wanted to marry her, though he was only twenty-one and she twenty. Her father had become impatient at the lack of 'progress', and her mother began to speak slightingly of David in her presence. Then came a chance for her to make a fresh start. Despite being awarded a CBE in the New Year's Honours list, Bobby Sharp had decided to retire prematurely from the RAF, apparently out of pique at receiving a reprimand from a superior (for conducting an affair with his secretary). He accepted a post with an American company based in Washington. Ann's mother and sister were also going, and put pressure on her to accompany them. David too urged her to go, arguing that this was an opportunity not to be missed. 'It might be good for him if I went,' she wrote in her diary, 'but six months is so long and him at university and so good-looking . . .' She was tormented by feelings of jealousy, which he fed with stories of adventures with other girls. In her diary she reported that she had tried to seduce him, 'and failed!'

Back at Tunmers for the Christmas vacation, he partied so hard that he made himself sick. On the night of 26 December he was involved in another car smash; though unhurt, he did not reach home until seven the following morning.

Eventually, after much hesitation, Ann succumbed to the pressure from her family: she would go to Washington and stay a minimum of six months, at least until her twenty-first birthday in the summer. She left England early in 1953, soon after the beginning of David's second term at Oxford. He encouraged her to 'live a full and happy life in the land of the Jumblies.* But please try to remember they are Jumblies – that truth is told by age and not by neon lights.'[11]

While Ann was away David saw plenty of other women; according to undergraduate contemporaries, he always seemed to have 'a girl in tow'. He was particularly fond of the attractive sister of his friend Colin Simpson, also called Ann, then at secretarial college in Oxford. In his letters to Ann Sharp while she was away in America he continued to play on her jealous feelings. 'Am leaping off to the most frightfully fashionable house party in Essex on Friday evening with all the gay young debs and whatnot,' he wrote to her in a typical throwaway line.[12]

Early in the Hilary term 1953 David presented a paper to the Canning Club. He had chosen to speak on the German opposition to Nazi rule, culminating in the attempt to assassinate Hitler in July 1944. His argument was that the Allies should have done more to encourage the conspirators. He was nervous, particularly when he discovered that the Senior Member present was to be the historian Hugh Trevor-Roper, an expert on Nazi Germany. Worse, it turned out that Trevor-Roper had made a study of this very subject. The Club had assembled in David's rooms, and he was about to begin speaking when a commotion announced the arrival of the very last person in the world he can have wanted to see there: his father, obviously the worse for drink, dressed in a too-loud pinstripe suit, accompanied

* Edward Lear's Jumblies 'went to sea in a sieve' and 'sailed to the western sea'.

by Percy Pratt, one of his cronies. Somehow David stammered through his paper. As soon as he had finished, Ronnie leaped up and asked an ill-informed question about the Allied policy of unconditional surrender, only to be ignominiously shot down by the Senior Member. Ronnie was furious to be snubbed in this way, and tried to continue the debate for a while before lapsing into silence. Trevor-Roper's subsequent comments on David's talk were dismissive. 'Typical undergraduate rehash' was his crushing verdict.

After the meeting had dispersed Ronnie took David and a group of undergraduate friends to dinner at the Taj Mahal, a restaurant in Turl Street. David suspected that his father had never eaten Indian food before. When the waiter arrived to take their order, Ronnie asked him with a smirk whether he had been lying too long in the sun. One of David's friends protested that this was a disgusting thing to say. The waiter himself was understandably offended, and the head waiter came over at his request, but Ronnie silenced them by handing over a wad of cash.

During the 1953 spring vacation David took a three-day walk across the Sussex Downs, accompanied by Hugh Peppiatt. Afterwards he made a trip to Paris on business for his father, before he 'pushed off' to Wengen, where he meant to dispose of a hoard of ski equipment he had accumulated. By chance he ran into Dick Edmonds, a fellow member of the DHO racing team, the editor of the Club journal who had commissioned him to produce a series of caricatures after his accident. The pair of them decided to exploit this serendipitous meeting by undertaking a four-day climbing expedition. On their second morning they climbed a col between two peaks, both more than 13,000 feet high, cutting steps in the glacier with an ice-axe as they ascended. A storm blew up, forcing them to rope together. Edmonds fell through the ice into a crevasse, but luckily his fall was broken by a ridge not far below the surface, and he was able to climb out again. They became lost in a blizzard, and groped their way forward until the clouds parted to reveal a tiny mountain hut, where they took shelter for the night. In the bitter cold David suffered some frostbite in his thumb. The next day they descended to Trümmelbach, where they spent that night at the von Almen family's hotel in what seemed 'obscene luxury', sleeping in proper beds, guzzling well-cooked food and drinking 'innumerable bottles of wine'.[13]

In the summer the two of them would return to the Bernese Oberland for another climbing holiday, which David would combine with more 'business' for Ronnie in Zurich and St Moritz.

Dick Edmonds would become a lifelong friend. Six years older than David, an Oxford graduate with his own Triumph Roadster, Edmonds was crown prince of Clements department store, 'the Harrods of Hertfordshire'. A young blade with an eye for the girls and a droll, self-mocking wit, he described the family business as 'flogging knickers on Watford High Street'. After borrowing £20 from Edmonds, David sent him a letter in mock cockney, addressed to 'My dear 'Erb, as ever was' and signed 'yer old mucker, 'arold'. He enclosed a 'chick', postdated, 'becos my dad 'as an 'orrible 'abit of forgettin my lolly for a couple of weeks or so.' Years later, David would characterise Edmonds as 'a fully paid-up closet rebel': especially once he became, in due course, a magistrate, and, eventually, high sheriff of the county.[14]

That spring the Australian cricketers arrived back in England for another Ashes tour. Once again Ronnie invited the visiting team to Tunmers. A marquee was erected on the lawn, and champagne served.[15] Besides the cricketers, there were 120 other guests of various kinds. The young Australian all-rounder Richie Benaud, then on his first overseas tour, remembered the party for his first encounter with aristocracy: a peer of the realm tried to jump an eighty-yard queue for the lavatory.[16] The Australians were without Don Bradman, who had retired from Test cricket at the end of the Ashes tour five years earlier; Lindsay Hassett had replaced him as captain, while Arthur Morris had taken over from Hassett as vice-captain. Morris had been the most prolific batsman on the 1948 tour, but he was to be less successful this time. Speculation linked his difficulties on the field to his personal relationships; during the tour he fell in love with Valerie Hudson, a showgirl performing in the Crazy Gang vaudeville show at the Victoria Palace Theatre, whom he married after a brief courtship. It seems likely that Ronnie made the introduction.

Ronnie was happy to oblige the visiting cricketers if they found themselves temporarily short of funds; it later emerged that he had lent £100 to Ray Lindwall and £150 to Keith Miller. He had bought a hundred cricket bats for the Australians to sign, which he had intended to distribute to the sons of potential or existing creditors; but in the commotion of the party this had proved impossible to organise. Ronnie was only briefly at a loss. He assembled a group of 'lovelies', and at six o'clock one evening sent them with the cricket bats round to the Strand Palace Hotel, where the Australians were staying. The players received the message that he had sent them a 'nice present', which they would find waiting for them in the hotel bar.

For all Ronnie's largesse, he was facing increasing financial difficulties, besieged by creditors demanding payment. His two principal lenders, the Skipton and Dudley Building Societies, had taken the management of the properties for which they had advanced loans into their own hands, leaving him with little room for manoeuvre. In the very same month that Ronnie held the garden party at Tunmers for the Australian cricketers, he applied for planning permission to build fifty-four houses on the site. This application was rejected. There was some relief, however, when Ronnie was able to buy the ticket agency Keith Prowse Limited and sell it on at a profit to Peter Cadbury, a former test pilot and Liberal Party candidate, then just beginning his career as an entrepreneur. It is possible that this deal, from which Ronnie realised about £15,000, was facilitated by Cadbury's godfather, Norman Birkett.

There was much public excitement about the forthcoming coronation of Queen Elizabeth II, who had succeeded her father on his death the previous year. Huge crowds were expected to line the streets, to watch the young monarch as she rode in her carriage between Buckingham Palace and Westminster Abbey. Privileged vantage points were at a premium; the Australian touring team had already been warned that there was no chance of their being able to see the procession. Nonetheless Ronnie was able to fix this, arranging seating for them on a building-site along the route.[17] David watched the coronation on television at Tunmers with his half-brother and sister. 'The children were bored stiff,' he wrote to Ann afterwards. 'But it was a beautiful thing to watch, full of royal tradition and splendour, full of terrifying solemnity; all the finality of a wedding-service, all the dedication of priesthood . . . a day to tell one's children about.'[18] News that two climbers from a British expedition had reached the summit of Mount Everest, the first ever to do so, had arrived in London on Coronation Day. David saluted the conquest of Everest as 'a magnificent and all-time achievement that we can be very proud of'. He celebrated by getting drunk.[19]

Gordon Richards, Ronnie's sometime adviser on horseflesh, had been knighted in the coronation honours list. Four days later he won his first Derby on the colt Pinza, beating the Queen's horse Aureole into second place, after twenty-eight years of trying and almost three decades as champion flat jockey. David, who had backed Richards, hailed this in a letter to Ann as 'a glorious – really glorious – victory'. A couple of weeks later he accompanied Ronnie to Ascot, dressed in 'a grey topper and a funny coat'.[20] And a few weeks after that both David and Tony were members of 'Mr R. T. A. Cornwell's XI' that travelled down to Poole to play the local cricket club, with which Ronnie had been associated for almost thirty years. His team included the former Test players Sidney Barnes and Learie Constantine, the promising young West Indian Roy Marshall (then playing for Hampshire) and the Sussex wicketkeeper, Jim Parks. Despite this talented line-up, Ronnie's XI could only draw the match.

David reported to Ann that 'life at home has been utterly chaotic', with 'all the family in a raging temper'. Ronnie was 'livid' with Tony, perhaps because he had announced he did not want to practise law. Tony had moved out of Tunmers to live in Hampstead – 'a very good thing because it paves the way for me to do the same thing myself if I want'. David fled back to Oxford, to gain some respite from 'the nervous tight-rope walking of home life and the endless bickering'.[21]

Nigel Althaus, one of Hugh Peppiatt's friends, then in his third year reading 'Greats' at Magdalen, invited David to play golf.

'I don't play golf,' said David.

'Well, walk round with me, anyway.'

As they strolled around the course Althaus sounded out David on his political views. 'I'd like you to meet a friend of mine,' he said before they parted. Though nothing had been made explicit, David understood that he was being recruited once more.

Althaus's 'friend' contacted David to suggest that they lunch together in Woodstock, a village outside Oxford where they were unlikely to encounter anyone David knew from the University. This was George Leggett, a man ten years David's senior, with whom he would form a lasting friendship. It helped that Leggett shared David's passion for German literature. The son of an English father and a Polish mother, Leggett had read modern languages at Cambridge during the war; he spoke Russian as well as French, German and Polish. While still in his early twenties he had served as an interpreter at the Potsdam Conference; it was said that Stalin had complained that Leggett spoke Russian with a Polish accent. Afterwards he had been recruited into MI5, where he had proved himself to be an analyst of outstanding quality.

Leggett asked David to adopt a left-wing persona. His task would be to infiltrate left-wing groups, to report back on who was present and what was said, and to identify previously unsuspected Communists. And in the process he was to trail his coat, attending meetings addressed by visiting cultural attachés from Communist bloc countries that might be on the lookout for disaffected undergraduates. David confided in Robin Cooke that he had been asked to keep an eye on subversive elements in the university.

His recruitment was part of a wider MI5 response to the discovery that Burgess and Maclean had been spying for the Russians. This pair had been recruited as long-term 'penetration agents' back in the 1930s. Where there were two, there might be more. Suspicion surrounded those who had associated with them at Cambridge, including the former Foreign Office official John Cairncross and the former MI5 officer Anthony Blunt, now an eminent art historian. Both would eventually be shown to have been Soviet agents – as would Kim Philby, a senior MI6 officer once considered a future 'C', head of the Secret Service. Philby was asked to resign from MI6, though he was given a golden handshake and several of his colleagues indignantly maintained that the evidence against him was purely circumstantial; and when, in 1955, he was named in parliament as the 'Third Man', the Foreign Secretary, Harold Macmillan, felt obliged to exonerate him.

Meanwhile the newly appointed head of MI5, Dick White, had ordered F Branch (responsible for counter-subversion) to infiltrate every left-wing organisation in Britain, including the Labour Party, the trades unions, the peace movement and student unions. White had appointed Alexander Kellar, a former president of the Scottish Union of Students, as the Branch's Director. MI5 enlisted students and trades unionists, who were told to express views sympathetic to Communism in the expectation that some of them would be recruited as Soviet agents themselves.

David showed a boy-scout enthusiasm for doing anything Leggett asked of him, just as he had done when 'Sandy' had recruited him in Bern. Once again he would answer the call to patriotic service, eager to atone for his father's dereliction of duty. His only reward would be a succession of furtive lunches in Woodstock. He maintained his cover even to his girlfriend. 'Forgive me if I wave the red flag at you for a while,' he asked Ann. 'I'm trying socialism now,' he told her; 'there must be an answer to all the utter waste of life and thought and energy – a creed that covers all the problems.'[22]

David joined the Oxford University Communist Club, which met, supposedly in secret, on Sundays at Lyons' café in Cornmarket. At least one member noticed that David seemed unusually inquisitive about others present. According to another member of the Club, David was different: 'he wasn't one of us'. This same witness, speaking forty years afterwards, remembered him as 'very withheld', with 'a terrifying reticence'.[23] At a meeting of the local branch of the Anglo-Soviet Friendship Society, David met the Soviet Cultural Attaché, who was often in Oxford, bringing Russian vodka to woo undergraduates. Since he seemed interested, David was invited to an evening party at the Soviet Embassy in London. This was one of several visits to the Embassy, which often put on showings of stirring films; David reckons that he must have seen *The Battleship Potemkin* three or four times during this period. At one stage in the courtship, the Cultural Attaché suggested that it might be 'more fun' to meet outside the Embassy, and suggested a rendezvous between the two of them at a pub in Victoria. Then, without explanation, David was suddenly dropped, perhaps because the mask had slipped.

He was unusual, though not unique, in being simultaneously a member of the Communist Club and the Grid. More unusual, perhaps, was to be a member of the Communist Club and to attend gatherings of the Cole Group, an informal discussion group of left-leaning undergraduates centred around the economist and political theorist G. D. H. Cole. Though sympathetic to Russia, Cole was not a Communist and steered his disciples away from what he saw as the Marxist cul-de-sac. Among those influenced by Cole were successive leaders of the Labour Party, Hugh Gaitskell and Harold Wilson.

David also joined the Socialist Club, which welcomed left-wingers of every hue, from pale pink to dark red. The Club's secretary was Caroline

Carter, often said to be the first woman undergraduate ever to be invited to speak at the Oxford Union. Attractive and charismatic, she was referred to around Oxford as 'the Body Politic'. At the time she was conducting a love affair with the Union president, Bryan Magee, who had joined the Socialist Club after falling for her, though she was believed to be a Communist and his politics were always on the moderate, anti-Communist left. David's constant presence at Club meetings and his obvious anxiety to please made the two of them uneasy. Furthermore Magee suspected David of having designs on his girlfriend.

Towards the end of his time at Oxford, Magee contemplated going into the Foreign Office. After performing well in the exams, he underwent a number of interviews, culminating in the final selection conference with a panel whose members included Walter Oakeshott, then about to succeed Keith Murray as Rector of Lincoln. Afterwards Magee was disappointed to receive a letter informing him that he had not been selected. Back in Oxford, he ran into Oakeshott in the street, who enquired how he was getting on 'at the FO'. Embarrassed, Magee explained that he had not been selected. Oakeshott expressed surprise. Years later, Magee would be told by a highly placed source at the Foreign Office that he had not been selected only because information had been received that he was likely to marry a member of the Communist Party. Magee suspected that this information had come from David.*

'It's time you met my superior,' said Leggett, and at their next lunch he introduced David to Maxwell Knight, a famous figure within intelligence circles: the inspiration, it is claimed, for Ian Fleming's 'M'. After joining MI5 in 1931, 'Max' Knight had recruited and run agents to infiltrate extremist organisations on both right and left, favouring attractive young women from 'good families'. At the end of the war Knight wrote a paper on agent-running, in which he had condemned the 'longstanding and ill-founded prejudice against the employment of women as agents'. Operating from a flat in Dolphin Square, Knight maintained a lively social life as professional cover. He had written two thrillers, and would meet his agents over dinner at the Authors' Club. In the inter-war years he had scored a number

* David cannot remember whether or not he did inform on Magee, and anyway thinks it unlikely that his word alone would have been enough to sway the selectors.

of notable successes, breaking the Communist spy ring in the Woolwich Arsenal and entrapping the American Nazi spy Tyler Kent in 1940; but his subsequent mishandling of the case of a pacifist accused of conspiring with the enemy had caused his judgement to be questioned. By the early 1950s he was a peripheral influence within MI5; he continued to run the agents whom he had recruited in the past, but the burden of agent-running and recruitment had fallen on his deputy, John Bingham. For David, however, Maxwell Knight remained the 'Pied Piper', a romantic and heroic figure, the inspiration for the character of Jack Brotherhood in *A Perfect Spy*. David himself has been named as 'one of Knight's protégés'.[24]

Soon after arriving in Oxford, David had become friendly with Newton Garver, an American exchange student at Lincoln reading for a postgraduate degree in philosophy. He invited Garver to Tunmers for the weekend. Garver had heard much from David of his ambivalent feelings towards his father, so he was fascinated to meet Ronnie. He was impressed by the 'posh set-up' at Tunmers, but was less taken with Ronnie himself, whom he found both 'right and wrong socially', a braggart who boasted that he could get tickets for any sporting event one might want to attend. Tony was at Tunmers that weekend too, and Garver observed Ronnie urging his eldest son to make a career in the RAF, promising 'I will get you promoted.' Afterwards, he deduced that David had taken him to Tunmers with a motive: he wanted Garver to meet his father so that he might understand him better.

Garver was a Quaker, with a strong social conscience. Like David, he had joined the Canning Club, though he never felt that he belonged there, as he was too critical of the established order. In debates at the Oxford Union, he expressed his horror at the prospect of nuclear war and his strong desire for reconciliation between the peoples of the world. He had been involved in the peace movement since 1947, when at the age of nineteen he had burned his draft card in San Francisco. In the following year he had written to President Truman to inform him that, 'as a carefully considered and conscious act of civil disobedience', he had refused to register for the draft as he was required to do by law. This was a symbolic gesture; but Garver's act of defiance in writing to the President had drawn attention to the case, and a federal judge had deemed it necessary to sentence the idealistic young Quaker to a year's imprisonment. Almost a decade after leaving Oxford, Garver would again be involved in peaceful protest, when he refused to sign a 'loyalty oath',* though threatened with dismissal from his post as a philosophy instructor at the State University of New York (SUNY) in Buffalo. Having served a jail sentence for his religious principles, Garver was not about to compromise himself by signing the oath. Several other professors joined Garver in refusing, and the case became a cause célèbre, being taken all the way to the Supreme Court, which ruled that the requirement to sign the loyalty oath was an unconstitutional infringement of academic freedom.

In his reports to MI5 on left-wing student activity David had mentioned Garver, whose name may have been forwarded to the FBI. Privately he wondered whether Garver might not be a CIA 'plant'. He searched Garver's rooms for evidence without finding anything incriminating, and suspected that Garver might have done the same to him. Years later David dimly recalled meeting a friend of Garver's at the Cavendish Hotel in Jermyn Street, who struck him as 'decidedly fishy'.[25]

Garver would be in intermittent contact with David after leaving Oxford. He believed that though unwilling to exhibit himself as a rebel, his young English friend shared many of his own ideals. And he observed how, in later life, David shed some of his inhibition and espoused progressive causes. So it was a shock when, more than half a century later, David confessed to having spied on him. Though startled, Garver did not allow this revelation to affect their longstanding friendship. In a 2007 letter, David applauded Garver's 'long, hard-fought campaign for sanity'. He continued: 'I'm almost ashamed I didn't fight it with you; but, of course, I secretly believe I did.'[26]

David shared French tutorials with Stanley Mitchell, a grammar school boy from Finchley who had won a scholarship to read modern languages at Lincoln. Mitchell enjoyed David's irreverent sense of humour, and they became close friends, close enough to undertake a walking holiday together along the Dorset coast. Like David, Mitchell had suffered at the hands of his father, a Yiddish-speaking immigrant from Russia. Mitchell noted David's 'flawless' German accent and his interest in people on the margins,

* This was the notorious 'Feinberg Certificate', a relic of the anti-Communist fervour of the McCarthyite era.

Jews in particular. He formed the conclusion that David was ill at ease in his own culture, and that he had immersed himself in German as a form of escape. A member of the Communist Party, Mitchell was impressed by David's anti-American sentiments, especially when he reacted passionately to the execution of the Rosenbergs.* It was Mitchell to whom David had explained his premature departure from Sherborne by claiming that his housemaster had tried to kiss him – or so Mitchell later said, though David has no memory of telling him this. Mitchell noticed that his friend recoiled when a visiting Communist lecturer, Arnold Kettle, took his arm. 'He's homosexual,' David explained. At the time, Kettle's homosexuality was secret, unknown even to his family; on the other hand his membership of the executive committee of the Communist Party was public knowledge. 'It has been suggested from a somewhat doubtful source that Dr Kettle may have homosexual tendencies,' Kettle's MI5 file noted in 1953. Perhaps David was that 'somewhat doubtful source'.[27]

After Mitchell became editor of a publication called *Oxford Left* in 1953 he persuaded his friend to contribute. David's first illustration for it was a cartoon that could easily be mistaken for the crudest of Soviet propaganda, showing a phalanx of hideous American soldiers marching past a crucified Jesus. His cartoons in the next issue, illustrating an article by the Oxford University Labour Club chairman Anthony Howard (later a much admired journalist, editor, broadcaster and political commentator), were subtler, though still satirical. He also contributed a story of his own, the whimsical tale of a socially self-satisfied mouse who inhabited the Oxford Union.

Towards the end of 1953 Mitchell co-produced a performance of *The Duchess of Malfi*, which took place in a panelled room within the college, and (like the play David had put on the previous year) was broadcast on the radio. Mitchell cast David in the leading part of Bosola, a malcontent and a cynic, a critic of Renaissance society. Though Mitchell rated his acting skills highly, it never occurred to him that David might be playing

* Julius and Ethel Rosenberg, an American couple convicted of passing atomic secrets to the Soviet Union. They were executed by electric chair in June 1953, despite worldwide protests, including an appeal for clemency to President Eisenhower from Pope Pius XII.

a role in real life. Evidently the anonymous *Imp* critic thought well of David's performance, since he mentioned him, together with the co-opted Somerville undergraduate who played the part of the Duchess, as worthy of special praise. The newly formed Lincoln Players, the critic suggested, 'clearly have a valuable asset in Mr David Cornwell, both as an actor and as a painter of striking posters . . .'[28]

In Trinity term 1954 *Oxford Left* brought out a 'Special Peace Issue', reflecting a wider concern about the new thermonuclear weapons then being developed. The Americans had tested a hydrogen bomb at Eniwetok Atoll eighteen months earlier; the Russians were not far behind; and in 1954 a British programme had begun. An Oxford campaign calling for disarmament and the complete abolition of the 'H-Bomb' attracted support from the University branches of all the main political parties; indeed, the text of the campaign's founding statement was proposed by the young Michael Heseltine,* then a prominent member of OUCA, the Oxford University Conservative Association. One of David's illustrations appeared on the opening page of the 'Special Peace Issue' of *Oxford Left*, a grim cartoon showing wounded figures stumbling across a devastated landscape. In a letter to Ann, David mentioned a 'rather good' radio talk by the Methodist preacher Donald Soper, in which the speaker had urged British unilateral disarmament as a prelude to universal disarmament. On the previous evening he had been with Mitchell to hear the evangelist Billy Graham – 'also good, but dangerously dramatic'.[29]

Visiting David in his rooms, Mitchell came across Hugh Peppiatt, and felt slightly surprised to find David in such company; he observed that their host seemed uncomfortable at this social juxtaposition. David was leading a double life, mixing with Stanley Mitchell and other left-wingers, while continuing to associate with much more conservative undergraduates. On 1 May 1954, for example, he attended a political demonstration with Mitchell during the day, and then in the evening had Robin Cooke, Colin Simpson and another friend, Sandy Llewellyn, round for drinks to his digs off the Abingdon Road. At tea with Llewellyn a few weeks later he became involved in 'a heated discussion about the Soviet Union', as he

* Though on different sides politically, Michael Heseltine and Anthony Howard were lifelong friends.

reported to Ann. 'It ended with one of Sandy's guests being very rude to me, and me getting very angry and leaving in a huff, which I suppose was silly. I'm afraid my friends are getting rather fed up with me,' he continued. 'Darling, is it so awfully wrong to be Socialist?'[30]

It is difficult to assess the sincerity of such remarks. Perhaps he was simply playing a part, or perhaps, as is often true of agents, David had absorbed some of the qualities of the person he was pretending to be. Even if this were so, it is probably fair to say that his political commitment did not run very deep. 'Talked much politics with Stanley M and Garver N and others you don't know,' he wrote to Ann at the beginning of the Trinity Term 1954, 'but ended by drinking beer, which is the answer to most political problems.'[31] It is worth noting that David possessed at least some of the characteristics that the KGB recruiter Arnold Deutsch had identified in Philby, Maclean and others, and had listed as attributes of a successful spy – an inherent class resentfulness, a predilection for secretiveness and a yearning to belong.

Looking back on this period almost half a century afterwards, David denied to an interviewer that he had ever been drawn into deceitful behaviour that would trouble his conscience.

> I don't know that it's such a disgraceful thing to have done, if you look at the record of people who were recruited at university from the ranks of Communist sympathisers and later turned traitors to their country . . . Largely the justification for what we did was one I accepted and still accept. That doesn't mean the work was pleasant. It could often be quite disgusting in the sense that you had to penetrate a settled organisation of people who trusted each other . . . but somebody has to clean the drains, and I found that I did do things that, although they were in some way morally repugnant, I felt at the time, and still feel, to have been necessary.[32]

During the Cold War there were others willing to supply information to the intelligence services about their fellow undergraduates – Neil Gow, for example, later a QC, who had done National Service in the Intelligence Corps and had known David at Maresfield Camp. Gow went on to Glasgow University, where he became secretary of the students' union;

when approached by MI5 and asked to provide information about left-wing students who might be considered subversives, he was happy to do so. 'I thought my duty to my country was higher than my duty to my fellow students,' he told a journalist many years later.[33]

But no amount of rationalisation can disguise the unpleasant taste left by such acts. Schoolboys dislike a 'sneak'; people shrink from informers. Some never forgave those who chose to 'name names' to the House Un-American Activities Committee, but at least that was public; David's reports were clandestine, and potentially more damaging because they remained secret. There is something especially troubling about informing on those one knows personally; it feels like a betrayal of the trust implicit in friendship. And befriending somebody in order to betray him is perhaps even more so.

After Stanley Mitchell's death in 2011, David reflected on their relations, in a letter of commiseration to his family. It seemed to him ironic that, as a Communist, Mitchell had nevertheless always insisted on placing personal friendship above political conviction. 'Was he really imagining that a bourgeois society would not spy on a revolutionary movement?'[34]

One could of course reverse David's paradox in assessing his own behaviour. Though perhaps not an ideologue, he had chosen loyalty to his country over loyalty to his friends. The dilemma continued to trouble him; it was a theme that would recur repeatedly in his fiction.

7

'This really is the end'

Ronnie was in the habit of opening his sons' post as it arrived at Tunmers. One morning he read a letter on Foreign Office notepaper from a vice-admiral, writing from an address in Buckingham Gate, inviting David to lunch with him at the Travellers Club in Pall Mall. A puzzled Ronnie telephoned his pal Sir James Barnes, who informed him that the Admiral was a representative of the Secret Intelligence Service (SIS, or MI6). Confused and upset, Ronnie confronted his son: 'What the hell are you doing with SIS?' David tried to placate his father, whose ambitions for his boys were fading. Over lunch the Admiral hinted at intelligence work without ever discussing it openly. 'I've been up to the Foreign Office for odd interviews preliminary to trying to get into the Diplomatic Corps,' David informed Ann in a letter written in June 1953. 'They were quite pleasant and things seemed to go well enough.'[1]

Later in the year, his tutor W. D. Williams submitted a confidential report in response to a 'vetting' enquiry. 'David Cornwell has given evidence of ability above the average,' he wrote. 'He has a discriminating mind with some power and subtlety and a good deal of imagination.' In this respect Williams rated him β+. For his character and general suitability to represent his country abroad, Williams rated him higher, α–. 'He speaks faultless English and has charm and poise,' Williams continued. 'He is a thoroughly likeable person and I should think would get on well with all with whom he came in contact.'

> There is, though, one point which perhaps should be borne in mind. He is of a somewhat unstable disposition, very much inclined to be swept off

> his feet for a time by some passing enthusiasm, inclined to let generous and idealistic impulses cloud the clarity of his thinking. He had, some time ago, considerable difficulty with his father when the latter learnt that he was associating with undergraduates of left-wing political views, and he eventually undertook to give up all activity on behalf of socialist groups. He is a man of integrity and has kept his undertaking, I think. Nor do I think that there is much danger of his succumbing to the blandishments of Communism on the continent, but he might be tempted to some equally silly course of action.[2]

The authorities at MI6 were aware of David's undercover work for their sister service, and discounted his tutor's warning accordingly. Indeed, had David really converted to Communism, his record of work for both services would have provided perfect cover. David's letters to Ann express confidence that he would join MI6 in due course; they contain several references to 'my future employer' and often allude to matters that could not be elaborated in writing, especially once she had returned to England and he had been able to put her in the picture. In one of the letters, for example, he refers to going 'on business' to Basel and Zurich 'for some "friends" of mine, who will pay my fare', during the University vacation: 'this is one of those things I warned you about'.[3]

While in Washington with her family, Ann had been working as a secretary at the British Embassy. The prevalent anti-Communist zealotry in America had scared her: actors and directors were being blacklisted, public servants smeared and books removed from library shelves, or even burned. To her it seemed like a witch-hunt, with disturbing echoes of what had happened in Germany in the 1930s. She sailed back to England with her sister at the end of August 1953, a week after her twenty-first birthday. Her mother would follow a few months later, having separated from her husband, weary of his philandering.

Meanwhile David undertook the regulation two weeks' training with the army at Maresfield, as did Gerald Peacocke. As members of the 'supplementary reserve', they were automatically given the worst jobs. Some senior officers present in the camp for a course invited the two personable young National Servicemen to join them for a drink in the officers' mess. The next morning they were summoned to the Adjutant's office and given a dressing-down. 'You behaved disgracefully,' the Adjutant bawled. 'You crowded the bar.' As punishment they were put on drill duty. Peacocke was upset, but David shrugged it off.

David was reunited with Ann over a meal at Verrey's, a smart restaurant in Regent Street dating back to Victorian times. She knew as soon as she saw him that she had been right to return. When she told him that she had received a proposal of marriage during her stay in America, and claimed to have fallen in love with a young American army officer, David seemed energised. He was in an emotional state, disturbed by 'the corruption, misuse, perversion or prostitution of real love' that he had witnessed in his family. In the attic at Tunmers he had discovered Jean's diaries, which revealed not only Ronnie's repeated infidelities but also his occasional violence towards her. Belatedly he understood why she always wore long sleeves, even in warm weather. He took to sleeping on a camp bed in front of his stepmother's door, to protect her when Ronnie came home late after drinking heavily. For David, Ann's upright principles contrasted with the moral chaos of home. 'I have always longed to find for myself among the complications and borders of our own rotten society the simple, true, unaffected love we deserve,' David wrote to her soon after term began.[4] Ann rejected his suggestion that they should become secretly engaged.

There was havoc at home, as Ronnie struggled to stay solvent and Jean threatened to divorce him. In the good times the cars with their personalised number plates had been ostentatiously displayed; now the only remaining car would often be hidden in the trees behind the house to prevent it from being seized by creditors, as had happened twenty years before, and the house lights switched off, to conceal the fact that Ronnie was at home. In November Jean's mother lent Ronnie £5,000 to keep him afloat; she had raised the money by a charge on her family business.

'I feel this really is the end so far as Tony and I are concerned,' David told Ann. 'There have been so many false climaxes, so many bits of cheap sensation and washing of dirty linen that nothing can depress me now except a false compromise based on the need for money and protection.'[5]

Towards Ann herself David blew hot and cold. Early in the new year, after she had spent Christmas with his family, he broke with her, but within a fortnight he was expressing feelings of sadness and guilt, and a couple of days later he sent her a letter by express delivery. 'Darling, I have made a mistake,' he wrote. 'I can't tell you how sorry I am, how wrong I have been in rationalising us into a kind of unwitting divorce.' His relationship with Ann offered security, a refuge from his crazy, unstable home life. Within a couple of months he was writing as if it was a given that they were to be married as soon as he was settled. 'Darling, when I write my first book,* I shall plonk on the fly-leaf in pompous capitals – "TO ANN, WHO UNDERSTANDS" – and mean it.'[6]

The supply of money from Ronnie dwindled and then ceased altogether, leaving David in a difficult position. 'For the past two terms I have been rather short of funds pending the transfer of a banker's draft from my grandmother's solicitor,' he wrote to the college bursar early in the 1954 Hilary term. He acknowledged that neither the term's college 'battels' (the college accounts for board and provisions), nor the £10 outstanding from the previous term, had been paid. 'My father is however attending to the matter and has told me that £250 will be forthcoming before the end of this term.' He enclosed a cheque for £35 in partial settlement of his debts.[7] But Ronnie was in a tight corner; on 10 March 1954, another petition for bankruptcy was served on him. Counsel had been asked to advise and guide the liquidator on the transactions of one of his companies, Reliance Properties Limited, and had advised that 'the whole conduct of this company's affairs strikes me as being flagrantly fraudulent'. In his submission to the Official Receiver, Ronnie claimed that the value of the properties owned by the companies in which he had an interest totalled £1.7 million, mortgaged to the level of £1.4 million, leaving a balance of £300,000, of which £190,000 was owed to him personally. The Official Receiver took a sceptical view of these figures. Notes in the Receiver's file estimated Ronnie's tangible assets at less than £200. 'The surplus from securities (£1400 or so) is very doubtful of realisation. So also are the many book debts (totalling £180,000 or so) due to him from his many companies, some of which are already in liquidation.' But, as the Receiver acknowledged, 'the case is enormously complicated'. Ronnie had admitted to being a director of about sixty limited companies with such names as Bedrock Investments, Universal Trading Corporation and Ground Rent Holdings, and had declared an interest in a further thirty-nine, 'for

* His second book, *A Murder of Quality*, was dedicated to Ann.

the most part involved in the acquisition, disposal and holding of real property'. A receiving order was served against him on 28 May, citing the Commissioners of the Inland Revenue as his principal creditors, with claims totalling £61,889 18s 2d. The value of Ronnie's assets had been reassessed at £129 12s 0d.[8] He tried in various ways to delay proceedings, but he was only postponing the inevitable.

Halfway through his second year at Oxford, David was beginning to doubt whether he could afford to continue. To make ends meet he had repeatedly borrowed money from Robin Cooke, but Cooke could help only to a limited extent. David discussed his predicament with Sir James Barnes, and with Vivian Green, now senior tutor at Lincoln, to whom he would increasingly turn for help and advice. A new possibility had arisen, now that his MI5 handler, George Leggett, had departed for Australia, where he would undertake an extensive debriefing of the KGB defector Vladimir Petrov. Dick Thistlethwaite, Head of Operations at MI5, was talking about 'taking him all the way through', meaning that David would masquerade as a secret Communist intellectual and become a double agent while pursuing a conventional career as a journalist, probably as a foreign correspondent. David was sent to see Denis Hamilton, then editorial director of the Kemsley Press, the newspaper group that included the *Sunday Times* as well as several tabloid and regional newspapers. Hamilton, a war hero known as 'the brigadier' by his staff, had strong intelligence connections, and expressed willingness in principle to employ David should he be forced to leave Oxford prematurely. Ann was indoctrinated by Thistlethwaite; as an air vice-marshal's daughter she was deemed suitable as a potential wife, and signed the Official Secrets Act.

A letter arrived from the Westminster Bank informing David that Ronnie's cheque for the term's fees had bounced. Since his account was overdrawn by eightpence, the letter continued, none of his own cheques would be honoured, including his payment for the term's battels. David feared that he might have to leave Oxford immediately.

Help came from an unexpected source. One of his contemporaries at Oxford, Reginald Bosanquet (later an ITN newsreader), had everything that David did not: a private income, a sports car and a seemingly continuous stream of beautiful girlfriends. He and David liked each other – but, as David has subsequently said, there is only so much time you can spend with someone who lives the life you dream of and can afford it, while you cannot. Bosanquet 'drifted into my room one day, probably with a hang-over, shoved an envelope at me and drifted out'. The envelope contained a cheque made out to David from Bosanquet's trustees, and a letter explaining that David should pay it back at his convenience, only when he was able. The letter further explained Reggie's wish that David should correspond directly with the trustees on all matters relating to the loan, since he did not hold with mixing money and friendship. David accepted the loan gratefully.[9]

Disenchanted with his father, David had begun to question everything that he had been told since early childhood. His German education had encouraged a determination to find solutions to all his problems, a sense of absolutism – what Germans call *Drang nach dem Absoluten*, the drive towards the absolute. He told Ann that he needed to get at the truth, so that he could sort things out with Ronnie once and for all. As part of this process he wanted to see his mother, for the first time since he was a little boy; but first he had to find her. Without telling Ronnie, he sent a letter to her brother, Alec Glassey,* whose terse reply provided an address on the outskirts of Woodbridge, near the east coast. David wrote to his mother, who responded by inviting him down to Suffolk for the weekend. Nervous about this encounter, he asked Ann to accompany him; they met at Liverpool Street station and spent the night together at the Great Eastern Hotel, where they became lovers for the first time. The next morning they took the train down to Woodbridge. Olive was waiting for them on the station platform; Ann's first impression was of a tall, middle-aged woman (she was forty-eight), recognisably like Tony.

Waiting outside in a blue-and-cream Jaguar was John Hill, a little man with a big moustache whom David addressed as 'sir'. He drove them to their small, suburban bungalow, where they were introduced to two little girls, his half-sisters, of whose existence David had been completely unaware. Conversation was polite but awkward. David noticed that his mother was very well spoken, talking in perfect paragraphs, albeit pompously formulated.

* Later he would find that Tony had done exactly the same.

There was no room for them in the house, so they slept in a local hotel. Later Olive took them to see a friend of hers who lived on a boat, a woman of masculine appearance whom David surmised to be a lesbian, and who gave them home-made advocaat to drink. On a nearby beach Olive turned cartwheels on the sands like a frisky schoolgirl. All weekend Ann had the impression that she was trying very hard. During a tête-à-tête Ann asked her why she had left the boys with a man whom she knew to be evil. Olive answered that she thought that Ronnie could give them more advantages.

Perhaps in self-justification, or perhaps because she believed that Ronnie had poisoned her sons' minds against her, Olive divulged some distressing details about her former husband. She told David of Ronnie's prison sentences, of the confidence tricks he'd played, of the money he had charmed out of her family. Some of this David either knew or suspected already, but some of it – such as her account of sharing a bed with Ronnie and Mabel George – was shockingly new. Perhaps most upsetting of all was her admission that his father had infected her with syphilis while she was pregnant with him, and that as a result he had been born with pus dripping out of his eyes. Afterwards David would have medical tests to ensure that he was free of infection. Olive spoke freely about Ronnie's sexual appetites, and presented her son with a tattered copy of Krafft-Ebing's *Psychopathia Sexualis* as a guide. David asked whether prison had changed his father. '*Changed*, dear? *In prison?* Not a bit of it! You were totally *un*changed. You'd lost weight, of course, well you would. Prison food isn't *meant* to be nice.' David noted that she used 'you' to mean 'he', identifying him with his father. She described Ronnie's 'silly habit' after his release of waiting humbly in front of a closed door, with bowed head, until someone opened it for him.

Back at Tunmers David confronted Ronnie with his Olive's disclosures, as he subsequently related in a letter to Vivian Green. 'After an awful lot of ducking and emotional side-tracking he said "so what?"' Though sickened by what he had learned about his father, David was reluctant to break with him altogether, which would necessitate leaving Oxford without a degree; but he told Ronnie that in future he wanted to be independent of him. 'He was terribly upset, and said that the irony of his life was that everything he had done for us (my brother & myself) had separated us further from him, that just at the very moment in his life when he most needed my companionship he should be denied it, etc. etc.'

A series of 'awful scenes' ensued. Typically Ronnie had resorted to moral blackmail, threatening that if David decided to leave home, he would sell up and divorce Jean. David felt responsible, knowing how difficult it would be for his stepmother to provide for herself and the children alone. However inadequate a husband and father Ronnie might be, he was better than nothing. They agreed a compromise: Ronnie would continue to pay David's allowance, but with no obligation for him to live at home. 'The thing that staggered him really was my apparent disinterest in the ultimate promise of plenty . . .'[10]

David escaped from Tunmers to spend a few days as a guest of Nigel Althaus and his family in their sixteenth-century rectory. On his return David found Ronnie tearful, rolling over and over in his bed and screaming, 'David's left me, David's left me,' again and again. 'Daddy has tried to make me recant everything I've said,' David wrote to Ann, then on holiday in Majorca with her mother and sister. 'I'm very tired of this awful business and his filthy habits. But I'm afraid that only the people who have lived with him know what a bastard he is.'[11]

Aside from his financial problems, Ronnie was facing prosecution for an offence committed some six or seven years earlier, of borrowing Swiss francs from an unauthorised dealer. He travelled to Switzerland over Easter, in a vain attempt to stave off conviction and the accompanying fine. Reluctantly David provided Kaspar von Almen's name as a possible source of legal advice.

Now very hard up, David gratefully accepted a commission from his skiing friend Dick Edmonds to paint a mural on a large area of wall in the main concourse of Clements, the department store owned by the Edmonds family. David painted a pageant of happy Watford shoppers trooping gaily through Clements's portals and emerging from them even happier. The mural survived a year or so, until Dick's father paid a rare visit to the store and summarily ordered it removed, on the grounds that it insulted the customers by making them look like a bunch of leering peasants.[12]

At the end of the working day, David would climb into Edmonds's roadster and together they would explore the open Hertfordshire landscape, coasting through still unspoilt country lanes. The village of Sarratt particularly impressed David, with its pretty village green, cosy redbrick cottages, half-hidden mansions and exquisitely beautiful twelfth-century church. It seemed to him some kind of secret haven, 'a forgotten piece of real England, just round the corner from subtopia'. He imagined himself living there, 'at the edge of the real world but safe from it'. Twenty years later, when he came to select a birthplace for his secret England, he chose Sarratt: he called his training school the 'Nursery', and he located it on the fringes of Sarratt, 'where I had once longed to live'.[13]

After two months with her mother and sister in Majorca, Ann returned to England and took a job in London working on the *Sunday Companion*, a Christian newspaper. Readers perplexed with scriptural difficulties or social problems were encouraged to write to the editor for guidance. (David would depict a very similar publication in his novel *A Murder of Quality*.) Ann, who earned £7 a week, loved her job and the independence that came with it. For the time being she shared a bedsit with a girlfriend, who set her cap at Dick Edmonds, unsuccessfully as it turned out. The fact that she and David were to be married once he left University was now public; the *Imp* congratulated him on their engagement. The plan was that she would continue working afterwards.

Back in Oxford for the Trinity term, David reflected on 'the strange life we shall live'. He warned Ann that they would be 'very unhappy now and again'. Their love, he told her,

> will have to see us through many storms. It will be exposed to a life you may grow to resent, for I know it, but you do not. A life where the borderline between fairness and treachery is so narrow that you will fear for your own integrity . . .
>
> I shall always appear to you a sort of watery Hamlet in some ways – my complete objectivity in all kinds of decisions has made a nasty impression on you, clouded the mouse brow on more than one occasion. It's my way, but I'll try to change it for you. It's not unnatural in someone who has been as intensely concerned in himself for so long.[14]

By early June it was obvious that David would not be able to continue at Oxford without further financial help from outside his family. Vivian

Green discussed his case with the new Rector; Oakeshott appealed to the Chief Education Officer for Buckinghamshire, who happened to be a friend of his. 'He is an intelligent and cultured man who should do very well in whatever career he adopts,' wrote Oakeshott. 'We think it probable that he would have won an open award in German had he stayed at his public school to the end of the course instead of going to a Swiss university.' He gave his opinion that it would be 'a real tragedy if, through his father's financial failure, he were forced to leave at the end of this year'. In a follow-up letter, Oakeshott estimated that 'Cornwell . . . ought to get a good Second; he might do something better though one knows only too well what the effect of family disturbances such as this can be on a young man's progress. He is, however, one of those who immediately catch the eye about this College, and his reputation in some of the University Societies stands, I find, very high indeed.' The Rector judged that 'he is the sort of man who might perhaps even make the very severe grade for the Foreign Service'. The Chief Education Officer asked to be put in contact with the young man's father, though he could not promise to help.[15]

David dreaded the scandal that Ronnie's impending collapse would bring. To escape the inevitable publicity Green suggested that they take a walking holiday together in the Swiss Alps, and lent the impecunious undergraduate money for the fare. The pair travelled there by couchette, a journey made memorable by their female fellow passengers, members of the Oxford Group for Moral Rearmament, who spent a restless night searching for the loo. Leaving the train at Sion, they backpacked from valley to valley.[16] Green told David that his path to God was through Nature; his intense response to the mountain scenery was obvious in his rapt expression as they walked together. He opened the younger man's eyes to the glory of landscape, which David today he considers his greatest consolation.

Though Green had known the Alps since childhood, David had never heard anyone mangle Swiss names in the way that he did, so that not even the inhabitants of a place would recognise it from his pronunciation.[17] In one remote hamlet they met a shepherd who innocently enquired whether they knew Winston Churchill and asked them to confirm the rumour that the war had ended. Crossing a high pass, they noticed a bearded man waving a red flag, which Green advised David to ignore. Moments later they dropped flat on their faces, as a blast shattered the silence of the mountain and boulders flew through the air above their heads. Green picked up his spectacles, cleaned off the mud and perched them comically on the tip of his nose. 'For a moment,' he said, 'I was tempted to invoke very different gods to the one my cloth professes.' They discovered that the explosion had been detonated by miners building a hydroelectric dam; Green was outraged by this desecration of the unspoilt valley. In the leisurely surroundings of a comfortable hotel, the walkers plotted 'The Bears', a children's story, to be written by the older man and illustrated by the younger, which would tell of the determined opposition of Alpine bears to the scheme of an exploitative capitalist to construct a dam and flood the valley where they live. With the help of other animals, the bears were able to foil his plan, by melting a glacier which destroys the workmen's huts and carries away their tools.

In the hotel register David was excited to find the name Pontecorvo, whom he took to be the British nuclear physicist who had defected to the Soviet Union while on holiday in Italy some years earlier. In fact, as he later learned, he had been mistaken: the man who had stayed in the hotel was not the defector, but one of his brothers.

The peace of the mountains was disturbed further by the Swiss army on manoeuvres; no sooner had the clatter of machine-guns died away and the artillery ceased its bombardment than the Alps rang to the sound of thousands of cow bells, as the herds made their way up from the valley below to their summer pastures. The two walkers fled to the relative calm of the upper Rhône valley. In the pouring rain they arrived bedraggled in Bern, where David's former landlady, Frau Schreuers, gave them salami and herbal tea for breakfast. Their last excursion was to the Lauterbrunnen valley, ending with strawberry tarts as guests of Kaspar von Almen at his family's Trümmelbach hotel, before he drove them at speed in his Jaguar to Interlaken, to catch the train to Calais.

This holiday was the beginning of an important friendship for David. Vivian Green appears to have been a remarkable man, someone whom one needs to have known in order to appreciate fully.[18] Perhaps those who did not have this opportunity can best understand him in the depiction of his fictional counterpart, George Smiley. Of course the two are not the same; but David would use many of Green's characteristics in his portrayal of Smiley – in the silences which punctuated his conversation, to take just one example. David acknowledged that Smiley's conscience derived from Green's 'strong moral intellect'. Green was famous in Oxford for his eccentric dress sense; Smiley 'appeared to spend a lot of money on really bad clothes'. Years later Green himself would identify some of his own qualities that David might have drawn on in his creation of Smiley: understanding of human nature, sympathy for human frailty and a capacity for listening – indeed David found him a natural confessor.[19] Even at Sherborne 'Gumboil Green' (so called by the merciless schoolboys because of an unsightly growth on his face, later removed) had been recognised to be vaguely seditious, a trustworthy bridge between the young and those in authority. Among his appealing qualities was that he appeared not to take himself too seriously. Green was a scholar with a well-stocked mind, with whom David could enjoy a stimulating intellectual discussion; but he was also an irreverent companion with whom to share a meal or a giggle. Above all David found him a firm friend, gentle, kindly, wise, tolerant, discreet, patient, dependable and honourable.[20]

One small sign of their growing intimacy was that until now he and Green (sixteen years his senior) had addressed each other by their surnames, as was usual for tutors and undergraduates in the 1950s; from this point on they would be on first-name terms.

The walking holiday had provided some relief from the troubles at home. 'What news of papa, I wonder?' David had written to Ann from an isolated village near the Italian border. 'I don't see much news here . . .'[21] A headline appeared in the *Daily Express*: 'Liabilities – £1,359,570 / Assets – a big smile and "lots more"'. Ronnie had been waylaid by a staff reporter as he left the bankruptcy court, outwardly jovial and even chuckling. 'Disaster? Not a bit of it,' he was quoted as saying – 'just the beginning of a fight after a temporary setback.'[22] A fortnight later he was adjudged bankrupt. Though the publicity was unwelcome, the immediate effects were few. Ronnie had been careful to place most of his personal assets in Jean's name, so that in the short term life at Tunmers carried on much as it had done before. Though he was forced to surrender his Mount Street offices, he remained unbowed, apparently confident that this was no more than another hiccup in his business career. But David was keenly aware of the damage Ronnie had wrought in the lives of others. Jean discovered belatedly that her husband had mortgaged her family business. One of her aunts had a cheque for £1,000 returned, marked 'account closed', in proposed repayment of an unsecured loan of almost her entire savings; she was left with only £28. The proximity of the Ansorges, just across the road from Tunmers, was an ever-present reproach. Perhaps worst of all was the case of Gordon Hobson, a sandy-haired, upper-class remittance man down on his luck who had attached himself to Ronnie like a lost dog. Ronnie had cleaned him out, but Hobson refused to recognise that he had been duped. He loved Ronnie, and believed that if he hung around him, somehow things would right themselves. 'I hope your father knows what he's doing,' he would say to the boys in his apologetic way, 'because he's had all my money!' Hobson appointed himself a member of Ronnie's Court and would run errands for him, place bets for him and lie for him, even as he was being lied to himself. He was a regular house-guest at Tunmers, referred to by Ronnie in patronising terms as 'dear old Gordon, a first-class chap and the salt of the earth, even if he is a bit too fond of the bottle'. But then David noticed that Hobson was no longer in attendance, his name ominously unmentioned. It would be a long time before he was allowed to know what became of him. Hobson had found himself a lady of the night and taken her to one of the grand London hotels, where they had signed in as Sir Gordon and Lady Hobson and enjoyed a splendid meal, fine wines, the best of everything; and then, in the small hours of the night, he had sent the woman home and killed himself.[23]

During the police investigation into Ronnie's business affairs, David was summoned to a meeting at the Royal Courts of Justice, to appear before the Receiver in Bankruptcy. He learned that he was a director of several of Ronnie's companies; his signature appeared at the foot of a clutch of company documents. He wondered: was that really his signature? And if he denied that it was, what would be the inference? David chose to tell the Receiver that yes, the signatures were his, and heard no more about it.[24] Typically he would make light of this episode in years to come, but at the time he found it worrying and upsetting.

Dick Edmonds offered David a holiday job during Clements's Grand Summer Sale. They agreed that he would work for three weeks in exchange for a charcoal-grey suit with two vents and narrow trousers. But on the very first day of the Sale he was fired from the towels and white linen counter for upsetting a customer, a tiny German lady. 'You'd better try carpets,' Edmonds told him – but David was no more successful there, selling the same carpet remnant to twenty different customers in the mistaken belief that there were plenty more knocking around the warehouse. Disappointed customers complained, threatening litigation; the inexperienced temporary salesman was rapidly laid off. For weeks afterwards, as Edmonds never tired of telling him, Clements was obliged to devote considerable resources to repairing the mayhem he had caused. Edmonds gave his friend a year to come up with the money to pay for the suit.[25]

By the end of the summer, when he was ordered back to Maresfield for his annual training commitment, David was in distress, repelled by his father's way of life and trying to find a moral basis for his own. In retrospect Ann felt that he underwent a 'mini-breakdown' at this time. 'I have just spent a terrible two weeks at home,' David wrote to Vivian Green, who had been providing him with pastoral counsel – 'so much so that I am positively relieved to find myself back in the Army for two weeks.' David's disenchantment with his father was now complete. 'His very existence is a complete mockery of any moral consideration,' David continued. He had already told Green of his plan to marry Ann as soon as possible, indeed had asked him to officiate. It seems that they had discussed married life in detail: Green had assured David that he and Ann would be able to give their children the stable family background which they themselves had both been denied. 'I've always wanted to become a Christian, and try & live like one,' David explained. 'Ann is a very religious girl and I think together we could manage.'

Green urged him to stay at Oxford, now that Buckinghamshire County Council was offering to pay his college tuition fees; but, for David, money was no longer the principal issue. Staying at Oxford, he argued, would mean remaining dependent on Ronnie – at least during the vacations. It also implied – though he did not make this point in his letter to Green – postponing his marriage until he had taken his degree, because undergraduates were forbidden from marrying without special permission. But that was a lesser consideration: David was focused on his father. What troubled him most was the fact that 'if I live with him or under him for another year, I shall be quite incapable of coming to any moral decision whatever'. He had come to appreciate that 'every time I take money from him, or even a meal, I am acquiescing to his way of life, and weakening my own position'.

> Having made a stand, and having tried to shake myself out of a state of indifference, I find I have slipped back into that horrible state of mind where I have no more resistance to his demands or his way of life. What do I do if he offers me five pounds, and I know that he has not only borrowed it from someone else, and owes it thousands of times over to people much more deserving than I, but also has refused the same sum to my stepmother for housekeeping?

For all these reasons David had concluded that he must quit Oxford immediately, without beginning his third year or taking a degree. He asked Green's forgiveness and understanding for this decision. 'I know it's all very impulsive and silly, and probably immature too, but what else can I really do?' David referred to the 'Kemsleys offer' – 'but again, I am committing myself to something I don't really want to do'. The offer was soon withdrawn in any case. Dick White asked to see David. He did not like the idea of setting up such a young man to become a double agent, which he felt might be putting too much pressure on him, a feeling which hardened into conviction during the interview.

'I love you so much that I am losing ambition for my job, which you must rekindle in my mind,' David wrote to Ann from Maresfield Camp. 'I seem to have all I ever wanted and money doesn't matter.' After a long talk with Sir James Barnes he warned her that 'the matter of immediate employment with the Kemsley Press' was by no means settled.[26]

Ann would later characterise David's state of mind at this time as wanting to run away from his father to a new family where he could hide and feel safe. He was now planning not only to leave Oxford but to leave the country altogether – 'as long as I stay in England I shall not be able to get away from him'.[27] He wrote to several friends in Switzerland asking them to find him work there. 'This is not an uncalculated and foolish flight from nothing,' he assured Kaspar von Almen, 'but a seriously considered plan to get away once and for all from things over here, and begin a new life.' He was willing to take any teaching job. 'Money is not the problem,' he insisted. 'The problem is to live happily with my wife away from the degrading publicity of the present court case, to live an intelligent life. I am miserably tired of trying to live for the future indefinitely. I want to live for the present.'[28]

In a further letter to von Almen, written from Oxford, David announced some good news: in principle Lincoln would allow him to 'go out of residence' for a year, and to return as a married undergraduate a year later to complete his degree, subject to the approval of the Rector.[29] David would spend a year teaching, not in Switzerland, but in Somerset, at Edgarley Hall, the preparatory school for Millfield. The suggestion had come from an old suitor of Ann's mother, George Turner. There was another link with Ann's family, in that her grandfather, George Wollen, had been teaching at Edgarley since 1948.

Vivian Green, in his capacity as senior tutor, provided an excellent reference:

> Mr Cornwell is an intelligent and serious student with a good knowledge of French and German; incidentally he speaks Swiss German fluently. He has wide general interests; and is a most promising artist with a real gift for caricature. Personally he is very presentable. I am quite sure that Mr Cornwell would be able to interest, control and teach any class and would prove a congenial, pleasant and loyal colleague.

A week later, after being accepted at Edgarley, David wrote to thank Green. 'I feel I must write and let you know that had it not been for your help and your friendship, I do not think I could have found anywhere near so satisfactory an answer to the present problem. I won't indulge in one of those awful Teutonic eulogies – but I do feel very deeply how much I owe to your help and understanding . . .'[30]

In the short term David had no access to funds, and relied on Ann to pay every bill. With the lack of money a pressing problem, there was a strong incentive for him to start teaching and drawing his salary of £8 a week straight away, rather than wait for the beginning of a new term. He gave up his digs in Oxford and moved down to Somerset, where he found a place to live in the 'dream-like village' village of Pilton (now the site of the Glastonbury Festival), about six miles from Edgarley Hall along the Glastonbury road. David cycled there and back every day of the week except Sunday, thereby saving the nine-penny bus fare, on a sit-up-and-beg bicycle given to them by Ann's uncle. On the few occasions when he took the bus, because it was raining or for some other reason, the conductor sometimes allowed the obviously impoverished young schoolmaster to ride free of charge. Steam trains could be seen puffing back and forth along a railway track running parallel to the road.

David's new home was Cumhill Farm, on the southern edge of Pilton, looking out over woodland towards the village church. Adjoining the stone farmhouse was a fine tithe barn, still in its original use. David rented four rooms within the main building for twenty-five shillings* a week, and filled these with borrowed furniture, most of it from Ann's mother. The idea was that Ann should join him as soon as they were married. She was loath to leave her job, but told herself that David needed her. And she would have time to concentrate on her writing.

When David wrote to tell Olive of his plan to leave Oxford and marry Ann, she cautioned him against doing so, arguing that his fiancée was a girl who had lived 'gaily and well', no wife for a humble schoolmaster without a degree. Ann was amused to be so misunderstood, but David was furious, and resolved to have no further contact with his mother. She would not be invited to the wedding, and he would not see her again for many years. Yet David himself was unsure whether he was right to marry. He had asked Robin Cooke to be his best man; when Cooke asked if he was certain that he wanted to go through with it, David said no, he was not. Apart from anything else they were still very young, he twenty-three and she twenty-two. But Cooke had the impression that there was more to it than that: he felt that David was slightly ashamed of Ann. She was a very proper young woman, with strong moral values, ill at ease in the company of David's sophisticated Oxford friends, none of whom would be invited to the wedding.

David had hoped for a private ceremony, and no reception, and told Vivian Green that Ann agreed with him; but her mother Alison insisted on a 'proper wedding' and offered to pay all the costs. Bride and groom were rationed to a limit of twenty-five guests (though Alison cheated and invited more).

Ann's father returned to England to inspect his future son-in-law. Bobby Sharp appeared to doubt whether it was sensible for his precious

* £1.25 in decimal currency.

daughter to waste herself on a young man with so few prospects; but he formed an immediate rapport with Ronnie, who had recently taken up with a woman claiming to be a former girlfriend of Guy Gibson* – 'a rather iffy South African blonde' in Ann's description. The two old roués went chasing after her together. According to David's later recollection, neither was invited to the wedding. Perhaps jaundiced by his exclusion, Bobby urged David not to marry Ann. 'Those Wollen women will destroy you,' he warned.

Ten days before the wedding, David sent Ann a round-up of his news. He had been decorating and had painted a mural in their new kitchen, but was not satisfied with it and had painted it over. Now that he had started teaching at Edgarley, he realised that he would not have much time for drawing during the term-time, but he was sure that he would be able to pursue his art in the holidays, just as she would be able to write. To that end, he had written to his father, asking for an old typewriter. While painting he had been mulling over their future:

> I don't somehow think that I shall ever get back to Oxford. I don't want to go particularly, and somehow there is something rather nasty in the idea of becoming a career man with the F.O. or Dick T† or somewhere – so it seems anyway. The most successful men in that line – in the office, not out of it, are competent and plausible, but dishonest and unscrupulous – and these are all qualities that I have, and are best suppressed rather than encouraged! So if I can find a good niche (dreadful word) at Edgarley, and a cottage to match, let's hang on down here, and draw and write and walk and fly kites and teach a little, and enjoy life.[31]

Within a month, however, David would tell Vivian Green that he was planning to return to Oxford 'if at all possible'.[32]

David and Ann were married at noon on Saturday 27 November 1954, at St Luke's Church, Redcliffe Square, in South Kensington. The bride was

* The original Commanding Officer of the RAF's 617 Squadron, the famous 'Dambusters'. He had died on active service in 1944, at the age of twenty-six.

† Dick Thistlethwaite of MI5.

given away by her uncle; David's half-sister Charlotte was bridesmaid and Ann's sister 'Winkie'* maid of honour. There was a reception afterwards at the Onslow Court Hotel, Queen's Gate. To keep the cost down Alison had provided white wine – but just before the toasts a waiter entered bearing a tray of champagne glasses, followed by a beaming Ronnie, dressed in a morning suit. 'Have this one on me,' he advised Alison, completely unrepentant at his intrusion into a reception to which he had not been invited. At any rate this is how David recalls the day: but in that case it is difficult to explain Ronnie's presence, with Jean on his arm, in the wedding photographs taken outside the church. Indeed there is a photograph of Ronnie inside the church, benevolently looking on as the bride signs the register.

Afterwards David thanked Green for conducting the service. 'Ann and I both felt most strongly that we had become part of a triple, not a dual, union,' he wrote. 'From the moment you began, it seemed as if only we three were in the church – Ann, myself and you as God's minister, and what we fully expected to be a gruelling and frightening affair assumed a very different character.'[33]

Alison had arranged for the newlyweds to stay that first night at the Avon Gorge Hotel in Clifton, where the manager, a friend of hers, had given them a special rate. Their bedroom balcony offered a prospect of Brunel's famous suspension bridge. They dined that evening in a private room, on turtle soup, caviar, sole, duck and *Poire belle Hélène*. The next day, after a lunch of smoked salmon, they took a taxi to Pilton. David was due to resume teaching at Edgarley the next morning.

* Always known as such, though her real name was Angela Wincombe, so named because she was born on the day her father was promoted to wing commander.

8

Poor but happy

Edgarley Hall was a comparatively new school when David arrived there in the autumn of 1954, founded only nine years before in order to accommodate increasing numbers of younger pupils arriving at Millfield. Indeed Millfield itself was less than twenty years old. Both had been founded by R. J. O. ('Jack') Meyer, whose nickname 'Boss' was an indication of his dominance. He was a keen sportsman, who had played first-class cricket. After leaving Cambridge in 1926 he had worked as a cotton broker in India and had once played for the Indian national side against a touring MCC team. He had returned from India in 1935 accompanied by seven Indian boys, six of them princes, entrusted to him for their education; he had founded Millfield to provide this, and would remain in charge for thirty-five years, becoming known as 'Britain's most progressive headmaster'. Meyer boasted that 'any subject you care to name we teach from 7 to 27'. Millfield grew steadily, gaining a reputation for sporting excellence, and for success in educating pupils with 'word-blindness' (dyslexia). In those days dyslexic children were regarded as 'backward'. To Meyer's fury, the boys at Edgarley produced a subversive magazine emblazoned with the motto: 'We're here because we're not all there'.

Stories proliferated about Meyer's eccentricity. He gambled on the horses with the school's money, and paid occasional visits to London casinos where he would wager large sums, often losing the lot.* (David told Ann that the

* Years later David would come across Meyer behind a pile of gambling chips at the White Elephant Club in Curzon Street.

bursar, a Brigadier Mackie, was 'absolutely hand-in-glove' with the headmaster.) Meyer was convinced that the Communist Party was systematically seeking out super-intelligent children in order to indoctrinate the leaders of the future; and that Mensa, the IQ society, was under Communist control. David was startled to learn that Meyer had written to the cellist Edmund Kurtz to complain that his son's behaviour was 'typical of the worst kind of Jew'. In later life David would characterise Millfield as 'a brilliant educational innovation, a shameless racket, a haven for millionaire misfits and a charitable madhouse run by a neo-fascist visionary who was also an enlightened liberal'.[1]

Edgarley was located on a separate site from Millfield, in a large house of Georgian origins but much altered since. When David was teaching there Edgarley took only boys, while Millfield was co-educational. Most of the other masters at the school were middle-aged or elderly, and included two veterans of the First World War who had been awarded the Military Cross; George Wollen was still teaching there in his eighties. One of the few younger members of staff was the mathematics master Dick Champion, who had been at Edgarley only a year. He and David became friendly; in later years he would recall that David had been so poor that he had to borrow some tennis shoes in order to play. There were more young masters at Millfield, among them Robert Bolt, later a successful playwright and screenwriter, whose wife Jo was the art teacher at Edgarley.

'I'm teaching 14 periods of Latin, 3 French & 2 German a week,' David wrote to Vivian Green soon after he arrived. 'I've forgotten *all* my Latin but will pick it up slowly as we go along. The boys here are awfully stupid, except one . . .'[2]

Among David's duties was to teach boxing, ironically enough since he had hated it at Sherborne and had given it up early. When he intervened to break up a fight, he received a punch from a tall Egyptian boy.

Despite his obvious lack of interest in organised games, David was a popular member of staff, reckoned by Champion to be 'very good with the boys'. One former pupil, John Warmington, remembers German lessons in which 'Mr Cornwell' told them about the 1944 plot against Hitler, and detailed how the Lord's Prayer was worded in a Wehrmacht paybook. He seemed to know a great deal about the German army and about British monitoring of German radio broadcasts, which led the boys to suspect that he had been involved in intelligence in some way.

The boys liked David, and he seems to have cared for them. He was offended when the mother of one of his pupils complained that her son was not more disciplined. 'When I send a horse to be broken, I expect him to come back broken,' she told him. 'I expect the same of my children.'

As he had done at Maresfield, David put on plays at Edgarley. One of these featured a wicked Uncle Jasper, who rowed his boat to an island to seduce a hapless girl; another (or possibly the same one) featured the lighthouse keeper's daughter Nellie, whose duty was to keep the light shining in the absence of her father. The actors' make-up was done by 'Mrs Cornwell', much admired by the boys, who relished the story of an occasion when her husband brought her into the school library. The joint headmaster, H. L. 'Charlie' Higgins, flustered by the presence of such an attractive young woman, hid himself behind a newspaper for several minutes, until the director of studies pointed out to him that he was holding it upside down.

On his first night as duty master, David was sitting in front of a large Victorian fireplace waiting for the boys to be put to bed when a prefect came to him and said, 'Excuse me, Sir, —— is trying to commit suicide.' A boy believed to have 'mental problems' had climbed over the banisters in the stairwell overlooking the front hall, and was threatening to throw himself off. While David hurried to the scene, another pupil seized him around the middle and dragged him to safety. David shot up the stairs and scooped him up. Afterwards, when they were alone, David asked the would-be suicide, 'What made you want to do a thing like that?' The boy, a small, fat child, explained that he could not stand the pace – 'I can't make my bed quickly enough, I can't eat breakfast quickly enough, I'm always late for class' – and that the others teased him about such deplorable failings.[3] David drew on the memory of this unhappy schoolboy for his portrait of Bill Roach, whose narrative frames the action of *Tinker, Tailor, Soldier, Spy*. 'I remember how deeply he got under my skin,' he would write, 'perhaps because I could not help thinking of him as myself, when I was fifteen years younger.'[4]

Ann's mother Alison and sister Winkie came to Cumhill Farm for Christmas 1954, together with her grandmother. In the early years of their marriage David was very affectionate towards Alison, treating her much as though she were his own mother, and addressing her as 'Dearest Mamma' or 'Alison darling'. She gave him the gold watch that she had presented to her husband as a wedding gift, retrieved when they had separated. But David was not sentimental about such matters: keen to raise money in any way possible, he sold the watch, together with the cufflinks Ronnie had given him on his twenty-first birthday.

On 14 October 1954 Ronnie had submitted himself for cross-examination in the bankruptcy court, a hearing that had to be adjourned when time ran out, and that continued in several subsequent sessions through into the summer of 1955. In all he answered more than 1,500 questions. As the lawyer acting on behalf of the trustees remarked, 'the estate is exceptionally complicated, the debts very large and the assets extremely difficult to identify. Mr Cornwell is the only person who really has any knowledge of the intimate working of the companies.' The case was very widely reported in the national evening papers, and also in the local papers in Skipton and Dudley, the locations of the two building societies from which Ronnie's property companies had borrowed the capital to fund most of their purchases. Ronnie repeatedly denied that he controlled these companies, under tough and prolonged cross-examination. ('I put it to you that this company is another of your creatures, is it not?'; 'You are not being frank with the Court, Mr Cornwell?'; 'Who is "we"? Kindly use "I" if you mean one human being'; 'Is this another case of Mr Cornwell the person and Mr Cornwell behaving as a company, doing things with one another . . .?') He also denied that the directors of these companies had been no more than his nominees, acting under his direction. ('You have been the guiding spirit, the general of this particular army, have you not?') Ronnie seemed to enjoy the jousting, though his demeanour was respectful throughout. The court was forced to admit that he had given his evidence 'with commendable clarity'.

The newlyweds kept Ronnie at a distance, even as he showered them with gifts, including forty-five shillings' worth of nylon stockings by Christian Dior. David learned from Jean that he was again becoming violent, and later that he had left her altogether. Just before the end of term he telephoned David at Edgarley, explaining that he was speaking from a callbox only a few miles away. He asked if he could join them at Pilton for Christmas, but David said no.

Around this time Ronnie went down to Poole to visit his mother, now eighty and very frail. The arrival of the Prodigal Son was enough to make a front-page story in the local newspaper. 'A man with a mission walked into my office today,' began the editor:

> His name: Ronald Thomas Archibald Cornwell, former Poole Grammar school boy, son of a Poole alderman. His mission: to clear himself from the stigma of bankruptcy.
>
> And it was the same ebullient, confident Ronald Cornwell whom I knew 20 years ago – plumper, perhaps, and grey, but still the same cheery personality.
>
> Yes, despite his rise to great heights in the real estate world, Ronald Cornwell has never forgotten his mother. 'And she still regards me as her boy,' he says.

The article was illustrated with a photograph of a smiling Ronnie. 'I'm determined to fight my way back,' the editor quoted him as saying.[5]

Some time later the Official Receiver's office received a clipping of this article from an anonymous source. 'THE SMILE OF THE MAN WHO WINS AGAIN AND AGAIN' was scrawled in blue ink across Ronnie's photograph. 'A FEW CROCODILE'S TEARS TO CLEAR WAY FOR NEXT EXPLOIT'.

Sharing a house with the farmer and his wife soon became irksome for the newlyweds. When an elderly villager came to the door and asked if they would like to rent an end-of-terrace cottage near by, they seized the opportunity, especially as the rent was considerably less, at seven shillings* a week. The 500-year-old cottage was small and basic; there was electricity and running water, but no drainage, so that dirty water had to be carried outside and poured down the drain by the front door. A path led from the back door behind the neighbouring cottage to a privy with two wooden seats; every couple of days David would collect the sewage and bury it in the back garden. Downstairs was a sitting room with a kitchen range, while the kitchen itself was equipped with a small electric cooker. The sink

* 35p in decimal currency.

drained into a bucket. They washed in a long tin bath, which they used perhaps twice a week, heating water in saucepans on the stove, and then emptying it down the steep slope behind the cottage after use. Upstairs were two tiny bedrooms: the one at the front was just big enough for a bed, a narrow wardrobe and a chest of drawers. The back room doubled as a spare room and as David's studio, where he painted an oil of Ann of which he was very proud. It also served as the resting-place for a stuffed tiger shot by Ann's grandfather, which suffered from its proximity to David's paints.

The Cornwells grew vegetables and kept chickens. They acquired a dog, a mongrel called Bobby who limped along on three legs after being hit by a car. Among their acquaintances in the neighbourhood was an old baronet, whose 'very Somerset' housekeeper kept him under her thumb. They were especially friendly with the Catholic family at Pilton Manor, Colonel and Mrs Phipps and their six daughters. The colonel made them laugh with his account of a cavalry charge in the desert; when the critical moment had come, he had been unable to draw his sword, which had rusted in its scabbard. The Cornwells played hide-and-seek with the Phipps girls in the old manor house; being dotted with priest-holes from the Civil War period, it offered plenty of hiding places. Another retired army officer whom they befriended drove them to a local race-meeting; when he found the course car park full, he rather mysteriously blamed 'the Jews'.

David mounted a production of Emlyn Williams's *Night Must Fall* for the Pilton Players, the village amateur dramatics group. Both he and Ann took parts: in David's case, that of the charming psychopath Danny, the character who had so intrigued him as a boy when he had been taken by his aunts to see the play.

They had no car, but they could get about locally by bus, and if they wanted to go to London or some other far-off place, they could take a train from Shepton Mallet, only three miles distant. Otherwise they hitchhiked, cadging lifts from passing lorries; in the mid-1950s there were still not many cars on the road, particularly in rural Somerset. In their free time the Cornwells would often take bicycle rides through the surrounding lanes; Ann remembered freewheeling at high speed down a steep hill, sending the water flying up high on either side as she sped through a flooded ford. On Sundays they attended church services – though, as David wrote to Vivian Green, the Pilton church was 'very high', so that they could not always understand what was happening. In the evenings David knelt beside Ann to say his prayers. 'We are really terribly happy,' David wrote to Robin Cooke.[6]

Green's story 'The Bears' was shown to a succession of publishers. None wanted it, though Edward Arnold liked the illustrations. Eventually the two co-authors agreed to abandon the project. Meanwhile Ann earned some pin money by writing short stories for the *Sunday Companion*.

At Easter-time the Cornwells took a belated honeymoon in Paris. They travelled by train to London and then on to the Gare du Nord, and found a clean but rundown hotel not far from the station. For several days they explored the city on foot, rarely eating out to save money. As they passed a grand hotel on their last evening, a voice rang out, bellowing their names: it was Reggie Bosanquet with his bride Karen, also on honeymoon. Reggie insisted that the Cornwells join them for dinner in a smart restaurant, where the four of them were entertained by Nellie Lutcher, a black cabaret artist, who sang a risqué song involving asparagus.

Early in May 1955 David asked formal permission from the Rector of Lincoln to return to Oxford later in the year to complete his degree as a married undergraduate.[7] For his final year he would drop French and concentrate on German. 'I had a very kind letter from Mr Oakeshott saying he would welcome us both,' he informed Vivian Green a few weeks later. His resignation from Edgarley had been 'very poorly received'; Meyer and Mackie had seemed genuinely upset, which seemed to David 'really quite funny', given his antipathy to both. Teaching, he said, 'has regenerated in me the thing I lacked since I entered this awful business with father – a desire (and I think a renewed capacity) for academic work'.[8]

Once again Oakeshott appealed to his friend on Buckinghamshire County Council for financial help. 'It would be a real injustice if this boy had to give up his course uncompleted,' he wrote.[9] David was awarded an exhibition, which would give him some measure of monetary security for the year ahead. 'I have rather strong views about Ann working in Oxford,' David told Vivian Green – 'would far rather she kept house and helped me by taking shorthand notes and typing them out and so forth.'[10]

In July, after he had finished at Edgarley, David took Ann to stay with Vivian Green in Minehead, where the bachelor don lived with his mother in the University vacations. From there they took long walks over Exmoor, and Green preached in the country churches that he loved the best: Selworthy, above Minehead, or the church on North Hill, or Lorna Doone's church at Oare. Together they walked up from the shore at Porlock to Culbone, where the smallest church in England stands isolated in a woodland combe, below the farmhouse where Coleridge wrote *Kubla Khan*. After Green's death in 2005 David could no longer remember a word of his sermons, but he was sure that they had been sensible, erudite, gentle and respectful of his feelings. 'Sometimes, in my youthful vanity, I supposed they were actually written for my benefit, which must be the definition of a good sermon. And perhaps one or two even were, because Vivian was fully aware that he was my lifeline.'[11]

Ann's father turned up at the cottage unannounced that summer, accompanied by Lynn, an American woman fascinated by English ways. His manner seemed to Ann unnaturally jolly; she was still angry with him, and unwilling to be reconciled. This would be the last time that she would see him, since he died six months later: only after his death did she discover that he and Lynn had married. Ann's mother had also remarried, and was living some twenty miles away in Taunton with her new husband, Guy Shacklock, a retired brigadier; later she would persuade him to buy a manor house near Chard in Somerset. This marriage too was short lived.

In September 1955 the Cornwells moved to Oxford, bequeathing Bobby, their mongrel puppy, to Green's mother. To begin with they rented a room in Summertown, from a landlady who soon yearned for David and vented her frustration on Ann, criticising her cleaning and telling her to be a 'proper wife'. After a few weeks they decamped to a furnished flat occupying the upper two floors of a house in Polstead Road, on the other side of North Oxford. It was owned by John Thring, of the family of Gabbitas-Thring, the agency founded in 1873 to recruit schoolmasters to public schools.* Thring knew Oakeshott, and had asked him if his prospective tenant was likely to have 'uproarious parties' in the flat, concerned for his nonagenarian aunt who lived with a housekeeper on the ground floor. The Rector replied reassuringly, and provided some family background. 'His father is one of those wild businessmen who is worth six

* A Mr Stroll, of the educational agency Stroll & Medely, appears in the opening chapter of *Tinker, Tailor, Soldier, Spy*.

figures one year and is an undischarged bankrupt the next three,' wrote Oakeshott. 'The boy, who went to Sherborne, has had a very rough time with the father, ending in a flaming row that was all to the boy's credit.'[12] His concerns alleviated, Thring accepted the young couple as tenants, and even allowed them to take a lodger to help with the rent. The Cornwells took in an undergraduate from a northern grammar school who spoke with a Yorkshire accent; in retrospect, Ann blushed with shame to recall how 'snooty' she and David had been towards him.

A disadvantage of the flat was that it lacked a double bed, but the young couple managed to share a single bed until David's finals, when they slept apart. On the other hand the flat had three bedrooms, which meant they could accommodate weekend visitors, among them the Bosanquets, Colin Simpson, Sandy Llewellyn and Hugh Peppiatt, who brought his glamorous Russian girlfriend.

David worked very hard in his third year. He wanted to vindicate the faith shown in him by Oakeshott and Green, though he found it more difficult because the syllabus had changed while he was away. Ann helped by typing his notes and essays, and by reading all his set books so that they could discuss them together. David would later describe their flat as being 'like an ops room', littered with Ann's files and card indexes. He confessed to Vivian Green that he found some of the work 'awfully dull'.[13] But as Green later recorded, he 'developed a lasting interest in seventeenth century German literature, especially that picaresque classic of the Thirty Years' War, Grimmelshausen's *Simplicissimus*, references to which are sprinkled through his novels'.[14] David's diligence was evident in his report for the Michaelmas term, in which he was awarded an α rating. 'Cornwell is a first-class man,' commented his tutor. 'He is industrious, thorough, and frequently brilliant.'

David had few friends to distract him from his work, since those whom he had known in his first two years had left Oxford; being married, and living out of college, he had little to do with other undergraduates, and had gratefully given up pretending to be a Communist. (MI5 had not reactivated him for his final year.) On most evenings David stopped working at about seven o'clock; he and Ann would then stroll to the pub at the end of the road, where he would have a beer, she would sip a ginger wine, and they would play bar billiards together. Sometimes they would go and see a foreign film at the Scala cinema in Walton Street. At weekends they would take walks, or fly kites on Port Meadow. 'We can't spend much money 'cause we haven't much,' David wrote to Robin Cooke, 'but we can still have a lovely time, can't we?' David addressed his old friend as 'sweetheart' or 'dear', and affected a camp manner: 'Do you see that Peter W has published his book "Against the Law"* and that we're *both* in it, with our photograph on the front page surrounded with irises and violets? Honestly, some people *sell* themselves.'[15]

Occasionally the Cornwells went to stay with friends; though they tried to avoid 'smart weekends' away because they felt obliged to tip the servants, which they found prohibitively expensive. Dick Edmonds invited them several times to The Round House, a former lock-keeper's cottage on the banks of the Thames at Lechlade, shaped like a windmill without the sails, that the family used as a country retreat. On one of these visits they met Dick's sister Susan and her Scots husband James Kennaway, a lively and good-looking couple. Kennaway was then working for a publishers; his first novel *Tunes of Glory*, based partly on his own experiences of National Service, would appear in 1956. He regaled his fellow guests with stories of the low-level and absurd tasks he had carried out at the request of an MI5 friend, Harold 'Hal' Doyne-Ditmas, who had summoned him to a rendezvous in Berkeley Square, which seemed to him a ludicrous place for secret meetings. After talking about this too openly Kennaway had been summoned by Doyne-Ditmas and given 'a hell of a bollocking'. Typically he made this into another amusing anecdote, complaining that 'For God's sake, they didn't even pay me!' Later David told Ann that he had reported this further indiscretion to his MI5 contacts.

David contemplated going to art school after leaving Oxford, reckoning that they could subsist on an inheritance Ann had received from her father's estate. Meanwhile he tried to supplement his meagre grant from Buckinghamshire County Council by obtaining commissions for drawing

* Peter Wildeblood's book *Against the Law* (1955) detailed the case which had led to his conviction for homosexual activities. His account of his experiences is said to have encouraged the setting up of the Wolfenden Commission, which in 1957 recommended the decriminalisation of homosexuality in the UK.

and painting. Dick Edmonds paid him £20 to illustrate the Clements annual catalogue. David was 'quietly optimistic' about his prospects of becoming a commercial artist on leaving Oxford, as he told Robin Cooke in a letter written soon after returning there. He had been seeing publishers and others, who had assured him that he could make a living from his work. The Bodley Head had already commissioned him to illustrate a book jacket,* for which he was paid £7. Ann found him an agent.[16] Through an acquaintance of Ronnie's, a commercial artist who drew a strip cartoon featuring a racehorse as a character, David was introduced to the principal of an art school, who inspected his folder and told him that he was far too intelligent to be doing 'this kind of stuff'.

Nothing had been heard from Ronnie for some time, but towards the end of the year he made contact and sought to persuade them to join him on a skiing holiday by offering to pay their costs. 'Ann, as you can imagine, is having a fit at the prospect of his turning up here with tickets to Davos, and frankly so am I,' David wrote to Vivian Green. 'I don't want to see him again.'[17] The offer must have been tempting to him nonetheless, as he could not afford to go skiing out of his own resources. At Green's recommendation David wrote to his father declining the offer. After a period of pained silence a note from Ronnie arrived, to say that the decision was as he 'had expected' and that he would 'make other arrangements'.[18]

Since the cottage in Pilton was so cheap the Cornwells had kept it on as a 'country seat', for use during the holidays. They invited Jean and the children, now evicted from Tunmers and living in a mean house in a bleak London suburb, to join them there for Christmas 1955. Despite his father's bankruptcy Rupert had been able to remain at his prep school, and would be able to go on to Winchester, because some years earlier, at a moment when his fortunes were high, Jean had managed to persuade Ronnie to pay his school fees in advance; but Charlotte would be compelled to give up her ponies and enrol in the local state school. Early in the new year Jean asked Vivian Green to christen her two children in Lincoln College Chapel. 'It was so nice also to be with David and Ann again,' she wrote to

* *They Fought for Children* (1956) by Peggy Chambers.

him in a letter of thanks afterwards. 'They're such a sweet pair and have been so good to the children and me.'[19]

As David's final year progressed, it became urgent to decide what he was going to do next. One possibility was to join MI5; but the Service preferred its officer recruits, however well educated, to have experience of the outside world and to be in at least their mid-twenties.[20] Early in the 1956 Hilary term, his penultimate as an undergraduate, David wrote to various schools about the possibility of a job after he finished at Oxford – despite having sworn to Ann after resigning from Edgarley that he would never again teach. It seems possible that, like MI5, his potential employers in the 'Foreign Office' may have encouraged him to pursue a conventional career for the time being. An indication of their continuing interest in David came the following March, when Green was asked to provide another written reference for him to the 'Foreign Office Co-ordination Staff'.

St Edward's School had the advantage of being only a short walk from their flat in Polstead Road. The Warden (headmaster), Frank Fisher, interviewed David and found him both pleasant and able. In response to Fisher's request for a reference, Oakeshott replied that 'young Cornwell is an attractive person who has already taught with success'.[21] Fisher also sought an opinion from R. S. Thompson, by now a headmaster himself. 'With the right kind of guidance, encouragement, and atmosphere, David will make an excellent schoolmaster,' replied Thompson. 'I don't suppose he has sorted himself out yet by any means. If he has married wisely it will be the making of him. But don't let the charm work too easily with you!'[22]

David had also applied to Eton and to Charterhouse, and went for interviews at both. The headmaster of Eton, Robert Birley, was looking for an assistant master to teach modern languages as a replacement for Gerald Peacocke, who had been teaching there for two terms on a temporary basis and was due to leave in the summer. Like Fisher, Birley was impressed by David and decided to offer him the job. The interview with the headmaster of Charterhouse, Brian Young, went less well. When Fisher offered him a post at St Edward's, with a higher starting salary than that available at either of the other two schools, David promptly accepted, and telephoned both Birley and Young to withdraw his application. 'I wouldn't have taken you anyway,' Young told him. Birley, however, was keen to have him and asked Oakeshott (himself a former headmaster) if he might persuade David to change his mind. 'I wonder whether Cornwell is not perhaps making a mistake,' Birley wrote to Oakeshott. 'If he wants to become a schoolmaster this is certainly a very good chance for him.' While he did not say as much, he meant of course that a post at Eton was more prestigious than one at St Edward's. Birley expatiated on the subject of Eton salaries, which he feared had fallen behind those offered at other public schools.* After Oakeshott convinced him to reconsider David extricated himself from St Edward's and accepted the offer of a job as an assistant master at Eton, teaching modern languages at an annual salary of £850.[23] By comparison, Ronnie would explain to the London Bankruptcy Court that summer that, though he had cut all unnecessary expenses, he had to do a great deal of entertaining and found it very difficult to get his household and domestic expenditure below £3,600 a year.[24]

'Though the salary isn't brilliant to begin with,' wrote Ann, in a letter to her recently widowed stepmother, 'it rises quite rapidly and of course one couldn't do better in the teaching profession than start there.' She outlined the thinking behind David's decision to become a schoolmaster. 'The chief thing about school teaching,' she explained, 'instead of the FO, which he was also thinking of, is that there are four months' holiday a year, in which he can do his painting. Eventually we hope he'll earn enough to stop teaching, but it will be a relief to have a regular salary, so that he can paint what he likes and not necessarily for the money.'[25]

In a 1999 interview, David claimed that he had been 'drawn to Eton by a great sense of service, which paradoxically I still feel'. He linked this decision to his ambivalence towards the institutions of the establishment, loving them and criticising them simultaneously.[26] At the time, however, it seems that his motives were less lofty; his principal aim was to earn an income to support himself and his wife.

David's reports for the Hilary term were less positive than for the previous term, though still good. 'He is not a brilliant linguist, and his work is not

* The Provost, Sir Claude Elliott, though an amiable man in private life, kept expenditure to the minimum: he was described by an Eton master as 'one of Nature's bursars'.

always free from illogicality,' wrote his tutor for German philology, 'but he is in general a man of very high intelligence and it has been a pleasure to teach him.' The tutor who had awarded him an α mark for the previous term now awarded him an α/β.

His reports for his final term at Oxford were perfunctory, as the focus for tutors and pupils alike was on the forthcoming final examinations (known in Oxford as 'Schools'). 'His knowledge is good, with, however, several gaps in it,' wrote one tutor; another reported that his work was 'intelligent and on the whole quite well balanced and he has obviously read with care and discrimination'. There was no doubt that he was working very hard: in May he decorated a hall in Oxford for a college 'Commem' Ball, in exchange for a pair of tickets, but then was too exhausted to go.

After Schools were over David characterised them in a letter to his mother-in-law as 'an awful strain for both of us'. The whole thing had been 'such a marathon – 30 essays, and commentaries as well, in a week; it seems potty as the climax to three years' work'. He had 'simply no idea' of how well he had done – 'certainly badly enough on the philology papers to exclude any thought of a *good* degree'.[27] He was wrong, as he would soon discover, when he was invited to undertake an oral examination (a viva) for a first-class degree; but he had been right to deduce that his lowest mark had been in his philology paper.

Towards the end of June David and Ann made the journey to Eton, to take tea with the Birleys, and to inspect a house that the Bursar had found for them in the then semi-rural hamlet of Eton Wick. Wheatbutts was a three-storey brick building dating from the early eighteenth century, almost smothered by a rambling rose; until recently it had been inhabited by the film star David Niven. Compared to the Somerset cottage, it seemed enormous, with two bathrooms, four bedrooms, one very large drawing room, a dining room, a kitchen and a study, and a large hedged garden outside, 'with lots of birds but no bees'. The upstairs rooms offered a distant prospect of Windsor Castle. In front was a village green; behind was a duck pond, with cows grazing in fields beyond. The rent of £80 a year was deducted from income at source, rather than from taxed income.[28] In a letter to Vivian Green, David portrayed Wheatbutts as 'unbelievably charming', and commented that it might be in the middle of the country. 'What a blessing we came back to Oxford!'[29]

As the house was unfurnished, they needed the furniture from the Pilton cottage, which they therefore decided to give up, a decision which Ann later regretted.

'I couldn't feel *less* like working for my viva but must I suppose,' David complained to his mother-in-law. 'It's so dismal going over the papers again and finding out what I should have said.'

The viva lasted more than an hour. David perceived it as a 'shoot-out' between his philology tutor, Olive ('O.L.') Sayce, and his literature tutor, Margaret 'Peggy' Jacobs. As he left the room, he was told to wait outside. After a few minutes he was joined by Jacobs, who shook him by the hand and then kissed him on the cheek. He was awarded a first.

The new Oxford Professor of Poetry, W. H. Auden, had delivered his inaugural lecture shortly before the end of term. In a crowded function afterwards, David became aware of a hand on his bottom and, turning around, saw that it belonged to the poet himself.

'Do you do this?' Auden asked.

'I'm afraid not,' stammered David.

'Ah well,' said Auden, 'it's nice to be fancied, isn't it?'*

* David recycled this line in chapter 7 of *Smiley's People*. As Smiley climbs the stairs of a house in Paddington, an old woman in a dressing-gown emerges from one of the flats, holding a cat against her shoulder. 'Are you a burglar, dearie?' she asks. 'I'm afraid not: just a visitor,' Smiley replies with a laugh. 'Still, it's nice to be fancied, isn't it, dearie?' 'It is indeed,' says Smiley politely.

9

'Milk in first and then Indian'

Eton is the grandest of English public schools. David would later refer to it as the 'spiritual home' of the English upper classes.[1] Eton College – always referred to as such, never as a school – was established in 1440. It had been founded, like so many other English public schools, to provide free education to poor boys, though this charitable intention had long since disappeared. In the 1950s the academic standard of entry was lower than it is today, which meant that boys from very wealthy and aristocratic backgrounds could be admitted even if they were not very bright. Among those whom David taught there were peers of various ranks and even one royal prince (Prince Richard of Gloucester). David told Vivian Green that he found life at Eton 'awfully expensive' and complained repeatedly about the difficulty of living on such a modest salary.[2] He resented that he was 'paid less than a road-sweeper' and was 'always in the red'. Much of his off-duty conversation with colleagues concerned schemes to make money: summer schools, guided tours for plutocrats, tutoring for the richest and thickest, and so on. It was perhaps especially galling to be struggling financially when so many of the boys he was teaching lived in mansions or castles, or on large estates in Scotland or Ireland.

Over the centuries Eton has preserved its traditions while adapting to social change – much like the aristocracy itself. Indeed the College was something of a hereditary institution, in that many of the masters had been educated there, and 60 per cent of its pupils were sons of Old Etonians.[3] Even today boys still wear tailcoats, with stiff collars and a black waistcoat underneath – except members of the privileged Eton Society ('Pop'), who are permitted to wear garish waistcoats of their own choosing. Eton has its own terminology: masters are known as 'beaks', terms as 'halves' (though there are three of them each year), cricketers 'dry bobs', rowers 'wet bobs', and so on. This was all Greek to David. He found many of the customs risible. 'I didn't know the language and I didn't know the ethic,' he would say later.[4]

Perhaps inevitably, the culture of Eton reflects the values and the manners of the class from which the majority of its pupils are drawn: including social ease, effortlessness, entitlement and an assumption of superiority, occasionally tending towards boorishness. As he walked along the High Street towards the College, a candidate for a teaching post at Eton in the late 1950s was indignant at being forced into the gutter by 'Pop' swells lounging on the pavement, canes in hand, and complained vociferously to Birley at his interview.

Birley himself was a large, clumsy, absent-minded man, whose earnest idealism was obvious to all. Known as 'Red Robert' because of his liberal views, he was believed to be a reformer, though this side of his nature was restrained by an innate cautiousness. He endeavoured to consult his staff, though some noted that he did so only in small matters. David thought him 'extraordinarily patient and tolerant': his 'great and probably only failing' being to 'talk incessantly and ineffectually whenever he gets a chance'.[5]

Some of the masters, particularly those who were Old Etonians, had never taught anywhere else and would spend their entire careers at Eton; naturally such men developed a strong attachment to the College and its traditions and tended to resist change. By contrast, there was a rapid turnover of young men, who left for more lucrative salaries and more exciting careers elsewhere. Under Birley's headmastership the proportion of masters who had not themselves been Etonians rose; such newcomers (like David) tended to be less taken with the College's mystique.

It was a custom that housemasters at Eton gave dinner parties to welcome newly arrived masters and their wives. These were formal, intimidating occasions. Dressing for dinner was de rigueur; at the end of the meal the ladies left the table to be entertained by the housemaster's wife while the port circulated among the gentlemen. At one of these dinner parties David encountered the Hartleys, sticklers for correct clothes, the correct ritual for a dinner ('Darling, you hand the vegetables from the left side') and correct forms of address, about which they cared passionately.[6] Hubert

Hartley had just retired after almost half a century at Eton; his wife Grizel was an Eton 'personality', kindly and cruel, mannered and snobbish. Their conversation went as follows:

> Grizel: 'Darling, are we by any chance related to the Cornwells of Shropshire?'
>
> David, bridling: 'No, actually my father is a self-made man.'
>
> Grizel, very pleased: 'Darling, how *sweet*!'

'There are *some* very sticky people,' David wrote to Vivian Green early in his first term, 'but a lot of awfully nice ones too – and obviously you can pick your company.'[7] With over ninety members of staff at Eton there was plenty to choose from. In general, David was welcomed by the other Eton beaks, who found him entertaining, even delightful, company. One of them, the history master William Gladstone, commented on David's skill in depicting their colleagues, observing that while some beaks were easily caricatured – the fat ones or the tall, cadaverous ones, for example – others were not: nevertheless David could capture the essence of a personality in a simple sketch, perhaps by drawing the person concerned in the act of a sudden, sardonic glance.

One of those whom David at first thought 'awfully nice' was his boss, Oliver Van Oss, another powerful Eton personality, who had been at Eton more than a quarter of a century. Depending on whom you spoke to, he was either a man of culture or 'a bullshitter of Olympic class'.[8] Van Oss was a large, rubicund figure, a wicked mimic whose eyelashes fluttered almost imperceptibly when he said something clever. Thanks to him, David had been allotted the brightest boys studying German. 'They are *very* good, & seem to learn by themselves', David told Vivian Green, though he complained that their essays were 'very clever-clever and crammed with idiotic careless mistakes'.[9] To his pupils, David's enthusiasm for the German language and German culture was obvious. Alexander Chancellor, later a successful journalist, thought him a very good teacher, even though David had 'torn over' (an Eton expression indicating poor performance) a piece of his work in front of the class because he considered it inadequate.

Before he arrived at Eton David had been warned that the boys would try it on with him at the start, to test his strength. Indeed his predecessor had been unable to keep control and had 'retired hurt', to go and teach in a girls' school. Sure enough, the boys began playing up in the first class he took. After about five minutes, a pile of books slid from one boy's desk on to the floor with a thump. 'Sorry, sir,' said the boy, affecting innocence as he picked up the books. About five minutes later another pile of books slid to the floor. 'Very sorry, sir.' And then again: '*So* sorry, sir.' After the third time, David announced, 'Very well, then. Now all of you can spend the rest of this class dropping your books on the floor and picking them up again.'

In one of his French classes, David discussed the French word *paysan*. 'How do we translate it?' he asked the boys. 'As you know, nobody in England talks about peasants any more.'

'Oh, Sir, Sudeley does.'

Later David would be told by one of the housemasters that Old Etonian fathers encouraged their sons to 'mob up' beaks when they arrived at Eton, 'to show them their place'. Ronnie had suggested that his boy might be 'out of his depth' at Eton, but David proved equal to the challenge.[10] When he caught a boy doodling grotesque heads in his exercise book, he turned the tables on the miscreant by telling him that he wanted 'five hundred of those by lock-up tonight'. Like his creation Jim Prideaux, David used the expression 'horrid little toad' to address any boy who was cheeky or who otherwise misbehaved. In response to a smart-ass remark in class, David asked: 'Is that another effort at wit, Marsh?'

'You think that you're superior to these grammar school boys with their caps on the back of their heads, but you're not,' David told one of his classes. 'Look at you. You're just a crowd of penguins.'

At this one of his titled pupils was stirred into a drawling response: 'But Sir, we dress better in the holidays.'

One of his former pupils, Ferdinand Mount, has written an account of David's early days at Eton:

> At first sight the new master looks quite innocuous, with a mop of corn-coloured hair and a soft, hesitant, slightly insinuating voice as though he means you to read between the lines of what he is saying. But from the beginning of the first lesson he is in control, apparently without making the slightest effort to exert authority. He switches on charm or menace

> at will and when the yobs at the back start to make trouble he delivers merciless and exact parodies of their arrogant, languid voices. For me David Cornwell also has the marvellous freshness of a born teacher who is teaching his subject for the first time . . .[11]

'The boys are collectively quite frightful, and individually variable and rather unnerving,' David told Green. He had been appalled by a colleague's report of an overheard conversation between two boys after one of them had been to tea at Wheatbutts:

> 'Had tea with Cornbeef the other day.'
> 'How was it?'
> 'Usual stuff. Milk in first and then Indian.'

'I don't think I've ever met *so* much arrogance,' David concluded. 'However, it's all right as long as you preserve the strength to resist.'[12]

Not for the first or last time, David found himself both attracted to and repelled by the institution he had joined. On the one hand he was enchanted by its good manners, by its ethic, by the civilised attitude to responsibility it instilled in its pupils. On the other hand, he found it objectionable that boys should be educated from an early age into privilege. He thought it wrong that they should dress differently and talk differently from the people that they were being trained to govern.[13] David was one of a small group of younger masters pressing for Eton to reform.

As an Eton beak David wore a white bow tie and stiff butterfly collar underneath a dark suit. Early each morning he would bicycle a mile and a half to the college to arrive in time for the seven o'clock lesson, returning afterwards for breakfast, before cycling back again. Ann was somewhat isolated at Wheatbutts, with no car and a long walk from town, but they acquired a new dog for company, a German Shepherd puppy called Barney, and a cat called October; and they quickly made friends with some of the other masters and their wives, the younger ones in particular. One of these, Geoffrey Marsland, also newly married, had been a contemporary of David's at Oxford. The Cornwells' closest friends also lived in Eton Wick, the assistant art master Oliver Thomas and his wife Sylvia, a chaotic bohemian couple, tolerated as eccentric by the College community. Oliver

Thomas was a painter, one of a group of artists who had experimented with painting under the influence of mescaline before the war.

The social life within the community of Eton beaks was not all formal. Ann remembered in particular a party at the Birleys', at which they played charades. One of the housemaster's wives rolled on the floor, emitting alarming groans: this was Jean Barker, the future Baroness Trumpington, who would become a Conservative minister and House of Lords whip, enacting *The Birth of a Nation*.

Most important of all for Ann, she had discovered that she was pregnant, a fact that became increasingly obvious towards the end of the year. David asked Vivian Green if he would act as one of the godfathers to the imminent baby (the other was Robin Cooke), and perform the christening. 'Impending parenthood finds me intrigued, apprehensive and extremely nervous.'[14]

The Suez Crisis, which reached its climax at the beginning of November 1956, only a few weeks after David's arrival at Eton, aroused passions now difficult to imagine. The emotions unleashed were even stronger than those caused by the invasion of Iraq in 2003. As in that case, the British government was condemned from both left and right. Those who disapproved of the use of force in international affairs were predictably opposed to the Suez expedition, but so too were many who took the opposite view. Some thought that the government had been panicked into action; others believed that action should have been taken more promptly. The denial of collusion with the Israelis looked like a dishonourable cover-up. In parliament, the opposition leader Hugh Gaitskell condemned the Anglo-French invasion of Egypt as 'an act of disastrous folly' which would do 'irreparable harm to the prestige and reputation of our country'. In a letter to his MP, the Conservative junior minister Edward Boyle, one Eton master expressed his 'complete abhorrence of the policy which the government is pursuing'. He informed Boyle that he had voted Conservative in the last three elections, but that his next vote would be for Labour.[15] Boyle himself would resign from the government in protest at the Suez invasion.

The Crisis divided opinion within the College as it did across the country, stimulating vehement debate on the dinner-party circuit and wherever masters met. The apparent duplicity and poor performance of the Prime

Minister, Sir Anthony Eden, caused particular pain, as Eden was an Old Etonian – as indeed was half his Cabinet. 'Eden has not taken the country into his confidence,' sighed Hartley, an ex-soldier and a dyed-in-the-wool Conservative. A letter to *The Times* protesting at the government's actions was strongly mooted. David was one of those masters keen to sign.

As headmaster, Birley was in a difficult position. Although regarded as dangerously left wing by some Old Etonians, he had an exaggerated respect for the judgements of politicians and statesmen. Moreover he was anxious about the danger of adverse publicity for the College. He persuaded those intending to put their names to a letter of protest to hear the government's case put by Lord John Hope, then serving as Under-Secretary of State for Foreign Affairs. Lord John was an Old Etonian, and closely involved with the College as the masters' representative on the Governing Body. He addressed the masters in Birley's sitting room. He was not especially convincing in defending the government's policy, but he succeeded in persuading his listeners to delay any letter to *The Times* until the situation cleared and until British troops were no longer in action.

The Suez Crisis ended in a humiliating withdrawal. It punctured British prestige and made painfully obvious the steep decline of British power in the decade since the war. British pride was hurt and national honour damaged. No doubt this was one reason why the Crisis aroused such strong feeling.

In a 2003 interview, David likened Tony Blair, the Prime Minister who earlier in that year had taken Britain into the Iraq War, to Anthony Eden. Like Eden, he argued, Blair had been adversely affected by his public school. In the course of the interview David mentioned the planned letter to *The Times*, and implied that John Hope had been despatched down to Eton by order of the Prime Minister. He suggested that Eden had been pre-occupied by Eton during the Suez Crisis: 'it was still all about school'. He told his interviewer that Eden had come down to Eton himself on several evenings to consult his old housemaster about what to do.[16] Clarissa Avon, Eden's widow, was furious at this allegation, which she knew to be false. She consulted Eden's biographer D. R. Thorpe, who was able to show that Eden's housemaster had retired long before the Suez Crisis erupted, indeed had died more than six months earlier. David wrote Thorpe a letter of retraction, and sent Clarissa Avon an apology that she thought fulsome.

Early in 1957, David wrote a long letter to Green in which he gave his impressions of Eton. In many ways, he said, his second 'half' had been very pleasant, 'without all the nervousness of starting from scratch'. But he was becoming more and more irked by what he called 'the "Herrenvolk" doctrine', which he felt was encouraged in the boys by the ruling body of masters: 'the free use of comparison with the "oik" classes . . .'

He noted a 'curious lowering of standards' in the aristocracy: for example, Lord Charles Spencer-Churchill, younger son of the 10th Duke of Marlborough, 'tells me that he spends his evenings with his father glued to the television, watching parlour games'. David had learned from a colleague who spent the holidays at Blenheim tutoring Lord Charles that the Duke continued to watch 'telly' while flunkeys served up meals to him and his family.

David fulminated to Green about the 'infuriating' Eton tradition 'of not being enthusiastic about anything, or surprised'. Discussion on painting, for instance, was limited by the extent to which a boy would admit to being impressed – 'and to be impressed by anything a "beak" does is pretty "wet" anyway'. He was dismayed by the lack of discipline: 'at concerts and so forth boys whistle and behave very badly, and leave before the speaker has been applauded'.

Yet David had to admit that Eton was astonishingly liberal in many ways – not the least of these being the number of boys who were terribly bad at games, 'whose lives remain unimpaired by this handicap'. This would never have been tolerated at Sherborne. David was impressed that the senior boys were allowed to drink beer at their own pretend-pub called Tap, a tiny bar room hidden behind the High Street. He told Ferdinand Mount that this was the most civilised thing he had heard about the school.[17]

David would later admit to 'a fascination with the mores of the Etonian class'. Some years after he quit teaching, he would have a bizarre encounter that seemed somehow characteristic, with a former pupil whom he found dead drunk on the corner of a street in Pimlico: the young man had laid out the family silver on a folding table and was trying to sell it to passers-by.[18]

Each Eton schoolboy chose a tutor for his last two years, with whom he could study almost anything that the two of them decided upon, in time set aside for 'private business'. David's 'pupils' liked the fact that he treated them as intellectual equals and did not talk down to them; of course it helped that he was younger than most beaks. But in any case he stood out from the other masters as someone with a sense of the wider world, 'a breath of fresh air'. He took pupils for walks, and lent them books. He introduced one of them, Bill Drummond-Murray, to Rembrandt, Vermeer and the other Dutch masters, showing him slides and talking them through. Ferdinand Mount related how during private business David talked 'about anything that comes into his head'.

> One of the things that I like about him is his irreverence towards the school and its encrusted traditions but at the same time his fascination with the place as if he was marking it all down for future use: 'Really, only Upper Boys are allowed to walk on that side of the road? I heard that but I could not believe it, and tell me, that business about who can wear the bottom button of his waistcoat undone, amazing.' Then we talk about Goethe or Schiller . . .[19]

David enjoyed his pupils, some of whom were exceptionally bright, though he was a little dismayed by their limited horizons, as he told Green. Of his first three, two, on being questioned about their future careers, 'replied that they were going to "manage the estate"! The other is going into "father's business".'

David mentioned to Green that there was 'a very considerable amount of perversion' in evidence at Eton. 'I have even heard a housemaster mention it with jocularity in connection with his own house!' He had learned from Nigel Althaus, an Old Etonian, of a 'tradition' that 'the needs of the "bloods" must be served by the smaller boys'. It seems unlikely that David would have written in these terms had he realised that Green himself was homosexual. Perhaps Green was unaware of this aspect of his nature at the time. To David, he was still the bachelor priest who had loved and been rejected by the assistant matron at Sherborne.[20]

As her labour drew near, Ann went to stay in a nursing home near her mother in Somerset. On 7 March 1957 she gave birth to a boy, whom they named Simon Anthony Vivian. 'Now we've both got a double first!' David exulted on hearing the news. While she was lying in, he attended a drinks party at Weston's Yard, part of the complex of College buildings. One of Birley's failings was an inability to draw an end to any social occasion. The party dragged on, and many of those present became tipsy. David had taken against one of the masters, the punctilious Julian Lambart, a man steeped in Eton, depicted by colleagues as 'an amazing relic' who had been pompous from an early age. When at last the party broke up, David stood outside swaying, shouting up at the windows, 'Lambart: come out and fight!' The Marslands took him back to their flat in the Vice-Provost's Lodge and fed him. Looking around the walls, David remarked that they did not have enough pictures, and lurched up from the table. Outside the flat was a corridor hung with pictures; he lifted them off the walls and returned with his arms full. Next morning he cut himself badly shaving.

The experience of fatherhood upset David's equilibrium. His difficult relations with his own father may have exacerbated his unease: he would come to feel that he had betrayed Ronnie by ostracising him. Whatever the cause, David became deeply depressed. Throughout his adult life he would suffer periodic 'black dogs', which would begin as a migraine and develop into a mood of hopelessness approaching despair, with thoughts of suicide and spasms of needless aggression. Looking back at this period, he has said that he felt 'absolutely no conviction', about either his marriage or his work. Though he could not persuade himself to believe in God, David contemplated going into the Church. In retrospect he would interpret this as a 'spiritual cover story', to provide a possible escape route from his marriage.

David was also considering a possibility that he might teach in a Borstal, a detention centre for delinquent boys – the very antithesis of Eton. In a letter to Ann he revealed 'feelings of insufficiency and waste'. During the summer vacation, while Ann went to her mother's house to present their infant son to 'masses of cooing female relatives', David returned to the Franciscan community at Cerne Abbas that he had first visited as a schoolboy at Sherborne, for a week's retreat.[21] During his stay he observed the 'Day hours', beginning with Matins at 5.45 a.m., followed by Holy Communion at 6.20, breakfast at 7.30, Terce at 8.15, and so on, becoming accustomed to the scent of incense. David was asked to refrain from joining the others in plainsong because he had such a poor singing voice.

Speech too was forbidden, except at weekends when one was free to talk outdoors between Sext and Compline (1.15 and 9.00 p.m.). He was however free to talk at any time to Denis Marsh, the Father Guardian, with whom he spent an afternoon in earnest communion.* 'There *is* no solution but prayer,' Marsh advised.

'I am seeing a lot of the Father Guardian,' David wrote to Ann the next day. 'I like it here v. much and I know that it has done me so much good in so many ways.' He had been passing the time doing lino-cuts and three-colour lino blocks. At the weekend he took a stroll in the mist with one of the friars, Father Gregory. 'He made it sound logical that one should pray for faith while having none,' David told Ann.

'Darling, I'm not suddenly getting religion, nor will I turn monk and leave you in the snow,' David assured her. 'I just feel, perhaps for the first time, that I am near to finding a way of life and a real faith.' As his stay at the friary drew to an end, David tried to summarise what it had meant to him. 'I have already reached a state of mind hard to express – a kind of spiritual purposefulness, not necessarily enthusiastic, not necessarily even Christian – though predominantly so.'[22]

On his way to the friary David had stopped for a night in Sherborne, where he had called on a retired schoolmaster and his wife, 'still obsessively mourning their elder son who was killed in the war'. In a letter to Ann he described this visit as 'spooky'. Afterwards, before going to bed, he had met an old schoolfriend called Palethorpe (a name which he would use in more than one of his books) for a drink in the Half Moon, a pub facing the Abbey. In the street the next morning he had 'bumped into' the head of the modern languages department at Sherborne, who was 'awfully keen that I should come and teach there, but the offer didn't attract me much'.[23]

Bankruptcy had not prevented Ronnie from operating in much the same way as he always had done. Around this time he encountered Colin Clark, younger son of the art historian Kenneth Clark, who had inherited a comfortable sum on reaching his majority. Clark would only belatedly

* Marsh had been James Thurber's confessor. He told David that he had required the entire sea-voyage back across the Atlantic to recover from Thurber's confessions.

appreciate that there were plenty of people ready to relieve him of this burden:

> The first of many people I found in my life who was willing to do me this service was called Ronnie Cornwell. Ronnie was the best con man ever. I had never seen anyone who looked so trustworthy in my life. He was your favourite uncle, your family doctor, Bob Boothby and Father Christmas all rolled into one. He was stout and beaming with white hair and bushy white eyebrows. He wore a black jacket and a waistcoat, and striped trousers like a faithful old family retainer, or Lord Reith. Ronnie knew how to fix anything – tickets for the Cup Final, a box at Ascot, dinner at the most exclusive restaurant in town. He had an attractive wife who hardly spoke but who obviously worshipped him. His accountant was perpetually on call to substantiate his claims to wealth and inside knowledge . . .
>
> In the face of this blast of confidence, flattery and bluff, I was as helpless as a baby. Ronnie invited me to Royal Ascot and gave me a few good dinners. Then he showed me a piece of derelict property, which he did not own, promised to double my money in three months, and took the lot. What was difficult to comprehend about Ronnie was that *everything* was fake. His office, his car, his chauffeur, his 'regular' box at Ascot, were all just hired for the occasion, and never paid for. His wife was not his wife,* and his accountant was just an accomplice.[24]

David tried to avoid any contact with his father, now reconciled with Jean and living with her in a modest house in Henley-on-Thames. Nor did he have anything to do with his mother, who around this time emigrated to Canada with John Hill and their two infant daughters. After the death of David's grandmother Bessie in November, Ronnie wanted him to attend the funeral. Jean too put pressure on him to come, which David resisted. 'I was very fond of the old lady etc., but feel that I can honour her at a distance,' he told Vivian Green. He agreed to write Ronnie a comforting letter. 'I feel rather like the man in "Lucky Jim" with all those different faces, and can't otherwise whip up any enthusiasm, remorse, affection or anything for him anywhere.'[25]

* Perhaps not so; see next paragraph.

One evening towards the end of the year the Cornwells returned late to Wheatbutts to find a familiar figure standing on the doorstep, holding a set of car keys in his hand. This was George Ellard, one of Ronnie's stalwarts. Parked in the drive was a brand-new Ford Popular, bearing the number plate RC 4.

'What's this?' David asked suspiciously.

'Oil, dear boy, on troubled waters,' replied Ellard.

It turned out that this was a present from Ronnie, who was due to sail to New York on the *Queen Mary* in two days' time.

David would have very much liked to have had a car, but he knew that if the Ford had been paid for at all, it could have been only with money owed to other people. When he examined the accompanying papers he discovered that it had been bought on hire purchase, in the name of Ronnie's secretary. The next morning he drove the car back to the garage in Wales that had supplied it, and left it there.

In New York Ronnie checked into the Plaza Hotel, announcing that he was in town to sell Bethlehem Steel, America's largest shipbuilder and second largest steel producer. He was given the fourth floor Frank Lloyd Wright Suite at the building's north-east corner, overlooking Central Park and Fifth Avenue. 'It's a nice pub, I must say, and they're treating me very well,' he remarked to his elder son, when they met for lunch a day or so later. 'You know, it's an amazing thing, Tony, my suite is not just a suite, it's half a floor of the whole hotel.' Then he asked, 'Who is this fellow Frank Lloyd Wright?'

Tony was by then married, with an infant son, living in the Bronx and working in Manhattan as an advertising copywriter. Ronnie asked for a loan of $500, to be repaid after a few days; and Tony naïvely agreed, though this was all the money he had saved. Within days Ronnie had inveigled himself into an ambitious scheme to build a large conference centre in the Bahamas.

By then he had moved out of the Plaza and into a beautifully furnished apartment on Third Avenue, where he remained some weeks without paying a cent, before returning to England.

David became restless in his second year at Eton. 'I wanted terribly to find myself an artistic life,' he would tell an interviewer many years afterwards. 'I knew by the time I left Oxford that I had a very robust intellect, and I also knew that I was extremely impatient with most orthodox forms of earning a living, and that I had a restless creativity within me.'[26] Among those who came to stay at Wheatbutts was Tony, on a visit from New York, who brought with him the manuscript of a novel he had written for the two of them to read. Ann appraised it as 'very stream of consciousness'.

The community of Eton beaks and their wives could seem parochial and inward-looking. John Wells, later an actor, writer and satirist, who arrived at the College to teach German soon afterwards, was warned, 'Don't be like Cornwell: he has too many friends in London.'[27] The feeling was mutual: David complained of the Eton beaks that 'we're all too broke, too comfortable, too smug. Bah!'[28] He disliked the uncharitable sniping that others either enjoyed or ignored. David had taken against Grizel Hartley, and had come to strongly dislike Oliver Van Oss, whom he saw as bogus. In January 1958 he began writing a novel, a murder mystery set in a fictional public school named Carne that he soon put aside and would not resume until several years later, when it would eventually be published under the title *A Murder of Quality*. On reading it, Grizel Hartley would recognise herself in the character of Shane Hecht, the snobbish and malicious wife of a housemaster; she was apparently very hurt by the portrayal, which David later regretted.[29] Colleagues suspected that she had spoken condescendingly to Ann, but this seems not to have been the case. For the background of the murder victim, the nonconformist Stella Rode, David drew on his childhood 'in the chapels and tabernacles of coastal Dorset, listening to a far humbler God than he who guided the untroubled conscience of the British ruling class'.[30] Her husband Stanley Rode, a grammar school boy striving for acceptance, may have been a satirical self-portrait. Others recognised Oliver Van Oss in the depiction of the villain Terence Fielding, and Julian Lambart in Felix D'Arcy, the 'self-appointed major-domo of Carne protocol'. D'Arcy's acknowledgement that he 'more than once was compelled to address Rode on the subject of his wife's conduct' is perhaps significant.[31]

David seems to have belatedly become aware that he risked a libel action, because he would add a specific disclaimer: 'There are probably a dozen great schools of whom it will be confidently asserted that Carne is their deliberate image. But he who looks among their common rooms for the D'Arcys, Fieldings and Hechts will search in vain.'

When Gerald Peacocke visited him at Wheatbutts, David indicated that he was thinking of moving on. He talked a lot about becoming a writer, though he feared that there was no immediate prospect of earning a living that way. The education department of The Bodley Head, the publishers who had commissioned him to do a book jacket, asked if he would compile a German reader, to be aimed at O-level examination students. David offered them a short story, about a pavement artist who one afternoon produced a masterpiece in pastels on the paving stones in Trafalgar Square, outside the National Gallery: and then the rain came, and washed it away.* In retrospect David saw this as a nice metaphor for his frustrated talent, lying on the ground unregarded by the hurrying passers-by. The Bodley Head declined to publish David's first venture into fiction.[32]

Though he seems not to have undertaken any duties for MI5 while he was teaching, he had kept in touch with his former colleagues and taken the odd lunch from Dick Thistlethwaite. Now he wrote to Thistlethwaite to say that he wanted to 'come inside'. Looking back on his decision to join MI5 from the perspective of almost half a century, David would say that it was like entering the priesthood, 'as if all my life had been preparing me for this moment'.[33] He was, he said, searching for moral certitudes that had so far eluded him – although, as he subsequently realised, 'I had come to the wrong address.'[34] At other times he admitted to baser motives. 'I relished the notion of appearing to be someone dull, while all the time I was someone terribly exciting,' he wrote in 1986. The lure of secrecy was that it provided 'a means of outgunning people we would otherwise be scared of; of feeling superior to life rather than engaging in it; as a place of escape, attracting not the strong in search of danger, but us timid fellows, who couldn't cope with reality for one calendar day without the structures of conspiracy to get us by'.[35] All this was written in retrospect, and reflects

* Leiser distracts his girlfriend with a version of this story in the closing paragraphs of *The Looking-Glass War*.

a cynicism about his own motives that he is unlikely to have felt at the time.

Though a strong patriot, David was certainly no Empire loyalist or hardline anti-Communist. 'I was vaguely left-wing but too polite to let it show,' he wrote in the piece cited above. In general his politics were moderately progressive. Dining with an acquaintance at the Colony Club one evening David said that he thought 'apartheid stank', whereupon his companion 'blew his top' – 'no one was helping his poor mother, so why should anyone help the bloody niggers?'[36]

It was agreed that David would leave Eton at the end of the 1958 Lent half. Somehow word got round the boys that 'Corns is going to be a spy.'

David made contact with John Shakespeare, to ask if he might be interested in taking over from him. He explained that he was 'not very happy' teaching at Eton, though he insisted that it was a 'wonderful job'. He invited Shakespeare down to stay at Wheatbutts, and took him to meet Van Oss. Shakespeare sat in on one of David's French classes and formed the view that his friend was a very good teacher. He was sufficiently tempted to return for a lunch with Birley, which resulted in his being offered the job, though he decided instead to accept an offer to enter the Diplomatic Service.

Writing to Ann while she was away staying with her mother in Somerset, David confided that 'I feel funny about returning to my old firm – rather relieved, as one might be returning to a crotchety wife after prolonged absence.' In another letter he asked Ann to tell her mother to be more discreet: 'she must get used to saying I'm doing something *dull*'.[37]

10

'A dead-end sort of place'

'Have you got over your father yet?' asked MI5's head of personnel, John Marriott, once David was seated in his office. It was a shrewd question. Marriott was a taut, upright man with the air of a country solicitor. During the war he had been secretary to the XX Committee, which supervised the double agents controlled by MI5. Like many of the older MI5 officers, Marriott had an impressive war record. From the beginning it was clear to David that there was an absolute distinction within MI5 between those who had served in the war and those who had not.

The interview took place in a seven-storey Mayfair office building: Leconfield House, where the Service had been based since 1948. The fact that this was MI5's headquarters was supposedly secret, though taxi drivers knew it, and as buses pulled up at the nearest stop on Park Lane conductors would shout, 'Curzon Street and MI5,' embarrassing the well-bred girls waiting to alight every weekday morning.[1] The surroundings were curiously mixed, with opulent town houses, embassies and hotels uncomfortably close to the seediness of Shepherd Market. Prostitutes patrolled the streets even in daylight.

Leconfield House dated from 1939, constructed perhaps to withstand bombing, since it had a large underground basement and a windowless ground floor. It was said that its angled corner, with windows pointing down Curzon Street towards Hyde Park, had been reinforced to support machine-gun emplacements, to counter the threat that German parachutists might land there. One entered the building through glass doors with a hessian screen behind, showing one's pass as one did so. The Registry occupied the whole of the ground floor; in the basement below were the 'Dungeons', a collection of storerooms and workshops; on the top floor was a canteen which served good food at cheap prices, and the staff bar, where officers could drink without fear that their conversations might be overheard by anyone from outside. In between were the six directorates ('branches') of MI5, designated A to F and divided into sections. The interior of Leconfield House had once been plush, with teak inlaid corridors and corniced offices, but by the late 1950s it had become as shabby as most other government departments. The inside had not been decorated in recent years, the windows were grimy and internal partitioning had left many of the rooms an awkward shape. A senior MI5 officer from the period remembers it as 'ludicrously overcrowded, with officers crammed four to a room'.[2]

Mrs Grist ran the listeners' room, a stuffed parrot on the wall above her. Her typists sat in cubicles muttering and occasionally giggling at the conversations they were monitoring through their headphones.

At the heart of MI5 was the Registry. Its central hall housed the main file index and the files themselves. Rooms leading off from the concourse held other specialist card indexes. The concourse was always busy, with trolleys transporting files from the shelves to special lifts. The trolleys ran on tracks so that files could be shifted speedily to case officers working on the floors above.[3] The Registry was the largest section of MI5, staffed entirely by women.[4] Known as the Registry Queens, they were traditionally recruited from upper-class families; a high proportion of them travelled in each day from Kensington. 'They were stunners,' David remembered. 'Country policemen, down for a couple of days to examine our methods, couldn't believe their luck.' At lunchtime the canteen was 'a showpiece for some of the best-looking women you ever saw, and they were all the prettier because we men were so dowdy by comparison'.[5] The desirability of these young women was thought to account for the high number of marriages within 'the Office', to the point where it was joked that the average career expectancy of a Registry Queen was nine months.[6]

David was twenty-six years old when he joined MI5 in the spring of 1958. His starting salary was £1,100 a year, a sizeable increase on his pay as an Eton schoolmaster, but still not a lot on which to support a family.* He and Ann lived frugally, drinking little at home beyond the occasional glass

* In 1958 the average male manual worker in the UK earned under £700 a year.

of Cyprus sherry. David told an MI5 colleague that he planned to supplement his salary by illustrating children's comics. When John Shakespeare came for lunch, it was obvious to him that David was struggling financially. He was particularly struck when David showed him a list of the life insurance policies that he had taken out to provide him with cash in old age.

Using Ann's inheritance from her father for the deposit, the Cornwells bought Orchid Cottage, a modest, two-bedroomed house on the fringe of Great Missenden, a village in the Chilterns. Each weekday David would leave home at 7.30 in the morning, bearing a thermos and sandwiches for lunch, and walk for half an hour down the hill to the railway station, served by the Metropolitan Line, not yet electrified and still running steam trains. A quarterly season ticket into London cost just under £14, roughly £1 per week. He would ride the sixty-five minutes into Marylebone, take a bus down to Park Lane and then stroll up Curzon Street, pausing to show his pass to the retired policeman at the doors of Leconfield House. In the evening he would make the return journey, this time taking a bus back up the hill to Orchid Cottage, usually arriving around eight o'clock, sometimes later.

At first Ann commuted into London too, finding a job as a magazine sub-editor, while a German au pair looked after Simon; but soon she decided that she would rather stay at home and care for her infant son herself. Dick Edmonds's bride Sarah remembers a happy atmosphere at Orchid Cottage when she went there for dinner, with Ann cooking while David put the baby to bed. Around this time Robin Cooke married, and David acted as his best man, just as Robin had done for David.

At home Ann began writing again, using an Olivetti portable typewriter which they bought on hire purchase. She submitted several short stories with such innocent and old-fashioned titles as 'The Incompetent Girl' and 'Summer Bazaar' to women's magazines, but none was accepted. Then she wrote a play about King Arthur entitled 'The Conscience of the King', drawn from Malory and intended to be broadcast over the radio. David read it through and annotated it extensively. 'How's the play going now, I wonder?' he wrote to Ann during a period when he was away for a few days on an operation. 'It was really quite funny watching you alternate between spontaneous pleasure and spontaneous rage at my suggestions!'[7]

Ann was obliged to concede that her husband's additions had substantially improved her play. When a couple from Eton came over to Orchid Cottage, the four of them read through it together, each taking different parts. Later there would be another read-through with another couple, one of David's MI5 colleagues and his wife. Once she was satisfied with it, 'The Conscience of the King' was submitted to the BBC; she received a kindly rejection, encouraging her to try again once she had written something else.

New entrants to MI5 had no formal training: just a ten-day immersion in the exercise of 'staff duties', which above all meant how to call up files from the Registry and how to use the amazingly efficient card index. For the average humble desk officer, it was the Registry, rather than their superiors, that ruled their destiny. 'Sh'd you l.u. sub's aunt and req. connected PFs?' an icy handwritten note might enquire (Should you look up the subject's aunt and request connected personal files?). In premises above an art gallery in Cork Street a chain-smoking former solicitor taught David how to apply for a Home Office warrant to tap a telephone, while talking incessantly about his children.[8] Applications for a warrant had to be signed personally by the Home Secretary; as David would discover, operations could be held up while awaiting his signature, though local police seemed able to ask whatever they wanted of the telephone exchange without one. There were four levels of warrant, permitting different levels of surveillance, starting with 'Return of Postage', which meant no more than a list of the letters delivered. Current and former members of the Service could be bugged without a warrant. There were ways of getting around the legislation, as the Americans, who had strict laws to prevent telephone tapping, had found: for example, by using an induction coil, which provided a means of monitoring calls without being connected to the telephone itself. The technical experts within MI5 tended to be mavericks, disdainful of the rules: MI5's principal scientific officer Peter Wright would boast in his memoirs that 'for five years we bugged and burgled our way across London at the State's behest while pompous bowler-hatted civil servants pretended to look the other way'.[9]

Soon after joining, David attended a talk given by Courtenay Young, head of D Branch (Counter-Espionage), in which he talked about 'illegals', agents of a foreign power living in Britain, often under false identities. Such men and women kept well away from their Embassies, so as not to attract the attention of MI5, and communicated directly with central command or with some controller by covert means. But Young (a close friend of Anthony Blunt, whom he would refer to as 'poor old Anthony') assured the young recruits that they need not waste time looking for 'illegals', because if there were any 'we would already know their names'.

MI5 was not a very impressive organisation. 'For a while you wondered whether the fools were really pretending to be fools, as some kind of deception,' David wrote later; 'but alas, the reality was the mediocrity. Ex-colonial policemen mingling with failed academics, failed lawyers, failed missionaries and failed debutantes gave our canteen the amorphous quality of an Old School outing on the Orient Express. Everyone seemed to smell of failure.'[10] Many of the older men seemed to be living on credit they had accumulated from their wartime records. David noted wryly that 'anyone who was old enough to have fought Hitler was deemed a hero'.[11] Stella Rimington, who would eventually rise to become MI5's first female Director-General, has related how, even at the end of the 1960s, 'the ethos had not changed very much from the days when a small group of military officers, all male of course and all close colleagues working in great secrecy, pitted their wits against the enemy'.

> Many had fought in the armed services during the war; some had performed heroically, and some, perhaps not surprisingly, seemed drained by their experiences. I remember one, who had been a Dambuster and had flown the most dramatic and dangerous sorties when he had been very young. He regularly withdrew into his office and locked the door after lunch. I used to jump up and down in the corridor to look over the smoked glass in the partition, to see what he was doing, and he was invariably sound asleep. No one thought it appropriate to comment.[12]

There were no Jews among the 150-odd MI5 officers, and certainly no black faces to be seen in Leconfield House. Nor were there many women in senior positions: one of the few was the fiercely loyal and hardworking Milicent Bagot, the Service's expert on international Communism, who had been with MI5 since 1931, the first woman within the Service to reach the rank of assistant director. Bagot was also one of the first to raise doubts about Kim Philby. Younger officers were wary of her as a stickler for meticulous office procedure; moreover she was a difficult colleague, whose robust opinions were expressed with passionate conviction. But her memory for facts was so extraordinary as to have passed into Service folklore.[13] Bagot has often been named as the basis for David's character Connie Sachs, the obsessive, eccentric spinster who first appears in his novel *Tinker, Tailor, Soldier, Spy* and seems to share many of Bagot's personality traits. He insists, however, that his inspiration for Sachs was not Bagot but Diana Mumford, a member of the English ladies' bridge team who had worked at Bletchley Park. Within MI5 there were several such women, who had sacrificed their youth to England in the struggle against Hitler.

To Stella Rimington, it seemed that the men in MI5 all lived in Guildford and spent their spare time gardening; David later commented that his colleagues all seemed to come from places like Tunbridge Wells or Gerrards Cross. Almost two-thirds of those recruited in the decade from 1955 onwards would come from the Colonial Service.[14] They joined in clusters as each of the colonies became independent, forming cliques known to their colleagues by such tags as the 'Malayan Mafia' or the 'Sudan Souls'. Most of these men were recruited in middle age; with no promise of a career progression, they lacked motivation or drive to exert themselves; many were merely serving out their time until they could collect their pensions. Perhaps as a result, some took refuge in drink, as Rimington recalled:

> I remember one gentleman, who was supposed to be running agents against the Russian intelligence residency in London. He favoured rather loud tweed suits and a monocle. He would arrive in the office at about 10 and at about 11 would go out for what was termed 'breakfast'. He would return at 12 noon, smelling strongly of whisky, to get ready to go out to 'meet an agent' for lunch. If he returned at all it would be at about 4pm, for a quiet snooze before getting ready to go home. Eventually, he collapsed in the lift returning from one of these sorties and was not seen again.[15]

For MI5 officers, a sense of humour was regarded as indispensable, both for preserving a sense of proportion when dealing with issues of national security and for maintaining team spirit.[16] The prevalent atmosphere when David joined seems to have been informal, jolly, almost schoolboyish. David remembers a wild Christmas party, when the police complained about bottles tossed out of upstairs windows into the street below. In his memoirs Peter Wright recalled that 'in the main, the 1950s were years of fun'. To a young recruit like David, much of what went on in the Office seemed ludicrous anyway. MI5 encouraged a level of secrecy that bordered on the absurd. New recruits curious about the identity of their mysterious employers were fobbed off – 'just the War Office, old boy'. A desk officer who shared an office with David had been at Leconfield House some weeks before David informed him, over coffee one morning, that he was working for MI5. Stella Rimington quickly learned that 'people regarded you with suspicion if you asked too many questions'. Indeed, she was not even certain whether she was supposed to know the name of the Director-General. 'There was a joke going around that you would know which was the Director-General because he was the one who always wore his dark glasses indoors so that he would not be recognised.'[17] Successive director-generals had maintained an aloof management style. In David's day the Director-General was Roger Hollis, a shy, kindly man who resembled an undertaker in his habitual dress of black jacket and striped trousers. He was having a long-term affair with his secretary, who had resisted opportunities for promotion so that she could remain working alongside him. Despite being one of the most junior officers in the building David would spend a fair amount of time with Hollis, carrying his bag at parlays with chief constables in regional cities, or crouching at the back of the room on the fifth floor when operations were being proposed. He recalls an operational meeting in which it was proposed to install a microphone in a suspect's bedroom; perhaps thinking of his own case, Hollis said that he could not easily reconcile such an invasion of privacy with his conscience.

During his time as Director-General Hollis would have to cope with the repercussions from a series of spy scandals. Such security failures, and the 'revelations' of Soviet defectors (some of them questionable), would convince Peter Wright and his colleague Arthur Martin that the Service had been penetrated at a high level.[18] Their fears had been fed by the CIA's James Jesus Angleton, who would come to suspect everybody, even Henry Kissinger. Angleton had been trained in the art of running double agents by

Kim Philby, and had become unhinged by the humiliation of being duped in this way, leading him to see the KGB's hand in everything – particularly everything British. The effect on MI5 was one of paralysis, 'a wilderness of mirrors',* in which nothing could be taken on trust and nobody, not even the Director-General himself, was above suspicion. Following his retirement in 1965 Hollis (who had been knighted in 1960) would be summoned back to MI5 to face a grilling by his former subordinates. No evidence against him was found, either in this investigation or in several subsequent reviews. In the 1980s, testimony from a senior KGB defector, Oleg Gordievsky, revealed that the Soviets themselves were baffled by the allegations against Hollis, and attributed these to 'some mysterious, internal British intrigue'.

Looking back at his career with MI5 more than thirty years afterwards David would write that 'it was witch-hunt time', when MI5 was 'riven with suspicion and rumour'. He was too junior to know the detail: 'I just smelt it, like death before you find the corpse'.[19] In another piece written around the same time David provided an account of the atmosphere in which he worked: 'Our senior officers hated each other for reasons we were not allowed to know. They hated our sister service even more. They hated politicians, Communists, and quite a lot of journalists. And, as we now know, they hated Harold Wilson and his kitchen Cabinet.'[20]

Perhaps David's memories should be treated with caution. Harold Wilson was not elected Prime Minister until long after David had left the Service; he was not even leader of the Labour Party at the time. David was remembering MI5 with the benefit of hindsight, with an insider's knowledge of the havoc to come. He had relived this havoc in his imagination, while writing his novel *Tinker, Tailor, Soldier, Spy*, which would evoke the paranoia prevalent within MI5 during the 1960s. There are reasons for doubting that the atmosphere was quite so noxious while David was serving there in the late 1950s, however. It was true that Peter Wright, then known as an expert on bugging, could be seen patrolling the corridors

* The phrase comes from T. S. Eliot's poem *Gerontion*. It was adopted by Angleton to refer to the labyrinthine world of espionage into which one is 'lured deeper and deeper . . . pursuing the traces of Soviet plots, both real and imagined, each step taking [one] farther into a bewildering world of intrigue'.

of Leconfield House while David was at MI5. But Wright himself has said that he did not begin to suspect the presence of a traitor within the Service until 1961, by which time David had left. Most of the security failures which were to arouse Wright's suspicions lay in the future, and the defectors who would hint at Soviet sources within the highest ranks of British intelligence had yet to defect. And though Philby's treachery was suspected, it would not be confirmed until January 1963, when he made a partial confession just before fleeing to the Soviet Union.

The distinction between MI5 and its sister service MI6 is not universally understood. MI5 is more formally known as the Security Service, while MI6 is the Secret Service, or Secret Intelligence Service (SIS). The function of MI5, as set out in a 1952 Directive from the Home Secretary that became regarded as its charter, is 'the Defence of the Realm as a whole, from external and internal dangers arising from attempts of espionage and sabotage, or from the actions of persons and organizations, whether directed from within or without the country, which may be judged to be subversive of the state'.[21] MI5 operates on home territory, which in those days included the colonies of the British Empire. The function of MI6, on the other hand, is to collect secret intelligence and mount covert operations overseas. Another way of looking at the difference between the two organisations is that MI5 is essentially defensive, whereas MI6 is offensive. MI5 is answerable to the Home Secretary, MI6 to the Foreign Secretary. In practice there has always been some overlap between the two intelligence services, for example in investigating the possible penetration of the services themselves by agents of a foreign power.

Another difference between the two services, which lingers today though it was then more pronounced, was cultural. Philby's most recent biographer has distinguished them thus: MI6 was White's, MI5 the Rotary Club. MI6 was upper-middle class (and sometimes aristocratic), while MI5 was middle class (and sometimes working class). 'MI5 looked up at MI6 with resentment; MI6 looked down with a small but ill-hidden sneer.'[22] The ethics of the two services reflected this class difference. MI5 was technocratic, whereas MI6 still cultivated the ideal of the brilliant amateur, effortlessly outwitting Johnny Foreigner without making a fuss about it.

MI6 officers tended to despise their Security Service colleagues as a bunch of civil service derelicts and plodding policemen.

Unsurprisingly, there has been a tradition of rivalry and mistrust between the two, at times bordering on hostility. 'It was natural that we should affect to hate our sister service,' David has written, 'because Six was trying to do to other countries what the Reds were trying to do to us: subvert, seduce and penetrate. Quite soon, a custodian's indignation infected my approach to SIS and, without knowing anything about them, I shared the common view that they were an untrustworthy, godless crowd.' He learned to refer to MI6 as Those Sods Across the Park – a reference to its headquarters on the far side of St James's Park.[23]

Like MI5, the Secret Service was still living on past glories – only more so. 'It stank of wartime nostalgia,' David would write later. 'People were defined by secret cachet: one man did something absolutely extraordinary in Norway; another was the darling of the French Resistance.'[24] After the end of the war SOE (Special Operations Executive) had been dissolved and its remnants absorbed into MI6, thus preserving a tradition of derring-do that would look increasingly dated as its wartime heroes aged. Lionel 'Buster' Crabb had made a name for himself as a frogman during the war, but by the time he disappeared during an MI6 operation in 1956, drinking and smoking had taken a toll on his health. Crabb had been asked to carry out a covert underwater reconnaissance of the hull of a Soviet warship berthed at Portsmouth Dockyard – the cruiser *Ordzhonikidze*, which had brought the Soviet leaders Nikita Khrushchev and Nikolai Bulganin on a diplomatic mission to Britain. A headless and handless body found fourteen months later was assumed to be his. The furore resulting from his disappearance was said to have embarrassed the British government, which distanced itself from the operation, and led the Prime Minister to decide that the Secret Service needed new leadership. Peter Wright wrote contemptuously that MI6 'never settled for a disaster if a calamity could be found instead', and deplored the 'senseless bravado about the way they behaved which I felt often risked the security of the operations'.[25]

One source of tension between the two services was the widespread belief within MI6 that Kim Philby had been unfairly treated. Several of his former colleagues vigorously protested his innocence; they felt that the career of an outstanding officer had been gravely damaged by smears.

Soon after his denunciation he was working for MI6 again as an agent. Within MI5, however, his guilt was largely accepted.

At the outset David's MI5 work was aimed at the most humble of targets, Commonwealth students in London. In the late 1950s the Chinese were avidly collecting industrial intelligence, using such students for low-level industrial espionage. Chinese Singaporeans and Malays were thought to be susceptible to inducements to spy for their mother country. David was dismayed to find that MI5's Chinese 'experts' were elderly retired missionaries, with an imperfect command of the language.

After cutting his teeth with the Commonwealth students David was promoted to F Branch, responsible for keeping a close watch on the Communist Party of Great Britain (CPGB). One of the most obvious sources of information about the CPGB's activities was the *Daily Worker*, the Party's newspaper (renamed the *Morning Star* in 1966). A vast number of copies were delivered to Leconfield House every morning. Indeed, after the Soviet Embassy, which subsidised it by bulk orders, MI5 was probably its best customer. The *Daily Worker* struggled to keep up its circulation; Party members were constantly being exhorted to spend time selling the paper on street corners, thus conveniently drawing attention to themselves.[26]

David worked in F2, the section responsible for 'positive vetting' of former Communists. MI5's responsibility for vetting civil servants, scientists and others who might have access to government secrets had originated in the early years of the Cold War. In March 1948, amid mounting anxiety about Communists betraying atomic secrets to the Soviet Union, the Prime Minister had announced the 'Purge Procedure', designed to exclude Communists and Fascists from work 'vital to the Security of the State'. The Procedure meant a significant expansion in MI5's responsibilities. Initially it involved only 'negative vetting', checking of those engaged in secret work against MI5 records, especially its increasingly complete lists of Communist Party members. But further security lapses had increased pressure to make the process more rigorous. Effective vetting required much more detailed and thorough examination, not least because real traitors were unlikely to advertise themselves by membership of the Party.[27] To assess the potential risk posed by such individuals meant careful scrutiny of confidential references solicited from present and former colleagues, employers, tutors and indeed anyone whose opinion was considered to carry weight, as well as a sifting of information obtained by other means.

A typical vetting enquiry might ask whether a trade union shop steward who had subscribed to *Soviet Weekly* for six months should be allowed to work for Hawker Siddeley, a firm that manufactured military aircraft and guided missiles for the armed services. The remit of one young desk officer, the lawyer Michael Overton-Fox, was to investigate Communists in the Post Office, for example by interviewing a postman who had been seen reading a copy of the *Daily Worker*. It was hard to take this kind of work very seriously. Special Branch reports were often unintentionally comic: 'I am informed that he is a voracious reader of westerns and keeps a parrot.' For a while Overton-Fox shared an office with David, together with several others; he portrays David as the funniest man he ever worked with, and recalls how he had the others 'in fits of laughter' every morning. Maggie Foster-Moore, who worked as David's secretary for a while, remembers him coming into the room where she and the other secretaries worked and regaling them with stories about their colleagues, exhibiting a gift for mimicry that seemed to her 'marvellous'.

As David much later recalled, this was 'a paper world'. He became practised in stripping intelligence of its source indicators, so that it was impossible to tell where it came from. Before being distributed outside MI5, his vetting reports were sent up the hierarchy as far as the Director-General, annotated with comments at each stage.

> A security service marches on its files, and I was one of the infantry. Like Bob Cratchit in his Tank, I toiled from morning and often till late into the evening at the dossiers of people I would never meet: should we trust him? Or her? Should their employers trust them? Might he be traitor, spy, lonely decider, a suitable case for blackmail by the unscrupulous opposition? Thus I, who seemed to have no adult understanding of myself, was being asked to sit in judgment on the lives and loves of others . . .

There was a voyeuristic character to this work, snooping on other people's lives. Indeed there was a sense in which the snoop was inhabiting the lives of others rather than living himself.

> The only tools I possessed were the possibilities of my own nature. These were of many sorts in those days, and the imaginative bridges I built to

> my paper suspects earned me a reputation for, of all things, perspicuity. Nothing could have been further from the truth. All I was doing was inventing people out of the meagre clay of telephone taps, purloined mail and investigators' reports. What else I gave to the subjects came from myself. It wasn't good intelligence work, but in that mediocre world it could easily pass for such. And it turned out to be excellent training for the career I had not yet consciously embarked upon: namely that of the novelist.[28]

But sometimes the paper suspects became creatures of flesh and blood. One of David's tasks was to interview people with a known or suspected Communist past who were being considered for higher positions within the civil service or government scientific establishments. The head of F Branch, David Haldane Porter, spotting that he was good at this sort of work, ensured that he was awarded the juiciest cases. The interviews would take place in rooms set aside for the purpose in every government department. David would begin by advising those whom he was interviewing that they were under investigation and that their telephones might be tapped. 'We know more than you think we know,' he would suggest, and would then recommend them to make a full disclosure. 'If we find that you have been lying, it's going to be bad for you: much better to tell me everything now.'

If an interviewee admitted to having been a member of the Communist Party in the past, David would ask him why he had joined, and who his friends had been; and try to ascertain whether he might be still secretly in the Party.

Such interviews could easily backfire if handled insensitively. A Labour MP would commit suicide after being interviewed by Peter Wright. In the late 1950s there were plenty of Britons working for the government who had been members of the Communist Party, or who had felt sympathetic to the Soviet Union, not least for its principal role in the defeat of Nazi Germany. This did not necessarily make them security risks. Often David encountered hostility from senior civil servants. Positive vetting was alien to the work culture of Whitehall. To interrogate a man's colleagues and friends about his background and to question his integrity was regarded as 'un-British'.[29]

One case involved a scientist who had written public letters supporting Communist positions. MI5 had evidence that he was, or had been, a secret member of the Party, though David could not reveal this. 'Can't you at least tell me something?' he asked, but the scientist stolidly denied all. David duly reported that he could not be cleared, and was surprised when his recommendation was ignored. He told Thistlethwaite that he thought this a case worth examining further. Years later, he discovered that the interviewee had been a British agent, who had feigned Communist sympathies in order to win the confidence of his comrades. The vetting process had been part of his cover story.

From time to time David took his turn as duty officer, tending the shop overnight or at weekends. In general there was not much to do; he had been briefed what to say if the Director-General's wife telephoned. For most of the time, as duty officer, 'the building was yours'. Once everybody else had left he was able to go down to the Registry and browse. David amused himself by looking up the file on Compton Mackenzie, who had served in British intelligence during the First World War: in it he found a letter from the head of the Secret Service, signed 'C' in green ink, fulminating that Mackenzie's *Greek Memories* (1932) had employed symbols of the Service, 'some of which are still in use!' – the symbol 'C' being one of these. Mackenzie had been convicted under the Official Secrets Act, and fined a token amount, while the book itself was suppressed.

It was always possible that a crisis might erupt, as happened when a Commonwealth leader from an African country contacted the newspapers, following a crude approach by an MI6 officer in a park. David denounced this to Ann as 'one of the biggest fiascos the office has had to cope with since the great defection'. He wrote to her that he had been on duty non-stop from ten in the morning on Saturday until midday on Sunday, without any sleep. 'Managed to raise the DG at 1 a.m. on Sunday and we opened up the office with all frills by 4 a.m.,' he told her. 'Nearly had to go to Chequers to find the Col. Office rep!'[30]

After a while David transferred to F4, the section responsible for agent-running. The term 'agent' is confusing, because it has different meanings in British and American parlance. In America, an 'agent' is used to mean an intelligence officer, as in 'FBI agent'; but in Britain, it means an individual who is paid or persuaded by an intelligence officer to provide information about the Communist Party, or any other organisation deemed to be subversive. David himself had been such an agent while an undergraduate at Oxford. Agent-running is the management (or 'controlling') of such individuals. It involves regular meetings between the agent and the case officer, sometimes after dark. Occasionally David would bring along his superior to meet one of his agents, just as George Leggett had brought Dick Thistlethwaite to meet David; but generally he was left to run them alone.

The most famous of all MI5's agent-runners was Maxwell Knight, by then retired, though he continued to run a handful of agents recruited long before and would appear at Leconfield House from time to time to hand in his expenses claims. Max Knight was considered unbalanced, partly because of his lingering conviction (which turned out to be correct) that the Soviets had penetrated MI5 during the war. Since his retirement in 1956, he had concentrated on writing and broadcasting on natural history. The British public, to whom the genial 'Uncle Max' was a familiar figure in the late 1950s and early 1960s, knew nothing of his earlier career as a spymaster within MI5. David was always on the lookout for ways to supplement his salary, so he seized the opportunity to illustrate a book of Knight's.* He spent some time in the pet department of Harrods, drawing parrots from the live models in the cages.

David shared a small back room at the end of a long corridor on the first floor of Leconfield House with Knight's former deputy John Bingham, a short, tubby, bespectacled man then almost fifty years old, the heir to an Irish peerage† and known as 'the Hon. John' as a result. His uncomplicated patriotism and vigorous right-wing opinions were tempered by his humanity, sweetness of character and sense of humour. He and David worked in harmony together and became close friends, socialising together outside working hours. 'Jack liked him very much,' Bingham's wife Madeleine would write in an unpublished memoir. She described David as 'a good-looking fair young man . . . intelligent and very funny'. With his excellent French and German, 'he seemed a very promising recruit to the Office, and well set to rise in the profession'.[31]

* Maxwell Knight, *Talking Birds* (1961). David also illustrated a subsequent book of Knight's, *Animals and Ourselves* (1962).

† In June 1960 Bingham became Lord Clanmorris on the death of his father, who had sold the family estate during the war.

Like Maxwell Knight, John Bingham wrote thrillers, stealing time to work on them during his lunch hours. His wife Madeleine was also a published writer, the author of a string of novels that she cheerfully categorised in her memoir as 'bodice rippers'. Bingham encouraged David to start writing again. Perhaps too the experience of correcting Ann's work stimulated him into thinking he could do better himself. 'I began writing because I was going mad with boredom,' he would declare later: 'not the apathetic, listless kind of boredom that doesn't want to get out of bed in the morning, but the screaming, frenetic sort that races round in circles looking for real work and finding none.' He wrote in penny notebooks, whenever he could find a spare moment: on the train to and from Great Missenden, in lunch hours, in the grey morning hours before going off to work, or when stuck for the night in London on some operational wild-goose chase.[32] Instead of resuming the story set in a public school which he had started writing at Eton, he began to write about the work he had until recently been doing for MI5. The initiating incident for his new novel would be the death of Samuel Fennan, a civil servant with a Communist past who has access to sensitive information. Fennan has apparently committed suicide following a vetting interview. George Smiley, who conducted the interview and knew that it had been innocuous, is asked to investigate; after intercepting a telephone call he comes to suspect that Fennan has been murdered. As the plot unfolds it becomes clear that Fennan has been the unwitting tool of an East German intelligence operation led by Dieter Frey, a former associate of Smiley's who had worked with him behind the lines during the war.

One aspect of the book, which would become a characteristic of David's writing, is the use of intelligence terminology – the term 'tradecraft', for example, to mean skill in espionage or intelligence work. Though this was standard usage in the intelligence world, David is credited by the *Oxford English Dictionary* as having introduced it to a wider public.[33] Such jargon accentuates the sense of verisimilitude, giving the reader the impression that he or she is being admitted into a select society, with its own private lexicon.

In the office canteen one lunchtime during 1958 David bumped into MI5's lawyer, Bernard Hill. On the Formica table in front of him was a mint copy of Graham Greene's *Our Man in Havana*. When David expressed interest in reading the novel, the lawyer sighed. The fellow Greene, he said eventually, would have to be prosecuted. As an ex-MI6 officer, he had accurately portrayed the relationship between a head of station in a British embassy and his agent in the field. It just wouldn't do.

'And it's a good book,' he complained, poking at the offending work. 'It's a *damned* good book. That's the whole trouble.'

The Service decided not to prosecute Greene, perhaps concluding that it was better to laugh than cry.[34] Some time later David was able to read *Our Man in Havana* himself, in a book-club edition. He was greatly entertained by the notion that the grandees of British intelligence could be taken in by bogus reports and a fictitious network of agents concocted by a humble vacuum-cleaner retailer, though he remembers feeling shocked that Greene had depicted a torturer (the chief of police, Captain Segura) as a comic character.

Bingham had determinedly resisted promotion, preferring to remain an active agent-runner rather than move into a managerial role. He was an experienced interrogator and field officer, who had served in Germany in the post-war period, interrogating refugees fleeing from the East, just as David had done in Austria; moreover he was extremely agile and sure-handed in the management of clandestine break-ins, surveillance and other tricks of the trade. But his greatest talent lay in running his women agents, some of whom he met several times weekly. One in particular lived under great stress at the heart of a target organisation and required debriefing every night after she came home from a day with the comrades. For her, and for his other agents, Bingham showed a pastoral concern that went far beyond the norm. 'The Service will be with you,' Bingham told them. 'We'll be walking at your side even when you can't see us.'[35] David, who often acted as his deputy, formed the opinion that Bingham's agents loved him, and worked for him rather than for their country or for any abstract ideal.[36]

Perhaps the most important of Bingham's agents within the Communist Party was Julia Pirie, a small woman whose unassuming demeanour masked a sharp intellect. She had infiltrated the Communist Party as a typist in the early 1950s and had worked her way into a position of trust, eventually becoming personal assistant to the Party's General Secretary. She was therefore in a position to provide regular reports and copies of documents to MI5, which she would pass to Bingham, during matches at the Oval in the cricket season. It seems probable that Pirie pinpointed the location of the membership files stored at the north London home of a wealthy Party member. The house was put under round-the-clock surveillance; when a wiretap revealed that the owner's wife had telephoned her husband to say that she was going out for an hour and would leave the key under the doormat, an MI5 officer grabbed the opportunity to take an impression. Armed with a copy of the key, the watchers waited until the occupants went away for a weekend in the Lake District, then let themselves in and copied the secret files. This was Operation Party Piece, one of a number of operations against the Communist Party that led Hollis to tell the Home Secretary that 'we had the British Communist party pretty well buttoned up'. Indeed, by the time David joined MI5, the Service no longer saw the CPGB as a major subversive threat. If it had ever been involved in espionage, it was not now. Henceforth the threat from the CPGB was seen as industrial rather than political.[37]

Pirie was also the most likely source for information that led to the successful bugging of the Communist Party's headquarters in King Street, Covent Garden. This had proved difficult because the Party leadership, suspicious of just such a possibility, had constantly changed the location of key meetings. An agent inside the building, probably Pirie, reported that meetings had been moved to a windowless basement room, apparently secure, but which could be reached by an old coal chute leading down from the pavement outside. The response was another MI5 coup, known as Operation Tie Pin, which took place on a Saturday night when no one was likely to be in the Party headquarters. The entire staff of MI5's A Branch surveillance team, known as 'the Watchers', was carefully choreographed to play the part of drunken revellers walking past the building in different directions, to disguise the noise made by an MI5 technician as he surreptitiously placed a false door containing a bugging device over the chute to allow continued monitoring of the meetings.[38]

At eleven o'clock one morning David was warned that an important woman agent he was running was in peril: a telephone tap had revealed that she had been blown. The priority now was to act swiftly to limit the fallout. David consulted Bingham, and within an hour they had devised a plan to suggest that she had been supplying information to a newspaper rather than to MI5. In the guise of an investigative journalist, David wrote a string of letters to his agent, thanking her for the information received so far and imploring her to reveal more details of her work. He and Bingham then had the forgery section provide stamped and postmarked envelopes, extending back in time over a period of weeks. They fed the letters into the envelopes, sealed them and slit them open again. All this was done in a single morning. Meanwhile David had sent a covert message to his agent, instructing her to tell her employers that she had toothache needing urgent treatment. At 'the dentist' she was handed the letters to place in her handbag and told to leave it on her desk when she next left the office, in the knowledge that it would be searched while she was out. Telephone checks confirmed that her employers had taken the bait. Though she was compromised the immediate danger had been averted, and she was gradually withdrawn.[39]

One of David's agents, John Miller, would become a lifelong friend. It was unusual for an agent and his case officer to become close, but Miller was an exceptional person. Over the years David developed an enormous respect for his personal qualities: his compassion, his unselfishness, his tolerance of the foibles of others, his common-sense wisdom, his sense of humour and his lack of sentimentality. David would come to rely on his judgement, always asking him to read his books before they were submitted to the publishers. Miller was a man of many parts: actor, restaurateur, soldier, architect, antique dealer and eventually artist. As a soldier on special operations he had suffered a terrible beating that had left him scarred but not embittered. His obvious spiritual qualities led to an invitation to become a lay canon of Truro Cathedral. Like David, Miller had spent time in retreat with the Franciscan community at Cerne Abbas; indeed he had a Franciscan approach to life, in his feeling for Nature and contentment with simplicity. At the Roman Catholic retreat of Walsingham he had met a confused and parentless young man, then being passed from monk to monk for sexual favours: this was Michael Truscott, who became his partner.

The Cornwell brothers cling to a maid, David (*left*) clutching a half-eaten apple.

David's father, Ronald Cornwell, sharply dressed as always.

David's mother, Olive.

Four generations of the Cornwell family, mid-1930s.

The Cornwell brothers in school uniform.

David (*far right*) is the only dwarf without a beard in a junior school production of *Snow White*.

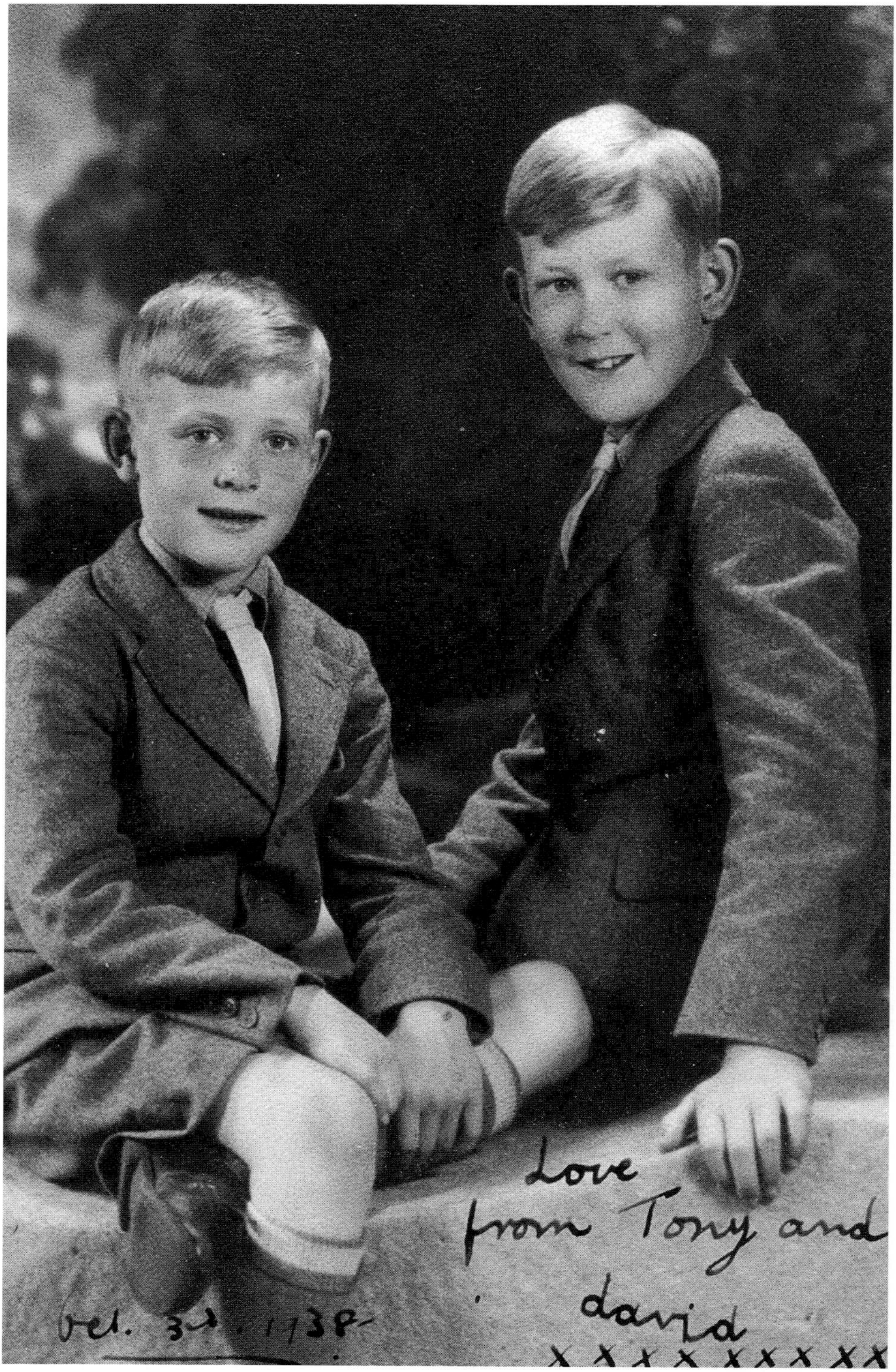
Love
from Tony and
david
XXXXXXXXXX

David (*left*) was a few weeks short of his seventh birthday when he and his brother posed for this studio photograph. He found the picture almost half a century later, while clearing out his mother's cottage after her death, and concluded that his father had sent it to her, after forging the inscription.

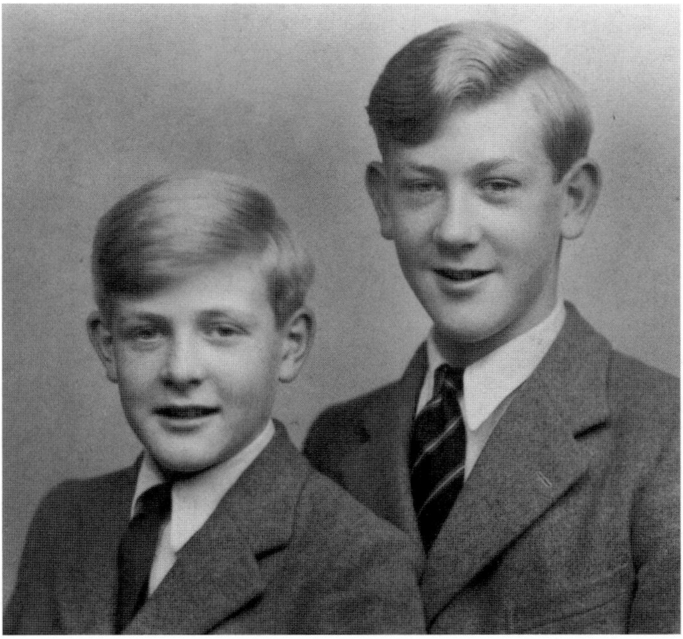

'I will be your mother.' David's older brother Tony took care of him after Olive abandoned them.

Westcott House, Sherborne School, 1947–8. David stands with arms folded in the back row, third from right; to his left is his friend Robin Cooke. David's housemaster R. S. Thompson is seated with an infant on his lap.

David in his National Service khakis, late 1940s.

In his mid-teens David fled boarding-school for Berne, where he wandered the cobbled streets, imagining himself as Young Werther.

At a dance with his girlfriend Ann, wearing his ceremonial 'Number 1' uniform.

David and Ann in the Alps. He is wearing his Downhill Only Club pullover.

The young couple in St Moritz with David's father and his stepmother Jean. Ann was suspicious of Ronnie from the outset.

'The best con man ever.' Ronnie at the races, apparently prosperous.

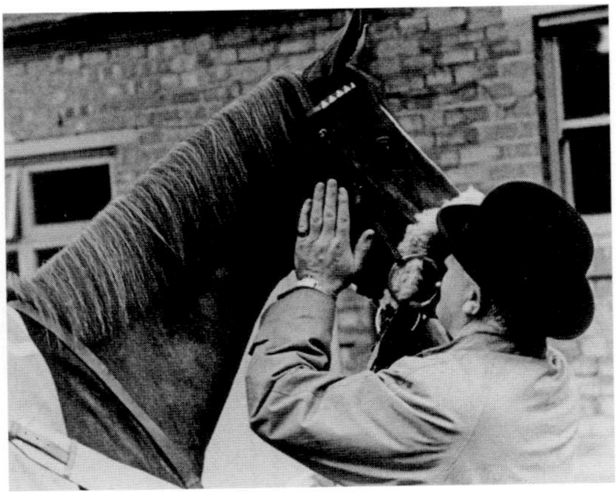

'Is it true that your father keeps racehorses?' asked David's housemaster, exasperated at the non-payment of school fees.

Ronnie throws a party at his house 'Tunmers' for the touring Australian cricket team, 1948. David and Tony stand on the left of the picture, next to Ronnie, with their half-brother Rupert in front; the great batsman Don Bradman stands next to their stepmother, Jean, holding aloft their half-sister Charlotte.

Ronnie and Jean with the boxer Sugar Ray Robinson in his Harlem nightclub.

Laughing all the way to the bank. Ronnie, David, Jean and Tony, *c.* 1950.

The committee of the Albany Club Sports Society celebrates after presenting a cheque for £8,000 to His Royal Highness the Duke of Edinburgh, in his capacity as patron of the National Playing Fields Association, 1949. Ronnie can be seen in the background, apparently trying to elbow his way alongside the husband of the future Queen.

Courtesy of Murray Glover

Lincoln College, Oxford, in the mid-1950s.

Courtesy of Murray Glover

David's friend and mentor, Vivian Green, a prototype for the character of George Smiley.

David and Ann, mid-1950s. Her parents became impatient at his failure to propose to her.

27 November 1954: the newlyweds sign the register, at St. Luke's Church, Redcliffe Square, in South Kensington, while Ronnie watches over them.

Outside the church: (*left to right*) Ronnie, Jean, the best man Robin Cooke, the bridesmaid Charlotte (*in front of the newlyweds*), Ann's mother Alison, her uncle (who gave her away in the absence of her father), and Ann's sister 'Winkie', the Maid of Honour.

David and Ann on holiday in North Devon.

The Pilton Players' production of Emlyn Williams's 'Night Must Fall'. David, standing in a bow tie, takes the part of the charming psychopath Danny, a character that had fascinated him since the late 1930s, when he was taken to see the play by his aunts.

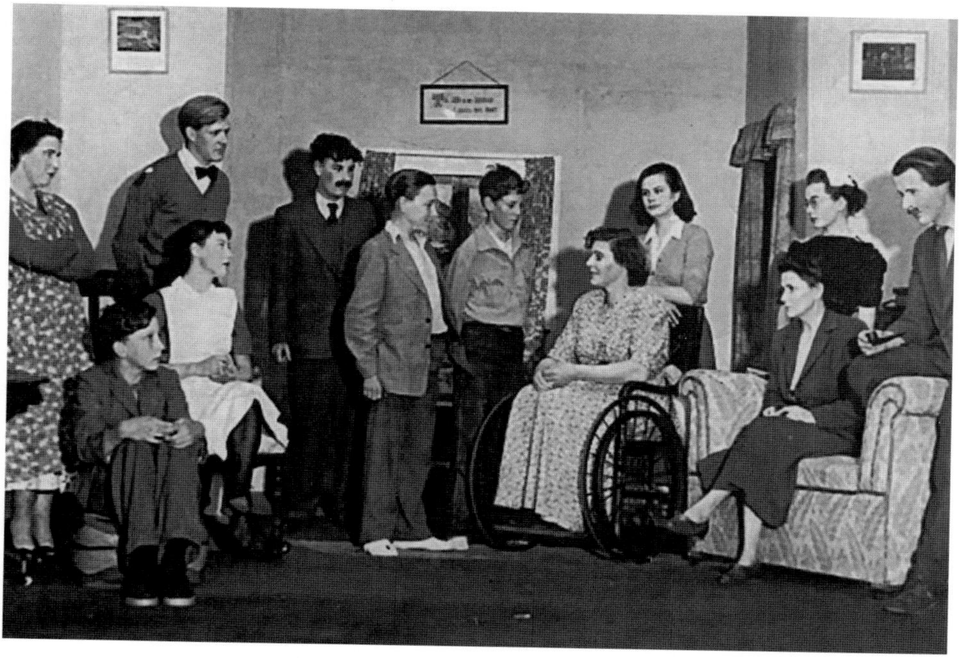

Broadway Buildings, headquarters of the Secret Intelligence Service (MI6) in David's day.

'The Circus', David's fictional equivalent.

Ralph Crane/The LIFE Picture Collection/Getty Images

David poses as a spy for a photographer from *Life* magazine, soon after he was outed as the author of *The Spy who Came in from the Cold*. At the time he claimed to be nothing more than an ordinary civil servant.

The successful author, *c.* 1964. David looks uneasy in this publicity shot, taken with Ann and the boys, (*from left to right*) Stephen, Timothy and Simon.

From time to time Miller would travel up to London from his home in West Cornwall to assist David on operations. He also joined the local Communist Party so that he could report back to David on its activities.

Another of David's agents was 'Harry', whom David would eulogise long after he left the Service as an 'unknown soldier of the Cold War'. Like Miller, Harry had joined the Communist Party in order to spy on it from the inside. 'All his energies from late childhood onwards had been directed at frustrating his country's enemies by becoming one of them,' wrote David. Harry had absorbed the Party's dogma until it was second nature to him; 'he had bent his mind until he scarcely knew its old shape any more'. With help from his MI5 agent-runners he had schooled himself to think and react as one of its faithful. Yet somehow he always managed to come up smiling for his furtive weekly debriefings.

Harry had volunteered for all the jobs that other comrades were only too glad to be relieved of, in the evenings and at weekends. He had spent countless hours on street corners trying to sell copies of the *Daily Worker*. He had acted as runner and talent-spotter for visiting Soviet cultural attachés and third secretaries, and had supplied them with harmless or inaccurate technical tittle-tattle about the industries in his area. Gradually, through diligence and apparent devotion to the cause, Harry had risen to become an influential and valued comrade, entrusted with semi-conspiratorial errands which seldom amounted to anything of substance.

Yet this lack of visible success did not matter, David would assure Harry during their weekly debriefings. 'If you didn't hear anything, Harry,' he had been taught to say, 'that means we can all sleep easier in our beds at night.' From time to time, perhaps to bolster Harry's morale, the two of them would rehearse together the plans for 'stay behind', after the putative Soviet occupation of Britain. Harry would retrieve his radio transmitter from its hiding-place in the attic, they would blow the dust off it, and then he would practise sending dummy messages to an imaginary resistance headquarters and receiving dummy orders in return.

David often pondered the motives of Harry and others like him. It seemed to him that Harry took no pleasure in duplicity, but bore it as a necessary result of his calling. MI5 paid him a pittance. 'If we'd paid him more, he'd have been embarrassed,' wrote David; 'besides, he could never have enjoyed his money. So we paid him a tiny private income and a tiny pension, and called it his alimony, and we threw in all the respect and friendship that security allowed.'[40]

David was becoming restless again. While away from home on operations he often stayed the night with his colleague Peter de Wesselow, a former RAF squadron leader who had a flat in Drayton Gardens.* As the officer with the day-to-day responsibility for handling the 'Venona' decrypts of Soviet telegrams, he had written a paper identifying Philby as the most likely candidate to be the Soviet spy code-named 'Stanley'.[41] But the 'Venona' material was handled with the utmost secrecy, and David knew nothing of it. A wealthy bachelor who seemed to be always between women, de Wesselow was an entertaining companion. Several letters to Ann relate enjoyable evenings with him. David was excited by such glimpses of a more sophisticated life. 'When I do all these things and see how many fascinating and stimulating places and people there are to be seen I long to bring you to London to live here – take a tiny unfurnished flat and a new lease of youthful energy,' he wrote to Ann. 'I feel you've nursed me through a period of stagnation, hopelessness and moribundity . . . I want to go with you to all the newest & loopiest theatres, go to beastly little night-clubs, listen to the speakers in Hyde Park.'[42]

In the summer of 1959 the Cornwells sold Orchid Cottage and moved to London. They rented a mansion flat on the first floor of a block on Prince of Wales Drive, which they found through a friend in the Office. David decorated the nursery with scenes from fairy tales, including elves that Ann considered too frightening for small children. A succession of lodgers helped them meet the rent of £8 per week, the first being a Nigerian called Richard, who was offended by the offhand manner in which his hosts spoke to him until he realised that they were treating him just as they would an Englishman; after that they got on very well together. Before leaving Richard offered to cook a traditional African dinner for the Cornwells and invited his glamorous Nigerian girlfriend. Ann returned home one afternoon to find a live chicken in the bathroom, feeding off corn on the floor.

* Peter de Wesselow was later accused of being part of the alleged MI5 plot to spy on Harold Wilson when he was Prime Minister.

The next morning Richard peeled off his shirt, grabbed the chicken and slaughtered it with a carving knife at the kitchen window.

One evening David and Ann went to see the film *On the Beach*, adapted from Nevil Shute's novel about the last days of humanity following an all-out nuclear exchange. Ann was so affected that, when she noticed representatives from the Campaign for Nuclear Disarmament (CND) in the street outside the cinema, she joined on the spot.

According to Madeleine Bingham, Ann adored David. 'She used to look at him as if he were some amazing piece of good luck which she had never thought would come her way.' There was something childlike about their relationship; in private they communicated in baby talk. Thus spies were referred to as 'pies' in their letters. But David often teased Ann, to a point where she would become upset. One letter written at this time suggests discontent within his marriage. 'You are an AWFUL pot,' he told her; '*please* don't any more or I *will* go loopy.' He pleaded with her to 'knock over the barriers, and be happy and *laugh*'. Something was evidently amiss, because he begged her, 'Oh please don't bleed me anymore.'[43]

Ann was already pregnant when they moved to Battersea. In March 1960 their second child was born, another boy whom they named Stephen – 'an agreeable youth with a large nose and no conversation', as David depicted him in a letter to his old friend Kaspar von Almen.[44] John Miller agreed to act as his godfather. Ann had chosen to have the baby at home, attended by her mother and a midwife. David stayed away from her throughout her labour. He suffered increasingly from disabling migraines. Ann feared that married life was beginning to pall for him, and that the responsibility of being a father of two children was more than he wanted. He would say later that, for him, writing was a way of breaking free. 'It was the gradual sense of hopelessness about marriage, of utter solitude, which first drove me to write.'

David would acknowledge his debt to Bingham by borrowing some of his traits for his most important character, George Smiley – his habit of polishing his spectacles on the end of his tie, for example, which became one of Smiley's trademarks.[45] Bingham had an inconspicuous, unassuming quality, which David appropriated for Smiley; his agent Peter Watt used to say of Bingham that he could 'lose himself in a crowd'. His skill as an intelligence officer was overlain by an endearing helplessness in everyday matters. Women liked to fuss over him, as they did over Smiley. Like Smiley, Bingham was squat and pudgy, almost toadlike in appearance.

Yet anyone familiar with Bingham could recognise that he was different from Smiley in significant ways. Unlike Smiley, Bingham was no scholar; his German was not fluent, and he had no love for German literature. Nor was Bingham a cuckold, like Smiley; on the contrary, Bingham was a lady-killer, one reason why he was so adept at managing women agents. Bingham was the heir to a peerage; Smiley was socially anonymous, 'without school, family, regiment or trade'. Nor did Smiley appear to share Bingham's robust right-wing views. Madeleine Bingham would come to believe that her husband was the model for Smiley, but she was mistaken; he was no more than a component. To David, Bingham was in some ways reminiscent of another and deeper influence, Vivian Green; the character of George Smiley drew on them both, but was not limited by their limitations. 'All fictional characters are amalgams,' wrote David, in a passage about his sources for Smiley. 'All spring from much deeper wells than their apparent counterparts in life. All in the end, like the poor suspects in my files, are remoulded in the writer's imagination until they are probably closer to his own nature than to anyone else's.'[46]

Smiley, the central figure in David's first novel *Call for the Dead*, would be one of several characters in the book to reappear in later books, including Smiley's wife Ann, his protégé Peter Guillam, the policeman Mendel and the villain Mundt. This was a deliberate ploy, picked up from reading Balzac, whom David had first read as a prescribed author on the French literature syllabus at Oxford. David would outline the strategy he had adopted in a letter to his accountant, written several years later. 'At an early stage I formed the notion of writing two novels, perhaps more, which would form a saga in which minor characters in the one would reappear in the second and assume greater importance.'

This 'second' novel would in fact turn out to be his third, *The Spy who Came in from the Cold*. 'I had begun as early February 1960 to sketch out on paper substantial scenes and situations which belonged to the second novel,' he continued. 'This is of course an inevitable practice if the two books together are to provide a single entity.' He drew attention to the fact that Mundt mysteriously disappears at the end of *Call for the Dead*, 'solely so that he may reappear in the sequel'. Mundt's reappearance and the role that he played in *The Spy who Came in from the Cold* were devised and written in the summer of 1960.[47]

David's secretary Maggie Foster-Moore typed the manuscript of *Call for the Dead*, which he had provisionally entitled 'A Clear Case of Suicide'. Bingham read the novel and introduced David to his literary agent, Peter Watt, the great-grandson of the founder of the firm of A. P. Watt which claimed to be the oldest literary agency in the world. Watt was a stylish dresser and an amusing man-about-town, whom David would come to know very well over the next few years. He submitted the book, under David's original title and the pseudonym 'Jean Sanglas', to Collins, then one of Britain's leading crime publishers.

On the afternoon that his son Stephen was born, David confided to Ann that he had applied for a transfer to MI6. He told Michael Overton-Fox that MI5 was 'a dead-end sort of place'. By contrast MI6 seemed smarter, more larcenous and more glamorous. The people were funnier, naughtier and raunchier than their counterparts in MI5.

David sat the Foreign Office examinations, successfully, and was interviewed by a selection board. He was appointed to start at MI6 on 27 June 1960, and promptly became involved in a wrangle with the pay office, about whether in assessing his rate of pay he should be considered as a new entrant to the service, or whether his work in Bern should be counted too. His claim was rejected.

11

A small town in Germany

The Secret Intelligence Service that David knew occupied Broadway Buildings, opposite St James's Park Underground station: 'conveniently located', as the official historian of the Service dryly records, between the headquarters of the London Missionary Society and the Old Star & Crown pub.[1] SIS had been there since 1926, and remained there throughout the war, though its subsidiary, the Government Code & Cypher School (GC&CS) had moved out of London to the comparative safety of Bletchley Park. Inside was a warren of confusing back staircases and dingy up-and-down corridors giving on to pokey little rooms. A fake plaque outside read 'Minimax Fire Extinguisher Company'. Here one was not required to show a pass to enter; the janitors would merely nod and say, 'Good morning'. Security was lax: at lunchtime David would go out to shop, bring parcels back, keep them beside his desk and take them out in the evening, without their contents being inspected. Kim Philby had exploited this trust by arriving on a Friday morning with a suitcase, as did many of his colleagues who were off to the country for the weekend – but while their suitcases contained nothing more sensitive than dinner jackets when they left on a Friday evening, Philby's was stuffed with secret documents, which he took home and photographed with his Soviet controller, returning with his suitcase on the Monday as if he had been in the country like the others.

Broadway Buildings backed on to the elegant eighteenth-century houses of Queen Anne's Gate; a secret internal passage ran to one of these, occupied by the Passport Office, while a bridge led to a flat occupied by the 'Chief' himself – Sir Dick White in David's day. The Chief's office could be found on the fourth floor, at the end of a creepy, spidery corridor and then up a small staircase. As the visitor approached, he saw himself distorted in a great fisheye mirror, in the eye-line of the beady women who protected their master.[2] Once admitted to the outer office, the visitor waited until a green light over the door was illuminated to indicate that 'C' was ready to receive him.

White was a skilful communicator, liked and admired throughout the intelligence world at home and abroad. Peter Wright likened him to David Niven: 'the same perfect English manners, easy charm, and immaculate dress sense'.[3] Incisive and persuasive on paper and in person, White understood how to work Whitehall. Appointed Director-General of MI5 in the disorder following the defections of Burgess and Maclean, he had restored calm. He had nurtured good relations with Commonwealth intelligence services, and earned both the respect of the Americans and the confidence of ministers. He had therefore been a natural choice to take the helm of SIS following the Commander Crabb fiasco. But, as he was the first to admit, he was an outsider, with no personal experience of running agents in the field. His appointment was greeted with hostility from some within the Service, particularly from those supporters of Philby who thought of White as one of his persecutors. Once he had imposed a necessary reorganisation, White concentrated on the Service's external relations and allowed his subordinates to get on with their jobs, a style which contributed to a perception among some field officers that he was aloof and out of touch.[4]

One of his fiercest critics was George Kennedy Young, Assistant Chief of MI6 since 1958: a very tall, red-headed, squash-playing Scotsman, seen as leader of the 'firebreathers'. (Young would be the model for the character of Percy Alleline in David's 1974 novel *Tinker, Tailor, Soldier, Spy*.) As head of MI6's Middle Eastern Operations, Young had played a part in the Iranian coup of 1953, and had been implicated in an unsuccessful plan to assassinate Egypt's President Nasser in 1956. His advocacy of aggressive covert action and his increasingly strident right-wing views contrasted with White's quiet moderation. New entrants to SIS were treated to a hair-raising lecture from him about the need for ruthlessness.

Another of the senior SIS officers who lectured on the new entrants' training course was Nicholas Elliott, whom David recognised as a member of the board that had interviewed him. In fact Elliott had been head of station in Bern when David had been recruited by 'Sandy' and 'Wendy', though he had been too senior to have concerned himself with such an insignificant agent. He had also been the officer most responsible for the Commander Crabb fiasco. He was now in charge of 'London Station', based at Londonderry House in Park Lane, which screened travellers to Soviet bloc countries for potential recruits.

At the start of the course David had arrived, as instructed, at a nondescript house in Palace Street, Westminster (now demolished). There he met the five other new entrants, a disparate bunch ranging in age from early twenties to late thirties.[5] The youngest, Barrie Gane, had come straight from Cambridge; he would remain within SIS until he took early retirement, having risen to director level and having been earmarked at one stage as a possible 'C'. One of the eldest was Rod Wells, a tough Australian who had been incarcerated by the Japanese after the fall of Singapore. In the notorious prisoner-of-war camp of Sandakan, Wells had constructed a working radio set out of scraps. When it was discovered he had been tortured and condemned to death, escaping execution only because of a clerical error. He had endured confinement in a tiny cell in which he could not even stand, while a naked light bulb shone down on him twenty-four hours a day. By the time he was liberated in 1945 he was blind from malnutrition; but within six months he was back at Sydney University studying for a science degree (his second).

Another of the more experienced entrants was Geoff Douglas, a former army officer and a Richard Hannay-like figure, member of an expedition to the Himalayas to look for 'Yeti', possibly as a cover for secret electronic interception. The officer in charge of the course was Gordon Philo, a kind, self-effacing man fluent in both French and Russian – an impressive individual, who had taken part in the Normandy campaign as a parachutist and been awarded the Military Cross, and who had afterwards taught modern history at Oxford before being recruited into MI6. Coincidentally he had just completed his first novel, a crime thriller set in Istanbul entitled *Diplomatic Death*.

'A Clear Case of Suicide' had been rejected by Collins. The obvious next step was to offer it to Bingham's publisher, Victor Gollancz. The firm was still dominated by the man who had founded it in 1927, and who had given it his name. 'VG' was an innovative and vigorous publisher, whose books in their distinctive yellow jackets with bold black type were instantly recognisable. He was also a public figure, active in CND and the campaign to abolish capital punishment. His commitment to the progressive cause was both good and bad for his business: though his Left Book Club had been a phenomenon of the 1930s, he had rejected *Animal Farm* because he was unwilling to publish a work critical of the Soviet Union. Like many of those who had founded their own business, Gollancz ran a tight ship. For him parsimoniousness was instinctive, indeed virtuous.

Peter Watt sold plenty of run-of-the-mill thrillers to Gollancz, who published them almost by rote. Yet perhaps this was the very reason for his hesitation. It was not until he had happened to bump into one of the firm's directors on the Underground, Gollancz's enterprising nephew Hilary Rubinstein, that Watt mentioned a novel 'by a friend of John Bingham's'.[6] Rubinstein combined good taste with commercial nous; in 1954 he had spotted Kingsley Amis's first novel *Lucky Jim* and had helped make it a bestseller. He expressed interest in seeing David's typescript, so Watt sent it over to him. The novel now had a new title, *Call for the Dead*.

David had also settled on a new pseudonym, John le Carré. The origin of this name remains obscure. For years he would claim to have spotted it on a London shopfront as he rode past in a bus, but more recently he has admitted that this was a fabrication. Carré means 'square' in French, and Madeleine Bingham would later interpret the name as a kind of backhanded tribute to her husband, who might have been styled 'a square' in 1960s parlance. But she had become jealous of David's success, to such an extent that her judgement on this subject was unreliable. There had been a Carré at Sherborne before the war; just possibly David had noticed this unusual name, perhaps displayed on a roll of honour, and had retrieved it from his memory; but since David himself has forgotten its genesis, one can only speculate. In 1980 he explained his choice thus: 'I thought that to break up a name and give it a slightly foreign look would have the effect of printing it on people's memories.'[7]

The new entrants' course was run partly in London and partly at SIS's field operations training centre on the south coast. As an exercise in basic tradecraft trainees were not told where they were going, but merely instructed to make their way to Portsmouth, catch the Gosport ferry and walk a few hundred yards down a particular street, where they would find a minibus waiting to take them to their destination. This turned out to be Fort Monkton, a battery constructed in the late eighteenth century to guard the approaches to Portsmouth harbour.

For the next few months the SIS trainees would undertake much of their training at 'the Fort' or in the surrounding area. Typically they would arrive on a Monday morning and stay at the Fort until Friday lunchtime, when they would rush back to London to maintain the fiction that they had been there all week. The Fort was connected to a London telephone number for the same reason. Another of the new entrants, slightly older than David, was John Margetson, who would make a distinguished career in the Diplomatic Service after completing five years in SIS. Margetson had a smart flat near Eaton Square and a convertible sports car; most weeks he would drive down to Portsmouth on the Monday morning, stopping in Prince of Wales Drive to collect David on the way. The two men formed a close and lasting friendship.

At the Fort David received a telephone call from Peter Watt, who assumed he was calling an office in Whitehall. There was exciting news: Gollancz wanted to publish the novel. Their chief reader, Jon Evans, had written an enthusiastic report, summarising the book as 'a Secret Service thriller of the first rank – by a born novelist'. Evans thought the characterization 'brilliant: & Smiley's immensely exciting duel with Elsa Fennan is something more than the stuff of which even the best thrillers are made. Le Carré is not merely the author of an outstanding "first": his will be a name to remember.'[8] There was an endorsement too from John Bingham: 'Mr le Carré is a gifted new crime novelist with a rare ability to arouse excitement, interest and compassion.' Bingham added a private aside to Rubinstein: 'I think that you are wise to take him on. I am sure he will write even better books in the future.'[9]

By the terms of an agreement made on 11 November 1960, Victor Gollancz agreed to pay an advance against royalties of £100, with an option to publish David's next two novels. This was a modest sum, not much more than a month's salary for David, but nevertheless it was a start, and he was delighted.

At Fort Monkton David and his fellow new entrants studied techniques of agent-running in enemy territory, and the tradecraft necessary to do so undetected: safe houses, dead letter-boxes, surveillance techniques, ciphers (coding and decoding) and clandestine wireless communication. They shot with 9mm automatic pistols at life-size pop-up targets. They were taught knife-fighting by an instructor who had been in the Shanghai police in the pre-war days of the Shanghai concession. 'Always keep the knife moving, sir, in a figure of eight movement,' he advised: 'keeps them guessing.' In lessons on unarmed combat they learned about target areas of the body, pressure points and how to kill a man with a single blow. They climbed telegraph poles, and detonated explosives in the wide moat of the Fort.

At night they were taken by Royal Navy motor torpedo boats to practise landing agents on and evacuating them from a hostile coastline – in this case a small bay on the Isle of Wight, part of the Osborne estate formerly owned by the royal family, where Queen Victoria and her children had swum from bathing machines. Another outdoor exercise required each entrant to find his way across a stretch of the New Forest at night, before climbing under a wire fence protected by searchlights and foot patrols.

As it turned out, David would never be at personal risk in his secret work – nor, to his knowledge, would the others in the intake, except one.[10] He would never again handle, let alone use, a 9mm automatic pistol. He would have little or no opportunity to use the skills he had acquired during his training – though they would provide a valuable source for his fiction.

The trainees undertook their tasks with youthful exuberance. In such a high-spirited environment the most trivial incidents took on a hilarious character. The point of one exercise was to kidnap an MI6 officer disguised as a passing cyclist and subject him to mock torture; unfortunately they chose the wrong cyclist, an innocent schoolmaster. As the climax to a map-reading exercise, a low-flying RAF aircraft was supposed to drop a wireless set by parachute. The young men below waited in eager anticipation as the parcel drifted to earth; but when they retrieved and unwrapped it, they were disappointed to find that their masters had not risked a precious piece of equipment on a mere training exercise. 'It's full of fucking stones!' exclaimed Rod Wells. On another exercise each of the trainees had to retrieve a cache of arms buried somewhere in the New Forest. David found a large car occupied by a pair of dozing tourists parked over the site where his cache had been buried. It required considerable charm to persuade them to move on so that he could begin digging.

Perhaps the most demanding exercise required each of the new entrants to go to a different town or city and live under a cover identity while performing various tasks that might be expected of an agent. David's cover was that of a German tourist in Brighton. By chance he bumped into Ann's aunt Kay, who was very tickled to be told that she must pretend not to know him, as he might be under surveillance. On his last day the local police arrested him and subjected him to an intense interrogation, after a cooling-off period in the cells. All this was done at the behest of SIS, to test whether the trainee could maintain his cover under pressure. Apparently David spoke in a convincing German accent throughout.

In London the trainees pondered at length the psychology of traitors, double agents and defectors, and how to obtain, motivate and control them. They were shown how to forge papers, make skeleton keys, pick locks and operate secret electronic equipment. They practised taking photographs from cameras concealed in special briefcases. They learned how to develop films, including how to measure the precise mixture of chemicals and to calculate the exact time required for the process to work. One evening, however, when David and John Margetson wanted to leave promptly to go the theatre, they estimated the amount of chemicals by eye and halved the time supposed to be necessary to develop the film. The result was just as good.

At the conclusion of their training the six new entrants were entertained to drinks by 'C' himself. White showed a keen interest in them, and solicited their thoughts about the training course just finished.

This agreeable occasion was followed by a shock. On the day of their initiation, they were summoned by a grim-faced Robin Hooper, head of Training, who told them that he must say something he never thought he would have to say: they had a traitor in their ranks, and his name was George Blake. Then he wept, and sent them home while it was determined whether they had been blown, or whether they were still employable under cover.[11]

Blake's unmasking came as a stunning blow to SIS. He had been a trusted officer, who had served in Berlin, perhaps the most sensitive of all SIS stations. It emerged that he had supplied his KGB controllers with the names of scores of agents operating behind the Iron Curtain, most if not all of whom had been arrested and executed. SIS's networks in Eastern Europe were in ruins. 'I don't know what I handed over because it was so much,' Blake later admitted. It was suspected that he had been responsible for the unmasking of a CIA mole within Soviet military intelligence, Pyotr Semyonovich Popov, who was arrested and executed in 1960. Blake's treachery appeared to confirm American suspicions that the British could not be trusted with important secrets. Another embarrassing discovery was that Blake had forwarded to the Soviet Union everything that George Leggett had reported back to London of his interrogation of the KGB defector Vladimir Petrov in Australia. Blake was put on trial, convicted of treason and sentenced to forty-two years' imprisonment.

David had been warned that he could not publish his book without the consent of his employers, because of the danger that he might expose something that should remain secret, without meaning to do so. He sent the typescript to Bernard Hill, who replied a couple of days later in a note saying how much he had enjoyed reading it. He asked for only one change, not for security reasons, but because he felt that the description of Maston, the Minister's adviser on intelligence, resembled his real equivalent too closely.*

Prompted by Gollancz's lawyer, David also changed the name of an East German assassin working in London under diplomatic cover from Wolff to Mundt, after discovering that the head of the East German Trade Delegation in London was called Wolf.† In his response to the publisher's libel reading David was careful to maintain the pretence that he was a simple civil servant, with no inside knowledge of the world in which his book was set.

> The Characters are wholly fictitious, and so is the Secret Service setting – so far as I am capable of judging. I know of no Govt office at or near Cambridge Circus, but I do not suppose that the Secret Service publishes the location of its offices. My reading on the subject has always led to the belief that Intelligence work is divided between separate services and you will notice that in my book there is only one service, which I suppose reduces the risk of a chance similarity.[12]

The publishers were not enthusiastic about the pseudonym David had chosen, and proposed that instead he should adopt one made up of Anglo-Saxon monosyllables suggesting an American provenance, such as Chuck Smith‡ or Hank Brown; but David resisted this advice.

Visiting him at the flat in Prince of Wales Drive, Rubinstein was puzzled by the drawings and poems pinned to the boys' bedroom door – until he realised that David himself had drawn and written them all, in a child's hand.

* According to the official historian of the Service, Christopher Andrew, this character was inspired by the flamboyant Alexander Kellar. In the novel Mendel lets slip to Smiley that Maston is known as 'Marlene Dietrich' within Special Branch.

† Not Markus Wolf, head of the foreign intelligence division of the East German Ministry for State Security ('Stasi'), which le Carré called the Abteilung, though it has often been erroneously suggested that Wolf, known as 'The Man without a Face', was the model for Mundt's rival Fiedler, or indeed for Smiley's arch-enemy Karla. David has repeatedly denied any such connection, for example on the front page of the *Guardian* on 6 May 1993.

‡ 'Chunk' Smith in David's account, but I suspect that this spelling originated in a typo.

Before the book was published David had received his first posting – to Bonn, capital of the Federal Republic. He would be 'undeclared', meaning that his presence as an MI6 officer would not be admitted to the German authorities, or indeed to any but his most senior Embassy colleagues. His cover was as a second secretary, reporting to the Head of Chancery, and his overt role would be to travel around Germany, trying to win support for Britain's application to join the European Economic Community, the precursor of the European Union, then generally known in Britain as the Common Market.

David took an advance on his salary to buy a car, a green Hillman Husky, which he drove to Bonn, taking the ferry from Dover to Ostend, with an overnight stay in Brussels. At the German border his diplomatic visa produced 'a comic show of deference', an indication perhaps of the respect still shown by Germans towards representatives of the former occupying powers. He arrived at the British Embassy in Bonn before lunch on 6 June 1961. 'I've got a nice office looking on to open fields,' he told Ann. She would remain behind in London with the two boys until he was settled. In particular he needed to find somewhere to live. Since David's job was a new one, he had no predecessor from whom he might otherwise have inherited a house.

The Bonn Embassy was large, with a minister as the Ambassador's deputy and several counsellors, plus a substantial MI6 station. The Minister would chair a meeting every morning to discuss recent events and the challenges of the day ahead, attended by seven or eight senior aides. There were five first or second secretaries in Chancery, plus Lance Pope, the Counsellor with special responsibility for German internal politics, who knew all the members of the Bundestag and was friendly with several ministers in the German government. David hugely admired Pope, who had worked in Germany during the 1930s, spoke flawless German and could sing German marching songs. During the war he had escaped from Colditz by dressing in a German officer's uniform that he had made himself. Before walking out of the gate, he had summoned the guard and reprimanded him for some minor misdemeanour.

The First Secretary (Political) in Chancery was James Bennett, who shared a house with another young bachelor diplomat, David Goodall: these two became David's closest friends in Bonn. Another of his Embassy colleagues, Tony Duff, though not a 'spook', would eventually become head of MI5. At a lower level were the ex-Control Commission local staff, including a small community of naturalised German Jews. David found them among the most hard working of the Embassy personnel and deplored the fact that these 'temporaries' had no employment rights or pension entitlement.

The Ambassador, Sir Christopher ('Kit') Steel, was a tall, heavily built, choleric man who had served in the British Embassy in Berlin before the war. When Ted Heath, the Cabinet Minister responsible for negotiating British entry into the Common Market, came out to Germany on a visit, Steel arranged a dinner party for him, to which the French Minister of Foreign Affairs, Maurice Couve de Murville, was also invited. It fell to David Goodall to explain to the Ambassador that Heath had come to Germany without bringing a dinner jacket. 'Bloody barbarian!' growled Steel.

Before leaving London David had had a morning coat made by a local tailor, which he wore for the first time at a garden party in Bonn. Various foreign diplomats introduced themselves, and David spoke convincingly about his work as a second secretary in Chancery. A Soviet diplomat took a particular interest, so David reached into his pocket and produced an engraved visiting card. On being handed the card, the Soviet diplomat scanned it with a puzzled expression – as well he might, because it bore the name of a Gentleman's Bespoke Tailor in Battersea.

The head of the MI6 station in Bonn was Peter Lunn, a devout Roman Catholic and fierce anti-Communist, who disapproved of David's more liberal political views. Lunn had been captain of the British ski team at the 1936 winter Olympics, and would seize every opportunity to ski, even in old age when he found it hard to walk. Slight in build, with blue eyes, he spoke in a soft voice with a lisp, every inch the gentleman spy, an image enhanced by the fact that he lived in a schloss down the Rhine, where he sometimes gave parties. During one of these David was shocked to overhear the Ambassador ask some German guests, 'What do you think of this thieves' kitchen?' There was a Foreign Office tradition that one *never* referred to clandestine activities in public.

The revelation of George Blake's treachery had hit Lunn particularly hard. Blake had been Lunn's protégé when he was head of station in Berlin; it had been Lunn's card index of agents which Blake had copied one night while acting as duty officer. As head of the SIS station in Vienna in the late 1940s, Lunn had masterminded a tunnelling operation that had enabled Soviet telephone lines to be tapped, providing a stream of valuable intelligence. It turned out that the Americans were planning something similar in Berlin, but on a much more ambitious scale. Lunn had offered to share the British expertise gained in Vienna; he acted as host for an Anglo-American meeting to plan the operation at a house in Carlton Gardens in London. Unfortunately he had asked Blake to attend and take the minutes. Blake's confession rendered the intelligence gathered from the Berlin telephone taps of questionable value. It now seemed obvious how the Russians had 'discovered' the tunnel, only eleven months after it had been dug. Blake later admitted that the full details of the operation, which would cost the Americans millions of dollars, had been known to the Soviet authorities 'before even the first spade had been put in the ground'.

The British were concerned about the security of their own communications in Germany. Diplomats were advised to close their curtains to minimise the possibility of electronic eavesdropping. While David was serving in Bonn it was decided to build a secure cipher room within the Embassy, with thick, sound-proofed walls and protected cabling.

'The work is interesting and by no means chairbound,' David wrote to John Margetson, soon after he arrived.[13] Until a suitable house could be found, he was billeted in a gloomy pension in Bad Godesberg, a short distance up the Rhine from Bonn, which he pictured to Ann as 'a pretty, dignified residential area . . . with expensive shops'.[14]

Bonn had been chosen in 1949 as the capital, rather than a bigger city such as Frankfurt or Hamburg, as a temporary measure, since the new Federal Republic took the line that the German Democratic Republic was an illegally constituted state, and that sooner or later Berlin would again become the capital of a reunified Germany. The choice of Bonn had owed much to the advocacy of West Germany's first Chancellor, Konrad Adenauer, a former mayor of Cologne and a native of the Rhineland, still in power after almost a dozen years, though by 1961 he was in his mid-eighties and nicknamed *der Alte* ('the Old One'). The city had been too small to accommodate all the necessary buildings, which stretched up the left bank of the Rhine towards Bad Godesberg. David would later provide a satirical portrait of the German capital in his novel *A Small Town in Germany*:

> To accommodate the immigration of diplomats, politicians and government servants . . . the townspeople have built a complete suburb outside their city walls . . . a jumble of stodgy towers and lowflung contemporary hutments which stretched along the dual carriageway almost as far as the agreeable sanatorium settlement of Bad Godesberg, whose principal industry, having once been bottled water, is now diplomacy . . . the seat of the Federal government and the great majority of the ninety-odd missions accredited to it, not to mention the lobbyists, the press, the political parties, the refugee organizations, the official residences of Federal Dignitaries, the Kuratorium for Indivisible Germany, and the whole bureaucratic superstructure of West Germany's provisional capital, are to be found either side of this one arterial carriageway between the former seat of the Bishop of Cologne and the Victorian villas of a Rhineland spa.

The British Embassy was an unlovely building, erected on the site of a former gravel pit to a specification from the Ministry of Works. Diplomatic staff complained about long corridors and poor construction standards.

> Imagine a sprawling factory block of no merit, the kind of building you see in dozens on the Western by-pass, usually with a symbol of its product set out on the roof; paint about it a sullen Rhenish sky, add an indefinable hint of Nazi architecture, just a hint, no more, and you have portrayed with fair accuracy the mind and force of England in the Federal Republic . . . Built as the Occupation drew to its premature end, it catches precisely that mood of graceless renunciation; a stone face turned towards a former foe, a grey smile offered to the present ally.[15]

David depicted Bonn as perpetually wreathed in the fog that clings to the Rhine valley, while teams of barges ground blindly up and down the river, shaking the buildings as they passed. Opposite Bad Godesberg on the right bank the Petersberg mountain towered above the resort town of Königswinter, capped by the hotel where Neville Chamberlain had stayed during the Sudetenland crisis, from which he had descended to Bad Godesberg to confer with Hitler. In *A Small Town in Germany* the looming mountain symbolises the past that everyone is striving to forget. 'We've got the big memory and the small memory,' observes Leo Harting, one of the few characters in the book with a conscience. 'The small memory's to remember the small things and the big memory's to forget the big ones.'[16]

Only sixteen years after the end of the war, Germany's past was hard to forget. Former Nazis were everywhere: in the police, the judiciary, the intelligence fraternity and the armed services, in industry and science and the teaching professions, and, most particularly, in the bureaucracy. Hans Globke, one of Adenauer's closest aides, had helped to draft the Nuremberg Laws. Reinhard Gehlen, head of the Bundesnachrichtendienst (BND), the Federal Intelligence Service, had learned his trade as head of German military intelligence in the killing grounds of the Eastern Front. Ernst Achenbach, a member of the Bundestag and a senior figure in the Free Democratic Party, had helped to organise the deportation of French Jews from Paris. And so on. 'Bonn in the early 1960s was a spooky place,' David would write in retrospect. 'Sometimes the very streets of the city seemed like a perilously thin surface laid hastily upon the recent dreadful past, like one of those nicely mown grass mounds at Belsen concentration camp, covering the mute agony of the innocent dead.'[17]

Bonn was a nest of spies. Former Nazis were vulnerable to blackmail: those with access to sensitive information were targeted from the East. Every prominent West German politician had contacts in the GDR. The BND itself was riddled with moles. Heinz Felfe had been head of its department of Soviet counter-espionage, until he was arrested in 1961 and shown to be a Soviet spy himself. He had risen rapidly within the BND because of his success in uncovering Soviet agents. It is possible that the cynicism of Soviet policy in sacrificing less important agents to further Felfe's career inspired the similar operation at the heart of *The Spy who Came in from the Cold*.

David's overt role required him to cultivate German politicians and journalists. For a sometimes idealistic young diplomat, the omnipresence of former Nazis was repellent. The fact that he was forced to consort with such people in his daily work was hard to stomach.[18] Many of his colleagues shared his distaste for their hosts. The British Embassy was 'a bastion of English phobias about the country in which it was situated', David would write in the foreword to *A Small Town in Germany*; it was 'a place made schizophrenic by Britain's continuing self-perception as victor in the '39–45 war, and by our much humbler and more realistic role as supplicant for German support for our belated entry into the European Community'.[19] Britain had only reluctantly supported America in endorsing and promoting German rearmament, which remained a controversial issue at home. Though officially committed to the goals of the Federal Republic, the British were nervous of any prospect of German reunification. 'I love Germany so much that I would like three or four Germanies,' quipped one British diplomat. When Hans Kroll, the German Ambassador to Moscow, proposed a unified, unaligned Germany, he was quickly replaced.

The action of *A Small Town in Germany* takes place against the background of a revival of the extreme right. As British diplomats struggle to negotiate entry into Europe, young Germans chant anti-British slogans and burn a library of British books. A neo-Nazi movement led by a figure 'from the old days' is poised to take power. In the early 1960s there were real fears that something like this might happen. With the benefit of hindsight we can now say that these fears were unfounded; but less than a generation after the most terrible war in human history, the prospect could not be ignored. Indeed in 1966 Kurt Georg Kiesinger, a former Nazi who had joined the Party within weeks of Hitler coming to power, would become Chancellor, though as leader of a cross-party coalition, not of the extreme right. At a political meeting in November 1968, Kiesinger would be slapped in the face by a young woman activist who shouted at him, 'Nazi!'

David's covert role had been created out of such fears.* His task was to investigate and detect potential Nazi cells or organisations, and to recruit German sleepers who would join any such groupings in order to provide information on them. But since the Germans were extremely sensitive about the possibility of any British interference in their politics, David's function had to be concealed from all but a very few senior members of the Embassy staff. Most of them were not even aware that he was SIS. Nor did he have much to do with the station itself, because his work was

* Readers should be aware that David prefers to remain silent on his covert role in Germany, though he is the first to admit that it was negligible. The information in this paragraph is gleaned from other sources, and he says that it provides an incomplete description of what he did.

peripheral to its main effort against the Eastern bloc countries, the Soviet Union in particular. He never had anything to do with running agents into East Germany, for example. His remit left him his own master, on his own for much of the time. As it turned out, there was very little for him to do, because the feared Nazi revival never materialised.[20] Parties of the extreme right failed to gain popular support, and at their rallies the neo-Nazis were usually outnumbered by the police.

After David had been in Bonn a month or so, Ann arrived with their two boys. At first they all lived together in the pension, but the landlady found them too noisy, so they moved first to a flat and then to a tiny, three-bedroomed house in Bad Godesberg, 42 Gringstrasse. David had enquired about housing in Königswinter, but had been warned that living on the 'wrong' side of the river was frowned upon. 'H.E. has more or less banned it on principle,' he had written to Ann while she was still in England. 'Apparently the Germans don't like it either – it's a bit like being asked to a diplomatic reception in Clapham . . .'[21] The last ferry crossed at 11.30 in the evening: if you missed that, you were forced to make a detour to the nearest bridge.

The difficulty in finding somewhere to live was exacerbated by David's anomalous position. The Head of Chancery resented the presence of an outsider in his domain. David had to overcome a general prejudice against 'Friends', as MI6 people were misleadingly known. Indeed some of those alongside whom he was working suspected that he might have been sent to spy on *them*. Despite these obstacles David soon made himself a popular member of the Embassy staff. His intelligence was obvious, and his quick wit appealing. Everything that happened to him became an anecdote, and he had an eye for everybody's foibles. One of his colleagues had a tic, which David imitated to entertaining effect. He did a faithful impression of the Ambassador's schoolboy German, which his German contacts found especially hilarious. One of his party pieces reproduced the conversation when the Prime Minister had come to Bonn in a forlorn attempt to solicit German support for Britain's Common Market application and was staying as a guest of the Ambassador. Both men drank steadily. After half a bottle of kirsch, Macmillan had become philosophical. 'Well, I see no hope,' he had said. 'We're the chaps of whom our children will say, we brought the world to ruin.' Afterwards David was charged with escorting the PM to bed, following his liver-spotted hand up the rail of the grand staircase. They reached the royal apartments, where the guest was sleeping.

'What did you say your name was, my dear fellow?' enquired the Prime Minister.

'Cornwell,' replied David, imagining promotion, even a knighthood. 'Corn*well*. David Cornwell.'

'Cornhill,' Macmillan repeated. 'I'll bear that in mind, my dear chap.'

The social life of the Embassy was conformist and restrictive, a caricature of the manners of the nation. 'Its styles and prejudices were informed by an expatriate vision of suburban England which was certainly long out of date, and had probably never existed anyway,' David would write in the foreword to *A Small Town in Germany*.[22] On at least one occasion he was taken aside and told that he was not behaving in the manner expected of a diplomat. When, at an informal dinner with colleagues, he congratulated the housekeeper on the dish she was serving, his host brought him up short. 'Can't you act like a gentleman and not talk to the servants?' David was stunned into silence; Ann wanted to leave immediately.

The British diplomatic community insisted on distinctions of rank: those on different grades were not supposed to mix socially. 'The A's . . . tend to have different tastes as well as different intellectual interests to the B's,' maintains one of the characters in *A Small Town in Germany*, the only senior woman in the Embassy, even as she confesses to an affair with a junior colleague.[23]

After she had been in Bonn a month Ann complained in a letter to John Margetson that she found 'the Embassy people *so* dull – wives especially – very concerned with their vanishing status socially and just as I imagine colonial wives to be'.[24] The women were as dutiful as their husbands in adhering to Embassy protocol. In *A Small Town in Germany* David provides an ironic description of how, 'with a little gesture of surprise', the senior wife present leads the others into the English Church on Sundays, and how they follow, 'quite by accident', in the order of succession which protocol, 'had they cared about such things', demanded.[25]

Several of the diplomatic wives made it obvious that they thought Ann an unsuitable partner for David. 'I wonder why so many clever men have such dull wives?' one of them murmured pointedly. David himself complained that she did not talk enough at dinner parties. He told her that it was embarrassing for a man in his position to receive CND mailings through BFPO (British Forces Post Office), and asked her to cancel her subscription.

In his first few months in Germany David's duties took him several times to Berlin, then in the front line of the Cold War. If armed conflict broke out between the superpowers, it was most likely to begin there. No longer the capital of Germany, it had become the world capital of espionage, with hundreds of agents passing back and forth between East and West.

Since the airlift in 1948–9 there had been constant friction between the Western powers and the Soviet Union over access to West Berlin. The Russians had found excuses to halt trains, to block the roads along which supply convoys were sent, to prevent barges sailing down the Elbe and to close the air corridors along which aircraft were permitted to fly into the city. 'Berlin is the testicles of the West,' the Soviet leader Nikita Khrushchev had told Mao Zedong. 'Every time I want to make the West scream, I squeeze on Berlin.'

For the Western Allies, Berlin was an island of freedom in a sea of Communist-controlled territory, with enormous symbolic significance. For the Russians, and their East German allies, it was a leaking wound. In recent years there had been a huge exodus of Germans from East to West, draining the young GDR of skills and talent. It was estimated that by 1961 a total of 3.5 million Germans, 20 per cent of the population of East Germany, had emigrated to the West. The East Germans were understandably anxious to block this outflow of talent. Though they were able to secure their principal frontier with West Germany, their citizens continued to escape through West Berlin in large numbers.

By the time that David arrived in Germany to take up his post at the British Embassy in Bonn, the position in Berlin had reached a crisis. That very month Khrushchev gave notice that at the end of that year he would terminate the agreement made between the four occupying powers guaranteeing unobstructed access to West Berlin.

In August 1961 David attended a rally of the Social Democratic Party (SPD) in Nuremberg. During the proceedings the mayor of West Berlin, Willy Brandt, made a dramatic announcement. 'We have a finger-tip feeling that something is about to happen in Berlin,' he declared. On the long drive back from Nuremberg David decided to file his report before going home, though it was late in the evening by the time he reached Bonn. He was surprised to find all the Embassy lights still burning. Brandt was right: something *was* happening in Berlin. The East Germans had closed the border with West Berlin, tearing up streets to make them impassable to vehicles and surrounding the Western sectors of the city with rolls of barbed wire, manned by armed soldiers. Within weeks, they began building the permanent concrete barrier that became known as the Berlin Wall. Passage between the Western sectors and the East was permitted only through strictly controlled checkpoints. Those who tried to climb the Wall, or tunnel underneath it, were liable to be shot.

The United States responded to this escalation by reinforcing its Berlin garrison, though President Kennedy knew that his troops would be unable to resist the much greater forces under Soviet command should they move to take control of the city. To keep his pledge to protect the people of West Berlin, his only recourse would be to threaten a nuclear attack against the Soviet Union – 'a hell of an alternative', as he told the Joint Chiefs of Staff. Berlin was a magazine, ready to explode at the smallest spark. The next few months were especially tense, culminating in a confrontation between Soviet and American tanks armed with live munitions, their engines running, at the main checkpoint.

David saw the Wall for himself when he arrived in West Berlin with his Foreign Office colleague James Bennett; they had flown in because of fears that the Soviets might close the roads. As they stared at the blank faces of the armed East German Volkspolizei ('Vopos') standing guard at the checkpoint, Bennett told David to wipe the grin off his face. 'I was not aware that I had been grinning,' he wrote later, 'so it must have been one of those soupy grins that comes over me at dreadfully serious moments.' Inside he felt nothing but disgust and terror, which he decided was exactly what he was supposed to feel; 'the Wall was perfect theatre as well as the perfect symbol of the monstrosity of ideology gone mad'.[26]

Call for the Dead had been published only a week after David had left England for Bonn. It was well received: the *Guardian* reviewer, Francis

Iles, found it 'outstanding'; in the *Observer*, Maurice Richardson praised it as 'highly intelligent, realistic'; Julian Symons, reviewing the book for the *Sunday Times*, thought this new young author 'undoubtedly a find'. Indeed the reviewer for *John O'London's* speculated that, because the book was so well written, it must be the work of an established author using another name.

'I have decided to cultivate that intense, worried look and to start writing brilliant, untidy letters for future biographers,' David wrote to John Margetson's girlfriend, Miranda Coldstream, signing himself 'The Author'.[27] He suggested to Rubinstein that a reprint might be needed because of the good reviews. The first impression of 2,500 copies soon sold out, to be followed by a second impression of 650 copies a couple of months after publication. Paperback rights were sub-licensed to Penguin for £250, and American rights sold to Walker & Co., which described itself as 'a small American house with a line in English mysteries', and which in turn sub-licensed American paperback rights to New American Library. French and German rights* were sold also. All in all, this was a very good start. David planned to write a thriller every year to supplement his salary. While living alone in the Bad Godesberg pension he had resumed work on *A Murder of Quality*, the book that he had begun at Eton. 'I wrote the book lying down, on beds, in notebooks, in the few snatched hours left to me by my family and the diplomatic life,' he would explain later.[28]

Once again George Smiley was his central character, this time acting as a private investigator rather than as an intelligence officer. *A Murder of Quality* is in many ways an old-fashioned murder mystery, though one with a strong undercurrent of social criticism. Carne, the school where the novel is set, is depicted as snobbish and self-satisfied. The chippiness that David had felt at Eton comes through strongly, and perhaps too his resentment of the treatment he and Ann had received from some of his colleagues in the Embassy. Physically the school resembles Sherborne, a risk that David would attempt to mitigate at the editing stage by altering the school motto he had devised for Carne to avoid any similarity

* The German edition was entitled *Schatten von Gestern* ('Shadow of Yesterday').

with Sherborne's. David showed the typescript to his colleague David Goodall, who protested that it presented a 'not altogether fair' picture of a public school. 'My dear chap,' responded David, 'I'm writing a novel, not a despatch.'

A Murder of Quality was submitted to Gollancz in January 1962. The publisher's reader, Sheila Hodges, clearly had mixed feelings about it, as did Gollancz himself. 'I agree with you entirely about this,' she wrote to him:

> you don't want to stop reading; the wit and the urbanity, and the generally civilized atmosphere, are extremely attractive; but the detection is thin and disappointing. Moreover, I became rather bored with all the U and Non-U business* . . . I only hope, though, that for his next book he will return to espionage, which he handles so outstandingly well.[29]

For this second book, Gollancz increased the size of David's advance from £100 to £150.

A Murder of Quality was published on 26 July 1962. Once again the reviews were favourable. Reviewing the book for the *Sunday Times*, Julian Symons rated it as 'the best crime story with a school setting since Nicholas Blake's first book, *A Question of Proof*, was published nearly thirty years ago'. Nicholas Blake himself (the pseudonym of Cecil Day-Lewis, who had been educated at Sherborne) found it 'vastly entertaining'. The *Illustrated London News* reviewer was perhaps extravagant in his praise. 'I believe that Mr le Carré is a phenomenon such as can be expected only in every two or three generations,' he raved. 'If he continues at this level, he will soon soar above any of the great names of this century.'

The first impression of 3,000 copies sold quickly, and a second impression of 600 copies was put in hand in the first week of publication.

At first Penguin did not want this second book, but reversed this decision and paid £250, the same amount as for *Call for the Dead*. Both books were published in the newly redesigned 'Penguin Crime' series, which

* Gollancz made this connection in their advance publicity, stressing the author's 'wit and urbanity' and claiming that 'he writes as ravishingly as Nancy Mitford'.

retained its distinctive green covers but added striking visual images. Once again American rights were sold to Walker.

Meanwhile the Crime Writers' Association had nominated *Call for the Dead* second on their list of the 'Best Crime Books of 1961'. David had been invited to the prize-giving ceremony, but the Foreign Office refused permission for him to attend. It was 'a relief really as the fares would have been excessive for such a venture', he argued in a letter to Ann. 'Peter Watt said it was really better to miss it than come second and Madeleine was slightly acid about John [Bingham] not having won it!!'[30]

David was writing from London, where he was escorting a party of young members of the Bundestag who were being encouraged to look favourably on Britain's application to join the Common Market. He took the opportunity to discuss his prospects with his employers. 'FO says don't worry about being a long time in Bonn,' he told Ann afterwards. 'We can stay as long as we can stick it, then probably East to Poland.' David reckoned that they should expect to remain in Germany another three or four years: long enough to make it worth looking for somewhere more comfortable to live.

The young German politicians whom David was shepherding around London enjoyed their stay. On the evening of their arrival, they insisted on being taken to a 'traditional English pub'. By the time the pubs closed, they had explored several, and sampled Scotch whiskies as well as warm English beer. On the steps to the hotel, they went into conclave and determined that the night was still young. 'We want to meet some girls,' they told David. In vain he argued that they would benefit from an early night. Consulting his conscience, he decided that it was his duty to see it through. He telephoned a contact at Special Branch, who recommended an establishment that turned out to be shut. Further research led to an address in Mayfair offering 'French lessons', then a common euphemism. The large lady who answered the doorbell wore a pink nightdress and a red bandana. She was not impressed to be confronted by an assembly of beaming Bundestag members, and was about to close the door on them when their leader stepped forward and made a solemn announcement: 'We are German, and we wish to learn French!'

While in London David went to dinner with Dick Edmonds's sister Susan and her husband James Kennaway, who lived in an elegant house in Highgate. Until this point David had known Kennaway only slightly, but now their shared experience of writing and publishing gave them more to talk about. Kennaway had achieved an enviable level of success, enough to enable him to give up his publishing job to concentrate on writing full-time. He had adapted his novel *Tunes of Glory* into a highly praised film, starring John Mills and Alec Guinness;* his screenplay had been nominated for both a BAFTA and an Academy Award (Oscar). As a result he was much in demand, and well paid. The Kennaways were able to spend long spells abroad, employing a governess to teach their four children. They were a glamorous couple, depicted by one of their friends as 'Scott and Zelda, with manners'.[31]

When David raised with his agent the possibility that he might tackle a 'straight' novel next, Watt warned that he would be 'bonkers' to do so if he wanted to make money out of writing. In fact David was already thinking about a new spy story, as he told Ann: 'I've just hit on a very good plot (I think) for another.'[32]

The plot for the new book was a fiendishly clever one. It concerned Mundt, a senior officer of the Abteilung, the East German secret service, who appears fleetingly in *Call for the Dead.* Unknown to the reader, Mundt has been 'turned' and is now working secretly for the British. To counter growing suspicion that he is a traitor, the Circus manipulates an innocent witness to testify against him, having planted evidence that will undermine the witness's testimony. The premise is that once an accusation has been made and the supporting evidence shown to be false, the accusation itself is discredited.†

Though the idea of a double agent highly placed within East German intelligence may have been founded on the Heinz Felfe case,

* Guinness himself apparently considered this his best performance on film.

† It has been suggested to David that he drew the idea for the book from Agatha Christie's short story 'The Witness for the Prosecution' (1933), which later became a play and then a film. (The play opened in London in October 1953; the film was released in 1957.) The premise of the story is that a witness has

David's central character was inspired by someone with whom he never spoke, whose name he never knew. He was seated at a bar in Heathrow Airport when a middle-aged man wearing a stained raincoat sat down near by. David noticed the deadness in his eyes; he looked as if 'he'd had the hell posted out of him'. The stranger fished in his pocket, drew out a handful of coins in different currencies and denominations, and slammed them down on the bar, demanding a large Scotch, in what seemed to David to be a faint Irish accent. Between him and the barman, they sorted out the money. In that moment, Alec Leamas was born.

At the beginning of *The Spy who Came in from the Cold* Leamas is a jaded British intelligence officer operating out of Berlin, whose agents have been rounded up by the East Germans one by one. Back in London he is ordered to trail his coat, posing as a heavy-drinking, burned-out former spy, willing to defect to the East – a bait which is duly taken. Until almost the end of the book he believes that his mission is to destroy Mundt. But Leamas has been deceived by his own masters: in reality, he is a mere instrument in what he eventually realises is a 'filthy, lousy operation' to divert attention away from Mundt at the expense of his rival Fiedler, a much more sympathetic character – 'to save him', as Leamas bitterly explains, 'from a clever little Jew in his own department who had begun to suspect the truth'. Two innocent people are sacrificed to protect Mundt's cover; the fact that both of them are Jews and Mundt a former Nazi makes an ugly operation hideous.

planted evidence that will discredit her own testimony, thereby discrediting the prosecution. In a letter dated 11 April 2012 to one of those who made this suggestion, US federal Judge Jon O. Newman, David admitted that he had seen the play, though he could not remember whether this had been before or after he devised the plot for *The Spy who Came in from the Cold*. 'But I am sure that the notion did not consciously present itself to me during the short and turbulent time of writing. I think there are a whole bunch of influences that kick around in one's head at such a time, and one draws on them because they are apposite, often without recognizing where they come from. Maybe that happened in this case, though I am inclined to doubt it. I had, for a short time in my life, been close to all manner of deceptions, and the process of inside-out thinking was very familiar to me!'

Leamas's boss, the subtle spymaster 'Control', head of the organisation known simply as 'the Circus',* is unabashed in admitting that the methods used by both sides in the Cold War have become much the same. 'I mean,' he muses aloud to Leamas, 'you can't be less ruthless than the opposition simply because your government's *policy* is benevolent, can you now?'[33] Control's cynical speech derives from the one given by George Kennedy Young to the MI6 trainees. *The Spy who Came in from the Cold* presents British intelligence as no better than the enemy, and in some ways worse. There is good and bad on both sides: Leamas and Fiedler alike are flawed individuals struggling to preserve their humanity, in a conflict without honour or principle.

Leamas's outburst at the end of the book is a fervent protest against the bad things he has been asked to do in the service of his country. 'What the hell do you think spies are?' he asks his distressed girlfriend: 'moral philosophers measuring everything they do against the word of God or Karl Marx? They're not! They're just a bunch of seedy, squalid bastards like me: little men, drunkards, queers, hen-pecked husbands, civil servants playing cowboys and Indians to brighten their rotten little lives.' This was a very different depiction of spying from the one presented in Ian Fleming's best-selling novels. The moral ambiguities of *The Spy who Came in from the Cold* are in marked contrast to the unquestioning certainties of the James Bond books, in which the goodies and baddies are clearly delineated. To readers in the early 1960s, accustomed to the messy compromises of the Cold War, they seemed far more truthful. Similarly, le Carré's squalid settings seemed more realistic than the glamorous five-star hotels, high-rolling casinos and expensive restaurants frequented by James Bond.

Overshadowing the novel was the image of the Berlin Wall, in all its stark, inhuman brutality: 'a dirty, ugly thing of breeze blocks and strands of barbed wire, lit by cheap yellow light, like the backdrop for a concentration camp'. The book opens at the Wall, when a man is shot while trying

* The Circus appears to combine the functions of MI5 and MI6. Its colloquial name is a reference to its supposed location in Cambridge Circus, at the intersection of Shaftesbury Avenue and Charing Cross Road in central London. The title 'Control' is perhaps a nod to the 'Chief' ('C').

to cross over to the West, and closes there, with two more corpses lying at the Wall's foot, raked by searchlights.

In retrospect David would link his revulsion against the Wall to his own inner misery:

> I know that I was deeply unhappy in my professional and personal life, and that I was enduring the extremes of loneliness and personal confusion.
>
> Perhaps some of that solitude and bitterness found its way into Alec Leamas. I know that I wanted to be in love, and that my own past, and my own inwardness, made this impossible. So, perhaps, the barbed wire and the machinations of the plot did duty for other obstacles that stood between myself and freedom.
>
> I had been poor too long, was drinking a lot, I was beginning to doubt, in the deepest of ways, the wisdom of my choice of job. The familiar process of embracing an institution, then fighting my way clear of it, was taking over my relationship to my marriage and my work. Staring at the Wall was like staring at frustration itself, and it touched an anger in me that found its way into the book.[34]

It was perhaps not surprising that Ann was less than enthusiastic about the novel. David would later tell people that she had interrupted him repeatedly and deliberately during the writing of it. For some time she had betrayed signs of envy of his success as a writer, the profession she had hoped to make her own. She had typed *A Murder of Quality* under protest, but this time she declined, so David had to rely on the Embassy secretaries instead. In a letter to Ann written in June, he complained that 'the new book drags along but the girls are all away and there's no one to type it'.[35]

Another spy scandal broke just as David was finishing the book. John Vassall, an Admiralty clerk who in the 1950s had served on the staff of the Naval Attaché in the British Embassy in Moscow, confessed to spying for the Russians. A homosexual, Vassall had been blackmailed after compromising photographs had been taken of him at a drunken party.

The Cornwells needed a bigger house, particularly as Ann was pregnant again. They were helped by the arrival in Bonn of a new head of station, a replacement for Lunn, who had moved on to another posting. This was Arthur Franks, always known as 'Dickie', who had served in SOE during the war: an SIS high-flyer who would eventually rise to become its Chief. He and David formed a lasting friendship. In January 1963 there would be a new ambassador too, Sir Frank Roberts, a small, bustling man who did not share his predecessor's lofty distaste for 'Friends'.

With Franks's help, the Cornwells secured a large house in Königswinter, with a garden running down to the Rhine. Under the new regime official disapproval of Embassy staff living on the 'wrong' side of the river had eased. The Königswinter house was equipped with counsellor-level furniture, much too good for a mere second secretary; when Ann accidentally stained the arm of a sofa, 'Admin' made a stink. Its dining room was capacious enough to seat a dozen; for dinner parties Ann relied on Frau Klampt, a refugee from the East, who at other times served as their housekeeper. Besides Frau Klampt they had a Spanish live-in maid, a daily woman who came in to clean and an old gardener, whose duties included stoking the large basement boiler that served the house. Ann's eighteen-year-old cousin had been acting as their au pair; she now returned to Scotland, to be replaced by a sensible English nanny named Janet.

Each day David crossed back and forth on the ferry, sometimes parking his modest Hillman with its diplomatic plates alongside Adenauer's huge armoured Mercedes as the Chancellor made his own way to and from work. There was excitement in Chancery when David was able to report which newspaper Adenauer was reading, and the press section was quick to deduce which leader writers might have influenced his mind. Sometimes David caught his eye, and occasionally it seemed to him that the Chancellor smiled at him; but the Old One was nearing ninety, and his lined face was as inscrutable as a Native American chief's.[36]

David snatched every available moment to work on his new book, rising very early in the morning to write for a couple of hours before setting out for work, and making use of odd moments at his desk in the Embassy when he was not otherwise employed. He began a habit of carrying a small notebook with him, which he kept on the passenger seat of his car and often scribbled in as he crossed the Rhine by ferry.

One day Ronnie turned up unexpectedly at the house, attended by one of his camp-followers. Ann was unwelcoming, but the boys were fascinated to meet their notorious grandfather. Parked outside was a strange-looking vehicle, which Ronnie explained was an 'Amphicar', a new concept in locomotion: an amphibious automobile which a German company had recently begun to manufacture, largely for export. The fact that it was not much of a car and not much of a boat did not deter enthusiasts. 'We like to think of it as the fastest car on the water and the fastest boat on the road,' one proud owner was quoted as saying. A sceptical writer for *Time* magazine suggested that the Amphicar 'promised to revolutionize drowning'.

No doubt Ronnie was trying to secure the concession to sell this radical new product in Britain – though it would have been impossible for him to do so in his own name. In 1962 another petition had been filed against him, presumably by someone unaware that he was already bankrupt. A receiving order would be issued against him in December 1963.

Keen to impress his grandsons, Ronnie looked longingly at the Rhine flowing past the end of the garden, but decided against an experimental dip – a prudent decision, as one disadvantage of the Amphicar was that it proved not to be watertight; its continued flotation was dependent on the ability of the bilge-pump to keep pace with the leakage.[37]

The winter of 1962/3 was the coldest for many years. The Rhine itself froze over, providing a welcome halt to the otherwise unending barge traffic. Ice stretched out five yards or more from each bank, and even in the middle where the sluggish flow prevented it from freezing solid, large blocks formed. Only the ferry continued to cut its way through the ice, carrying David back and forth to work.

On 22 October 1962, President Kennedy delivered a nationwide televised address, in which he revealed that Soviet missiles equipped with nuclear warheads had been deployed in Cuba. America would not tolerate the installation of nuclear weapons so close to its mainland: Kennedy demanded their withdrawal. The President announced a blockade of shipping bound for Cuba, enforced by the US Navy.

This was the most dangerous moment of the Cold War, when tension between the superpowers stretched almost to breaking point. For Kennedy, the crisis in Cuba was intertwined with the crisis in Berlin. In his speech to the nation he explicitly linked the Cuban blockade to the Russian blockade of West Berlin in 1948–9, and declared that the United States would not deny Cubans 'the necessities of life', as the Soviet Union had done to Berliners.

There was a general perception that, should war break out, Germany would be 'the first place to go'. When news came through of Kennedy's ultimatum, decorators working on the Cornwells' dining room quietly washed their brushes, packed up and went home, to prepare for Armageddon. Meanwhile senior Embassy staff met in secret conclave to discuss contingency plans for evacuation.

The stand-off ended when Khrushchev backed down. He agreed to dismantle the offensive weapons in Cuba and return them to the Soviet Union, in exchange for an American agreement never to invade Cuba. Secretly, the United States also agreed to dismantle its missiles with nuclear warheads deployed against the Soviet Union in Turkey and Italy.

The Cornwells' marriage had been under stress for a while. When a married woman of the Bonn expatriate community made a pass at him during a dinner party, David, after some hesitation, had reciprocated. This was a love affair rather than a flirtation, although it had no sexual outcome; but it was a source of anguish rather than joy, since the lovers could only rarely arrange to be alone together, and then usually in public places such as on the largely deserted Eifel hills outside Bonn or in municipal parks.*

David was tormented by guilt. He felt 'unfrocked' by the affair; he became a pariah in his own eyes, and the self-hatred in Alec Leamas reflected the tumult in his own mind. Indeed Leamas's decision to allow himself to be killed at the end of the book could be interpreted as a manifestation of David's own death-wish. As Leamas falls from the Wall in the final sentence of the book, an old nightmare recurs to him: the image of a small car crushed between two lorries, with children waving cheerfully through the window. During the Cuban Missile Crisis, which was raging as David was finishing the book, he had been full of apprehension for his boys. More generally, the sense of futility pervading the book may stem from his sense of being trapped in an unhappy marriage. Tellingly, when the novel was complete he gave it to his would-be lover to read before showing it to his wife.

* 'We were lovers but we hadn't been to bed. It was very grown-up,' says Hazel Bradfield, the unfaithful wife of the Embassy's Head of Chancery in *A Small Town in Germany*.

It seems that in its original draft *The Spy Who Came in from the Cold* was much longer than its finished form. Among the passages that David cut were those dealing with Leamas's failed marriage.[38] In subsequent years David has often said that he wrote the book over a period of about five weeks, but the record suggests that it took him considerably longer.[39] It would be more than eight months from the letter in March 1962 in which he mentioned to Ann hitting on 'a very good plot' for a new book until he delivered the typescript to his agent in November. Indeed its origins went back further than March: he had planned Mundt's reappearance in print while he was writing *Call for the Dead*, two years earlier. And the building of the Berlin Wall in August 1961 had stimulated him to start thinking seriously about a new book in which the Wall would play a symbolic part.[40] In a television interview in 2000 he suggested that he had written the book in response to the news of the Wall going up. 'I think for forty-eight hours I didn't sleep at all,' he told the interviewer. 'When I got back to Königswinter where we lived, I was in a state of what I think shrinks called "fugue",* I was tremendously high, and in five weeks I wrote a huge, overlong version of what became *The Spy who Came in from the Cold*.'[41] This seems to be another example of false memory: when the Wall went up in August, David was still working on *A Murder of Quality*, which would not be delivered to the publisher until the following January.

More than half a century later Michael Horniman, an agent at A. P. Watt in the 1960s, remembers the proprietor coming into the office one morning, tired but excited after staying up late into the night reading the typescript of David's new book. 'I think we've got something,' Watt told his colleagues.

* In fact the term 'fugue', as used by psychiatrists, is a disorder associated with amnesia.

12

Becoming John le Carré

Peter Watt's submission letter conveys his sense that the new book, provisionally entitled 'The Carcass of the Lion', was special: 'to my mind, this, his third novel, fulfils all the promise of the first two'.[1]

Hilary Rubinstein had wearied of his uncle's autocratic rule and was on his way out of the firm, so Watt had submitted the novel to Victor Gollancz himself. Though now in his seventieth year, Gollancz had lost none of his zest for the book business. Recognising that the new novel was a leap forward from its predecessors, he argued that it should be published in a different form. 'After a second reading (by another of my directors) and a thorough discussion, I have come to the conclusion that we ought to make the gamble of taking this right out of the thriller and le Carré category, and of launching it as a high spy-adventure story by a completely new name,' he wrote to Watt. He proposed publishing it under the title *The Spy who Came in from the Cold*, picking up on a phrase used by Control early in the novel, as he briefs Leamas on his mission: 'We have to live without sympathy, don't we? That's impossible, of course. We act it to one another, all this hardness; but we aren't like that really. I mean . . . one can't be out in the cold all the time; one has to come in from the cold . . . d'you see what I mean?'[2] Control tells Leamas that he wants him to stay out in the cold a little longer.

The new title was an inspired suggestion, a gift to tired sub-editors, who have drawn on it ever since. Gollancz also proposed that the book should be published under the name 'Leamas', rather than le Carré. On behalf of his client Watt accepted the first of Gollancz's suggestions but not the second.[3] David had responded to the latter by telegram: 'RELUCTANT PUBLISH AUTOBIOGRAPHY DEAD SPY'.

Arguing that this was 'in effect, a "first novel"' for David, Gollancz offered an advance of £150, no more than he had paid for *A Murder of Quality*. Under pressure from Watt, he grudgingly increased his offer to £175.

In the meantime the book had been cleared by the authorities. On a visit to London at the end of January, David had been informed that it had been passed for publication by MI5. 'It will now go to the F.O. for a final vet,' he told Ann: 'no trouble expected there.'[4] He was right: MI6 raised no objection either. It was perhaps surprising that neither of his two previous employers objected to the novel, since it presented British intelligence as devious and unscrupulous. In retrospect, David felt that they had allowed the book to be published because they had known that it was not based on authentic experience – the very antithesis of what the public would come to believe.

'I have just finished another book which will be coming out in July,' David wrote to Vivian Green early in February 1963. 'We expect to stay here for a year or two longer, and while the present mess continues, I for one am content to see it out. We now have three sons (the third called Timothy).* They are all down for Westminster, and two of them will be going to the Dragon School first, providing that the royalties keep rolling in.'[5]

David was in England again in late February, to act as escort for Fritz Erler, the deputy leader and leading political intellectual of the SPD, tipped as a future defence minister in an SPD administration. (Indeed it was believed that Erler might have risen to become Chancellor had he not died prematurely of leukaemia.) During the war he had been interned in Dachau as punishment for his opposition to the Nazi regime.

Erler spoke good English, but nevertheless wanted David to act as interpreter. He had come to England to discuss the control of nuclear warheads sited in West Germany with the Prime Minister, Harold Macmillan, a subject he had already discussed with President Kennedy. In David's company Erler also met other prominent British politicians, including the leader of the opposition, Harold Wilson, and the Minister of Defence, Peter Thorneycroft. Immediately before seeing Macmillan,

* Born in November 1962, while they were living in Königswinter. His godfather was John Margetson.

Erler had been to see the Lord Chancellor, Lord Dilhorne, formerly Reginald Manningham-Buller,* at the House of Lords. The limousine that was supposed to take them to Downing Street afterwards did not turn up. As there were no taxis either, David decided that drastic action was necessary. He stepped out into the road and stopped a passing car, a modest vehicle with a working-class couple inside. 'We're going to see the Prime Minister,' David explained to the incredulous duo. Erler produced his card in supporting evidence. 'Oh go on, let them in,' said the wife.

The door of 10 Downing Street was opened by Macmillan's private secretary, Philip de Zulueta. They were shown in to see the Prime Minister, whose opening statement set the tone for an unsatisfactory exchange. 'Well,' Macmillan began, 'I suffered in the First War and you suffered in the Second War, so we have a lot in common, don't we?' Erler tried to steer the conversation towards the topic he had come to discuss. Flustered, Macmillan consulted a sheet of paper on his desk, shielded beneath a thick plate of glass. 'Well,' he began again, 'I suffered in the First World War, you suffered in the Second.' When Erler tried to press the point, Macmillan became more vague: 'You know, bombs fall here and bombs fall there, and you never can tell what they are going to do . . .' Embarrassed, Erler thanked the Prime Minister and terminated the conversation. On the way out he whispered to David, '*Dieser Mann ist nicht mehr regierungsfähig*' ('This man is no longer capable of government').†

Zulueta, who was escorting them to the door, whirled around. 'I understood that!' he said.

London was abuzz with rumours of an affair between the Secretary of State for War, John Profumo, and the call girl Christine Keeler. The pair had been introduced by the society osteopath Stephen Ward, with whom Keeler was living. What gave the rumours extra spice was the allegation that Keeler had simultaneously been involved with a senior naval attaché

* Apparently one of the inspirations for the character of Widmerpool in Anthony Powell's sequence of novels, 'A Dance to the Music of Time'. Bernard Levin nicknamed him 'Bullying-Manner' because of his rudeness in court; after Manningham-Buller's elevation to the peerage as Lord Dilhorne, Levin had dubbed him Lord Stillborn. His daughter Eliza became Director-General of MI5 in 2002.

† Macmillan resigned as Prime Minister on 9 October 1963.

at the Soviet Embassy in London. It was an alarming possibility that a senior Soviet diplomat and the British Secretary for War had been sleeping with the same indiscreet young woman. Ward was supposed to have asked Keeler to pump Profumo about the very question that Erler had come to England to discuss: when West Germany might be granted control over American nuclear weapons stationed on German soil. In fact Ward did tell her to ask Profumo this, but only as a joke.[6]

Journalists had been eagerly looking forward to Keeler's testimony at the trial of her former lover Johnny Edgecombe, accused of trying to break into Ward's flat while Keeler was there and firing several shots. At Erler's request, Dilhorne arranged for him to attend the opening of the trial, with David as his escort. They sat directly behind Stephen Ward, who turned round during a break and asked them, 'How am I doing?' David said, 'Fine'; Erler made no reply. In parliament Profumo tried to brazen it out: in a statement to the House of Commons he avowed that 'there was no impropriety whatsoever in my acquaintanceship with Miss Keeler'. In due course he would be forced to admit that he had 'misled' the House, and resigned.

A couple of months later David was again in London, this time to act as John Margetson's best man. The pair arrived at the church near Chalk Farm far too early, so they drove up and down Haverstock Hill to pass the time. David diverted the groom with a rendering of the spoof sermon delivered by Alan Bennett in *Beyond the Fringe*. This kept Margetson laughing so hard that he had no opportunity to become anxious about the ordeal ahead.

In April there was exciting news from Peter Watt: an American publisher was willing to pay 'a small fortune' for the rights in *The Spy who Came in from the Cold*.

Jack Geoghegan had recently been appointed president and editor-in-chief of Coward-McCann, a publishing house with a lacklustre recent history. Geoghegan had been hunting for a high-profile bestseller to revive its flagging list. He would later say that he had been searching for 'something well written that would sell'. Aware that it would be difficult to persuade American literary agents to offer their best authors to him, he reckoned that England was the most likely source of such a bestseller.

His first scouting trip to London had proved a disappointment – but his hunger had impressed Watt. Geoghegan had employed Lena Wickman, a Swedish woman living in London who was close to Watt, to act as his scout. Some months later, back in New York, he received a parcel containing the typescript of *The Spy who Came in from the Cold*. In subsequent years he would always remember reading it with mounting excitement. This could be the bestseller for which he had been searching. His principal reaction was a churning sensation in the pit of his stomach, a fear that he had come across something really good, which would in the end, as had happened several times before, go to another publisher.[7]

The Spy who Came in from the Cold was under option to Walker & Co., the small American publishing house which had published David's first two books, and had done satisfactorily but not spectacularly with both. Walker wanted the book and bid for it, but David decided to accept Coward-McCann's slightly higher offer of $4,500* for the American rights, mainly on the strength of Geoghegan's obvious enthusiasm.[8]

The ball was rolling. Not long after the deal had been concluded with Coward-McCann, Paramount Pictures made an offer for the film rights. Peter Watt presented the contract to David over lunch at the Savoy. Paramount proposed an outright purchase, giving the studio control over any future use of the characters on film. They were offering to pay £7,500, with two further top-up payments of £2,500 each linked to sales of the American edition. 'It would be so wonderful to feel what it was like to have ten thousand pounds,' sighed David. Watt told a colleague that though he was loath to accept such a restrictive deal, David's excitement at the large sum of money on offer had overcome his qualms; David does not recall any reluctance from Watt. In any case the contract was signed. This mistake would cause David a great deal of trouble further down the line. Soon afterwards he replaced his small Hillman with a large Humber.

In a letter to Vivian Green, David described *The Spy who Came in from the Cold* as 'a sort of Quiet American story set in Berlin'.† It had already 'made a fortune', he continued, 'but of course I don't know how we can

* Just over £1,600 at the exchange rates then prevailing.

† He no longer knows what he meant by this comparison.

keep at least enough of the money to justify my getting out of the F.O. I would very much like to talk to you about all this.' The rates of tax then prevailing penalised high earners. 'We want to get out of the F.O. but daren't quite take the plunge – I think they may chuck me out after this book which would simplify things.' He urged Green to make haste if he had any intention of visiting them in Germany, 'as we may well abandon the F.O. for the lusher pastures of the Perfecto-Zissbaum Corporation'.[9]*

During another official trip to London David stole away from his duties to meet Martin Ritt, the director who would be making the film for Paramount. He was in town escorting another set of German dignitaries, which explained why, when he arrived at the Connaught Hotel to have lunch with Ritt, he was wearing the then standard diplomat's livery of a tight black jacket, black waistcoat, silver tie and striped grey-and-black trousers. Fortunately he had left his bowler hat in the cloakroom. As they shook hands, Ritt enquired of him cordially, 'What the hell possessed you to dress like a maître d'?'

Ritt himself was wearing a black shirt buttoned to the neck and a pair of baggy trousers held up by elastic and nipped at the ankles, unusual dress in the Connaught's Grill Room; and – to David's astonishment – an artisan's flat cap with the peak turned up where it should have been turned down, *worn indoors*. He had the bearish frame of an old footballer run to fat, with a broad, bronzed, mid-European face etched with the pain of ages, thick, swept-back greying hair and pitch-dark, watchful eyes framed by black-rimmed spectacles.

'Didn't I tell you he was going to be young?' Ritt demanded proudly of his four associates.

Originally an actor, Ritt had been a member of the radical Group Theater in the 1930s, a disciple of Elia Kazan's. After serving in the American armed forces during the war, he had worked in television as a director, but had been blacklisted in the early 1950s because of his strong left-wing sympathies. Over lunch in the Connaught Grill, it quickly became clear to David that Ritt saw in *The Spy who Came in from the Cold* some kind of crossing

* The Perfecto-Zissbaum Motion Picture Corporation features in the novels of P. G. Wodehouse.

point from his earlier convictions to his present state of impotent disgust at McCarthyism, at the cowardice of many of his peers and comrades in the witness box, at the failure of Communism and at the sickening sterility of the Cold War.

Ritt admitted to David that Paramount's purchase of the rights had been 'a steal'. The script was being written by Guy Trosper, the writer and producer of *Birdman of Alcatraz* (1962), who had been nominated for an Oscar for his 1952 film *The Pride of St Louis*. Ritt asked David who he thought should play Leamas. David felt strongly that this was a British story, which required a British actor to play the leading part. He suggested Trevor Howard – or perhaps Peter Finch, who, though Australian, could play an Englishman convincingly. Ritt said that he took the point, liked both actors, but feared neither was big enough to carry the budget.

A few weeks later David again flew to London, this time at Paramount's expense, to take part in a tour of locations with Ritt, who told him that the role of Leamas had been offered to Burt Lancaster. 'Burt will play it Canadian,' he explained.[10]

Towards the end of June President Kennedy came to Berlin. Together with Chancellor Adenauer and Mayor Brandt he rode in an open-top car, cheered by waving Berliners who lined the route into the city centre from the airport. The President paid a visit to Checkpoint Charlie, where he stood facing a group of East Berliners too cowed to acknowledge his presence. Later he was photographed on a raised platform gazing across the Wall into East Berlin. Afterwards, in front of the City Hall, he spoke to a huge crowd, estimated at several hundred thousand strong. His impassioned speech, which was punctuated throughout by rapturous cheers of approval, declared the solidarity of the people of the United States with the citizens of West Berlin. Again and again he challenged those who defended the actions of Communist regimes: 'Let them come to Berlin.' He ended with a stirring peroration: 'All free men, wherever they may live, are citizens of Berlin, and therefore, as a free man, I take pride in the words, *Ich bin ein Berliner*.'

A few days after Kennedy's speech, Kim Philby surfaced in Moscow. It turned out that he had been the 'Third Man' after all. Six months earlier he had gone missing: a message had been sent out from London to all SIS stations abroad, announcing that a former member of the Service had disappeared and was suspected of being a Soviet spy. Though the name of the suspect was encoded, Dickie Franks realised immediately that it must be Philby, who had been living in Beirut since 1956. Ostensibly Philby had been working as a stringer for the *Observer* and the *Economist*, but this was cover for his work as an intelligence agent, arranged by his old chum Nicholas Elliott, who served a term as head of the local MI6 station, until succeeded by Peter Lunn.*

Dick White had long suspected Philby. When he had taken over as Chief, he had been shocked to find him back on the books. As more intelligence implicating Philby had accumulated, White had decided to act: he had ordered Elliott back to Beirut, to see if he could extract a confession from his old friend. For years Elliott had defended Philby, but even he had come to recognise that the evidence against him had become undeniable. In Beirut, Elliott had confronted Philby, offering him immunity from prosecution in return for a full confession. Philby had agreed in principle but asked for more time, and Elliott had returned to London without him. Later this would be seen as a blunder, though perhaps it had been a ploy. 'My dear boy, nobody wanted him back here,' he would tell David long afterwards. Lunn had then telephoned Philby and ordered him to report to the British Embassy in Beirut. For the next few days Philby continued to stall, until two o'clock one morning, when Philby's wife Eleanor had telephoned Lunn to tell him that her husband had failed to return home from a party. Lunn had hurried round to the Philbys' flat, fearing the worst.[11]

The revelation that Philby had indeed been a traitor renewed public interest in spies. That he had been publicly exonerated seven years before

* David has often claimed that his own name was passed by Philby to his Russian controllers. It is difficult to understand how this could be so, since Philby was unlikely to have had access to the names of new entrants by the time David joined SIS in 1960. In a television interview in 2000 Mikhail Lyubimov, a former KGB officer in London, stated that Philby had passed David's name to his Russian controllers in the late 1940s, after he was recruited as an agent by the Bern SIS station. Lyubimov's assertions should be treated with caution.

by no less a person than the Prime Minister suggested a lack of security bordering on incompetence.

Always a clever publicist, Victor Gollancz skilfully exploited the topical nature of the book. The advance publicity for *The Spy who Came in from the Cold* quoted from a recent review by Julian Maclaren-Ross of Len Deighton's *The Ipcress File* in the *Times Literary Supplement* that had argued for spy fiction to be more true to life: 'How peculiar . . . at this time of the Vassall Tribunal, with so many real-life parallels from which to draw, that our spy fiction should be at such a low ebb . . . the really realistic spy novel, as prefigured by Ashenden and Mr Ambler, does not as yet exist.'[12]

Gollancz put a red jacket on *The Spy who Came in from the Cold*, to distinguish it from the yellow jackets usual on his books. He wanted to convey to readers and reviewers that this was a work of literary merit, far above the general run of spy stories. To support this message he solicited endorsements from prominent literary figures, sending each a set of proofs. 'It is very far from being an ordinary "spy story", even if of a superior kind,' he wrote in his covering letter. 'I think you will find in it an unmistakable (and quite terrible) authenticity. For that reason, and quite apart from its thrilling quality, it seems to me of great social and political importance in the present situation.' Puffs came in from Alec Waugh – 'I was held spellbound by it' – from J. B. Priestley – 'A superbly constructed story with an atmosphere of chilly hell' – and from Graham Greene – 'The best spy story I have ever read'. This last was perhaps the ideal publisher's quote, from the ideal source.

Advance copies were due on 9 August; publication was set for 12 September 1963. Towards the end of July Gollancz sold the paperback rights to Pan for £1,750, ten times as much as he had been bullied into paying for the book overall. The Pan royalties were split equally between the author and hardback publisher, ensuring a handsome dividend for Gollancz. Soon afterwards a book club, the Book Society, made it one of their choices for September. Though the royalties per copy from book-club editions were much smaller, their print runs were larger. By this time it was clear that Gollancz's efforts had been successful. Advance orders were such that the book was reprinted three times before publication. Sales were boosted by some excellent reviews. For the *Daily Telegraph*'s literary editor,

David Holloway, it was 'a brilliant, bitter novel'; for the *Time and Tide* reviewer, it was 'a masterpiece'; for Phyllis Bentley, writing in the *Yorkshire Post*, it was 'the spy story to end all spy stories'. Anthony Price, reviewing the book for the *Oxford Mail*, judged that the book set 'a new standard by which to judge spy thrillers'. The sole discordant note in this chorus of praise was heard in the pages of the *Times Literary Supplement*; the anonymous reviewer complained that 'the author . . . overstresses the thriller element in his story . . . It is to be feared that we still have to wait for the genuine unromanticised article foreshadowed by Mr Somerset Maugham's Ashenden stories . . .' The reviewer was Julian Maclaren-Ross.

Several of the reviewers suggested that the book provided an insight into the normally hidden world of espionage. 'Here is no bogus superman stuff, but what must be something like the real thing,' wrote the reviewer in the *Sunday Times*. 'This is really it,' proclaimed the *Scotsman*. 'The truth about the spy sub-world, the secret war between East and West that is always hot, may be revealed in a book out today,' speculated Kenneth Allsop in the *Daily Mail*, under the headline, 'Is this the Private Nightmare of a Master Spy?' The *Glasgow Herald* reviewer thought the book 'probably as convincing as any spy story ever written'. The bleakness of *The Spy who Came in from the Cold* helped to persuade the media that it must be authentic.

There was a further boost when it was taken by the Reprint Society, in an edition of 55,000 copies. The book continued to gather momentum in the period leading up to Christmas, entering the British bestseller lists some months after publication, when sales of novels usually flagged. Its sales were boosted further when the *Sunday Express* began to publish extracts, having bought serial rights for £500. The press baron Lord Beaverbrook, then in the last year of his life but still hungry for the latest new thing, had instructed the newspaper's editor, John Junor, to serialise the novel in full. These factors had helped to make *The Spy who Came in from the Cold* the most talked-about book of the season. By early October it was into its fifth impression, with 17,500 copies in print. It would continue to sell throughout the following year. By the middle of February 1964, some 30,000 had been sold, with 40,000 in print.[13] By the end of the year the book had reached its twentieth impression.

David consulted an accountant, Horace Hale Crosse (always known as 'Hale'), who advised him to stay out of England until at least 6 April 1965.

He would be allowed brief visits, but he should continue to live abroad if he wanted to avoid paying a very large tax bill. Among the objectives which David outlined to his new accountant was his desire to resign from the Foreign Service 'as soon as possible'.[14]

At some point after the film deal had been announced Ronnie arrived in Berlin, introducing himself as his younger son's 'professional adviser'. He graciously accepted a VIP tour of West Berlin's largest film studio, enjoyed a great deal of the studio's hospitality, and no doubt a starlet or two, and listened to a lot of earnest talk about tax breaks and subsidies available to foreign filmmakers. Neither his son nor anyone at Paramount had the least idea of what he was up to.[15]

Ronnie's movements in this period are hard to trace. He had once again separated from his second wife Jean, this time permanently. David believed that he was on the run from the police at this time. Perhaps too he was on the run from violent 'business associates': there is anecdotal evidence that he had become embroiled with the slum landlord Peter Rachman, whose property dealings were at root not wholly dissimilar from his own. Rachman had entrusted a West End nightclub to Reggie Kray, one of the Kray twins who would later become notorious as gangsters, though in the early 1960s they were often seen in the company of showbusiness and sporting celebrities, sexually adventurous politicians and raffish members of the aristocracy. It seems possible that Ronnie had had some dealings with the Krays which frightened him. There was certainly some connection. In the late 1980s, David's half-sister Charlotte, by then a well-known actress, was given a leading part in a film about the Kray twins, for which their brother Charlie was retained as a consultant. In an idle moment during the shooting, Charlotte allowed Charlie to show her an album of family photographs. Only half her mind was engaged as he leafed through the album – until she spotted a snap of her father, an arm around each twin.

For whatever reason, Ronnie left England, and would not return for several years. For a while he based himself in New York. The city's estate agents and their clients were offering a month's free accommodation to first-time tenants in new developments; Ronnie took a free month here, a free month there, using different names for each rental contract.

Around the time that *The Spy who Came in from the Cold* was published, David was posted to the Consulate-General in Hamburg. Within MI6 it has been claimed that he was willing in principle to leave the Foreign Office once the book had proved a success, but had asked to be kept on for tax reasons. David emphatically denies this story, which has the stink of disinformation. In any case his overt role, of trying to win German support for the British application to join the Common Market, had become redundant in January, when the French had vetoed the British bid. There are hints that the Foreign Office disapproved of *The Spy who Came in from the Cold*. Tony Duff likened writing to a dog returning to its vomit. David wrote to the Margetsons that he would have dedicated the book to the two of them, 'if Aunty FO didn't have such a stern look'.

The Cornwells moved into a house on the outskirts of Hamburg. They took walks along the nearby Upper Alster, and picked apples from trees in the garden to make juice. David's restlessness was obvious in a letter to Vivian Green, written in November 1963. He seemed to be contemplating returning to England to teach, 'as I am tired of the FO and tired of abroad. I don't really need to earn very much but we would like to buy a pleasant house almost anywhere rural and beautiful, and do something a bit useful . . .'

> I had in mind one of the new universities, and wondered if you know anything about them . . . Almost anything considered really, provided it enables me to settle Ann and the children in a decent, permanent home not too far from where I work, and let off political steam without offending anyone – that is, anyone who employs me. I would of course need time to write.[16]

Hale Crosse again warned him against coming back to England too soon: the very idea, he wrote, 'gives me cold shivers!!'[17]

Around this time Green's views of David were solicited for a fresh security check. The most likely explanation is that his security was being reassessed, prior to his becoming established in the Service after three years of probation. His unconsummated love affair in Bonn had come to the attention of SIS colleagues; perhaps this stimulated concern. David was no happier in his marriage, and spent much of his time away from home. Since the woman he loved had left Bonn, he was rarely able to see her, though they would keep up a passionate correspondence for the next two and a half years.

Around this time John Shakespeare ran into David in St James's Park. 'What are you doing here?' he asked. David explained that he was back from Hamburg, and busy writing his next book. 'How do you find the time?' asked Shakespeare. David explained that he worked through his lunch hours, and rarely went out in the evening. He was in England for a Gollancz publicity tour – 'a disgraceful flop', he wrote gloomily to Ann. He would not be the last author to find none of his books in the shops when he arrived after a long journey, and to be dismayed by interviews with ignorant journalists. He told her that he was 'quite flaked' and warned that 'there's going to be a row'. At the end of the letter he referred to the assassination of President Kennedy the previous day. 'I can't write any more after the Kennedy thing: it's just too dreadful.'[18]

Gollancz was impatient for another book like *The Spy who Came in from the Cold*. He told Peter Watt that he was 'exceedingly anxious' to have a long talk with David. 'After all, I have run *The Spy who Came in from the Cold* on a terrific scale – heaven knows how much I have spent on advertising! – and I am extremely anxious to confer about his future.' He held out the prospect that, 'provided we can establish the right kind of co-operation here, we may have a permanent best-selling author . . .'[19]

But David was not at his ease with Gollancz, who was forty years his senior. High-minded and energetic, Gollancz was either lovable, indeed saintly, or insufferably self-regarding, depending on your point of view. At Christmas he sent David a copy of a book he had recently published, E. P. Thompson's *The Making of the English Working Class* – perhaps an odd choice to give to an author who had just hit the big time. David invited Gollancz to join him for lunch to celebrate the success of *The Spy who Came in from the Cold*. It was unusual for an author to entertain a publisher, but David wanted to make a handsome gesture to show his appreciation, and he reserved a table at the Savoy Grill, unaware that his publisher lunched there almost every day. As they entered the restaurant the maître d'hôtel came forward. 'Good morning, Mr Gollancz. Your usual table by the window?' In vain David protested that he was the host, that he had made a reservation. They were led through the tables to one overlooking the river. As soon as they were seated, a waiter presented the menu. 'I'll have my usual,' said Gollancz, waving it away. And so the meal progressed. David felt afterwards that the occasion had not lived up to his expectations.[20]

David's response to the sudden acclaim had been to question his own talent. A number of critics had hinted that *The Spy who Came in from the Cold* had been a fluke. It was in this mood of self-doubt that David began writing the follow-up. Moreover he had come to perceive the intelligence community, on its knees after a succession of disasters, as a measure of the hapless state of the country. *The Looking-Glass War* is a story of incompetence and self-delusion. A washed-up unit of military intelligence, sustained only by the memory of wartime heroics,* decides to mount an operation: an ill-equipped agent is sent into East Germany to investigate insubstantial rumours of missile deployment. The agent, Leiser, is sacrificed to feed the fantasies of the ageing men in control of 'the Department'. The narrative of the final part of the book, 'Leiser's Run', bears some resemblance to 'Freedom', a short story David had written while in Bonn, about a Czech who tries to escape across the frontier into the West.†

David's misery in his marriage was high in his thoughts as he began planning the book. The protagonist, Avery – like David, a man in his mid-thirties – becomes alienated from his wife Sarah, who repeatedly questions the value of his work; his response is to suppress his own doubts. Ann came to believe that he had based the character of Sarah on her. 'There was a tension in her expression, an anxiety, and incipient discontent, as if tomorrow would only be worse,' he wrote of Sarah; 'somehow marriage had made her childish.' At one point Sarah snaps at her husband, 'don't try to run me like one of your wretched agents'.[21] Avery's middle-aged colleague, Woodford, is similarly undermined by his wife, who is both bitter and sarcastic in her disdain.

* The fact that 'the Department' was based in Baker Street during the war suggests an identification with SOE.

† The story has never been published.

Rubinstein's replacement at Gollancz was James MacGibbon, co-founder with Robert Kee in 1948 of a lively publishing house, which had recently been sold and broken up. Once he joined Gollancz as the next heir apparent, MacGibbon strove to woo their bestselling author. During a visit to America early in 1964, he wrote to David referring to 'the great sensation The Spy is creating in New York – I got reflected glory from being the English publisher'.[22] When David complained that he had heard reports of books being unavailable and bookshops saying that *The Spy* was out of print, MacGibbon wrote two letters of reassurance.[23] But David had private reservations about MacGibbon, a former member of the Communist Party who had worked in senior positions in military intelligence during the war. He knew that MacGibbon had passed secret information to a Soviet handler.[24]

David's discontent with Gollancz caused him to contemplate switching publishers. This was a delicate business, as the 'option clause' of the contract for *The Spy who Came in from the Cold* required David to give Gollancz the first offer of his next novel. Through Peter Watt he made a discreet approach to Charles Pick, managing director of Heinemann since its purchase by the conglomerate Tilling in 1962. Pick was a suave figure with a reputation for wiliness, known affectionately as 'Big Daddy'. He had begun his career in publishing at the age of sixteen as one of Gollancz's sales representatives, after his father's bankruptcy had left the family destitute. He and David met on a very foggy afternoon at a flat in Lowndes Square. David said he would like to join Heinemann, they shook hands, and he disappeared into the fog. Pick would hear nothing more from him for almost a year.

The success of *The Spy who Came in from the Cold* led to speculation about the author's identity – even from Graham Greene. 'I'm so glad that *The Spy who Came in from the Cold* has proved a winner,' he wrote to Victor Gollancz, soon after the book was published: 'it certainly deserved it.' He then asked about the book's author. 'I suppose it's asking too much of you to tell me even in confidence what his real name is? My only possible guess is that Blake has taken to writing novels during his first year sentence!'[25]

Perhaps it was inevitable that the press would uncover the real John le Carré sooner or later, especially as David had not concealed his identity from the *Observer*'s Bonn correspondent Neal Ascherson, and perhaps not from other members of the local press corps either. Early in the new year 1964 David was at his desk at the Hamburg Consulate when he received a telephone call from Nicholas Tomalin of the *Sunday Times*, who had been tipped off by the paper's Bonn correspondent, Anthony Terry. David felt forced into a half-truth: he readily admitted to being John le Carré, but protested that he was no spy. 'Any expertise I have on espionage is just a gimmick,' he claimed. 'If you sit in Government offices you pick up experience which can be translated to other spheres.' He conceded that his diplomatic work had given him 'great knowledge of the political situation in Germany'. Asked if he planned to leave the Foreign Service, he said that he had no such intention at present, though if he ever made a lot of money from his writing he might think about it. He denied that the Foreign Office was worried about his book. 'I won't say that they approved it, but I sent it to them first and they passed it, so they didn't disapprove.' The reason for keeping his name hidden was 'the usual Civil Service one', he told Tomalin. The *Sunday Times* printed an account of the telephone conversation in its 'Atticus' column, accompanied by a recent passport photograph of the author.[26]

David's 'outing' as John le Carré stimulated a fresh burst of attention from the press and renewed speculation that the book was based on real experience. The more that he denied this, the more the conviction grew. The timing of the revelation was propitious, only two days after his book had been published in America. The *New York Times* ran a story on him. *Time* magazine sent a photographer, who snapped David pressing against a wall and crouching self-consciously behind a bush in his garden as he pretended to play hide-and-seek with Ann and the boys; while the celebrated *Life* photographer Ralph 'Rudy' Crane shot pictures of a moody David standing outside a shop window in a dark backstreet, and a purposeful David striding out across some tracks against the background of the Hamburg docks. Press harassment increased to the point that the Cornwells were forced to flee their home, taking refuge with the Consul-General and his wife, while most of their possessions went into store. The switchboard at the Hamburg Consulate was kept busy with unwelcome enquiries. Such publicity was incompatible with the anonymity required of an SIS officer.

In an interview with the Chief back in London, he was told that he could no longer continue as a diplomat, but might carry on with some other form of cover, for example as a journalist or an academic. Apparently White told him that he was highly thought of within the Service, and even that he might be a candidate for 'the top job' in due course. David declined the offer of a role as a travelling interrogator.

White would deplore the impression of the Service left by *The Spy who Came in from the Cold*. 'John le Carré hasn't done us any good,' he is said to have told his American opposite number during a dinner in the 1960s. 'He makes all intelligence officers look like philanderers and drunks. He's presenting a service without trust or loyalty, where agents are sacrificed and deceived without compunction.' Le Carré's portrayal of cynicism, betrayal, defeatism and lack of conviction, he added, suggested that sacrifice for the good fight was not worthwhile. 'He's getting his revenge on the old-school ties in British intelligence,' White continued. 'He wants to show them who's on top.'[27]

In subsequent years David would often say that his resignation from SIS had been prompted by a cable from his accountant. He had given Hale Crosse instructions to inform him when his net worth reached £20,000; and when a cable had arrived confirming that his earnings had reached this target, he handed in his resignation.

Watt relayed a message from Jack Geoghegan that things were going very well across the Atlantic: an offer had come in from the Book of the Month Club. This was significant in itself, as the Club had more than a million members; but it also carried prestige, suggesting that the chosen book was a potential bestseller. Income was accumulating from the sale of book-club rights, condensed-book rights, serial rights, talking-book rights and omnibus editions, and from sales of foreign rights. The agency had now sold foreign-language rights in ten countries, with more offers coming in all the time; eventually the novel would be published in such comparatively obscure languages as Icelandic and Afrikaans. Many of the publishers bought rights in David's earlier books also. 'It seems as though The Spy is scooping the entire pool,' wrote Watt.[28]

A few weeks later David gave power of attorney to Hale Crosse, including the power to buy and sell investments in his name. He used his newfound wealth to provide for his relatives, many of whom had of course been cheated by his father: buying a flat for his stepmother, Jean; arranging for allowances to be paid to Ann's mother and sister; and employing his brother Tony as a part-time 'proof-reader', for an annual retainer of

$2,000. His mother was threatened with eviction from the cottage where she was living; he bought it, so that she could stay there.* Hale Crosse confessed to being 'rather shaken' at the number of dependants for whom he seemed to feel responsible.[29]

Around this time David met his old friend John Bingham for a cup of coffee in a Wimpy Bar. He described success on the scale which had come to him as 'like being in a car crash'.

Coward-McCann's publication of *The Spy who Came in from the Cold* was the culmination of months of planning. From the start Geoghegan had been determined to prove that a small, aggressive publishing house could do as well as a bigger one, given the right book. To persuade the trade to take *The Spy who Came in from the Cold* seriously, he had to overcome the widespread prejudice against 'suspense' novels. At the time, the market for these was dominated by cheap paperbacks. Geoghegan decided to put a quiet grey jacket on *The Spy who Came in from the Cold*, to indicate that it was a serious novel rather than a pulp thriller. He took advertising space in *Publishers Weekly*, comparing the book to Arthur Koestler's *Darkness at Noon*.

Geoghegan told his salesmen that *The Spy who Came in from the Cold* was the book to push. They were allowed to offer booksellers one free book for every ten ordered. He urged them to read it; having spent fourteen years on the road selling books himself before landing his own imprint, he knew the importance of personal commitment from the individual selling the book. Geoghegan also sent advance copies to salesmen in other publishing houses – an unusual measure, intended to generate talk within the trade. He announced that $10,000 had been earmarked for publicity, an extraordinary amount for a book by an unknown author. When

* Olive had been left destitute in Canada, when John Hill had run off to Las Vegas with a couple of girls and spent everything they had; but after she sent him a photograph of herself Ronnie had come to her rescue, providing £100 in travellers' cheques and air tickets back to England, both for her and for her daughter Alex. He had set her up in a Suffolk cottage; but some while after she had moved in, she received a letter informing her that she would have to leave, as the property was now in the hands of the Official Receiver.

the Graham Greene quote came in, he made full use of it, in advertisements and window streamers, on 35,000 matchbook covers (apparently the first time a book had ever been promoted in this way) and on an orange wrapper put around the jacket.

It was slow going to begin with. One major book club turned it down twice, before the Book of the Month Club took it, originally just as a 'mystery' for its 'One Dollar' book club, upgrading at the last moment to the more upmarket Literary Guild Alternate Selection. The *Reader's Digest* took it for its Condensed Book Club, after David's political views had been pronounced acceptable by contacts in the CIA. Serial rights were sold to *Show* magazine for $2,000, a respectable though not spectacular sum. Dell picked up the paperback rights for $25,000, which seemed a lot at the time but would come to look relatively modest.

Geoghegan reckoned that he needed to sell 50,000 copies to break even. By the end of November Coward-McCann had almost 60,000 on order – though of course these were orders from the bookstores, not sales. Geoghegan dropped another $10,000 into the promotion kitty, enough to fund a series of full-page advertisements.[30]

Publication on 10 January 1964 coincided with a major snowstorm over the New York area, by far the most important region for book sales. Potential buyers were reluctant to venture out to the stores. But the reviews vindicated Geoghegan's faith in the book. The *New York Times* reviewer praised it 'both as a compelling and dazzlingly plotted thriller and as a substantial and penetrating novel of our times', acknowledging that the book had raised the genre to a higher level: it was 'a light year removed from the sometimes entertaining trivia which have (in the guise of spy novels) cluttered the publishers' lists for the past year' – perhaps a reference to Ian Fleming's *On Her Majesty's Secret Service*, which had been a fixture on the American bestseller list for the previous six months or so.[31] This was one of several reviews to suggest that *The Spy who Came in from the Cold* had rendered the James Bond novels obsolete. In fact *On Her Majesty's Secret Service* would be the last of Fleming's books to appear in his lifetime, since he was to die of a heart attack that same summer.

As the storm lifted, orders began to pile in by the thousand, so that Coward-McCann's sales manager was forced to ration stock on hand. Within a month 45,000 copies had been sold.[32] *The Spy who Came in from the Cold* entered the American Bestseller List at no. 7 on 26 January 1964; four weeks later it reached no. 1.

Now that he had quit his job, David was footloose, though he had to remain abroad another fourteen months to avoid paying tax. He decided that the family should head for Agios Nikolaos in Crete, perhaps an unlikely destination – chosen, according to Ann, on the recommendation of a man whom David had met in a swimming pool. But Ann had always dreamed of going to Greece, and at the time it seemed as good a choice as any other. Neither of them spoke Greek.

In mid-March the Cornwells, with their three children and a new nanny, travelled by train from Germany to Venice, where they were eventually able to board a boat bound for Crete – but not before David was obliged to bribe customs officials to release their impounded luggage.[33] Four days after leaving Hamburg, at six o'clock on a grey March morning, they found themselves at the end of a long jetty in the port of Heraklion, surrounded by four large trunks and about twenty suitcases, while the children clutched various soft toys. Nobody else had disembarked. Agios Nikolaos was forty miles distant, across a mountain range. David left his family on the deserted quay and set off on foot, eventually returning with two taxis. A couple of hours later they arrived at their destination in torrential rain. Their youngest boy, Timothy, had been sick during the drive.

Agios Nikolaos was not then the busy resort it would later become. In 1964 it was still a quiet little fishing port, shabby and dusty, with few facilities and only basic accommodation. Food was sparse. The local women were clad in black from head to foot, and the men often carried guns. Today thousands of tourists descend on the town every summer; in the early 1960s only a handful of foreigners ventured there, mostly what were then known as drop-outs.

The plan was to spend a few days in a hotel while they looked for a house to rent. Still reluctant to spend too much money, David had reserved rooms at a modest pension rather than at the one smart hotel in town; since it had no restaurant, the Cornwells ate their meals at the simple café next door. David rashly let it be known that he was looking for a house to rent; within two hours he was standing on the steps of his pension, besieged by importunate locals like Gordon facing the mob at Khartoum. It seemed that every house in town was available for rent.

After a few days they moved into an apartment: the top floor of a stone Venetian-style building set well into the rocks, with a long balcony overlooking the caiques moored in the bay below. The local sponge fishermen spread out their catch for sorting on a grassy slope beside the house. The view was splendid, the amenities less so. Running water was available for a maximum of three hours each day. Their landlady, who lived downstairs, scattered holy water around the house with a branch and crossed herself whenever Ann raised her voice; obligingly she informed them that their maid was a thief. Scorpions invaded the house and hid under the furniture, or crawled into the boys' shoes. One night, while Ann was reading in bed, a large centipede dropped on to her book and scuttled away.

For David, the months that followed were the most wretched of his married life. He regretted coming to this remote and inaccessible part of Greece, where no amount of money could procure comfort. He was repelled by the prevalent deprivation. 'I find I cannot live close to poverty,' he wrote at the time. 'I cannot get used to the dispassion with which wealthy Greeks contemplate their impoverished compatriots; to the arid, crumbling villages where only the very young and the very old remain, waiting for their different kinds of release . . .'[34]

As David did not feel rich enough to buy a second-hand car – and in those days there were no cars available to hire – they were dependent on buses and taxis to get around. It would take him a while to grasp that he could now afford almost anything he wanted. In the decade since he had broken with his father he had lived carefully; the habit took some time to wear off.

Until the sun began to shine in May it was surprisingly cold, made worse by a strong wind; it snowed in mid-April. David found the apartment itself noisy and difficult to work in. There was little congenial company in the area, and it seemed that he and Ann now had nothing to say to each other. She wanted them to explore the Minoan sites on the island; he was determined to work. 'I hate ruins,' he admitted to a friend. During the months they spent in Greece he often went abroad, leaving Ann on her own with the children for weeks on end. While on Crete, he took long walks dreaming of his beloved, and telephoned his agent on the slightest pretext, though making overseas calls involved long waits in a booth at the local post office. A local official accused him of spying for the Turks and asked for a bribe as the price of his silence. Somebody claiming to be a Czech writer insisted on coming out to Crete to see him. Each time they met in local cafés, David was certain that they were under surveillance. He deduced that Czech intelligence was trying to recruit him, and felt sufficiently concerned to consult the head of the Athens station. It was as if he were Alec Leamas, just discharged from prison; life was imitating art.

David had been in Crete only a few weeks when he received a terse telegram from Geoghegan: 'COME OVER NOW'. He left the island with relief, stopping in London to collect two literary prizes, the Crime Writers' Association Gold Dagger* and the Somerset Maugham Award,† and flew on the next day, his head already reeling, to New York.

His plane had already landed and was taxiing to its resting-place when he became aware that a 'Mr Lee Carr' was being paged. David identified himself to a stewardess and learned that special arrangements had been made for him on the ground: a limousine was waiting at the foot of the steps. Inside was his publisher, a handsome man in his mid-forties with dark wavy hair. The bemused young novelist was driven straight to a packed press conference at the Plaza Hotel. As cameras flashed and microphones were pushed towards his face, David realised that he was famous.

At the press conference and in interviews afterwards, he tried to maintain the line that he had been nothing more than a simple civil servant. He was therefore thrown when a journalist 'with connections' told him out of the corner of

* The Crime Writers' Association (CWA) has long taken the view that thriller writers qualify for their awards. In 1988 David would be awarded the CWA's Diamond Dagger, only the third writer (after Eric Ambler and P. D. James) to receive it. The award, a silver book with a diamond-encrusted dagger plunged into the pages, has become recognised as the highest accolade a crime writer can earn. It is given for a lifetime of achievement: the career of the winner 'must be marked by sustained excellence', and he or she 'must have made a significant contribution to crime fiction published in the English language'. To celebrate the golden jubilee of the Gold Dagger in 2005, CWA members voted for the 'Dagger of Daggers'; the winner was *The Spy who Came in from the Cold*.

† Awarded jointly to John le Carré for *The Spy who Came in from the Cold* and to Dan Jacobson for *Time of Arrival*.

his mouth that White himself had blown his cover to the former Director of the CIA, Allen Dulles, who had made free with the information.[35]

For the next week David was in 'fairyland'. His book was already a sensation; now everything he said was news, or so it seemed. He couldn't go into restaurants without being recognised. Wherever he went, people wanted to shake his hand. Everyone wanted a piece of him. He was interviewed in the press and on television. Women propositioned him. It was intoxicating, flattering and terrifying.

One evening Geoghegan escorted David to the 21 Club for dinner. As they were being shown to their table, David was startled to spot Ronnie seated in a corner, behind a large brandy and ginger. It was immediately obvious to him that this was an ambush: his father had prevailed on his publisher's good nature to arrange a rendezvous. Sure enough, Geoghegan suggested that Ronnie join them for dinner. Proudly patting David's arm, with tears in his eyes, Ronnie told him that he hadn't been a bad father, had he, son? And we've done all right together, haven't we, then? Throughout the evening, as the champagne flowed, Ronnie made repeated and unsettling references to '*our* book'. His line seemed to be that, having paid for David's education (or at least some of it), he was now entitled to share in the rewards. After all, Geoghegan added, 'he put you through college, didn't he?' Out on the sidewalk afterwards Ronnie gave David one of his bear-hugs.

'You may be a successful writer, son,' he said through his tears, 'but you're not a *celebrity*.' And leaving David with this warning, he set off nobly into the night.

Arguably, Ronnie's judgement was vindicated when David appeared with two lookalikes on the popular CBS television programme *To Tell the Truth*, sponsored by the manufacturers of 'Easy-Off' oven cleaner. Panellists were entitled to cross-examine three Englishmen before guessing which of them was the real John le Carré. One of the four panellists claimed to have read *The Spy who Came in from the Cold*, which, she judged, was 'just peachy'. Nonetheless she, with all her fellow panellists, identified the wrong man.[36]

Some while earlier, Burt Lancaster had withdrawn from the film of *The Spy who Came in from the Cold*. While David was in New York, it was reported that Richard Burton had been signed to play Alec Leamas instead, for a fee said to be more than a quarter of a million pounds, against 29 per cent of the gross take. David received the news in a telephone call from an ecstatic Jack Geoghegan. Burton was then a major movie star, not least because of his romance with Elizabeth Taylor, which had made the pair perhaps the most famous couple in the world at the time. Their affair had begun when they co-starred in the big-budget epic *Cleopatra*, attracting enormous publicity. Since both were married, this created a public scandal, resulting in lurid headlines across the globe. Burton had since divorced his wife and married Taylor.

He was in New York at the time, playing *Hamlet* in a production directed by John Gielgud, who spoke the part of the Ghost. This was one of the most talked-about shows on Broadway. After each night's performance crowds gathered outside the theatre to catch a glimpse of Burton, and sometimes Taylor. An excited Geoghegan told David that he would take him to see the show, and afterwards introduce him to Burton.

In his dressing room Burton was very charming and spoke graciously about the book. David responded that his Hamlet was better than Olivier's – better even than Gielgud's, he went on recklessly, though amid this torrent of mutual compliments he was secretly uneasy about the prospect of Burton playing Leamas.[37]

While in New York, David replied to a 'wonderful letter' from C. P. Snow, who had written to say that he and his wife (the novelist Pamela Hansford Johnson) 'rejoice in your success'. Snow had already given Gollancz a favourable quote for *The Spy who Came in from the Cold*, but in this letter he went much further. 'People don't seem to realise what a deep novelist in the deepest and fullest sense, you are,' Snow wrote tautologously. 'You make most writers look like ignorant and bad-mannered school children.' Snow was then at the height of his fame, an influential figure in the worlds of literature, politics and academia, bestowing patronage on young novelists of whom he approved. Attention from such a source was flattering; David sent an effusive letter of thanks. 'There is no one, no living writer, whose judgement I value more than your own,' he replied; and suggested that he might call on Snow once he returned to England from Greece the following year.[38]

David's arrival in America to promote the book boosted sales of the novel, which by mid-May approached 180,000. Eventual sales were well over 200,000 in hard cover. *The Spy who Came in from the Cold* remained at the top of the US bestseller list for thirty-five weeks, becoming the best-selling novel of 1964. It was still one of the top ten bestsellers more than a year after publication. No other spy novel had ever done so well. For Coward-McCann, which became Coward, McCann & Geoghegan, it was the best year in the firm's history. Even for Walker & Co., the book proved a bonanza. On the back of its success, they were able to sell paperback rights in David's first two novels for a substantially higher price than they might otherwise have expected. Walker reissued them in a single omnibus volume entitled *The Incongruous Spy*, which became a Book of the Month Club Alternative Selection.[39]

The Spy who Came in from the Cold changed David's life irrevocably. As he was slowly coming to appreciate, he would never again be short of money, provided that he kept writing. While this opened up many possibilities, it also created problems. His enormous success would attract envy, even in those who loved him. An early indication of this came at Coward-McCann's stylish party for David, held at the 21 Club. Among the guests was David's brother Tony, who had protected him at school and comforted him throughout his motherless boyhood. Tony aspired to write the Great Novel; for years he had tried to save his earnings to buy himself time to write. By a strange coincidence he dreamed of escaping to a Greek island where he could work undisturbed. But the ambition seemed more elusive than ever; he had become a husband, and then a father, and now had a steady job in advertising to pay the mortgage. It was painful for him to watch David being lionised as a novelist, the very thing he wanted most for himself. It seemed to Tony that his little brother had left him far behind. At the party Tony tried to drown his jealousy in drink, with predictable results. Distressed to see him in such a state, his wife dragged him away.

Afterwards Tony was mortified by his behaviour. Almost half a century later he wrote David a letter in which he tried to explain his feelings, and apologised 'with all my heart'.

13

Naïve and sentimental love

David flew back to Crete via Rome, laden with presents for the family. Ann met him at the airport, obviously tense: she lost her temper with a young woman at the counter when David's luggage appeared to have gone astray. On the drive back to Agios Nikolaos, she showed no interest in what had happened to him in New York, and spoke only of scorpions.

Ann's attitude to David's success felt to him grudging and ungracious. His achievement apparently meant nothing to her. She seemed anxious to reclaim him, from a life of excitement and glamour to one of tedium and routine. In New York he had been fêted; in Crete he received nothing but disapprobation, or so it seemed. She gave him no credit for the restraint he had shown in resisting advances from other women while he was away – though she could hardly have done so, because he had not told her about it. Ann was wary of the brash, moneyed, 'Americanised' milieu into which he had been introduced, which seemed alarmingly like Ronnie's world, the world from which she had rescued him. For her, *The Spy who Came in from the Cold* was a source not of pride but of danger; in later years she would say that its success had ruined their marriage. Nevertheless she undertook to type the first draft of his new novel.

Both were appalled when an American agent, Alvin Ferleger of Ashley-Famous, followed David to Crete in an attempt to persuade him to write an outline for a television series – one that, he promised, would 'net you millions'. Ferleger and other similar suitors were all too reminiscent of Ronnie's business associates. David felt confused and alienated at becoming 'a property'.

Ann's mother was a further strain, now divorced from her second husband and a regular visitor to the Cornwell household. David's initial affection for her had become replaced by a strong dislike. To him, she appeared preoccupied with needless feminine detail that sheltered her from having to recognise the important things in life. Her experiences with men had led her to brand them as innately unreliable, callous, lecherous and brutal; and David felt that she was perpetually looking for signs of these qualities in him. Her repeated presence in Crete was one of the reasons why he fled abroad on the slightest pretext.

Besides, there was a new lure to draw him away. David had become closer to the Kennaways, to James in particular. Earlier in the year he had stayed with them at the manor farmhouse in Gloucestershire which they rented from Susan's father. Writing about this visit years afterwards, Susan recalled 'lots of jokes, funny voices, excursions . . . David telling stories to the boys, conjuring shillings out of their ears and generally making himself an extremely amiable guest'. The two young writers talked all the time, 'discussing George Orwell or Ortega y Gasset* or the novel or the film, or just themselves'.[1] Repeatedly they explored ways to 'beat the system'. James saw himself as an artist, perpetually at war with the crassness and corruption of the commercial world. Under James's influence, David began to refer to agents, publishers, accountants and other professional advisers as 'con men'.

James Kennaway was a handsome, virile, charismatic man, three years older than David, with easy charm and a winning manner, strongly committed to his writing, determined to 'blaze in every direction'. His father had died suddenly in his mid-forties, leaving him with a powerful sense of urgency; he had resolved not to 'sink with too much left undone, too much never tried, too many sensations missed'.[2] He had become a much praised novelist, and a successful and highly paid screenwriter.

Susan was a stylish beauty, her dark hair set in a fashionable bob. David found her enchanting – though somewhat in James's shadow. The Kennaways' marriage seemed to him to have everything that his own lacked. In fact it was tested by James's repeated infidelity. From boyhood Kennaway had recognised two sides to his nature, 'James' and 'Jim'. James

* José Ortega y Gasset (1883–1955), influential Spanish philosopher and essayist.

was quiet and studious, enthusiastic and eager to please, a domesticated man constrained by society; Jim was an actor strutting the stage, often outrageous and exuberant, the master manipulator, a boy who should be allowed unlimited licence, above all the freedom to sleep with as many women as he wanted. 'You need a different woman for each book,' he would tell David. To Susan, he would justify his philandering as 'an essential part of the creative process of his writing, a necessity'.[3]

Kennaway claimed a philosophical underpinning to this thirst for experience. From Ortega y Gasset he had absorbed the idea that the novelist is involved in the process of writing his own life. He had come to believe that in order to write about triumph and disaster, he had first to experience them himself. There was therefore a tendency in him to push things to extremes.[4] He often quoted Scott Fitzgerald's dictum that the obligation of early success is to lead a romantic life.* David understood this to mean that one should identify one's own private standards, and adhere to them.[5]

Kennaway had been in New York while David was there, researching a possible film about the life of the war photographer Robert Capa (another energetic womaniser). David had sought his advice about a screenplay for *The Looking-Glass War*, which seemed certain to be adapted into a film. Already a large sum had been offered for the rights, sight unseen. Guy Trosper's changes to *The Spy who Came in from the Cold* had made David uneasy: in particular that Leamas, instead of punching a grocer and going to jail for this, was to be confined in a psychiatric hospital. David resolved to script the film of the new book himself, or at least not to allow it outside his control. In New York he and Kennaway had 'cooked up' a plan to collaborate on a screenplay.

The relationship between the two men quickly became very close. Shortly after returning to Crete David wrote to James, addressing him as 'my new mate and mucker'; the letter's margin has 'CORNCRAKE AND KENNAWAY ARE SOUL MATES' written in large capitals in the margin, between a succession of cartoons.[6] He expressed confidence that they would soon be working together on a screenplay for *The Looking-Glass War*. The producer/director Karel Reisz was interested in adapting

* 'The compensation of a very early success is a conviction that life is a romantic matter. In the best sense one stays young.'[7]

it. David liked what he had heard about Reisz, best known for *Saturday Night and Sunday Morning*, based on Alan Sillitoe's novel. His most recent feature had been a film of *Night Must Fall*, the Emlyn Williams play that had so enthralled David when he saw it as a boy in Bournemouth.

On 30 May 1964 David reported that his new book was finished. 'It should be in my hands next week,' Peter Watt wrote to Victor Gollancz on 11 June. As Gollancz was leaving imminently for a holiday on the Continent, it was agreed that the typescript should be submitted to his daughter Livia. She forwarded a copy to her father at the Hotel Danieli in Venice, with a note explaining that only the first two-thirds was finished. 'The last third is, he considers, in a very rough state indeed.'[8]

Jack Geoghegan, who saw the typescript first, thought it too dark, and requested rewriting. He wanted more action and less gloom; for his sake David introduced a sub-plot of rivalry between the Department and the Circus, and tried to brighten up the book in various ways that he has since forgotten – though it remains a very bleak book, so either this attempt failed or it must have been even more depressing in its original form. *The Looking-Glass War* would be the only one of David's books altered radically at an editor's request. He would come to regret making these changes:

> I should not have pulled my punches. I should have let the Department exist where I was convinced . . . that Britain herself existed, and in some eerie way contrives to exist until this very day: in a vapour of self-delusion and class arrogance, in a gung-ho world of 'we've-never-had-it-so-good' bordered on one side by our supposed external enemies – the Europeans, the Russians, you name it – and on the other by an illusory conviction that our island can live off its colonial heritage and the favour of its American Cousins for all time.[9]

Later, in an attempt to explain what he was trying to say in the book, David would write an open letter to his American publisher, which Geoghegan printed and distributed in advance of publication. As originally written, the plot drew on David's perception (which proved true) that the Western intelligence services in Germany had been penetrated to the hilt: agents inserted into East Germany were rarely seen again.

One minor change was that Coward-McCann preferred to do without the hyphen in the title. 'Do it your way and vive la différence,' David cabled Geoghegan. More recent British editions have appeared without the hyphen.

Gollancz was keen to publish the novel, whatever its shortcomings. From Venice he wrote David an enthusiastic letter in his own hand. *The Looking-Glass War* was 'quite magnificent', he wrote. 'It's every bit as exciting as Spy.' David was in London to discuss film rights in the new book. Again he stayed with the Kennaways. He left a typescript of *The Looking-Glass War* with James, and arranged to spend the second half of August with him working on a treatment.

Gollancz was still abroad when David met his daughter Livia and James MacGibbon at a publishing party in London. A few days later Peter Watt came to see them. Obviously embarrassed, Watt delivered a succession of complaints: David felt that they had published *The Spy who Came in from the Cold* badly and sold far fewer than they ought to have done; Victor himself was paternalistic and always giving advice; David had heard a rumour that the firm was up for sale. Watt then told them that David wanted a commitment to three books, with an advance of £6,000 for each. Consulted by telephone, Gollancz immediately agreed to the proposed terms, and was disconcerted when these were not immediately accepted. On his return from Venice, he was incensed to learn that Watt was negotiating with Heinemann. 'I can remember nothing since I started publishing in 1922 that has astonished me so much,' he wrote in a furious letter to David. He threatened legal action if the option clause was not honoured, and desisted only after Watt persuaded him to back down.[10] Even then he continued to fulminate. The *Evening Standard*'s 'Londoner's Diary' reported him as saying: 'In my own time, I shall tell the whole story of the le Carré affair – an affair of the gravest import to every publisher in the land.'

It rankled with Gollancz that his bestselling author had been poached by a man to whom he had given 'his first chance in publishing': he found it difficult to accept that David had chosen to go to Charles Pick rather than stay with him. 'Why would anyone want to leave a West End Jew for an East End Jew?'*

* One of Gollancz's more endearing qualities was his apparently inexhaustible stock of Jewish jokes.

David returned to Crete, to resume work on a second draft of *The Looking-Glass War*. He had hired Liz Tollinton,* who had worked at MI5, to be his secretary; she came to Agios Nikolaos and was billeted in a hotel a few hundred yards away. Early in August the Margetsons arrived for a visit. Miranda was by this time three months pregnant, and John was naturally very attentive to her. Though David was an entertaining host, as charming and amusing as ever, he was noticeably frustrated not to have more time alone with his friend. In mid-August, he left for Paris, to join James Kennaway.

The fortnight that followed was bacchanalian. Kennaway was exhilarating if hair-raising company: David trailed in his wake as he prowled the pavements for prostitutes, brought woman after woman back to their hotel and explored bars, nightclubs and brothels. Kennaway was capable of taking two women to bed in an afternoon, drinking all night and being ready for work the next morning. He argued that an active sex life, far from being a distraction, was a stimulus to his writing. For David, this seemed almost too good to be true. James was a *real* writer, whose life expressed his art: a philosopher, a poet, an adventurer. He was reckless where David was timid; James embraced life, while David stood on the sidelines. James goaded him to take advantage of the sexual opportunities available on every street-corner, urging him to shed his bourgeois scruples, but David held back, still shy and fearful.

Kennaway had brought with him to Paris the manuscript of a play adapted from his novel *Household Ghosts*, due to be tried out in Stratford, Ontario, that autumn.† In a letter to Susan he boasted that David 'loved the play'. If this was true, the admiration was mutual. 'I'm truly amazed by David,' wrote Kennaway. 'Believe me, he didn't get here by luck. The head is strong and the heart a much hunted one.' A subsequent letter suggests that he felt his talent inferior to David's. 'As much as possible I'm trying to

* In November 1963 David had given her a copy of *The Spy who Came in from the Cold*, inscribed 'To Liz, with love from John le Carré' and illustrated with cartoons of 'Rugged Leamas' and 'Mixed-up Liz', which suggests she may have been the inspiration for Leamas's girlfriend, Liz Gold.

† After many changes *Country Dance* was eventually staged at the Hampstead Theatre Club in 1967 by the director James Roose-Evans, and afterwards had a short run at the Lyceum Theatre, Edinburgh. It was adapted into a 1970 film starring Peter O'Toole and Susannah York, released in the USA under the title *Brotherly Love*.

get it all out of him, and sometimes I feel I'm way behind,' he admitted. 'David has a very big nut, good for plotting with.' The fortnight together had cemented their friendship. 'David and I are inseparable chums.'[11]

By contrast, Karel Reisz, who joined them in Paris, was obviously irritated by Kennaway's self-indulgence. Although only a couple of years older, Reisz was more mature and serious: he had escaped from Nazi-controlled Czechoslovakia as a child; his parents had died in Auschwitz. In the late stages of the war he had served as a pilot with one of the RAF's Czechoslovak squadrons. 'Some of us seem to find it very hard to grow up,' he snapped at Kennaway in a difficult moment. Stung by this rebuke, Kennaway was doubly upset that David did not immediately spring to his defence. It was clear that Reisz saw him as more of a nuisance than a help. Relations between them deteriorated to the extent that David contemplated telling Reisz to leave; but they patched things up enough to continue. From a letter that David sent afterwards to his publisher, it is clear that the discussions between the three men in Paris were at least as much about the novel as about the film. 'I have spent the last eight days with Karel Reisz and James Kennaway talking of nothing but the book, and in doing so I have considerably clarified in my own mind what I am trying to say,' he wrote.

> The outer story of incompetence, ministerial rivalry and self-interest, the echoes of war, the restlessness of old soldiers, is pretty well told, I think. But the inner story of ritual sacrifice is not quite effective because of the lamb – Leiser. If the half-people, the impotent and inward-looking men, are to destroy a life, a life-force almost, it seems to me mistaken to have him almost half spent. I think Leiser must be a young man and someone we can really love. We must watch the destruction of someone far more vigorous than Leiser as he now is.[12]

'JIM, you have done more for me in a week than I have done for anyone else in a lifetime,' David wrote on Kennaway's draft of the script, though one suspects that he was referring more to his friend's liberating influence than to his assistance with the writing.[13]

When the time came for Kennaway to go back to England, the two could hardly bear to part, so David decided to accompany Kennaway on the drive to the Normandy coast, where he would take the ferry back to

England. Near Barfleur they dozed for a while in the car, and on waking he confided to Kennaway some of his most intimate secrets, revealing how miserable and lonely he felt in his marriage. The only other person with whom he had shared his innermost feelings was the woman in Bonn: she and James were his two loves, as he then saw it.

David returned to Paris for a day or two before flying back to Greece. A dreamy letter written shortly afterwards gives a sense of the euphoria of that fortnight together in Paris. 'Cher Jeem, I think you went off with both copies of the treatment you lovely boy,' wrote David. 'Paris was empty without you, quite empty . . . It was all *lovely* . . . bonne, bonne chance with your play you great big *positive person*.'[14]

Kennaway had returned to his wife in England 'with many tales of happy, funny, outrageous and awful days spent together with David'. He told Susan that his new friend did not seem to be a very happy person, dissatisfied with his marriage and until recently very short of money. The success of *The Spy who Came in from the Cold* had taken him by surprise, 'and he was quite unprepared for it'. From what James said it appeared to her that David's life up to this point had been comparatively restrained. She deduced that he had professed to need help with the scriptwriting only as an excuse to get to know James better.[15]

Hale Crosse had come over to Paris to meet David while he was there. His efforts were concentrated on attempts to reduce the amount of tax his client would have to pay. The top rates of tax at the time were considered by many punitive: 88.75 per cent in the UK on income in excess of £15,000 a year, and an even higher rate, 91 per cent, in the USA – with surtax or supertax (tax on tax) on top. In reality very few of those on large incomes paid these rates, as accountants devised intricate schemes to minimise their liability. After consulting a specialist lawyer and 'an intensive period of brain flogging', Hale Crosse had found a loophole in David's tax position, which he thought might be exploited to considerable advantage: to sell *The Looking-Glass War* to Heinemann outright.[16] Coward-McCann would underwrite Heinemann's purchase of the rights by guaranteeing $370,000 of the cost. They could well afford to do so, having received an offer from Dell of $380,000 for the paperback rights alone. The British paperback publisher, Pan, contributed a further £50,000, an exceptionally large advance for paperback rights, encouraged by the huge sales of their edition of *The Spy who Came in from the Cold.** The eventual sum paid by Heinemann for English-language rights in *The Looking-Glass War* was approximately £145,000:† a remarkable increase on the advance of £175 paid by Gollancz for *The Spy who Came in from the Cold.*

At Hale's recommendation a company was formed, to take over David's income once he returned to live in the UK. David became an employee of le Carré Productions Limited, to which he assigned all his copyrights.

The Cornwells' stay on Crete was coming to an end; Ann had found a house to rent from the beginning of September on the fashionable island of Spetsai, which was less remote, being only two hours from Athens by hydrofoil. David wanted the Kennaways to join them and take the house next to theirs; but even if they had been tempted to do so, James was in no condition to travel, having succumbed to glandular fever on his return from Paris.

Over the next couple of months David sent him several further letters, addressing him affectionately as 'lovely boy' and 'golden boy'. He was reading Kennaway's novels for the first time, and his letters glow with praise. 'Jeem boy, you really got it,' he wrote in one of these. 'In a big way. Far bigger than most of us lot. So for Gawd's *sake* take your silly finger out and give. Write bigger books with more crap in them . . . But oh Jim if you love us at all write.'[17]

David's faith in his talent was clearly important to Kennaway, who was struggling to write a new novel himself, without much success. Looking back at this period a year later, he acknowledged that David's appearance in his life 'had several effects – envy, love, the idea that I was after all an artist of integrity who could help, and a man to set others free . . .'

The Cornwells stayed in Spetsai only a few weeks before moving on to Vienna for the winter. They rented the top floor of a grand house on the Hohe Warte, an apartment recently vacated by the conductor Herbert von

* By 30 December 1966 the Pan edition had sold 850,000 copies.

† A payment of £99,714 on signature of the contract, followed by the sterling equivalent of $70,000 on 31 March 1966, plus a further £22,500 in two more stages.

Karajan, who had lived there during his tenure as director of the Vienna State Opera. Ann was told that the Maestro would order his minions to telephone from the theatre as he left, so that when he arrived all the doors would be open and the household gathered to greet him.

In Vienna David was soon being lionised by the Austro-Hungarian nobility. It helped of course that he spoke fluent German. At one dinner party a countess laid her hand on his knee and left it there through the meal. Ann was uncomfortable at such grand gatherings. She felt neglected by her husband, having to fight off unwanted advances by other men without his protection.

They had moved to Vienna because David thought that he might set a novel there. He had clear memories of his visits to the Austrian capital fifteen years earlier, when Austria was still occupied by the Allied powers, and Vienna itself was divided into sectors like Berlin. It was in many ways a suitable setting for a spy story: a melodramatic city of intrigue and scandal, unforgettably evoked in Carol Reed's 1949 film *The Third Man*, conceived and written by Graham Greene. For his new novel, David planned to write about a revived German nationalist movement, drawing on his experiences while stationed in Bonn. He consulted the Nazi-hunter Simon Wiesenthal, who helped him to construct a convincing past for the movement's leader, Karfeld. In Vienna David was able to hear first-hand the language of uninhibited anti-Semitism, which in post-war Germany was rarely heard in public, from embarrassment if not from decency. 'If you are studying the disease,' Wiesenthal advised, 'you have to live in the swamp.'

In mid-November David returned to London to deliver the final version of *The Looking-Glass War* to his agent. Among those thanked in the foreword was 'my friend James Kennaway, to whom this book is dedicated, for his generous advice'. (This acknowledgement was removed before the book was printed, though the dedication remained.) The end of the book had been rewritten, to include an appearance by George Smiley, rather as he appears at the end of *The Spy who Came in from the Cold*.

While in London David met the new scriptwriter for *The Spy who Came in from the Cold*, Paul Dehn, a replacement for Guy Trosper, who had fallen ill. Dehn was an Englishman; David was relieved to find that he had no patience with psychiatric hospitals and no compunction about punching grocers. An experienced screenwriter, a gay man nicknamed 'King of the Queens', Dehn had won an Oscar for his film *Seven Days to Noon*, and had recently adapted Ian Fleming's *Goldfinger* for the screen. David particularly admired his film *Orders to Kill*, about the assassination of a suspected double agent in the French Resistance. Dehn had been in SOE during the war, and for a while had been stationed at SOE's training camp (Camp X) in Canada, so he knew his subject. When in due course his script arrived, David was not surprised to find that he liked it.

David had arranged to spend a weekend with the Kennaways at their house in Highgate before going back to Vienna.[18] On his first evening they were due to go out to a formal dinner and pressed him to come too. David was reluctant, saying that he had nothing suitable to wear; but James devised two outfits from one, lending David his dress trousers and a velvet jacket, while he wore the dinner jacket and a pair of worn blue trousers. The pair of them spent the evening joking and privately sending up their stuffy hosts.

The three went on to a nightclub, where they found some friends in celebratory mood. James invited a couple of girls from the club to join them. In the smoky gloom the group could not find a table large enough to seat them all; David gripped Susan by the hand and steered her to a separate table some distance away from the others, where they sat talking. While James was out of earshot, she confided that she wanted a 'small revenge' on her husband for his womanising.[19] She had never taken a lover, she said, though James had often suggested that she should do so. 'What about me?' asked David. Until that moment it had not occurred to Susan that he might be interested in her; she assumed that she was merely confiding in a friend. But the look in his eye, and the way he clutched her when they stood up for a last dance, caused her to feel a sudden thump of excitement.

Eventually the three of them left. Though by now quite drunk, James took the wheel of the car to drive home; David and Susan sat in the back seat, holding hands in the darkness. When they arrived at the house James was tired, so he went straight to bed. David and Susan stayed up talking for a while before saying goodnight. She found it difficult to sleep and rose early, to find David awake too. At dawn they stood by a window together, watching the sun come up over London. By now they were impatient to be alone. David was about to leave for Vienna, but he promised to return soon. In the meantime they would write to each other poste restante; David would send his letters to the post office in Curzon Street, just along the road from MI5. Susan stumbled through the rest of the day in a daze. That evening the three of them went to see Truffaut's 1962 film *Jules et Jim* – perhaps because Oskar Werner, the actor who played Jules, had been cast to play the part of Fiedler in *The Spy who Came in from the Cold*. The film tells the story of two men determined to preserve their friendship despite being in love with the same woman. Susan sat between James and David in the darkened cinema, each clasping her nearer hand.[20]

From Vienna, David wrote to thank James for a 'glorious' and 'splendid' weekend:

> How super it all was; and – can I say it? – what a lease of life you've given me. How much more *difficult* you make writing for me, which must be a good thing; how much more worth while . . . I'd take your talent for my success any day – because your prose has the tension of someone really at the edge – glimpses of the unbound – and I know, if I know anything, that there will be more . . . I don't think I can give you anything like all this in return . . . while I don't think I can offer you much more than admiration for your own work, I think I can still be trusted to pick you off the street if ever you need it . . .
>
> Your mate Corncrake[21]

David returned to London early in December, and met Susan at a smart hotel near Oxford Street. He was very nervous, terrified of exposure, divorce and scandal. At lunchtime they drove out to Heathrow Airport and drank cocktails. Almost fifty years later Susan remembered David telling her how unhappy he was with Ann, complaining that she was glum and moody; according to him, she would sit for hours listening to music, neglecting the children and the housework. He said that he had married her only because instructed to do so by MI5, as an entrée into left-wing circles. This, of course, was untrue.

When Susan arrived home that evening, James told her that David had just telephoned 'from the airport' and was coming to dinner. Susan could not face seeing her husband and her secret lover comfortable in each other's company and began drinking again to calm her nerves. She downed so many martinis that she was forced to take to her bed early.

Over the next few days she and David saw each other whenever they could. London was crowded with Christmas shoppers. 'I remember you best in your black coat and boots – they were new then,' David would write afterwards: 'a little, perfect aristocrat, indignant with the mob that had roughed you in Selfridges'.[22] They spent whole days together, driving about London in Susan's green Morris Traveller, walking round the Tower of London hand in hand and drinking tea at the Ritz. Once David pointed out an old-fashioned shopfront which, he said, reminded him of the shop from which he had taken the name le Carré.

Before Christmas he returned to Vienna, but soon after Christmas he was back in London, to spend more time with Susan while James was away in Paris. By now they were talking about running off together and marrying. They spoke about James incessantly; their shared love for him was a chain that bound them together.

After returning again to Vienna David tried to end the affair. 'Still drunk with love and still deeply hurt with the pain,' he wrote to Susan.

> Your marriage is sane and real; I love your marriage and James almost as much as I love you, because I love your way of living and understanding, I despise what you despise . . . I don't want to take or destroy, I want to give. If you can see any other way, if you can honestly see any other hope, tell me. But I will *not* destroy what you have.[23]

James had come back from Paris in good spirits, just in time to set off for the Alps. For the past few years the Kennaways had taken a chalet for several months each winter; James would spend the morning skiing and the afternoon working. This time they had rented the Haus am Berg, a lodge above the Austrian ski resort of Zell am See. Oblivious to what had been happening between his wife and his friend, James invited the Cornwells to join them for a few days. In theory there was something to be said for this arrangement, as the two families had boys the same age.

The Haus am Berg turned out to be a gloomy lodge on the mountain-side, about half an hour's walk from Zell am See. David was uncertain what to expect, not knowing how he and Susan would cope with the strain, but hoping that Ann might find some of the same delight that he found in the Kennaways' company. Susan was welcoming towards Ann; perhaps predictably, James made a pass at her. Afterwards he took David to one side and told him that he thought she was awful. The lovers managed to snatch only a few brief moments alone and the odd furtive kiss. One evening, as the four of them sat around the fire and talked, David took hold of a locket around Susan's neck and asked her about it in a way that aroused Ann's suspicions. That night in bed she asked him if anything was wrong. He told her not to be silly, that she was imagining things.

David presented his hosts with a copy of *The Spy who Came in from the Cold*, in which he scrawled a schoolboyish inscription, in large lettering:

> CORNGuilt hiz Book
> CORNGuilt luvs KennawayS and is called le CarRé
> January 1965

A few nights after the Cornwells had returned to Vienna, Martin Ritt telephoned from Ardmore Studios in Ireland, where *The Spy who Came in from the Cold* was supposed to have started shooting. His voice had the strangled throb of a man taken hostage.[24]

'Richard needs you, David. Richard needs you so bad he won't speak his lines till you've rewritten them.'

'But what's wrong with Richard's lines, Marty, they seemed fine to me?'

'That's not the point, David. Richard needs you and he's holding up the production till he gets you. We'll pay your fare first class and give you your own suite. What more can you ask?'

David flew to Dublin, taking Ann with him. On the set it quickly became obvious that the director and the star were barely speaking. Ritt had come to despise Burton, whom he saw as a spoiled and self-indulgent actor dissipating his talent. After it was all over, when Ritt called 'wrap' on the last day of shooting, he would turn to Burton and say bitterly, 'Richard, I've had the last good lay in an old whore, and it had to be in front of the mirror.'

One further factor complicating their relations was that Ritt had cast Claire Bloom as the female lead, rejecting Burton's suggestion that his wife might play the part instead. (The thought of Elizabeth Taylor in the role of a serious young Communist was perhaps too much for him.) More than fifteen years earlier, while still a teenager, Bloom had acted opposite Burton, himself then only twenty-four, in Christopher Fry's stage play *The Lady's Not for Burning*, and the two had become lovers. She had then played Ophelia opposite Burton's Hamlet. A decade later their affair had resumed during filming of *Look Back in Anger*, until Bloom had broken it off. Now she was once again playing opposite Burton, as Leamas's girlfriend. It was scarcely surprising that Elizabeth Taylor, to whom he had been married less than a year, should be jealous of her. This is said to have been the reason why the name of Bloom's character was changed from Liz Gold to Nan Perry for the film. Calling the leading lady Liz was not an option.

'I can't go to a pub any more,' Burton complained to David: 'Elizabeth is more famous than the Queen. I wish none of it had ever happened.' Perhaps to find his way into the role of Leamas, Burton was drinking a lot, though (unlike the character he was playing) he had a comparatively weak head for alcohol; as Bloom recalled, 'sometimes he was drunk, yes; sometimes he wasn't'. Taylor had insisted on accompanying her husband to Dublin for the filming, bringing an entourage reputed to be seventeen strong: composed, as David understood it, of children by different marriages, tutors for these children, hairdressers, secretaries and, in the words of one waggish member of the unit, the fellow who clipped their parrot's claws. These occupied one whole floor of the Shelbourne, Dublin's grandest hotel.

In the final sequence of *The Spy who Came in from the Cold*, Leamas and his girlfriend attempt to escape from the East over the Berlin Wall. A grim likeness of the Wall had been mocked up in breezeblock and barbed wire in a floodlit Dublin Square, attended by a crowd of Irish onlookers craning for a glimpse of the stars.* Burton was not supposed to emerge until it was fully dark, so, at Ritt's request, David kept him company in a basement

* Some of the desolate scenes of East Berlin were shot in London's Docklands, then of course still undeveloped.

room, sharing a half-bottle of whisky. To stop Burton from becoming so drunk that he would not be able to climb the Wall, David tried to consume most of it himself, but he wasn't sure that he had succeeded. Outside, set designers and technicians were having a last fidget. There was a point where iron bolts formed a crude, barely visible ladder. The director and the cinematographer were studying it together.

Suddenly, to delighted cheers from the assembled crowd, a white Rolls-Royce appeared, driven by a chauffeur, bearing the most famous film star on the planet on to the set of a film in which she played no part. Roused by the clamour outside, Burton bounded up the basement steps into the square, roaring 'Oh Christ! Elizabeth, you *fool*,' and raging at the French chauffeur, who threw the Rolls into reverse and drove away. Furious, Marty Ritt called off the shoot.

That night Burton came out for dinner with the Cornwells on his own. Back at the hotel, David was already in his pyjamas when the telephone rang. It was Burton. 'Come up for a drink,' he said. 'Elizabeth wants to meet you.' So David and Ann dressed again and went up to the fourth floor. They found him, sitting alone in a vast sitting room. Suddenly they heard a seductive, disembodied voice, speaking through an intercom: 'Richard?'

'Yes, darling?' he answered.

'Who's all there?'

'The writer.'

Burton went into the bedroom to fetch her. The Cornwells tried not to listen to the sounds of an obvious altercation coming through the intercom. Eventually Taylor emerged, barefoot, dressed in a fluffy, wraparound dressing gown. Extending David a little-girl handshake, she managed a brief 'How d'you do?' before turning tail and going back to the bedroom. The Cornwells decided to leave. Burton, obviously embarrassed by his wife's rudeness, walked his guests to the lift. As they said goodnight he told Ann that she was very pretty.

Taylor made her presence felt at Ardmore by bellowing 'Richard!' across the set. Claire Bloom tried to keep out of the way, staying in her caravan much of the time. One evening, however, she was persuaded to go out to dinner with her co-star and his wife, with David making up the four. The Burtons became very drunk and fractious with each other, she recalled almost half a century later. Though Burton was an excellent raconteur, 'David was better,' and 'Liz didn't like that at all.' Bloom was so uncomfortable that she ducked out midway through the dinner.

David's notional task was to rewrite Burton's lines, which meant reworking scenes to make them play as the star wanted. But Burton's way wasn't always Ritt's way, with the result that David became, for this brief period, their go-between: sitting down with Ritt and fixing a scene, then sitting down with Burton and fixing it again, then scurrying back to Ritt. This process lasted only a few days, until Ritt declared himself satisfied with the revisions and Burton stopped complaining. In fact, Burton's lines remained largely unchanged. Some of the most significant new lines that David wrote were not for Burton at all, but for Oskar Werner in the part of Fiedler, when he turns on Leamas and angrily reminds him that he is a traitor, in no position to demand anything.

One evening the Cornwells dined with Claire Bloom in a private room in her hotel. During the meal David was called to the telephone; it was Susan from the Haus am Berg, in a panic. James knew everything. He had found a letter that she was writing to David, which had made it obvious that she and David were having an affair. Distraught, he had taken the car and driven south across the Italian border. From a progression of Italian hotels and bars he was bombarding her with letters and telegrams, one moment saying that he never wanted to see her again and the next begging her to come back to him. He had cancelled their joint bank account, instructed his solicitor to sell their Highgate house and written to his father-in-law, telling him that they no longer needed the house in Gloucestershire. Meanwhile he telephoned various friends for solace. The publisher Mark Longman warned him that, given his record with women, he didn't 'have a leg to stand on' in complaining about Susan's behaviour. But James was beyond reason. The discovery of his wife's infidelity had unbalanced him. It seemed that James, who had taunted David for being 'weak' in his unwillingness to inflict pain on others, could not take it himself. One especially crazy letter to his wife referred to 'a plot afoot, a plot of the gods whereby everybody in my life for nearly a year has been sent to destroy me'. He raved about knives and a gun, seeming to suggest that he planned to kill both his wife and her lover. It was this letter which had frightened Susan into telephoning David in Dublin.

The next morning David took Ann for a walk into the countryside surrounding the studio. Leaning on a five-bar gate, he confessed to being in love with Susan. He told her that he felt stifled in their marriage. Ann was shocked; though she had sensed that something was wrong at Zell am See, she had known nothing of the affair. He ducked admitting that he had slept with Susan, but warned that he was considering whether to run off with her.

Back in Vienna, David received a series of threatening telephone calls from James, now consoling himself in a Marseille brothel. Trying to calm his friend, David proposed that they should meet and talk.

Susan was due to travel back to Britain for her daughters' half-term. She broke her journey in Vienna, for one last meeting with David. He drove her to the airport; both were tearful and shaky. David presented her with his fountain pen as a memento, but in her confusion she left it behind. When she arrived in England she found a telegram from him declaring his love for her, followed by a letter. 'This place is full of you – oh Susie, love, dearest heart, I love you,' he wrote: 'I seem to miss you more with each day that passes.'

A week later she returned to Zell am See, accompanied by James's Oxford friend Denys Hodson, who had been his best man at their wedding. Up at the lodge they found James, who had returned from France while she was away. A series of terrible rows followed. Susan had been a quiescent wife; now she was raving and shouting back at her husband. In a ghastly way James seemed to find the confrontation stimulating. He insisted that David join them at Zell am See. In retrospect, Susan would conclude that her husband 'didn't want the drama to end just yet, and was setting in motion acts to complicate the plot still further, so that he could write a better script for us'.[25]

A series of minor misunderstandings followed. James had arranged to pick up David from the station by car, but returned to the lodge without him, bringing instead a case of wine that David had sent as a thank-you for the skiing holiday. Then he decided to drive back to the station. Meanwhile David had arrived in Zell am See, having missed his intended train and taken the next one. Finding nobody there to collect him, he had started up the mountain on foot. By now it was getting late in the afternoon and the snow was thick on the ground. Trying to take a short cut to the lodge, he found himself on the wrong side of a high wire fence. Susan spotted him through a window and dashed out into the snow in her slippers. The fence kept them apart: the lovers could only touch fingers through the wire mesh. Eventually, with Susan's help, David managed to clamber over it, tumbling into the snow beside her. The two of them trudged back to the house.

Hodson tactfully left them alone. A few minutes later James burst into the room, having driven back from the station. At first it seemed as if all would be well. James began opening bottles, laughing and joking, as ebullient as he had ever been, while the others sat in comparative silence. In his heightened state James had decided to make a present of Susan to David, and wanted them to go off together that very night. There was more than an echo of *Jules et Jim*, in which the husband, anxious that his wife will leave him, gives his blessing for his friend to begin an affair with her, so that the three of them can remain living together. James seemed to relish such parallels: he had already accused Susan of 'behaving like a bloody dentist's wife', a reference to Graham Greene's play *The Complaisant Lover*,* in which both lover and husband (a dentist) gallantly agree to indulge the wife's desire for a dalliance. Indeed the adulterous triangle was a recurrent theme in his own novels.[26] 'How wonderfully close fiction and life have suddenly become,' James would write in his journal, a few weeks afterwards.[27]

With an embarrassed Hodson making up the four, the party descended the mountain to a restaurant in Zell am See. The atmosphere was restless and uneasy. Neither David nor Susan challenged James, not wanting to upset him further. Towards the end of the meal James began to discuss the practical arrangements for their departure: train timetables, packing, had she remembered her passport? When David betrayed signs of hesitation, James was quick to suggest that maybe he did not want Susan after all. Abruptly he stood up from the table, asserting that David should pay for the meal as he had more money. He grabbed Hodson and the two of them left the restaurant.

* In his journal he referred to this play as *The Complaisant Husband*.

Stunned, Susan and David remained seated, uncertain what to do next. Then Hodson returned. There was a train in about an hour's time, he told them. James was ensconced at the station bar. Susan accepted Hodson's offer to escort her up the hill to collect her things. At the lodge she hurriedly packed a bag and changed into going-away clothes. Then she and Hodson made their way back down the hill, Susan slipping and sliding in the snow. They found James and David together at the bar, 'old chums, old friends, comforting and swearing and laughing and crying all at once'. James called out to her that she ought be ashamed of herself, leading a young man like David (who was only a year or so younger than her) by the nose. 'My God, this is going to make a good book,' he said to David, and the pair of them started laughing. Irritated that they were ignoring her, Susan flounced out, and had to be persuaded to return. By this time it was late and the train had left. Eventually they found themselves in the lobby of the deserted station, shouting and screaming at each other in the cold, James pulling Susan by one arm and David tugging her by the other. 'It isn't *Jules et Jim*, can't you see,' Susan raged through her tears: 'it's James and Jim.' James began howling. Hodson dragged him away. The two lovers slunk round the corner and found a hotel, where they spent a miserable, sleepless night. Susan sensed that David was anxious about James and needed to see him again. It was now obvious to her that she would not be leaving with David the next morning.

It was therefore with some relief that, as they were sipping coffee at breakfast, they saw Hodson walk into the hotel. Shaking the new snow off his shoes, he told them that they had better come back to the house. 'I think James is going mad,' he said. The three of them climbed the hill again to the Haus am Berg. More than a decade later Susan related what happened when they arrived:

> we went into the big bedroom, where James was lying curled on the bed in his vest and pants unshaven, in the foetal position, crying. It had been snowing in the night and the white flakes piled up high against the window panes caused both a strange lightness and a shadowless gloom in the room. David went straight to the bed and sat across the end of it. 'Old Jim, old chumbo, old chum, come on,' he said, and James peeped through his fingers, and their conversation began.[28]

Susan left the two friends alone. She locked herself into an attic bedroom, took some sleeping pills and fell asleep. By the time she woke it was dark and David had gone.

Their affair had not ended: over the months that followed they continued to see each other from time to time, while she lived apart from James. But the crisis was past. Susan increasingly came to believe that David would never leave his wife. When her father was dying, James came to the nursing home to support her. Eventually the two of them were reconciled. They sold the house in London and began living together again in the house in Gloucestershire. 'The difficult years are behind,' James would write to Susan in 1967.[29]

In a confessional letter David had told Susan that he wanted to give his family 'a home and land before I burst out, if I do . . . Once home is established I am going to travel for six months or so – I have to collect for a new book, that's the story.'[30] He portrayed ghastly scenes of sobbing and 'small madnesses', interspersed with 'massive statements of generosity' from Ann and spells of coolness and detachment – 'not so different from James actually'. David tried to explain to Susan why he could not commit to her:

> I'll tell you what I am: a painkiller, a concession man, grown-up on negotiating other people's emotions. A great big fat fraud. Poor love; I've been more brave with you than with anyone, and still I've been a coward. I can't hurt – it's as simple as that . . . I can't bear discord; you can blackmail me any time with the simplest disapproval . . . I *tried* to warn you; I love you, but take care; I love you, but I'm a hollow oak . . . I am filled with the smell and energy of you, the life and the courage, sheer beauty and friendship; but I *can't destroy*.

Later in the letter he reflected on his relations with James. 'I suppose I am growing up – I can't cope with him any more.' He commented sadly that 'it's certainly my own fault and it's certainly true; I've lost the best friend I ever had'.[31]

He wrote a letter of remorse to Kennaway himself, addressing him as 'Dearest James'. David insisted that 'I failed you most terribly,' and asked forgiveness. 'I describe you in conversation as my best friend,' he wrote. 'If you can, say the same.' He would never see Kennaway again.

The affair with Susan set a pattern that would recur in David's life: the compulsive search for love. He felt he had been swept up in a piece of bad theatre, that he had protested emotions he did not afterwards feel, had betrayed those whom he most loved and had paid a heavy price for it. He had said the unsayable, things that had been banking up in him and then poured out, that he was a stranger to happiness, and all the rest. He could not take the words back, any more than the deed. In his own words, one part of him longed for a return to captivity, for the children's sake, and for Ann's. But the other half yearned to make up for his womanless youth, his sexual inexperience and his longing for real connection. There would be other Susans, some brief, some more enduring, a few even rewarding. But David's longing for stability was as powerful as his longing for experience and his thirst for knowledge, and it would lead him to search for a partner who could manage these seemingly irreconcilable needs, and give them a home.

It was little consolation to Ann that her husband had not left. She believed that she was no more than 'a tie from the past he hasn't the heart to cut'.[32] She accused him of being cold and calculating, an emotional eunuch, incapable of real passion. For her, as for James, only 'real' emotion counted. Privately, David suspected that she despised him for not having the guts to go off with Susan. In his lowest moments he felt that he had been branded by all three of them as a sexual inadequate, an opinion that he shared.

Ann loathed James, and felt if anything more jealous of him than she did of Susan. She formed the theory, which she expressed to David often, that he had consummated a homosexual love affair with the wife of his lover. Susan too came to believe that there had been a homosexual element in their friendship, though she compared them to David and Jonathan, more like brothers than lovers.[33] David himself could not accept Ann's theory, though he thought about it a lot; he said that he had never felt physically attracted to James, even if he had been enormously stimulated by Kennaway's energy and zest. James too addressed this idea, in a letter to his wife. 'Nothing clearer has come out of this than that neither he nor

I are queer, not one bit. We are men. You're woman, and we've all pushed ourselves to the edge of civilization, the case being special only in that we all love each other.'[34]

Theories of homosexuality were never far from Ann's thoughts as she tried to analyse her errant husband. He was attractive in a boyish, almost feminine way, and he used his charm effectively on men as well as women. Denys Hodson remembered him as simply the most charming man he had ever met. There is some evidence that David may have enjoyed playing on Ann's suspicion that he could be homosexual. For example, in a letter to her from Bern, where they had been staying together, written just after she had left, he mentioned picking up a twenty-three-year-old boy in the Casino for 'a lark'. Together they had gone to a homosexual restaurant, where they 'sat around and got minced at for a bit'. A few years later in Bath he and Robin Cooke judged it prudent to quit a pub abruptly, after their exuberant behaviour had led them to be taken for 'a couple of queers'.

Ann told him frequently that he knew nothing of women, having grown up in a family in which women were absent. She argued that the poverty of the female characters in his books showed his ignorance. It was certainly true that there were far more men than women in his novels, as they were set in a world in which men predominated. *The Looking-Glass War* depicted a platonic love between Leiser and Avery; these two men make a closer connection than they are able to make with the women in their lives. But the women who did enter this world – Elsa Fennan, Shane Hecht, even Liz Gold – were vividly drawn. The most enigmatic of them was a character introduced in the opening paragraphs of his very first book, who nonetheless had yet to appear in person in his fiction – Smiley's wife, Lady Ann. It was curious that David should have used his own wife's name for the wife of his principal character. On the face of it, they were as unlike as could be: Ann was conventional, monogamous and middle class, while Lady Ann was bohemian, promiscuous and aristocratic. Perhaps Ann was right in at least one respect: Lady Ann represented the essential unknowableness of women to Smiley, and by extension to David.

14

Caught in the machine

In March the Cornwells' landlady in Vienna gave them notice; she wanted the apartment for the opera director Wieland Wagner, the composer's grandson. Ann took the children back to England, while David remained to serve out another month of tax quarantine. 'I know I am a great louse, but Mousey I do so love you still,' he wrote to her while they were apart.[1]

David's German publisher, who also published Graham Greene, told him that Greene was coming to Vienna and wanted to meet him. David was in awe of Greene. While still in Agios Nikolaos he had received a letter from him, writing in his capacity as a director of The Bodley Head: he had enquired whether David might be interested in publishing his next book with the firm. Presumably he was responding to gossip in the publishing business about David's discontent with Gollancz. He seemed unaware that The Bodley Head had rejected David's work in the past. In response, David had said that he feared it was now too late, as he was in negotiation with another publisher, though he promised to get in touch if the negotiations fell through. Greene's letter was very welcome nevertheless:

> You have given me an opportunity to write to you, which I have long wanted to do, to thank you most sincerely for your support: I do not need to tell you what this has meant to me, both practically, since it contributed immeasurably to the success of my last book, and morally, because there are few writers, living or dead, whose support I would appreciate more.[2]

In a letter to Ann, David referred to Greene's *In Search of a Character: Two African Journals*, which he said was 'really his notebooks while collecting material for his novels: very interesting to compare Greene's with my own way of looking at people, his technique of slipping into the role of the character he's putting together, his horror of being affected by other writers, e.g. Conrad'.[3]

Greene turned out to be a tall man, with very pale blue eyes and a trailing voice, with a stammer like Philby's. They lunched together with their German publisher, and later spent a 'pissy' evening *à deux*. Mischievously Greene asked David whether he had been in SIS, and when David denied this, commented that he was quite right to do so: 'You never know where these conversations will lead.' He mentioned that he kept a flat in Paris, and extended an invitation to David to call on him when he was there.

David was still working on a script for *The Looking-Glass War*. Film rights had been sold to Columbia for $150,000,* plus a further $12,500 for the screenplay. Karel Reisz had dropped out, but another director had taken his place: Jack Clayton, whose first film, *Room at the Top* (1959), had pioneered the British 'New Wave' in cinema, incidentally picking up two Academy Awards. David met Clayton in Paris, where Susan joined him for a few days. Afterwards he travelled to Bad Godesberg, where he stayed with his former Foreign Office colleague Julian Bullard and his wife Margaret while trying to make progress with his new book. He was finding it a struggle to write anything at all, and what he did produce seemed to him 'wretchedly bad'. One problem was the number of distractions. Now that he was a bestselling author he was in demand to give talks and interviews and to broadcast on radio and television. At first this was new and exciting, but the glamour quickly palled. Moreover he received a steady stream of requests to write short stories, feature articles and book reviews, all of which were less daunting to undertake than a full-length novel. For example, in 1967 he would be persuaded to contribute a short story to the first number of *Student* magazine, edited by the seventeen-year-old Richard Branson.

Like James Kennaway, and so many other novelists, David was tempted by the allure of screenwriting. He was fascinated by cinema and relished the challenge of adapting his talent to this different form: in the next few

* More than £50,000; the conversion rate was then $2.80 to the £.

years much of his time would be spent scripting his novels. He dabbled in television, too, and put forward a rather perfunctory proposal for a series of four television plays under the umbrella title 'The Face of Conflict'. This was not taken up. In 1969 Thames TV would broadcast his hour-long drama *End of the Line* in its 'Armchair Theatre' slot, after it had been offered to the BBC and unexpectedly declined. 'I must say that I admire your courage in turning down a play by John le Carré,' commented his agent.[4]

As well as *The Looking-Glass War*, Columbia had bought the rights in *Call for the Dead*. The film would be directed by Sidney Lumet, from a screenplay by Paul Dehn, the scriptwriter of *The Spy who Came in from the Cold*. This time David was not involved with the production.

One evening David was taken by his French publisher to a beautiful house on the Île St Louis, home of James Jones, the American author of *From Here to Eternity*. There were about thirty people present and the atmosphere was self-consciously bohemian. At the centre of the enormous living room was a medieval pulpit; the rule of the evening was that anybody who had something important to say should step into the pulpit, and everyone else must shut up. David recalled that Jones spent most of the time in the pulpit, while he himself lounged beside Françoise Sagan, talking quietly to her amid the hubbub. Sagan's first novel *Bonjour Tristesse* (1954) had made her famous at the age of only eighteen. The two young authors discussed the effect of success on their work, and agreed that it was negative.

While in Paris, David took the opportunity to call on Greene. His host offered him a drink; David noticed with amusement that the Great Writer drank green Chartreuse. On the bookshelves of his tiny flat David spotted many of the erotic and avant-garde books published by Girodias: works by Henry Miller, Frank Harris, Anaïs Nin and others.

David would be in occasional contact with Greene over the next few years. Early in 1966, for example, he wrote a letter praising Greene's *The Comedians*, which he had just finished reading for the second time. 'I find it quite excellent – for my taste, your greatest novel,' he wrote. 'I do hope you realise that that is the common talk of everyone one meets.' He had been 'disgusted' by Kingsley Amis's mocking review,[5] which seemed to me the cheapest thing I have read for a long time. Why does no one dwell on the construction? There can be few plots in our time which can so perfectly *move* the idea, and few characters which so innocently move the plot. It was, is a really wonderful book. I am too stuck with German ideas I know, but I could not help equating the thesis of the book to that of the Thomas Mann short stories – the notion of the 'artist' and his relation to 'citizen'.* You say quite casually in humanist terms what Mann contrived in mechanical terms; what Mann blared at us with an orchestra you play gently in clear, solitary themes, and having established your distinctions you continually rearrange them. You have also done strange and marvellous things with motive: 'I am behaving like this because people are watching me' is not an easy notion to express!

Although it is a book which will provide critics with endless interpretations (the Germans will run on forever) it is also wonderfully entertaining. I do believe it is a masterpiece – that is all I am trying to tell you.

Don't bother to reply to this, and please believe that I am neither trying to requite your generosity to me, nor secure it for the future. I am spellbound by a great novel in our own time and wanted to tell you so.[6]

Before returning to England David gave a magazine interview in which he outlined his working day:

> Between 8 and 12 every morning is for original work. Always longhand – I never mastered the typewriter. First draft in blue Biro, revisions in red, final copy in green. In the afternoon, my secretary types out the sheets with green on . . .
>
> I prefer to lunch alone, without the boys. My wife understands that. Then, in the afternoon, cutting, revision, selection. A lot of that . . . When I am working full steam, I suppose I am writing fourteen, fifteen hours a day.

* Mann's *Tonio Kröger* (1903) and *Death in Venice* (1912) explore the feelings of the artist as an outcast from respectable, bourgeois society. 'To be an artist,' Kröger comes to believe, 'one has to die to everyday life.'

> I never pre-plot a book, plan what is going to happen in advance. For me, that would destroy the unpredictable, the surprising. The books take place around a theme and some characters, as *The Spy* shaped around a phoney defection. I haven't yet had to *search* for themes that generate tension in me.[7]

One legacy of David's involvement with James Kennaway was a feeling that he ought to be writing 'serious' novels. Kennaway shared the prevalent prejudice against genre fiction, believing it to be innately inferior. While acknowledging David's talent, he was occasionally disparaging of his work. The enormous sales of *The Spy who Came in from the Cold* made it easier to dismiss. Like Ann, Kennaway saw popularity as vulgar. He may have felt sensitive about David's success, especially once he appreciated that the two of them were in competition for Susan's love. To Kennaway, his writing was bound up with his manhood. 'More than David, I have connected living and writing, which is why I am writing more profoundly *at the moment*,' he had written to Susan immediately after the crisis at Zell am See.[8]

Kennaway's lack of enthusiasm for spy fiction seems to have influenced David. While still abroad he suspended work on the neo-Nazi thriller. One reason was his lack of conviction that Vienna was the right setting. 'It is a city of incident, but no plot, a no man's land after the war is over,' he would write. 'The tension is gone; only the clichés, like the incidents, remain.'[9] But anyway he had a new idea, 'which I think could be super,' he told Ann. 'I don't want anyone much to know I'm on it – let the *world* think I'm doing the Nazi thing.'[10]

Almost half a century afterwards, David can no longer remember anything about this new novel, beyond a feeling that he was trying to find a way of addressing the central realities of his past: his father, his spying and his sense of utter isolation, as well as his sense of self-contempt about his involvement with the Kennaways.

At the beginning of May 1965 he was at last able to come back to England. Apart from brief visits, he had been away for almost four years. He told an interviewer that he had come home to settle. 'I've made so much money that I can afford to live in Britain,' he joked.

Since returning to England with the children, Ann had been living with her mother in the North Somerset village of Chew Magna; but, knowing that this would not suit David, she found a house to rent in Essex while they searched for a permanent home – 'the Forever House', as David referred to it in letters to the children. They looked at castles and stately homes, and one of the most beautiful houses in Bath, Widcombe Manor; at one stage they seemed set on moving to Wales, or at least to Herefordshire, on the Welsh border. Soon after they came back to England their eldest son, Simon, aged eight, started boarding school. Ann afterwards regretted the decision to send him away, and suggested that she had surrendered to pressure from David. Given that he had reacted so strongly against his own schooling, it seemed curious that he should have chosen to send his sons away to be educated; in retrospect David regards this decision as a tragic mistake. The preparatory school they chose for Simon, Frilsham, was only a few miles from St Andrew's, the school which David himself had attended during the war.

While Ann and the children were in the country, David spent much of his time in London, working on the film script; he bought a penthouse on the thirteenth floor of a tower block in Maida Vale, a stone's throw from Lord's Cricket Ground. He had several jolly meals with Len Deighton, whose life had been similarly transformed by a string of bestselling books, all made into films. They used to eat at Mario & Franco's Terrazza in Soho, then the most fashionable restaurant in 'Swinging London', patronised by actors, models and photographers. The two young writers marvelled at their shared experience of success. Deighton was the first person David knew who had a telephone in his car.

He and Ann exchanged recriminatory letters. To her, he was heartless, selfish and juvenile: 'how I wish for a mature relationship'. To him, she was demanding, jealous and possessive: 'blackmailing me with your tantrums'. In a letter written on the back of an estate agent's circular, Ann complained that she was lonely and depressed. 'I am looking for houses you are too busy to see,' she wrote. 'Even if we find a house, will you be there? There will always be someone else, a film, anyone more important than us. You'll always be away.' While Ann hated to be admired as Mrs John le Carré, she was furious about being ignored; she referred to her husband sarcastically as 'the Great Man'. She wrote that she was thinking of leaving him. 'It's a pretty lousy life you offer me.'[11]

In the run-up to publication there was intense interest in *The Looking-Glass War* – especially in America, where *The Spy who Came in from the Cold* had been such an enormous success. Could he do it again?

One of the biggest book clubs in America, the Literary Guild, had already chosen *The Looking-Glass War* as its September Choice, splashing out the largest advance it had ever paid. *Ladies' Home Journal* bought the serial rights for a staggering $75,000 – presumably sight unseen, since it is hard to believe that they could have thought it an appropriate choice had they read the book.

David was invited to give an address to the annual convention of the American Booksellers Association (ABA), the largest English-language book-related event in the world, to be held that year in Washington in early June. On Memorial Day 1965 (the last Monday in May), he arrived in New York, accompanied by Ann. They stayed at the Plaza Hotel; Coward-McCann hosted a reception for him at the Canadian Club in the Waldorf-Astoria. An interviewer from the *New York Times* wanted to know how the success of *The Spy who Came in from the Cold* had affected David. 'I am only slightly less happy than I was before it happened,' he said. Asked if he planned to continue to write spy stories, he replied, 'I'm not going to plod like an old athlete around the same track because it makes money.' Although his next book would probably not be a spy story, it would retain the element of suspense.* He would like to write all kinds of things, including plays, he said; but he intended to remain 'a storyteller'. He told the *New York Times* that he admired Graham Greene's work: 'the marvellous search for moral values, mixed with the adventure story'.[12]

David and Ann stayed with the Geoghegans in Weston, Connecticut, as he had done on his previous visit. From the start Geoghegan treated David with exceptional care. In later life Geoghegan's son could not remember any other author being invited to the house, let alone coming to stay.

One weekend they took a jaunt across Long Island Sound to stay at the Sea Spray Inn, on the dunes facing the ocean in East Hampton. Everyone seemed to be in a good mood: there was lots of storytelling, laughter, good food and wine. After dinner, they strolled out on to the beach in the darkness to watch the Gemini space capsule pass overhead. Geoghegan was clearly anxious about something; that night he stayed up late, while his

* Later in the year he would tell the American men's magazine *Playboy* that his next book would 'definitely not be in the suspense/spy genre'.

wife tried unavailingly to calm him. Later he would tell his son that he had been worried by David's desire to stop writing spy thrillers.

David's speech to the ABA, entitled 'The Book Machine', was perhaps not what his audience was expecting. Instead of the upbeat rallying-call usual on such occasions, they were given introspective angst. David teased his audience briefly by dilating on the parallel between the writer and the spy: 'like a spy his real work is done alone . . . like a spy he needs secrecy'. But this was a digression from his main theme, which was to warn of the hazards of success for the writer: he becomes 'caught in the machine . . . he has become a property'.

Geoghegan was impatient with David's soul-searching. He led David to a high vantage-point above the cavernous central concourse of Grand Central Station. It was rush hour, and the station was thronged with hurrying commuters. 'Look down there,' Geoghegan commanded: 'do you want to be one of them?'

British publication of *The Looking-Glass War* was set for 21 June 1965. To commemorate the occasion Charles Pick threw a party at his Knightsbridge flat. David was apprehensive about the critics: rightly so, as it turned out. Maurice Richardson in the *Observer* thought it 'slightly disappointing . . . I got the impression that le Carré had been attempting an exercise that was just a little too difficult for him';[13] in the *Sunday Telegraph*, Anthony Curtis confessed that he had found the middle section of the book 'tedious to a degree . . . Mr le Carré, mistakenly, sacrifices danger to irony.'[14] Much of the review coverage could be summarised as 'jumped-up thriller with not enough thrills'.[15] The most damaging review came in the *Times Literary Supplement*. 'In *The Spy who Came in from the Cold* Mr le Carré's talents were held in poise: character, theme and plot worked together,' began the reviewer. 'Here they have fallen apart disastrously.'

> The spy thriller in this case just does not seem the right vehicle for him, and his prose style is too thin as fuel. He may have been hit over the head with Graham Greene. On this showing, he deserves to be coshed again. Far too much reads like a pastiche of *England Made Me* or one of the later entertainments.[16]

The anonymous reviewer was Alexander Cockburn, then just twenty-four years old.

David was very hurt by the criticism. He characterised *The Looking-Glass War*'s reception in Britain as 'outright abuse'.[17] In fact the book was reviewed favourably in the *Financial Times*, the *Daily Telegraph* and the *Sunday Times*, and the *New Statesman* had plenty of good things to say about it too.[18] But the good reviews failed to soothe the wounds he received from the bad.

It was a similar story in America, where Orville Prescott, writing in the *New York Times*, described the book as 'even harsher and angrier than its predecessor, but not nearly as interesting as a novel'.[19] The *New York Times Book Review* gave the book faint praise:

> In *The Looking-Glass War*, le Carré has written a story with some of the suspense of the spy thriller and also with some of the psychological, social density of a novel. But the two modes do not mingle well . . . As the writer of a thriller that says something about the world, le Carré ranks with Greene and Chandler. But as a true novelist he has a long way to go.

By contrast, the *Atlantic*'s notice was favourable, and the reviewer in the *New York Review of Books* hailed le Carré as 'the legitimate heir of Greene'.[20] In *Life* magazine, the veteran spy novelist Eric Ambler went out of his way to praise the book as 'very well written and very exciting indeed'.

> With *The Looking-Glass War* John le Carré may not exactly have done it again but he has done something almost as reassuring. He has made it plain that *The Spy who Came in from the Cold* was not a fluke, and that those of us who like good spy novels and good writing may expect a long and mutually profitable relationship with him.[21]

A review of the German edition in the *Frankfurter Allgemeine Zeitung* speculated on what lay ahead for le Carré. The reviewer thought it 'barely conceivable' that he would be prepared to write spy novels again. Like so many of the Anglophone reviewers, she suggested that he might well be 'a worthy successor to Graham Greene'.[22]

A quarter of a century later David would feel able to joke bitterly that the book had been received, in Britain, 'with such wholesale derision from the critical community that, had I taken it to heart, would have persuaded me to follow a different profession, such as window-cleaning, or literary journalism'.[23] But there was nothing funny about it at the time. At this stage in his career it was natural for him to feel sensitive towards suggestions that *The Spy who Came in from the Cold* had been a one-off; he could not know what he might be capable of in the future. He gave Susan a copy, inscribed thus: 'Susie, from David with Love. Rotten reviews all round; le Carré no good any more, but what was good, you had. D.'

In publishing terms, *The Looking-Glass War* was far from being a flop. Coward-McCann's edition was thirteen weeks in the *New York Times* best-seller list, reaching number 5; while Heinemann's edition sold almost 50,000 copies. But sales fell short of the very high expectations raised by *The Spy who Came in from the Cold*. After three years Heinemann still had almost 10,000 copies of the first printing unsold, plus a further 15,000 unbound sheets.

The general view among the Cornwells' friends was that he had written a dud. 'I expect you are now rather relieved you didn't get "The Looking-Glass War",' John Bingham wrote to Gollancz a couple of months after it was published.[24] Bingham disliked the bleakness and the nihilism of the book. *The Spy who Came in from the Cold* had presented the Circus as fiendishly cunning, if disturbingly amoral; *The Looking-Glass War* portrayed the Department as incompetent and deluded. For David's former colleagues in MI5 and MI6, his satirical depiction of a botched operation by fools living on past glories made uncomfortable reading. Some of them resented it, or found it offensive. 'I suppose it is better to foul one's own nest by remote control after one has left it,' Bingham commented to his wife.[25]

David decided to dispense with Peter Watt's services. 'I feel that the emphasis in my affairs is now so altered as to make the services of an agent redundant,' he wrote to Hale Crosse.[26] Increasingly he was asking his accountant to perform the tasks normally done by a literary agent. He had come to the conclusion that 'John le Carré' was a business, requiring professional management. He felt that Watt was not equipped to handle movie deals; in particular, he held Watt responsible for the problems caused by the Paramount contract for *The Spy who Came in from the Cold*, which had given the film company control over the use of his characters in film or television. The restriction on the use of the characters elsewhere had proved a continuing irritant, jeopardising the sale of film rights in both *The*

Looking-Glass War and *Call for the Dead*. This was exasperating, as these sales were much more lucrative than the original Paramount deal. There was a particular problem with the character of George Smiley, who had appeared in all David's books. Though Smiley plays only a small part in *The Spy who Came in from the Cold*, the contract applied to him as it did to the central characters in the story. Michael Horniman, one of Watt's colleagues, suggested that the problem could be overcome by changing Smiley's name; David did not like this at all, but it was the solution eventually adopted.

He was an exacting client, requiring rapid and repeated attention, always pushing at the boundaries of conventions generally accepted in the business. Like James Kennaway, he wanted to 'beat the system'. He had formed the view that the publishing world, once you stripped away the literary veneer, was as grasping and unprincipled as Ronnie's, 'and dreadfully incompetent'. According to Bingham, David had been riding his agent very hard to obtain better terms.[27] Though Watt liked David and indeed had become fond of him, he had come to dread his telephone calls. The agency maintained the tradition of 'morning prayers', when incoming letters were opened and shared among the principals. Horniman remembered a letter arriving from David in Vienna, insisting on a reply on the issue of the Paramount contract; 'You've got to deal with this, Peter,' he had said, but Watt had merely shrugged his shoulders.

Nevertheless Watt was distressed when he learned that David no longer wanted him to be his primary representative. The agency would continue to handle routine business on a reduced commission, but would not be involved in the most important negotiations, which would henceforth be handled by Hale Crosse, as David's personal manager. For Watt, this meant a severance in their personal relations. Not only had he lost the agency's most valuable client: he had lost contact with a man whom he had come to think of as a friend. A few weeks after receiving David's announcement of his departure, Watt died suddenly of a stroke, at the age of only fifty. His early death was perhaps not altogether surprising, given that he was a heavy drinker and a chain-smoker; nonetheless his widow sent David an angry letter, accusing him of responsibility for her husband's death. 'I imagine David may be slightly blaming himself, justly or unjustly, for poor Peter's demise,' Bingham wrote to Gollancz.[28] A few years later David would receive a similar letter from Gollancz's widow.

David's morale was further dented when Jack Clayton rejected his screenplay. He received no comfort from Ann, who thought screenwriting unworthy of a serious novelist. Understandably she associated the project with James and told her husband that he had been ill advised to undertake it in the first place. The combined effect of several blows – the poor reviews (as he saw them) for *The Looking-Glass War*, his inability to make progress with another novel and Clayton's rejection of his script – plunged David into despondency. His involvement with the Kennaways had stripped away his protective covering, and the continuing unhappiness in his marriage kept him raw. He felt a failure. Secretly he feared that the critics might be right, that he had nothing left to give and that his talent had run dry.

After ceasing work on his script David was suddenly unemployed. In a few weeks' time he was due to fly out to America to promote Coward-McCann's edition of *The Looking-Glass War* and to appear at a trade fair in Chicago. Meanwhile he could not face resuming his novel. For want of anything better to do, he accepted an invitation from his Danish publisher to address a student meeting. In a Copenhagen hotel he came near to despair and had thoughts of suicide. But he delivered his talk, and caught the ferry across the straits into Sweden to speak at Lund University; there he met a very beautiful young student, with whom he went to bed. It was his first sexual experience that was wholly gratifying, and it made him astonishingly happy. The next morning she sent him off to Stockholm, where he was due to give a television interview; and there, half in a frenzy, he emulated James's exploits in Paris the previous summer, taking woman after woman to bed, barely sleeping, drinking and drying out in saunas. Then he returned to Lund to spend three more blissful days and nights with the young woman who had finally awakened his dormant sexual appetite.

From Stockholm he had written several despairing letters to Ann: 'I'm sick of England and English institutions, I'm sick of our neuroses & the flesh-eating & the infantilism, of all the painful, wasteful, sterile dishonesty – I'm in a fury and I don't want to come back, certainly not before Chicago . . . You can say I'm ill or something – film or something . . .'[29]

In Chicago, taking part in a lacklustre campaign to sell British goods abroad, David received an urgent message from John Margetson, now serving as a diplomat in the Foreign Office. A telegram had been received in London from the British Embassy in Djakarta: 'BRITISH CITIZEN, [illeg] CORNWELL, ARRESTED FOR GUN RUNNING AND CLAIMS TO BE FATHER OF A MEMBER OF YOUR STAFF'. Tony Cornwell had already been contacted and had declined to help.

This was the culmination of a sequence of memoranda and telegrams from Djakarta, informing London that it might be necessary to repatriate Ronnie from Indonesia urgently at public expense, in order to keep him out of detention. A memorandum from the British Embassy in Djakarta on 31 July 1965 provided a summary of a conversation between Ronnie and an Embassy commercial officer. Ronnie had mentioned that he had already signed a contract with the Indonesian government for the supply of 8,000 trucks from Italy, and that other contracts would come for two million barrels of oil to Japan from Indonesia and for the building of three ships. 'When I asked him why, in the case of the oil deal, he was being used as an intermediary,' the Commercial Officer reported, 'he said that in government-to-government contracts there was nothing in it for anybody, whereas in private deals individuals could make a handsome profit.' Ronnie had told the Commercial Officer that he had seen the President of Indonesia and presented him with a copy of his son's book, *The Spy who Came in from the Cold*. ('I should think this would get the prize for the most inappropriate gift of the year,' the Commercial Officer added in parentheses.) Ronnie had further told the Commercial Officer that the President had paid for a trip to Algeria out of his own pocket and that, as a result of the truck deal, half a million pounds had been deposited in the President's private bank account in Geneva. 'Cornwell strikes us as a somewhat shady character,' the memorandum concluded.

'Perhaps, if things are desperate, I might after all be able to help,' David replied to Margetson.[30] He asked how much was needed to keep his father out of an Indonesian prison: it was only a few hundred pounds, an alarmingly small sum for a man of Ronnie's ambition. David undertook to guarantee the required amount, and the local Embassy paid it.

For the past couple of years Ronnie had been wandering around the globe, chasing the big deal that would clear his debts and put him on top again, leaving a trail of unpaid bills. From New York he had moved to Canada, where he set up a bogus property company in a scam to take a Chicago building company for millions of dollars. A firm of lawyers just across the border in Buffalo was also involved.* His notional plan was to build a satellite town outside Toronto. Discussions continued for months while the interested parties sat around tables, looked at models, listened to projections and raised funds. Eventually it emerged that Ronnie had never had planning permission for the development; he did not even own the land; the whole project had existed only in his imagination.

After this scheme had collapsed, he had moved on to Hong Kong. For some months he took suites at the best hotels, before renting a villa in Repulse Bay. Ronnie presented himself as someone very rich, discreet and well connected. Modestly he let it be known that he was John le Carré's father. He consented to sign copies of *The Spy who Came in from the Cold* for friends and business associates, inscribing them 'with best wishes from the Father of the Author of this book – my son, David'. While Ronnie was resident in the Far East, David received a succession of typed letters from him: beseeching, commanding and some even threatening blackmail. In April 1965 Ronnie had written to Gollancz, explaining that he had been living in Hong Kong since Christmas. He offered his services in placing the publication rights for *The Spy who Came in from the Cold* in China and Japan.[31]

Ronnie was next heard of in Kuala Lumpur, renting a house from expatriates who had gone back to England for a sabbatical while he tried to start an airline. He soon moved on to Singapore, where he busied himself in trying to set up a football-pools scheme. Through an assistant in the Prime Minister's office who happened to be a mason he obtained an official interview, presenting himself as the representative of the two largest (and rival) British football pools. 'I represent Vernons and Littlewoods,' he announced by way of introduction. He proposed that the state of Singapore should take a commission on earnings from the scheme. Satisfied that he had secured an understanding, Ronnie proposed a similar arrangement to

* One of the lawyers involved contacted David after the publication of *A Perfect Spy*. They had laughed so much and had such a good time with Ronnie, he wrote, that they had not resented being taken for a ride, but had simply written it down to experience.

the Tunku of Malaysia. To cover his accommodation needs while staying in that part of the world he offered to cut the owner of the Mandarin Hotel in on the deal, thus obtaining the use of a suite. When all seemed to be falling into place Ronnie returned to Liverpool via Ireland,* presenting himself in succession to the top brass of Vernons and Littlewoods. 'I represent the Prime Minister of Singapore and the Tunku of Malaysia,' he began.

Back in England, David embarked on a period of 'six months' madness', when he slept with any woman who would have him. Some knew Ann, some did not; he avoided becoming emotionally entangled with any of them. Gradually, he thought, he could accumulate what he needed: a standard of reference by which to judge his own marriage. He envisaged that, by careful selection, he might return to his wife while keeping a mistress in London. He told himself that even if he did not learn to love Ann again, he would honour her as the mother of his children, learn to respect her again and perhaps find a new tranquillity. David was briefly reunited with the woman whom he had loved in Bonn; in a private moment she told him that she still loved him, but it seemed hopeless, and he realised that he had aged emotionally by at least fifteen years in the eighteen months or so since they had last seen each other.

After looking at many different houses in various parts of England and Wales, Ann at last found one that she wanted to buy: Coxley Manor, a former farmhouse of Jacobean origins a few miles outside Wells, facing south over the Somerset levels; Glastonbury Tor was visible through the trees. A prosperous farmer had added a Georgian façade, a grotto and a ha-ha to keep the livestock at a distance. There were also various cottages and outbuildings. It was a marked contrast to the Pilton cottage, only a few miles off, where they had lived ten years before. The family moved to Coxley in December 1965; David cautiously agreed to come for a fortnight at Christmas. 'We are both hurt and wary, I suppose,' he wrote to Ann beforehand, 'and I for one don't know what I am or feel, except that things can never go on as they were before we parted.'[32]

* No doubt it was more prudent for Ronnie to come home via the back door.

In mid-December David wrote to the Margetsons from Coxley. 'It's been a bleak year for the Cornwells, and I'm afraid that with the selfishness of self-absorbed people we have visited some of our troubles on you,' he began. He thanked them for their loyalty and understanding, sent his abiding love and hoped they 'would be able to know us in the future with less pain and more reward'.

> Things are still a bit shaky but less tense and I hope that you will fairly soon come and see us in our house, which turns out to be dry-rotted, wet-rotted, beetled and plain dangerous, so there's masses to be done.[33]

While still in America David had been shown a rough cut of the film version of *The Spy who Came in from the Cold*. He told the television talk-show host Merv Griffin that he was in an unusual position for an author whose novel had been turned into a movie, of having nothing to complain about. The film remained true to the essence of the book: the dialogue of the script followed the text of the novel closely and in places even improved on it. Though by the mid-1960s most big feature films were being made in colour, Ritt had taken the bold decision to shoot the movie in black and white, evoking the bleak, colourless world it portrayed. The film would be a critical success, winning a string of BAFTAs as well as being nominated for two Academy Awards. Oskar Werner won the Golden Globe award as Best Supporting Actor for his performance as Fiedler.

Princess Margaret attended the premiere of the film in Singapore. Hospitality in the Mandarin Hotel was provided by Ronnie, who wrote a long account of the party to his son. The cost was borne by the hotel itself, defrayed against the owner's share in the football-pools scheme. It turned out that Ronnie's activities were being monitored by the local Special Branch. A telegram to London from the High Commission in Singapore stated that a British citizen named Ronald Cornwell was trying to bid for £1 million worth of tin, apparently unconnected with the football-pools scheme. A short while later he was once again arrested, this time for illegal currency dealing.

While Ronnie was languishing in the Far East he received a handwritten letter from David, asking if he wished to return home – 'Can you?' – and how much would be the sums involved. 'Knowing you, I suspect you want to return as a conquering hero rather than merely a solvent citizen – but surely there are things to be said for a less ambitious plan, if one can be devised. Will you lift the veil a little?'[34]

'I am a slow writer and it seems that with each new work it becomes more painful,' David told an interviewer from *Playboy*.[35] Following the knock to his confidence from the reception of *The Looking-Glass War*, he seemed to struggle to find his equilibrium. The mayhem in his personal life cannot have made work easy. 'I am so terribly incomplete and you have been so good while I was looking for the other bits,' he wrote to Ann. 'I don't suppose I shall ever find what I am looking for, because if biographies are to be believed, no one does.'[36]

After a tentative start, David remained at Coxley with Ann, and gradually settled into a routine. One of the two cottages was converted into a studio for him to work in, while his secretary lived in the other. David renewed contact with Robin Cooke, now living in Bath. Though they would see each other regularly over the next few years, David never told his old friend much about what he had been doing: Cooke came to the conclusion that he kept different parts of his life very much separate.

David began buying antiques from a dealer in Wells, Eddie Nowell. The Cornwells carried out alterations to the house, installing new ceilings and fireplaces, and landscaped the garden; David had the ha-ha lined with concrete and flooded to make a canal. He bought the field to the south of the house and a horse to keep in it; for a while he went out riding regularly, until the day the horse threw him and he decided to stop playing at being a country squire. Ann acquired a large white dog, and kept geese.

As he had done in Germany, David would rise very early to write and then go for a long walk, before returning to eat breakfast and resume work. On one of these walks across the fields he came across a pigeon that had been eviscerated by a bird of prey, but not finished off; it was fluttering on the ground, struggling to get airborne, in evident distress. David could not bring himself to end the poor creature's suffering by killing it, and walked away. His cowardice in failing to act haunted him thereafter.

When he was working on a novel it preoccupied him, even during convivial dinner parties. One friend from this period remembers him rising to his feet at the coffee stage, with the apology, 'I'm sorry, but I have to leave,' and later that night finding him seated in a deserted railway station, as he scribbled in his notebook.

His relations with Ann continued to be strained, especially after she found some condoms in his studio. She protested that while he was at Coxley he seemed to avoid being alone with her, and that while he was away he could seldom be bothered to telephone or write. 'Your accountant, your lawyer, your secretary, your acquaintances, all rank before me,' she complained: 'I can't exist on such scraps.'

An unexpected visitor appeared at the door, soliciting donations for a local charity: Sir Roger Hollis, David's former boss at MI5, now retired, who lived near by. David invited him in; Hollis stayed an hour, and over coffee he talked distractedly and at length, without ever once asking his host anything about himself. At the time he was under investigation as a suspected Soviet agent: he bore the ordeal stoically, but it was clearly telling on him. He dropped by again, a couple of days later, and sat in an armchair reading *The Times* while David worked; and then three or four times more over the next few weeks. It dawned on David that Coxley Manor was a refuge for Hollis, a safe house.

To the relief of his publishers, David had abandoned his intention to write a novel without spies or suspense; he had reverted to his original concept of a spy thriller against the background of a neo-Nazi revival. He would set the story in Bonn rather than in Vienna. The plot would take the form of a hunt for Leo Harting, a low-ranking diplomat who has gone missing from the British Embassy with its most sensitive file. Harting is ex-Control Commission, one of the put-upon 'temporaries', a dogsbody treated with condescension by his senior colleagues. Alan Turner from 'Security' is sent out from London to investigate Harting's disappearance. His interviews with Embassy staff strip them of their protective covering, to reveal underneath their vulnerability, snobbery, duplicity and hypocrisy. In retrospect David would say that he had planned to write a black comedy about British political manners. Secretly he allocated to himself the role of the driven and unhappy Turner, whose abrasive style grates against diplomatic decorum.[37]

In May 1966 Charles Pick proposed David for membership of the Savile, a London club in the heart of Mayfair founded in 1868 by some of the most distinguished writers and artists of the time, which had retained something of its literary and artistic flavour. In his letter of proposal Pick outlined his candidate's qualifications for membership:

> I have no reservations in proposing Cornwell for the Savile as he is a brilliant conversationalist, extremely modest, and, as one would expect from his writing, highly intellectual. I believe he would make friends very easily in the Savile and would contribute to the general spirit of the Club.
>
> Cornwell is a generous person and I happen to know of two occasions where, anonymously, he has given help urgently needed. He is a person to whom friends could turn for sympathy and is quite unspoilt by his success as a novelist.[38]

David's half-sister Charlotte, then sixteen and a pupil at Windsor Grammar School, came to him for aid. She had become pregnant after sleeping with her best friend's elder brother, her first sexual encounter. Abortion was then illegal; besides, she was already six months pregnant. Her parents were no help: Ronnie was abroad somewhere, and Jean resisted her daughter's attempts to discuss the matter; she moved house, rather than face the shame of her daughter's pregnancy. David offered Charlotte a refuge at the penthouse during the later stages of her pregnancy. Ann offered to bring up the child herself, but Charlotte chose instead to give up the baby for adoption. David supported her throughout this ordeal.

Charlotte began working as a sales assistant at Harrods, followed by a stint as a trainee fashion buyer at Jaeger, but her heart was not in it. 'Come on, Sis, what are you going to do?' asked David. 'I think you're creative – have you ever thought about acting?' With his encouragement, she applied to drama school. This was the beginning of a successful career. Within a few years she would be playing leading roles at the Bristol Old Vic. For Charlotte, David was 'the best brother a girl could have'.

Some time in the mid-1960s David was staying in a small hotel in Schleswig-Holstein, near the East German border,* when his telephone

* He was researching locations for *The Looking-Glass War*.

rang. 'Is that David Cornwell?' David said yes. 'My name is Clark. Your father ripped off my brother. I'm downstairs – do you want a drink?' In the hotel lobby was a tall, handsome man, radiating an almost violent vigour: the young Alan Clark, later a Conservative politician and author of candid diaries. He explained that he was in the area doing a story on the Iron Curtain for the *Telegraph*, and had spotted David's name in the visitors' book. Parked outside was a huge gleaming Mercedes 600, a prototype according to Clark. As they climbed in David noticed a packet of Bath Oliver biscuits and a bottle of Malvern water on the back seat. 'I don't eat foreign food very much,' muttered Clark.

Over a drink he told David the story of how his younger brother Colin had been defrauded by Ronnie, with many amusing details. Far from resenting what Ronnie had done, he seemed to relish it. The two Englishmen found plenty to talk about. Clark was only a few years older than David: he too was married, with young sons. Like David, he kept a flat in London, where he spent much of his time, while his wife and children lived in a manor house in the West Country. And like David, he pursued other women – though, unlike David, he had no scruples about cheating on his wife. He was a wealthy young man, with extravagant tastes; in particular, he adored fast cars, which he drove with a gambler's appetite for risk.

David was lonely, living apart from Ann for much of the time and telephoning home every night to talk to his children. He was making little if any progress with his novel. So when Clark suggested that they might drive down to his chalet in Zermatt together, David accepted. This was the beginning of an unlikely friendship, which continued for several years after they returned to England. Clark was a dashing, impatient, amusing figure, who could be disarmingly frank. David found him exciting, often outrageous company: a man's man. He wrote him affectionate letters, addressing Clark as 'lover boy' or 'golden boy', in much the same terms as he had written to James Kennaway.

Clark was trying to establish himself as a writer. His military histories had attracted considerable success, though he lacked application, as his Oxford tutor, Hugh Trevor-Roper, had often complained. 'Let's face it, David,' Clark remarked, 'when you get to your desk in the morning what you need is a bit of a hangover, then you read through all the shit you wrote the day before, then you add a bit, then really you're screwed and you want to go out for a couple of hours, so actually what you do is about a page a day.' Clark's novels had been less well received. He had read and admired *The Spy who Came in from the Cold*, and in some superstitious fashion he seemed to think that getting to know David might help him to become a more successful novelist.

Like David, he had a difficult relationship with his father, the eminent art historian Kenneth Clark. Both felt damaged by neglect; together they discussed the point at which an unhappy childhood should cease to be an excuse for adult misbehaviour. David perceived an unreconciled anger in his new friend, and sensed that he too was trying to come to terms with the injuries that he felt had been done to him as a boy.

Clark was an Old Etonian, with the sense of entitlement familiar to David from his time teaching there. Unlike David he had been born into privilege and had never known want; towards underlings he behaved with contempt. He embarrassed David by his rudeness to waiters – 'he treated them like shit', David would later recall[39] – refusing to leave even a modest tip.* Clark made no attempt to conceal his extreme right-wing views, though when he expressed these, most people assumed that he was not serious, merely trying to shock. But they were sincerely held. For him, the most important question about Hitler was not whether he was good or evil, but whether he was a competent military commander. 'Alan knew some appalling people,' David would recall after his death. 'He was great mates with Enoch Powell.' Clark mixed with members of the neo-fascist National Front, and admired the right-wing historian David Irving. Together with a fellow backgammon player he joined a syndicate which aimed to buy Göring's Mercedes.

David detected in his friend an unusual capacity for evil. For him, Clark was a kind of Mephistopheles, whose wicked example he found both fascinating and repellent. Clark chased women with a predatory zeal that seemed to mirror his reckless driving, though except in bed he preferred men's company. Reflecting on him after his death, David would observe that 'women were the enemy for him'. Clark's rooms in Albany were too

* According to Madeleine Bingham, after David had taken them out to dinner in the first flush of his new success, her husband had remarked on how rude he had been to the wine waiter. But she was far from being a dependable witness.

public for him to feel comfortable about taking women there, so he often borrowed David's penthouse flat for his assignations. This put David in an awkward position when he drove over to visit the Clarks at their pretty Georgian manor house in the Wiltshire village of Seend.

The film of *Call for the Dead* was released towards the end of 1966. Columbia had renamed it *The Deadly Affair*, apparently because some high-up had decided that the original title suggested a horror movie. David was not involved in the production, so the first he saw of the film was in a huge and almost empty cinema in Kilburn one winter's afternoon. The central character of George Smiley, played by James Mason, had been renamed 'Charles Dobbs', to circumvent the obstacle of the Paramount contract. The changed title reflected a radical change to the plot. In the film Dieter Frey, played by the handsome Maximilian Schell and no longer a cripple as he is in the book, has cynically seduced Dobbs's wife in order to penetrate his guard.* The interplay between husband, wife and lover is at the centre of the movie. Dobbs's wife Ann, who never appears in the novel, is present for much of the film, played by Harriet Andersson as a kittenish child bride, not the mature and sophisticated aristocrat of the novels. The sturdy Simone Signoret played Elsa Fennan, quite unlike the slight, frail figure David had depicted. Nonetheless he was enchanted by her performance, which would be nominated for a BAFTA award. Afterwards he walked all the way home, dreaming of tearing up the book and rewriting every scene, just for her.

The Deadly Affair often feels more like an early James Bond than a le Carré. The mood wavers between early 1960s faux-sophistication and gritty realism, reflected in the settings, which vary from the self-consciously modern Serpentine restaurant to grimy Victorian backstreets. The combination is an uneasy one. The cool, jazzy score by Quincy Jones and the bossa nova theme tune are at odds with the seriousness of the story. Nevertheless the film was reasonably well received, attracting five BAFTA nominations. David would develop a cynical attitude towards film adaptations of his books. 'You sit there and watch this great cow you've designed

* This plot device recurs in le Carré's later and more famous novel *Tinker, Tailor, Soldier, Spy*, which was not published until almost a decade later. David himself resists the speculation that he may have taken the idea from the film.

reduced to a bouillon cube,' he would tell an interviewer, years later – 'and then you have to drink it.'

In August 1967 David informed Charles Pick that he was now the proud owner of a Mercedes 250SE. He had been personally attended to by Mercedes UK's head of sales. 'We finished up on Christian name terms, with luncheon at the Caprice at the expense of Mercedes-Benz. Nobody could ask fairer than that.'[40]

Pick forwarded to David a message asking him to contact his father's 'Austrian lawyer'. It seems that Ronnie was being held in custody for his old trick of failing to pay his hotel bills. There was a further complication, in that he had gulled a rich old lady into allowing him to get her paintings cleaned for her, and had sold them instead. David flew to Vienna to bail him out. Afterwards he gave him lunch in the grill room of Sacher's, one of the city's most elegant and luxurious hotels. Ronnie outlined a succession of business proposals; when David showed little interest, he came to the point: '£20,000 would get me out of all my difficulties'. David refused, privately noting that his father seemed pretty well informed about how much money he was earning. Ronnie then invited his son to reimburse him for the cost of his education, plus interest of course; David again refused, protesting that he had not selected those schools and would not have done so. Ronnie reverted to a favourite topic, his dream of a pig and cattle farm in Dorset. David offered to buy him a farm in which he could live rent-free, and to give him an allowance on top of any income he made from farming, but insisted on retaining ownership, aware that if his father owned any property he would instantly mortgage it. 'You want to pay your own father to sit on his arse,' protested Ronnie. He burst into a torrent of tears, in full view of waiters and other diners. No matter how many times David had seen this performance, it never failed to stir him, and he began to feel tearful himself. 'You go back to your wealth and family and all the advantages I gave you,' his father sobbed. 'All I want now is for you to put me in a cab.' With David's arm around his shoulders, Ronnie allowed himself to be led out of the hotel, sweating and heaving. Outside David helped him into a taxi. Still in tears, Ronnie wound down the window. Father and son sobbed at each other for a while, until Ronnie said, 'I've nothing to pay the cabbie with.' David paid the driver direct.

Earlier that summer there had been glimpses of Ronnie in Beirut, and in Cairo, where he had introduced himself on his arrival as 'John le Carré's father'. It was the time of the Six Day War between Israel and the Arab nations; David suspected that Ronnie might have been trying to get into arms dealing.

Following his arrest in Singapore Ronnie had been given the airfare to Hong Kong, where he was once again arrested, briefly imprisoned and then deported. David had next heard from him in a letter from Delhi. Ronnie recounted a hunting expedition he had just made in the company of a famous maharajah. 'His Highness asks me to assure you that you will be royally welcome at the Palace whenever the winds of fate cast you on these lonely shores,' wrote Ronnie. David would be pleased to hear that the Maharajah had appointed him 'sole administrator, manager and bailiff' of his affairs, with powers to do whatever he deemed best, on behalf of himself and his heirs. A postscript to the letter asked for a thousand pounds in cash ('no cheques please') to be cabled as soon as possible, care of Mrs d'Arcy, whose late husband, the colonel, had tragically died some years back. Understandably sceptical, David had made enquiries about the Maharajah at the Indian High Commission in London. He learned that the Sultanate about which he was asking had ceased to exist in the year 1948. Within twelve months of its abolition the sole heir to the title had been killed in a motoring accident in the south of France.

Years later, after Ronnie's death, David tried to reconstruct how his father had come to write that letter. He imagined Ronnie driving out from Delhi to the Maharajah's derelict palace in Mrs d'Arcy's decrepit car. He pictured broken statuary, grand staircases leading to gutted upper rooms, ant-infested carpets, great halls full of giant bats hanging from the rafters, all gradually succumbing to the encroaching jungle. He heard Mrs d'Arcy telling Ronnie how her husband used to shoot tiger from the back of the Maharajah's elephant. He imagined the feasts that went on all night, all the little attentions that the Maharajah had showered on the honoured guests, the diamonds that he pressed on Mrs d'Arcy, which she had been obliged to refuse. Perhaps she had even let slip that his highness had asked the colonel to abandon his military career and take on the role of 'sole administrator, manager and bailiff' of his affairs.

David saw his father sitting at the colonel's desk, having done his duty by Mrs d'Arcy, an enormous brandy and ginger by his side, composing the letter to his son.

> And by culling her images and adapting them to himself, by placing himself upon the Maharajah's elephant, he allows himself to be fired by the grandeur of that elusive vision, to be assumed by it, possessed by it, to the point where, if the bedroom door were flung open, and a pair of murderous Dervishes burst in – why, he would be on his feet in a second, his military revolver in his hand; he would have felled the brutes where they stood, plugged them with a shot apiece, before returning to his dispatch.

He mused on this 'process of heady abstraction, of deliberately controlled vertigo, in which life's components break and remake themselves according to a wished-for formula and become a story, to be understood as truth and allegory at once'. And he reflected, not for the first time, that Ronnie, in his own way, had been as much of an addict to the process of artistic creation as he was himself.[41]

15

Rich but restless

The news that Kim Philby had written his memoirs, soon to be published in the West, prompted a fresh wave of interest in him. An investigation by the *Sunday Times* Insight team revealed that he had risen much higher within MI6 than had previously been acknowledged; his treachery had been correspondingly more damaging. Philby's personal life also came under scrutiny, as a book was due too from his estranged American wife, Eleanor. She had followed her husband to Moscow, and then had made a humiliating return to the West after he began an affair with Melinda Maclean, wife of his friend and comrade Donald Maclean. This double betrayal – of Maclean as well as of Eleanor – fed the appetite for stories about Philby.

David was asked to write a long article about him for the *Sunday Times Magazine*. It was too good an offer to refuse, though his novel was still unfinished and he could ill afford the distraction. 'I have put the book aside,' he confessed to Charles Pick. 'I'm afraid I just have too much to contend with – most of it of course of my own making!'[1]

His piece on Philby was an attack on the complacency and stupidity of 'the Establishment'; but it was also autobiographical. He envisaged Philby as his 'secret sharer',* as the person he might easily have become himself. Though they had never met, he felt that he understood Philby's motivation because it mirrored his own. Like David, Philby had a monster

* A favourite phrase of David's, deliberately ambiguous, deriving from Conrad's novella *The Secret Sharer*. David generally used it of a character within his novels with whom he identified.

for a father; like David, Philby had served out time in institutions from which he felt alienated. 'Philby, an aggressive, upper-class enemy, was of our blood and hunted with our pack,' he wrote:

> he could hardly fail, when his father delivered him over to the Establishment for his education, to feel already that he was being trained in the enemy camp . . . Through his father, and the education which his father gave him, he experienced both as a victim and as a practitioner the capacity of the British ruling class for betrayal and polite self-preservation. Effortlessly he played the parts which the Establishment could recognize – for was he not born and trained into the Establishment?

David thought that he understood Philby's relations with women: 'Women were his secret audience. He used them like he used society: he performed, danced, phantasized with them, begged their approbation, used them as a response for his histrionic talents, as a consolation for a manhood haunted by his father's ghost. When they came too close, he punished them or sent them away . . .' Philby himself he referred to as 'spiteful, vain and murderous'. He had given himself body and mind 'to a country he had never visited, to an ideology he had not deeply studied, to a regime which even abroad, during those long and awful purges, was a peril to serve; he remained actively faithful to that decision for over 30 years, cheating, betraying and occasionally killing'.

David's piece articulated a theme that he would later develop, of the secret services 'as a microcosm of the British condition, of our social attitudes and our vanities'.[2]

David's *Sunday Times* article was used as the introduction to a book based on the Insight team's revelations, *Philby: The Spy who Betrayed a Generation*, which became a no. 1 bestseller. Due to a mix-up at the newspaper Hugh Trevor-Roper, who had served alongside Philby in MI6 during the war, had been commissioned to write the same article. The literary editor, Leonard Russell, was forced to send him a cringing letter of apology, explaining that the le Carré piece had already gone to press. Trevor-Roper was mortified to be displaced in this way. His Philby article was published in *Encounter*, and later expanded into a short book.

David happened to be in one of the two wooden telephone booths in the Savile when he overheard his own name mentioned, and realised that the eminent Oxford don was speaking in the other. 'I think his introduction is ridiculous,' he heard Trevor-Roper say, 'and I look forward to confronting him.' David deduced that he was speaking to the book's publisher, André Deutsch. He crept away unnoticed. Soon afterwards he met Deutsch, a dapper Hungarian émigré, fondly described by one of his authors as a 'mid-European leprechaun'.[3] When David came to write his novel *Tinker, Tailor, Soldier, Spy*, he would draw on Deutsch for his character Toby Esterhase, who like his original would speak his own form of English.

'First of all fantastic,' enthused Deutsch. 'I am huge admirer.' He referred to Trevor-Roper's *Encounter* article, implying that there was a large measure of agreement between the two men. 'I should like you to appear on platform together for launch of book in Oxford,' he said.

Graham Greene reviewed *Philby: The Spy who Betrayed a Generation* in the *Observer*. Like Trevor-Roper, he had worked alongside Philby during the war, and he remained loyal to his old friend. Greene's biographer Norman Sherry, who interviewed his subject at length, recounts that he responded very angrily to being questioned about Philby, apparently the only time in all their interviews that he lost his temper.[4] Philby's memoir *My Silent War* had appeared with an affectionate foreword from Greene, who played down Philby's treason. To the charge that Philby had betrayed his country, Greene answered, 'Yes, perhaps he did, but who among us has not committed treason to something or someone more important than a country?' Though Greene was not blind to Communism's faults, he nevertheless seemed to favour the East over the West. 'If I had to choose between life in the Soviet Union and life in the United States of America, I would certainly choose the Soviet Union,' he had written in a letter published in *The Times* in 1967.[5]

In his review, Greene mocked the fact that the term 'Establishment' was used seventeen times in an introduction of fifteen pages. 'It is true that the introduction is written by someone who calls himself John le Carré,' he continued, '. . . but there is no copyright in pen names, and I can hardly believe that these wild Phillips Oppenheim* speculations and the vulgar

* E. Phillips Oppenheim (1866–1946), prolific and successful author of cliché-ridden spy thrillers.

and untrue portrait of Philby at the end are by the distinguished author of *The Spy who Came in from the Cold*.'[6] This clash between the two spy novelists over Philby was itself the subject of an article in the American magazine *Time*.[7]

Nineteen-sixty-eight was a year of upheaval, when the hopes of the Prague Spring were crushed by Soviet-led tank squadrons, when students fought running battles with policemen in the centre of Paris and when protests against the Vietnam War deeply divided the American public. The clashes in the streets, and the shocking assassinations of Martin Luther King and Bobby Kennedy, both leaders advocating peaceful change, suggested a disastrous spiral of revolution and counter-revolution. Some interpreted the events taking place across the world as a conflict between the generations. It was also a time of radical innovation in the arts, when existing conventions were subject to challenge. Perhaps this background helps to explain David's blank-verse poem 'The Night of the March', published on the 'Opinion' page of the *Telegraph Magazine* in July of that year: though surely it has autobiographical origins also. Addressed to his father (the boss of a corporation) by a son who has died in some form of apocalypse, it is a remonstrance for his neglect. Indeed the son is a Christ-like figure:

Father, don't weep I beg you
I can't stand your tears . . .

I heard these hammers beating, driving in the nails . . .
. . . My vision
is a little indistinct
and my side is aching painfully . . .

Look, please don't be upset
Because there is the age gap
We will very soon
Be cleared away.
Truly. What are three bodies in a town like this,
Two murderers and me?[8]

Around this time David wrote another blank-verse poem, entitled 'It's a Long Way Home, Dickie Ann'. This does not seem to have been published anywhere. Perhaps the most impressive attribute of this almost entirely incomprehensible poem is its length: thirty-six manuscript pages.* What it suggests is a restless creativity in David, seeking a new outlet.

It had been frustrating for Pick to see the Philby book, with David's introduction, at the top of the British bestseller list in the early months of 1968. He had been hoping for another le Carré long before this – as had Jack Geoghegan. *The Looking-Glass War* had been published back in 1965. In January 1967, when Pick had spent a weekend with David, he had been led to believe that the next novel was imminent. 'It is finished, but David needs another four to six weeks before letting me see it,' Pick wrote confidently afterwards.[9] But weeks passed, with nothing to see. 'I must ask you to bear with me patiently a little longer,' David wrote to Pick in mid-May. In the summer of 1967 he spent a fortnight with Pick and his family at their London flat,† working hard on the book. In the autumn he took his new secretary with him to California to try and make progress away from any distractions. But the novel remained unfinished. Several times he was close to abandoning it altogether.[10]

Geoghegan urgently wanted another le Carré bestseller. He had already told David that *The Looking-Glass War* was not the follow-up he had been looking for. In February 1967 he had hinted that 'the next le Carré' must be commercially a 'big book' so that a scheme to offer Coward-McCann shares to the public would be successful – a suggestion that David found 'very unattractive'. His American lawyer, 'Mort' Leavy, warned they were in for a considerable struggle with Coward-McCann 'on the financial side'. Geoghegan missed no opportunity to tell him that prices were going down.[11]

Eventually David took himself off to Germany in great secrecy, with a briefcase weighed down by hundreds of pages of handwritten manuscript, and worked in a hotel room overlooking the Rhine in Remagen, about

* David has suggested that he may have been drunk when he wrote it.

† Pick's daughter (then twenty years old) gave up her room for him.

a dozen miles upriver from Bonn. There, with the help of a 'kind angel', he at last succeeded in bringing the book to a completion. He entitled it *A Small Town in Germany*, an ironic reference to the anomalous status of Bonn as the Federal Republic's capital.

David left for New York soon after delivering the typescript of *A Small Town in Germany* to Heinemann. 'I am going away at once to write a book and come to terms with life,' he wrote to Ann. He referred to 'my great failure to find happiness'.[12] It was implicit that he would not be coming back to Coxley. He had found sanctuary with his friend and former agent John Miller, who lived at Sancreed House, not far from Land's End, a former Georgian vicarage surrounded by subtropical gardens. David took the top floor on a semi-permanent basis. 'It was because of you that I came to Cornwall at the lowest point in my life,' David would say in his funeral oration for Miller in 2002, 'just as so many others came to you in their distress.'

At the time Miller and his companion Truscott were selling antiques; Miller, who would become a renowned and successful artist, was then just beginning to paint, selling his work in pubs for a fiver a time, while Truscott would become an accomplished potter and picture restorer. Miller's beloved mother 'Reni' lived in the converted barn next door. It was a warm, welcoming set-up: a place where David could relax, work and bring his children and other guests, confident that they would be welcome. At the centre of this alternative extended family was Miller himself, a calm, benign presence, while Truscott cooked delicious meals and entertained them with sharp one-liners. Neither was especially camp, which was perhaps just as well, because David expressed dislike of 'fairies'. But he felt comfortable in their company, and relaxed about addressing each of them as 'lover', a term of affection his male characters would use towards each other in the novel he was writing.

In the gardens at Sancreed were a number of wooden cabins that served as holiday homes. Most of those who came to stay were male couples. The Sexual Offences Act 1967 had decriminalised homosexual relations between adults, but nevertheless this remained a furtive, underground activity, tolerated but not altogether accepted. Sancreed

House was a haven for homosexual men, a place where they could relax and be themselves, without having to hide. David observed some surprising visitors to the 'fuck huts' at Sancreed, including prominent married politicians and other famous figures accompanied by their boyfriends.

The break-up of a marriage is seldom tidy; typically it is a tangle of departures and returns, quarrels and reconciliations. The Cornwells' was no exception. That summer he took a villa not far from Venice and invited Ann to join him there with the children, though his invitation seemed half-hearted: 'we can put the world's affairs to rights'.[13] In any case she chose not to go. Afterwards he moved on to Paris, where he worked on a film treatment for his new novel. Again he suggested that Ann joined him there, and again she declined the invitation. She had been very upset to discover a love letter from a woman whom she knew; he tried to assure her that the liaison was 'brief, worthless and forgotten'.[14] In an undated letter she referred to the 'extremely painful' possibility of 'hearing about fresh adulteries, possibly with other acquaintances'.

David's letters at this time repeatedly stressed his concern for his children. He asked John Margetson to act as an intermediary with Ann. He hoped to live at Sancreed when he was in England, to visit the children at school and receive visits from them in the holidays. 'I have no attachments outside the family,' he wrote to Margetson. 'I like to work in Sancreed, and have no intention of remarrying or getting closely involved with other women for a good time; I want to spend a bit of time each year abroad.' David asked Ann to consider an arrangement that would allow him to return to Coxley for specific periods of the year, according to a predetermined and fairly strict routine. 'I have had a lot of affairs whereas she has had none. I know that sustained affection/love is beyond me and I have chosen a fairly lonely road. But I also have conditions to make: that she sees her mother when I am not there; that she does not punish me and rebuke me because it is not a *whole* relationship . . .'[15]

In an attempt to understand why his marriage was failing, David had consulted a psychiatrist, to whom he sent a long document of self-analysis. He wrote that he did not think he was capable of 'that total abdication of intellect which real passion, or love, may demand'; instead he was searching for 'a relationship which is dignified, and liberates me for my work and protects me a little at the raw points'. He admitted that he had found:

> a mistress who might very well provide me with the happiness I speak of – and whom I in turn can please with my success, if it returns, and my talent, if it has not left; but she has the rare gift of not pressing me, and we have no particular plans. In the time we have been together – admittedly never long – I have been content, and have written a great deal. When this last book was in shreds, it was she who helped me piece it together and make something of it. I find her compassionate, understanding and remarkably intelligent.

This was (Valerie) Jane Eustace, the 'kind angel' in Remagen who had helped him bring *A Small Town in Germany* to completion. They had met at an otherwise dreary books event in Birmingham. The daughter of a dentist, she was then aged thirty (seven years younger than David), unattached, and living alone in a flat in Primrose Hill. A friend described her as 'a pretty pink-and-white English rose who looked as though she had been raised in a vicarage'.[16] For the past decade she had worked in publishing, first as secretary to the literary agent George Greenfield, and then in publicity for the publishers Hodder & Stoughton. After six months she had been promoted to become foreign rights manager. At her first Frankfurt Book Fair, a German publisher came to the Hodder stand asking for 'Miss Eustace' which he pronounced 'Oystace': a story that later amused David, and 'Oysters' became his nickname for her, often abbreviated to 'Oy', or sometimes just 'O'. Modest and retiring, she nevertheless knew her own mind and could be forceful when required. 'She carried out her duties with warmth and exemplary efficiency, and became well known in the publishing trade,' wrote Greenfield.[17] Though she was not, as she has often been mistakenly identified, an editor, she possessed qualities that would be very helpful to David: practical and organisational skills, combined with publishing savvy. Most important of all, she had an unshakeable faith in David's writing, a faith that would sustain him through periods of self-doubt.

Jane understood that David's work was sacred to him. If the truth had to be lived to be discovered – as it did for Faust – then live it, and pay the price. In Jane, David had found a helpmeet, a companion, who would support and encourage him in his writing for the rest of his days. She recognised from early in their life together that she would have to share him with other women. The restless, self-destructive search for love is part of his nature. It has led him into impulsive, driven, short-lived affairs; none of them has threatened the stability of his relationship with Jane. 'I think we're more monogamous than most couples,' he told one guest. For him, she would always be his best friend, his wise counsel and his anchor through every storm.

David's infidelities have created a duality and a tension that became a necessary drug for his writing, often brought about by deliberate incongruity. The secrecy involved and the risk of exposure have themselves been stimulating, bringing a dangerous edge to the routine of everyday existence. From an early stage in their relationship Jane has suffered David's extramarital adventures, and tried to protect him from their consequences. Though it has not been easy for her, she has behaved with quiet dignity. 'Nobody can have all of David,' she said recently.

In October 1968 David received a letter from an unexpected source: Stanley Thompson, his old housemaster. Thompson had been prompted to write after hearing David take part in the long-running BBC radio programme *Any Questions?*, as one of a panel* answering questions from the public at Poole Technical College. David wrote back on Coxley notepaper. 'I lead an odd life, partly here, partly in Paris, and partly in the States,' he told Thompson. 'It is mainly films which take me away so much, and a desire for change I suppose.'

> I hated teaching at Eton, was deeply depressed by the Foreign Service, and still have my gloomy memories of Sherborne. Isn't it odd? I suppose that after shaking off all those gruesome family ties, and then getting out of Sherborne, I have just been determined not to accept any institution at face value any more.

* The other members of the panel were Quintin Hogg MP, Malcolm Muggeridge and the progressive writer and teacher Baroness Stocks.

He mentioned the satisfaction he gained from writing. His was, he wrote, 'a curious, godless, lonely life all the same, and still treading that arrogant moral search!'[18]

Heinemann's edition of *A Small Town in Germany* was published on 28 October 1968. Ominous political developments in the Federal Republic suggested that the book might be prophetic in predicting a revival of the extreme right. In March the neo-Nazi National Democratic Party* had secured a markedly increased proportion of the votes in municipal elections; polls suggested that it might rise high enough in the forthcoming national elections to straddle the 5 per cent hurdle for parties aspiring to send delegates to the Bundestag. 'To my mind this is the finest novel he has ever written,' Heinemann's editorial director Roland Gant wrote to Malcolm Muggeridge a week before it was published, 'and it looks as if events in Germany are going to catch up with his fiction.'[19] A German translation of the novel was rushed through. The *Frankfurter Allgemeine Zeitung* noted both le Carré's ability 'to observe and listen' and his understanding of German political psychology, 'particularly hurt pride'. The writer thought that it would only be possible to judge the accuracy of his vision of the near future in ten or twelve years' time.[20] Just before publication it was announced at a press conference in New York that film rights had been sold to Avco Embassy Pictures. David would be writing the screenplay.

Once again David had been dreading what the critics might say. In a letter to Vivian Green, he quoted his publishers as claiming that *A Small Town in Germany* was 'my most ambitious book, whatever that means . . .'[21] He had been demoralised by Heinemann's offer of an advance against royalties of £22,000, which had fallen far short of his expectations.[22]

'The book is, quite simply, too long,' wrote the anonymous *Times Literary Supplement* reviewer.† 'Like Greene (he must be sick of the comparison) he can be glib. But like Greene he has the right obsessions, and works on them with the right mixture of device and rawness.'[23] Writing in *The Times*, the crime novelist H. R. F. Keating seemed to find the novel pretentious. 'The

* Then led by Adolf von Thadden, enabling David's quip: 'one Adolf is enough'.
† Francis Hope.

whole structure is ridiculously undermined by one omnipresent vice. The writing is overpoweringly literary.' Keating diagnosed that 'Mr le Carré has too much time on his hands now that he no longer needs to work for his bread-and-butter.'[24] Even Neal Ascherson, who as an *Observer* correspondent in Bonn had become friendly with David, thought *A Small Town in Germany* 'overloaded'.[25] On the other hand C. P. Snow, in an article for the Book of the Month Club, considered him to be 'on the peak of his form'; he is, he wrote, 'one of the most interesting writers alive'.[26]* The publisher Tom Rosenthal, reviewing the novel in the *New Statesman*, pronounced it to be 'certainly at least a near masterpiece' (a piece of curiously qualified hyperbole).[27] And the English critic Richard Boston praised it in the *New York Times* as 'an exciting, compulsively readable and brilliantly plotted novel'.[28]

A Small Town in Germany was far from being a commercial failure. By the end of the year Heinemann had sold more than 50,000 copies, plus a further 20,000 to a book club. In America, the book went straight into the *New York Times* bestseller list and remained there for twenty-eight weeks, reaching no. 2. Its net hardback sales in the USA would be 66,000, an improvement on the 59,000 sales of *The Looking Glass War*. But after the phenomenal success of *The Spy who Came in from the Cold* this seemed disappointing. Jack Geoghegan had taken to telephoning David late at night, often when he had been drinking. On one of these occasions he told David bluntly that he hadn't 'had the balls' to follow up *The Spy who came in from the Cold*.

A few days after publication, David wrote to Charles Pick about the reviews:

> I know you are terribly disappointed at the reception my book has received; deep down, you seem to be more depressed than I am. I *know* it is my best book by far, and I know what I have to do for the future. Equally, it is not a perfect book, and I am one of those writers whose imperfections are a great deal more interesting than their virtues. To be honest, I am even alarmed at how seriously the reviews affect you: and by now *The Times* will have

* In 1970 David repaid his debt to Snow with an elegiac *Sunday Times* piece looking back at his 'Strangers and Brothers' sequence of novels.

driven in the extra nail; it is an unanswerable charge, and therefore cheaply made, that I am too rich, too pretentious, too much all the rest. For critics, you *must* try and realise, I am simply too much altogether: too fluent, too young, and too capable. This is why, after 'The Spy', I recognised, as I believe you must, that personal publicity about me is very ill-advised . . . This is something Jack and I have learnt at great cost in the States: I *am* in an extremely equivocal position. A thriller-writer with pretensions? A novelist who hasn't the guts to drop the thriller form? An FO smoothie doing his upper-class PR and [illegible] the Establishment he lampoons . . . At the moment, this is the anti time.[29]

With some further financial help from his sons, Ronnie had returned from the East. While remaining an undischarged bankrupt, he resumed business as a 'property and financial consultant'; and though now based in England, he continued to pursue interests overseas. He telephoned David from Zurich, reversing the charges.

'Son, it's your old man.'

'What can I do for you, father?'

'You can get me out of this damned jail, son. It's all a misunderstanding. These boys just won't look at the facts.'

Ronnie had been arrested for hotel fraud. 'How much?' David asked wearily. There was no answer, but a long pause, and then the gulp of a man fighting back tears. David found himself weeping too.

'I can't do any more prison, son.'

In March 1969 Ronnie made a triumphant appearance at a dinner held to celebrate the fortieth anniversary of the Poole Round Table. As its founding chairman, he was an honoured guest. He brought with him good wishes from 'Tablers' across the Channel, having met the President of the French Round Table while travelling back from Vienna. His scintillating speech produced a standing ovation.[30]

David mentioned Ronnie in a letter to John Margetson that June. 'Not long ago Father surfaced with a "this-is-it, seven-thousand-quid-or-I'm-in-the-workhouse" touch,' he wrote, 'and in the end we gave him a thousand in old ones and he promptly pushed off to Madrid and, so far as I can make out, blew it in a fortnight.'[31]

Ronnie was not above resorting to blackmail in between the pleading. When he heard about David's involvement with a woman, he demanded payment of £1,000 as the price of his silence. On another occasion he threatened to sue David for failing to mention him in a television interview. One Christmas he telephoned David at Coxley, to say that he was just down the road, in Wells. Could he drive over to spend Christmas with his grandsons? David felt torn. It was a turbulent time in the marriage, and Ronnie was the last person in the world that Ann wanted as a visitor. With a heavy heart he told his father that he was not welcome at Coxley.

From time to time over the next few years Ronnie would turn up at Westminster, where Simon was now boarding, and take his eldest grandson out to lunch at Simpson's or the Savoy. Such occasions were an ordeal for Simon, who found that he had very little to say to his grandfather.

Ronnie had taken the opportunity of his return to England to divorce his second wife, Jean, from whom he had been separated for almost a decade. His first wife, David's mother Olive, was living in the cottage David had bought for her near Woodbridge. One day her daughter Alex, by now a young woman, answered the doorbell, to find herself facing a huge bunch of flowers. Ronnie's large head appeared from one side. He seemed vexed to see her there, rather than her mother. 'I'd like you to make yourself scarce,' he said.

Some years later Ronnie would marry for a third time. His new wife was Joy Folland, a longstanding mistress of his, who had two children from a previous marriage. David had been billeted with her during the war. She wore twinset and pearls, and appeared to those who met her to be 'county'. The day after the wedding, Ronnie took her to the Derby.

John Miller led David on a walk to Tregiffian, where he and Truscott had lived when they first came to Cornwall. Their house, which lacked electricity and running water, had been one of three clifftop cottages forming a terrace facing out to sea, down a long track from the nearest road. The original occupants had been cliff workers, producing crops from the meadows that descended the cliff in steps; in the mild Cornish climate flowers bloomed and vegetables ripened earlier than anywhere else in the kingdom. The opening of the London–Penzance railway had placed a big premium on early crops, until refrigeration crippled the market. Now the cottages were derelict, their roofs falling in. But the location was spectacular, facing south over a vast expanse of sea. Walks led across the clifftops in both directions along rugged paths. David was so taken by the place that he accosted the farmer who owned the cottages, then out ploughing his fields. He arranged to buy them, including nearly a mile of cliff, for £9,000: a substantial sum, almost twice the price of an average house, but maybe a small amount to pay for somewhere to settle. Once they were his, work started to convert the three cottages into a single dwelling.

By coincidence, another successful writer lived in a simple cottage only a short distance away. Derek Tangye wrote the 'Minack Chronicles', a series of books celebrating the pleasures of living in rural Cornwall, often featuring animals as characters; his books were all bestsellers, and it became a long-running joke between the two authors that his were more popular than David's. Over the next thirty years Tangye's admirers would often turn up at Tregiffian, roosting in the garden or lurking by the door, some mistaking David for Derek. 'That way,' David would explain patiently, 'about a mile.'

Tangye and his wife Jean (known as 'Jeannie') were unlikely neighbours in that remote part of West Cornwall. Before they had settled there in the early 1950s he had worked in Fleet Street as a gossip columnist on the *Daily Express* and elsewhere, while she had been an agony aunt on the *Daily Mirror*, and before that press officer for the Savoy Hotel Group. Their friends, who included Danny Kaye, Beverley Nichols, A. P. Herbert, Noël Coward, Bing Crosby and Tyrone Power, had been amazed when this good-looking and sophisticated couple chose to exile themselves to a simple cottage in such an isolated place. Tangye had served in MI5 during the war, in a press section set up by John Bingham, and had worked closely with Bingham on the deception plan surrounding Operation Torch, the Allied invasion of North Africa. It has been alleged that he continued to work for MI5 secretly after the war, and even that he was a Soviet agent, though the case has not been proven beyond doubt.[32]

He was a small man, touchy and jealous, a rogue and a troublemaker; he and David would develop what David would call 'an adversarial friendship', lubricated by often refilled glasses of whisky. Though David was sceptical at first about the sincerity of Tangye's pose as the plain man's philosopher, and shuddered at his purple prose, he came to accept that

Tangye's books were written from the heart, and that 'you could never quite deny the magic'. Despite his execrable style, Tangye 'gave more comfort and joy to more readers in his lifetime than most writers dream of'. David would sometimes visit Tangye when his own writing was not going well, and found that 'within an hour his strength, heart and energy had bounced me back to life'. As David would reflect after Tangye's death, they had 'an almost ridiculous amount in common': the same love of Cornwall; the same 'places and faces from the secret world of the post-war years'; the same need for solitude, 'interspersed with bouts of random, crazy conversation'; even the same drinking habits. Perhaps Tangye was a foil to David, reflecting back at him his fraudulent self, or the self that he feared becoming. Tangye was libidinous, sometimes drunken and not always clean; Jane did not enjoy his company, but David described him as 'a wicked, adorable man'. In 1996 David would deliver the eulogy at Tangye's funeral, surveying a friendship that had lasted more than a quarter of a century: he concluded that he had 'loved him greatly', despite the fact that Tangye's final words to him were 'bugger off'.[33]

Miller introduced David to a fellow artist, Karl Weschke, who would become another lifelong friend. Indeed David was an important patron to Weschke, who would have to wait until the 1990s before he began to get the wider recognition he deserved. A small man with piercing eyes and more than a passing resemblance to Picasso, Weschke seemed haunted by the past; indeed his disturbing work appeared to draw on the terrible things he had witnessed in his youth. 'The artist's eye must shrink from nothing,' he would say. He lived on a cliff overlooking the sea at Cape Cornwall, an idyllic spot in complete contrast to his home-town of Gera, an ugly industrial city in what was now East Germany. Weschke's childhood had been scarred by poverty and degradation. The son of a prostitute, he had embraced the ideology of National Socialism and served in the Luftwaffe. He had been brought to England as a prisoner-of-war and had lived there ever since, with a succession of wives and partners (several of them Jewish), though he would remain a German citizen to the end; indeed he remained aggressively himself. This was a characteristic that David relished about him: 'the Karl who from Year Zero set out to build a brain and a heart and a talent; the Karl who stuck to his Germanness, and built on it through thick and thin . . .'[34] Most of all he valued his dedication to his calling.

'Like many artists, and like many of the world's strivers, Karl readily identified with Goethe's Faust, whose mission was to find out what the world contains at its inmost point,' David would write in drafting a eulogy for Weschke after his death in 2005, 'and everyone knows that means there will be bodies along the path.'[35] For David, Weschke was a slice of Germany on his doorstep in Cornwall, a man still raw from his early experiences: combative and sometimes difficult, but also warm and often charming.

Around the same time as he bought the cottages at Tregiffian, David bought a piece of land in Wengen and built a chalet, fulfilling a childhood dream. His purchase was made possible by his old friend Kaspar von Almen, at that time chairman of the local parish council. The chalet would be ready to inhabit by the autumn of 1969. Some time afterwards David invited Robin Cooke to a party there, but Cooke declined, explaining that he could not afford to come. 'I suppose that the super-rich are different from other people,' David commented apologetically.

Earlier in the year he had taken the boys for a skiing holiday in Zermatt, staying with Alan Clark and his wife Jane. 'They don't go out at all, are fundamentally anti-social & terrifically rich,' David wrote to Ann. Clark's friends were 'ghastly'. He had endured an evening with an earl and his wife, 'louche, thick and arrogant'. The Earl had offended him by praising the 'benevolent dictatorship' in Argentina.[36] David was startled to receive a bill afterwards. It seemed outrageous for Clark to charge him for staying at his chalet when he had so often borrowed David's penthouse flat. Clark himself seemed to realise this, because he rang up and apologised. 'I shouldn't have sent you that bill,' he said. 'Jane is furious with me.'

'I eventually found him too rich for my blood,' David would tell Clark's biographer. 'He offended the last of the Puritan in me.' The final straw came when Clark had once again borrowed the penthouse while David was away. Afterwards his charwoman handed in her notice. Investigating on his return, he discovered that when she had gone in there to clean up, she had found blood on the wall. She had consulted the concierge, a former Scottish policeman; together they had decided to have the flat redecorated before he returned. The concierge was entirely silent about it. David never asked for details. In retrospect he thought that the girls were much younger than he had realised: 'there was some very dark stuff going on'.

So far as David was concerned, that was the end: he broke contact. By this time he was living in Cornwall. Clark drove down there and put a note through the letterbox, but David did not reply.

The film of *The Looking Glass War* was released in September 1969. It was written and directed by Frank Pierson, who had taken on the project after it had been abandoned by Jack Clayton. This was Pierson's first feature film; previously he had worked in television, and written screenplays for such films as *Cat Ballou* and *Cool Hand Luke*. Unfortunately his script missed much of what the book was about. He showed the East German rockets as real, whereas the book had suggested that they were a fantasy, a piece of wishful thinking on the part of Leclerc, head of the Department. The script downplayed the rivalry between the Department and the Circus, thus making Leclerc's longing for an intelligence coup difficult to understand. The character of Smiley did not appear at all, perhaps for contractual reasons. Pierson had assembled a strong cast, including Ralph Richardson, Timothy West, Susan George, Ray McAnally and Anthony Hopkins, playing Avery. The part of Leiser was taken by the American actor Christopher Jones, whose voice had to be dubbed to make him sound convincing as a Pole living in England; even so, his long hair and rock-star good looks made him an implausible choice for an undercover agent in 1960s East Germany. The jazzy score seemed more suited to a summer-holiday idyll than to a doomed operation behind the lines.

Once Clayton had rejected his script, David had no further involvement in the movie, which he would rate in a retrospective interview given at the National Film Theatre in 2002 as 'truly bad'.

The film had taken a long time to reach the screen. Before it appeared there had already been discussions about a film version of David's next book, *A Small Town in Germany*. Robert Shaw's menacing demeanour and intimidating physical presence made him an obvious casting as the hardbitten security man, Alan Turner; Shaw himself was so keen to play the part that he offered to write a script himself. As well as being an actor Shaw was a novelist, who had already adapted two of his own works for the screen; but he led an undisciplined life, with competing demands on his attention. After a succession of delays he promised to finish the script while on location in Spain, where he had rented a villa belonging to Orson Welles. Unfortunately the villa was destroyed by fire while he was staying there, and with it his script.*

After this setback David decided to undertake the job himself. His failure with *The Looking-Glass War* increased his motivation to succeed next time around. His treatment for *A Small Town in Germany* was intended to show how the essentially intellectual chase of the book could be translated into a physical chase more suitable for film. In particular the treatment incorporated an important structural change: the physical presence, for a substantial portion of the film, of Leo Harting himself. In the book he appears only as an unnamed figure in the prologue and then is absent from the rest of the narrative until glimpsed from a distance on the final page. David produced a first draft of the script in March 1969. The plan was to shoot the film in the autumn, but by June there was still no director attached to the project. Karel Reisz had shown initial interest, but then told David that he thought that the script debased the book; another director branded it 'professional suicide'. Eventually Sydney Pollack came on board. Pollack was a young director, whose first big feature film *They Shoot Horses, Don't They?* would be released later that year, winning five Academy Awards. David worked closely with him on the script, at Coxley, in the Swiss chalet and at a beach house in Malibu, and completed a second draft in November.

Pollack's upbringing in a small town in the mid-west had been hard: his father left the family home while he was still an infant and he had been raised by his alcoholic mother, who had died when he was only sixteen. Unsurprisingly his schooling had been rudimentary, but he made a virtue out of his unsophisticated background. 'I'm from South Bend, Indiana,' he would say. 'If I get it, everyone gets it.' David took him to Bonn, where the novel was set, and showed him the hotel where Chamberlain had stayed when he came to confer with Hitler. Pollack was puzzled. 'I know who Hitler was, of course,' he said: 'but who's this Chamberlain cat? The only Chamberlain I know is Wilt "The Stilt" Chamberlain.'†

* It has been suggested that the fire was caused by Shaw smoking in bed, after he had had too much to drink.

† A basketball player of the 1960s and early 1970s, considered one of the greatest ever. His nickname derived from the fact that he was over seven feet tall.

Frustratingly, the plan to make a film of *A Small Town in Germany* came to nothing.* More than twenty years later Pollack had a reason to re-read the script. 'Jesus, there's some good stuff in those pages,' he wrote to David afterwards. 'With all the groaning I think we came very, very close.'[37]

In Malibu, just before Christmas, David received a curt telegram: 'James Kennaway is dead. Ann.'

The full details of what had happened would not be known until later. Kennaway had gone to London to see Peter O'Toole, who had been cast in the lead role of 'Pink' in *Country Dance*, the film based on his novel *Household Ghosts*. After lunching with O'Toole, Kennaway had left London in the early evening to drive to Gloucestershire. He was due back in time for a dinner with Susan and friends to discuss setting up a restaurant in Fairford. On the newly built M4 motorway his Volvo had spun out of control, veering across the lanes before breaching the central reservation into the paths of oncoming cars. According to the coroner's report, he had suffered a massive coronary: he was probably already dead by the time his car collided with the others.

As Kennaway himself had so often predicted, he had died young. His death lent a grim irony to the title of his most recent novel, *Some Gorgeous Accident*. Published in the year before he died and set in Swinging London, the book had explored a triangular relationship. Two men love each other like brothers, but one (ironically named 'Fiddes', suggesting faithfulness) betrays the other by seducing his woman, 'a smooth-walking, cool-talking, coon-meeting, all-happening chick' – named Susie, though the character, an American photographer, was based on another woman. There were numerous echoes of what had happened two years earlier between David, Susan and James, including a confrontation at a railway station in which both men take Susie by an arm and try to pull her in different directions. David said that he had not read the book, but even if this were so, it seems likely that he had a notion of its content, if only from the reviews. So his horror and distress

* Pollack borrowed the name 'Turner' for the protagonist (played by Robert Redford) of his 1975 film *Three Days of the Condor*.

at the death of his friend was mingled with feelings of confusion and, perhaps, resentment.

His new novel could be interpreted as a response to *Some Gorgeous Accident*. It seems that he may have started writing it before Kennaway's death; he had told Ann some six months later that he had begun 'a long novel quite unlike the one I meant to write and no sort of suspense'.[38]

Susan hoped that David might invest in her new restaurant, which she planned to name Pinks as a tribute to her husband's memory. They arranged to meet a few weeks after the funeral, but David pulled out at the last moment when he had to go abroad at short notice. Instead they spoke on the telephone. 'I have felt very little but anger since our telephone conversation,' he wrote to her afterwards:

> I have thought long and deep about what you said, and I know that I don't want to put money into your restaurant . . . there is just too much in me that objects: the knowledge, perhaps, that I have been laughed at a little too much in the last four years . . . the whole three-cornered game, as I remember it, still sings in my ears. To give you money is to dance again to the same music . . .[39]

Susan seems to have written him a letter of remonstrance, if not rebuke, because in his next letter he acknowledged that 'everything you wrote was true'.

> I was mad to write as I did – God knows what lunatic notions were going round my head. Please try to forgive me – put it down to a momentary madness in my own kind of bereavement which I know, I *do* know, is absolutely nothing beside yours. I shall keep your letter because I deserved it. Please try to get rid of mine and try to forget it. Forgive me.[40]

Some months later David was in New York, staying at the Plaza Hotel, when he learned that Susan was in town. He telephoned her and they arranged to meet. When she arrived at his hotel, she found him with Sydney Pollack. She chatted happily with Pollack until David became impatient and dragged her away. They spent that night together in his hotel room. Afterwards he relented and agreed to put money into her restaurant after all. He sent her a cheque for £3,000 with a note wishing her luck, to which he added a jokey postscript alluding to their night in New York – 'the most expensive one since Liz Taylor in her prime!'*

At Susan's request David provided a quote† for Kennaway's posthumous novel *The Cost of Living like This* (1969), though afterwards he admitted that 'of course' he had not read the book. 'I couldn't possibly,' he wrote to her. 'I didn't read the last one either. I haven't changed *that* much!'[41] Susan was keen to explore the possibility of publishing James's letters and diaries, though to do so was potentially explosive, as they dealt in detail with his reactions to her affair with David. After consulting James's agent, she wrote to David suggesting that they should meet for lunch to discuss the matter; she appears to have proposed that he might help edit the diaries. David replied that he did not want to 'bury myself' in them, because then 'I shall be thrown completely for the book I'm now writing, and lose that very concentration which is my strength.' He could only write without interruption or distraction.

> I have lived and relived those ghastly scenes, and now they are pretty well asleep in me . . . I've a good idea what he has written about me, and for myself I simply don't care . . .
>
> It is like this for me: I feel a sentimental affection for you from old times. It simply doesn't go beyond that – I haven't a large register of emotion, some people are made like that, & I have made a fool of myself several times by playing in the league which I don't belong to . . . I am weak, a sort of tart who pays, and the one thing I'm gradually learning is to keep to my own track. I have one ambition which makes me quite ruthless: I *am* going to get these books written, and I am *not* going to be walked over any more . . . I may say other things, think of other things for a few hours at a time, but the one bedrock of resolution is this: I am not in search of an ultimate in my life, but only in my work. I have that responsibility to an unfulfilled talent. There is nothing dishonourable to that – it's simply a different scale of values from the one you're used to.

* Susan repaid the loan in 1973.

† 'More than any other of his books, it testifies to his extraordinary poetic talent and the power of his insight. The theme is man's triumphant conquest over his own insufficiency: he was equal to it.'

> You say I'm for me, well, that's another way of putting it. Who isn't, at the end of the day?[42]

'I think we should dissolve our marriage,' David had written to Ann from Malibu. 'I have played too many parts in the hope that I became one of them and now I must accept the pain of trying to live honestly.' She was jealous of the fact that he would be able to take the boys on expensive holidays while she could not afford these; he protested against her plans to keep the children away from him. 'You seem to see my father's shadow everywhere: you seem to think that I'm going to fill them with champagne and urge women on them . . .'[43] Their correspondence became increasingly strained. 'Dear, dear Ann forgive me, I can't go on and keep my dignity,' David wrote a few months later, early in 1970. 'I can't, from moment to moment, face the life I lead and it is driving me to destruction. I am desperately, hopelessly sorry.' After he had written to her from Wengen about the practical arrangements for a divorce, Ann reacted angrily. 'You are surrounded by yes-men and have perhaps lost a little contact with reality.'[44]

David informed Vivian Green that he had left Ann. He had been putting off telling him as long as he could. 'It's all very sad and reprehensible but really I feel much better for my decision,' he wrote. 'It seemed to me that we had reached a very low point and that staying together was doing neither of us (nor the children) any good.' He invited Green to come and stay at the chalet later in the summer, and explained that he might have a girlfriend staying. He was 'wrestling with a book and dare not leave it for the time being'.[45] Ten days later he wrote to Margetson to say that he was 'now deep in a new novel which is going fast and quite well'.[46] Around the same time he reported to Pick that he was 'working very hard on the new novel. I put the thriller thing aside finally – it was just too brittle – and am working very happily on something more ambitious.'[47]

This was the story of Aldo Cassidy, a prosperous entrepreneur who lives a conventional married life until he becomes involved with Shamus and Helen, a bohemian couple, and embarks on a journey of self-discovery.

The novel is obviously autobiographical, a reworking of his involvement with the Kennaways. Shamus, a dissolute writer who constantly goads

Cassidy to discard his inhibitions, is clearly based on James Kennaway; indeed his very name is Gaelic for James. Many of the scenes read like re-enactments: a riotous adventure in Paris; a catharsis in the snow-covered Alps, when Shamus offers Helen to Cassidy in a mock wedding; even a climax at the railway station. In many ways the novel is a love letter to his dead friend. Though Cassidy becomes involved sexually with Helen, his relations with Shamus – who calls him 'lover' throughout – seem much more vivid. At the end Cassidy withdraws. Though he is sent a copy of Shamus's novel *Three for the Road*, he never reads it – just as David claimed never to have read *Some Gorgeous Accident*. 'As to Shamus, with time Cassidy forgot him entirely,' the book concludes. 'For in this world, whatever there was left of it to inhabit, Aldo Cassidy dared not remember love.'

In retrospect, David felt that *The Naïve and Sentimental Lover* had more in common with the rest of his work than the critics acknowledged:

> Aldo Cassidy, like Smiley, is a naïve Hamlet, constantly havering between institutional commitments and unattainable hopes. Like Smiley, or another character close to me later in my work, the luckless Magnus Pym of *A Perfect Spy*, Cassidy seems to invent inside his own head the dilemma from which he can never escape, since it is made up of the unfordable gulf between dream and reality.[48]

Like *Some Gorgeous Accident*, *The Naïve and Sentimental Lover* is very much a novel of the 1960s. It is packed with autobiographical elements – not least Cassidy's father, an old monster like Ronnie. Cassidy himself is a motherless child, who finds difficulty in relating to women. His success – 'the sudden wealth, the fame, the recognition of his talents' – has led to 'a deep and tragic change, a frightening loss of appetite for life'. It is hard not to believe that David felt at least some of this himself. 'There's no fun any more,' says Cassidy. 'Having money takes all the joy out of achievement.'

But Cassidy's angst is undercut by self-parody throughout. Though most critics would fail to recognise it, the book is meant to be funny. 'I wrote it as a sad comedy about the hopes and dreams of a middle-class, inhibited, senior management, public-school Englishman caught in a mid-life crisis at a moment in our social history when followers of the sexual revolution saw themselves locked in mortal combat with the slaves of convention,' he would write later.[49]

Even the philosophical idea behind the book is subverted by being articulated by Helen, remembering what Shamus has told her.

> Shamus had developed a theory, she said, which he had worked into his latest book. It was based on someone called Schiller who was a terrifically famous German dramatist actually but of course the English being so insular had never heard of him, and anyway Schiller had split the world in two.
>
> 'It's called being *naïve*,' she said. 'Or being *sentimental*. They're sort of different kinds of *thing*, and they interact.'
>
> Cassidy knew she was putting it very simply so that he could understand.
>
> 'So which am I?' he asked.
>
> 'Well, Shamus is *naïve*,' she replied cautiously, as if remembering a hard-learned lesson. 'Because he lives life and doesn't imitate it. Feeling is knowledge,' she added rather tentatively.
>
> 'So I'm the other thing.'
>
> 'Yes. You're sentimental. That means you long to be *like* Shamus. You've left the natural state behind and you've become . . . well part of civilisation, sort of . . . corrupt.'[50]

Versions of Schiller's dichotomy, a recurrent theme in German literature, had long interested David. 'Thomas Mann was obsessed by the attraction/repulsion, mutually, of the artist and the citizen,' he had written in one of his last, anguished letters to Kennaway, though typically he had lightened this with a joke: 'I've bored you with this before . . .'[51]

David toyed with a variety of titles for the new novel before settling on *The Naïve and Sentimental Lover*. Some of these other titles were drawn from his own past, reflecting the autobiographical nature of the book. Among those he considered were 'The Two-Stroke Lover', 'All My Life I Have Been Terrified of Ridicule', 'The Pigeon Tunnel', 'The Love Thief' and 'The Death of Christopher Robin'. The book would be dedicated 'For John Miller and Michael Truscott, at Sancreed, with love'.

Early on, David had formed the habit (which continues to this day) of sending copies of the typescripts of his novels to people for comment.

Those to whom he regularly sent typescripts tended to be friends whom he trusted, not necessarily those with any special literary qualifications; among them were John Margetson and Eddie Nowell. He sent the typescript of *The Naïve and Sentimental Lover* to his old friend Robin Cooke, who was slow to react, distracted by the demands of a young family and the business he had started with his wife Charlotte, the toy retailer Tridias. There had been some suggestion that David might put money into Tridias, to fund its expansion, but Hale Crosse had discouraged the scheme. Another reason for his delay was that Cooke was offended by what he took to be thinly disguised references to Ann, and was hesitant about how to respond. When David telephoned for the second or third time to ask what he thought of the novel, he was unsparing in his criticism. 'I think I've hurt David,' he told Charlotte after the telephone conversation ended. Some while later he received 'a 'letter of dismissal' from David, terminating their friendship.

It had been clear for some time that the arrangements for David's representation were not working satisfactorily. Though Hale Crosse was competent to handle the most important negotiations, he had neither the time nor the expertise to deal with the multitude of lesser matters which arose day to day. An author of the stature of John le Carré, published in numerous different editions around the world and constantly in demand to write short pieces and give interviews, needed a first-class agent who would give concentrated attention to his affairs. David was discontented with the service provided by Watt's successors in the agency, particularly in his foreign markets.[52] One minor grievance lodged in his memory. During a period when he was living in Paris, one of the agents had proposed coming over to see him. David had booked a table at Laserre, a gastronomic restaurant in the *huitième* frequented by artists and film stars. When the bill came, it was very large. 'I'm terribly sorry, I can't pay for this,' said the agent, with obvious embarrassment. David had no option but to settle the bill.

David's German agent, Rainer Heumann, could not have been more different. 'He was generous without limit,' David would say at his memorial service in 1996; 'it took me years of tough negotiation to buy Rainer my first meal.' When David first visited him in Zurich, where his agency, Mohrbooks, was based, Heumann had taken him to dinner at the Kronenhalle, one of the finest restaurants in the city. David found him to be excellent company, a man of great warmth and sophistication, an Anglophile who dressed beautifully and enjoyed the good things of life, without being possessed by them. Afterwards David had remarked that 'Rainer was the kind of man with whom one could steal horses' – a German expression, meaning a dependable ally.

Heumann's life story fascinated David. He had been born in Saxony, in the city of Chemnitz (known since 1953 as Karl-Marx-Stadt), into a cultured family, and had been raised in a household surrounded by books and paintings. His father, who had a fine collection of German Romanticist art, would be killed trying to rescue his treasures during an Allied bombing raid. As the product of what the Nazis would call a 'mixed marriage', his father a Jew and his mother a gentile, Heumann had been denied higher education, and instead had accepted an apprenticeship in a factory in Munich: there he had been briefly imprisoned for distributing poems by Erich Kästner, whose books had been burned by the Nazis. Being a half-Jew in Nazi Germany, Heumann was living on borrowed time; in 1944 he had been deported to a forced-labour camp in the Harz mountains, from which he had escaped and gone into hiding until the Americans arrived. In the months following liberation he had made repeated crossings into the Russian zone, risking both his freedom and safety, to bring the surviving members of his family back to the West, together with his father's precious art collection.[53]

'Rainer spoke to the middle European in me,' David would say. 'I knew who he was and I understood his enthusiasms and his endearing determination to be a gentleman – his passion for beautiful English cars and his interest in people and in the world at large.' The two men became intimate friends. 'I loved him & looked up to him as my elder brother at least, and always as the most wise and honourable and stylish friend,' David would write to Heumann's son Andreas after his death in 1996.[54] 'We spoke about everything in our lives,' Heumann would say of their friendship. 'I think those two guys are gay,' Heumann's second wife Inge once remarked half seriously, perhaps a little jealous of their closeness.

Heumann became David's primary agent throughout the world. The decision to ask Heumann to handle his business affairs was founded on friendship and trust, but it also reflected the increasing significance to David of the German market. The fact that his books often had German subjects, his fluency in the German language and his strong feeling for German culture combined to make him one of the biggest-selling foreign authors to be published there. His most recent novel, *A Small Town in Germany*, had of course been especially topical to German readers.

But though Heumann became David's lead agent, he still needed an English-language representative. Jane's former boss George Greenfield was a shrewd, foxy operator, with a mischievous streak. 'There were as many Georges as he had books inside his head,' David would write after Greenfield's death in 2000:

> The raffish exterior, the beastly little brown cigars, the David Nivenish urbanity, concealed a multitude of identities and a silent credo. There was the secret sceptic who was never surprised by human foible. There was the Cambridge double first and Leavis disciple who liked to keep his intellectual gifts out of sight until he saw the whites of his adversaries' eyes. There was the imperturbable officer and gentleman who would have you think that he had pottered his way across the Western Desert complaining about the people and the noise. And there was another man – though he very seldom declared himself – who too often felt that he had risked his life and lost good friends for values he could no longer see around him . . . At 25 he knew more about the world than most men of 50, and it gave him an edge on people a few years younger than himself. If you had served as a peacetime soldier, as I had, George was your senior captain with a bunch of campaign medals across his chest.[55]

As Greenfield sold more books to Hodder & Stoughton than to any other publisher, it was natural for him to keep in touch with Jane Eustace after she had left the agency to work there. They occasionally lunched together, and once or twice she had invited him to make up the numbers at her dinner parties. But Jane had kept her relationship with David secret, so he was surprised when he arrived at her flat one Friday evening to find David present. Greenfield had been introduced to him before, at a publishing party for Jack Geoghegan, and he would have recognised him anyway from press photographs. The three of them passed a relaxed evening at an Italian restaurant. The following week David telephoned Greenfield at his office to propose that the three of them meet again, this time for lunch.

After a long and convivial meal, washed down with three bottles of good wine and several glasses of malt whisky, David asked Greenfield whether he would be interested in becoming his agent. For a moment Greenfield wondered if it was the wine talking; but once he realised that David was serious, he readily accepted the offer.[56] Soon afterwards Jane resigned from Hodder and was taken on to the books of le Carré Productions, initially as a secretary, later as an editorial assistant. Subsequently Georges Borchardt was appointed David's representative in America.

Since becoming his British publisher in 1964 Charles Pick had become friendly with David. Their relationship had widened to embrace the two families; David enjoyed the company of Pick's children, both in their early twenties, while the Picks were happy to entertain David's eldest son Simon on half-holidays. David would sometimes stay in their Knightsbridge flat; he liked to work there because it was empty during the day, and quiet. Pick had learned that it was pointless to press David to deliver a book until he was ready to do so; he had become accustomed to periods of silence while David was immersed in writing. In April 1970 Pick received a note from Sancreed House: 'a voice from the wilderness to say that I am writing happily . . .'[57] In another letter two months later David was writing 'with subdued excitement', and said that he hoped 'to have something for you not too long away'. In the same letter he explained that he had separated finally from Ann.[58] 'My dear David,' Pick replied, 'I am sorry this has happened but I do so understand how you are feeling.' Several times over the past year he had been tempted to get in touch, he continued, 'but I felt that you knew I was here and if I could be any help, you would always call on me.' He offered to come out to Wengen to read the book when it was ready.[59]

Pick had no reason to think that anything was amiss. It was with a shock, therefore, that he received a letter from David that November terminating their professional relations:

> This is a very sad and difficult letter for me to write. I think it is time that I had a change of publisher. I have reached a moment in my writing career where, for good or ill, I have taken leave of the type of book that has made my reputation, and as never before I need to have absolute confidence in the way the transition is handled. In the last two months, as the book

> neared completion, I found myself worrying more and more about whether I was really suited – in this new role – to the house of Heinemann. The last two books, it seemed to me, had found no real acceptance outside the framework of 'The Spy' – I even remember your telling me in Paris that had you known me better you would have perhaps dissuaded me from publishing *The Looking-Glass War* at all. Just what it is that I fear for the new book I don't know; perhaps that very commercialisation which is also the admirable strength of Heinemann . . .

In his letter David acknowledged the 'close and friendly personal relationship' which the two of them had always shared. 'I do not deceive myself that this news will not be a great blow to you,' he wrote. 'I know that I mean a lot to you, and I am very, very sorry to cause you personal distress . . . But I believe that, with the great professional wisdom you have always brought to publishing, you will find it in you to agree that when an author feels he needs a change, he should make it.' In conclusion, he emphasised that this had been his decision, and his alone. No doubt he wanted to stress that he had not been influenced in his decision by his girlfriend.[60]

David's departure was 'completely unexpected' for Pick. 'How could I help feeling embittered?' he told an interviewer almost twenty years afterwards. 'I think I now knew what Victor must have felt when he moved to us.'[61]

David would say later that he had been dismayed by the 'shoddy' production values of the Heinemann edition of *The Looking-Glass War*. It was also true that Heinemann's list was essentially middlebrow – fine for spy thrillers, but perhaps not ideal for a novelist attempting something more serious. In retrospect, Pick felt that a dispute over the division of paperback royalties had contributed to the break, though David had made no mention of this in his letter. Now that most hardback and paperback publishers are integrated, authors usually receive full paperback royalties. But in those days, when most hardback and paperback publishers were separate, it was customary for the hardback publisher to retain a percentage of the royalties received from the paperback publisher. The standard authors' rate was 50 per cent; David received 60 per cent, as much as any other author on the Heinemann list, but even that was not enough for him. David told Pick that he wanted to 'break the system'. In an emotional telephone call from New York that lasted more than an hour, David begged Pick to relent and pay even 5 per cent more. Pick told him bluntly that, with so many top authors on the Heinemann list, he could not afford to make exceptions.

Pick's point of view was understandable, but then so was David's. One only had to consider the Pan edition of *The Spy who Came in from the Cold* to see his point: it had sold around a million copies, earning tens of thousands of pounds in royalties, of which half was retained by Gollancz as the original hardback publisher – though their original advance of £175 had been earned many times over in sales of the hardback edition.

David left Heinemann without knowing his destination. He had some thought of moving to a smaller, more literary publisher. Greenfield produced a shortlist of likely British publishers, listing the pros and cons as he saw them. As it turned out, Jane's former employers fulfilled most of David's requirements. Like most British publishers in the 1960s and 1970s Hodder & Stoughton was still a family firm, run by the Hodder-Williamses and their cousins the Attenboroughs. The company had been famous between the wars for publishing thriller writers such as John Buchan, 'Sapper' (author of the Bulldog Drummond stories), Edgar Wallace and Leslie Charteris (the Saint). Under the leadership of a new generation the company was beginning a resurgence that would make it one of the most powerful forces in British publishing by the early 1980s. Jane thought especially highly of Robin Denniston, Hodder & Stoughton's managing director. David too warmed to him; he seemed more bookish and less corporate than other publishers. According to Greenfield, Denniston could almost have been a character out of a le Carré novel himself:

> Westminster and Oxford, a trained parachutist from National Service days, the son of a Royal Navy officer who served with real distinction in the Secret Intelligence Service during the Second World War,* he had that vague, slightly shambling air that concealed a sharp and incisive mind. Untidy, with the knot of his tie screwed round almost under one ear and,

* Alastair Denniston, head of the Government Code & Cypher School (Bletchley Park), 1919–42.

> more often than not, a spot of blood on his collar where he had nicked himself shaving, he did not resemble the prototype of the smart young executive. He kept a harmonium in his room at St Paul's House* and played it at times of high emotion.[62]

After David had dined with Denniston and Greenfield at Boulestin, Hodder became his choice. For his part, Denniston jumped at the opportunity to publish John le Carré. A colleague had never seen him move as fast as he did when she told him, 'There's somebody called David Cornwell on the phone'.

Jack Geoghegan read the typescript of *The Naïve and Sentimental Lover* with dismay. The book did not work for him; he was certain that there was no market for it in America. He felt strongly that David was not ready to write an autobiographical novel and had taken a wrong turn; he should have stuck to the genre which he had created, the literary spy thriller. Geoghegan was in a quandary: on the one hand, he was desperate not to lose David as an author; on the other hand, he had no confidence in the book. He was so upset that he asked his wife to read it; she felt as he did. They discussed the dilemma for days, in the kitchen, in the library, even in bed at night. The problem was exacerbated by David and Jane's imminent arrival in America; the Geoghegans had been close to Ann, and felt awkward about meeting the new woman in David's life. Geoghegan did make an offer, but this was rejected. No doubt his misgivings about the new novel had become obvious.

Jane introduced David to Bob Gottlieb, editor-in-chief at Alfred A. Knopf, perhaps the most prestigious literary publisher in America. He had built a reputation both as an effective publisher and as a dedicated and skilled editor, reckoned by many to be the best in his time. Some years before he had met Jane on a scouting trip to London, and the two of them had become friends. But he had lost contact with her after she left Hodder, until they were reunited at a dinner party given by Tom Rosenthal. Jane had telephoned him beforehand, to say that they would be meeting at Rosenthal's and that she was bringing David Cornwell, with whom she had been living. Afterwards, on the way back to where they were staying, Gottlieb told his wife of his suspicion that the evening had been orchestrated so that

* The offices of Hodder & Stoughton in Warwick Square, near St Paul's Cathedral.

he and David could meet. 'This is a guy who is so cloaked, so armoured, so deep,' he said of David. 'This guy's mind is a lot more complicated than mine – than anyone's – so, whatever this is about, I'm not ever going to try to out-think him, because I can't.' The next morning Jane telephoned to ask if he would like to read 'the new le Carré'. He had been vetted, and presumably had passed muster.

Jane explained that she could not give Gottlieb the typescript because it could not be allowed out of David's hands; so he came over to her flat to read it there. Afterwards he told David that he liked the book very much and wanted to publish it, but asked him to understand at the outset that it couldn't possibly have the success of his previous books. David took the point. This was the beginning of a satisfying relationship with Knopf, and with Gottlieb in particular, which would continue for the next quarter of a century.

Geoghegan was devastated by the loss of his star author. It felt like a death in the family. Though he would go on to publish other eminent authors, David remained the most important. For the rest of his career in publishing Geoghegan kept a photograph of the two of them on his desk, sitting in a Cornish field, having a picnic together. His son never once saw his father without the subject of David coming up in the conversation. He was still talking about him on the day before he died.

On 13 March 1971, a diary piece appeared in the trade magazine the *Bookseller*. The diarist, a hack who went under the pen name 'Whitefriar', had read a typescript of *The Naïve and Sentimental Lover* and pronounced it a 'masterpiece'. 'I'm going on record to say that this book may be hailed as the Great English Novel. It is funny, sad, poignant, and, I believe, absolutely wonderful as a publishing proposition. Lucky old Hodder.'[63]

Two days later David wrote to Pick, expressing cautious willingness to meet if it would serve any useful purpose. 'I don't quite know how matters lie between us,' he began, and continued by saying that if Pick was going to make the easy point that 'Jane has simply lined me up with her old associates, I don't think we have much to discuss'.[64]

Some months before *The Naïve and Sentimental Lover* was published in September David sent a copy to Susan Kennaway, perhaps at her request. His accompanying letter has been lost, but a deleted extract from a draft gives some idea of his thinking:

> Please try to remember that my book is absolutely *not* a portrait of you, James and me.* I showed it to you because it had obvious resonance, but neither the events nor the relationships nor the characters have *factual* similarities with [passage missing] . . . not least a year's preoccupation with the Fitzgeralds – let alone the processes of creation themselves – which make the novel in fact and in theory totally different from the events which set it in action. I don't need to tell you that – but perhaps you *have* mistaken the baying of the trade for a true word upon the book itself.

'I'm totally bewildered but I think delighted about it,' Susan responded. 'The thunderous Seamus† rang a lot of bells; likewise Cassidy.' She did not recognise herself in the character of Helen, though she accepted that some of the scenes in the novel resembled ones which had actually taken place. 'I was more worried about what you might have written about James,' she continued, 'but in fact you seem to have written about the shit-Shamus with a degree of admiration – might even say love?'

Susan had discussed her late husband's diaries and letters with a potential editor, Lynn Hughes, who received a warning from George Greenfield. 'Would you tell George to stop panicking about the letters?' asked Susan. 'I'm not that mad!'[65] David expressed the hope that his own letters would be destroyed. She told him that a publisher wanted to bring out James's diaries to coincide with 'a major publishing event in the autumn', that is *The Naïve and Sentimental Lover*. David discouraged this proposal. 'You can be sure that a book which is published "in the slipstream" of another book is never going to be a prestigious publication,' he advised.

> Most relevant of all the slipstream, by the sound of it, is created by misinformed gossip, by people who have read neither my book nor James's. The very nature of the offer makes their venture inappropriate. My book is not what they seem to think it is. I cannot speak for James's since I have not

* Years later, while watching the quiz show *University Challenge* on television, Denys Hodson would be startled by a question, posed by the quizmaster Bamber Gascoigne, asking for the names of the real people on whom the fictional characters in *The Naïve and Sentimental Lover* were based.

† She misspelt the name.

read it, but I'm sure it deserves better than to be published for such vulgar and tenuous reasons.[66]

'*The Naïve and Sentimental Lover* is widely regarded as the blip in my work, the aberration, or, more baldly, the turkey,' David would write almost thirty years later. 'British critics fell gleefully on it, welcoming it almost with one voice as the proof, if proof were needed, that I should stick to the "genre" novel and not aspire to "real" literature, to which they alone held the golden key.'[67]

The tone of bitterness is understandable, given the savagery of some of the criticism. 'The book is a disastrous failure,' was the verdict of the anonymous reviewer* in the *Times Literary Supplement*.[68] 'The narrative limps along,' according to the *Listener*'s critic.[69] 'Sporadically dazzling, but running to fat,'[70] wrote Claire Tomalin in the *Observer*. In the *Spectator*, Auberon Waugh condemned the novel as 'the product of self-indulgence and intellectual laziness'.[71]

On the other hand H. R. F. Keating, who had found *A Small Town in Germany* overblown, welcomed le Carré's decision to abandon spy novels as 'wonderfully liberating', when he reviewed *The Naïve and Sentimental Lover* in *The Times*. 'It has enabled him to give us a mainstream novel at once both delightful and considerable.'[72] To the *Sunday Express*'s Graham Lord it was 'the most interesting novel I have read this year'.[73] Frederic Raphael's review in the *Sunday Times* gave as it took away:

> *The Naïve and Sentimental Lover* is an interesting experiment and it is often painfully funny but its tone is so world-wearily whimsical and so cutely acute that there is something platitudinous, *déjà vu* even, in its originality. Paradoxically, entertainments like *The Spy who Came in from the Cold* and *A Small Town in Germany* can seem more serious, more passionate and more pertinent than this highly personal and doubtless genuine *cri de coeur*.[74]

The reviewer for the *Frankfurter Allgemeine Zeitung*, Jochen Schmidt, read *The Naïve and Sentimental Lover* as a satire, both of those who 'attempt

* Julian Symons.

to give their lives a deeper meaning through the love of art and artists' and of 'those who – under the guise of artists – exploit society without contributing one iota to its development'.[75] For Georg Hensel, writing in the *Süddeutsche Zeitung*, the book dragged, to the extent that by the time he reached page 100 he was 'gripped by a wild yearning for secret agents'; he claimed to have been delighted by the discovery of an agent on page 300, 'even if it was only an insurance agent'.[76]

The response of American critics was similarly damning. Writing in the *New York Times Book Review*, Geoffrey Wolff saw many virtues in the book. 'All that's missing from the novel's inventory of virtues is the most important thing,' he wrote: 'it doesn't do what Le Carré thinks it does. It does not penetrate the character of Aldo Cassidy.' Wolff went on to suggest a problem in the depiction of Shamus, and was by no means the only critic to do so. 'It is a sign of this novel's fundamental indecisiveness that we cannot know whether the value Shamus's wife puts on his work, "he's altering the course of world literature", is played straight or for laughs.'[77]

The *New York Times* critic Christopher Lehmann-Haupt concluded that 'le Carré has simply failed to transform life into art':

> What we are left with is really what it sounds like in summary – a slapstick potboiler about a London businessman being conned by a pair of overwrought aesthetes – a story shy of deep symbolic meaning, penetrating psychological insight, genuine wit, or any other quality that might have enriched its all-too familiar theme. In other words, it is a triteness disguised as something more, but finally most interesting for the time it takes to reveal itself as something less.[78]

The Naïve and Sentimental Lover is a raw book: perhaps too raw. There is a sense that the writer has not yet fully digested some very distressing experiences. Perhaps Geoghegan was right to think that it was too early for David to write a novel which drew so directly on his own experience. Of course the very fact that it did so made the criticism feel more personal. David had opened up his private feelings to public scrutiny and been mocked for it. Small wonder that he was 'extremely hurt' by the book's reception.[79]

Nevertheless he put on a brave face. In a letter to an American friend, he affected not to care about the reviews: 'I am sick of reading them anyway, they just annoy me.'[80] When the book appeared he had just written a long and generous tribute to one of his favourite authors, P. G. Wodehouse, for the *Sunday Times*, due to be published to coincide with the Master's ninetieth birthday; he wrote from Tregiffian to thank the literary editor, J. W. Lambert, for sending him a copy of the piece.[81] David's message was defiant: 'Weather's gorgeous, reviews foul, but the weather wins every time. A pox on Raphael et al – it's a marvellous book.'[82]

16

Keeping the bitterness at bay

'My hardest duty to myself was to keep the bitterness at bay,' David would recall of this time twenty years later. Those who have not published a book may not appreciate how destructive critical reviews can be. Years of effort can be dismissed in a few glib sentences. *The Naïve and Sentimental Lover* was his third novel in succession to receive a critical pasting. Much of the criticism had been *ad hominem*; it was even suggested that le Carré's career had run its course. To be denigrated in print is painful, of course; but more dangerous was the threat to his self-belief. Without confidence that what one produces is worthwhile, it is difficult, if not impossible, to write. David's recovery from the drubbing he had taken would be as much a test of character as of talent.

But he remained resilient: bruised, but still standing. And he refused to succumb to resentment. 'I love it all far too much to let them fuck it up for me,' he wrote of his critics, in a letter of advice to a young novelist.[1] In his next novel he would return to the genre in which he had made his name, the spy thriller. It would prove to be one of his most accomplished performances to date.

No doubt it helped that his personal life had stabilised. Jane's unwavering belief in his work bolstered him. They were now settled at Tregiffian, spending holidays at the Wengen chalet. He sold the penthouse, using her flat in Primrose Hill when they came to London. In 1971 he had divorced Ann; on 2 May 1972 he and Jane were married in a private ceremony, with only John Miller and Michael Truscott present as witnesses. (The four of them spent their honeymoon together at the Budock Vean Hotel on the Helford River, playing a four of ping-pong before retiring for the night.) He gave up smoking, having realised after almost twenty years that he didn't enjoy it. On advice from his accountant, he bought 'a filthy great Rolls': perhaps not the ideal car for negotiating the narrow lanes and bumpy tracks of West Cornwall.* Six months later Jane gave birth to a boy, whom they named Nicholas, and asked Truscott to act as his godfather. That same year Ann married Roger Martin, a diplomat whom she had met through the Margetsons. A little later she too gave birth to a son, whom they named Adam. She and David continued to meet from time to time, and talked regularly on the telephone. He sent her copies of his typescripts for comment. In due course Ann and Roger would come to stay at Tregiffian, and David and Jane would visit them at Coxley. If there was such a thing as a civilised divorce, they had achieved it.

The three children of his first marriage were welcome at Tregiffian, where Jane worked hard to make them feel at home. Perhaps the greatest tribute of all was that David put aside his writing while they were there. Simon remembers terrifying games of tennis with him on the local courts. At David's instigation John Miller came over and taught Simon and Stephen to paint. All three boys were now boarding at Westminster. Simon had won a scholarship, though David insisted on returning the scholarship money to the school. In 1976, Simon would go up to Oxford, to read physics at Wadham, switching after his first year to French and German, the same languages that his father had studied at Oxford twenty years earlier. In due course the youngest of the three brothers, Timothy, would follow him to Oxford; earlier the middle brother, Stephen, had taken a degree in photography, film and television at the London College of Printing.

In 1974 the Cornwells bought a Georgian house in Islington. One of David's motives was to provide a base for his sons from his first marriage. Ann and her husband were soon posted abroad, so it was no longer practical for the boys to spend weekends and other short breaks with their mother. Though pretty, the Islington house was small, and in 1977 the Cornwells would move again, to a larger house in Hampstead, close to the Heath.

Jane provided practical as well as moral support. She acted as David's gate-keeper, protecting him from the outside world by screening telephone calls

* The 'social baggage' that came with driving a Rolls-Royce made him uncomfortable, and he soon got rid of it.

and dealing with routine business herself, which of course her background in publishing equipped her to do. He developed a disciplined routine for writing, which has persisted, largely unchanged, to this day, though the development of word-processing has made Jane's typing less laborious. As before, he writes in longhand, often scribbling fragments of text on scraps of paper (sometimes headed paper), which Jane types up; he then cuts these into strips and arranges them as he wants by stapling them on to a fresh sheet, with handwritten interpolations, which Jane retypes into a fair copy. This process is repeated several times through a succession of drafts, often half a dozen and sometimes considerably more. One of the most impressive aspects of his work is his willingness to jettison dozens and even hundreds of pages if he thinks them unsatisfactory, and to keep revising for month after month until he reaches a text with which he feels content.

David is at his best in the morning. He rises early,* working through until lunchtime. In the afternoon he sets out on a walk on the Heath or along the cliff-top paths, carrying a notepad to jot down sentences as they occur to him. These are often snatches of dialogue, which he perfects by speaking them aloud; in Cornwall, locals have become used to hearing him apparently talking to himself in a variety of accents, and have learned not to interrupt him as he passes. Back at the house, he pours himself a Scotch, takes a look at what his wife has typed out and fiddles with it further. When he is working he retires early, at eight-thirty or so. He tries to go to bed while there is still something unresolved, so that he knows roughly, though not exactly, where to start the next morning; and sleeping on the problem always seems to deliver the answer. He has learned to respect the 'black' days, because they are usually an indication that something is wrong which he hasn't yet recognised.

Usually he starts a novel without knowing how it will develop, though like a film director he often has a vision of what the audience will see at the end, the last image in their minds as they emerge from the cinema. By allowing the story to advance spontaneously, in unexpected and unpredictable directions, David hopes to feel the same nervousness and excitement

* When he was younger he would often start work at four-thirty or five o'clock in the morning; nowadays eight o'clock is more typical.

as the reader at the twists and turns of the plot. At each stage he aims to live the part of his characters like an actor preparing for a scene, trying to evoke internally the tension that he or she might feel at that particular moment. 'When I write as an Ingush, I try to *be* an Ingush,' he wrote to a reader who asked whether he shared the anti-Russian prejudice expressed by one of his characters.[2]

David likes to begin a book with at least one strong character in conflict with something or somebody. '"The cat sat on the mat" is not the beginning of a story,' he often says, 'but "the cat sat on the dog's mat" *is*.' His characters are often torn between loyalty to individuals and loyalty to institutions. He writes far more than he can use, particularly about the minor characters, with the result that he has to cut much of what he has written to keep them in scale. But this effort is not wasted because he sweeps up the discards – which he calls 'industrial waste' – to use again in future books. 'I promise them a treat in the next book,' he told one interviewer, 'if they'll just keep quiet now.'[3]

David collects characters, whom he stores for future use. 'They mature in the bottle, sometimes for decades,' he would tell an interviewer in 2008. For instance, there was an old man he met in St John's Wood, seated on a bench with a week's shopping at his feet, weeping. When David asked him why, he replied that his wife's scolding had become unbearable to him and he couldn't find the courage to go home. He has tried to fit the old man into one of his novels, but has yet to find a place for him.[4]

When a novel is going well, he writes fast; it is not unusual for him to write a chapter in a day. The first hundred pages, and the first chapter in particular, always take much longer than the remainder. If a novel curdles in the middle, it's the first chapter that he returns to. He likes to come into the story as late as possible; the later the reader joins the story, the more quickly he or she is drawn in. But beginning late requires a lot of retrospection, which creates its own problems.[5]

David is not one of those writers who telephones his editor at two in the morning to say that he's going through a crisis and about to slit his wrists. 'I don't want to see my publishers, editors or anybody until I've produced my baby,' he says. This ensures that, when they do read his book, they will respond like ordinary readers, without any prior knowledge of its content. Even if he is struggling to make his story work, he will never seek help, but always continues until he has resolved the problem somehow himself.[6] The exception to this rule is Jane. When he is writing a novel, they 'talk book' at every opportunity. She still types his drafts, and then they work through them together. She is reluctant to criticise what he has written, though he knows how to read her responses. He speaks wryly of Jane's 'hairy eyebrow' rising in mute disapproval; but that is the full reach of her influence.

As soon as the editing process is finished he likes to get the next one under way as quickly as possible, so that he is undaunted by the pessimism of publishers or negative reviews. He tends to start his novels in London, and then continue in Cornwall. For a while he kept a flat in London where he went to write, whose whereabouts he kept secret so that he could not be disturbed there, first in St John's Wood and then nearer at hand, in Hampstead High Street.

David is a professional, who expects that same professionalism from his publishers and representatives. His attitude is encapsulated in a letter from Jane to a new publisher, written in the 1990s:

> His standards for himself, and for everybody around him, are the highest. He was Foreign Office trained and wants the world to function at that level. He is meticulous about everything; he hates to be late; he hates inaccuracy; he double checks everything; he follows up everything; he has fallbacks if things should, in spite of everybody's efforts, go wrong.[7]

For David, writing has been both a vent for the unrest within him and a source of misery. It has provided him with fulfilment and frustration. It is often a way for him to bring himself up again out of depression. He recognises that he is obsessive about his work, that it is a kind of 'joint madness' into which he has drawn Jane. Spells of over-excitement about what he has written have been followed by periods when none of it has pleased him.

David's new book was planned as the first in a sequence of interlinked novels. He talked of seven, or even more: perhaps as many as ten or fifteen.[8] The overall theme would be the struggle between the Circus and the KGB, in particular the contest between George Smiley and Karla, the mysterious and apparently all-powerful head of the 'Thirteenth Directorate of

Moscow Centre'. The 'Thirteenth Directorate' was an imaginary body, though 'Moscow Centre' was real slang used by KGB agents themselves.

For David, the actions of the intelligence services revealed the true, hidden nature of the state they represented. The Circus was England in miniature, looking back with nostalgia and contemplating the future with foreboding. Smiley's generation of senior officers, now approaching retirement, had been among England's most gallant knights in the crusade against Nazism; their reward had been to see their country reduced to the status of a second-class power, humiliatingly subservient to America. 'Poor loves,' laments a drunken Connie Sachs, the Circus's dismissed head of research. 'Trained to Empire, trained to rule the waves. All gone. All taken away. Bye-bye world.' She is nostalgic for a golden past, of the exploits of courageous young men; she does not want to hear that one of them might have betrayed his country. 'I want to remember you all as you were. Lovely, lovely boys.'

Taken as a whole, therefore, the sequence of novels provided an opportunity to train a light not just on the secret state but on the state itself, in its painful attempt to come to terms with its post-imperial role. This was a scheme that went far beyond the limits of the genre, on the scale of similarly ambitious projects in post-war fiction by such 'literary' writers as Paul Scott, Anthony Powell and C. P. Snow.[9] Once again David's inspiration was Balzac. 'I had originally intended to do an espionage *Comédie humaine* of the Smiley–Karla stand-off, and take it all over the world,' he would tell an interviewer in 2002, 'a kind of fool's guide to the Cold War.' This of course was a throwaway comment: his real aim was to examine the state of the nation, by exposing its secret underside.

It is revealed in the opening pages of the first novel that there is a Soviet 'mole' at the heart of British intelligence, controlled by Karla. 'A mole is a deep penetration agent so called because he burrows deep into the fabric of Western imperialism,' explains Irina, an unhappy Russian agent wanting to defect. The unidentified mole, code-named 'Gerald', is said to be 'a high functionary in the Circus'.* This discovery presents the authorities with a dilemma. 'We can't move,' laments the Minister's adviser, Lacon:

* Among the suspects for 'Gerald' in early drafts of the book are characters called Delaware, Greville, Zacharay and Swinburne. None of these appears in the final version.

> We can't investigate because all the instruments of enquiry are in the Circus's hands, perhaps in Gerald's. We can't watch, or listen, or open mail . . . We can't interrogate, we can't take steps to limit a particular person's access to delicate secrets. To do any of these things would be to run the risk of alarming the mole.

'It's the oldest question of all, George,' Lacon says to Smiley: 'Who can spy on the spies?' The answer is of course Smiley himself, who has been sacked from the Service for suggesting that there was a traitor in their midst. He is called out of retirement to lead the mole-hunt.

In this first novel of the sequence, which would be published as *Tinker, Tailor, Soldier, Spy*, David wanted to explore 'the inside-out logic' of a double-agent operation. He would show the mayhem that could be caused by such an agent in a strategic position within the intelligence services, as Philby had been. For all the startling revelations about Philby, Blake and others, few people fully understood what David called 'the pushme-pullyou nature of the double agent's trade':

> For while on one side the secret traitor will be doing his damnedest to frustrate the efforts of his own service, on the other he will be building a successful career within it . . . The art of the game . . . is therefore a balancing act between what is good for the double agent in his role as loyal member of his service, and what is good for your own side in its unrelenting efforts to pervert that service, to the point where it is doing more harm to the country that employs it than good; or, as Smiley has it, where it has been pulled inside out.[10]

Instead of burying himself below ground, the mole Gerald has been hiding in plain sight, as controller of a supposed double agent within the enemy camp named Polyakov, source of the much prized 'Witchcraft' material. Gerald has persuaded his colleagues that he should provide Western secrets in exchange, supposedly so that Polyakov can maintain his cover by claiming to have access to an agent within the Circus. Thus Gerald is overtly playing the part of a double agent while secretly acting as one, and each side is supplying the other with secrets to keep up the pretence. 'The only problem arises when it transpires that you've been handing Polyakov the crown jewels and getting Russian chicken-feed in return,' says Smiley.

In fact Smiley does not appear at all in the first draft of the novel. A letter to Vivian Green written more than two years later, after the book was finished, suggests why. 'My demon American lawyer has at last liberated George Smiley from the lock of Paramount Pictures so that I was able to use him, and can do so in the future, without them owning anything. . .!'[11]

The evolution of the book through successive drafts demonstrates two of David's qualities as a writer: his ability to develop and manage an exceptionally complex plot without a pre-planned scheme, and his commitment to rework what he has written over and over again until he achieves the result he wants. 'Tinker, Tailor was the most difficult book I ever wrote,' he would recall five years after it was published. He claims to have destroyed two versions of it in despair before he came up with one that he thought worked.[12]

As usual, David had begun with a character, in this case 'a big, rugged fellow with a limp', a schoolmaster colleague of his at Edgarley with some connection to MI5, who provided the outer shell for the character of Jim Prideaux, originally known as 'Billy'.[13] In the first draft Billy is living on a Cornish cliff, embittered and alone, discarded by the Service after he had been wounded in a disastrous operation behind enemy lines in Czechoslovakia. It is clear to him that he had walked into a trap, but he does not know who has betrayed him: as he eventually discovers, it was someone he loves. As the book opens he is holding a bucket in his hand, on his way to feed the chickens; he has paused to stare up at a black car weaving down the hillside towards him. This brings 'Rod' Tarr, the troubled Chief of the intelligence service known as 'the Tank', who suspects the existence of a mole within the organisation. Tarr is a closet homosexual, married to a 'dragon' wife; one of the early drafts opens with him picking up another man in a south London park. Billy is interrogated by Tarr in a safe house, just as in the finished version Tarr (now named Ricki) is questioned by Smiley.

David's original plan had been for Tarr to put Billy back in harness, to provoke the traitor into trying his hand again, thereby revealing himself. The story would be narrated by Billy in the first person. David intended to tell the whole story in real time, without flashbacks, but found that he was painting himself into a corner: 'I could think of no plausible way to pursue a linear path forward while at the same time peering back down the path that had brought my man to the point where the story began.' After months of frustration, he took the manuscript out into the garden and burned it.[14] Or so he says, though if he did this was a departure from his usual practice, which was to keep rejected drafts. Perhaps he burned a copy of the manuscript as a symbolic gesture, in the knowledge that another identical or similar copy had been preserved.

In what appears to be the second draft of the book, dated November 1971 and still told by Billy in the first person, he has relocated to Thursgood's, a boys' preparatory school in the West Country, where he is happily involved with Sal, the school's assistant matron. Only in a later draft did he revert to being the gruff, damaged loner who inspires the devotion of the unhappy schoolboy Bill Roach. The published book opens and closes with these two, though the relations between them are irrelevant to the main narrative – a device which adds humanity and perspective to the whole story.

Gradually, through successive drafts, the book took shape. A draft dated January 1972 is told in the third person, and begins with Billy, now renamed Jim, arriving at Thursgood's. The Tank has become the familiar Circus, and Smiley has assumed the role of investigator, while Tarr is no longer the ageing Chief but the younger semi-hooligan Ricki Tarr, whose encounter with Irina in Hong Kong starts the mole-hunt. Tarr follows Smiley back from his club and accosts him on his doorstep – until a draft dated October 1972, which introduces the character of Peter Guillam, first seen in *Call for the Dead*. In this and subsequent drafts Tarr tells his story first to Guillam, who alerts Lacon.

Guillam becomes an important secondary character in the sequence of novels. A man of David's generation, he admires his senior colleagues who have fought in the war. Being younger, Guillam is a more plausible man of action than Smiley, capable of subduing Tarr when he turns violent. Several of the chapters are told from Guillam's point of view, which enables the reader to observe Smiley in action without revealing his thoughts. In the book's denouement the reader shares in Guillam's confusion, when the man whom he has always idolised is unmasked as a traitor.

In its final form, the novel centres on Smiley: indeed some of the late drafts are headed 'The Reluctant Autumn of George Smiley, being the first volume of The Quest for Karla'; only in the final version is the title *Tinker, Tailor, Soldier, Spy* used. Smiley's continuing love for his adulterous wife is his weakness, exploited by Karla to divert his attention from the mole. Guillam's failure to understand his enigmatic girlfriend Camilla mirrors Smiley's perplexity at Lady Ann's unfaithfulness.

One of the strengths of the book is a vivid sense of the Circus itself. Some of the most compelling scenes are set there. In David's previous novels the Circus had been comparatively nebulous, but here it springs sharply into focus. The anonymous entrance, the garrulous janitors, the dingy interior, the warren of corridors and the clanking lifts – all create the illusion of a real place: as well they might, because the interior of the Circus is based on Broadway Buildings, the headquarters of the Secret Service in David's time (though in 1964 MI6 had moved to a characterless modern office block in Lambeth). David carefully reconnoitred his locations, and recorded them in photographs taken from different angles. He modelled the Circus's exterior on an unassuming building (since demolished), which, he told an American journalist, 'had some of the same qualities of dilapidation and anonymity'.[15] His concern for detail extended to identifying individual rooms within.

As in David's previous books, but to a much greater extent, the sense of authenticity is made keener by the use of intelligence jargon, some of it genuine but much of it invented – 'the Cousins' (Americans), 'the competition' (MI5), 'scalphunters' (specialists in dangerous operations), 'babysitters' (bodyguards), 'pavement artists' (specialists in active surveillance), 'lamplighters' (specialists in watching and listening), 'reptile fund' (a secret account to finance intelligence operations), and so on. Some of David's coinages have subsequently been adopted by intelligence professionals – for example, 'honey trap', to mean enticing an enemy into a sexually compromising situation for the purposes of blackmail. On the other hand the term 'Moscow Rules' was an established term used by Western intelligence agencies to mean a set of principles to guide those operating in the enemy capital; but in this novel and in its successor *Smiley's People* David would extend its meaning, to include inconspicuous signals such as chalk marks and drawing pins, as part of the procedure for arranging a clandestine rendezvous.

The word 'mole', in the sense defined by Irina, has gone into general usage, extending beyond the limits of espionage, to mean a person who betrays confidential information from a position of trust, especially over a long period. So apposite is the term that one feels it must have been in use for many years. In 1981 the editor of the *Oxford English Dictionary* wrote to say that its appearance in *Tinker, Tailor, Soldier, Spy* was the earliest printed use of the word that he and his colleagues could find; he asked David to confirm that he had invented it. David had a vague memory that the equivalent Russian word *krot* had been used in this sense by the KGB during the period when he was an intelligence officer. But perhaps this was a false memory, as the *OED* editors were unable to trace it, either in Russian dictionaries or from other sources.[16] In his memoirs the Soviet agent Michael Straight, one of the 'Cambridge ring' of spies recruited in the 1930s, suggests that it was in use within their circle.[17] It is used in John Buchan's *The House of the Four Winds* (1935). Indeed one of David's former SIS colleagues wrote to inform him that Francis Bacon refers to 'moles perpetually working and casting to undermine' the monarch in his *Historie of the Reigne of King Henry the Seventh*, written in 1622 and published posthumously in 1641.[18] But the latest edition of the *OED* recognises that 'earlier uses appear to be isolated' and 'lack the specificity of meaning' which the term acquired after it had been popularised in *Tinker, Tailor, Soldier, Spy*.

As some reviewers would be quick to notice, the mole's story was similar in a number of ways to that of the real-life double agent Kim Philby. David incorporated details of real incidents into the narrative which played on this similarity – such as the Volkov affair, when a would-be Soviet defector was returned to Moscow bandaged and under sedation, and then executed, just as Irina had been. Volkov had been betrayed by Philby.[19] In his evocation of the paranoia within the Circus as the fear grows that they have a traitor in their midst, David may have drawn on the experiences of his friend and former controller George Leggett, with whom he had remained in intermittent contact. Leggett himself had been suspected of treachery after a Polish defector had indicated the presence of a Soviet spy within MI5.* Ironically the suggestion had emerged during an interview conducted by Leggett himself. On his return from sabbatical leave in 1968,

* Information provided by the defector, Michal Goleniewski, a colonel in Polish military intelligence, had led to the arrest of George Blake, and the rounding up of the Portland spy ring. Some of the intelligence he provided was much more questionable; like so many defectors, he may have embellished or even invented what he thought his interrogators wanted to hear in order to demonstrate his continuing worth. In public he claimed to be the Tsarevich Alexei, only son of Tsar Nicholas II, adopting the name Romanov while living in exile in New York.

he had been subjected to a humiliating interrogation by Peter Wright.* Instead of taking up his designated post as head of one of the counter-espionage sections, he had been unexpectedly sidelined to another branch of the Service. In 1971 he had retired early, at the age of only fifty, deeply upset at his treatment after thirty years' loyal service with MI5. David employed him as a fact-checker for several of his books.

David had kept in touch with his former station chief in Bonn, Dickie Franks, who would become assistant chief in 1977, and who would succeed Maurice Oldfield as chief ('C') the following year. It was Franks who mediated David's continuing connection with his former employers over the years. David was amused to observe how closely his own statements were monitored. Journalists who came to interview him would report what he had said to them to contacts in the intelligence services; often his remarks would come back to him with surprising speed. Around this time, for example, he had a chat with the journalist Anthony Sampson, who was giving a barbecue to celebrate publication of his latest book, on the oil companies.† David suggested that Sampson might like to write next about the intelligence community. Forty-eight hours later Franks was on the phone complaining to him.

Though David finished what he referred to as 'the complete working draft' of *Tinker, Tailor, Soldier, Spy* in the early summer of June 1973, he would not deliver the final text until the winter, another indication of the care he took in rewriting and revising. 'My book went on for ever and ever and has only just gone to the publishers,' he told Vivian Green on 9 December. 'I wrote the book three times in all, and it was still rushed at the end.'[20]

In fact David would revise the text yet further in response to the comments he received, from Bob Gottlieb in particular. In March 1974 he sent another bulletin to Green. 'I have done a lot since that draft to clarify and dramatize the book, and the professional consensus seems to be that it is much improved.'[21]

* There is a misleading account of this interrogation in Wright's *Spycatcher* (pp. 320–5), which is inaccurate throughout.

† *The Seven Sisters: The Great Oil Companies and the World they Shaped* (1975). Sampson's next book would be *The Arms Bazaar: From Lebanon to Lockheed* (1977).

David learned to trust Gottlieb's judgement. He would tell an interviewer working on a piece about Gottlieb that the editorial process at Knopf was 'streets ahead' of its British counterpart. In his experience British publishers tended to print what they received, misspellings and all; the American equivalent was much more rigorous. 'I'm always putting commas in, and he's always taking them out, but we know that about each other,' Gottlieb would tell the same interviewer. 'He'll say, Look, if you absolutely need this one, have it. And I'll say, Well, I would have liked it, but I guess I can live without it.'

Though erudite and intelligent, Gottlieb was not the heroic kind of editor who tried to write the book for the author. 'Bob knows how much to tell me and how much to leave to me,' said David. 'Bob is like a good movie director with an actor – he's just trying to get the best out of you.'

> Bob will tell me how he understands a story, and where he feels slightly disappointed, perhaps . . . He will say to me, I'm going to draw a wavy line down these pages; for me, they're too lyrical, too self-conscious, too over-the-top. And I will say, OK, for the moment I disagree because I'm in love with every word I've written, but I'll rake it over and lick my wounds, and we'll see what happens. Or he'll say something like, Actually you didn't need this beautiful passage of description here . . . Occasionally I'll say I disagree, in which case we will leave the matter in suspense until I recognize that he is right. In no case have I ever regretted taking Bob's advice . . .

Gottlieb found David 'unbelievably sensitive' to editorial suggestions: 'he'll take the slightest hint and come back with thirty extraordinary new pages'. In response to just such a suggestion, David expanded and developed the chapter in which Smiley visits Connie Sachs in Oxford, which became one of the most vivid and telling scenes in the book.

Gottlieb did not believe in mollycoddling his authors. 'I don't think writers need all that sympathy,' he would say. 'They need to be told when their books are bad.' He was very much a hands-on editor, who preferred to roll up his sleeves and get down to work, rather than making a fuss of an author. 'Most publishers, when you arrive in New York with your (as you hope) best-selling manuscript, send flowers to your suite, arrange for a limo, maybe, at the airport, and then let you go and put on the nosebag at some great restaurant,' said David. 'With Bob you did best to arrive in jeans and sneakers, and then you lay on your tummy side-by-side with him on the floor of his office and sandwiches were brought up.' Gottlieb preferred not to pay huge advances, not even when other publishing houses were offering twice as much. 'Negotiations were always tight with Bob,' David would say. 'He felt that for half the money, you got the best.'

After they had worked on several books together, David exacted a small revenge:

> My agent called me and said, Okay, we've got x-zillion yen and whatnot, and I said, *And lunch*. My agent said, What? I said, *And lunch*. When I get to New York I want to be taken, by Bob, to a decent restaurant for once and not eat one of those lousy tuna sandwiches lying on my tummy in his room. Bob called me that evening and said, I think we have a deal; and is that true about lunch? And I said, Yup, Bob, that's the break point in the deal. Very well, he said. Not a lot of laughter. So I arrived in New York, and there was Bob, a rare sight in a suit, and we went to a restaurant he had found out about.* He ate *extremely* frugally, and drank nothing, and watched me with venomous eyes as I made my way through the menu.[22]

Jane took David to lunch at the Savoy to celebrate the completion of the novel. They were enjoying a glass of champagne before the meal when Ronnie unexpectedly appeared, as always immaculately dressed in a dark pinstripe suit, bold red braces, handmade shoes and shirt, silk tie and chunky cufflinks. 'What the hell are you doing in the restaurant, son?' he asked. 'You should be in the Grill, it's far better. Come and join us.'

Ronnie was now operating from plush offices in Jermyn Street, using such names as Trans World Trading. A large telex machine stood in the foyer. Glenda Voakes, who joined him as his secretary at the age of only seventeen, quickly learned to address him as 'RC'; she was delighted to be earning more than twice as much as in her previous job, though surprised

* In elaborating this story, David has Gottlieb grudgingly taking him to his local 'diner'. Gottlieb insists this is an embellishment. 'It wasn't a diner, it was a perfectly respectable Indian restaurant.'

to receive payment in cash. She fended off his advances (he was her senior by half a century) with no ill feeling on either side. Once he gave her instructions that he should not be disturbed while he entertained his guest, described as an Austrian countess, and firmly closed his door; over the next half-hour or so she overheard scuffling sounds coming from inside, until the pair of them emerged, both flushed, and left for lunch at Wheeler's; afterwards she found a pair of tights discarded in his wastepaper bin. Occasionally she was invited to join her boss for lunch at Jules Bar, where he sat at his regular table, 'the Royal Box', surrounded by cronies such as the snooker champion Joe Davis, the wicketkeeper Godfrey Evans, and an RAF chum, Group Captain Harry Summers. Sometimes he would give her chips from the casino at the Sportsman, just north of Marble Arch, where he would go two or three times a month to play roulette. Other visitors to the offices included the racehorse trainer Paddy Prendergast and the Brylcreemed cricketer Denis Compton, as well as a variety of business associates, some seedy and others sinister. Recently Ronnie had been trying to involve his son in a deal to sell 5,000 tons of scrap metal to an overseas buyer.

In the Savoy, David explained that they were celebrating a special occasion. Nevertheless, he and Jane were persuaded to join Ronnie and his guests for a drink. They were introduced to a middle-aged couple from Poole, who owned 'a fine bit of land overlooking the sea, son'; Ronnie was advising them how best to develop it. A bottle of champagne was cooling in an ice bucket. David noticed that it was Dom Pérignon, reflecting wryly that he and Jane had settled for the house bubbly, sold by the glass.

Like *Tinker, Tailor*, the second novel in the 'Quest for Karla' sequence pitches Smiley against his Soviet opponent, though this time much of the action takes place in South-east Asia, a region then in turmoil. The Vietnam War, which had begun in 1945 as a Communist-led revolt against French colonial rule, and had continued as a struggle against American 'imperialism', was in its last stages. Back in 1954, as the French prepared to pull out, President Eisenhower had warned that if one country succumbed to Communist insurgents, its neighbours could fall like dominoes. Now his prediction seemed set to come true. The Americans had withdrawn, abandoning the beleaguered pro-Western government in South Vietnam to fight the North Vietnamese Communists alone. The Vietnam War had spilled over into the adjoining Kingdom of Laos, where the government had been fighting the Communist Pathet Lao on and off for more than twenty years. A fragile truce now threatened to break apart. Cambodia too was tottering: by 1974 the Chinese-backed Khmer Rouge controlled much of the Cambodian countryside and had begun laying siege to the cities. French Indochina was a rotten fruit, ready to drop into Communist hands.

David wanted to see what was happening at close hand. In any case he felt that he needed to alter his way of working, though it meant extended periods away from Jane and his young son Nick. 'I had become too sedentary, too much the desk officer, not enough the field man,' he wrote of this decision more than twenty-five years later.

> Imagination and deliberately falsified memory were no longer enough. I deserved, and needed, to share the misfortunes I was writing about . . . Henceforth, I promised myself that if I wanted to write about a place I would go there . . . In a word, I started writing on the hoof, in the company of whichever secret sharer I had appointed as my main character, and to this day that's what I like to do.[23]

When David travels for his research he invariably does so 'in character', playing the part of his secret sharer, and seeing the places he is visiting through the sharer's eyes rather than through his own.

Early in 1974 David arrived in Hong Kong. He had come east of Suez, he said, to get his 'knees brown', a self-mocking reference to the days when white men wore shorts in the tropics.[24] He had already been to Singapore, where he had originally planned to set much of the novel, but found it uninspiring as a location. There especially, he had dreaded coming across anyone who might associate him with Ronnie, remembering in particular the ill-fated football-pools scheme which had led to his father's arrest and deportation. All over the Far East, it seemed, there were people whom Ronnie had defrauded in some way. It therefore came as something of a surprise when, at the Happy Valley racecourse in Hong Kong, David ran into somebody who spoke warmly of him. This was a colonial policeman, his father's ex-jailer; from their brief conversation it became obvious that even in prison Ronnie had been fattening his victim for the pot. 'Mr Cornwell, sir, your father is one of the finest men I ever met,' the innocent policeman told him. 'I'm retiring soon, and when I get back to London, he's going to set me up in business.'

According to Richard Hughes, the most senior of the foreign correspondents based in Hong Kong, David saw 'everyone here who mattered' within a short time.[25] In his novel he would provide a 'shamelessly exaggerated' portrait of Hughes as Old Craw, doyen of the Hong Kong Foreign Correspondents' Club. 'Some people, once met, simply elbow their way into a novel and sit there till the writer finds them a place,' David would write later. In fact Hughes had form, since he had been the model for the character of 'Dikko' Henderson, chief of Australian intelligence in post-war Japan, in Ian Fleming's *You Only Live Twice* (1964).

From a very early stage David had an idea that the protagonist of his next novel would be a journalist. He found such a character in Peter Simms, an Englishman who in an earlier generation might have been running the Empire instead of recording its demise. Simms was married to a Burmese princess, whom he had met when they were both students at Cambridge. He was a very tall man, and broad, 'with a laugh like a rolling artillery barrage that you could hear across any crowded bar in Southeast Asia'. His bluff manner concealed a more complex interior; like so many British foreign correspondents, he worked on the side for British intelligence. To David, Simms was instantly recognisable as 'Office', as a 'UA'* (Unofficial Assistant). 'It was as if the British Empire had been boiled down to the last drop, and there in the bottom of the cup you would find Peter,' a fellow journalist would write. 'Sometimes I thought of him as Fowler in Graham Greene's "The Quiet American", the cynical old British journalist whose face had seen a thousand betrayals and compromises. At other times he reminded me of Conrad's Lord Jim, idealistic and vulnerable, perhaps trying to redeem, if not himself, then the white race for its sins east of Suez.'[26]

Simms became the prototype for Jerry Westerby, second son of an ennobled press magnate, the eponymous 'honourable schoolboy' of the

* An 'occasional' in le Carré's parlance.

novel, with the same distinct gestures and mannerisms. Westerby's grubby shirt, buckskin boots and old-school vocabulary ('Gosh, super, Sport') were instantly recognisable to anyone who knew Simms. Westerby had appeared briefly in *Tinker, Tailor, Soldier, Spy*, but without any of these distinct characteristics. In the new novel he would move centre stage, and in the process emerge as a complex, tragic character. At first he is an uncomplicated patriot, ready to do the bidding of his masters without question; but as the novel progresses he comes to recognise the human cost of the operation of which he is the spearhead. Finally Westerby, like Lord Jim, sacrifices himself to atone for the wrong he has unwittingly caused.

Simms had given David the name of H. D. S. (David) Greenway of the *Washington Post*, who had been reporting on the region out of Hong Kong for a number of years, as someone who might be able to 'show him around a bit'. David would later acknowledge his gratitude to Greenway, and his 'huge good luck' in being able to slipstream behind him, 'for he had a reporter's courage, and a reporter's canniness'.[27] Greenway's initial impression of David was of 'a large, rather shy man with enormous eyebrows that gave him a rather quizzical air'. At their first meeting David was soft-spoken and polite; only later did the zany side of his personality emerge. 'A master raconteur and a mimic, he turned out to be like a cooler Scaramouche, "born with the gift of laughter and a sense that the world was mad"'* – highly desirable qualities if you wanted to spend any time trying to work in South-east Asia in those days. They agreed that David would travel with Greenway, posing as his photographer; to support this cover story he equipped himself with an SLR camera in a metal camera case. In due course his photographs began to appear in the *Washington Post*, credited to 'Janet Leigh Carr'. Greenway's foreign editor sent him a stuffy letter, rebuking him for travelling around South-east Asia with this unknown woman when he had a wife back at home.[28]

After a look round Hong Kong and Macao, the two men took a swing through Thailand, Laos and Cambodia. Under his arm David carried an enormous bookkeeper's ledger, in which he jotted down every mood and anecdote that caught his imagination. These jottings would then be typed up into notes, consisting of (as one member of the Foreign Correspondents'

* Rafael Sabatini, *Scaramouche: A Romance of the French Revolution* (1921).

Club remembered) 'descriptions of terrain, jungle, villages, hot and bouncy journeys in local buses, character sketches of people he'd met, possible plot developments which could grow out of these travels – an impressive demonstration of why his books are set so firmly in their landscapes and carry such conviction'.[29]

David was willing to take risks that even most journalists would shirk. In Vientiane, capital of Laos, he choked on opium pipes in one of the city's most sordid dens. In those days of uneasy cease-fire, Vientiane was a centre of intrigue, where American, Russian and Chinese diplomats circled round each other at cocktail receptions. David was entertained to dinner by the British Ambassador, Alan Davidson, known for his serious interest in food;* on the menu that evening was a local speciality, *pa beuk*, a giant catfish found only in the Mekong.

From Vientiane Greenway planned to spend a few days driving around northern Thailand, one of the poorest regions of the country, the scene of a low-level Communist insurgency. They would be escorted by the local *Washington Post* stringer, a young man called John Burgess. Crossing the Mekong on a small wooden ferry, they arrived at an immigration post on the far bank, at the top of some steep steps. From there they were pedalled on tuk-tuks to a waiting car. Their first stop was a village that had been largely burned down by the Thai army in January in the belief that it was harbouring insurgents. It was eerily quiet. Wandering through the charred stilts and twisted corrugated roofing, they came across a farmer searching through the wreckage of a house. Later Burgess took them to another village, known as a centre of insurgent operations. They drove in from the east, passing roadblocks and covering stretches of deserted and very dusty road. Burgess took them to meet the local commander, an American-trained colonel from Thai Special Forces. The taciturn colonel received his guests dressed in fatigues, his house protected by sandbags and armed guards. Burgess noticed some spy novels, in English, on a shelf: thinking this might break through their host's reserve, he was on the point of revealing the identity of his English companion when he became aware

* Among his books was *Fish and Fish Dishes of Laos* (Charles E. Tuttle, Rutland, Vermont, 1975).

that David was silently signalling him not to do so. The interview with the Thai colonel would provide another scene in David's novel.

Throughout the trip Burgess occupied the front seat of the car, while the two older men sat behind. He remembers the atmosphere as relaxed and friendly, with plenty of jokes coming from the back. It impressed him that David was willing to mix with the local people and eat at roadside stalls, unlike some visitors from the West.

Back in England, David wrote to Vivian Green that his six weeks' tour of Asia had been 'fascinating and stimulating'.[30] Within a month or so he was back there. For a while he based himself in Chiang Mai in northern Thailand, exploring the illicit growing and refining of opium poppies in the 'Golden Triangle', the mountainous area that spans the highlands of Thailand, Burma (Myanmar) and Laos. Much of this trade was controlled by armed rebels fighting against the Burmese government. Through the offices of one branch of the Shan State Army David succeeded in getting himself escorted along its supply line into the heart of the opium-growing area. For this privilege he was obliged to make a contribution of $1,000 to their fighting fund. He also found it prudent to make a donation to the remnants of the Kuomintang (Chinese nationalist) army, which supplied the bodyguards for the opium caravans.*

In Vientiane David made contact with an ex-Air America (CIA) pilot, who was running heroin and diamonds into Cambodia. For a contribution of $500 he allowed David to fly with him as far as Pailin in north-western Cambodia, near the Thai border. In another plane David then accompanied the merchandise on the short hop to the regional capital of Battambang. From there he took another flight across Communist-controlled territory to Phnom Penh, flying with the grandly named Royal Air Lao, in a rackety DC-8. As David would subsequently try to explain to his accountant, Royal Air Lao operated on an informal basis, issuing neither tickets nor receipts.[31]

By this time Cambodia was an archipelago. The Khmer Rouge held the countryside, while the government, with American support, clung to the

* Troops from the Kuomintang army had invaded the Shan States of Burma in 1950, after the Communist victory in the Chinese civil war. Their progeny remain there to this day.

towns. Phnom Penh itself was ringed by Khmer Rouge forces, in a radius of three to six miles from the centre. There were nightly artillery bombardments and incoming rockets. Hundreds of thousands of refugees from the countryside had sought safety in the city, with more arriving all the time as the defence perimeter steadily collapsed. These people were helpless and desperate, with little food, shelter or medical care. Their condition worsened as Khmer Rouge forces gradually gained control of the banks of the Mekong. From the riverbanks, their mines and gunfire deterred the river convoys from bringing relief supplies of food, fuel and ammunition to the slowly starving city. Many of the foreign residents had left, fearing the worst.* The wealthier journalists stayed mostly at one big old hotel with gardens and a swimming pool. David took shelter with an old friend from his Bonn days, Baron Walther von Marschall, now the most senior of the few diplomats remaining in the city, whose residence was only a hundred yards from the Presidential palace. One night the artillery was especially loud, and von Marschall became concerned for the safety of his guest. He knocked at David's door and suggested that they move to a cellar, where they would have some protection from the incoming fire. The disadvantage was that they would have to sleep in armchairs. Weighing danger against discomfort, David chose to remain in bed. They discovered the next morning that it had been outgoing fire anyway.

On another evening, over a stylish dinner at von Marschall's house, served to the clatter of machine-gun fire, David met a Frenchwoman in her mid-thirties, whose small stature belied her toughness and energy. This was Yvette Pierpaoli, whom he would describe as 'by turns vulnerable and raucous, and enormously empathetic'. David was fascinated by her:

> She had all the wiles. She could spread her elbows and upbraid you like a bargee. She could tip you a smile to melt your heart, cajole, flatter, and win you in any way you needed to be won.
>
> But it was all for a cause. And the cause, you quickly learned, was an absolutely non-negotiable, visceral requirement in her to get food and money to the starving, medicines to the sick, shelter for the homeless, papers for the stateless, and, just generally, in the most secular, muscular, business-

* The city would fall to the Khmer Rouge the following spring, on 17 April 1975; less than a fortnight later Saigon fell to the North Vietnamese.

> like, down-to-earth way you could imagine, perform miracles. This did not in any way prevent her from being a resourceful and frequently shameless businesswoman, particularly when she was pitched against people whose cash, in her unshakable opinion, would be better in the pockets of the needy.

Pierpaoli and her companion Kurt ran a trading company called Suisindo, which owned a couple of clapped-out, twin-engined cargo planes, used to fly supplies into places cut off by road or rail. (David would depict a similar partnership in the novel he was writing, between the bush pilot Tony Ricardo and his girlfriend Lizzie Worthington.) With Pierpaoli, David flew the delivery round of the besieged towns of Cambodia, each one swelled with refugees from the countryside. 'Mme Yvette' was greeted everywhere as a patron saint, the adoptive mother of delighted children, the quiet friend of the bereaved, the bringer of hope and courage, as well as of the necessities of life.

Members of the local press corps reckoned that flying in such planes was more dangerous than playing Russian roulette, especially as the Chinese pilots appeared to be high on opium most of the time. David remembered returning to Phnom Penh at night, to land on a bomb-pitted, unlit runway 'while the city winced with gunfire'.

> I was never quite sure what we carried on that plane, and I don't think Yvette knew, either. But I know that while the plane was slaloming between craters, and I was praying to whatever divinity came fleetingly to mind, Yvette was laughing like a child at a fireworks party.

She and David became intimate friends, and would remain so. 'Over time he has become part of me,' she would write in her autobiography, published almost twenty years later. In due course she would become a friend of Jane's as well as his, and visited them more than once in Cornwall, though never, to her disappointment, during an Atlantic storm. She would write or telephone the Cornwells from outlandish places, preferably with outlandish news, at all hours of the day or night, confident that they would be happy to hear from her, which they always were. 'Dearest Jane and David,' she would write, twenty years later, 'I wanted to tell you that you are the most precious companions of my life, even if we don't see each other much.'[32]

After the fall of the Western-backed regimes in South-east Asia, she returned to France, but continued to devote her formidable energy to helping the world's wretched, particularly the women and most of all the children, in Guatemala and Bolivia, in Mali and Niger, in Burma and Bangladesh. In 1992 she published her autobiography, *Femme aux Mille Enfants*; while writing it she had kept faxing passages to David, impatiently expecting his immediate comment. She was a profound influence on him, his 'constant muse'. He was touched by her courage and her commitment, and delighted by her vitality and flirtatiousness. After her death he would write that she, 'like almost no one else, had opened my eyes to constructive compassion, to putting your money and your life where your heart was'.[33]

In Phnom Penh David again linked up with David Greenway. The pair of them decided to go and find the fighting. It was the habit of journalists during that time to hire taxis to drive them out into the countryside, at a rate rising according to the distance travelled and the hazards they might endure on the way. It was dangerous to venture out of the towns; more than thirty journalists lost their lives in this way, but it was a risk most judged acceptable. The fight for Cambodia then was a fight for the roads. The Khmer Rouge would block them and the government would send out troops to open them again. Reporters covered the war by 'running the roads': by following the government soldiers in their armoured personnel carriers, they would sometimes run into a firefight. The rule was that you turned back if you didn't see any traffic coming the other way, because that meant the Khmer Rouge was somewhere up ahead.

Yvette Pierpaoli resolved to come with them. She had heard of a woman capable of amazing predictions who lived in a Khmer village a few miles into the jungle. Greenway was less than keen, and David was too ignorant to know whether to be keen or not, but 'when Yvette was determined to have her way there wasn't much you could do about it'. As the only Khmer speaker, she gave the driver instructions. What happened on that drive would appear in the novel – 'not just the way it was', Greenway recalled, 'but with the drama heightened to show the pointlessness and, in the end, the hopelessness of all that was happening in Cambodia'.

In a tribute to Yvette Pierpaoli after her death a quarter of a century later, David would recall an incident on that drive:

> We drove for an age. The road was a dead-straight canyon cut through mile-high teak trees. Tropical rain was falling in sheets. Through the teeming windscreen, we saw a sinister brown lorry roll out of the jungle in front of us. It stopped, blocking our way. Two boys with guns dismounted, inspected us, and returned to the lorry, which rolled back to let us pass. We were not the quarry they were waiting for. Abandoning our search, we returned to Phnom Penh. I was still shaking when we reached the hotel, and even Greenway looked a little sallow. But Yvette was in a state of grace. She had touched the high mark. She had lived another day.[34]

Greenway's recollection is different. He remembers 'passing a truck', but not being looked over by boys with guns. He is certain that, had they been stopped, they would have been killed. Nor, according to him, were they ever close to any fighting during that drive. Perhaps, then, in recalling what happened on that day, David was recalling his own fictional recreation of the incident, rather than what really happened.

Later Greenway was present at a dinner when David related one of their adventures together. After the meal was over, he took David aside. 'That wasn't the way it happened,' he said.

'Your job is to get things right,' David replied; 'mine is to turn them into good stories.'

The two men returned to Vientiane, before taking the ferry across the Mekong to catch the overnight train back to Bangkok. As they queued for tickets, they pondered the choice of travel: third class, on slatted wooden seats, among saffron-robed monks sitting cross-legged eating rice out of lotus leaves, Thai soldiers drinking beer, and the odd scruffy young Westerner; or first-class, in a modern sleeping-car with beds and air-conditioning. Greenway recalls telling David that if they went third class, he would get a real feel for South-east Asia, even if they had to sit up all night. It was David who suggested that they should travel first class. 'Let Jerry go third class and tell us about it later.'

Tinker, Tailor, Soldier, Spy was about to be published. David had asked Greenway to look through the segments set in Hong Kong. Early in the novel Ricki Tarr describes to Smiley his anxiety after Irina has failed to appear at a rendezvous: on a hunch he had decided to go down to the airport. The airport was then in Kowloon, across the water from Hong

Kong Island. 'I took the Star Ferry, hired a cab, and told the driver to go like hell. It got like a panic,' Tarr tells Smiley.

'Does this novel take place in the present?' asked Greenway.

'Yes, why?'

'So if he's so anxious to get to the airport quickly, why doesn't he just jump in a cab and go through the tunnel?' The Cross-Harbour Tunnel linking Hong Kong Island to Kowloon had been opened in 1972.*

'Oh God!'

As soon as they reached Bangkok, David contacted his publishers: though the American edition had already gone to press, it was not too late to change the passage in the British edition.

He found a pile of telegrams waiting for him in Bangkok, with encouraging updates on the prospects for the novel. After the battering that *The Naïve and Sentimental Lover* had received, such news was especially welcome. Still grubby and frayed from the rigours of their tour, he promptly checked into the Somerset Maugham Suite of the Oriental Hotel and ordered up bottles of champagne. The suite overlooked the swimming pool; afterwards Greenway could recall a serious discussion between the two of them, of the ballistics and trajectory necessary to bombard the German stewardesses lounging by the pool in their bikinis with corks from well-shaken bottles of Mumm.[35]

Tinker, Tailor, Soldier, Spy was published in America a few weeks before it appeared in Britain. This was partly for complex reasons to do with book clubs, but it was also a reflection of economic realities. 'When I publish a book, the English reaction, apart from personal pride and so on, is absolutely secondary to the American reaction, the German reaction and even the French,' David told an interviewer. 'The French market is probably more important to me financially than the English one.'[36]

Another reason why David preferred his books to be published first in America was that he felt he was taken more seriously there. In this case the American reviews were generally positive, though not unequivocally

* In *The Honourable Schoolboy*, Westerby breaks out of a car stuck in the tunnel and escapes by bounding though the stationary traffic towards the exit.

so. The anonymous reviewer in the *Wall Street Journal* thought the novel 'a stunning story'. The British critic Karl Miller described it as 'very lively throughout' in an otherwise lukewarm *New York Review of Books* piece.[37] The *New York Times* reviewer, Richard Locke, provided the kind of quotes that help sell a thriller: 'thoroughly enjoyable . . . the plot is as tangled and suspenseful as any action fan could require . . . keeps one guessing right to the end'. In an assessment of le Carré as a novelist, Locke condemned *The Naïve and Sentimental Lover* as 'a pretentious romantic story about a businessman, a writer and the woman they share – an inept psychosexual portrait of the bourgeois and the bohemian soul'. For him, this had been 'a book that failed with both critics and public'. *Tinker, Tailor, Soldier, Spy*, on the other hand, was 'a full recovery, which in many ways consolidates le Carré's career':

> It reconfirms the impression that le Carré belongs to the select company of such spy and detective story writers as Arthur Conan Doyle and Graham Greene in England and Dashiell Hammett, James M. Cain, Raymond Chandler and Ross Macdonald in America . . . When le Carré tried for depth in his last novel, he failed; modernism and the ironies of the literary novels of the 1960s are beyond him; but when, as in this new book, he shows the surface of experience in that good old-fashioned way, he is thoroughly entertaining.[38]

Reviewing the novel for the American magazine the *New Leader*, the critic Pearl K. Bell acknowledged that le Carré was more sophisticated than other thriller writers, but argued that 'it is myopic and unjust to link le Carré with high art'; it was more appropriate to evaluate him as a 'master craftsman of ingeniously plotted suspense, weaving astoundingly intricate fantasies of discovery, stealth, surprise, duplicity and final exposure'. David was moved to reply, even though he had 'always thought it foolish to take up correspondence with critics'; he thanked her warmly for her piece, 'which touched me, and gave me a sense of usefulness'. He accepted the description of his books as '"historical" novels, as near as I can make them, but above all stories. I would not wish anything better. I creep around miserably when I read that I am Sartre, or Camus, or anti-Fleming, or whoever; I am sure I don't want to be anything but what you so kindly say I am.'[39]

There were mixed opinions of the book in Britain. The anonymous reviewer* in the *Times Literary Supplement* declared that *Tinker, Tailor, Soldier, Spy* showed the author to be 'at the height to his powers'. The reviewer recounted how *The Naïve and Sentimental Lover* had been 'vilified in a striking display of small-mindedness. Perhaps wounded by this reception, Mr le Carré in his new novel reverts to the world of British intelligence; he does so, however, in a wholly original manner.'[40] Many of the other reviews were equally favourable. 'The spinner of spy stories and the poet of fantasy have met to produce a spy story that shoulders its way into the front ranks of the art,' wrote H. R. F. Keating in *The Times*.[41] For the *Spectator*, this was 'a great thriller, the best le Carré has written';[42] for the *Financial Times*, it showed le Carré to be 'the great master of the spy story'. The young Timothy Mo, whose first novel *The Monkey King* would be published in 1978, was another enthusiast. 'I find it difficult to be temperate in saying how much I enjoyed John le Carré's new spy story,' he wrote in the *New Statesman*.[43] Though he had some reservations about the book and thought it 'far too long', the *Observer*'s critic Maurice Richardson nevertheless thought it 'the best book Mr le Carré has written since "The Spy Who Came in From the Cold"'.[44] But for Derek Mahon, writing in the *Listener*, the novel was 'twice as long as it needed to be'.[45] In the *Sunday Times* Edmund Crispin agreed that it was 'lengthy and diffuse, far more than its essentially simple material might have dictated'.[46] The *Guardian*'s reviewer, Matthew Coady, was especially damning. 'Mr le Carré strives for what Graham Greene called the sharp touch of the icicle in the heart. He never achieves it.'[47]

Whatever some of the critics might have said, the public liked the book. *Tinker, Tailor, Soldier, Spy* took le Carré back to the top of the US bestseller lists for the first time since *The Spy who Came in from the Cold*. It became a no. 1 bestseller in both the UK and the US, selling strongly for month after month, and was still in the bestseller list on both sides of the Atlantic almost a year after publication. Looking back at the novel sixteen years on

* The names of most writers of unsigned *TLS* reviews have subsequently been revealed, but this one has not.

from its first publication, David felt vindicated by its success. 'It restored my spirits after the miserable critical reception given to its predecessor,' he wrote. The effort and care that he had put into writing *Tinker, Tailor, Soldier, Spy* had paid off.

17

'You treated your father very badly'

David began writing the novel that became known as *The Honourable Schoolboy* immediately after the publication of *Tinker, Tailor, Soldier, Spy*. It takes up the story where the last book left off. After the exposure of a Soviet mole at the highest level of British intelligence – 'the fall' in Circus parlance – Smiley takes 'back bearings' from intelligence that 'Gerald' had downgraded, distorted or suppressed, reasoning that this might uncover secrets that Karla did not want revealed. One of these is a 'gold seam', clandestine payments from Moscow that traced a tortuous route from one account to another. Smiley sends Westerby to Hong Kong, where he finds the end of the seam in the bank account of Drake Ko, a prominent if crude local businessman. This leads to the discovery that Ko's beloved brother Nelson, one of the most important officials in Communist China, is a Soviet agent. Smiley launches Operation Dolphin, intended to secure the services of Nelson Ko for British intelligence.

Like its predecessor, the book went through numerous drafts, altering considerably in the process. Originally it was told in the first person by Steve Mackelvore, a character who had appeared briefly in *Tinker, Tailor, Soldier, Spy* as head of the Paris SIS station. In the early drafts Mackelvore performs several of the actions undertaken by Westerby in the finished book, for example the 'burning' of the hapless Hong Kong banker Frost. Another character featuring in the early drafts and later omitted is Ailsa Brimley, who had played a substantial role in *A Murder of Quality*. She is one of several veterans whom Smiley brings back into the Circus following 'the fall'. Smiley also co-opts Ribble, the junior Foreign Office official who had the temerity to question the 'Witchcraft' material in *Tinker, Tailor,*

Soldier, Spy, though he too is later dropped. Among the scenes that David wrote and then discarded is one in which Ko's English mistress Lizzie Worthington comes to London and shops in Bond Street. The character of Lizzie – known by Ko as 'Liese' – was modelled on a German woman with a Chinese-Thai husband whom David met on one of his trips. He contemplated a Taiwanese dimension to the plot, and undertook a research trip to Taipei, though in the end he thought better of this.

As always, David took great care with the details. For the meeting at the Foreign Office in which Smiley seeks authorisation to launch Operation Dolphin, he drew a diagram of the table to show where everyone present is seated. He had the usual difficulty in settling on a title: among those he considered were 'Operation Limberlost', 'The Twelfth Direction',* 'The Pigeon Tunnel' (again), 'The London Occasional' and 'A Spy for Reasons of Politeness'.

Once again, Guillam is used to provide a perspective on Smiley, who is portrayed as both masterly in his handling of the operation and fatally innocent in his lack of political nous. The story is narrated as if in retrospect by a Circus insider, who at various points poses rhetorical questions, suggesting what might have been. One effect is to imply from the start that things are not going to end well. Operation Dolphin itself is a complete success; but the prize is snatched from Smiley at his moment of triumph. The novel provides the reader with a vivid impression of South-east Asia on the verge of collapse, in its last days before the Communist deluge.

David made several further trips to the region while researching the background to the novel. In Saigon he re-read Graham Greene's *The Quiet American*, which drew on Greene's experiences in French Indochina as a war correspondent in the early 1950s. In his bookkeeper's ledger David recorded that 'Greene is my influence, not Hemingway. The difference between Greene and myself (and between our characters) is the weight of ignorance on my shoulders. G writes as someone who oversees his landscape, with an assured wisdom. I write without any knowledge of what lies on the other side of the mountain, let alone under it.'

On returning to England in November 1974 he contacted Greene. 'After our passage of arms over Philby a while back it is a little difficult for me to

* Refers to a section of Moscow Centre directed at the Chinese target.

write to you,' he began. 'But I should hate you to think that the dispute either soured my gratitude to you ten years ago, nor [sic] – for what it's worth – my admiration for your work.'

> I am moved to write by my visits to the Far East this year, and particularly to Indo China: The Quiet American which I re-read in Saigon seems to me still as fresh as it did nineteen years ago, and it is surely still the only novel, even now, which does justice to its theme. But the sheer accuracy of its mood and observation, is astonishing. The book seemed more real on location, even, than away from it; I was really very moved and felt I had to tell you. It is, of course, all quite hideous in Saigon. Phnom Penh is still beautiful, but not for much longer, and the rest of Cambodia is heart breaking.

Greene replied that he had 'never for a moment felt that our little passage of arms over Philby was a serious one'. He had been asked to return to Vietnam by the *Sunday Times* only a month before, but 'felt a strong disinclination'.

> I had enjoyed so much – in so far as one can enjoy a war – life in Saigon and Hanoi and the beautiful countryside and I knew I would be made miserable by the present Saigon. It would be a great pleasure if one day you were down near Antibes and I could hear from you about Indo China. I wonder whether the bowler hat with an ostrich feather is still in the Royal Museum in Phnom Penh!

In a further letter, David reported that the museum had closed after a rocket had fallen near by. 'The new Saigon is absolutely unvisitable,' he wrote, 'the present regime is even more frightful than one would suppose, but above all the charm is dead. You are an extraordinarily cherished absentee there, a reminder of times lost. "He sat here, he sat there," at the Continentale.'[1]*

Back in England, David was having dinner at the house of his friend Eddie Nowell one Sunday evening when he was called to the telephone. It was

* Greene was a long-term resident of this hotel; several scenes in his novel *The Quiet American* are set there. It was a popular rendezvous for foreign correspondents, politicians and businessmen.

his stepmother Jean, to tell him that Ronnie was dead. He had suffered a heart attack while watching cricket on television, after a hearty lunch of roast lamb, pudding and cheese. He was sixty-nine years old.

David returned to the dinner table, where a fellow guest was holding forth about the BBC, which he labelled the Communist Broadcasting Corporation. David sat silent, keeping his news to himself. He felt no sadness, no loss; on the contrary, he would later claim that he felt liberated, even jubilant. 'I never mourned him, never missed him. I rejoiced at his death,' David would write to Tony, many years afterwards.[2] Yet that night he ran a high fever, and vomited repeatedly. Before going to bed he telephoned some members of the family, including his sister Charlotte, who was tearful. 'Father was in good shape, really,' he assured her: 'he's beaten the system.'*

Next afternoon David arrived at Ronnie's flat in Tite Street, Chelsea, which he was curious to see. He noticed only one of his books on the shelves, a copy of *A Small Town in Germany*, though he knew that in the past Ronnie had ordered his books by the boxful in order to be able to sign them 'from the author's father'. Charlotte was already there, with Ronnie's third wife Joy and her daughter by an earlier marriage. David advised them all not to pay any bills. 'How can you talk about money at a time like this?' asked his sister. In death as in life, David was made to feel in the wrong for his coolness towards his father.

Joy did not share Charlotte's reticence. 'He's taken everything I've got,' she told David. Ronnie had bought the flat in her name, but neglected to inform her that he had raised a loan on it, at compound interest, so that more was now owed than it was worth, and the outstanding amount was increasing all the time. Over the months that followed, she would be hounded by the building society that had supplied the loan. After she

* The following passage describing Jerry Westerby's feelings about his father was cut from *The Honourable Schoolboy* during the editing process: 'I think that was what amazed him: the *licence* that his father had enjoyed with what these days we call the institutions. I think that deep inside he surveyed his father's life and saw it not as a failure at all, but as a statement of personal freedom: freedom to strive, to love, even the freedom if necessary to fail . . . And I do believe that the part of his father which Jerry loved was the part that beat the system.'

appealed to David for help, his lawyer succeeded in persuading the lenders that it was pointless to pursue her further, because 'the poor woman is destitute'. David would be nonplussed therefore when, six months later, she revealed that she owned a couple of Old Master paintings, and asked his advice on the best auction-house through which to sell them.

At Ronnie's office in Jermyn Street David had found a scene of chaos, reminiscent of one near the end of the film *Zorba the Greek*, when the villagers plunder the rooms of Madame Hortense as soon as she is dead. Arthur Lowe, Eric Bent and other members of Ronnie's Court were ransacking the place, searching through papers on their hands and knees. Eventually someone found the key to the safe, which proved to be disappointingly empty. David was amused to learn that two 'working girls' inhabited the top floor of the building, known affectionately as 'Sausages' and 'Mash'.

It turned out that most of Ronnie's 'assets' – the house in Maidenhead, the two cars, the racehorses – were owned by one or other of his bogus companies, all of which of course were insolvent. In fact there was no money anywhere, not even enough to pay his employees at the office to the end of the week. Ronnie had been living on air. In recent years he had pinned many of his hopes on a valuable piece of land in Cobham, which he had obtained planning permission to develop. He had sold it on to the house-builders Wimpey (now Taylor Wimpey), but the local council had withdrawn the planning permission and Wimpey had refused to pay. Since then Ronnie had been pursuing parallel lawsuits against both the council and the house-builders. 'One day I'll be paid for that land and everyone will be seen right,' had been his refrain. Indeed he had mortgaged his anticipated pay-out to fund his legal costs. Soon after his death the case came to court, and was decided in his favour. At Ronnie's moment of posthumous triumph a man stood up and identified himself as a representative of the Inland Revenue. As 'preferential creditor', the Revenue had first claim on the estate; and in settlement of their claim they took the lot.

David paid for his father's funeral costs. He attended the cremation in London, but chose not to go to the subsequent memorial service, held at the Parkstone Baptist Church. Charlotte was so offended by David's absence that she refused to speak to him for almost two years afterwards. Tony did not come back to England at all after his father's death. The service was otherwise well attended: among the mourners were members of the family and a solid phalanx of local businessmen in black suits and ties, many of them seemingly masons. It was conducted by David's cousin Brian Haynes, wearing clerical robes. In his address he recalled being similarly attired on another occasion, when he had been officiating at a wedding. Ronnie had come breezing up to him and quipped, 'I may be the Prodigal Son but you're certainly the Black Sheep.'

Not long after his father's death, a woman in Brussels contacted David. Her name was unfamiliar to him, though it rapidly became obvious from her communications that she believed them to have conducted an affair together, on the train from Rome to her native city. After a while the penny dropped: his father had been passing himself off as the world-famous author, John le Carré.

Ronnie continued to haunt his son, who learned to dread such questions as 'Are you by any chance related to Ronald Cornwell?' He braced himself for trouble whenever an immigration officer hesitated over his passport. More than a decade after Ronnie's death he handed his credit card to a clerk at the Imperial Hotel in Vienna.

'Cornwell, Cornwell,' the man mused. 'Is that a common name in England?'

'Spelt that way, no, not very,' replied David.

'But John le Carré's father was called Cornwell.'

'Yes, I believe he was,' David conceded, meaning to leave it at that, before softening and admitting that he was John le Carré. The reaction was not the one he had anticipated.

'You treated your father very badly,' the clerk observed. '*Ja*, such a nice gentleman, you could have given him money.'[3]

In 1975 the Western-backed regimes in Cambodia, Vietnam and Laos collapsed in a line of dominoes. There was a succession of excruciating scenes as Western diplomats clambered aboard helicopters taking them to safety, while those poor locals who had cooked their meals and cleaned their rooms clutched desperately at the gates outside. David was still writing *The Honourable Schoolboy*. In a bitter passage cut from the final version of the book, David satirised the indifference of the London literary world to the terrible events taking place on the other side of the world. Over lunch at the Garrick, Westerby's literary agent is preoccupied with cricket, and advises his client against writing a novel set in South-east Asia. 'Absolute death, to be frank, the East these days. Only have to *whisper* Vietnam to a publisher and you won't see the fellow for dust.'

If David deplored the lack of interest his own countrymen showed in the tragedy unfolding in Indochina, he was still more critical of American interference in the region. As Graham Greene had done a generation before, he blamed American meddling for the developing disasters. In his notebook he poured out his loathing of the CIA men he had encountered: 'I hate them more than I hate myself, more than I hate a hangover. They're the one bunch I hate morally: I only have to see their Mormon haircuts and listen to their open-plan charm. I have only to hear them call Europe "Yurrp" and I start sweating at the joints.' While staying at one of the Bangkok hotels he expressed his disgust at being served 'one of those ghastly American sandwiches, full of wooden spikes'.

In *The Honourable Schoolboy* the Americans enjoy the fruits of Smiley's success, thanks to the duplicity of those on the make in Whitehall – especially Smiley's eventual successor as head of the Circus, Saul Enderby, whose mannered speech seems to Peter Guillam 'the last stage of linguistic collapse'. Enderby appears in the follow-up book, 'drawling in that lounging Belgravia cockney which is the final vulgarity of the English upper class'.[4] Several bad eggs in later le Carré novels speak the same way.

The Honourable Schoolboy was the first of a succession of novels exploring the unequal relationship between the Circus and its American 'Cousins', with their much greater resources and longer reach. American bullishness, naïvety and eagerness to please are contrasted with British cynicism and world-weariness.

Knee-jerk anti-Americanism was latent in Englishmen of David's generation; resentment of American influence was endemic in British culture. Anti-American sentiment is certainly present in David's novels. One of his characters in *Tinker, Tailor, Soldier, Spy* states openly that he hates America very deeply – though this sentiment is undercut by being voiced by the traitor Bill Haydon. In his apologia Haydon echoes Greene:

> He had often wondered which side he would be on if the test ever came; after prolonged reflection he had finally to admit that if either monolith

had to win the day, he would prefer it to be the East. 'It's an aesthetic judgement as much as anything,' he explained, looking up. 'Partly a moral one, of course.'

'Of course,' said Smiley politely.[5]

In January 1976 David gave a long television interview to Melvyn Bragg, broadcast on his book programme *Read All About It*. When Bragg asked if he had been a spy himself, he evaded the question. The interview explored the character of Smiley as 'a committed doubter'. *Tinker, Tailor, Soldier, Spy* reflected David's own view of life that every human relationship is 'necessarily insecure . . . fraught with all kinds of nerve-wracking tension'.

> I think all of us live partly in a clandestine situation. In relation to our bosses, our families, our wives, our children, we frequently affect attitudes to which we subscribe perhaps intellectually but not emotionally. We hardly know ourselves – nine-tenths of ourselves are below the level of the water. One of the greatest realities is sex, but we almost never succeed in betraying our sexuality to one another fully.[6]

In September David wrote to tell Vivian Green that he was 'just putting the finishing touches to my novel', and planned to leave for South-east Asia at the end of October 'to check out a few details'.[7]

On this trip he would once again spend time with Yvette Pierpaoli, based in Thailand since the Khmer Rouge had overrun Cambodia in April 1975. She had begun visiting the refugee camps near the border, where tens of thousands of Cambodians who had fled from the Khmer Rouge were living in squalid conditions. Plying the border in a small car, she brought them food and medicine, and took back to her house in Bangkok as many children as she could carry.

One evening Pierpaoli took David to meet her friend and fellow countryman François Bizot, one of the few Westerners to survive capture by the Khmer Rouge. Bizot was then living in northern Thailand, in a wooden house of his own design surrounded by enormous trees. They stood outside as the sun set, sipping whisky. Gradually Bizot let go of his reticence. Pierpaoli had already told David the outline of his extraordinary story, but it was another thing altogether to hear of his ordeal from this brooding, volatile figure in the gathering darkness. Back in 1971, while working as an anthropologist in the ruins of Angkor, Bizot had been taken by the Khmer Rouge and held captive in a jungle camp, chained to a post, accused of being an agent of 'American imperialism'. After three months of deliberation, during which his every word was weighed and his life hung in the balance, he had suddenly been released. This terrible experience convinced him of the genocidal tendencies of his captors, at a time when other Western intellectuals often praised them as leaders of a 'liberation struggle'. Four years later he had witnessed the entry of the Khmer Rouge troops into Phnom Penh, astonished to find themselves unopposed and standing about perplexed as they waited for orders. As a fluent Khmer speaker, he had become the primary point of contact between those sheltering in the French Embassy and the ruthless new masters of the city. He told David of a succession of surreal encounters, each a tragedy in itself, of frantic individuals seeking entry to the French compound, most of whom he had been forced to turn away to protect those inside. David would contribute a foreword to Bizot's powerful memoir *The Gate*, published in 2003.

In the summer of 1977 the Cornwells took a family holiday in Corfu. Sitting outside at an open-air beach restaurant David overheard a familiar voice talking at a nearby table.

'Reg?' he asked tentatively.

'What if I am?'

'It's David.'

The suspicious glare melted. 'Ronnie's boy!'

Reg had been one of the most faithful members of Ronnie's Court. Several drinks later, he tearfully gave David what he called the bottom line: he had 'done time for your father'. So had George-Percival, another courtier. So had Eric and Arthur. All four had taken the rap for Ronnie at one time or another, rather than see the Court deprived of its monarch.

> And d'you know what, David? If your father rose from his grave today and asked me to do another stretch for him, I'd do it again, the same as George-Percival and Eric and Arthur would. So far as Ronnie was concerned, the whole lot of us was soft in the head.

'We was all bent, son,' Reg admitted, before adding a final admiring tribute. 'But your dad was very, very bent.'

Since the mid-1960s David had been an employee of le Carré Productions Limited, on the advice of his accountant Hale Crosse. In 1973 there had been inconclusive discussions about selling the company to Booker-McConnell, to whom Hale had sold Georgette Heyer's company in 1966. (Booker already owned rights in the works of several other bestselling authors, including those of Dennis Wheatley and much of Agatha Christie.) In 1977 Hale came up with a new wheeze, setting up a company based in Switzerland, Authors Workshop, of which Rainer Heumann was sole shareholder and director. David became an employee of this company, as in due course did Jane too. All publishing and other contracts for David's work were made direct with Authors Workshop, which therefore owned the copyrights. In exchange for these valuable assets, Authors Workshop paid David a salary with an annual bonus, and settled most of his work-related expenses direct. By the late 1970s he was receiving total payments of between £100,000 and £150,000 annually,* though this was considerably less than the earnings from his work, which accumulated in Switzerland. In 1978, for example, Knopf paid Authors Workshop $2.5 million in a two-book deal.

David would later say that he had been talked into these tax-saving arrangements and felt ashamed of having done so. But at the time he was unsure of his capacity to continue to turn out bestselling books and feared that his income might decline rapidly in the future. For his own financial security, and for that of his dependants, he felt the need to minimise his tax liabilities while his earning capacity lasted. This was a period of exceptionally high tax rates: in 1974 the top rate of income tax in the UK had been raised to 83 per cent, with a further 15 per cent surcharge on investment income. Any doubts that David may have felt at the time were allayed by the fact that the scheme had been approved by a leading firm of accountants, legally tested at an advanced level, and was widely used by corporations.

* In 1979, average 'original household income' in the UK was little more than £5,000 a year.

For the scheme to be acceptable to the Inland Revenue, it was necessary to maintain that David's assets had been transferred to the company for sound commercial reasons, not for the purposes of avoiding liability to tax. It was a condition of the Revenue's acceptance that David had no interest in the company, either present or future. There was an element of sleight-of-hand in this, of course: in his management of the company Heumann could be relied upon to act in David's interests. In that sense he was a trusted nominee, not unlike those nominees that Ronnie had used to control his property empire.

Before *The Honourable Schoolboy* was published David hosted a party at his house in Hampstead for the Hodder sales force. Nowadays much bookshop buying is centralised, and the importance of salesmen has diminished; but in the 1970s they could still make a significant contribution to a book's success. Publishers' representatives, known as 'travellers', were the footsoldiers of the forces of publishing, in the front line; David recognised their value.

The British edition was published in September 1977, with the American edition following a few weeks later, so that the critical response came almost as a single chorus. The reviews tended to reflect the background of its critics: literary reviewers and political journalists slapped it down, while crime aficionados praised it.[8]

The most unstinting praise came from one of le Carré's regular reviewers, H. R. F. Keating, writing in *The Times*. 'I think it may justly be said that with this book the spy novel comes of age,' Keating wrote. 'Le Carré has produced something on a whole new scale. He has used a spy story . . . to penetrate a whole world in the way of the great comprehensive novels of the nineteenth century.'[9] For the crime-writer and academic T. J. Binyon, reviewing the book for the *Times Literary Supplement*, le Carré had 'triumphantly succeeded in . . . writing a thriller which is at the same time a substantial novel in its own right'.[10] Similarly, the novelist Thomas Hinde, writing in the *Sunday Telegraph*, argued that the book 'is not merely a splendid example of the genre but offers more in the way of characters, setting [and] relevance to life than the majority of ordinary novels'.[11]

Some reviewers complained that *The Honourable Schoolboy* was too long, with too much padding. The *Observer*'s Maurice Richardson grumbled about 'a mass of topographical detail'.[12] The *New Statesman* deplored 'a deadeningly spun-out display of unassimilated guide-book information'.[13] For Clancy Sigal, writing in the *Guardian*, the book was 'overlong and fussily written'. Sigal argued that le Carré had 'stumbled this time because he's bent on creating "serious literature" à la Graham Greene'.[14]

Anthony Burgess, writing in the *New York Times Book Review*, came to a similar conclusion about *The Honourable Schoolboy*. 'Does it have anything to do with literature?' he asked: 'the answer has to be no.' He complained that the book was too long and boring, and he was one of several reviewers to compare it unfavourably with Greene's *The Quiet American*.[15] But Rudolf Walter Leonhardt, writing in *Die Zeit*, reckoned that the novel held its own alongside *The Quiet American*, as novels 'that provide us in the West with a better understanding of the Far East'. For Leonhardt, 'le Carré's development from *The Spy Who Came in From the Cold* to *The Honourable Schoolboy* represents a literary gain, bought at the cost of a loss of suspense'.[16] To Jürgen Busche, the reviewer for the *Frankfurter Allgemeine Zeitung*, *The Honourable Schoolboy* was an 'exquisite' thriller. 'John le Carré has significantly extended the genre with this book.'[17]

The most mocking review came from the British-based Australian critic Clive James, writing in the *New York Review of Books*. He branded *The Honourable Schoolboy* 'tedious' and its prose style as 'overblown'.

> Le Carré's new novel is about twice as long as it should be. It falls with a dull thud into the second category of le Carré's books – those which are greeted as being something more than merely entertaining. Their increasingly obvious lack of mere entertainment is certainly strong evidence that le Carré is out to produce a more respectable breed of novel than those which fell into the first category, the ones which were merely entertaining. But in fact it was the merely entertaining books that had the more intense life . . .
>
> There is no possible question that le Carré has been out there and done his fieldwork. Unfortunately he has brought it all home . . .
>
> But the really strength-sapping feature of the prose style is its legend-building tone . . .
>
> Outwardly aspiring to the status of literature, le Carré's novels have inwardly declined to the novel of pulp romance . . . Raising le Carré to the plane of literature has helped rob him of his more enviable role as a popular writer who could take you unawares.[18]

But David could afford to snap his fingers at the critics. *The Honourable Schoolboy* was awarded the James Tait Black Memorial Prize, Britain's oldest literary award. The British edition of the book sold 78,500 copies in hardback, a substantial increase on the 52,000 copies sold of *Tinker, Tailor, Soldier, Spy*. The paperback edition would sell more than half a million copies, which made it the third highest-selling paperback of the year.[19] The American edition of the novel reprinted twice before publication; it was selected as the October main selection for the Book of the Month Club, a very big deal in those days; and *Time* put him on its cover, an accolade only very rarely granted to writers. Paperback rights in *The Honourable Schoolboy* were sold to Bantam for a million dollars – a huge sum, more than half a million pounds, at a time when average annual earnings in the UK were less than £3,000. In the wake of this success George Greenfield claimed to have received 'sight unseen' offers from reputable American publishers offering almost $5 million for the next two books from le Carré.[20]

'I have ordered *The Honourable Schoolboy*,' Kim Philby wrote to Phillip Knightley, one of the co-authors of the book based on the *Sunday Times* Insight team's investigation. 'From le Carré's introduction to your book, I get the vague impression, perhaps wrongly, that he didn't like me. But we are generous, and have no objection to contributing to his vast affluence.'[21]

To coincide with publication of *The Honourable Schoolboy* David wrote a piece for the *New York Times Magazine*, 'In England Now', in which he looked back over his childhood with quite startling bitterness. 'Like many writers, I consider myself to have been born in captivity,' he began. 'And after 46 years I am still there, still have not tired of examining in wonder the bars and stones that incarcerate me: their blemishes, which are like the claw marks of my own hands, their truly terrible homeliness.' The article concentrated on his schooling, which he depicted as barbaric and cruel. Even now, David told his readers, he still shuddered as he drove past his preparatory school on the motorway.

That was thirty years before; but the public schools were doing brisker trade than ever. He admitted to sending his own sons to them. The result was disillusion, a sense that nothing would ever change. The prison is in our minds, he believed.

> All my adult life I have watched, you see, in the institutions which I have served – whether they be educational, or administrative or, as now, artistic – the same sourceless, unled bigotry at work that characterised the bedlam of my childhood. I have watched how it poisons communication between British men and women . . . how the knotted shadows of our childhood become the very snares with which we trip our own children.

'How many more generations of honourable schoolboy must we produce', asked David in a rhetorical finale, 'before we can finally achieve the maturity to look each other in the eye?'

It was not entirely clear what he was trying to say in this piece. David's contemporaries thought his portrayal of his schooldays distorted to the point of caricature. What was obvious was his continuing sense of alienation from the society in which he lived, notwithstanding his enormous success. The anger ignited within him as a boy still blazed fiercely.[22]

By this time David had scaled down his plans for 'The Quest for Karla', from the original seven or more novels to a quartet.[23] The third book would be set in the Middle East, another turbulent region. The Arabs had never accepted the creation of the state of Israel in 1948. Hundreds of thousands of Palestinians had been displaced and were still living in refugee camps, demanding the right of return. A succession of wars between Israel and the surrounding Arab states had failed to improve their plight. Palestinian militants had mounted a succession of high-profile terrorist operations, especially against Israeli citizens abroad. The Palestine Liberation Organisation (PLO) had established itself in southern Lebanon, drawing strength from the refugee camps, which came under its control. The PLO constituted a state within a state, challenging the authority of the Maronite Christians who had traditionally dominated the country. From 1975 onward there had been civil war in Lebanon. Beirut had been devastated by the fighting, and by repeated Israeli air attacks.

David Greenway had left the *Washington Post* and had begun covering the Middle East for *Newsweek*, working out of Jerusalem. He received a telephone call announcing the imminent arrival of 'ace photographer Janet Leigh Carr'. This was the first of a dozen or more trips David would make to the region over the next few years. On this occasion he and Greenway undertook a perilous drive to the extreme south of Lebanon, only a few miles from the Israeli border, where the PLO was ensconced in the old Crusader castle of Beaufort, perched on a cliff high above the Litani River. Greenway had obtained an interview with the PLO's military chief Khalil al-Wazir – also known as Abu Jihad, meaning 'Father of the Struggle' – a man responsible for planning a succession of military operations in Israel and elsewhere. As they climbed into the mountains the passengers were alarmed, both by the sporadic Israeli sniper fire from the valley below and by the technique of their Druze driver, who grunted a prayer each time he flung them into another hairpin bend.

Greenway took David on a tour through Lebanon, Syria, Jordan and Israel.[24] By the time they reached the Allenby Bridge, then the *de facto* frontier between Israel and Jordan, David was stricken by dysentery. A long line of lorries stood between them and the checkpoint. As David crouched miserably in the back of the car, Greenway strode confidently down the line of stationary traffic and, by throwing out the name of every local dignitary he knew, persuaded the guards to let them jump the queue.

In Israel, the two men went in search of an old prison on the outskirts of Jerusalem where Jewish paramilitaries had been held during the British mandate, since converted to a museum. They stopped to ask the way of an old man. 'Have you come to see where they hanged the Jews?' the old man angrily demanded. From David's tropical suit and polished brown shoes, he had taken him for a former policeman who had come back to his old haunts to gloat.

In reality David had felt sympathetic towards Jews from an early age, and had consistently portrayed Jewish characters such as Fiedler or the Fennans sympathetically in his novels. Like many of his contemporaries, he supported the creation of a Jewish national home and admired the energy and courage with which the Israelis had built a modern state. But his visits to Palestinian refugee camps showed him the other side of the story. He came to believe that 'a great injustice' had been done, to salve the conscience of Europeans for their own crimes against the Jews. 'We gave them a country which was not ours to give,' he would say later. A people had been first driven from their homes and then demonised as terrorists. In his new novel David resolved to put 'a human face upon the Palestinians'.[25]

Around the New Year David went back to Israel with John Miller. They stood side by side on the Mount of Olives, gazing wonderingly at old Jerusalem, still intact despite everything. David found Miller an ideal travelling companion. 'Few creative people have much natural company within their own profession, least of all when they are actually at work,' David would write. 'But the accident of my friendship with John Miller has taught me that between a painter and a writer a wonderful harmony is possible.'[26]

The intended starting-point of David's novel would be the Circus's receipt of intelligence from a highly placed source about an imminent Israeli attack on Lebanon. The premise was prescient: in 1978 Israel would indeed invade Lebanon, provoked by Palestinian raids launched from across the border. In the winter of 1977/8 David wrote three chapters in which he tried to develop this theme. Yet again he planned to call the book 'The Pigeon Tunnel'. But he found himself unable to write convincingly about Smiley in such a setting. 'I couldn't find the right plot for him there,' David would say later; and indeed it is hard to imagine Smiley operating in such an environment. Eventually David scribbled 'poor stuff' on the manuscript and abandoned the attempt.

Undeterred by this failure, David began another novel, the last in the 'Quest for Karla' sequence, now reduced to a trilogy. The story was one of small beginnings leading to a momentous conclusion. Ostrakava, a Russian woman living in Paris, is approached by the KGB hood Oleg Kirov, ostensibly to ask whether she would like her daughter to join her in exile. Her suspicions aroused, she contacts Vladimir, formerly a general in the Red Army, now leader of a group of exiles campaigning for independence for the Baltic states. Vladimir despatches Villem, son of one of his former comrades and now a long-distance lorry-driver, to Hamburg to collect 'proofs', evidence with which he hopes to ensnare his enemies. He tries unsuccessfully to contact Smiley, known to him by the code-name Max. 'Tell Max it concerns the Sandman,' he insists – 'the Sandman' being the code-name for Karla. He is murdered by the KGB on Hampstead Heath, but not before he has hidden a negative print, which Smiley retrieves. From this single clue Smiley accumulates evidence that Karla is 'making a legend' (a cover story) for a young woman, who turns out to be Karla's own daughter, being treated for schizophrenia in a Swiss sanatorium. Karla has abused his position to place her there and misappropriated state funds to pay for her keep, through a harmless stooge, Grigoriev; Smiley is able to exploit these facts to induce his great rival to defect. The book reaches its climax in Berlin, when Karla crosses the checkpoint between East and West, into the arms of Smiley's people. In the first book of the trilogy Smiley tells Guillam that fanaticism is Karla's weakness, though ironically it is Karla's humanity, his love for his daughter, that proves his undoing.

The spur to the novel in its final form was an encounter on the Heath with an old Russian gentleman, an émigré who had escaped from Petrograd in the early days of the Revolution, the inspiration for the general, called Valentine in early drafts and only later changed to Vladimir. (Villem was originally called Stefan.) His Estonian wife reminded David of the sadness of small exile groups, waiting with diminishing hope for the day when their homeland might once more be free. Madame Ostrakava was inspired by an old lady whom he found slumped over in a Paris street near the Gare de Lyon. When David offered his help, she answered in what seemed to him a Russian accent: *Je souffre d'une manque d'haleine.*

This time there would be few wrong turnings. Once he started writing, he went hard at it and threw comparatively little away. Indeed, some deleted scenes from *Tinker, Tailor, Soldier, Spy* were incorporated into this new novel. Even so, he wrote at least one chapter that he decided not to use, in which Smiley goes to see Lacon to seek protection for Villem and his family. Both Prideaux and Mendel appear in early drafts of the book but are later eliminated, as is Ostrakava's son Nikita.

While writing the book David allowed himself visits to Paris and Hamburg to scout locations, rather as Smiley journeys to Hamburg on Karla's trail. In the novel Smiley boards the ferry across the Alster, retracing Villem's route. An old friend, the journalist Haug von Kuenheim, took David to Amphore, a sex club on the Reeperbahn, the model for the Blue Diamond, the club where Kirov is framed, and where Smiley follows after Vladimir's murder. David's own feelings are detectable in a passage later redrafted, describing Smiley's emotions on arriving in Hamburg seems to reflect his own feelings: 'he felt the involuntary sensations of kinship, assimilation and dread, which assailed him like old friends whenever he set foot on German soil. Germany was his second nature. Its literature was in his blood and in his childhood. He put on the language like a uniform . . .'*

The first draft of the novel was completed in ten months. 'I've just finished my new book, which is not the one we discussed, not the Middle East one, but a totally different story which ran away with me,' David wrote to John Margetson in December. 'I'll revise it through the winter and deliver it in late March.'[27] The first reaction from his publishers was enthusiastic. 'It is magnificent,' wrote Michael Attenborough, one of Hodder & Stoughton's directors who ran the Coronet paperback imprint. 'We have a major bestseller on our hands.' In April David would make another trip to Germany and Switzerland, to check on locations. As so often in the past, he wanted to entitle the book 'The Pigeon Tunnel' or, failing that, 'The Giant Hunter'. He settled on *Smiley's People* only at a late stage.

One of the revisions David would make after finishing the first draft was to introduce Ostrakava at the start of the story; originally her encounter with Kirov had been described second hand, as part of her debriefing to Guillam, near the end. In the process of revision David tightened up the text: for example, the insistent 'Tell Max it concerns the Sandman' replaced the much less powerful 'Inform Max the Sandman has a Little Girl.' At proof stage, David decided to rewrite the 'burning' of the hapless Grigoriev with meticulous care, making small changes to almost every sentence.

Many of the late changes highlight similarities and contrasts between Smiley and Karla. A number of them came in response to Gottlieb's comments. Originally the book had ended, 'They walked slowly towards the car, shirking the halo on their way.' In the final version, the ending was more characteristic of Smiley.

* The final version, from the opening page of chapter 16, reads as follows: 'Germany was his second nature, even his second soul. In his youth, her literature had been his passion and his discipline. He could put on her language like a uniform and speak with its boldness.'

'George, you won,' said Guillam, as they walked slowly towards the car.

'Did I?' said Smiley. 'Yes. Yes, well I suppose I did.'

Three of the first four le Carré novels had been made into films, but none since. Various directors showed an interest in filming *The Naïve and Sentimental Lover*, but nothing came of these discussions. As for *Tinker, Tailor, Soldier, Spy*, its complexity was said to have been the deterrent. In a letter to a friend who had offered to raise money to purchase the rights and finance a screenplay, Karel Reisz said that it was 'not for me'. Though he thought the book 'brilliant', it was not, in his opinion, a movie. 'David's plots are enormously intricate and complex, and adapting them always involves one in very painful and unsatisfactory reducing, which I don't think ever quite works,' he wrote.[28] Movie producers judged *The Honourable Schoolboy* even harder to adapt. One studio executive asked his script department to produce the customary one-page synopsis of the novel, only to receive the reply that this could not be done.[29]

Barry Levinson, then just beginning his career in the industry after working in television, had approached David about the possibility of filming *Tinker, Tailor, Soldier, Spy*, but after the two of them had lunch together, David had the feeling that 'this cannot go to America'. Having wasted, as he saw it, the better part of a year in the late 1960s working on film projects that failed to come to fruition, he was 'very leery then of the short form' and feared that the novel could not be compressed to the necessary length.[30] 'I have had film offers but they stank,' he had told Margetson early in 1975.[31]

London Weekend Television (LWT) wanted to make *Tinker, Tailor, Soldier, Spy* as a series, with Paul Scofield playing Smiley, or perhaps James Mason again, and a script by Harold Pinter, later replaced by another writer specialising in television adaptations, Julian Bond, a contemporary of David's from Sherborne. LWT made a deal with Paramount, but the project stalled because David did not like the scripts.[32] So the matter remained for some years, until a succession of chance occurrences brought *Tinker, Tailor, Soldier, Spy* to the television screen.

18

'Does anyone know what's going on?'

For years the BBC had been negotiating with the estate of Evelyn Waugh for the rights to adapt *Brideshead Revisited* into a drama series. Jonathan Powell, then in his early thirties, had recently been appointed staff producer for BBC's 'Classic Serials'; he wanted to adapt more contemporary novels for the small screen, but had been frustrated to find rights in many of them owned by American film companies. This was one reason why securing *Brideshead Revisited* was so important to the BBC, which jealously guarded its dominant position as the broadcaster of quality television. Powell was sitting in his little office overlooking Shepherd's Bush Green when his boss Graeme MacDonald burst in. 'We've got a problem,' he said: 'we've lost *Brideshead*.' At the last moment the Waugh estate had sold the rights to Granada, the only commercial television company that really frightened the BBC.[1] Powell himself had worked at Granada before joining the corporation. The loss left a hole in the BBC's schedule. 'You've got to do something,' MacDonald told Powell.

It so happened that Powell had recently read *Tinker, Tailor, Soldier, Spy*, perhaps because he was dating Emma, daughter of James and Susan Kennaway. It had struck him at the time that it could make 'an amazing piece of television'. The next day he took the book along to MacDonald's office and proposed it as a possible replacement for *Brideshead Revisited*. 'Nice idea,' replied MacDonald, before adding that, as in so many other cases, the rights were not free: the BBC had made enquiries back in 1976, only to discover that LWT owned them. Powell decided to check. He telephoned George Greenfield, who rang him back with the message, 'David will see you this afternoon.' It turned out that LWT's option had expired the previous day. Powell went home and changed into a suit before going to meet David. A tall man, he squatted on his haunches as he attempted to convey his enthusiasm for the story. 'We will do your book properly,' he told David. He tactfully kept quiet about his involvement with Emma Kennaway; nor did he mention that he too had been at school at Sherborne.

The BBC paid a fee of £14,000 to make *Tinker, Tailor, Soldier, Spy* in seven fifty-two-minute episodes. It was stipulated in the contract that American rights must be offered to Paramount, and that the choice of the producer and the writer of the series were to be 'subject to our client's approval'. In fact David would be involved at every level of the production. Powell reassembled a team with which he had worked successfully at Granada, bringing in John Irvin as director and Arthur Hopcraft as writer. Irvin was a dynamic young television director with a background in documentary filmmaking; Hopcraft was a former football journalist who had come to scriptwriting late, whom David would describe as 'ex-*Manchester Guardian*, north country and very unyielding'.[2] When they met for supper at David's house in Hampstead, everyone present agreed that casting Smiley would be crucial to the project. As David put it, 'the plot, narrative and heart are all sustained by one character – George Smiley'. They were unanimous that Alec Guinness would be ideal in the role, if he could be persuaded to take it on, but Irvin doubted that he would be willing to make the six-month commitment necessary for a series. Though one of the most highly regarded of all living screen actors, who had starred in innumerable successful films, Guinness had done very little television. In 1958 he had won the Best Actor Academy Award for his role in *The Bridge on the River Kwai*; in the following year he had been knighted for services to the arts. More recently, in 1977, he had achieved a new prominence for his part as Obi-Wan Kenobi in the first of the *Star Wars* trilogy.

With Powell's agreement, David made the initial approach to Guinness. It was of course highly unusual for the author of a novel being adapted for the screen to take the initiative in this way, but the tactic would prove successful. 'I write to you as an unbounded admirer of your work for many years,' David began, before stressing the importance of the part to the story: 'Smiley is the "motor", as the Germans call it . . .' He identified the key members of the production team. 'All of us are agreed on one thing:

that if we were to cry for the moon, we would cry for Guinness as Smiley, and build everything else to fit.' You, he said, have the right 'existential manner' for Smiley. He asked Guinness to read the book and consider the proposal. 'The truth is that ever since I started writing about Smiley, I dreamed of your playing him one day.'[3]

Guinness replied the next day. He was 'thrilled' at the prospect. 'There is no question but that I would love to have a shot at playing Smiley,' he wrote, despite 'a few reservations' about his ability to do so satisfactorily. He feared that at sixty-four, as he would be shortly, he was too old for Smiley, though he supposed that make-up and acting could make him appear younger. He had a further concern about his appearance. 'Although thick-set I am not *really* rotund and double-chinned . . .' Perhaps more serious was the problem that he had done very little television, and never a series. 'What worries me about the likely schedule, so far as a series is concerned, is my slow memorizing.' He had no trouble in the theatre if he could get the script two or three weeks before rehearsal started, but was anxious that 'hasty learning would fuss me no end and interfere disastrously with performing'. He professed also to be 'rather anxious' about the fact that Arthur Lowe, 'an actor I greatly admire', had recently played Smiley on television – though this had been no more than an eight-minute dramatised sequence from *Call for the Dead* in a BBC 2 programme about le Carré's work. 'I must add that I've enjoyed *hugely* your books I've read – all but three I think,' Guinness concluded.[4]

David hastened to allay the concerns of the distinguished actor. At sixty-four Guinness was the 'ideal' age, he wrote. 'Smiley can't be less, arithmetically, and I fear that he may be more, though I deliberately arrested the passage of time in the later books!'* David acknowledged that Guinness was neither rotund nor double chinned, 'though I think I have seen you in roles where you have, almost as an act of will, acquired a sort of cherubic look!' But, apart from plumpness, Guinness had all the other

* Smiley first appears in *Call for the Dead*. In 1928 he is due to reply to an offer from All Souls (a college open only to graduate students) when his tutor Jebedee persuades him to attend an interview with a board from the 'Overseas Committee for Academic Research', which recruits him into the Circus. The fact that he had completed his undergraduate studies by 1928 suggests that by the time of the exchange with Guinness he would be into his seventies.

necessary physical qualities: 'a mildness of manner, stretched taut, when you wish it, by an unearthly stillness and an electrifying watchfulness. In the best sense you are uncomfortable company, as I expect Smiley is.'

> An audience wishes – when *you* wish it – to take you into its protection. It feels responsible for you, it worries about you. I don't know what you call that kind of empathy but it is very rare, & Smiley & Guinness have it: when either of you gets his feet wet, I can't help shivering. So it is the double standard – to be unobtrusive, yet to command – which your physique perfectly satisfies . . .
>
> Smiley is an Abbey, made up of different periods, fashions, and even different religions, not all of them necessarily harmonious. His authority springs from experience, ages of it, compassion, and at root an inconsolable pessimism which gives a certain fatalism to much that he does . . . If I may say so, you communicate to me many of his pains, and the almost *archaeological* authority of so many lives and identities. He is also a guilty man, as are all men who *do*, who insist on action. To this, you add another, more practical sort of authority terribly important in the several interrogations, in the research, and in the dénouement of Tinker Tailor: the authority of plain *intellect*. We shall believe Guinness when he tells us things from the past, when he theorises, when he acts in accordance with unstated predictions – because, simply, the intellect is patent, and commanding, yours and Smiley's both.

Guinness's intelligence, David argued, was 'pure gold, because it gives such base to the other things – the solicitude, the moral concern, the humanity of Smiley – all, because of the intelligence of his perceptions, grow under our eyes and in your care'.

David assured Guinness that he would be given plenty of time to memorise the scripts. Powell had promised him over the telephone that they could be ready well in advance.[5]

Guinness agreed to meet them a few days later to discuss the project. He suggested lunch at the Mirabelle, a long-established restaurant near Berkeley Square favoured by film stars. When an excited Powell told his boss of this coup, MacDonald warned him that he could not take anybody, not even the most distinguished actor of his generation, to lunch at the Mirabelle on licence-fee payers' money. Instead they went to L'Etoile in Charlotte Street instead, another classic but less expensive French restaurant.[6] By the end of the meal, it was clear that Guinness would accept the part.* 'We sat bemused after you left, savouring the pleasure of lunching with George Smiley – an absolute conquest,' David wrote to Guinness afterwards.[7]

A friendship began between the two men, carefully delineated. 'If you are incurably fond of him, as I am, you do your best to keep your feelings to yourself,' David would write after he had known Guinness for almost twenty years. He acknowledged Guinness's kindliness, but stressed too his punctuality, self-discipline and professionalism. 'Form is desperately important to him,' David would write; 'he treasures good manners and good order.' Nevertheless they did exchange 'horror stories' about their families at an early stage, which perhaps helped to cement their friendship. Guinness never knew his father, and felt nothing but contempt for his mother, whom he described as a prostitute. David identified in Guinness a trait he recognised from his own childhood, the need to take centre stage and to entertain the adults around him.[8]

It was fascinating to observe a great actor feeling his way into a role. 'Watching him putting on an identity is like watching a man set out on a mission into enemy territory,' David observed.[9] Guinness took meticulous care with the details, trying on one pair of spectacles after another from trays of samples provided by Curry & Paxton† until he found one that he felt was appropriate for the part. David described what Guinness did as a process of 'self-enchantment . . . a kind of controlled schizophrenia', and likened it to his own method of devising a character, trying on his clothes and experimenting with his accent. Of course David was something of an actor himself. 'He really *is* an actor, in my opinion,' Guinness would say of him, after they had come to know each other, 'he has an actor's instinct, and his imitations of people are extremely good.' Indeed David's

* There is some doubt about this. David remembers one of those present saying to Guinness, 'Were you to do this . . .' and receiving the reply, 'I thought that was understood.' Elsewhere it has been suggested that only subsequently was Guinness persuaded by John Irvin to take the part.

† Long-established spectacle makers, since bought by Boots. Curry & Paxton also supplied the spectacles worn by Michael Caine for his role as Harry Palmer in the films of Len Deighton's thrillers.

imitation of Guinness himself would become one of his party pieces.[10] He had shown his quality as an actor by reading *The Spy who Came in from the Cold* on Radio 4, broadcast in January 1978 on the 'Book at Bedtime' slot in fourteen-minute episodes, to a highly enthusiastic reception. The actors' union Equity had raised the matter with the BBC, asking why the task had not been given to a professional. The producer, Maurice Leitch, defended his choice on two grounds: first, because David was able to convey the sense of his own material better than anybody else, and second, because he was a better reader in this genre than 90 per cent of available actors.[11] Following this success, David's readings of many of his novels would be recorded and sold as audiobooks.

Three months after they had first met, Guinness and his wife contrived to borrow the house at Tregiffian for a holiday. They were supposed to stay a fortnight; but after only two or three days Guinness telephoned with an unconvincing excuse to say that they were cutting short their stay. 'We adore it here, but a very dear friend of ours is ill in London and we have to go back to look after him.' Later David learned what had caused Guinness to leave so prematurely. Soon after he arrived, he had taken a call from the British Embassy in Bonn, to say that the Ambassador wished to speak to John le Carré. Guinness was already in the process of becoming Smiley, so this call seemed to him somehow significant. Then there was another semi-official call that aroused his suspicions further. Walking along the clifftop paths he happened to meet Derek Tangye. Guinness confessed to feeling uneasy about the amount of electronic equipment at Tregiffian. Tangye convinced him that the house was bugged.

Once Guinness had agreed to take the part, the rest of the casting was easy; other actors jumped at the chance to work with him. 'The moment we had Guinness, we could empty the National Theatre for *Tinker, Tailor*,' David would say later. The outstanding cast would include Hywel Bennett as Tarr, Ian Richardson as Haydon, Siân Phillips as Ann, and Michael Jayston as Guillam. Lacon was played by Anthony Bate, who had played Kim Philby in a 1977 ITV drama about the Cambridge spy ring. One of Irvin's boldest decisions was to cast Ian Bannen as Jim Prideaux, as Bannen's career had been almost ruined by drink. This choice was vindicated: Bannen would give an outstanding performance, perhaps bringing to the role some of the damage from his own past. Another controversial decision was to give the part of Connie Sachs to Beryl Reid, best known as a music-hall comedienne.* Guinness detested acting with her, fearing that he would be upstaged; 'Nobody can act with a clown,' he said. But the scene between the two of them, when he visits her in Oxford, is one of the most effective and moving in the whole series.

Guinness took a close interest in the scripts, comparing notes with David, who passed on the results to Powell. At first this caused a degree of frostiness with Arthur Hopcraft, a well-organised writer, known to turn in highly polished scripts. Guinness expressed admiration for Hopcraft's work, and offered what he hoped were merely constructive suggestions. To take one small example, he was anxious that Smiley was introduced 'far too weakly and too passively' in the first episode of the series, when he is waylaid in a bookshop by the appalling Roddy Martindale (an old Foreign Office hand) and reluctantly agrees to have dinner with him. To deal with this concern, David suggested that Smiley should make a mild protest as he buys a book – 'Barabbas was a publisher,' a phrase of Byron's, one of George Greenfield's favourites.† This minor change satisfied Guinness.

Hopcraft made two significant changes for the final episode of the series. He wrote a new scene at the very end to show Prideaux's recovery and reintegration into the life of Thursgood's Academy through the eyes of the schoolboy Roach, a process that David had described but not dramatised. The preceding scene in the book has Smiley travelling by train for a reconciliation with his wife, and ends with his first glimpse of her as she waits for him at the station. Hopcraft shows their subsequent conversation, as they stroll together through the countryside. Smiley appears surprised when Ann denies ever having been in love with Haydon. 'Poor George,' she says. 'Life's such a puzzle to you, isn't it?'

Perhaps appealing to Guinness's religious sensibilities, David had stressed Smiley's role as a confessor, 'as sort of Father Brown figure'. In fact this side of Smiley would be more evident in *Smiley's People* than it was in its predecessor. As David reported to Powell, Guinness was anxious that 'Smiley's passivity, or weakness, reaches a low point at the end of the Karla

* Elizabeth Spriggs and Peggy Ashcroft were both considered for the part.

† Also attributed to the poet Thomas Campbell. It is a variation of the Gospel of John 18: 40, 'Now Barabbas was a robber.'

sequence where he confesses that he was not equal to the confrontation, that he shed his professionalism, and at a crucial point in his career, started maundering on about his own wife, and staged a sort of psychological breakdown.' Guinness was 'very uncomfortable having Smiley talking and thinking Ann', and felt that 'he is much too confessive towards Guillam'.[12]

Eventually it was decided that all seven scripts should be discussed at length between producer, director, writer and star, with David also present. They spent a week together in a room at the BBC's Lime Grove studios in Shepherd's Bush, revising the script as Guinness acted out the lines. 'Guinness was extraordinary,' Powell recalled, 'inhabiting the rooms and corridors of the script in his mind.' It was obvious that he was keenly aware of every aspect of every scene. 'No film director, producer or screen-writer of my acquaintance has a better eye for structure or dialogue,' David would write of Guinness. 'Working on scripts with him is what Americans call a learning experience. One scene may go through a dozen revisions before he is persuaded by it. Another . . . is nodded through without debate.' Guinness was ruthless in eliminating lines that he felt he did not need; he cut so many that the episodes became too short, which is one reason why the opening credits are so protracted. These depict a succession of Russian dolls, one inside the other, an image taken from the novel itself. The last doll has a blank face, to reflect Smiley's belief that only Karla could perceive the real Haydon.

To win approval for the series, Powell had said it would be made in the studio in the conventional way; but as the project gained momentum he was able to gain the extra funding to make it on location, though they did economise by relocating the scenes between Tarr and Irina to Portugal rather than Hong Kong. Irvin decided that he wanted to film in winter, which was more expensive, as shorter days allowed less time for shooting. Guinness was encouraged to say that he could only really work in the fluid (but expensive) medium of film, rather than on videotape like most other TV drama at the time.[13]

In researching locations, Powell asked David what the Circus looked like. Irvin, who was always concerned about authenticity, wondered if it would be possible to arrange for him to be shown round the offices of MI5 or MI6. There was no need, David said, looking about him: the Circus, with its dusty rooms, long corridors, shabby paintwork, decrepit furniture and even the cranking lifts, was just like the BBC. As it turned out, and by pure chance, the Circus interiors would be shot on location in a building in Cork Street formerly occupied by MI5, the very house where David had undergone his training. He was delighted by this coincidence.

David helped the series designer, Austen Spriggs, to ensure that everything looked as it should. For example, he explained that 'Top Secret' material was usually handwritten because it was too sensitive to be entrusted to a typist; and that the word 'GUARD' on a file was Whitehall code for 'Do Not Show to the Americans'. He described files, code-books, 'one time' encryption pads and the other paraphernalia of spying, so that Spriggs could depict these realistically.

'When he is composing characters, he steals shamelessly from those around him,' David wrote of Guinness. In due course he would be amused to note that the actor had appropriated his own habit of kneading his brows with his knuckles. To help him assume the role of Smiley, Guinness asked if he could meet a real spy. David arranged a lunch with Sir Maurice Oldfield, the recently retired 'C'. When serving with MI6 David had had a brief operational connection with Oldfield, and since then they had met a few times for drinks, though they had never discussed anything secret. Recently he had received 'a furious ticking-off' from Oldfield for publishing 'distorted versions' of the Firm.[14]

Oldfield was a small, tubby man with spectacles, who carried an umbrella; his superficial resemblance to Smiley would lead to repeated speculation that he was the original for the character. In fact there was nothing in this: David had not met Oldfield when he invented Smiley.* Guinness would add to the confusion by claiming to have met 'the real Smiley' for lunch, as well as incorporating aspects of Oldfield into his portrayal of the part.[15]

* David slightly muddied the waters when he claimed, in a letter to *The Times*, to have 'never heard of Sir Maurice, either by name or in any other way, until long after the name and character of George Smiley were in print' ('Unlicensed to quote', 17 March 1981). This was true, though Oldfield had been an unidentified member of the selection board that had interviewed him when he applied to join MI6. David had written *Call for the Dead* by then, though it was not in print and had not yet been accepted by a publisher.

David arrived at the restaurant in Chelsea to find his guests already seated in a private room, chosen by Guinness 'for security reasons'. In his mind, David surmised, Alec had already joined the Secret Service. During the lunch the two older men did most of the talking. 'I think young David here has gone a bit over the top about this spying stuff,' Oldfield remarked at one point. 'Oh, I do so agree,' said Sir Alec. When Oldfield left at the end of the meal Guinness hastened out into the street to watch him waddle away, swinging his umbrella as he went. Then he turned to David, who had followed him out. 'Could we do a quick brandy?' Back in the restaurant, Guinness demonstrated how Oldfield had run his finger along the inside rim of his wine-glass. 'Do you think that he was checking for the dregs of poison?' he asked.

'I liked him very much and had the impression of a good man,' Guinness wrote to David afterwards.

> The dreadful necktie was beyond any wildest dreams. The ginger shoes, I felt, had been put on to shock quite deliberately. I see what you mean about his shirts. The cuff links were surprisingly flashy but I couldn't see their design very well . . . The suit was good though – well, goodish.
>
> I shall not follow that footwear, or the mahogany dark nicotine stains on his fingers. The glasses I've got are very similar to what he was wearing. I must adapt my wig a bit.
>
> I don't know yet what I absorbed from watching him or sensing him. A few gestures which I probably won't use. But having met him, and noting I'm not desperately dissimilar physically, I feel more confidence than I have done in the past few days.[16]

Guinness became very nervous as shooting drew near. David had to persuade him that it had not been a mistake to accept the part. He was a superstitious actor, who kissed the camera lens each time he arrived on set. He was especially self-conscious about the way he looked; he was too tall to play Smiley, and all his efforts to put on weight failed. To compensate for this he bulked out his figure by wearing heavy pullovers and extra coats. After about three weeks of shooting he again lost his nerve, and suggested to Irvin that he should withdraw in favour of Arthur Lowe. Irvin, who had seen the rushes by then, assured him that he had nothing to worry about.

David and Jane went down to the 'safe house' in Camden Lock to watch the filming of the climax, when the identity of the mole is revealed. It was a cold night, and they found Guinness in his long johns, 'making friends with the pistol' that he would grip as he unmasked the traitor. To their astonishment, he was speculating on who the mole might be. David realised that he was working himself into the mode of believing that he didn't know and was about to make a discovery – although, of course, Smiley had really known all along.

A couple of months later David relayed a telephone message from Jonathan Powell, who had seen the rough cuts and said that they were 'wonderful'. At last, in late June, David was able to view the first episodes himself. 'Smiley is marvellous,' he wrote to Guinness. 'You carry it all. What more can I say? Immense range, yet all within the difficult bounds of the character: heart; humour; occasional surprising fury. It's amazing, and I'm sure that Smiley will be heralded as one of your great parts.' A private screening was organised, to which 200 guests were invited, including publishers, agents and Hodder's 'travellers'. Afterwards David wrote to Guinness that 'even such hard-boiled characters as Mort Leavy, and Jaffe, the head of Bantam Books,* used adjectives like "wonderful"'. He reported on comments from the audience:

> he leaves Smiley alone . . . leaves his enigma intact, yet allows us to love him . . . allows Smiley to be defined by the characters who bounce off him, till gradually you realize he is sort of reluctant confessor of all their sins, a moderator . . . what a terrible limbo he lives in . . . makes the bleakness bearable but is part of it.

In fact Guinness had subtly altered Smiley, as David acknowledged. 'Somewhere in the middle air between myself and Smiley, you have interposed your own marvellous assimilation of the two of us, and added those delicate and illuminating brush-strokes.' He outlined some general criticism of the production as a whole, though the reaction was overwhelmingly favourable. 'I have to tell you,' he wrote, 'it really was, in all of our views, your day . . . Dear Alec, thank you again – forgive this slightly emotional letter, but finally, I am deeply moved, so why not?'[17]

* Marc Jaffe, the long-serving editorial director of Bantam.

After the screening David sent a similar tribute to Arthur Hopcraft. 'Seeing it all put together, I was overwhelmed by how well served I had been; by the quality of the acting, direction, and, of course, your script, which seemed to me to work with quite amazing ease,' he wrote: 'just as we could not have had a better Smiley, so we could not have had a better writer than yourself. Thanks for your craft, & the ingenuity, and the beautifully done additions – Ann at the end, Roach in the chapel, etc.'[18]

Before the series began the BBC gave a grand lunch for the cast and the crew. Everyone had arrived and was standing around, drinking champagne, except Bernard Hepton, who played the part of Toby Esterhase, one of the four suspected of being the mole. Guinness became impatient, suspecting that Hepton was deliberately late, as actors so often are. Eventually Hepton arrived, wearing a green tailored suit. 'Oh Bernard,' said Guinness, 'you came as a frog.'

Tinker, Tailor, Soldier, Spy was due to be broadcast on BBC 2 on Monday evenings at 9.00 p.m., and repeated on Sunday evenings at 10.30. The first episode went out on 10 September 1979. There was much uncertainty about how it would be received: especially whether viewers would tolerate such a complex plot. Early comment was cautious, with some exceptions. ('Don't dream of missing it,' wrote Nancy Banks-Smith in the *Guardian*.) Gradually, though, the critics began to realise that this was an exceptional piece of television. The fact that some of the critics as well as many of the viewers found much of the story incomprehensible merely added to its mystique. Terry Wogan, then presenting the breakfast show on the BBC's Radio 2, ran a quiz, 'Does anyone know what's going on?' The series became a national talking-point. Its success was enhanced when the Association of Cinematographic Television and Allied Technicians called its members working for the ITV companies out on strike, taking the ITV channels off air and leaving the BBC free of competition for viewers. This helped the series achieve viewing figures of eight and a half million, plus a further three million watching the repeats.

The music accompanying the end-credits by the composer Geoffrey Burgon, an arrangement of *Nunc Dimittis* ('Lord, now lettest thou thy servant depart in peace') from the Book of Common Prayer, became a top 10 hit in the UK singles chart, an indication of the popularity of the series. Burgon would win an Ivor Novello award for his score.

Despite the evident success of the series David was nervous. Richard Ingrams, television critic of the *Spectator*, had labelled it 'pretentious':

> Le Carré, who started out as a writer of excellent espionage and murder stories . . . grew more prolix the more successful he became, and began to fancy himself as a cut above the mere writer of thrillers. The flattery which has been accorded to him by people like Melvyn Bragg, who called him in a recent interview 'one of the two or three leading novelists of his generation', has not been good for him . . .
>
> The adaptation suffers from the same fault as the Melvyn Bragg interview in that it seriously over-rates le Carré's talent.[19]

After a long talk with David, the chairman of Hodder & Stoughton, Philip Attenborough, reported that 'there is much on his mind':

> The knives are out, and the articles in the New Statesman* and The Spectator have hurt, and the stuff in the Express about his connection with Sir Maurice Oldfield (ex head of MI5)† has brought back old rumours, all inaccurate, that he thought were forgotten . . . He is beginning to be nervous (in the light of the above) about the critical reception for the new novel and implores us to warn our salesmen not to be disappointed . . .

'This very sensitive man is forever feeling on behalf of others, particularly those in the front line,' commented his brother, Michael Attenborough.[20]

Once the final episode had been screened, David wrote a letter of tribute to Guinness. 'Dear Alec,' he wrote, 'how perfectly marvellous it was. I shed tears over the last episode, not least because the lights seemed to have gone out on your wonderful, wonderful Smiley; but of course they never will.'

> Nothing to report except the clear and belated recognition of a triumph. There are just too many indications around that the public was flattered,

* In fact the *New Statesman* article ('The endless quest for Supermole', 21 September 1979) by its editor, Bruce Page, had concentrated on the authenticity of the series, and was otherwise uncritical. The magazine's cover showed three partly masked men: Philby, Bond and Smiley.

† Sic. Oldfield had been head of MI6, not MI5.

> finally, to have its intelligence appealed to; responded, & ended up very, very pleased with itself in consequence. I've stopped reading the reviews, but I'm astonished by the correspondence columns & the continued (posthumous now) radio comment . . . Le tout St Buryan* – which is where it really counts – was ecstatic, & everyone is your personal friend there, & your longstanding advisor on Cornish affairs, drama, & intelligence matters. My bank had a sweepstake on who the mole was, so did my accountants; Hugh Trevor-Roper, a lifelong enemy, wrote nicely about it in the *Mail,*† & so it all ends – happily & with the clear message that we've set new standards, broken new ground etc. etc.[21]

The critics had been won over. 'Baffling, slow moving, uncompromising and ultimately completely gripping, it was far and away the serial of the year,' wrote Bill Grundy in the *Evening Standard*, and this comment was typical of many.[22] 'Quite obviously, it's been the best drama serial of the year,' was the judgement of the anonymous *Time Out* reviewer.[23] The high quality of the production, and of the acting, would be formally acknowledged when the series amassed nine BAFTA nominations, with Guinness taking the award for Best Actor and the cameraman, Tony Pierce-Roberts, the award for Best Film Cameraman.

Soon after the television series had ended, a letter arrived from – Smiley. Colonel David Smiley had been an army officer, who had served with distinction with SOE in Albania and South-east Asia. After the war he had been seconded three times to SIS and had trained agents to infiltrate Albania (all of whom had been betrayed by Kim Philby).‡ He asked in his letter what had made David choose the surname Smiley. 'I had

* The Cornish village closest to Tregiffian.

† In his *Daily Mail* review of the television series, Trevor-Roper described le Carré as 'a sensitive and thoughtful writer . . . Inevitably his mole, Gerald, recalls to me my old friend Kim Philby.'

‡ Smiley recorded in his memoirs that he had cried only once during the war, in 1940, when he had to have his terrier put down after being posted overseas. In a poignant passage of *A Perfect Spy*, Jack Brotherhood takes his ailing dog outside and shoots it.

two sons at Eton when you were a beak there* and wondered if you had picked the name off the school list?'† David admitted that he could not provide a definite answer:

> Well, now, I just don't know! Maybe I *did* pinch your name from the school list, but it would only have been unconsciously, since Smiley was not a twinkle in my eye till a year after I gave up teaching. But the memory plays strange tricks, and I have no other solution to the choice . . . I embarrassed myself by stealing one name wholesale from The New Statesman (Roy Bland, their writer on East European educational affairs). He wrote to me very sweetly, rather than suing me, and wished me luck.
>
> So I'm inclined to believe, on balance, that your hunch is right, and that I owe you, if not an apology, at least a debt of thanks! And thanks, too, for writing – I'm glad you like my books, & hope you enjoy the new one, just coming out, called – what could be more apt? – 'Smiley's People'!

Smiley thanked him for his reply. 'Incidentally you have done me a good turn as shops now know how to spell my name correctly!'[24]

The series was a big commercial success, being sold to more than thirty countries, including Argentina, Australia, Belgium, Canada, Egypt, France, Germany, Gibraltar, Greece, Hong Kong, Ireland, Israel, Italy, Japan, Jordan, Philippines, Portugal, Trinidad, Turkey, Venezuela and Zambia. But it was thought to be too demanding for the US networks, so Americans had to wait a year before it was shown, compressed into six parts, on the Public Broadcasting Service (PBS). Each episode was introduced by the Canadian journalist Robert MacNeil, whose function was to explain the workings of the Circus to the baffled but fascinated American viewers. *Newsday* announced it as 'the big event of the public TV season', and so it proved, attracting almost universal praise. The *Washington Post* reviewer was not untypical in describing the series as 'one of the most madly atmospheric and enjoyably literate films ever done for television'.[25] On the other hand the series was reckoned a 'disastrous flop in France',

* Both his sons were too young to have been at Eton when David was teaching there.

† It was said that Ian Fleming took the names of Bond's enemies Blofeld and Scaramanga from his contemporaries at Eton.

and far too complex for the Germans to bother with, despite excellent reviews.[26]

One of the few who did not share in the general enthusiasm was the *Observer*'s television critic, Clive James. Following his mocking review of *The Honourable Schoolboy* in the *New York Review of Books*, James had taken another swipe at David in a review of Graham Greene's *The Human Factor*, which he likened to 'one of those good, solid early le Carré novels, plus the moral overtones which the later le Carré vainly tries to add by cramming on hundreds of extra pages, but what [sic] Greene can't help generating from the first sentence, simply because he sees life in a certain way'.[27] By contrast, T. J. Binyon had compared *The Human Factor* unfavourably with le Carré's works. 'With this novel Graham Greene has ventured into territory previously explored by John le Carré,' he wrote in the *Times Literary Supplement*. 'If the map he has brought back is sharper in its outlines, surer in its delineation of major features than those of le Carré, it lacks their detailed topography, their shading and their relief.'[28]

As the television series of *Tinker, Tailor, Soldier, Spy* began broadcasting, James renewed the attack on le Carré in his *Observer* column. 'The first instalment of "Tinker, Tailor, Soldier, Spy" fully lived up to the standard set by the original novel,' he wrote after the first broadcast. 'Though not quite as incomprehensible, it was equally turgid.' Two weeks later he had another go. 'What's going on is a concerted attempt to inflate this book into a fat series,' he alleged. 'It might have made two mildly riveting episodes on television. Spaced out over a whole series, it grips you like a marshmallow.' The following week he tried again. 'Anything can improve, even "Tinker, Tailor, Soldier, Spy" of which the latest episode was marginally better than the first three. People have written to ask whether I am conducting a personal vendetta against John le Carré . . .'

> Le Carré's early books were excellent genre fiction – a far better thing for a book to be than third-rate literature. The kind of book-reviewers who are daunted by real literature, and who are always on the lookout for a more easily readable substitute that they can call literature instead, called them literature.

> In the resulting climate of worship le Carré's sense of proportion, it seems to me, became somewhat scrambled. The books became bigger and bigger with less and less in them . . .
>
> I shall watch to the end but I fear that what should have been a thriller is turning out to be only marginally better than plain dull.[29]

David was provoked into writing a letter of response to the *Observer*, in which he scoffed at James's television reviews as 'no more than a warmed-up rehash' of his review of *The Honourable Schoolboy*. 'I look forward to reading it again when my new novel appears next February.' Perhaps he decided in the end not to send this letter, because it was never published. Later he wrote a spoof letter to the *Guardian* suggesting that there never had been a mole within the Circus, and that the whole thing had been a devious trick on Control's part.[30]

David's sensitivity to criticism was evident in a letter he wrote to Mary-Kay Wilmers, co-founder of the new *London Review of Books*, which was established while the *Times Literary Supplement* had suspended publication because of an industrial dispute. Explaining his decision not to review a novel by John Cheever, after originally agreeing to do so, he outlined 'a firm principle which I made when I first became a full-time novelist – namely, never to get involved in the London reviewing scene, never to confuse the production industry with the service industry'.

> I think that Cheever is a magnificent story-teller, but I know that when I say that in the context of a London literary journal, I appear to be making a case for narrative writers like myself to the detriment of more fashionable trends . . . I suppose what I am saying really is that I find the business of being a successful English novelist living in England hard enough already – there is nothing like the flak of home guns – without walking into the minefields of the London literary scene as well.[31]

Even as the *Tinker, Tailor* series was still being filmed, there was talk of a follow-up. The BBC passed on *The Honourable Schoolboy*, on the basis that it would be too expensive to shoot on location. David sent a typescript of *Smiley's People* to Guinness. 'Of course I'm thrilled at the idea of having another and better stab at Smiley – but you should see the whole of Tinker Tailor before morally committing yourself,' replied Guinness.[32] By June 1979, more than six months before it was published, David's representatives had already received two offers for the film rights in the new book. It was taken as self-evident that Guinness would play the part in any feature film. But the discussions dragged on. 'The waiting is such a bore, and half of me at least says let's do another BBC TV thing & to hell with movies,' David wrote to Guinness as the *Tinker, Tailor* series reached the end. 'But I hope sincerely that we shall be able before long to present you with a choice between one & the other, best of all with John [Irvin] once more at the helm.'[33] Guinness had been very comfortable with the team that had made *Tinker, Tailor* and 'tremendously pleased' with its reception. He disliked the thought of the project being touted around Hollywood; he was acutely conscious that he was not regarded as a big enough star to carry a film on his own, and he became increasingly unhappy at the thought that other 'name actors' would have to be dragged in to shore up the production. He announced that he would rather go back to the BBC.[34] Mort Leavy asked £40,000 for the television rights in *Smiley's People*; the BBC offered £18,000, and they settled on £25,000.

Smiley's People was due to be published early in 1980. A few weeks beforehand the Cornwells moved again, just a hundred yards or so closer to the Heath, to Gainsborough Gardens, a gated enclave of private houses arranged informally around communal gardens. The new house, dating from the late Victorian period, was a large redbrick building in the Arts and Crafts style.

This time the American edition was published first. *Publishers Weekly* had already announced that *Smiley's People* was 'superb, with le Carré writing at the height of his powers'. Knopf's first printing was 150,000 copies. In Britain, subscription sales* amounted to 79,224, then the highest total for a fiction hardback published by Hodder & Stoughton since the firm was founded in 1868. 'The book sells prodigiously,' David wrote to an old friend a few weeks after publication: '93,000 so far, plus 120,000 book clubs – I've never known such figures in England.'[35] *Smiley's People* turned out to be the bestselling novel of the year, according to the

* Orders taken in advance of publication.

Sunday Times. It may have helped that both Canada and Australia screened *Tinker, Tailor, Soldier, Spy* in January, and the series was repeated on BBC 1 as two 150-minute episodes in February/March. Sales may also have benefited from the excitement surrounding the revelation that Sir Anthony Blunt, the former Surveyor of the Queen's Pictures, had spied for the Soviet Union. The 'mole' Bill Haydon was an amateur painter who appreciated fine art, as of course did Blunt, and who had a homosexual side, like Blunt. The actor who had played Haydon, Ian Richardson, resembled Blunt physically. Haydon even had something of Blunt's hauteur – albeit redeemed by a mischievous wit. Several of the reviewers commented that life was imitating art.

The critical reception was mixed. In the *New York Times Book Review*, Michael Wood judged the writing 'a little tired, and the whole book a little bland'.[36] In his *Guardian* review, Matthew Coady described the novel as 'an unexpectedly old-fashioned adventure'.[37] The *Times Literary Supplement* gave the book to the Professor of German Language and Literature at Oxford, who criticised Smiley's taste in German literature.[38] For C. P. Snow, on the other hand, writing in the *Financial Times*, this was 'the best single thing that le Carré has done'.[39] Also very positive were the reviews in *The Times* and the *Sunday Times*; in the former, Michael Ratcliffe likened 'The Quest for Karla', in its scale and ambition, to 'A Dance to the Music of Time'.[40]

The book was generally well received in Germany. 'George Smiley has now become a figure with few equals in the literature of our time,' wrote Rudolf Walter Leonhardt in *Die Zeit*. Commenting on reports that le Carré had taken his leave of Smiley and of spy stories, he asked 'Who or what can replace him?'[41]

Perhaps the most interesting assessment came from the writer and critic Al Alvarez, a neighbour of David's in Hampstead with whom he had recently become friendly. Alvarez was wary of reviewing a book by someone he knew socially, but David assured him that nothing he wrote would make any difference to their burgeoning friendship.[42] Fortunately Alvarez thought *Smiley's People* 'a marvellous book, stylishly written, intricate, absorbing'.

> Yet although it is bound to be a vast popular success, there is still a tiresome intellectual snobbery which fixes a gulf between strong plot and psychological

depth, what Graham Greene called 'entertainments', and serious novels. It has, I think, always been a spurious distinction, and we have the novels of Walter Scott, Conrad, Hammett and Greene himself to prove it.

Alvarez rightly stressed le Carré's 'mimic's ear for variations in pitch and cadence', which gives each of his characters 'his distinct, recognizable voice': 'One of the many pleasures of reading le Carré's novels is in hearing the different voices come argumentatively and irrepressibly to life on every page, like the instruments of an orchestra heard through a very good hi-fi.'[43] Alvarez and his wife Anne, a psychotherapist, held lively dinner parties at their house in Flask Walk, to which David and Jane were often invited. There David met his fellow spy writer Len Deighton, whom he had not seen since the 1960s. Afterwards Deighton wrote to Alvarez that it had been 'wonderful' to see David again. 'I feel a curious affinity with him, like two people who have shared some weird experience.'[44]

Soon after *Smiley's People* was published, David received an appreciative letter about the book from Vivian Green. 'My dear Vivian,' he replied:

> I was so glad you picked up the references. I felt diffident about them, & it always amused me, secretly, that you didn't seem to notice where so much of Smiley came from – his humanity, at least, his perception of human frailty & his difficulty about buying clothes! Nobody ever did so much to set me on my feet as you did, and probably nobody gave me the feeling of seeing me so clearly . . .[45]

But Green was not his only source for Smiley. In an interview broadcast on BBC Radio's *Kaleidoscope* programme, David was asked how he came to invent his most famous character. 'I don't really know,' he replied.

> But I think that there was one prototype originally, certainly in appearance there was one man who had his features, his looks and many of his mannerisms – particularly the one of removing his spectacles and polishing them on the inside of the fat end of his tie. 'He was one of London's meek who do not inherit the earth'* – an absolutely forgettable man, the most

* From the opening paragraph of chapter 2 of *Tinker, Tailor, Soldier, Spy.*

> forgettable man I ever met, who was also very intelligent. I worked with him for a while in the Civil Service. Then I think gradually, as with most of one's characters, he becomes a vessel into which you put other things, and I think Smiley changes very much from book to book.[46]

It happened that Bingham heard this interview. His reaction is unknown, but a woman who was with him at the time, one of his subordinates, protested on his behalf. In a letter to David, which she copied to Bingham, she deprecated his 'sneering and belittling attitude' and his 'hurtful and cheap jibes'. She paid tribute to Bingham's 'unswerving loyalty to his friends and colleagues – even to you who hold loyalty in such contempt'. Though the letter was unsigned, the writer mentioned that 'many years ago, before you transferred to other work, you did take me out to dinner'. She concluded, 'I just wish you had never been part of us.'

David thought the letter 'loony'. He sent an emollient letter to Bingham, addressed from 'Tax Haven, Hampstead', a jokey reference to a jibe about his tax status. 'You know the creative process as well as I do,' he wrote, 'so perhaps you can persuade her that no good character was ever made without deep affection (which, as I'm sure you know, endures blithely to this day).' Bingham sent a good-humoured reply, as from 'The Slaves' Galley'. Somewhat awkwardly, he referred to himself in the third person:

> Smiley has never minded being called a Forgettable Man, and has even regarded it as a mild professional compliment to a man who can merge into the general background. He thinks that that and keeping a low profile are quite useful traits.
>
> On the other hand, to be perfectly frank – always difficult for Smiley – he has often been puzzled as to why you so frequently and harshly attacked his mob, directly in interviews or obliquely in books.
>
> You are far from being pro-Soviet Russia or pro-Communist, but I would think the attacks gave comfort and even pleasure and glee in some places.[47]

There was no doubt that Bingham felt strongly about this. In a taped conversation with his wife,* Bingham acknowledged David as his friend,

* From internal evidence I deduce that this conversation took place around 1980.

with the qualification that 'I deplore and hate everything he has done and said against the intelligence services.'* Years afterwards, in an introduction to a new edition of one of Bingham's novels released posthumously, David attempted to analyse the irreconcilable differences between the two of them, which he ascribed in part to the conflict between the generations. He paid generous tribute to his old friend's qualities, both as an intelligence officer and as a novelist.[48]

Bingham's abhorrence of the way in which the intelligence services were represented in David's novels was widely felt. David had repeatedly to endure the accusation that he had dragged the good name of the Service (or the Services) through the mud. 'You *bastard*!' a middle-aged intelligence officer, once his colleague,† yelled down the room at him, as they assembled for a diplomatic dinner in Washington. 'You utter bastard.'[49]

Such criticism focused on *The Spy who Came in from the Cold*, which portrayed the Circus as unscrupulous, and *The Looking-Glass War*, which had perpetuated that depiction and portrayed the Department as incompetent. That these were works of fiction, and that neither the Circus nor the Department existed, was little considered. It was the old problem of authenticity that had confused discussion of David's work from the outset. Of course David had benefited from such ambiguousness; but it exposed him to the charge of disloyalty. Those who made such accusations failed to acknowledge Smiley's triumphs in 'The Quest for Karla' trilogy. Indeed, one might make a case that in these novels David had exaggerated the significance and the effectiveness of British intelligence. According to the CIA agent Miles Copeland, George Kennedy Young had referred sourly to *The Spy who Came in from the Cold* as 'about the only bloody double agent operation that ever worked'.

As the years passed, John Bingham's wife Madeleine had convinced herself that George Smiley was nothing other than her husband under a pseudonym. In her mind, David owed his success to Bingham. It seemed to her therefore that he should be entitled to share the wealth that had accrued from the Smiley novels. The fact that he disapproved of the books themselves was for her no obstacle. Nothing could shake her from this opinion.

* These remarks were quoted in a letter to the *Telegraph* from the Conservative peer Lord Lexden on 3 March 2014. David responded the next day.

† This was Guy Maurice Bratt, who served under diplomatic cover in the British Embassy in Washington in the late 1970s.

But if Bingham was Smiley, it followed that she was Lady Ann, the unfaithful wife, a characterisation that she resented.* She wrote a memoir, 'Smiley's Wife', which Hamish Hamilton agreed to publish in 1980. A letter from Michael Attenborough to a colleague in New Zealand asked to be kept informed of any information that Hamish Hamilton put out about the book. 'Our author is more concerned than we are about the book's publication, although I dislike the title intensely.' As it turned out the Office refused permission for the book to be published. Aggrieved, Madeleine Bingham wrote 'Smelly's People', described by Bingham's biographer Michael Jago as 'a farcical, outdated story about a Polish defector whose memoirs were banned by MI5'.[50] This too remained unpublished.

David encountered the Labour politician Denis Healey at a dinner party given by the lawyer and former minister Hartley Shawcross. As a former Secretary of State for Defence, Healey knew more than most politicians about security matters. 'I know who you are,' cried Healey, hand outstretched, as he walked towards David from the doorway. 'You're a bloody Communist spy, that's what you are, admit it!' So David admitted it, and everybody laughed, including their startled host.[51]

Out of the blue David received an invitation to lunch with the Queen. Jane drove him down to Buckingham Palace and dropped him by the pedestrian gate, which had to be unlocked to let him in. 'You should have driven in,' the policeman on duty told him. There were eight people at lunch. David sat at the Queen's left; on his other side was the Dean of Windsor. On the Queen's right was the actor Alec McCowen, who was enjoying a success in performing his own adaptation of St Mark's Gospel on the stage. Ten days later a letter arrived offering David a CBE. He wrote back, courteously declining. Another letter arrived, this time from the Prime Minister's office, renewing the offer. David wrote again, saying that he 'would like to go on record as not wanting that sort of award'.

Interest from a Canadian academic had revived Susan Kennaway's ambition to edit James's letters and diaries. She undertook the task herself, adding extracts from his novel *Some Gorgeous Accident*, and interspersing

* It has been suggested that her feelings stemmed from her attraction to David, or from his towards her. He strongly denies any such feelings on his part.

the material with her own memories of the time. In doing so she felt an obligation not to censor what he had written to suit herself or anybody else. She had little thought then of commercial publication. 'I wanted to write a love story, about James and me, and how such frightful scenes could end in a sort of peace and reconciliation,' she wrote recently. 'I wanted to show, I am ashamed to say, that it was me that he really loved.'[52]

When James's agent asked to read the typescript, she innocently gave it to him, scarcely imagining that he would offer it for sale. She was therefore disconcerted by a telephone call from Tom Maschler, editorial director of Jonathan Cape, who told her that he wanted to publish the book. Susan warned him that the material was very personal: she was especially concerned at the danger that the character identified only as 'David' might be revealed as the world-famous author, John le Carré. According to her, Maschler was adamant that this would not happen. 'Why would I put Cape in jeopardy by letting the name get out?' he asked.

Susan allowed herself to be convinced. Maschler was offering an advance of £3,000, a tempting sum at a time when she was short of money. She was tempted too by the opportunity to give her own version of the story. 'Both James and David had written fantasies that some people believed to be the truth,' she wrote; 'why not let the little pig in the middle write what really happened?' Moreover she felt a duty to promote her late husband's writing. Believing in its importance, she was keen to do everything possible to bring it to public attention. 'Most of all I hope that the publication of these papers will lead to a revival of James's work,' she told a reporter.[53]

When Susan wrote to David suggesting that they should meet to discuss the proposed book, he replied that he would prefer to read 'whatever material you would like to publish' before discussing it. In sending him 'the unexpurgated version', she expressed her willingness to 'alter some of the more obvious things'.

David responded promptly. 'I think about 500 different things,' he wrote, 'but let me try to separate them, some of them.'

> Firstly, it was about people I no longer know, and in some ways, perhaps, never knew. To that extent, I don't really care what anybody writes about me all those years ago, or wrote about me . . .

> The professional in me, incidentally, questions the viability of the material at any level except the most prurient. James may be a great literary name in fifty years, but at the moment, like so many writers after their deaths, he is temporarily unknown, too young to be a classic, too old to be fashionable. In case the publishing world doesn't say those things to you, perhaps I should. This puts his connection with *me* in a far more commercial light than my connection with *him* . . .
>
> As James's friend, sometimes familiar, admirer, fan – what you will – lover – I think I disagree with you quite deeply about the quality of the diaries (where you quote from them) and their significance. Much of what you include is plain bilge, in my view . . . The diary is worst, I think, where it is most self-conscious and aware of other, later eyes.
>
> I think you have succeeded in doing yourself and James an injustice, and leaving me – very sweetly – blank but intact, which is probably how James would have described me anyway![54]

Susan wanted to call the book 'James and Jim', but Cape preferred *The Kennaway Papers*. The book attracted a number of positive reviews, though ironically several of them commended Susan at the expense of her late husband. 'His continual self-dramatizing and self-justifying, coupled with boasts of sexual conquests, add up to an unattractive personality blinded by a sense of his own importance,' wrote James Campbell in the *Times Literary Supplement*. For Campbell, 'the most engaging parts of the book are written by Mrs Kennaway herself. Her writing has a frankness and simplicity and sense of humble regret which her late husband evidently never achieved.'[55] In the *London Review of Books* the Scottish novelist Allan Massie praised her 'rare candour', as well as 'the beautiful lucidity of her writing'.[56] Philip Oakes, writing in the *Sunday Times*, judged it 'a courageous and healing book', and 'truth-telling of a high order'.[57] But others disapproved of putting so much private material into the public domain. 'Strictly for snoopers', sniffed Paul Bailey in the *Observer*. 'Only a person addicted to the sight and smell of old, dirty linen could possibly take pleasure in the revelations.'[58] In *The Times*, Philippa Toomey speculated on whether the book was 'an act of homage, reparation or revenge'.[59]

Even before *The Kennaway Papers* appeared, Susan's belief that David's anonymity could be preserved was shown to have been naïve. The *Sunday*

Times was due to serialise the book; a listing of their forthcoming features included one entitled 'John le Carré: his secret love'.[60] On seeing this, Susan failed to make the connection with her own book; she assumed that it must refer to some other dalliance. But when she telephoned the newspaper to ask whether they needed photographs to illustrate the serialisation, she was told, 'Oh, we already have a very nice one of John le Carré.' She was disconcerted, and then horrified when she learned that the extracts they planned to publish were almost all about David. Much to Maschler's annoyance, her solicitor obtained an injunction preventing the *Sunday Times* from publishing material from the book. But soon it was obvious that David's identity was widely known. The *Daily Express* ran a story on the book, predictably entitled 'The Lover who Stayed out in the Cold'. The *Evening Standard* review, by Valerie Grove, had been headed 'The Wife who Came in from the Cold', illustrated with photographs of Susan, James and David.[61] George Greenfield was quoted as saying that his client had gone away and would make no comment. Susan could not understand how everybody in the press seemed aware that her character of 'David' was John le Carré. At a dinner with friends she met the journalist Jill Tweedie, who told her why this was: copies sent out to reviewers had contained a note, to the effect that 'Mrs Kennaway doesn't want you to mention that the person named David in this book is really John le Carré.' Susan felt that she had been deceived: she found it difficult to avoid the conclusion that Cape had taken on the book in the hope of its becoming a *succès de scandale*. Afterwards she could not stop crying. A doctor told her that she was having a nervous breakdown. Her attempt to pay homage to her late husband's memory had become 'a nightmare'.

Alec Guinness consulted David about the choice of title for his autobiography, which he proposed to call 'A Halfway Man'. David protested that this was over-modest. Expanding on the theme, he declared it absurd that Graham Greene should have entitled his autobiography *A Sort of Life*, 'as if being a bestselling novelist for 50 years, living in the South of France, having lots of money & ladies *and* discovering God into the bargain added up to very little. Whereas for most people, pains and all, his life is the nearest man can get to perfection. I think one has to remember that somehow.'[62] Perhaps chastened by this outburst, Guinness adopted a new title, *Blessings in Disguise*.

Later in the year, David wrote to Greene 'in great embarrassment' after an interview had appeared in *The Times*, 'in which I appear to claim a far greater and more significant acquaintance with you than was ever the case'. The interviewer, Nicholas Wapshott, had referred to 'a close friendship' between the two novelists; and had written that Greene had 'dumped him' after David's introduction to the Philby book had appeared in 1968. Another of Wapshott's howlers was a reference to the novel *The Dishonourable Schoolboy*.[63]

The embarrassment may have been exacerbated by the fact that David had taken part in a BBC radio tribute to Greene on his seventy-fifth birthday in 1979, produced by the film critic Philip French. Greene had written to French afterwards to say that he had found David's tribute patronising. Shortly thereafter Greene's brother Hugh had written a hostile review of the television adaptation of *Tinker, Tailor, Soldier, Spy*.

A few days after Wapshott's piece, a letter from Greene was published in *The Times*. 'I am only too accustomed to the errors which appear in almost every interview to blame Mr John le Carré for what has been put into his mouth by your reporter,' he began.

> Certainly Mr le Carré would never have described Sir Maurice Oldfield as the head of MI5 and I am sure that Mr Wapshott (perhaps I should describe him as Mr Badshott) is responsible for his description of my relationship with Mr le Carré.
>
> I think Mr le Carré and I have only met twice – once over drinks with our German publishers in Vienna, and once by chance when we sat together at a musical in Paris in which our French publishers had an interest . . .*
>
> I never took him 'under my wing' (I haven't wings wide enough) and we have never been 'close friends' – 'casual acquaintances' would be more accurate – nor have we ever drunk 'for hours', 'swapping stories', any more than I have ever 'dumped' him.[64]

Greene replied privately to David's letter of apology. 'Of course I never for a moment imagined that you were responsible for that interview, and

* They met on at least one other occasion, when David called on Greene at his Paris flat.

it was amusing to stick a knife into the ribs of Mr Wapshott,' he wrote. 'I have suffered too much from people of that kind myself to attribute it to the person interviewed.' He expressed the hope that one day 'our friendship will be a less casual one'.[65]

In his embarrassment about this matter David had consulted Greene's publisher, Max Reinhardt. Afterwards he wrote to Reinhardt to thank him for his good offices. 'GG wrote a very super letter,' he began. 'I owe him *so* much, in spirit, in sheer literary scale, and it made me sick to think that I seemed to be chucking his name around. It makes me fairly sick to be compared to him too; for I am content to *know* he is an immeasurably greater talent. Period.'[66] A little later Greene received a letter from Moscow, from his old friend Kim Philby, who referred to Wapshott's interview with le Carré in *The Times*.

> I had been startled by the news that you had broken up a close friendship for so trivial a cause as le Carré's attack on me. I was happy to learn that there had been no close friendship and therefore no breach. I don't think that le C's preface could have added much to his reputation, except perhaps as a writer of fiction. Over confident, long-range analysis of someone you have never met, is a risky business. Some time ago, he was quoted (I think in the NYT Review of Books) as saying that I had described his novels as nonsense; he was pleased, he was alleged to have said, because it showed that he had 'stung' me. In fact, I never said anything of the sort. What I actually wrote was that, although his plots were more complicated than anything within my own experience, they were good reading after all that James Bond nonsense – a rather different judgement. Actually, I have all his books, and have enjoyed them all, except The Honourable Schoolboy; it was so long and so far fetched that it faded long before the end . . . [67]

19

'The Love Thief'

By the time that the long-drawn-out arrangements had been concluded for the BBC to make *Smiley's People*, neither Irvin nor Hopcraft was available. Jonathan Powell brought in John Mackenzie, director of *The Long Good Friday*, but he proved unacceptable to Guinness, and was replaced by Simon Langton. John Hopkins, writer of the innovative quartet of television plays *Talking to a Stranger* (1966), produced a script which was thought much too long and wrong in various other ways. By this time the cast had been assembled and the BBC was ready to start shooting, so David was obliged to rewrite the scripts himself, very quickly, with help from Jane and input from Guinness. Once again, the BBC assembled a strong cast, including Eileen Atkins* as Ostrakova, Curd Jürgens as Vladimir, and Michael Lonsdale as Grigoriev. Several of the actors from the *Tinker, Tailor* series were available to play the same roles, including Bernard Hepton and Beryl Reid, but sadly not Michael Jayston, who had played Guillam. Once again, the series was made almost entirely on location, except for the final scene at the Berlin Wall, which was shot at Nottingham's Lady Bay Bridge. *Smiley's People* was broadcast in six parts on BBC 2 on Monday evenings at 8.00 p.m., starting on 22 September 1982, and on PBS a month later. Like its predecessor, it was greeted with general acclaim. 'It has just opened in the States to a triumphant reception,' David wrote to Vivian Green in October.[1] In America the series was nominated for three Emmys; in

* Judi Dench had accepted the part, before she snapped her Achilles tendon during rehearsals for *Cats*. Simone Signoret was also considered.

Britain, it was nominated for ten BAFTAs, and won four, including Best Actor for Alec Guinness (again) and Best Actress for Beryl Reid.

As John Irvin remarked, Guinness had made Smiley his own. In a sense he had stolen the character from David. Henceforth it would be an effort for David to think about George without picturing Alec. 'Guinness had taken over the part, and his voice was in my ear,' David would tell an interviewer in 1989. 'I was writing Guinness cadences, and giving him Guinness mannerisms.' When he tried to imagine his character, 'it wasn't my Smiley, it was his Smiley'.[2] It was time to leave Smiley behind. He was getting too old, anyway; there were only so many times that he could be brought out of retirement.

David had re-established contact with a friend from his Bonn days, David Goodall. In 1979 Goodall had been posted back to Bonn, this time as Minister. David visited him there in October of that year, after passing the proofs of *Smiley's People*, and would go back to stay with him at least once more in the next couple of years. During a walk along the Rhine, David outlined his thoughts about what he might tackle next. He was nerving himself to write something 'agonising' and 'completely different': he wanted to break away from the espionage genre and write 'something really good'.

Within a few months, however, he had gone back to planning another spy story. He already had a character in mind, based on his sister Charlotte, whose early experiences had made her an angry young woman. Passionate by nature, with a strong social conscience, she was drawn to radical causes. Though David thought her politics naïve, he was never dismissive. 'Oh Sis, calm down,' he would say. This was a period when the far-left Workers Revolutionary Party (WRP) attracted a disproportionate number of actors, including the Redgrave siblings Vanessa and Corin. When Charlotte had been at the Bristol Old Vic Theatre School, she had heard Vanessa Redgrave proselytise. David came to believe that Charlotte had joined the WRP and been sent to a radicalising school for 'training', though in fact she never joined this or any other political party.

One evening, while staying down in Cornwall on his own, David went to a local sports centre to see Charlotte play Beatrice in a touring Royal Shakespeare Company production of *Much Ado about Nothing*. Watching the cast shouting their lines in order to be heard above the din of rain drumming down on the metal roof, David was suddenly inspired. Afterwards he invited his sister and two other cast members back to Tregiffian, where they chatted beside a blazing open fire while drinking warm red wine. David's close involvement with the two television series, and with Guinness in particular, had caused him to reflect on the parallels between acting and spying. He now saw a possibility to combine the two in a single story. Charlie, a beautiful young actress with a radical background, would be recruited by the Circus to penetrate a terrorist organisation, after a British minister has been killed by a bomb. She would be offered a role in the 'theatre of the real': to become a double agent, playing the part of a young woman only slightly different from herself. Charlie would be 'taken all the way through', just as it was once suggested that David should have been. The suspense would come from the difficulty of maintaining her cover, and the risk of exposure, which would put her in peril; the psychological tension would derive from her own confused loyalties. The book would be told in the first person by Charlie's case officer.

'I'm writing a novel about an actress,' David told Charlotte. 'Would you be an advisor on that?' He did not elucidate the plot. Charlotte agreed, and talked at length about her experiences of radical politics. He supplemented what he learned from his sister by talking to others with similar experiences and by visiting radical bookshops in Islington. With John Miller he travelled to Mykonos, the setting where Charlie would be recruited at the beginning of the novel. Charlie's back-story, as envisaged by David, was comparable if not identical to Charlotte's own. Her father goes bankrupt and is imprisoned for fraud; she has to leave boarding school because of unpaid fees; she comes home to chaos, with a furniture van being loaded up in the drive; her beloved pony has been taken away. When her father comes back from prison, he waits humbly for doors to be opened before passing through, just as Ronnie did.

After a while David changed direction: instead of being recruited by the British, Charlie would be recruited by the Israelis to penetrate a Palestinian terrorist cell. Rather than a British minister, it would be an Israeli diplomat whose Bonn residence is blown up by terrorists at the beginning, one of a succession of attacks mounted by Khalil, a terrorist mastermind. Charlie's mission would be to locate Khalil, so that the Israelis could assassinate him. This aspect of the plot was reminiscent of real operations mounted by

Mossad, which had a policy of seeking out those responsible for terrorist atrocities against Israeli citizens and eliminating them.

It was difficult to explain Charlie's motive for risking her life in the service of a cause about which she felt ambiguous, to say the least. Then as now, the default position for radical leftists was pro-Palestinian and anti-Zionist; indeed, this was how Charlotte felt. But David perceived in her, and in other idealists like her, a longing for 'a direction, a purpose, a mission'; he had felt the same way himself. 'Although she's rejecting,' he told an interviewer who quizzed him about Charlie's motivation, 'she really wants to join.'[3]

With this change of direction David introduced another human element into the story: Charlie's relationship with her Svengali-like controller 'Joseph', who becomes her lover. Joseph's unease about what Israel has become ('an ugly little Spartan state') grows as Charlie surrenders to his manipulation.

David shuttled back and forth to the Middle East, using Cyprus as a staging post. He began with the Israelis, because he found them much more open and accessible. In the foreword to his book he would pay special tribute to General Shlomo Gazit, former head of the Military Intelligence Directorate, a man who personified for David 'the enlightened Israeli soldier and scholar of his generation'. The Israelis allowed him to see anyone he wanted to see, without conditions, including members of special forces and people who had served in secret units. He was also given the opportunity to meet a captured terrorist: someone who really was what Charlie would only pretend to be. Like Charlie, the German terrorist Brigitte Schulz was in her mid-twenties; she had been arrested by agents of Mossad in the process of trying to shoot down an El Al airliner as it came in to land at Nairobi's Kenyatta Airport. Because the plot had been detected, the plane had been empty of passengers; it had returned smartly to Israel with only Brigitte on board. In Israel she had been sentenced to ten years' imprisonment. David visited her in a secret prison set in a fold of the Negev desert, known colloquially as the 'Villa Brigitte': a cluster of low green military huts surrounded by barbed wire, with a watchtower at each corner. He was driven there in a jeep by a helpful young colonel in Shin Bet, the Israeli equivalent of MI5. Inside the compound the colonel led David up an outdoor staircase, rapped on a door and called out a greeting. They were received by the prison governor, a sturdy woman in late middle age with bright brown eyes and a pained but kindly smile, who addressed David in English.

A few moments later Brigitte was led in. She was a striking young woman: tall, clear-eyed and beautiful. David introduced himself in German and they sat facing each other across a table, while the prison governor seated herself in the corner of the room, patiently prompting her ward from time to time in English. In his questioning, David tried to elicit how a young woman from a good family in one of the richest countries in the world could have reached the point of being willing to cause the deaths of hundreds of innocent Jewish passengers. She told him that she was a resister and a liberator. The Federal Republic was a Nazi country run by state fascists of the Nazi generation. She was opposed to armed capitalism, the remilitarisation of Germany and American colonialism. The foundation of Israel was a trick to force innocent Arabs to pay the price for Nazi atrocities.

David sympathised with much of what she said. He too had been disgusted by the ubiquity of former Nazis in positions of power in West Germany; by the refusal of the older generation to discuss what had happened in the Nazi period; and by the willingness of the occupying Western powers to overlook Nazi crimes in return for German subservience. He too had come to believe that the Palestinians had been forced to pay the price for Western crimes against the Jews. Nevertheless he found her espousal of terrorism inexcusable and repellent. And though he said none of this to Brigitte, it was clear to him that in her eyes he was just another lackey of the bourgeoisie, a voyeur, a terror tourist. Even as he admired the beauty and the boldness of this young woman, he sensed her cool assessment of him as an inadequate.

She terminated the interview. After Brigitte had gone, David remained seated for a moment, confused by his reaction. The prison governor asked him whether he had got what he had come for. He replied lamely that it had been very interesting. Then it struck him that she had spoken to him in German. Seeing his surprise, she answered his unasked question. 'I speak only English with her,' the woman said. 'I cannot allow her to know. When she speaks German, I cannot trust myself. I know the voice too well.'

Then she added, by way of explanation: 'You see, I was in Dachau.'[4]

David found the Israelis both friendly and approachable, almost disarmingly willing to talk. It was much more difficult to get to know the other side. He had begun by making an appointment to see the PLO's London representative, only to be stood up when he arrived at the appointed time. This was the first of many frustrations. David put out a number of feelers to the PLO without making contact. Eventually, however, he was granted an interview with Salah Ta'amari, one of the most dashing of their military commanders, a tall, handsome man who spoke ardently. They met over a late lunch in Odin's restaurant in Devonshire Street. 'I had my first taste of Salah's passionate oratory over a Dover sole and Perrier water,' David would write later; 'the people at the surrounding tables were spellbound.'[5]

The lunch was a success: one meeting led to another. David tried to make it clear to those whom he met that he wished to be entrusted with no secrets; he wished only to hear the arguments and meet the people. Nevertheless it became obvious to him that he was taken for more than he claimed. His protestations to be a mere novelist looking for a story were listened to with knowing politeness; he was assumed to be a conduit to the British Foreign Office.

Most of all David wanted to meet the PLO's charismatic chairman, Yasser Arafat, head of the comparatively moderate faction known as Fatah. This was not easy to arrange: Arafat lived in fear of assassination, by agents either of the Israelis or of a rival Palestinian faction. David endured infuriatingly long waits in the anteroom of the Fatah offices in the wrecked city of Beirut. A group of boys with machine-guns lounged nervously outside. A ring of cement-filled barrels shielded the entrance; most of the street had been wrecked by a car bomb, which the Palestinians claimed was Israeli.

'You will be contacted at your hotel,' David was told. 'Remain in your hotel, please, and wait.' Day after day passed. David spent long hours in the hotel bar, where the sound of incoming and outgoing gunfire was so common that the resident parrot had learned to imitate it. From his unlit bedroom window David would listen to the evening fusillades and watch the long, slow flashes behind the hilltops. At night he ate jumbo spring rolls in the empty Chinese restaurant. It was there that a maimed waiter limped towards him through the empty tables, his young eyes shining with excitement. 'Our chairman will see you now,' he announced, in a conspiratorial murmur. 'Now, please.' The summons was so sudden, and from such an unexpected source, that David took him to mean the chairman of the board of the hotel. He followed the boy across the lobby, wondering if he might have stayed too long without paying his bill, or whether he might be asked to sign one of his books. It was not until he saw the small group of fighters at the front door, with their coats worn like capes over their shoulders, and their hands out of sight in the folds, that it dawned on him that he was being taken to see the chairman of the PLO.

David was led outside to a sand-coloured Volvo with a whip aerial and sandwiched between machine-gun-bearing guards. This was the first stage of a hectic journey through the Beirut night, driving at speeds of up to ninety miles an hour, hurriedly switching cars in little courtyards, passing through checkpoints manned by armed men crouched around braziers, and at one stage bumping across the central reservation of a dual carriageway before continuing in the wrong direction down the opposing side with lights flashing. Their destination was a half-bombed, half-restored high-rise apartment building, the staircase lined with armed men, all smoking. As they reached the tenth or twelfth floor, and the fighters came forward to frisk David for the umpteenth time, he lost his temper and announced that he was sick of being searched. Smiling apologetically, they drew back and bowed him into Arafat's presence.

The chairman's face was that of an over-sensitive little soldier who had lost his horse, David would write later, 'and you felt an irresistible urge to go and find it for him'. He was wearing a silver-coloured pistol and a perfectly pressed uniform. And he smelled of baby powder. The stubble on his cheeks, as they entered the traditional embrace, was silky, not prickly.

'Mr John, why have you come here?' he demanded, placing his hands on David's shoulders, while scanning his eyes like a worried doctor.

'Mr Chairman,' David said, 'I've come to put my hand on the Palestinian heart.'

Arafat seized David's hand and pressed it to his breast. His own hand was as soft as a girl's. 'Mr John, it is here, it is here.'

As David was finishing his novel, real events threatened to overtake his fiction. In London, the Israeli Ambassador to the United Kingdom was shot and seriously wounded by members of the Iraqi-backed Palestinian group run by Abu Nidal. The Israelis took this as sufficient provocation to launch air strikes against Palestinian targets, including the refugee camps, followed by a full-scale invasion, aimed at driving the Palestinians out of southern Lebanon. The fact that Abu Nidal had been expelled by the PLO, that the British police reported that PLO leaders were themselves on the hit list of the attackers, and that the Abu Nidal organisation was based in Syria and not in Lebanon, did not deter the hardline Israeli government. Some of the fiercest fighting took place around Fort Beaufort, the PLO's strongpoint above the Litani River where David had gone with David Greenway some years before. The old Crusader castle was reduced to rubble.

David had returned to Israel via the Allenby Bridge. On the day before the invasion, he visited the northernmost kibbutz in Israel, a strongpoint often targeted by cross-border raids from Palestinians based in southern Lebanon. The following night, while Israeli bombers pounded Lebanese cities, he was back in Jerusalem, being gently lectured by a distinguished diplomat on why it was quite impossible for the Palestinians ever to make peace. David stayed in Jerusalem to watch the funerals of the first Israeli soldiers killed in the war, their bodies returned from Lebanon. A journalist stepped out of the crowd and greeted him, almost manic with grief. He had lost a son in the war of 1973 and had come to the funeral because he knew the family of one of the dead men. 'In '73 we fought for the peace that was around the corner,' he told David. 'What do we fight for now? It goes on, and on, and *on*.'

In an article for the *Observer*, David condemned the attack on Lebanon as 'a monstrosity, launched on speciously assembled grounds, against a people who on the Israelis' own admission constitute no serious military threat'.[6] David would incorporate the invasion into the final chapter of his novel.

> And in the late spring at last, as soon as the Litani basin was dry enough for tanks . . . the long-awaited Israeli push into Lebanon occurred, ending that present phase of hostilities or, according to where you stood, heralding the

next one. The refugee camps that had played host to Charlie were sanitised, which meant roughly that bulldozers were brought in to bury the bodies and complete what the tanks and artillery bombing raids had started; a pitiful trail of refugees set off northward, leaving their hundreds, then their thousands, of dead behind. Special groups eradicated the secret places in Beirut where Charlie had stayed; of the house in Sidon only the chickens and the tangerine orchard remained.

By midsummer David was able to inform Goodall that he had finished his novel – 'which includes blowing up your house in the Fasanenstrasse, which I knew you'd like'.[7] As so often in the past, David toyed with a number of titles before settling on *The Little Drummer Girl*: among them 'The Twice-Promised Girl', 'The Piper and the Tune', 'The Cage on the Roof', 'The Girl on the Casino Roof' and 'Taking One All the Way Through'.

There was intense excitement about the book in advance of publication, especially in America, where the Palestinian point of view was rarely enunciated. Warner Brothers bought the movie rights. The Book of the Month Club made *The Little Drummer Girl* a main selection. Bantam bought the paperback rights for $1 million, the same sum they had paid for *The Honourable Schoolboy*. CBS ran a feature on the book on the evening national news. This was the kind of publicity that no amount of money could buy. 'It seems to be a book whose time has come,' commented Knopf's director of publicity. 'Rarely is a novel as tied in to current headlines as le Carré's is,' commented George Will in his syndicated column.[8]

Newsweek made it a cover story, meaning that David had achieved the rare double of cover stories in both the major American news magazines. *Newsweek*'s reporter Ed Behr spent no fewer than eight days with David in Wengen, and accompanied him to Beirut. Behr was a seasoned foreign correspondent who had covered the conflicts in Algeria, Indochina and Lebanon and had been *Newsweek*'s bureau chief in Hong Kong.* He described David as 'tall and handsome, with the offhand, self-deprecating

* In 1978 Behr published a volume of memoirs, memorably entitled *Anyone Here Been Raped and Speaks English?* To his irritation his American publishers insisted on giving it the much blander title *Bearings: A Foreign Correspondent's Life behind the Lines.*

charm and marbled accent of the well-born Britisher' – a strange expression for Behr to use since, though he wrote for American periodicals, he was English, with connections that he was able to exploit in writing his piece.

The Little Drummer Girl sold more copies in a single day (59,000) than any previous book published by Knopf in its sixty-eight-year history. David's American agent Georges Borchardt claimed that it was the fastest-selling novel by an English writer ever to have appeared in America. Knopf had ordered a bullish first printing of 200,000 copies, but nevertheless the book reprinted three times before publication, bringing the number in print to 400,000. Naturally it went straight in to the US bestseller list at no. 1.[9]

In the *New York Times Book Review* the conservative columnist and broadcaster William F. Buckley Jr praised *The Little Drummer Girl* as a spy novel 'that transcends the genre':

> 'The Little Drummer Girl' is about spies as 'Madame Bovary' is about adultery or 'Crime and Punishment' about crime. Mr le Carré easily establishes that he is not beholden to the form he elects to use. This book will permanently raise him out of the espionage league, narrowly viewed . . . He is a very powerful writer. His entertainment is of a high order. He gives pleasure in his use of language. And his moral focus is interesting and provocative.[10]

Acclaim from this source was especially sweet because Buckley was himself a prolific author of espionage novels. Some reactions were less favourable. In the conservative, Jewish-themed magazine *Commentary*, the historian Walter Laqueur accused David of being 'a PLO propagandist' who took 'a pro-Palestinian line'.[11] George Will suggested that he had acted as a conduit of Arab propaganda. To David Pryce-Jones, who reviewed the book in the *New Republic*, it was obvious that he believed 'the Palestinians are good, the Israelis are bad'.[12] In an introduction to a subsequent edition of the book, David recorded that he had endured 'the cheap jibe that anyone who criticizes Israel is anti-Semitic'. He had received 'some foul letters from American Jewish organisations, but some remarkably moving ones from individual Jews'. In a discussion on CBS news Chaim Herzog,

President-elect of Israel,* praised the book as 'realistic'; while the leading Arab-American commentator Edward Said dismissed it as 'the usual stuff about Arabs as terrorists'. Within Israel itself, the response had been largely positive.[13]

A few weeks later *The Little Drummer Girl* was published in Britain. Here too the excitement was considerable. On ITV, Melvyn Bragg devoted a whole edition of *The South Bank Show* to an extended interview, built around it. The *Observer* serialised the book on three consecutive Sundays, beginning with an interview by Hugh McIlvanney. Perhaps unsurprisingly their reviewer, John Gross, praised it as 'a first-rate piece of story-telling', though he admitted to being puzzled by Charlie's motivation.[14] Writing in the *Sunday Times*, Julian Symons admitted that he had disliked all le Carré's books since *The Spy who Came in from the Cold*. 'Happily "The Little Drummer Girl" is different and far better, perhaps the equal of "Spy",' he wrote. 'A few years ago he had not yet written the book he would want to be buried with. Perhaps he has done so now.'[15] The *Guardian*'s reviewer, the novelist Robert Nye, could not share in the enthusiasm, dismissing the book as 'an agreeable if somewhat turgid yarn'. He thought that 'the melodramatic if downbeat conclusion reads (not for the first time in le Carré) like a parody of Graham Greene'.[16]

In Germany *The Little Drummer Girl* was published under the title *Die Libelle* ('The Dragonfly'), an allusion to a Heine poem. Here too the critical response was uneven. Alfred Starkmann, reviewing the book for the pro-Israeli *Die Welt*, argued that the book was slanted in favour of the Palestinians. He was one of those reviewers who felt that le Carré had outgrown the genre of the spy thriller. 'In literary terms le Carré is treading water,' wrote Starkmann. 'If he really means to be a great writer he will have to leave this milieu.'[17] Peter Laemmle, reviewing the book for *Süddeutsche Zeitung*, admired his technical skill. 'Nobody in Germany could write a book like this,' he asserted.

> That the atmosphere of the book sometimes becomes so oppressively close has something to do with le Carré's subtle powers of observation, with his photographic eye which puts seemingly insignificant details into the

* He took office two days later.

> picture, thereby making them significant. It is not surprising that the screen adaptations of his books, which are themselves so filmic, have so far never been able to satisfy him.
>
> The book leaves one with a sense of pointlessness and absurdity. Events take their course inevitably, inexorably. Le Carré's pessimism, with which we are familiar from his previous books, has reached a peak here. It is as if he has lost belief in human reason once and for all.[18]

The *Newsweek* profile had confirmed what many had suspected for a long time: that David had been a 'spook' himself. 'I have nosed around the secret world,' Behr quoted David as saying. 'But it was a long, long while ago.'[19] In the simultaneous *Observer* profile, David expressed an anxiety that if his activities with British intelligence were to be disinterred, he should at least 'be known as a writer who had been a spy rather than as a spy who became a writer'.[20]

For David, this was 'a kind of exorcism'. Over the years interviewers had often quizzed him about whether he had been a spy, but he had either denied it or deflected the enquiry.* In his James Tait Black Memorial Lecture in 1978, he had raised the question himself – without answering it.

> When people ask me whether I am a spy – *'are you now, or have you ever been?'* – I am tempted to reply with a hearty – *'Yes, and since the age of five.'* For a state of watchfulness must surely be the first requisite of a writer, as it is of a secret agent. A writer, like a spy, must prey upon his neighbours; like a spy he is dependent on those whom he deceives; like a spy he must somehow contrive to keep a distance from his own feelings and by doing so conjure up a package that will meet with the approval of his masters. Like a spy, he is not merely an outsider, but implicitly a subversive . . .[21]

Despite his enormous success, David remained sensitive to negative reviews. Though he claimed not to read these, he was obviously aware

* For example in 1980, when, during an interview for the *Observer*, Miriam Gross asked him if he had 'ever been talent-spotted for the Secret Service', he replied, 'No, but I've stopped beating my wife.'

of them, as his former pupil, Old Etonian Alexander Chancellor, was to discover. Chancellor was then editor of the *Spectator*, which had republished from the *New Republic* David Pryce-Jones's ferocious attack on *The Little Drummer Girl*, this time under the heading 'Drumming up Hatred'.[22] Oblivious to any offence this might have caused, Chancellor approached David, reminding him of their connection and asking him if he would like to write a piece for the magazine. Of course I remember you, David replied: 'how could you possibly expect me to write for *The Spectator* after you published that review?' Some time later Chancellor tried again, and received the same response: 'I've told you already!'

Shortly before *The Little Drummer Girl* was published, David received an abrupt telephone call from 10 Downing Street inviting him to lunch with the Prime Minister, Margaret Thatcher. Though he had never voted anything but Labour, he had been impressed by the Conservative leader, who, he believed, had shown courage and determination in sending a task force to retake the Falkland Islands when many of her Cabinet had been willing to accept the Argentine invasion as a fait accompli. A friend of David's from Sherborne, the historian Hugh Thomas, was chairman of Mrs Thatcher's think tank, the Centre for Policy Studies. Some months before the lunch at Downing Street, he had given a dinner for Mrs Thatcher to meet writers and intellectuals at his house in Ladbroke Grove. Among those who came were Al Alvarez, Isaiah Berlin, Philip Larkin, V. S. Naipaul, Anthony Powell, V. S. Pritchett, Stephen Spender, Tom Stoppard and Mario Vargas Llosa. David was invited, but declined, pleading a prior commitment, and asked Thomas to give his good wishes to the Prime Minister if the opportunity arose. 'I never thought I would find her admirable, but I do somehow, even though the immediate consequences, at least, are so wretched,' he wrote in reply to Thomas's invitation, 'perhaps because I really *do* believe she is an honest & extraordinarily brave person.'[23]

There were eight people at the Number 10 lunch, which had been arranged for the visiting Dutch Prime Minister, Ruud Lubbers. David was seated next to Mrs Thatcher, facing Lubbers on the other side of the table. 'Now Mr Lubbers, you may not know that Mr Cornwell is John le Carré,' Mrs Thatcher explained – 'surely you've heard of John le Carré?' Lubbers said no, he had not. Nobody said much except David and the two prime ministers. It became obvious to David that Mrs Thatcher had 'tuned into'

The Little Drummer Girl. At one point she turned to him and asked if there was anything that he wanted to say to her. He said yes, he thought that the Palestinians deserved greater sympathy from the British government. The Prime Minister's face darkened. 'They were the people who trained the people who killed my friend Airey Neave.'*

If *The Little Drummer Girl* marked the apogee of le Carré's career as a best-selling novelist, the film of the book, directed by George Roy Hill, which appeared a year later, represented the nadir of his movie career. It was blighted above all by a disastrous piece of miscasting: Diane Keaton in the central role of Charlie. The public was asked to believe that the ditzy New Yorker was a young radical, capable of convincing suspicious Palestinian terrorists that she was one of them. Very few of those who saw the film were able to make this leap of imagination.

David had lobbied for his sister or, if not her, some other English actress to play the part, but the studio's desire for a big star in the central role overruled any other considerations. As a result Charlie's character was transformed from a twenty-something Englishwoman into a thirty-something American. The only other actress seriously considered was Meryl Streep. Keaton's stock was high as a result of her performances in *Annie Hall* (1977), for which she had won an Oscar, and in *Reds* (1981), for which she had received an Oscar nomination. Here, she received sole name above the title, a mark of her importance to the movie. Hill found himself unable to resist her demands, which extended to choosing her own costume designer after she had told him, 'My fans would not want me to be seen in these clothes.' Fatally, there was no chemistry between Keaton and the Greek actor playing Joseph, Yorgo Voyagis.

Like many directors, George Roy Hill had been an actor first. He had played a cameo in his own film *The World According to Garp*, a fact that may have inspired him to suggest that David should do the same. Hill was

* Airey Neave, an ally and close associate of Mrs Thatcher's, was murdered by Irish republicans in 1979, shortly before the general election that brought the Conservatives to power. It has been suggested that the explosives that killed him may have originated from Palestinian militants, supplied through a German far-left terrorist group. Mrs Thatcher's assertion that the bombers had been trained by Palestinian militants may have been based on secret intelligence; it does not seem to be supported by any published sources.

best known for his two very successful 'buddy' movies with Paul Newman and Robert Redford, *Butch Cassidy and the Sundance Kid* (1969) and *The Sting* (1973). By the time of *The Little Drummer Girl*, he had begun to suffer the first symptoms of Parkinson's Disease, though he concealed this from the studio. One effect was that he struggled to maintain his concentration. Nevertheless before shooting began he was still able to take David through the whole movie, script in hand, a tour de force that impressed everyone present.

The screenplay was by Loring Mandel, a close friend of Hill's, who introduced him to David in New York. It was obvious to Mandel that David would have preferred to script it himself. He was dismissive of previous films adapted from his work. At an early stage in the process they took a trip to Beirut, putting up at the Commodore Hotel, where they spent long hours in the bar, a favourite meeting-point for reporters. Mandel observed that David never seemed happier than when 'rubbing shoulders with the journos'. As they travelled around the ruined city by taxi, they were stopped every few blocks at checkpoints and scrutinised by armed men. 'Let them see your hands,' David advised his fellow passengers. Together they visited the Sabra and Shatila refugee camps, where only months before hundreds and perhaps thousands of civilians had been massacred by Lebanese militiamen after the camps had been overrun by the Israeli army.* As they were walking down the street, a gunshot rang out; David shoved Mandel to the ground.

David was present on the set during much of the filming. One morning on location in Munich, Hill invited several of the crew, plus David and Mandel, up to his apartment, which was reached through a garden from the hotel where most of them were staying. Hill had gone ahead: a door had slammed shut behind him, leaving his followers stranded. 'Well, there's nothing for it,' said David reluctantly, and he set about picking the lock. He had it open in seconds.

Once the film was in rough cut, Hill brought it to London for a screening to an invited audience. Afterwards he asked whether anyone had any

* The ensuing scandal forced the Defence Minister, Ariel Sharon, to resign from his post, though he was soon active again in Israeli politics and became Prime Minister in 2001.

comments. A fourteen-year-old girl whispered into her father's ear. When she had finished he raised his hand and said, 'My daughter can't understand why the police went to Charlie's flat.'

Hill never spoke without using the F word. He turned to David and asked, 'Why did the fucking police go to Charlie's flat?'

'Well, we had it in, George, it was in the script, but it got taken out.'

'What do we do about that?'

'Well,' David said, 'we'll have to put a scene in.'

'What kind of fucking scene would that be?'

David explained, and suggested that a new character was required to explain why the police were there.

'Well you write it. And you fucking well play it.'

So the cast was reassembled for a night shoot. David played a plainclothes policeman, in raincoat and fedora hat. He had only one sentence to speak,* but Hill was not satisfied with the way he delivered it, and by the end he had been humiliated by having to do seventeen takes.†

In 1983 David's sister Charlotte became involved in a legal action for defamation. Her performance in the ITV television series *No Excuses* (written by Barrie Keeffe) had been denigrated by Nina Myskow of the *Sunday People*, in Myskow's 'Wally of the Week' column. An indication of Myskow's qualities as a critic was provided by the byline she used in her subsequent incarnation as television critic for the *News of the World*, 'The Bitch on the Box'. In this case she had written of Charlotte: 'She can't sing, her bum is too big and she has the sort of stage presence that jams lavatories.'

Charlotte was outraged by the review, which she thought malicious. She had a professional reputation to defend. Her performance in the 1976 television series *Rock Follies*, together with her fellow members of the girl band the Little Ladies, Julie Covington and Rula Lenska, had shown that

* 'She's running, if that's what you want.'

† Graham Greene played a cameo in *La Nuit Américaine* ('Day for Night'). According to the film historian Philip French (*Guardian*, 25 July 2010), he was introduced as a retired English businessman living on the Côte d'Azur, and the director François Truffaut was unaware of his real identity until the shooting was well under way.

she could sing. Though David's lawyer advised her not to sue, and so did David, she persisted. The case came to trial in 1985. Counsel for the plaintiff alleged that this had been 'a vulgar, vindictive, personal attack'; the defence pleaded fair comment. The barrister acting for Charlotte caused hilarity in court when he quoted a remark made by her solicitor, the libidinous and flamboyant Oscar Beuselinck, 'I've looked at the bottom and it's beautiful.' The court found that the words used by Myskow were malicious and awarded Charlotte damages of £10,000, later increased on appeal to £11,000. This was a pyrrhic victory: the damages were nowhere near enough to cover Charlotte's legal costs. She was forced to sell her flat to pay these; together David and Charlotte's brother Rupert bought the flat and put it in trust for Charlotte's daughter.

After the trial Charlotte restated her belief that Myskow's article had gone way beyond fair comment. She hoped that the action would help to define 'the limit between what is fair, however adverse, and what is mere personal abuse'.[24]

For a quarter of a century or more David had wanted to write about Ronnie. The notion had been with him long before he became a professional author. Even as a young man he had scribbled and plotted. For David, writing about Ronnie was part of his wider struggle to establish an identity distinct from that of his overpowering father. It was a form of autobiography, illuminating the secret places of his childhood, the influences that had shaped him into the man he had become. In exploring what had made him who he was, he would surely produce his masterpiece. Again and again he tried to write such a book, but in vain. His first effort, dating from 1959, was written in the self-conscious manner of Gosse or Ackerley,* 'willing the reader to believe that I was a tender soul crushed by a tyrant'. The son assumed a kind of weary cultural superiority over his father, as if the sheer effort of living in the parental shadow had left him exquisitely drained. In retrospect David would view these early drafts as 'perfectly sickening'.[25]

* Edmund Gosse, *Father and Son* (1907); J. R. Ackerley, *My Father and Myself* (1968).

Over the ensuing twenty-five years, whenever he was between books, David would return to the yellowing heaps of manuscript that testified to his frustrating inability to write about his father – until his next novel took hold and he would shove them aside once more. He took consolation in proxy father figures, in George Smiley most of all, and burdened them with his unfocused broodings on love and loyalty. Successive failures caused him to despair of ever writing the 'big book'; all his other novels seemed to him satellites, circling round a missing centre. Nevertheless he did make the occasional feint at the subject. Aldo Cassidy's father in *The Naïve and Sentimental Lover* is a watered-down version of Ronnie – so much so that he had threatened a libel suit, until David paid him off.* It had been difficult to write honestly about his father during his lifetime, but his death in 1975 had removed this obstacle. Jerry Westerby's father in *The Honourable Schoolboy* is another study for the finished portrait, as is Charlie's father in *The Little Drummer Girl*.

Autobiography is risky for David. He has examined himself closely, with a penetrating writer's eye; his observations have not always been favourable. He often quotes Graham Greene's aphorism that childhood is the credit balance of the writer, a balance not to be drawn on too heavily lest it be exhausted. Rainer Heumann cautioned him against draining the reservoir from which all his success has been drawn.

In a whimsical draft, David imagined a bestselling author, born like himself in 1931, contemplating a saga of his childhood, written as if posthumously in the Dickensian style. The ghost of the narrator expresses guilt for his philandering, doubts his own talent and expresses the 'sad conviction' that he lacks 'the dignity of labour'. He is not comforted by his agent's cry of 'Jesus Christ, John, *you're* not just a great artist, *you're* a great industry!'

In 1979, after finishing *Smiley's People*, David had made yet another attempt on Ronnie. He was again planning a memoir, perhaps stimulated by Geoffrey Wolff's book about his father, *The Duke of Deception*, a runner-up for the Pulitzer Prize, which Greenway had sent him. (This was the 'completely different' book that he had discussed with Goodall during

* Ronnie withdrew his threat of a libel suit only when David paid him $14,000. In another version of this story (interview with *Lire*, summer 1986) Ronnie threatened to sue when David failed to mention him in an interview.

their walk along the Rhine.) He considered hiring a researcher to follow Ronnie's trail through his years of his exile abroad, but he soon lost faith in this idea. Ronnie was a slippery figure; as soon as one tried to grasp him, he slid away. David told himself that since his father's view of the world had been essentially imaginative, the truth about him was more likely to emerge through a work of fantasy than through the specious arrangement of documentary detail. Besides, David was a novelist; even as he wrote fact, it blended into fiction. The notes he made for a memoir became the skeleton of a novel. In an opening chapter, set in 1930 and rich in period detail, a young man named Rick, obviously based on Ronnie, welcomes worshippers to Sunday-morning service at a Methodist chapel.

Once again David became distracted, by writing the novel that became *The Little Drummer Girl*. In doing so, he proved to himself that he did not need Smiley any more. Afterwards it would occur to him that by elbowing Smiley aside, he had made space to write about Ronnie. The proxy father made space for the real thing. Once *The Little Drummer Girl* was finished, he returned yet again to his father, but this time by a completely different route – as a play. He wrote a first act, which he sent to George Roy Hill for his opinion; though Hill made constructive comments, he never heard anything more from David. No doubt this was because David had thought better of the idea. He had found yet another way forward: he would write about his relationship with Ronnie in a spy novel – or to put it another way, he would write an autobiographical novel in an espionage setting. Until this moment he had resisted connecting the two sides of his life, but now he saw a link that made sense to him. He had long recognised that his own exaggerated rush into marriage, respectability and a conventional career had been a flight from his father, and from his father's way of life. Now he saw too that as a young man he had given himself to his country to expiate Ronnie's misdeeds; he had dedicated himself to a life of service to atone for a life of selfishness.

David recognised that portraying Ronnie as the villain of the story was problematic. Books that set out to denigrate one character to the advantage of another had an unhappy way of producing a contrary effect, as he had discovered. Readers find their sympathy flowing in the opposite direction from the one intended. The villain becomes the hero, while the narrator become less and less appealing. David could not find a way to write about his father's wrongdoings without appearing unpleasantly self-satisfied, even sanctimonious. There had to be a balance of culpability between father and son. There had to be love in the midst of revulsion, pity in the midst of revenge, and humour in the midst of resentment. With this realisation he was at last able to write the book that he had been contemplating for so long.

The story begins with a telephone call, from which the son Magnus Pym, head of the MI6 station in Vienna, learns of the death of his father Rick, a bewitching con man. 'I'm free,' he tells his wife, who doesn't understand. Magnus subsequently disappears and is assumed to have defected. In fact he has sought refuge in a boarding house in a south of England seaside resort, run by the motherly Miss Dubber.* Much of the narrative takes the form of an extended confession, in which Magnus tries to explain what has brought him to this point to his own son, the schoolboy Tom. Magnus visits Tom at school after Rick's death, as Tom later tells Magnus's Circus patron, Jack Brotherhood. 'I think he was telling me that if I was unhappy I should run away,' Tom says. He quotes from 'a great long letter' Magnus has written him. 'He said Granddad had gobbled up the natural humanity in him and he didn't want to gobble it up in me.'[26] In a farewell letter, written just before he shoots himself, Magnus tells Tom, 'I am the bridge. I am what you must walk over to get from Rick to life.'†

Magnus writes about his younger self with amused detachment, switching between the first person and third person to heighten this effect of dissociation. For years he has been betraying his country – but out of love for his friend Axel, not out of ideology. Axel grants Magnus an imaginary knighthood, and tells him that he is 'a perfect spy'.

> For once nature has produced a perfect match . . . All you need is a cause. I have it. I know that our revolution is young and that sometimes the wrong people are running it. In the pursuit of peace we are making too much war. In the pursuit of freedom we are building too many prisons. But in the long run I don't mind. Because I know this. All the junk that made you what you are: the privileges, the snobbery, the hypocrisy, the churches, the schools, the

* Robin Cooke's landlady, when he was an undergraduate living in digs, was a Miss Dubber.

† See the last paragraph of the book, on page 602.

> athers, the class systems, the historical lies, the little lords of the countryside, the little lords of big business, and all the greedy wars that result from them, we are sweeping that away for ever. For your sake. Because we are making a society that will never produce such sad little fellows as Sir Magnus.[27]

Axel understands an essential truth about his friend. 'Magnus is a great imitator, even when he doesn't know it,' Axel tells Mary, Magnus's wife. 'Really, I sometimes think he is entirely put together from bits of other people, poor fellow.'

Magnus has betrayed Axel too, and his father, and his friend Jack. 'Love is whatever you can still betray,' he reflects at one point.* 'Betrayal can only happen if you love.'[28] Thus the son is as guilty as his father; and as innocent.

Betrayal becomes an obsession for Magnus. 'We betray to be loyal,' he writes in his unfinished novel, as his wife discovers when she sneaks a look at the manuscript:

> Betrayal is like imagining when the reality isn't good enough . . . Betrayal as hope and compensation. As the making of a better land. Betrayal as love. As a tribute to our unlived lives. On and on, these ponderous aphorisms about betrayal. Betrayal as escape. As a constructive act. As a statement of ideals. Worship. As an adventure of the soul. Betrayal as travel: how can we discover new places if we never leave home?[29]

Rick is recognisably Ronnie. Magnus's SIS career is similar to Philby's, but his background is almost identical to David's – so much so as to tease the reader into speculating whether David himself may not have been a traitor. 'How much of Magnus is in le Carré himself remains a tantalizing speculation,' wrote one of the reviewers, and several others would pose the same question. After reading the book Ann would say that she had always suspected David of working for the other side. But, unlike David, Magnus is no novelist; he tries to write, but fails. 'If Magnus's writing had ever worked for him, he'd have been okay,' suggests Grant Lederer III,† the CIA

* An echo of *The Looking-Glass War* (chapter 18): 'Do you know what love is? I'll tell you: it is whatever you can still betray.'

† To Gottlieb's complaint that Lederer read like 'a parody American', David replied, 'You don't meet the ones I meet.'

man who is both friend and enemy to Magnus. 'There is just too much inside him. He has to put it somewhere.'[30]

David succeeded where Magnus failed. A few years later he would tell an interviewer that he had never been to 'a shrink';* but writing the novel about his relations with his father 'is probably what a very wise shrink would have advised me to do anyway'. In *A Perfect Spy* he was able to externalise aspects of his past about which he had felt extremely uncomfortable. Finishing it at last, after so many failed attempts, was 'a tremendous catharsis' for him: 'I cried and cried when it was over.'[31]

After the worldwide success of *The Little Drummer Girl*, David was very much in demand. Penguin made a 'blind bid' for the new book, offering to buy it sight unseen. Though this was rejected, the management at Hodder & Stoughton was conscious of the need to work hard to keep him. The new novel from le Carré would be the first to be published in Hodder's paperback imprint, Coronet. This was a bold move, since Pan had published every le Carré novel since *The Spy who Came in from the Cold*, selling more than 650,000 copies of *The Little Drummer Girl*. For the new book Hodder set a target of 100,000 sales in hardback and 750,000 in paperback.† They paid an advance against royalties of £525,000, rising to £600,000 if Canada was included: 'a cool half-mil', as Michael Attenborough put it to George Greenfield.[32] By 1985 Hodder had a string of bestselling authors, including Jeffrey Archer, James Clavell, Stephen King, Harold Robbins, Maeve Binchy, James Herbert and Fay Weldon. But none of the others commanded such serious critical attention as John le Carré.

This would be the last le Carré book to be sold by George Greenfield, who announced his intention to retire in September 1986. He had prepared for his departure by merging his firm, John Farquharson, with the biggest literary agency in Britain, Curtis Brown, back in 1982. Nevertheless David decided that he did not want to remain with Farquharson after Greenfield had left. After consulting Rainer Heumann, who recommended several agents, he picked Bruce Hunter to represent him in the traditional British Commonwealth area,

* This was not strictly true; in the late 1960s he and Ann had consulted a psychiatrist about their marriage. But he has never been psychoanalysed – except by himself.

† By 29 April 1988 they had exceeded this target.

including Canada and Australia. In a way the choice was ironic, as Hunter worked for the firm co-founded by David Higham, described by Greenfield in his autobiography as 'the only really unpleasant agent I met in those post-war years'.[33] But Hunter was a very different character from Higham, who had in any case died in 1978. A Canadian, Hunter was a large man, whose studious demeanour was undercut by a mischievous twinkle. David made it clear to him that he wanted a business rather than a social relationship. He did not mix in literary circles; he did not want to be invited to parties, especially those at the newly formed Groucho Club; he valued discretion highly and loathed gossip. David made it obvious to Hunter that he was not looking for an agent to discuss what he was writing and provide comments on what he had written; he wanted him to reach lucrative deals, and to ensure that his publishers were doing everything they could and should be doing for his books. Hunter set up a system to this end: for the period from the delivery of a new book until three months after paperback publication (that is, about eighteen months for each book) he would attend a monthly meeting at Hodder, at which every detail of the publishing process was discussed. It was extremely unusual, and possibly unique, for an author's agent to be admitted into a publisher's decision-making operation in this way.

Hunter began a process of reverting rights in the earlier le Carré books from Gollancz and Heinemann, and licensing them to Hodder & Stoughton, who began reissuing them in 'Lamplighter' editions with new forewords (redesignated in later editions as introductions). He obtained considerably better terms in the process, while Hodder were able to market the books much more effectively once they had all of le Carré's backlist in Coronet paperback editions.

At the same time that he moved to David Higham Associates, David moved to a new agent in America, Lynn Nesbit of International Creative Management (ICM), a close friend of Bob Gottlieb's.*

'As I told George, the book seems to me to be some kind of a summation of all my work till now,' David wrote to Attenborough after the deal was made, 'and it was very expensive of spirit, which I hope doesn't show too

* ICM was the product of a merger between the Creative Management Agency and Ashley-Famous, the agency that had courted David back at the time of his first success.

much! I have no confidence at all that it will be sympathetically reviewed here: to the contrary, a sort of inverse ratio seems to exist which should guarantee us the usual critical misery . . .'[34]

The novel was dedicated to 'R' – Rainer Heumann, 'who shared the journey, lent me his dog, and tossed me a few pieces of his life'. David used some of what Heumann had told him of his experiences in the war and afterwards under the occupation in forming the character of Axel, Magnus's controller and his dearest friend, known by his code-name 'Poppy'.

Until this point in his career David had always submitted his novels to his former employers for clearance, and in all these years he had only once been asked to make a change, to his very first book, *Call for the Dead*. Now he chose not to submit his new book, arguing that by this time, twenty years after he had resigned from MI6, he was 'out of quarantine'.

In editing the book, Bob Gottlieb identified passages that seemed more reminiscence than fiction. It was not easy to write a novel that drew so deeply on personal experience without it becoming embarrassingly autobiographical. 'What we left on the cutting room floor still makes me blush,' David would say afterwards. [35] As usual, he hesitated between several titles. The original working title was 'Agent Running in the Field'; others he considered included 'The Burn Box', 'A Man with Two Houses' and 'A Spy with Excellent Manners'. All were rejected in favour of 'The Love Thief', which remained his preferred title right up to the editing stage, when Gottlieb suggested *A Perfect Spy*.

A Perfect Spy was published first in Britain, to a mixed reception. For Julian Symons, reviewing the book in the *Guardian*, it was 'a flawed, overlong but still very interesting novel'. He acknowledged that le Carré was more than just a writer of 'spy stories', but questioned whether he was 'a major modern novelist'. The psychiatrist Anthony Clare, writing in the *Sunday Times*, was less stinting in his praise. 'This is a psychological study and it copes well with the burden of such a label . . . without doubt it is his masterpiece.'[36] But Anthony Burgess remained unconvinced. 'Mr. le Carré's talents cry out to be employed in the creation of a real novel,' he pronounced in the *Observer*. Burgess's review inspired letters of protest from Ann Alvarez, and from another friend of David's, the journalist William Shawcross, son of Hartley Shawcross.[37] In a perceptive review in the *Times Literary Supplement* Blake Morrison praised *A Perfect Spy* as a rich work, adorned with 'unerringly suggestive' social detail. He recognised that this was a spy thriller overlapping with a *Bildungsroman*, and dismissed criticism of le Carré as a mere espionage writer. 'To say that *A Perfect Spy* is about the intelligence service is like saying that *The Mayor of Casterbridge* is about the Corn Laws,' wrote Morrison. 'There is enough here to silence those who have urged le Carré to abandon spy fiction and write a conventional novel, a plea which ignores the fact that he has already beaten the genre trap – not, though, by venturing outside, as in *The Naïve and Sentimental Lover*, but by finding unexpected room within, as in *A Perfect Spy*.'[38]

The German critics were equally divided. Jochen Schmidt, reviewing *A Perfect Spy* for the *Frankfurter Allgemeine Zeitung*, judged the novel to be 'by far le Carré's best'.[39] But Eberhard Falcke, writing in *Süddeutsche Zeitung*, thought it 'overly long'.[40]

In the *New York Times* Frank Conroy, who in 1967 had published his own highly acclaimed memoir *Stop-Time*, assessed *A Perfect Spy* as 'a first-rate espionage novel, perhaps the best of his already impressive oeuvre'.[41] In the *Los Angeles Times*, Morton Kamins suggested that le Carré had been stalking Proust – successfully, as he had come home with his trophy, 'the masterly welding of an intricate page-turning spy thriller with the infinitely complex exploration of time and a man's memory'. Kamins reckoned that *A Perfect Spy* was 'easily le Carré's best book'. He went further, believing it to be 'one of the enduring peaks of imaginative literature in our time'.[42] Noel Annan reviewed the novel for the *New York Review of Books*, rating it as 'le Carré's most brilliant achievement'. As a grandee of English academic life with connections everywhere, whose book *Our Age* (1990) would provide a 'portrait of a generation', Annan was well placed to make a wider evaluation of le Carré's work. 'For some time astute judges have seen in le Carré far more than a writer of spy stories,' wrote Annan. 'He seems to be capable of leaving the allegory of the spy story and evoking in fiction his society and spelling out Britain's decline.'[43]

A Perfect Spy was another no. 1 bestseller in America, muscling its way to the top past such blockbusters as Robert Ludlum's *The Bourne Supremacy* and Judith Krantz's *I'll Take Manhattan*. In Britain the novel outsold Wilbur Smith's *Power of the Sword*. Thus a novel considered by serious reviewers to be a work of the highest literary merit had sold at least as well as the most unpretentious airport fiction. It was a remarkable achievement.

When the telephone rings in the opening chapter of *A Perfect Spy*, the maid who answers the call has instructions not to disturb 'Herr Pym' unless it is essential. Magnus is busy telling a funny story to his dinner-party guests, 'in that perfect German of his which so annoys the Embassy and surprises the Austrians'. He is like David as a young diplomat, who could delight his hosts in Bonn with his irreverent impression of the Ambassador's German. Like David too, Magnus can do an Austrian accent on demand or, funnier still, a Swiss one.

> Herr Pym can put you a row of bottles in a line, and by pinging them with a table knife make them chime like the bells of the old Swiss railway, while he chants the stations between Interlaken and the Jungfraujoch in the tone of a local stationmaster and his audience collapse in tears of nostalgic mirth.[44]

Over the years he has expanded his repertoire and perhaps polished his technique, but David is still doing the same thing that he did as a boy, when he entertained Ronnie's guests with his stories and his mimicry.

'You go to a dinner-party with David,' Al Alvarez has said, 'and he will put on a show for you.'

> He always sings for his supper, in a very amusing way, telling stories tirelessly. I have been with him at parties where we've both been clearly bored out of our skulls, and David has never ever let up. He's terribly well-mannered, but it's purely an act so the evening won't sink into some slough of despond.[45]

But in his own ears David's comic turns ring hollow. Often he is filled with self-disgust after excelling in one of these performances.

Through Alvarez, David had become friendly with Philip Roth, then living in London with his long-term companion Claire Bloom. Like David, Roth was an entertaining mimic. The two novelists met regularly at dinner parties, where they would urge each other on. They admired each other's work; Roth thought highly enough of *A Perfect Spy* to rate it as 'the best English novel since the war'.[46] From the publishers' point of view, this was as good an endorsement as could be, comparable to the quote that Graham Greene had provided for *The Spy who Came in from the Cold* more than twenty years before.

'Dad would have been delighted to have a book,' Charlotte told an interviewer from the *New York Times*. Mimicking Ronnie's voice, she uttered his imaginary protests. 'I don't know where he got the idea for this,' she said huffily: 'it's absolutely not true.' Reverting to her own voice, she said, 'Deep down, he would have been thrilled.'[47] She respected David for his honesty.

David had sought Charlotte's agreement, and that of his other siblings, before publishing a long piece in the *Sunday Times*, 'Spying on my Father', one of a pair about the truth behind the fiction of *A Perfect Spy*.[48] The article upset Ronnie's sisters Ruby and Ella, who expressed their distress in a letter to David. In reply, he told them that he had consulted 'just about everybody except yourselves' before publishing the book. He had sent it to all three of Ronnie's wives, and to his own first wife, Ann. 'My mother felt that it was a fairy-tale by comparison with the reality,' he wrote. 'Jeannie admired it greatly, and Joy, on second thoughts, waived her initial objection.' In retrospect he was sorry not to have consulted his aunts also. 'Perhaps I knew subconsciously that you would not approve, although I believe that I have written about Ronnie with tolerance and love, both in the article and the fictionalised portrait of him.' His good relations with his aunts continued undamaged, and they subsequently visted him at Tregiffian. Though he was sorry to have upset them, he defended his actions, referring to the pain Ronnie had caused to those around him. 'In writing as I have done, I believe that I have not only alleviated my own pain, which has been prolonged and crippling, but lightened the burden of others.'[49]

A BBC mini-series based on *A Perfect Spy*, co-written by David and Arthur Hopcraft, was screened in the year after the book was published. Hopcraft noticed how fact and fiction had become intermingled in David's imagination. 'Rick is a character in his own right,' he said, 'but it's noticeable that since finishing the book, when David's talking about Rick, he's really talking about Ronnie. In his mind, the two have merged.'[50]

By this time Jonathan Powell had been promoted twice, first to become head of drama and then controller of BBC 1, so his involvement was limited to that of executive producer. In the view of most dispassionate observers this third BBC series adapted from a le Carré novel lived up to the very high standards set by the first two, though David disagreed. 'Did you see "A Perfect Spy" on the telly and did you find it as embarrassing as

I did?' he wrote to Alec Guinness a couple of years afterwards. 'Somehow they took all the bounce out of it in the first hour and never put it back. I shall always remember it, along with the film of "The Little Drummer Girl", as one of the unadulterated disasters of my professional life.'[51]

It was perhaps not to be expected that le Carré would be comfortable with a film that so closely depicted his own life, especially as the main disappointment in an otherwise excellent cast was the actor playing the adult Magnus Pym, the character le Carré had modelled on himself.* Ray McAnally won both BAFTA and Royal Television Society awards for his outstanding performance as Rick.

Around this time David was presented with another chance to act himself. The German director Wim Wenders wrote to him, having seen his face on the back of a book. Knowing that David spoke fluent German, Wenders wanted him to play the part of the sea captain Dollmann, in a television film based on Erskine Childers's novel *The Riddle of the Sands*. 'It was a distraction that I couldn't resist,' David would tell an audience at the National Film Theatre: 'I thought it could be a second profession.' It was arranged that David would meet Wenders and a friend for lunch at the Connaught Grill. Waiting for them to arrive, he was startled to see two 'Neanderthals' come in, wearing frayed jeans with bite-marks in them. 'I got them out of the Connaught immediately.'

Wenders insisted on speaking English, despite a thick German accent. 'Vot is required here is six months in ze Baltic,' he said. 'Zere vill be no women. Also you vill have to fall about sixty metres off ze back of ze boat, into ze water. Is zat OK?'

'Of course,' David replied politely.

He took the script home and read it; then made an excuse to withdraw.

The more evasive David was, the more people suspected that he had something to hide. His authority on intelligence matters was assumed, however much he protested his ignorance. As a result he was sometimes placed in a false position. Such experiences made him feel a phoney and caused him to avoid, whenever possible, interviews in which he was to pose as an

* Magnus as a boy was played by twins, Jonathan and Nicholas Haley; and as a young man by Benedict Taylor. The adult Magnus was played by Peter Egan.

intelligence expert. They also made him suspicious of others who professed such expertise.

Soon after the publication of *A Perfect Spy* David received a telephone call from the Italian Cultural Attaché: apparently President Francesco Cossiga was a huge fan of his novels and wished to invite him to lunch at the Quirinal Palace. This was an offer David could not refuse. Before flying to Rome to meet the President David had a copy of *The Spy who Came in from the Cold* specially bound for him. The lunch itself was a bemusing experience. On emerging from his hotel David found a limousine waiting for him, with an escort of police motorcyclists; he was driven the short distance to the Palace with the ceremony befitting a head of state. As he walked up the steps of the Palace itself halberdiers stood to attention, while photographers snapped his picture. Inside he was shown into an enormous and beautiful room, where a crowd of men assembled at a distance. Nobody spoke to David until an elegantly dressed man, whom he took to be his host, approached him. 'Mr le Carré,' he said, without introducing himself, 'such a pleasure . . . All my life.' He proceeded to entertain David with some talk about their surroundings. 'In this room we are keeping Galileo while he considers his future.' At the appropriate moment David produced his gift. 'I brought this for you,' he explained; but his interlocutor declined the offering. 'Why don't you give it to the President?' Belatedly David realised his mistake.

He was led up to the penthouse, where a table was set for twenty-four, and seated next to the President, a weaselly-looking man who wore spectacles with lemon-tinted lenses. He spoke poor English, but he and David found that they could converse in French, so they were able to dispense with interpreters. It seemed that David was the guest of honour, perhaps the only foreigner present, and that the others were senior representatives of rival Italian intelligence services; every time he or the President spoke, they all fell silent, which inhibited the free flow of conversation. A succession of delicious dishes arrived, but were whisked away before he could take his fill. Then the President departed. David was left with the grey men of Italian intelligence, who studiously ignored him. He felt like 'a performing flea'.*

* P. G. Wodehouse's *A Performing Flea* (1953) was a volume of letters to his friend from schooldays, William Townend. The title alludes to a disparaging comment about Wodehouse made by Sean O'Casey, in a letter to the *Daily Telegraph* in 1941.

20

Moscow Rules

David felt that he had 'touched the limits of my ability' in *A Perfect Spy*, and feared that he might have written himself out. It seemed to him important 'to put another card down fast'.[1] He decided to set his next novel in the Soviet Union, where a new leader had instituted a process of change. Soon after taking office in 1985 Mikhail Gorbachev had announced the need for 'new thinking': he introduced policies of *perestroika* ('restructuring'), *glasnost* ('openness') and democratisation. David's book would be written as these changes gathered momentum. Gorbachev took a much more positive approach in international affairs, recognising that foreign relations and internal reform were linked. After the long winter of the Cold War there were signs of a thaw. A visit to the Soviet Union by the British Prime Minister, Mrs Thatcher, had helped to melt the frosty relations between the two nations.

Nevertheless it remained difficult for most Britons to travel within the Eastern bloc countries. Except for a few forays into East Berlin while he was serving in Germany, David had never been behind the Iron Curtain. His previous attempts to obtain a visa to visit the Soviet Union had met with stony silence. The Soviet press had demonised him for 'elevating the spy to the status of a hero in the Cold War'. Only two of his books had been judged acceptable enough to be published there: *A Murder of Quality*, which explored the class tensions in a 'bourgeois' public school; and *A Small Town in Germany*, which predicated a resurgence of nationalism in 'fascist' West Germany.

David sought the help of Sir Bryan Cartledge, British Ambassador to Moscow, taking advantage of a personal connection: half a lifetime before they had been officer cadets in the same platoon at Eaton Hall. Cartledge put him in touch with John C. Q. Roberts, director of the Great Britain–USSR Association, a body funded by the British government to promote and facilitate cultural and other non-political contacts. Roberts was in a position to introduce David to people he would never meet through the normal diplomatic channels. When the two men met for lunch at the Connaught Grill in January 1987, David explained that he wanted to find potential prototypes for characters in his new book, literary apparatchiks as well as dissidents.* Roberts agreed to do what he could to help through his contacts in the Soviet Writers' Union. 'Selling the Soviets the idea of a le Carré visit is not proving easy,' Roberts wrote in his diary; but in April, after weeks of silence, a message arrived from Russia confirming that they were expected in mid-May.[2]

David's first experience of the Soviet Union was a long wait while the KGB frontier guard at Moscow airport scrutinised his documents. 'Why do you look older than the photograph in your passport?' he asked. 'Because I have been disappointed in love,' replied David. Not even a flicker of a smile greeted this quip. Eventually allowed through into the baggage hall, David found that his suitcase had gone missing. Two days later it appeared unannounced beside his hotel bed, obviously ransacked. His room was crudely searched every time he left it, and he was followed everywhere by two watchers – except after a dinner with a group of Western journalists, when they followed his half-brother Rupert (then Moscow correspondent for the *Independent*) by mistake. On another evening, at the home of a dissident journalist on the outskirts of Moscow, David stayed up drinking into the small hours of the morning, until his host fell asleep on the sofa. David emerged from the house rather drunk, with no idea how to find his way back to his hotel. Fortunately the two watchers were still outside, sitting bleary-eyed on a bench. Communicating by sign language, David explained his predicament. His tails became his guides: they led him through the Moscow streets to the steps of the hotel, where the three men shook hands.[3]

* In the foreword to the book David would state misleadingly that Roberts 'knew nothing of my dark intent'. He wrote this to protect Roberts from the reproaches of his Russian contacts.

Most nights David would stay up late in his room recording his impressions while they were still 'oven-fresh': the omnipresent reek of petrol, the procession of anonymous grey buildings, the rusting ironmongery of Communist insignia, the hostility of those serving meals. One especially grim morning, when David joined John Roberts in the hotel canteen to queue for breakfast, they found that the only knife had disappeared, they were forced to share a plate, there was no tea or coffee, and the woman behind the counter seemed to be deliberately taking her time to open the tin of orange juice so as to needle them. The two Westerners found this both hysterically funny and a sad metaphor for the economic mess of the Soviet Union. From such trivial incidents David deduced 'that a country so congenitally inefficient, extraordinarily incompetent and frequently lazy could not nurse at its centre a flawless, superefficient military capability'.[4] This insight would be central to the plot of his new novel. Since the 1950s the superpowers had assumed that each possessed the retaliatory power to destroy the other, even after a surprise attack, the so-called 'first strike'. This was the ultimate nuclear deterrent, the doctrine of mutually assured destruction, which had (according to its proponents) kept the peace throughout the Cold War. To question this capability was therefore profoundly disturbing to both sides.

Notwithstanding the frustrations of his stay, David developed a strong sympathy for ordinary Russians. 'Nobody who visits the Soviet Union in these extraordinary years, and is privileged to conduct the conversations that were granted to me, can come away without an enduring love for its people, and a sense of awe at the scale of the problems that face them,' he would write in the foreword to his novel. One of their most endearing qualities was their earnestness. When the cleaning lady came to his hotel room to settle up for the laundry, she astonished David by mentioning that she had seen his picture in the *Literary Gazette*; Roberts hazarded the thought that not many of her British counterparts read the *Times Literary Supplement*. 'You go for a walk in the countryside and end up arguing with a bunch of drunk poets about freedom versus responsibility,' David has his British hero say of the Russians. 'You take a leak in some filthy public loo, somebody leans over from the next stall and asks whether there's life after death.'

Both men attended a lunch hosted by Genrikh Borovik, the Writers' Union board member responsible for international contacts. A typical member of the *nomenklatura*, Borovik behaved aggressively towards Roberts and unctuously towards David. He explained that he was a friend of the 'patriot' Kim Philby, and invited David to meet 'Kim' over a glass of wine.* David declined, explaining that he was attending a reception given by the British Ambassador the following evening; he could not possibly sup with the Queen's representative one night and the Queen's traitor the next. Borovik spluttered that Philby was no traitor. They could continue the discussion at the reception, he said; David agreed, but pointed at the chandelier, warning that they would have to be very careful of the microphones. 'For a lovely moment, he gave a stage nod, and the complicity was absolute,' David wrote of this exchange in a letter to John Margetson. 'Then to his credit, he let out a wild whoop of laughter, remembering too late they were his mikes.'[5]

The reception was held in the white-and-gold ballroom on the first floor of the Embassy, offering a view of the Kremlin across the river.† The Ambassador had agreed with David to invite as many KGB operatives as possible to the reception, and they all came; nobody could remember such a large KGB presence in the building. It seemed that they were all le Carré fans, despite the difficulty of obtaining his books in Russia. In Cartledge's view, David handled the situation superbly; he had the KGB people 'eating out of his hand'. He was both charming and polite, 'a born ambassador'.

One afternoon David spent a couple of hours answering questions from a select audience of postgraduate students and literati at the Library of Foreign Literature, repository for books thought to be too 'dangerous' for the Soviet public. The atmosphere was excitable, almost euphoric. 'What is your idea of good government?' someone asked him. 'One that gives the greatest freedom to the greatest number of people,' he replied, to greedy applause. Questions came thick and fast. 'What do you think of Marx,

* Though neither of them could know this, Philby had not long to live; he would be dead within a year.

† The building is no longer the British Embassy, and is now used as the Ambassador's residence.

Lenin, Engels?' asked someone else. 'I love them all,' David said, prompting a burst of laughter. Another member of the audience asked him to define the line between individual conscience and social responsibility. How far could one go in defending a society and be sure it was still worth defending? The question went to the heart of David's work. Afterwards a group of students took him downstairs to a common room and showed him a television set where they had covertly watched a video of the series *Tinker, Tailor, Soldier, Spy*. David has recently described this occasion as 'one of the most moving moments of my life'.[6]

David had arrived in Russia with only a misty idea of his two central characters, nothing more; but by the time he left he had accumulated enough material to begin writing on his return. As usual for him, the first chapter was the most demanding, and he was still revising it three months later. Gradually the plot took shape. Barley Blair is a small-time, middle-aged publisher who comes to Russia for a book fair. He becomes expansive during a boozy lunch at a Moscow dacha with a group of Russian intelligentsia. 'If there is to be hope, we must all betray our countries,' he tells his listeners round the lunch table. In particular he quotes the American poet May Sarton: 'One must think like a hero to behave like a merely decent human being.'[7]

'Sovs are the only people daft enough to listen to my bullshit,' Barley remarks ruefully afterwards. One of his listeners is Yakov, a brilliant physicist racked with guilt about his work on weaponry and longing for peace. He is stirred into action by Barley's careless talk. Through his former lover Katya, an editor in a Soviet publishing house, Yakov sends Barley a manuscript, which is intercepted by the Circus. Yakov hopes to influence the West not to start a dangerous new arms race. 'The American strategists can sleep in peace,' writes Yakov. 'Their nightmares cannot be realized. The Soviet knight is dying inside his armour.' The message is both exciting and alarming to the inhabitants of the 'Russia House', the section of the Circus that spies on the Soviet Union, and to their American 'Cousins': exciting because, if verified, it suggested that their assumptions were mistaken, and the enemy was less formidable than they had thought; alarming, because it might be part of a deception operation, intended to undermine Western resolve to invest in a new generation of weapons.

Western assessment of Soviet missile capabilities was of crucial strategic significance in the 1980s, once President Reagan had announced the Strategic Defence Initiative (SDI), an ambitious plan to provide a comprehensive defence against all-out attack. This required a vast increase in military spending: planners envisaged using space-based weaponry to shoot down incoming missiles. The plan was thought by many to be unrealistic, even unscientific, and was derided in the press as 'Star Wars'. But it raised the prospect of a new arms race, threatening to destabilise the 'balance of terror' that had kept the peace between the heavily armed superpowers. The Russians feared that they would be unable to compete. Without their own equivalent missile defence system, they would be vulnerable to nuclear blackmail by the West. They could scarcely be expected to argue that SDI was unnecessary because their existing weaponry was outdated and decaying.

Barley is sent back to Russia to establish Yakov's bona fides, in an operation designated 'Bluebird' by the Russia House. Despite several failed marriages Barley remains a romantic; he falls headlong in love with Katya, a single mother with two children. In the end Barley is faced with a choice: whether to betray his country and save Katya and her family, or to remain loyal and lose the woman he loves. For him the decision is obvious: 'real people in exchange for unreal arguments':

> As to his loyalty to his country, Barley saw it only as a question of which England he chose to serve. His last ties to the imperial family were dead. The chauvinist drumbeat revolted him. He would rather be trampled by it than march with it. He knew a better England by far, and it was inside himself.[8]

As David acknowledged, his story bore some resemblance to that of Oleg Penkovsky, described by authoritative sources as 'the most important Western agent of the Cold War'.[9] Though not a scientist, Penkovsky had supplied invaluable intelligence about the inadequacy of Soviet missile systems. During the Cuban Missile Crisis, Penkovsky's assessments of Khrushchev's capabilities and intentions had directly influenced President Kennedy's decisions. His conduit had been Greville Wynne, like Barley Blair a businessman with only sketchy training in intelligence operations.

David had written about the case in a review of Wynne's autobiography back in 1967.[10]

During the writing of the book David broke with his usual practice by consulting the American journalist and Soviet specialist Strobe Talbott, whom he had met in Israel in the early 1980s while gathering material for *The Little Drummer Girl*. Talbott provided handwritten notes on David's draft chapters.

He made a second visit to the Soviet Union in September 1987, in time to attend the Moscow Book Fair, where he would set a scene of his novel.

The publisher Robert Bernstein, founder of Human Rights Watch, offered him an introduction to the most eminent dissident of them all, Andrei Sakharov, awarded the Nobel Peace Prize in 1975 *in absentia* because the authorities had refused him permission to attend the prize-giving ceremony. As a young physicist Sakharov had played a key role in the development of Soviet thermonuclear weapons; subsequently he had become concerned about nuclear proliferation. In the 1960s, twenty years before Reagan's SDI, Sakharov had written a paper urging 'bilateral rejection by the USA and the Soviet Union of the development of anti-ballistic missile defence', to avert an arms race in this new technology which would increase the danger of nuclear war. He had not been allowed to publish his arguments and had suffered persecution by the state; he and his wife, the human rights activist Yelena Bonner, had spent the early 1980s in internal exile, before Gorbachev had allowed them to return home. David met them both for lunch in a busy restaurant in Leningrad, where they were forced to shout to be heard above a loud gypsy band, as KGB hoods circled them, taking photographs with old-fashioned hand-held flashbulbs. Sakharov questioned David about those British nuclear physicists who had spied for the Russians – particularly Klaus Fuchs, whom he had evidently met in East Germany. David did not ask why Sakharov was so interested in Fuchs and could only speculate afterwards on his reasons. 'He was thinking that in an open society Klaus Fuchs had chosen the path of secret betrayal; and that Sakharov, in a closed society, had suffered torture and imprisonment in order to speak out.'[11]

On his return to England, David decided to tear up the beginning of the book and start again.[12] In sculpting the character of Yakov, David imagined how a younger Sakharov might have chosen to do as Fuchs had done, to betray his country for the sake of a higher principle.

The pianist Alfred Brendel and his wife Irene, neighbours of the Cornwells in Hampstead, introduced David to the poet Joseph Brodsky, who was staying with them. David invited Brodsky to lunch at a local Chinese restaurant. They had arrived, and were seated chatting, when 'Reni' Brendel burst in, with the news that the house was under siege by the media.

'Joseph, come home immediately,' she said. 'You've won!'

'Won what?'

'The Nobel! They've given you the Nobel!'

As a young man in Russia, Brodsky had been publicly denounced and then confined to a psychiatric hospital before being sentenced to five years' hard labour in Siberia for 'social parasitism'. His case became a cause célèbre in the West, attracting protests from prominent Russian intellectuals as well as foreigners. In 1972 he had been suddenly expelled from the Soviet Union. Brodsky was savagely critical of Western fellow-travellers; he would write a celebrated essay condemning the decision of the Soviet authorities to honour Kim Philby with a postage stamp.

Brodsky looked miserable at the news, but David ordered champagne. 'Joseph, if not now, when?' he asked. 'We've got to be able to celebrate our life at some point.'

In the street outside Brodsky hugged David. 'Now for a year of being glib,' he said.[13]

'I hope it is not too much of a shock hearing from me after so long,' wrote Charles Pick. He explained that before retiring three years earlier he had commissioned John St John, a director of Heinemann who had been with the firm thirty-five years, to write its official history, in time for it to be published in the company's centenary year, 1990. 'As a courtesy Johnny is showing authors who are mentioned in the book the relevant pages,' Pick continued. 'As he has never met you he asked if I would send you the enclosed.' His letter ended with an invitation to David and Jane to 'drop in for a drink one day'.[14]

St John's text quoted at length from two of David's letters. Commenting on David's letter to Pick about the disappointing critical reception of

A Small Town in Germany, St John wrote, 'le Carré was highly sensitive of his reviews'. The other letter cited was the one David had written to tell Pick that he had decided to leave Heinemann. 'Pick recalls his shock on opening this letter,' stated St John. He suggested that le Carré had left Heinemann 'at least partly because of a refusal to meet his financial demands', though he hinted that 'there were in addition complex personal reasons'.

If Pick assumed that David would have little or no objection to such matters being aired after twenty years, he was soon disabused. 'I find the piece thoroughly offensive,' David told him.

> I am astonished that your ethical judgment, and that of Heinemann's, will allow you to make free with house correspondence, in which incidentally I have the copyright, and with confidential matters relating to finance and taxation in the case of a living author.
>
> I also find the entire passage contemptible in its selection of that correspondence, and in its tendentious presentation of my behaviour towards Heinemann; and most of all my reasons for leaving.

He sincerely hoped that Pick would take steps to correct 'what I regard as a cavalier abuse of a trusted if brief professional relationship'. He referred to Pick's invitation to drop in for a drink. 'I am always happy to drink with anyone who was my publisher, confidant and friend,' he wrote. 'Let me know.'[15]

Pick's suggestion of a meeting between the three of them was rebuffed by David. 'I wish for no part of this book,' he said. He continued to insist that his letters and verbal confidences should not be quoted, and that his 'contractual, financial, taxation or other business details should not be aired'. He warned that unless Pick desisted, and provided him with an assurance that he would henceforth give him the protection to which he was in honour entitled, he would take the matter formally to Heinemann through his solicitors, and, 'since a very large matter of principle is at stake', to the Publishers' Association.[16]

St John then appealed to David 'as one author to another' – which seems to have enraged him. 'My position is unchanged and will remain so,' he responded. 'I find the project totally dishonest, and I wish no part of it. I find it unethical and, in a "fellow author", uncomradely. And I shall exercise the rights I have in order to protect myself.'[17]

Best Seller List

An analysis, based on reports from more than 125 bookstores in 64 communities throughout the United States, showing the sales rating of the leading fiction and general titles. Sales through outlets other than bookstores are not included, and figures which are shown in the right-hand column do not necessarily represent consecutive weeks appearance on the list.

August 2	August 9	August 16	This Week		Weeks on List
				Fiction	
1	1	1	1	The Spy Who Came in From the Cold. *Le Carré*	32
2	2	2	2	Armageddon. *Uris*	10
6	5	5	3	The Rector of Justin. *Auchincloss*	4
5	3	3	4	Julian. *Vidal*	10
3	4	4	5	Candy. *Southern and Hoffenberg*	13
4	6	6	6	Convention. *Knebel and Bailey*	22
9	7	7	7	The 480. *Burdick*	7
10	9	10	8	The Group. *McCarthy*	51
			9	This Rough Magic. *Stewart*	1
7	8	9	10	The Night in Lisbon. *Remarque*	19
				General	
1	1	1	1	A Moveable Feast. *Hemingway*	14
2	2	2	2	The Invisible Government. *Wise and Ross*	8
5	3	3	3	Harlow. *Shulman*	6
4	4	4	4	A Tribute to John F. Kennedy. *Salinger and Vanocur*	9
3	5	5	5	Four Days. *U.P.I. and American Heritage*	28
9	7	6	6	Mississippi: The Closed Society. *Silver*	5
6	6	7	7	Diplomat Among Warriors. *Murphy*	23
10		8	8	Crisis in Black and White. *Silberman*	4
	10		9	The Kennedy Wit. *Adler*	2
8	9	9	10	The Naked Society. *Packard*	20

The *New York Times* bestseller list, 23 August 1964. *The Spy who Came in from the Cold* remained at number 1 for thirty-five weeks, becoming the bestselling novel of the year.

The Ronald Grant Archive

David and Ann on the set of *The Spy who Came in from the Cold* in Dublin, February 1965; he confessed to her there that he was having an affair with Susan Kennaway.

Courtesy of Susan Vereker

Courtesy of Susan Vereker

Susan Kennaway and her husband, the novelist and screenwriter James Kennaway.

The Kennaways pose on the balcony of their house in Highgate for American friends.

MI5 agent-runner John Bingham, who shared an office with David for a while; he was the physical model for George Smiley.

The Ronald Grant Archive

The Ronald Grant Archive

Murray Close, by courtesy of Portobello Productions / Eric Abraham

Four screen Smileys: (*clockwise from top left*) James Mason, Rupert Davies, Denholm Elliott and Gary Oldman.

David and his second wife Jane, with their son Nick, mid 1970s.

Tregiffian, *c.* 1980.

Courtesy of Andreas Heumann

David with his American publisher, Jack Geoghegan, in an English field. Geoghegan kept this picture on his desk for the rest of his career.

Central Press / Getty Images

Courtesy of Martin Pick

'Why would anyone want to leave a West End Jew for an East End Jew?' After the success of *The Spy Who Came in from the Cold*, David left his British publisher, Victor Gollancz (*left*), for Charles Pick of Heinemann (*right*).

© Pascal Parrot / Sygma / Corbis

Yvette Pierpaoli, 'the constant muse', and the inspiration for Tessa Quayle in *The Constant Gardener*.

Courtesy of Andreas Heumann

David's agent and close friend, Rainer Heumann, 'the kind of man with whom one could steal horses'.

Bodleian Library

19.2.79 Retyped by me 27/28/Feb 22/1

22.

Tricky Tony

~~Sand~~ sandbagging ~~SALAMANDER~~

The ~~snatching~~ of ~~Anton Gerdov~~, as it afterwards became known in the Circus mythology, was one of those ~~rare~~ operations where luck ~~and~~ timing ~~combined to make a~~ perfect marriage. The problem ~~had been~~ to find Gerdov alone, at a moment ~~and a place where he would not immediately be missed, whether at work or at home, and~~ which ~~also~~ allowed for his speedy reintroduction into normal life a few hours later, ~~preferably~~ with ~~an unimpeachable~~ cover story to explain his absence. ~~None of Toby's~~ researches into Gerdov's behaviour pattern ~~over the last four weeks~~ had produced ~~any~~ obvious pointers ~~as~~ to when this moment might be. ~~To~~ snatch ~~Gerdov while he was walking the~~ few hundred metres between his house and the Embassy ~~was unthinkable.~~ ~~He~~ would be missed immediately; worse ~~still~~, the sandbagging would quite likely occur under the full gaze of the diplomatic community and even its police patrol: for who was to say that Gerdov would not resist his abductors? ~~Yet when else was Gerdov to be found alone? Practically never.~~ His wife, in the gloomy view of the watchers, ~~supervised his every movement; they were certain~~ she suspected him of a tenderness for little Natasha. Their fears ~~was~~ confirmed ~~by sporadic bursts of telephone surveillance mounted against the Gerdov domestic line, which~~ Toby's listeners ~~had~~ contrived ~~by~~ meddling with the junction box at the corner of the road. Gerdova telephoned her husband at the Embassy three times ~~in one day, apparently to make sure he was actually there.~~ ~~She had~~ even enquired of the Ambassador's private secretary whether a conference over at the trade delegation's

A page of typescript from the book that became *Smiley's People*, with David's handwritten corrections, and a note in Jane's hand. This is a draft of the opening page of chapter 24 (not 22 as shown here); readers may be interested to compare this with the final version. Gerdov was renamed Grigoriev at a later stage.

© Michael Lionstar

David's longstanding American editor, Bob Gottlieb. 'I don't think writers need all that sympathy,' he would say. 'They need to be told when their books are bad.'

David Montgomery / Getty Images

With Richard Burton in Dublin during the shooting of the film of *The Spy Who came in from the Cold*.

TopFoto

With Alec Guinness on Hampstead Heath during the shooting of *Smiley's People*.

Two cameos, in *Tinker, Tailor, Soldier, Spy* (*above*), where David is glimpsed among the revellers at a Circus party; and *A Most Wanted Man* (*below*), in which he sits back-to-back with Philip Seymour Hoffman in adjoining booths of a Hamburg bar. David grew a beard for the part. He also plays a cameo in the film of *The Little Drummer Girl* and is due to play another in the forthcoming adaptation of *The Night Manager*.

Courtesy of John Burgess

Surveying the charred ruins of a village destroyed by insurgents, north-east Thailand, February 1974, while in south-east Asia researching *The Honourable Schoolboy*. With David is H. D. S. Greenway of the *Washington Post*.

Moscow, 1987, collecting material for the book that became *The Russia House*. This was David's first visit to the Soviet Union.

© Judith Herrin

Marching to protest against the visit to Britain of President Bush, following the invasion of Iraq in 2003. With David is Anthony Barnett.

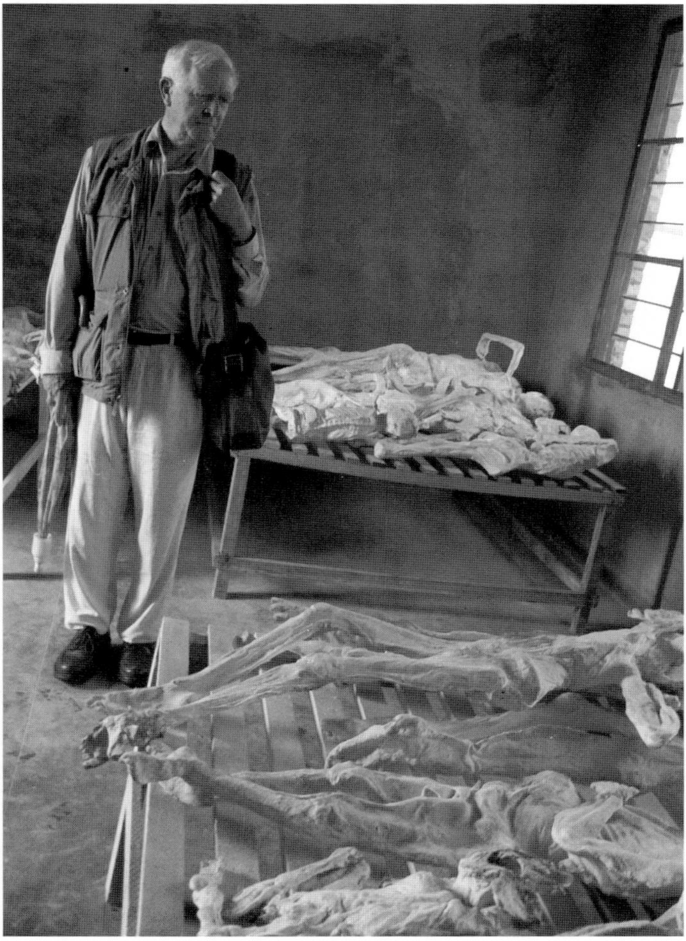

Courtesy of Michela Wrong

Inspecting the mummified corpses of people slaughtered at Murambi in the Rwandan genocide, while on a research trip to Africa for *The Mission Song*, spring 2006.

Simone Casetta / Anzenberger Agency

Flying low over south Sudan in a Buffalo cargo plane, while collecting material for *The Constant Gardener*, July 1999. David is seated on soy oil cartons carried for World Food Programme.

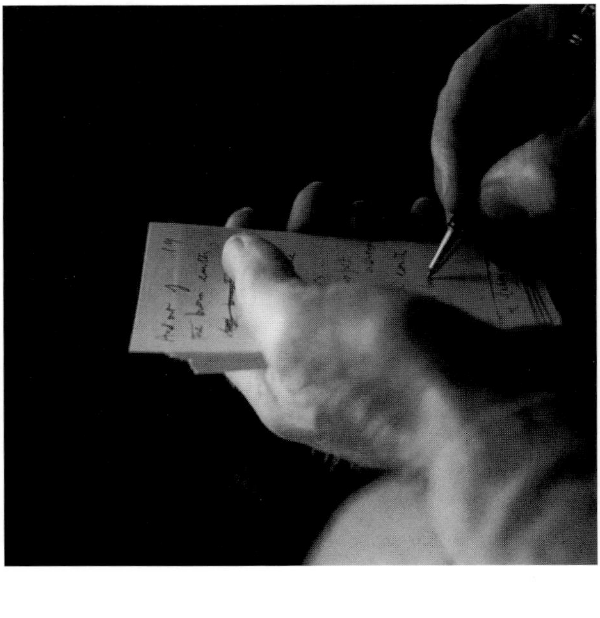

Simone Casetta / Anzenberger Agency

After David had complained to St John that he had not received a response from Pick, the retired publisher wrote to point out that he was no longer employed by Heinemann and did not control the Heinemann archives. (It was perhaps a little disingenuous of him to disclaim responsibility in this way, since he had commissioned the book in the first place.) Pick argued that he had forwarded the relevant passages from St John's text in good faith. He promised David that 'I have not revealed (and would not do so) any of the confidences you shared with me during our few years [sic] association.' He understood that St John had agreed 'to remove the passages about your financial matters, which I agree are confidential, and he assures me that he always intended to ask permission to quote from your letters'.[18]

There would be no quotations from David's letters in the final text of St John's book, nor would there be any explanation of his decision to leave Heinemann.[19]

In 1987 an inquiry into David's affairs had been launched by the Special Office of the Inland Revenue. The arguments on both sides were highly technical, but essentially the Revenue contended that the company that owned David's copyrights, Authors Workshop, was no more than a device for avoiding tax. Though David defended his position, it became clear to him that he should make a change. He and Jane had become deeply uncomfortable with the existing arrangements, even if they were justifiable on legal grounds; and they were concerned about the future of the copyrights in his books. Moreover, there was less incentive for such a scheme now that the tax regime had changed: under Margaret Thatcher the top tax rates had been reduced to 60 per cent, and would be reduced further, to 40 per cent in 1988. David's relations with Hale Crosse, once close, had deteriorated over the years, and he sought advice from a new accountant, Gordon Smith of Citroen Wells, who negotiated with the Inland Revenue on his behalf. It was with a sense of relief rather than resentment that at the end of these negotiations David signed a very large cheque for back-dated tax liabilities. Authors Workshop was wound up, and he became a self-employed UK taxpayer.

David's distress at the position in which he had found himself led him to want to give something back. Previously he had made ad hoc donations to family and friends, rather as Ronnie had always claimed to want to 'see everybody right'; but now he aimed to make philanthropic donations on a more systematic basis, both privately and, increasingly, through a registered charitable trust, set up in 1992. Gordon Smith advised him that 'if you were Jewish, it would be 10% of your gross income', which seemed to David an admirable principle; to date he has paid into the Trust approximately two and a half million pounds. The Cornwell Charitable Trust particularly favours local causes: providing the entire cost of a playing field, and a Community House in St Buryan, or a new wing on the village school; and has funded other local institutions such as the air ambulance service in Cornwall, one of Britain's poorest counties. But the Trust's donations are by no means confined to Cornish causes: for example, it has made substantial pledges to Lincoln, enabling the college to provide bursaries to undergraduates from poor families who might otherwise be deterred by the costs involved; and it has financed a charity founded by Yvette Pierpaoli to undertake humanitarian work.

In 2000, after a bruising battle with the farmer who in the 1960s had sold him Tregiffian and who now wanted to erect a large cattle shed overlooking the coastal path, David donated most of his land to the National Trust, with an endowment to help preserve it from 'human predators'. He retained only the gardens surrounding the house itself.

The Inland Revenue inquiry into David's affairs had been precipitated by its investigation into the affairs of another author, Noel Barber, who had become a successful novelist in his seventies following a career in journalism. Like David, Barber had been represented by George Greenfield, and he had attempted to make similar arrangements to minimise his tax liability. When the Inland Revenue questioned his tax status, Barber pleaded, 'Well, they told me it worked for John le Carré.'

By October 1988 David had finished a first draft of the new book. He had considered entitling it 'The Biggest Toys in the World' or 'Thinking Like a Hero', before deciding on *The Russia House*. He still had a number of changes to make in the final stage of the revision. The novel is narrated by Harry Palfrey, the Circus's lawyer, a decent man who has settled for a safe pension and a loveless marriage. In the final rewrite David made much more of Palfrey and his wife Hannah. 'I hope the effect will be to contrast

Barley's redemption by love with Palfrey's permanent imprisonment by compromise,' he wrote to his Hodder editor, Ion Trewin. 'By extension, I hope the two parallel love stories will point up the looming political choice that faces us: have we the courage to grasp the chance of peace in the future, or do we prefer the status quo?'[20]

David was uncertain whether to give the novel a happy ending. In the final pages of the story, Barley is in Lisbon, decorating his apartment in preparation for the arrival of Katya and her family. He seems confident that the Soviet authorities will honour their agreement to allow her to join him in the West. In some drafts Katya and her family arrive at the end. David was still hesitating about this when he delivered the book to the publishers, and revised the ending afterwards. Eventually he decided to leave the outcome open. The novel ends with the sentence 'Spying is waiting.'

The Russia House is dedicated to Bob Gottlieb, 'a great editor and a long-suffering friend'. There is no doubt that David greatly valued Gottlieb's input into his books. But the dedication was double-edged, because in 1987 Gottlieb had become editor of the *New Yorker*, in succession to the long-serving William Shawn. He had been replaced by Sonny Mehta, who had earned a reputation in London publishing as an editor with taste and flair. The arrangement was that Gottlieb would continue to edit David's books in parallel with his new role, though inevitably he would not continue to influence every stage of the publishing process as he had been able to do as editor-in-chief.

Knopf's first printing was 350,000 copies. Once again David's timing was fortuitous. *The Russia House* was published in America in June 1989, just as the first cracks had appeared in the Iron Curtain. In May the Hungarians began dismantling their border fence with Austria, allowing thousands of people from neighbouring Eastern bloc countries to cross freely into the West. Meanwhile partially free elections in Poland had demonstrated overwhelming popular support for the non-Communist trade union movement, Solidarity. A series of revolutions followed, which would overthrow Communist governments throughout Eastern Europe, ushering in a 'New World Order'.

David's novel was set two years earlier, and contained no suggestion that Communism was about to collapse. But in 1989 anything to do with the

Soviet Union seemed topical. *Newsweek* again made it a cover story. 'John le Carré, master of the spy story, ushers in a new era with a remarkable – and surprising – thriller,' trumpeted the news magazine. 'The days of Smiley and Karla are over.' It predicted that *The Russia House* would shoot up the bestseller list like a Minuteman missile.[21] In fact the novel went straight into the bestseller list at no. 1, and remained at the top for twelve weeks. This was le Carré's third no. 1 US bestseller in succession.

For *Newsweek*, *The Russia House* was 'faster and leaner than anything le Carré has done in years – a taut spy story embracing a lean romance'. Its rival news magazine *Time* also praised the book, as 'a thriller that demands a second reading as a treatise on our times'. The *New York Times* critic Christopher Lehmann-Haupt, who had written a damning review of *The Naïve and Sentimental Lover* eighteen years before, admired the 'superb' dialogue and the 'convincingly authentic' settings; but felt that the love affair between Barley and Katya seemed 'forced'. Not every reader, he suggested, would agree with the underlying assumption that 'only American militarism stands in the way of world peace'.[22] The Irish writer Conor Cruise O'Brien also thought the book marred by anti-American bias, though he rated it as 'vintage le Carré':

> . . . much of the story hinges on the fraught relationship between the British and American 'intelligence communities'. The Americans come across as hard-boiled and cynical, the British as decenter, in their own devious way, but having in the end to take their lead from the Americans. Significantly, the only character who is consistently presented as despicable, in everything he says and does, is Clive, a senior figure in British intelligence, who is entirely in the pockets of whichever American intelligence faction appears to be on top.
>
> Early on in the story, the narrator establishes the Britons' view of their domineering cousins. The Americans, in the view of Harry Palfrey, think of themselves as 'the larger beneficiaries . . . the majority shareholders'. The Americans throw their weight around in a manner distressing to British sensibilities, since the British have more refined and cryptic ways of throwing their weight – as we Irish know. Palfrey despises the American 'frank enjoyment of power and money'. Americans, he thinks, 'lack the instinct to dissemble that comes so naturally to us British'.[23]

In advance of the American publication David had given a long interview to *Vanity Fair*, recently revived by a new editor, the ambitious young Englishwoman Tina Brown. Lord Snowdon was commissioned to photograph David for the piece.

'Do you mind if we use Christian names?' asked Snowdon.

'Well, no,' replied David, 'you've got more to lose than I have.'

T. J. Binyon reviewed *The Russia House* for the *Times Literary Supplement*, as he had done *The Honourable Schoolboy*. 'The sentimental strain which marred the conclusion of The Little Drummer Girl and ruined The Naïve and Sentimental Lover, re-emerges,' wrote Binyon. 'As an optimistic fairy story the book still perhaps works; but not as a novel which engages reasonably seriously, as the earlier novels did, with reality.'[24] The novelist Salman Rushdie reviewed the book for the *Observer*. 'John le Carré . . . wants to be taken very seriously indeed,' he wrote. 'Much of the trouble is, I'm afraid, literary. There is something unavoidably stick-figure-like about le Carré's attempts at characterization.' His summary damned the book with faint praise. 'Le Carré is as serious a writer as the spy genre has thrown up. Close, but – this time anyway – no cigar.'[25]

David had met Rushdie some years earlier, when he had been persuaded by his sister Charlotte to take part in an event in support of the Nicaragua Solidarity Campaign, on a Sunday night at the Piccadilly Theatre. The show had been delayed, so the participants, including Rushdie and Harold Pinter as well as David, had all spent some time in the Green Room, chatting amiably about writers and their political involvement as they waited to go on stage.

By the time he reviewed *The Russia House* Rushdie was living in hiding, under police protection. Earlier in the year the Ayatollah Khomeini, the spiritual leader of Iran, had declared his novel *The Satanic Verses* to be 'blasphemous against Islam', and issued a fatwa, calling for the death of Rushdie and his publishers. Iranian officials had offered a bounty for his death. The book had drawn mass protests in Muslim countries and firebombings of bookshops in the West: several people had died as a result.

In a letter published in the *Guardian*, David suggested that Rushdie should have known better. 'Anybody who is familiar with Muslims, even if he has not had the advantage of Rushdie's background, knows that, even among the most relaxed, you make light of the Book at your peril.'* He indicated that Rushdie had, 'perhaps inadvertently', provoked his own misfortune. 'His open letter to the Indian Government seemed to me to be of an almost colonial arrogance.' Free speech was always curtailed, David insisted. 'Nobody has a God-given right to insult a great religion and be published with impunity.' He argued that anyone who wanted to read *The Satanic Verses* had already been given ample opportunity to do so. To David, Rushdie's attitude was a mystery. 'How can a man whose novel, for whatever twisted reasons, has already been the cause of so much bloodshed, insist on risking more?' He failed to understand both why Rushdie had not withdrawn the book until a calmer time and why he was 'inviting further bloodshed' by insisting on its publication in paperback. 'It seems to me that he has nothing further to prove except his own insensitivity.' David noted the 'elitism' of Rushdie's most vociferous defenders, who claimed 'great literary merit' for the book, even that it was 'a masterpiece'. He saw this as a dangerous and self-defeating argument. 'Would the same people have leapt to the defence of a Ludlum or an Archer? Or are we to believe that those who write literature have a greater right to free speech than those who write pulp?'[26]

A few weeks later Rushdie retaliated in a *Newsweek* article, in which he implied that David was an isolated critic. 'Slowly, slowly a point of view grew up, and was given voice by mountebanks and bishops, fundamentalists and Mr John le Carré, that I knew what I was doing,' wrote Rushdie. 'I must have known what would happen; therefore did it on purpose, to profit by the notoriety that would result.'[27] In his autobiography *Joseph Anton*, published more than twenty years later, Rushdie would single out le Carré as 'one of the few writers who had spoken out against him when the attack on *The Satanic Verses* began'.[28] He seemed to have forgotten that at the time plenty of other prominent people were calling for *The Satanic Verses* to be withdrawn, or for the paperback to be postponed: among them such varied figures as the former American President Jimmy Carter, the writer and critic John Berger, the novelist Roald Dahl and the political

* The letter had been written three months before it was published, in response to an enquiry from W. J. Weatherby, the *Guardian*'s correspondent in New York, who was writing a biography of Rushdie. It is not clear how this private letter came to be published.

journalist Hugo Young.[29] In December 1990 Rushdie himself would make a volte-face: he signed a declaration affirming his Islamic faith, and publicly called on his publisher neither to issue the book in paperback nor to allow it to be translated – a call he retracted once it became obvious that the fatwa would not be lifted. His estranged wife, Marianne Wiggins, told the *Sunday Times* that Rushdie was not man enough to fill the role history had given him.[30]*

It was later suggested by the journalist Mark Lawson that David's criticism of Rushdie had been provoked by his review of *The Russia House*.[31] This explanation was generally accepted, though David himself describes it as 'sheer nonsense'. One could equally well argue that it was the other way round, that Rushdie's review was itself the product of a grudge. In May 1989, a couple of months before it had appeared, David had spoken about *The Satanic Verses* in an interview with the *New York Times*. He condemned the fatwa as outrageous. But he also expressed mystification that Rushdie had not withdrawn the book, given that people were dying because of it. 'I have to say that would be my position,' David told the *New York Times* reporter.[32]

The Russia House was a worldwide bestseller. Since *The Spy who Came in from the Cold*, each new le Carré novel had been published in at least thirty languages. The French, German and Italian editions of David's books, for example, sold in large quantities, and attracted serious review attention – more serious, arguably, than the English-language equivalents. One mark of David's status in France was an invitation to appear on the prestigious television programme *Apostrophes*. This was a French institution, of a kind hard to imagine in English-speaking countries. For the past fifteen years its presenter, Bernard Pivot, had been interviewing many of the world's most highly regarded authors, including Umberto Eco, Milan Kundera, Norman Mailer, Vladimir Nabokov, Alexander Solzhenitsyn, Susan Sontag and Tom Wolfe. Despite its dauntingly highbrow content,

* Rushdie's publisher, Viking Penguin, was reluctant to issue a paperback edition. Eventually the rights were returned to the author, and a paperback edition was issued in March 1992 (four years after the book had first appeared in hardcover) by an anonymous consortium, formed by Rushdie's agent, Andrew Wylie.

Apostrophes went out live at prime time and regularly attracted six million viewers, making it one of the most watched shows on French television. It was recognised that an appearance on the programme could generate thousands of book sales.

As well as Pivot, there were two other journalists present, a man and a woman. David's French was good enough for him to be able to cope with the ninety-minute interview, helped by the fact that the loquacious journalists' questions were often longer than his replies. The talk was not confined to intellectual matters. Pivot was interested to know why David had chosen a French nom de plume: David provided two replies, the dull *vérité* and the more entertaining *mensonge*, of seeing the name on a shop-front from a bus window. Pivot himself gave an account of a ceremony in Capri, at which both he and David were to receive a prize; he told how he had been mortified to find himself at this formal event 'sans cravate', in contrast to David, who was immaculately turned out. 'Voilà John le Carré,' Pivot told his audience, 'un vrai Anglais . . . il connaît savoir vivre.' He explained how David, 'dans une geste magnifique', had taken off his own tie and handed it to him: at this point Pivot removed the tie from around his own neck and showed it to the viewers. It was this very tie, he said, and offered it back to his guest. 'Vous pouvez le retenir,' said David, laughing.

The broadcast was still winding up as he left to have dinner with his French publishers, Laffont. Emerging on to the street, David commented that it was empty. 'Where is everybody?' he asked. 'Tout le monde regarde la fin d'*Apostrophes*,' his publisher replied.

David's mother died in 1989. For some years she had been a resident in a nursing home, once ill-health had forced her to give up the cottage that David had bought for her. In clearing out the cottage he retrieved the white hide suitcase which Ronnie had given her for their honeymoon, and which she had taken with her when she slipped out of Hazel Cottage that night so many years before, leaving her boys sleeping innocently upstairs. Beneath the leather handle were the initials O.M.C., for Olive Moore Cornwell, a relic of a life left behind. David took it back to his house in London and kept it there, an object of intense speculation, perhaps a key to his lost childhood.

In a dark drawer in Olive's cottage David found a studio photograph of his brother and himself, aged seven and five, posing with carefully combed hair in their new uniforms of St Martin's boarding school, inscribed with handwritten greetings from each of them, David's signed 'love from david', with a small 'd'. This made no sense to him: if Olive had fallen into immoral ways, and perhaps died as a result, which was what Ronnie had suggested to them at the time, why would they have signed the photograph for her? David could remember posing for the photograph, but he had no memory of writing such a message. He speculated that his inscription, and maybe his brother's too, had been forged by their father.

In recent years he and Jane had been more regularly in contact with Olive, visiting her from time to time, sending her presents at Christmas and on her birthday, and letters or faxes full of his news. These were written in affectionate, even sentimental terms, and usually addressed to 'my dearest mother'. It might seem that he had forgiven her for all the hurt she had caused him; but the tone of the letters rang false, as though he was striving for feelings that he could not find. The truth was that he found her irritating. He paid her nursing-home fees, and, after her death, distributed handsome gifts to the matron and her assistant. As a dutiful son he came to her funeral, though he discouraged his brother from flying across the Atlantic to attend. Indeed he organised it and gave an address. 'Why didn't you ever buy me orchids, darling?' his mother had asked him at their final leave-taking, as so often in the past mistaking him for Ronnie. He placed an enormous bunch of orchids on her coffin. Some of the mourners were comparative strangers, who apparently came merely to gawp at the famous author. His Canadian half-sister commented sourly that it was like a 'dog-and-pony show'.

In January 1989 the East German leader, Erich Honecker, had predicted that the Berlin Wall would stand for another fifty or even a hundred years. But only months later, following the outbreak of mass demonstrations across the country, Honecker was forced to resign. The chorus of discontent rose to a climax in early November, when half a million protestors gathered in East Berlin's Alexanderplatz. It became obvious that the East German authorities were no longer willing to authorise the use of force to prevent people crossing into West Berlin. The vastly outnumbered soldiers started to open the frontier checkpoints to allow free movement back and forth. Demonstrators began to climb the Wall, and to take chunks out of it with sledgehammers. The unnatural division of a city, and of a people, was ending. Within the year Germany would be reunified. Across Europe there were celebrations as a succession of uprisings brought down hated regimes. The Cold War was over. Less coherent than usual, David wrote happily to Alec Guinness: 'if life and politics ever give a chance to celebrate, which they don't, we really should. Because, for all our faults, WE were right, and for all their proclaimed ideals, THEY were a bunch of corrupt, foul-minded piglets. Which is a calumny against piglets. So please read, swine.'[33]

MGM had bought the film rights in *The Russia House* early, and the movie had gone into development while the novel was still in manuscript form. This would be the first major film production from the West to be filmed substantially in the Soviet Union with full permission from the Russian government. Early in October the crew began shooting scenes in Leningrad.

The movie was produced and directed by the Australian Fred Schepisi, best known for *A Cry in the Dark*, *Six Degrees of Separation* and *Last Orders*. The cast included Sean Connery as Barley Blair and Michelle Pfeiffer as his leading lady, Katya Orlova, despite the fact that she was almost thirty years younger. Pfeiffer's performance would earn her a Golden Globe Best Actress nomination, though she would lose out to Kathy Bates for her performance in *Misery*.

Connery had been attached to the movie from an early stage, and his participation was considered crucial to its prospects. His contract gave him casting approval for the other parts. He had become a major movie star from playing James Bond; to those who noticed such things, it was amusing that he should play the leading role in a movie derived from a le Carré, given that his novels were so often contrasted with Ian Fleming's. Other members of the cast included Roy Scheider, James Fox, Michael Kitchen, Martin Clunes and Ken Russell, with Klaus Maria Brandauer as Yakov.* Connery and Brandauer had previously worked together on the 1983 James Bond film *Never Say Never Again*.

* Yakov's code-name was changed from 'Goethe' to 'Dante' for the film, because the latter was thought to be easier for audiences to spell.

Tom Stoppard was hired to write the screenplay. When David met Stoppard to discuss the project, he found him 'enchanting' and 'extremely intelligent', as he told Alec Guinness. The two of them went together to the Park Lane Hotel, to go through the script with Sean Connery. The film star had a suite on the top floor. On the way up Stoppard warned David to expect some tension between the two of them, arising from Connery's withdrawal from the film version of Stoppard's play *Rosencrantz and Guildenstern are Dead.** 'You must be young Mister David,' Connery said as he met them at the lift.† He was noticeably cooler towards Stoppard. He led them into his luxurious suite. 'A hundred pounds a night is the negotiated sum,' he told them proudly, 'and free minibar.' As soon as they began talking Connery tore into the script, alleging that it was overwritten and too long. 'If anyone said that to me,' the star said of one line, 'I'd kick them in the balls.' The meeting ended abruptly. Connery walked them back to the lift; just as the door was closing, while Connery was still within earshot, Stoppard turned to David and said, 'I think that I need to invent a new typeface for irony.'

Stoppard's response to the criticism that his script was too long was to print it out in smaller type. In fact his script was largely faithful to the original, so that many of the best lines in the film are versions of lines in the book. Perhaps predictably, the end was altered. While the novel ends with Barley waiting in Lisbon in the hope that Katya will come, the movie shows her arrival, in a scene that provides the big emotional pay-off so beloved by Hollywood.

Early in 1990 Michael Attenborough reported to his colleagues on an idea for 'a new le Carré'. David had written the Maugham-like tale of 'Jungle Hansen', a British agent held in captivity by the Khmer Rouge, drawing on the experience of François Bizot – though David would be at pains to stress that Bizot had never been a spy, and that he had been 'nobody's creature but his own'. David proposed to publish this short story as a novella; but after some discussion with Ion Trewin and a review of discarded material from previous books, he devised a new formula, a volume of loosely

* The part was taken by Richard Dreyfuss.

† Connery is fourteen months older than David.

linked short stories in the manner of Somerset Maugham's *Ashenden*.[34] His provisional title was 'Plain Tales from the Circus'.*

The stories would be narrated by Ned, former head of the Russia House, who has been sidelined after the failure of Operation Bluebird and is now running Sarratt, the Circus's training centre in Hertfordshire. David identified himself with Ned: he imagined what might have happened to him had he remained within MI6, 'life's mystery left somehow untouched'.[35] Ned has invited Smiley to address the passing-out class on the closing evening of their new-entry course. In his talk Smiley scoffs at the idea that spying is a dying profession, now that the Cold War is over. The occasion is portrayed like a college feast, with those present dining in evening dress, in a candle-lit room lined with old photographs; as guest of honour Smiley is seated at high table. After the meal the diners gather in a panelled library around a blazing log fire, smoking cigars and cradling balloons of brandy, the older ones reclining in cracked leather armchairs, while the students lounge at their feet. Smiley's appearance reminds Ned of scenes from his past, which form the short stories. At various points in this sequence of memories Smiley interjects a few sagacious comments. 'It's over, and so am I,' he says at the close of the evening, as he swirls the last of his brandy. 'Time you ran down the curtain on yesterday's cold warrior. And please don't ask me back, ever again. The new time needs new people.'[36]

In the final story, which takes place outside the envelope of the Sarratt evening, Ned is sent to confront Sir Anthony Bradshaw, a cynical, amoral arms dealer, living like a country squire on a sumptuous estate. His unrepentant attitude stimulates Ned to an epiphany: 'For a moment it was as if my whole life had been fought against the wrong enemy . . . I remembered Smiley's aphorism about the right people losing the Cold War, and the wrong people winning it . . . I thought of telling him that now we had defeated Communism, we were going to have to set about defeating capitalism.'[37] The book ends with Ned's retirement.

The idea for the novel, if it was a novel, had been inspired by Smiley himself. Back in 1982 Alec Guinness had proposed to David that they might devise a one-man show, in which he would play Smiley lecturing at

* An allusion to Kipling's *Plain Tales from the Hills* (1888), and perhaps to the successful BBC Radio 4 series *Plain Tales from the Raj*, broadcast in 1974.

Sarratt. The two men had discussed the concept over a period of months without reaching a resolution. 'Smiley's lecture remains a wonderful idea and I should write it,' David had written to Guinness in 1983. 'But then again, I'm not sure. I think we maybe really *should* just hang up his boots.' When he returned to the idea seven years later he acknowledged its paternity in a letter to Guinness. 'I set to work on Smiley's speech to the passing-out at Sarratt and it ran away with me and became a novel,' he wrote.[38] The book was dedicated to Guinness, 'with affection and thanks'.

Once David had settled on this formula, he wrote the book very fast. Much of it was written by hand and faxed to a typist from Wengen, or wherever else he happened to be at the time. This was the first of his books to be typed on a word processor. By May 1990 he had a first draft of the whole.* Originally the stories had separate titles, which were replaced by numbered chapters, an indication of how the separate stories became unified into a single novel. At least two of the stories included in early drafts were later omitted. After abandoning the working title of 'Plain Tales from the Circus', David contempleted calling the book 'Agent Running in the Field' (a title he had considered for previous novels) and 'The Interrogators' Poll', before choosing 'The Case Officer'. At a late stage this was changed to 'The Silent Pilgrim', before he fixed on the title *The Secret Pilgrim*.

In America *The Secret Pilgrim* went straight to no. 1, le Carré's fourth consecutive book to reach the top of the US bestseller list. The English novelist William Boyd praised it in the *New York Times*. 'The many ingredients are skillfully marshalled: story elides into story; flashback and flash-forward, reminiscence, analysis and prognosis are lucidly and elegantly controlled,' wrote Boyd. 'Indeed, "The Secret Pilgrim" is, technically, Mr le Carré's most magisterial accomplishment.'[39] The Anglo-Dutch writer Ian Buruma, reviewing *The Secret Pilgrim* for the *New York Review of Books*, deplored what he saw as the 'crude anti-Americanism' in le Carré's work. Like Boyd, he reflected on what le Carré would write, 'now that the cold war is apparently over'.

> Much is made in interviews with le Carré and reviews of his last two books of the supposed end of the cold war. Can he still go on writing his spy

* On delivering the book David learned that Ion Trewin was on his way to Australia, to attend the local sales conferences and see another of his authors, Thomas Keneally. He telephoned Michael Attenborough. 'Get me a new editor,' he said.

> novels? Must he look for another enemy, another subject? In fact, I think too much is made of this. The cold war was never more than a frame for his stories anyway. His real subject is rather like Graham Greene's: man's, especially Englishman's, struggle with his soul. But, if not the cold war, le Carré does need some kind of model for his stories. Like Raymond Chandler, he is at his best when he expands the limits of his chosen genre. But without the genre he is at sea. In his latest book, the frame is barely there; instead we have a series of episodes, knitted together by Smiley's speech. It is little more than a loose bit of string to tie up various good ideas for stories that never made it into his other books.[40]

In the spring of 1991, David published a long essay in the magazine *Granta*, about Brigadier Jean-Louis Jeanmaire, a Swiss army officer who in 1977 had been sentenced to eighteen years' imprisonment for passing military secrets to the Russians. The outside world had paid little attention to the case. Jeanmaire was just another KGB mole, and not a very interesting one at that. Why would one spy on the neutral Swiss? Did they have any secrets worth stealing?

It was difficult to comprehend Jeanmaire's motives. He had not done it for money, because in fourteen years of spying he had received only occasional gifts, worth in total a couple of thousand dollars at most. Nor had it been for ideological reasons: Jeanmaire was a traditionalist, profoundly conservative in his politics. He was above all a proud soldier, to whom the army mattered more than anything. So why had this deeply patriotic man betrayed his country?

After Jeanmaire's release, David visited the eighty-year-old widower in his tiny flat on the outskirts of Bern. They passed an evening together. Over whisky and schnapps and a simple meal of cheese fondue that the old man had himself made for his English guest, he told his story. 'It is a journalistic conceit to pretend you are unmoved by people,' David wrote afterwards. 'But I am not a journalist and I am not superior to this encounter. Jean-Louis Jeanmaire moves me, deeply, with a fascination that I can't escape.'

David showed a Smiley-like ability to empathise with this damaged and vulnerable man. His interview with Jeanmaire would be as compelling as any of the fictional stories in *The Secret Pilgrim*. In his hands Jeanmaire's case became a touching psychological study, revealing the naïvety and even the innocence of the spy.

Jeanmaire denied that he had ever passed information to the other side that could harm his country. 'All I ever did was give the Russians harmless bits of proof that Switzerland was a dangerous country to attack!' he insisted angrily. 'C'était la dissuasion,' he bellowed. His case officer, the Soviet Military Attaché and GRU intelligence officer Vassily Denissenko, had understood that. 'We were working together against the Bolsheviks!' He had convinced himself that his friend 'Deni' was a man like himself, with similar values. Deni was cultivated, charming, honourable, a gentleman! Deni was a hero of Stalingrad, with medals for gallantry! Deni was a horseman, a Tsarist, an officer of the old school! Far from resenting it when Denissenko had seduced his wife, Jeanmaire had been indulgent, indeed understanding. 'But Deni was an attractive man!' he protested. 'If I'd been a woman I'd have slept with him myself!' He spoke lovingly of Marie Louise herself, who had died while Jeanmaire was still serving his prison sentence: 'she was a good, sweet, dear comrade'. She had girlishly displayed to him the 'beautiful bracelet that Denissenko had given her'. Jeanmaire had taken this as 'a gift of love', 'a beautiful gesture'.

He had been reluctant to offend his Russian friend. When Denissenko offered him an envelope stuffed with banknotes, he had flung it to the floor in indignation. He spurned what he saw as a bribe. But afterwards Jeanmaire had given Denissenko the Swiss order of battle, to show him that there were no hard feelings.

David sensed that Jeanmaire's relationship with Denissenko had become compulsive. 'Again and again you sense that it is Jeanmaire, not Denissenko, who is forcing the pace,' he wrote. 'Jeanmaire, you feel, needed Denissenko a good deal more than Denissenko needed him.'

In David's sympathetic account, Jeanmaire emerges as a tragic figure, a 'flawed, latter-day Dreyfus', more deserving of pity than of punishment.[41]

Though Smiley had left the stage, he would return for one last bow. In April 1991 ITV screened an adaptation of David's early novel *A Murder of Quality*, made by Portobello Films for Thames Television and directed by Gavin Millar. This was a prestigious production, shown at prime time, between 8.00 and 10.00 p.m. on a Wednesday evening. Six months later it would be shown in America, on Channel 9's 'Masterpiece Theatre', in two parts, introduced by Alistair Cooke. Much of it was shot on location at Sherborne – an ironic choice, given how David had been at pains to distance the fictional school of the story from his own *alma mater*. It featured a fine cast, including Glenda Jackson as Smiley's friend Ailsa Brimley; Billie Whitelaw as the madwoman Janie who is initially suspected of the murder; Joss Ackland as the real murderer, the schoolmaster Terence Fielding; Ronald Pickup as his snobbish colleague Felix D'Arcy; David Threlfall (who had played a small part in *The Russia House*) as the bereaved husband Stanley Rode; and the young Christian Bale, in one of his first parts, as the schoolboy Perkins, Fielding's favourite. Another newcomer was Samantha Janus, who plays D'Arcy's young mistress.

On behalf of the production company David had written to Alec Guinness to ask if he would like to reprise his role as George Smiley. At first he showed interest in the idea, but after some months of wavering he withdrew. 'In my bones (or gut, as everyone now says) I feel I am right,' he wrote to David. 'All along, I must confess, I have felt there would be huge difficulties with scripting the book. I am sorry. Anyway there should be two or three or six acceptable Smileys to be found. I shall have a twinge of jealousy, of course, but no envy.'[42]

A year later, as shooting drew near, Guinness's prediction that the book would be difficult to adapt seemed to be coming true. The original writer, the experienced Hugh Whitemore, asked for his name to be expunged from the credits after David had rewritten his screenplay. David Elstein, Thames's director of programmes, admitted that there had been problems with the script because, he said, the novel's plot did not translate naturally to television.[43]

Anthony Hopkins, who had been cast to play Smiley, pulled out of the project only a week before shooting was due to begin, reportedly because he was unhappy that his role had been diminished by the rewrite. With nobody to play the lead, the project was in jeopardy; the programme-makers were desperate to find a replacement. Then the producer, Eric Abraham, had an idea. He had heard an audiocassette of David reading one of his novels, doing the voices of all his characters, and thought, 'This man can act.' After discussing it with the director, Abraham proposed to David that he should play Smiley himself. For a brief moment there was the enticing possibility that le Carré might take the part of his most famous character. But David decided not to accept the role, remembering his humiliating experience of playing a cameo in the film of *The Little Drummer Girl*. With just three days until production was due to start, the producers approached Denholm Elliott, a much loved character actor best known for playing Marcus Brody in the *Indiana Jones* films. Elliott, who was living in Spain, turned down the part initially, but accepted when offered a larger fee. He claimed not to be intimidated by taking the part of a character so much identified with Alec Guinness. The great actor had been 'brilliant' as Smiley, he was quoted as saying, 'but I wanted to play him with more comedy, something that was missing from Guinness's portrayal'.

Elliott had no time to prepare before filming commenced. On his arrival at Sherborne, he was introduced to someone called Cornwell, whom he failed to connect with John le Carré. 'I though he might be the headmaster of the school we were filming in,' Elliott admitted afterwards. 'When he started giving me notes about playing Smiley, I thought, "Who is this geezer?"'[44]

21

'Whatever are you going to write now?'

It was often said that le Carré lost his subject when the Cold War ended. Friends stopped him in the street to commiserate. 'Whatever are you going to write now?' they would ask. No matter how often or how emphatically he rejected the idea that the destruction of the Berlin Wall meant the death of the spy novel, the impression persisted. In 1994 a cartoon by Jeff Danziger in the *Christian Science Monitor* showed David bowing his head to his Maker in grateful thanks at the revelation that Aldrich Ames, a CIA counter-intelligence officer, had been supplying secrets to the Russians.

To some extent David was a victim of his own success. To most people, the name John le Carré was synonymous with the Cold War; more than any other writer of his generation, he had shaped the public perception of the struggle between East and West. 'I saw the Berlin Wall go up when I was thirty and I saw it come down when I was sixty,' David told an interviewer from the *Guardian*. 'I was chronicling my time, from a position of knowledge and sympathy. I lived the passion of my time. And if people tell me that I am a genre writer, I can only reply that spying was the genre of the Cold War.'[1]

David resented the notion that he was finished. He did not relish reading his own obituary. He argued that the spy story had been born long before the birth of the Cold War, and would not die with its demise; spy writers would just have to adapt.[2] He pointed out that at least three of his novels (*A Murder of Quality*, *The Naïve and Sentimental Lover* and *The Little Drummer Girl*) had nothing whatever to do with the Cold War, and a fourth (*A Small Town in Germany*) not much. Communism might have been vanquished, but other enemies remained. There was still plenty of territory left for him to explore in the future. In 1989 he identified Angola, El Salvador, Sri Lanka, Cambodia, Burma, Eritrea, Ethiopia, Chad and Libya as just some of the places where 'spooks, arms dealers and phoney humanitarians' were active. His next novel, *The Night Manager*, would describe an undercover operation by a branch of British intelligence against one such arms dealer, a man contemptuously indifferent to the victims of his trade.

As David pointed out, the collapse of Communism did not mean the end of the Russian threat. 'The Russian Bear is sick, the Bear is bankrupt, the Bear is frightened of his past, his present and his future,' he said in a speech delivered in the summer of 1990, as the Soviet Union was already beginning to break up into its constituent parts. 'But the Bear is still armed to the teeth and very, very proud . . .'[3]

David was restless. In several letters to friends* he talked about leaving London for good and settling in Cornwall; or leaving England altogether, to live abroad, which he hoped might enrich his writing. Around 1990 he took out Swiss residency, because, as he would later tell a friend, 'I really didn't think that I could stand being English for another day, or in England.'[4]

He had lost touch with John Shakespeare, along with almost all his other University friends, within a few years of leaving Oxford. In 1989 he received a letter from Shakespeare's son Nicholas, then in his early thirties, who had just been appointed literary editor of the *Daily Telegraph*: he introduced himself as the son of John and Lalage, and asked David to consider reviewing Germaine Greer's memoir *Daddy, We Hardly Knew You* – no doubt thinking of David's troubled relations with his own father. To Shakespeare, David had been 'a small speck on the windscreen' all his life, whose outrageous stories and skills as a mimic and raconteur were fondly recalled by his parents. His silhouette of a boy stretching out towards a crescent moon, which he had given them as a wedding present, had accompanied the family around the world, from one Foreign Office posting to another.

* 'I hate London,' he told Vivian Green in 1987, 'and have decided more or less not to be there much more.'

In a warm reply, David congratulated Shakespeare on his new appointment. Though he declined to undertake the review, a year later he gave Shakespeare an interview, to coincide with publication of *The Secret Pilgrim*. The two men formed an immediate rapport, despite the difference in their ages.* 'In his company, I felt exhilarated and engaged,' Shakespeare recalled. 'I found him courageous, generous, complicated, competitive, touchy, watchful, suspicious, and incineratingly honest, although perhaps not in every single instance about himself, but then who is?' Afterwards Shakespeare invited his new friend for a reunion with his parents over dinner at his North Kensington flat, where David entertained the party with a succession of hilarious stories, staying until 1.15 in the morning.

At the time Shakespeare was struggling with a dilemma that must have sounded familiar to David: whether to give up his safe job in literary journalism for the hazardous existence of a full-time writer. In 1989 he had published his first novel, *The Vision of Elena Silves*, a critical success which had been translated into several languages; he had received the Somerset Maugham Award, a prize that David himself had received back in 1964 for *The Spy who Came in from the Cold*. Shakespeare wanted to press on with his second novel, but to do this he knew that he would have to leave the *Telegraph*, and he had no money. He found David 'hugely supportive' at this pivotal moment. As well as writing to Shakespeare to say that he had read *The Vision of Elena Silves* and believed in his talent, he offered practical help, in the form of a 'safe house' at Tregiffian, to borrow when he was not there, and to share occasionally when he was. This was the Long Barn, one side of a courtyard in the neighbouring farm, about 300 yards across the field from his own house, which the Cornwells had bought and converted into a two-storey cottage for their guests, with underfloor heating beneath the flagstones. There were two bedrooms upstairs, and a study downstairs looking over the field towards the sea.

For Shakespeare, this generous gesture was enough to tip the balance, and he resigned from his job at the *Telegraph*. 'I am pleased if I gave you a little extra shove,' David wrote to him in reaction to the news, 'and I wish

* Shakespeare was the same age as David's eldest son, Simon.

you from the heart the fulfilment of your art, and all the pleasure & magic of the journey.'

> I hope you will not be pulled too often by the quick fixes of journalism, but you'll work out a balance between the sprint & the marathon. I hope you get the right woman to write with, and to. And I hope you keep your generosity of spirit when they (the hacks & worst of all the fellow novelists) go for you, because your writing has great humanity, & so have you.[5]

Shakespeare arrived for his first visit a few months later. On his first evening the two men sat up talking until 2.00 in the morning, over malt whisky.

David had proposed that they should write separately during the day and meet in the evenings, but on his very first day Shakespeare found himself invited to join David's regular post-lunch walk along the coastal path, which lasted an hour and twenty minutes. Jane collected them in the car. As she strode across the field towards them, an elderly whippet trailing by her side, David smiled wryly. 'I always have this fantasy', he said, when she joined them, 'that you're coming to tell me that I've won the Nobel Prize.'

He took Shakespeare to visit Derek Tangye. 'He's the local writer,' David explained; women knocking on the door at Tregiffian and asking for 'the writer' invariably wanted him. One had said to David, 'Aren't you in one of his books?' – 'thereby reducing me to the level of Raulo the fisherman and Ambrose the cat'.

This was the first of at least a dozen visits Shakespeare made to Tregiffian over the next twelve years, as he wrote his next two novels, *The High Flyer* and *The Dancer Upstairs,** and his highly praised biography of Bruce Chatwin. He would usually stay for about a fortnight, working hard, invariably joining David on his daily afternoon walk when he was there, and often having dinner with him and Jane, or whoever might be staying. They played pool together, or, in fine weather, croquet (David always won both). They would walk along the cliffs to see Tangye, or drive over to see John Miller or Karl Weschke. On several occasions Shakespeare brought a girlfriend with him; David likened one of these, the novelist Donna Tartt, to the elfin Françoise Sagan. 'I was always utterly candid

* Both titles suggested by David.

with him about almost every aspect of my life,' Shakespeare recalled, 'and he reciprocated.'

> We had interests and prejudices in common, knew many of the same countries, were intrigued by similar people. There was also his sense of humour. He was one of the funniest mimics I'd met, and it was impossible not to rejoice in most of his targets. He put an extraordinary amount of himself into his performances (and I gathered from Jane that he felt drained at the end of them). He was an exhibitionist and charmer who moulded himself according to his audience in a way that reminded me of Bruce Chatwin, of whom one friend memorably said: 'Think of the word seduction, it doesn't matter if you are male, female, an ocelot or a tea cosy.'

Shakespeare sensed that this was not a friendship that could be taken for granted. Though the two men became very close, David was not someone whom he felt able to ring up and have a chat with. While very open with him when they were together, David was at the same time immensely private, and guarded his privacy to a ruthless degree, frequently changing his telephone numbers to exclude unwanted callers. Shakespeare appreciated that this ruthlessness derived from David's commitment to writing, a quality that would become even more apparent as he came to know him better. He rationed his time in the city: 'ten days at a time are all I can handle before I want my solitude again,' he wrote to a London friend, and explained his need to escape to Cornwall:

> Mostly, my withdrawal has to do with the husbanding of resources. We follow a strict regimen; I'm always asleep by 10.00 pm. I know that if I shine at dinner I don't shine next morning; I walk, loaf, plot new stories, do not neglect the bottle, thank God, and read only sparingly because my best hours go to the work. The price I/we pay is that we have lost almost all our friends, or lost touch with them; we are up to date on almost nothing in the way of theatre, movies & the rest, which to many people is incomprehensible.[6]

'For me, he was a model to follow, in terms of his discipline, his respect for plot, and his narrative technique,' wrote Shakespeare. He learned certain tips from the older man: begin the story as late as you can; write out key sentences and put them on the wall; rewrite; don't be afraid to throw away eighteen months' work. Shakespeare never forgot coming back to his London flat to find a handwritten fax from David, about three yards long, curling out of his study into the hallway; he had just read a draft of *The Dancer Upstairs* and was keen to point out ways in which it could be improved. His advice ran to twelve or more pages, 'all of it good'. He urged Shakespeare 'to go the extra mile', commenting that 'there have been times in my own career when I wish someone I trusted had been able to say the same to me . . .'[7]

David affected a kind of rivalry, itself a form of compliment. 'I told Jane if that fucker's writing a masterpiece, he can go,' was how he greeted Shakespeare on one of his arrivals at Tregiffian. The pair held passionate discussions about those writers whom they admired (Marquez, Waugh, Wodehouse) and those they didn't (Anthony Powell, for example). They shared a special interest in Graham Greene, whom Shakespeare admired greatly and had met several times, as of course David had done. On Greene's death in 1991, David wrote to Shakespeare about him:

> First to Graham: yes, it's a big gap, the General is dead, and he won. He won his war, if not all his battles; he left imperishable work and the self-perpetuating memory of a very large man with all sorts of fascinating smallnesses – a lot of them sprang from boredom, from too much ease with his talent, but a lot of them were diligently tended by himself in order to keep the child in him alive. I think that was why he was such a writer's writer: he was all of us, but more so. To write to you this way is already to pray to him: he woke the agnostic in all of us! – and put it to work.[8]

'I have made no friends in Oxford I have kept,' David told Shakespeare. 'I have no nostalgia for it.' On one occasion, when David and Jane were elsewhere, Shakespeare's parents came to stay a weekend at Tregiffian, with the Cornwells' blessing. In a letter of thanks, John Shakespeare wrote that he would love to meet again some time, and invited David to lunch at his club, the Garrick. 'I'm afraid that the Garrick is one of my no-go areas,' replied David. The friendship was not resumed.

David celebrated his sixtieth birthday in October 1991 by inviting guests to a dinner at the Savoy, cooked by the hotel's *maître chef des cuisines*, Anton

Edelmann. Toasts were called by Ann's husband, Roger Martin. Vivian Green made a speech proposing David's health, David proposed the health of the guests, and David Greenway responded for the guests, who were invited to respond for themselves, 'or not'. John Margetson did respond, and afterwards David wrote to thank him for his 'elegant and affectionate speech'. He confessed that he had been tempted to publicise how they had met, though it would have been a breach of the Official Secrets Act – 'but who's counting, these days?' He would love to have told the guests how Margetson had been at his elbow when the news came through to Fort Monkton that *Call for the Dead* had been accepted for publication by Victor Gollancz – 'if only VG had known where we were at the time, what a scoop! And what a giggle.'[9]

In a similar letter of thanks to Vivian Green, David commented on how the age gap between them had shrunk:

> I was so struck by the circularity of our acquaintance – it must happen to you all the time, and the Savoy was no place to speak of it that night. But we touched on it – how much I owe to you, how much of my life you have been able to observe and even share and then suddenly the age gap between us is academic: we both have made our main experiences, and have only the conclusions to draw. So very strange, and interesting. How the autobiography does pull![10]

David's next novel followed on from *The Secret Pilgrim*, in that Sir Anthony Bradshaw, the 'entrepreneur' whom Ned confronts but fails to shame in the final story of *The Secret Pilgrim*, becomes a minor character in the new book, which David would call *The Night Manager*. In fact he had begun the novel back in November 1989, before he wrote most of the stories that made up *The Secret Pilgrim*, but had then laid it aside for twelve months or so to concentrate on them. David had originally intended Bradshaw to be the villain of the new novel, but came to think better of the idea: through a succession of drafts he mutates into the sleek and loathsome arms dealer Richard Onslow Roper, 'the worst man in the world'. Roper is unequivocally evil, lacking any redeeming virtue; there is never any doubt in the reader's mind that he should be destroyed if possible. In *The Night Manager* the goodies and the baddies are clearly differentiated; there is none of the moral ambiguity that had marked David's books from the very beginning.

Like several of David's villains, Roper speaks 'Belgravia slur, the proletarian accent of the vastly rich'. He justifies his deadly trade with a brutal, survival-of-the-fittest philosophy, using such Thatcher-era terminology as 'the bottom line'. The book shows how Roper and his ilk corrupt government officials to allow them freedom to inflict suffering on innumerable defenceless victims. It is permeated with disgust for Roper and his cronies, amounting to a physical revulsion:

> And after the Frequent Flyers came the Royal & Ancients: the sub-county English debutantes accompanied by the brain-dead offshoots of the royal bratpack and policemen in attendance; Arab smilers in pale suits and snow-white shirts and polished toe-caps; minor British politicians and ex-diplomats terminally deformed by self-importance; Malaysian tycoons with their own cooks; Iraqi Jews with Greek palaces and companies in Taiwan; Germans with Eurobellies moaning about Ossies; hayseed lawyers from Wyoming wanting to do the best by *mah* clients and *mah*-self; retired, vastly rich investors gleaned from their dude plantations and twenty-million-dollar bungalows – wrecked old Texans on blue-veined legs of straw, in parrot shirts and jokey sunhats, sniffing oxygen from small inhalers; their women with chiselled faces they never had when they were young, and tucked stomachs and tucked bottoms, and artificial brightness in their unpouched eyes . . .
>
> After the Royal & Ancients came . . . the Necessary Evils, and these were the shiny-cheeked merchant bankers from London with eighties striped shirts and white collars and double-barrelled names and double chins and double-creased suits, who said 'ears' when they meant 'yes', and 'hice' when they meant 'house' and 'school' when they meant 'Eton' . . .[11]

Pitched against Roper is Jonathan Pine, 'the night manager' of the novel's title. At the beginning of the novel Pine is working for a smart Zurich hotel,* when Roper and his entourage arrive. A former soldier, without family or ties, Pine allows himself to be recruited by British intelligence in

* David has said that his model was the Dolder Grand, 'before it was developed and ruined'.

an operation against Roper. To entrap his victim Pine must first win his trust, going undercover at risk of his life. In the process he falls for Roper's much younger mistress, Jed.

The earliest surviving draft of the book is told in the first person by Pine, though subsequent versions are told in the third person. Nevertheless David seems to have awarded Pine aspects of his own story. 'You give the air of looking for someone,' a girlfriend tells him. 'But I think the missing person is yourself.'[12] Like David, Pine has undergone 'a locked-up childhood', one devoid of women: 'the friends and sisters of his youth he had never had, the mother he had never known, the woman he should never have married, and the woman he should have loved and not betrayed'.[13] Pine's memories of his youth seem to draw on David's own experiences:

> He relived his fear of everything: of the mockery when he lost and the envy when he won; of the parade ground and the games field and the boxing ring; of being caught when he stole something for comfort – a penknife, a photograph of someone's parents; of his fear of failure, which meant failing to ingratiate himself; of being late or early, too clean, not clean enough, too loud, too quiet, too subservient, too cheeky. He remembered learning to be brave as an alternative to cowardice. He remembered the day he struck back, and the day he struck first, as he taught himself to lead from weakness into strength.* He remembered his early women, no different from his later ones, each a bigger disillusionment than the last as he struggled to elevate them to the divine status of the woman he had never had.[14]

In a foreword to a reissue of the book, which appeared eight years after its original publication, David paired it with his later novel *Single & Single*, the story of a son, who for reasons of conscience, finds himself spying on his father. Although Pine is not Roper's son, writes David, 'he does come to look and feel like one, and Roper for his part assumes the father's role'. To most readers this is a surprising interpretation: the two men are enemies, and not obviously from a different generation. David characterises their relations as 'ambiguity, sexual rivalry and the submerged craving for one another's destruction' – though it is hard to see that Roper cares

* A favourite phrase of David's.

much about Pine one way or the other. The contest between the two of them, David writes, is a duel between 'a father figure and a son figure fighting over the same young girl'.[15] Perhaps this understanding of the book refers back to its original conception, before it was extensively rewritten. While the finished version of Roper is quite unlike David's own father, the early sketches of his character (sometimes known as Sir, and later as Mr, Archibald Duffy) are reminiscent of Ronnie: 'proletarian but senatorial . . . genial but menacing'. It is perhaps relevant that David had suspected Ronnie of trying to find an opening in the arms trade at the time of the Six Day War.

There is some evidence that the book was still more autobiographical in its original draft, which has not survived. In the summer of 1991 David stayed with his friend, the film studio executive John Calley, and his partner Sandy Lean (widow of the director David Lean), at Calley's thirty-five-room mansion on Fishers Island in Long Island Sound. Afterwards he wrote to thank them for their hospitality, and 'all the generous help with the book . . . for the faxes and maps and creative hints, the everything'. His letter suggests that he discussed the book in detail with his hosts:

> The book has everything to thank you for. Gone is the wimp factor & the self-flagellation; enter a Jonathan renewed and a new stable of characters, a new Baddie and much more zip. You midwifed a much better, stronger baby, which now cries healthily for attention. I'll contemplate my soul later, do the book now.[16]

In his research for the book, David consulted his friend and neighbour Anthony Sampson, who had written about the arms trade in his book *The Arms Bazaar* (1977). He wandered the halls of Miami gun fairs, chatting to healthy young saleswomen in short skirts and groomed young men in suits and ties. He flew to Panama to talk to semi-legitimate arms dealers. 'The thing you quickly learn about arms dealers is that they're always the good guys,' he wrote afterwards. 'The bad guys are somewhere totally else, and the good guys wouldn't touch them with a bargepole.' The arms trade in the Americas in the early 1990s was interlinked with the multi-million-dollar drug trade. David spent time with operatives of the US Drug Enforcement Administration, watching with them through one-way mirrors at Miami airport as they scrutinised passengers and baggage emerging from planes out of Bogotá. He lay in wait with them in disused airfields for drug shipments that failed to materialise.[17]

As always, David took enormous care with his prose, tirelessly rewriting until he was satisfied. Nicholas Shakespeare, who witnessed the process, was impressed by his capacity to go back to the start after writing more than 300 pages. Surviving drafts of typescript show that he produced at least sixteen different versions of the opening sentence of the book, one small indication of his diligence.

David had his usual difficulty in settling on a title for the novel. Among those he considered before settling on *The Night Manager* were 'A Woman of Cairo', 'The Junior Leader', 'The Unknown Soldier', 'The Underground Soldier', 'The Last Clean Englishman' and 'The Camel's Nose'. In a jokey fax to John Calley, David listed some variations on his eventual title, including 'Knight Manager', 'He Managed by Night' and 'One Flew over the Night Manager'.

In 1992 David became involved in what *Newsweek* described as 'a celebrity slugfest'. An item in the *New Yorker*'s 'Talk of the Town' column poking fun at his friend William Shawcross had offended him. The short piece, by the English journalist Francis Wheen, referred to Shawcross's biography of the newspaper proprietor Rupert Murdoch, published in Britain but not yet available in America. It suggested that in Shawcross Murdoch had found his 'Boswell', that Shawcross had become Murdoch's 'hagiographer', that he had been 'beguiled' by Murdoch, had been 'wooed and flattered and given every kind of assistance', and that in return he had produced 'a remarkably sympathetic' study of his subject. Wheen had already reviewed the British edition of the book in the September number of the *Literary Review*, where he had characterised Murdoch as a 'pornographer' who had made billions selling 'excrement' in his newspapers. The book was 'a long tedious chronicle', Wheen had commented, 'written in a species of American thrillerese which is as euphonious as a pneumatic drill'.

The *New Yorker* item had appeared in only the second issue edited by Tina Brown, who had recently replaced Bob Gottlieb. Her appointment had caused consternation among traditionalists, startled that someone whose experience had been entirely in lightweight glossy magazines should have been handed control of such a revered American institution.

In a faxed letter, David labelled the 'Talk of the Town' item 'one of the ugliest pieces of partisan journalism that I have witnessed in a long life of writing'. He deplored what he saw as a decline in the 'noble standards' of the venerable magazine. 'God protect *The New Yorker* from the English,' he thundered. David was enraged at Wheen's 'vulgarity' in dragging in the subject of Shawcross's 'lovelife', by referring to the fact that Shawcross had recently left his second wife for Olga Polizzi, daughter of the property tycoon Lord Forte. He argued that the new editor should have revealed that the book being mocked in the 'Talk of the Town' piece was critical of her husband Harold Evans, who had worked for Murdoch as editor of *The Times* before being sacked. Shawcross, who had once worked for Evans, had portrayed him as a bad manager and a capricious editor, sycophantically willing to do his master's bidding.

Tina Brown called this a 'sexist' accusation: 'the idea that I would bang the drum for my husband is silly'. She offered to publish David's letter of protest if he would condense it to a single paragraph, which she argued 'might pack a little more punch than sounding, as a couple of the editors here thought, like a choleric Colonel in Angmering-on-Sea'. In a further fax David refused to allow this. 'Within weeks of taking over *The New Yorker*, you have sent up a signal to say that you will import English standards of malice and English standards of inaccuracy,' he wrote. 'Mr Wheen's piece may be as trivial as the common cold, but my subject is the ethics of the great magazine of which you are now the editor.'

The spat was covered widely in the American press; a *Washington Post* story was headed 'The Tiff of the Town'. The *Boston Globe* quoted Ms Brown as saying, 'le Carré has somehow gone very choleric.' Asked by the *New York Times* if it was unusual to publish an item about a book not yet published in America, she said that the book had been the object of much talk in New York as in London. 'It was much discussed in the Hamptons this summer,' she told the *Times* reporter. For *Newsweek*, 'the flap at *The New Yorker* had all the dignity and relevance of a vice-presidential debate'.[18] It was one curiosity of this row that, with the exception of Murdoch, all the principals concerned – Wheen, Brown, Evans, Shawcross and David – were British.

David's defence of his friend was commendable, though perhaps he took the item too seriously; 'Talk of the Town' pieces were supposed to be humorous, whimsical or eccentric vignettes. To some observers it seemed incongruous that he should appear to be siding with those who defended Murdoch, generally regarded with horror by the British intelligentsia. But only a year before David had complained privately to Murdoch about an item in *The Times* (which had misleadingly suggested that he had demanded an extortionate copyright fee from a small Polish theatre company) and received a courteous response. In recompense Murdoch had bought him lunch, at the Savoy Grill (Ronnie's favourite).[19]*

As for Shawcross, he was best known for his book *Sideshow* (1979), about the bombing of Cambodia. Handsome and charismatic, he had once been regarded as 'a poster boy of the anti-Vietnamese war Left'.[20] In the 1970s he and his first wife, the writer Marina Warner, had made a glamorous couple in leftist London. But by the 1990s he was moving to the political right, just as David seemed to be moving left. In due course he would become one of the most vociferous British supporters of the Iraq invasion; the scourge of Nixon and Kissinger would become a cheerleader for George W. Bush and Dick Cheney. Wheen implied a connection between his rightward drift and his new girlfriend, a Conservative councillor and a friend of Mrs Thatcher's. 'Some say that Shawcross's turnabout is genetically programmed,' Wheen had written: 'his father, Sir Hartley Shawcross, was a socialist politician who veered off to the right in the 1950s and earned himself the nickname Sir Shortly Floorcross.'

From time to time aspiring biographers surfaced. In 1989, for example, the prolific Jeffrey Meyers recognised the potential in a life of le Carré, set to work with characteristic zeal and then responded ungraciously when his subject chose not to co-operate. A couple of years later David was

* Murdoch amazed David by asking him about Robert Maxwell. Only days before their lunch, the naked body of the publishing tycoon had been retrieved from the sea, after disappearing over the side of his yacht, the *Lady Ghislaine*, then cruising off the Canary Islands. 'Who do you think killed Maxwell?' Murdoch asked David quietly. David recalled this as 'a gorgeous moment: Rupert, the man of hard fact, imagining that I knew what had become of Maxwell!'

approached by Robert Harris, a journalist who wrote a weekly column for the *Sunday Times*. Though only in his mid-thirties, Harris had already written or co-authored five books, including an authoritative and highly entertaining account of the 'Hitler Diaries' affair, *Selling Hitler* (1986). 'I have long been an admirer of your work,' wrote Harris. 'Apart, perhaps, from Graham Greene, it seems to me that you are the only modern British writer who has tackled the big themes of our time and country – most notably, our position as a declining power, poised between the American and Soviet empires.'

David thanked Harris for his interest, but declined to collaborate, explaining that he didn't believe in 'authorised' biographies or 'authorised' critiques. He mentioned that 'half a dozen or so' studies of his work had already been published. 'I'm very leery of the critical process anyway, & prefer where I can to stay completely clear of it: even to the point of not reading what is written about me when I can avoid it, which is the case with all the books that have so far appeared,' he wrote. 'But of course I would not obstruct you or discourage you.' Harris was sufficiently heartened to persist.[21] Through his agent, Pat Kavanagh, he sold the book to his publisher, Hutchinson. Subsequently the biographer and his subject met by chance in a Fitzrovia restaurant, where Harris was dining with a friend, the writer and publisher Robert McCrum. At the time Harris's first novel *Fatherland* was at the top of the bestseller list. 'You must be on a roll,' the older man said in an avuncular way. Harris said that he still wanted to write the biography, and suggested meeting for a drink. 'A drink, yes,' said David, 'but not an interview.'

Towards the end of 1992 another journalist, Graham Lord, put himself forward. He had recently retired as literary editor of the *Sunday Express*, a post he had held for more than twenty years. In this capacity he had interviewed David back in 1971, and had been one of the few reviewers to write favourably about *The Naïve and Sentimental Lover*. 'For a couple of months afterwards there was a flicker of friendship between us,' claimed the Pooterish Lord, 'but the budding friendship foundered when I wrote unflattering reviews of two of his books.' He suspected that as a result he had been on le Carré's 'blacklist' for a while, 'but more recently we have maintained a wary truce'. After writing to David and receiving a not unfriendly response, Lord set out his credentials for prospective publishers in an outline entitled 'The Quest for le Carré'. He referred to his recent success with a biography of the hard-drinking journalist Jeffrey Bernard. Le Carré too was 'a ferocious drinker whose capacity for booze astonishes even other heavy drinkers', he revealed.

Lord showed a commendable critical distance from his subject. 'I admire some of his books but find several of them grossly overwritten and a touch pretentious,' he declared. Nevertheless he thought his biography certain to be 'a huge bestseller'. Among the 'many secrets' he promised to expose was 'le Carré's weird, three-in-a-bed, adulterous, semi-homosexual relationship with author James Kennaway and his wife Susan'. He had been in touch with Susan, and with Liz Tollinton, who had acted as an intermediary between Susan and David. 'A le Carré biography and I are made for each other,' he boasted.

Lord's agent, Giles Gordon, submitted the outline to nine publishers. The covering letter from Gordon stated that Harris had abandoned his plans to write a biography. 'This was, to say the least, disingenuous,' wrote *Private Eye*'s columnist 'Grovel'.[22] It was true that Harris had written to David, offering to drop the idea of a biography if that was what he wanted; but, far from accepting his offer, David had encouraged the scheme. Hutchinson issued a statement declaring that any publisher interested in Lord's biography should be aware that Harris fully intended to proceed with his. Kavanagh insisted that Gordon make this known to the publishers considering the proposal, some of whom consequently withdrew bids. Lord maintained that it had been a misunderstanding. 'Robert and I have talked about this, and sorted it out between us,' he told the *Bookseller*.[23] At least two publishers were undeterred. Little, Brown bought the book for a sum reported to be £75,000.

'I'd be very glad if they would both do something different,' David said when contacted by the press about the furore. He affirmed that he would provide no assistance to either writer. But then he added, 'I'd rather be written about by a winner than a loser.'[24]

Lord seemed surprised by the controversy, and belatedly alarmed. He wrote to David avowing goodwill towards him. Meanwhile a copy of his outline found its way into its subject's hands. One of the publishers to whom it had been submitted, Simon Master of Random House,* had telephoned Bruce Hunter to enquire about David's attitude to the biography and had subsequently sent him the proposal, in confidence. Hunter showed it to David, without revealing its source. After some deliberation, David decided to try and stop the book. 'I didn't want him gumshoeing around my children, my ex-mistresses, my everything,' he would say, years later.[25] He wrote to Susan Kennaway (now using her married name of Vereker), proposing a 'united front' against Lord – 'not to speak to him at all, not even to say one doesn't want to speak to him!'[26] His solicitors served a writ on Lord, alleging libel.[27] Not only was the outline defamatory of their client, it also appeared to defame his ex-wife, by suggesting that she, like Smiley's Ann, had been unfaithful, and as a result she too took legal advice. Nor was this the limit of Lord's woes; *Private Eye* reported that his solicitors had received a letter from solicitors acting for Susan Kennaway.[28] 'If your client relies on the novel *The Naïve and Sentimental Lover* by le Carré and/or *Some Gorgeous Accident* by James Kennaway as evidence,' their letter warned, 'you should remind him that these novels are works of *fiction*.'

Faced with such pressure, Lord backed down. He abandoned the biography, and signed a letter apologising for the false imputations in his outline and undertook not to repeat them. In a letter to the *Bookseller* he fulminated that a publisher had acted 'utterly shamefully and unprofessionally' by 'leaking' a copy of his outline. This had been a 'disgraceful breach of confidence, causing me to lose a legitimate book contract and costing me thousands in legal costs'.[29] (At one point Lord's solicitors threatened to sue David for spoiling his contract, but this was mere bluster.) Harris commented that Lord was 'incredibly stupid to pinch my idea without giving me a call, and incredibly stupid to circulate an outline that was libellous – just mad'.[30]

By the early 1990s Hodder & Stoughton was struggling to maintain its position. During the previous decade British publishing had

* Harris's publishers, Hutchinson, were part of Random House; it was perhaps incautious of Gordon to have submitted Lord's proposal to another publisher in the same group.

been transformed, from being an industry largely composed of small, family-run concerns to one controlled by vast international media conglomerates. Hodder faced relentless competition from well-financed groups such as Rupert Murdoch's brutally named HarperCollins. Its bestselling authors were lured away one after another. In 1993 the company accepted a buy-out by a smaller publisher, Headline, founded only seven years earlier by the dynamic Tim Hely Hutchinson, who became chief executive of the newly merged Hodder Headline PLC. The takeover took place just as *The Night Manager* was published. The book reached no. 1 in the UK hardback fiction bestseller list, but only briefly. It was unfortunate that Jeffrey Archer's first book for HarperCollins, *Honour among Thieves*, appeared almost simultaneously, and reportedly subscribed four times as many copies. The *Sunday Times* reviewed the two books alongside each other, with a cartoon showing the two bestselling authors as duellists. In fact both were outsold by Delia Smith's latest cookery collection.[31] David was irked by a succession of minor problems, which he felt had damaged sales. 'I cannot remember an unhappier publication,' he complained to Hely Hutchinson. 'I don't honestly know whether I can muster enough conviction for the future to remain with Hodder's.'[32]

Understandably Hely Hutchinson was keen that John le Carré should stay. 'He is indeed the jewel in Hodders' crown,' he wrote to Jane. For a while he dealt with David personally, before Roland Philipps, a capable and experienced editor, took over.[33]

With the support of a fresh promotion effort, *The Night Manager* re-entered the UK bestseller list in October, and sold strongly through the Christmas period. The Coronet paperback edition, published the following May, reached no. 2 in the UK bestseller list, selling almost 600,000 copies in the first three months, fewer than *The Russia House* (670,000), but more than *The Secret Pilgrim* (470,000).

The American hardcover of *The Night Manager* reached no. 3 in the *New York Times* bestseller list: a disappointment, given that the four previous John le Carré novels had all gone to no. 1. Knopf reported to the trade magazine *Publishers Weekly* 'a respectable in-print figure' of about 350,000 hardcover and one million softcover, but suggested that these figures fell short of the sales necessary to make the book profitable, given that it had been purchased for an advance of $5 million.[34]*

Perhaps predictably, many of the reviews of *The Night Manager* had addressed the question of what the future held for le Carré now that the Cold War had ended. 'John le Carré's marvellous new novel leaps free of Smiley's Circus entirely,' wrote Michael Ratcliffe in the *Observer*.[35] Julian Symons, reviewing the book for the *New York Times*, rated it more highly than its recent predecessors, 'a brilliant performance, executed with an exuberance, a richness of detail and a narrative drive that have been absent from Mr. le Carré's writing for a decade . . .' Nevertheless he thought it marred by an implausible conclusion, and a 'romanticism about women that leads to the creation of a pipe-dream fantasy rather than a character in Jed, Roper's mistress'.[36] Several other reviewers made the same criticism: Penny Perrick in the *Sunday Times*, for example, wrote that 'weaving unconvincingly through this otherwise formidably authentic account of wheeler-dealer weapon supply is a love story that Dame Barbara Cartland might find a trifle over the top . . .'[37]

Soon after the book was published David received an unexpected letter of appreciation, addressed to him as John le Carré. 'I just wanted you to know the pleasure you have given this retired Prez, the retired CIA guy,' wrote George H. W. Bush, who had been President of the United States, 1989–93, and Director of the CIA, 1976–7. In due course there would be another letter from Bush, thanking David for an advance copy of his next novel.[38]

In the *New York Review of Books*, David Remnick took the opportunity to review David's oeuvre. 'So much of the pleasure of le Carré's cold war novels lay in the way he created a shadow world that the reader imagined, somewhere, to exist,' he wrote. 'Now it has cruelly and suddenly disappeared. I can think of no other novelist associated with a specific atmosphere – not Faulkner, not Waugh – who ever had to deal with such complete and instantaneous obliteration.' In Remnick's reckoning *The Night Manager* was 'as taut a spy novel as one could hope for'. But it lacked some of the qualities that had made le Carré's novels of the Cold

* By comparison, Hodder had paid an advance of £525,000, against hardback royalties of 20 per cent and paperback royalties of 12½ per cent, in each case considerably higher than the norm.

War so fascinating: 'shading, ambiguity and doubt'. For Remnick, the warring parties in *The Night Manager* were, 'by le Carré's standards, stock figures'. Like other reviewers, he saw Jed as a caricature, albeit 'numbingly gorgeous'. At moments *The Night Manager* seemed to Remnick like a James Bond novel written by a superior Ian Fleming, 'a Goldfinger for grownups'.[39]

Remnick complained of being dazzled by the 'glittering locations' and 'establishing shots that speak too clearly of the screenplay to come'. They seem to have spoken to Sydney Pollack, who persuaded Paramount Pictures to buy film rights in the book and hired Robert Towne, best known for scripting *Chinatown*, to write the screenplay. But Pollack was notorious for falling in love with novels, getting the studio to buy them and then losing faith in the project: he had already done this with *A Small Town in Germany*, and now he did it again with *The Night Manager*, quoting Towne to the effect that there was no way to end the movie. To prove him wrong David wrote an ending to the story himself and sent it to Pollack for Towne's use. Subsequently the three men held brainstorming sessions in Los Angeles, but failed to reach a satisfactory outcome. 'We bought some sculpture and some pictures for Tregiffian after Paramount paid me a stupid amount of money for "The Night Manager" and then promptly ditched the project,' David told Alec Guinness in a letter afterwards.[40]

Before Pollack had become interested David had given first option on the film rights in *The Night Manager* to Stanley Kubrick, whom he had known since 1980. After some discussion Kubrick had passed, saying that he could not find a way to compress the plot into a two-hour movie 'without flattening everybody into gingerbread men'.[41] Ten years earlier he had passed on an opportunity to film *The Little Drummer Girl*. Kubrick, who was obsessed with guns, sent detailed technical notes to David about the weaponry used by Roper. 'Isn't he an *asshole*?' David scribbled on one of these before forwarding it by fax to their mutual friend, the studio boss John Calley.

It was Calley who had introduced David to Kubrick. At the time Kubrick had recently finished filming *The Shining*, which was due to be released a few weeks later. He invited David to a private screening at Shepperton Studios, followed by dinner at his Hertfordshire manor house

Childwickbury. Kubrick, who expressed great enthusiasm for David's work, talked about Arthur Schnitzler's novella *Dream Story*, which he had wanted to film ever since first reading it in 1968. Would David be interested in adapting it for the screen? After reading the book David spent a day with Kubrick outlining his ideas: he wanted to set the story in an inhibited, priest-ridden, walled city such as Wells and play upon the hypocrisies of a small community and its sexual obsessions. Kubrick listened and then politely declined; he had already decided to set the story in New York.

Later he tried to interest David in scripting a film based on research which suggested that a network of British agents operating in France during the Second World War had been betrayed as part of a massive deception operation. David didn't believe the story and didn't want to put his name to it. Then Kubrick wanted to make a film of *A Perfect Spy*; when David told him that the BBC proposed to adapt it as a series, he said, no problem, he would direct it for them. David passed this suggestion to Jonathan Powell, who 'had a fit': Kubrick was certain to go vastly over budget, he said, and would probably take seven years to make the series anyway.

Also present at the Childwickbury dinner had been Michael Herr, author of *Dispatches* (1977), described by David in a quote given to the publishers as 'the best book I have ever read on men and war in our time'. Herr was living in London at the time, and he and David had become friendly; David had suggested to Kubrick that he might join them. In due course Herr would collaborate with Kubrick on the script of his film *Full Metal Jacket* (1987), and Kubrick would try to interest him too in the Schnitzler novella. 'His idea for it in those days was always as a sex comedy,' Herr recalled, in a memoir of Kubrick. 'He'd talked about this book with a lot of people, David Cornwell and Diane Johnson* among them, and since then David & Diane and I later talked about it among ourselves.' But none of them was seriously tempted to adapt it for him.† 'Stanley was a terrible man to do business with, *terrible*.'[42]

* Diane Johnson had collaborated with Kubrick on the screenplay for *The Shining*.

† The Schnitzler novella formed the basis of Kubrick's last movie, *Eyes Wide Shut* (1999). The writer was Frederic Raphael, who wrote a rueful memoir of working with Kubrick (*Eyes Wide Open*, 1999).

In an interview with the journalist Zoë Heller,* David claimed to have read not a single English review of *The Night Manager*. 'I never do,' he said. 'I cannot make it sufficiently clear that I have never been part of that world. I don't know the people who review me, I don't go to their parties – I never will . . . I have the most profound contempt for the system – a total alienation from it.' In her profile of him, Heller referred to 'an aura of spikey dignity – of lonely honour and unassailable privacy' attached to his public image. 'His writing has occupied an uneasy position, at the very perimeter of literary respectability,' she suggested, citing Rushdie's jibe that 'le Carré wants to be taken seriously'. She attributed David's 'fabled spikiness' to his sensitivity to critical opinion. 'Le Carré affects not to be bugged by the literary caste system,' she wrote, quoting his statement that his novels were influenced by the German Romantics. 'They are for me a kind of *Bildungsroman*,' he told her. 'I don't really expect, on an intellectual level, to be understood here anyway.' He wrote for the average reader rather than the critics. In his experience, he said, his readers were 'a great deal more responsive, sensitive and understanding than the people who presume to speak for them'. When Heller took issue with his avowed populism, David insisted that the opinions of ordinary people were worth more than the 'corrupt' literati. 'If you move in those circles,' he told her, 'you trip over connections at every point. You feel – I always feel – that every time I've put one foot in front of the other in English life, I've made an enemy. I know the scale of the envy market. I know the way such minds work . . .'[43]

David told Zoë Heller that he did not compete for literary prizes. A profile in the *Sunday Times* deplored the fact that none of le Carré's novels had been nominated for the Booker Prize, 'though his best stories are indisputably superior to most Booker winners'.[44] This prompted a letter to the newspaper from Martin Neild, Hodder's managing director. 'The reason that his books have never been nominated is that author and publisher have always agreed not to submit them,' wrote Neild – omitting to mention that Booker Prize judges are entitled to 'call in' novels not submitted by the publishers if they think them worthy of consideration.

* Daughter of Caroline Carter, whom David had known and admired when they were both undergraduates at Oxford, though neither of them made the connection.

In a comment omitted from the abbreviated version of his letter published in the paper, Neild referred to 'John le Carré's determination to let his work be judged solely on its own merits, unhampered by personal relationships and prize aspirations'.[45]

The starting-point for David's next book would be a visit he made to Russia in 1993 with his son Nick, then just twenty and a Cambridge undergraduate.[46] Since his first visit in 1987 the country had undergone radical change: in those few years both the KGB and the Soviet Union itself had ceased to exist, after several of its constituent republics had declared themselves independent. David was curious to see how the rump of the Russian Federation was holding itself together, now that the ideological glue provided by the Party had come unstuck and the control exerted by the forces of state security had been relaxed. Several of the Islamic states of the North Caucasus were clamouring for autonomy; Chechenia, the most strident of them all, was demanding independence.

He arrived in Moscow with suitcases full of gifts: ballpoint pens, Harrods ties, American cigarettes and packets of tea, coffee, soap and toilet paper, all products hard to obtain in Russia the last time he was last there. But the country had changed beyond recognition in the previous six years. Where there had been scarcity, now there was excess: the shops were crammed with luxury goods, albeit priced far out of reach of ordinary citizens. The economy was in free fall, but the new rich were prospering. A line of Mercedes and Rolls-Royces waited outside GUM, the old state department store, while inside millionaire wives chose and chattered and left their chauffeurs to pay their bills in dollars. 'I began to feel more like a disenchanted Communist than a victorious westerner surveying the people he had notionally helped to free,' David wrote in an article about his visit.

He already had some useful contacts in Russia, including Mikhail Lyubimov, a retired KGB colonel with literary ambitions, a former head of the Residency in London, and Vladimir Stabnikov, at that time involved with Moscow PEN. He told them that he wanted to meet the bosses of the new Russian Mafia, former KGB men and cops – 'and not too many writers, thank you'. David found himself in a nightclub in the small hours of the morning, squatting on his knees before a huge bald man wearing pitch-black Ray-Ban sunglasses. This was Dima, chief of one of the Moscow area's most ferocious criminal gangs. While Nick gyrated on the dance floor with a beautiful Russian girl, David was forced to yell to make himself heard above the pounding music. Dima's minder Sergei, a former special forces man with a rearranged face and a shoulder-holster, had already asked him where he got his ideas from, and whether his father had been a writer before him. After extracting from Dima the detail that his rackets had made him worth in the region of $50 million, David was emboldened to ask, 'When are you going to start putting something back?' The interpreter relayed this rash question to Dima, before pausing for the gangster's reply. Then Dima began speaking, so softly that the interpreter had to lean close to his mouth to hear, and continued for a long time. When at last he was done, the interpreter appeared embarrassed as he searched for the right reply. 'I regret to tell you,' he said finally: 'Mr Dima says, "Fuck off".'

David was taken to meet the former KGB general Oleg Kalugin, at his opulent apartment in the Moscow hills. As a young KGB officer, Kalugin had served under cover in Washington, posing as a journalist and later as a press officer. He had been rapidly promoted to become the youngest general in the agency's history, and had risen to become head of foreign counter-intelligence (K Branch of the First Chief Directorate). 'My friend, you are welcome!' he said to David when they met. 'Listen, do you know I am your best fan?' David was persuaded to sign several of his books in Kalugin's collection. Over Scotch, pretzels and hors d'oeuvres, his host reminisced about his 'dear friend Kim'. He had been one of Philby's principal minders in Moscow. 'Kim was fine man,' he assured David. Kalugin went on to boast of his part in the murder of Georgi Markov, the Bulgarian émigré writer assassinated in London (with a poison pellet fired into his leg, via a gun disguised as an umbrella). David was repelled, but as a guest felt too embarrassed to do more than protest that he did not think Markov a good topic of conversation.*

Through Lyubimov David gained an introduction to the last chairman of the KGB. Vadim Bakatin had never heard of John le Carré, but after

* Kalugin disputed David's account of this interview (*New York Times*, 19 February and 2 April 1995). 'I was then and still am his fan,' insisted Kalugin, 'for few writers are so convincingly good in their description of the intricate world of espionage.' David wrote a robust riposte.

Kalugin had persuaded him to read *A Small Town in Germany*, he agreed to meet in the offices of David's Russian publishers. Bakatin was not a career spy; an engineer by profession, he had been a member of the Communist Party Central Committee and Minister of Internal Affairs before being appointed by Gorbachev to clean up the KGB. 'You know far more about spying than I do,' he suggested to David.

'But that's not true,' David replied, 'I really don't. I'm a novice too. I did the work for five minutes when I was young, nothing spectacular happened except that we discovered a clutch of KGB spies in our ranks and I got out. That was more than thirty years ago. I've been living off my wits ever since.'

'So it's a game,' said Bakatin, shaking his head. David asked him how he felt about the post-Communist era; not too good, Bakatin replied. He seemed to David a decent, honourable man, bewildered and indignant about what was happening to his country. Though he condemned the mistakes made by the Communist movement he remained loyal to the cause, still believing that 'we were the moral force for good in the world'.

'I believed in Communism then, and I believe in it now,' he said with dignity.

In place of the watchers who had followed him everywhere during his previous visit, David now had his own private bodyguard: Pusya, an all-Abkhazia wrestling champion broad enough to require two seats on an aeroplane, and so short that he seemed to skim the ground as he walked. As well as being immensely strong, Pusya was also a scholar and doctor of philosophy; while he escorted his British charges around Moscow he lectured them on the plight of Russia's Muslim minorities. This was a recurrent theme during David's stay in Russia: everywhere he went, it seemed, he encountered prejudice towards the Muslims of the Caucasus mountains, the 'black-arses', hounded and harassed when they were not being actively persecuted. One of those whom David interviewed was Issa Kostoyev, the policeman-turned-politician who had caught Andrei Chikatilo, supposedly the world's most prolific serial killer. Kostoyev came from Ingushetia, a tiny Muslim republic* within the Russian Federation

* Its population was then fewer than 300,000.

bordering Chechenia. He described his career within the police as a constant fight against Russian racism.

To David, it was self-evident that the oppression of the indigenous peoples of the Caucasus could be lifted only by freedom from Russian rule. 'Their recent history is so terrible,' David would write, 'and their cry for land and self-government so unanswerable, that even with the entire armoury of modern sophistry and news distortion to help us, it is hard to see another side to their argument.'[47] He felt bitterly that the West had failed in its duty to such peoples. One of the principles on which the Cold War had allegedly been contested was the right of self-determination for small nations, the liberation of the victim from the tyranny of the bully: this was for him 'a cornerstone of our anti-communism'.[48] But, now that the Cold War was over, Western politicians could safely abandon them to their fate.

His euphoria at the defeat of Communism had been shortlived. After his return from Russia he would argue that 'we have squandered the peace that we won with the end of the Cold War'. The struggle against Communism had provided some kind of vision, some sense of purpose, even if, as he would say, 'we distorted our own minds'. With its end, there was a desperate need for a 'new romantic dream', a crusade to unite the world in a common purpose, perhaps a new Marshall Plan or Peace Corps. He felt strongly that the West had failed to rise to the moment. He looked in vain for leadership from Western statesmen, and feared that this was 'a time of absolute moral failure by the West to perceive its own role in the future'.[49] His idealistic engagement with the West's cause during the Cold War made his disillusionment afterwards hard to bear.

David had found a subject for his next novel: the struggle of the Ingush for independence. In England he cultivated the company of expatriate Chechens and Ingushis, and established contact with the community of impassioned scholars 'who talked and breathed nothing but the North Caucasus'. Meanwhile he arranged to visit Ingushetia and Chechenia with Issa Kostoyev, travelling by rail from Moscow. Though they planned to take several bodyguards, Kostoyev advised David to bring a few pieces of gold or other valuables to satisfy the bandits who inevitably raided the train on the way down to the Caucasus. David obtained a visa, and in Penzance he bought a rucksack and a money belt in anticipation of his trip, and attempted to get fitter, so that he would not disgrace himself in the highest mountains in Europe. Only forty-eight hours before he was due to leave, however, Kostoyev telephoned to advise him that his visit had been deemed 'inappropriate' for the time being. 'The authorities would not be responsible for my safety, and wished me not to come until things had settled down,' David wrote afterwards. 'Which authorities, I never quite knew.'

Though David was obliged to write the novel without having seen Ingushetia, this would not be a significant obstacle, as most of the story is set in England, and the action moves to the Caucasus only at the very end. In the foreground is the unstable triangle of three English characters: the narrator Tim Cranmer, a prematurely retired officer of 'the Service'; his gorgeous young mistress, the waiflike Emma; and his former secret agent, Larry Pettifer.* Cranmer's repression is contrasted with Pettifer's exuberance: while Cranmer has retreated from the problems of the world into his Somerset manor house, Pettifer embraces the cause of the Ingush with Byronic zeal. The two men have known each other since their schooldays; though lifelong friends, they are also rivals for Emma, even enemies. Pettifer's goading of Cranmer is reminiscent of Shamus's mockery of Cassidy in *The Naïve and Sentimental Lover*. The novel explores themes of personal betrayal, the addictiveness and destructiveness of a life of deceit, and the responsibility that people must bear for their manipulation of others. Eventually, it is implied, Cranmer will take up the cause for which Pettifer has sacrificed his life.

A letter written while David was immersed in the book gives a sense of his engagement with the subject. 'If this is age, give me more of it,' David wrote to Sydney Pollack. 'I'm having a wonderful time writing, the calm and the anger are both nicely in place.'[50] He delivered the first draft to his publishers in September 1994. His provisional title was 'The Passion of his Time', picking up a remark made by Cranmer's superior Jake Merriman at his leaving interview. 'Done your job, Tim old boy,' drawls Merriman. 'Lived the passion of your time. Who can do more?'† Roland Philipps

* Physically Pettifer is a reincarnation of Jerry Westerby, with dangling forelock and 'disgraceful buckskin boots'.

† See page 478 for David's own use of this phrase.

suggested that this was not as instantly memorable as a title ideally should be. Among other titles David considered were 'The Road to Honeybrook Farm', 'A Man of the Caucasus' and 'The Free Servant'. They settled on *Our Game*, a reference to the special form of football played at Winchester,* the school where Cranmer and Pettifer had met; and perhaps to Bakatin's remark about spying being a game.

As so often in the past, his timing was fortuitous. When he turned in the first draft of the book, his American agent asked him in good faith whether Ingushetia was a made-up name or really existed. Two months later she had her answer. The simmering tension on Chechenia boiled over: Russian troops entered the republic and began laying siege to the capital under the gaze of television cameras. 'Le Carré continues to stay ahead of the news,' reported *Publishers Weekly*.

'Poor David needs friends,' Ann told Robin Cooke. At her suggestion, he wrote David an apologetic letter, though he remained unconvinced that he had done anything that required an apology. David replied by fax: 'don't give it another thought'. Despite this civil exchange, the friendship was not resumed.

David contributed an essay to a volume of tributes to Alec Guinness, published to mark the actor's eightieth birthday on 2 April 1994. Guinness was not grateful for his birthday present, indeed he was annoyed, though he did consider David's essay, entitled 'A Mission into Enemy Territory', 'remarkably perceptive' – so much so that he used it as a preface to a volume of his diaries published two years later.[51]

David's sixty-third birthday in October 1994 was celebrated in an upstairs private room at a restaurant in Hampstead, the Villa Bianca. The guest of honour was Strobe Talbott, now US Deputy Secretary of State in President Clinton's administration, with a special brief to manage the consequences of the break-up of the Soviet Union. Talbott brought along his Russian opposite number, Georgiy Mamedov, whom he knew to be a le Carré fan. Talbott's bodyguards sat at one table, the Russian bodyguards sat at another. Other bodyguards prowled the street.

* David consulted Nicholas Shakespeare, who had been at school there – as had his father John and Hugh Peppiatt, as well as David's brother Rupert.

Mamedov had been suspected of being a KGB spy when he had served in the Soviet Embassy in Washington during the 1970s. In the course of a toast David cited the evident camaraderie between the two senior diplomats, the Russian and the American, as evidence of why he had been obliged to look beyond the Cold War in seeking raw material for his novels.

A few years later Yevgeny Primakov, the Russian Foreign Minister and former head of the Russian intelligence service, would visit London as part of a Russian effort to warn against Nato expansion. The British Foreign Secretary, Malcolm Rifkind, presented him with a copy of *Smiley's People*, inscribed by the author. That evening David arrived in person at the Russian Ambassador's residence in Kensington Palace Gardens for a private dinner with Primakov, his Estonian wife and a handful of other Russian diplomats.[52]

A couple of months afterwards Talbott and his boss, the US Secretary of State Madeleine Albright, were guests of Primakov's at his apartment in Moscow. Over vodka and dumplings Primakov reminisced about his dealings with Donald Maclean, while serving as a KGB agent in Washington under journalistic cover. The conversation turned to espionage in fact and fiction. Primakov mentioned his dinner in London with David. His knowledge of David's plots and characters was evidently comprehensive, and he appreciated the way in which they had captured an era that he had known well. The Secretary of State asked him if he identified with Karla. 'No,' he replied; 'I identify with George Smiley.'[53]

22

'He makes us look so *good*'

In February 1995 David sent a pre-publication copy of *Our Game* to Stephen Fry, then taking part in warm-up performances of *Cell Mates*, about to open in the West End. Written and directed by Simon Gray, the play centred on the spy George Blake and his former cellmate Sean Bourke, who had helped him escape to Moscow after five years in prison. Fry had been cast as Blake and his fellow comedian, Rik Mayall, as Bourke. The pair had appeared together in a previous play of Gray's, *The Common Pursuit*, in 1988.

Our Game seems to have appealed to a strong strain of romantic nostalgia within Fry; for him, it was 'a Greenmantle* for the 90s'. In a letter thanking David he compared Larry Pettifer to the volunteers who had joined the International Brigades to fight in Spain:

> . . . Englishmen who wanted to *do* something. The fire has gone out and fanning the dead embers of Englishness may be regarded by some as fatuous. At least, however, at least there is one spark alive; the language and the 'culture' still contain enough to produce works like 'Our Game'. You are all we have left to be proud of – and your message is how ashamed we should be.

The two men had been in intermittent contact since 1991, when Fry had sent David a fan letter. 'Dear Mr. le Carré,' he had begun, 'I felt I simply had to write to you, after finishing, this morning at 3.00, *The Secret Pilgrim*. The English dam can withstand the pressure of fifteen years of

* In John Buchan's novel *Greenmantle* (1916), set during the First World War, his dashing hero Richard Hannay foils a German attempt to foment a general Islamic uprising that threatens turmoil throughout the Middle East, India and North Africa.

admiration and affection no longer and I have done the unthinkable and taken up my keyboard to pester you.' Fry praised *The Secret Pilgrim* as 'your most magnificent work to date', rivalling Flaubert. 'The only writer I've ever written to apart from yourself was P. G. Wodehouse, when I was twelve,' he revealed; 'I'm afraid, twenty years on, I've reverted to schoolboy gushing.' He claimed 'a small connection' in Simon Langton, the director of the television series of *Smiley's People*, who had directed the second series of *Jeeves and Wooster*, in which Fry played Jeeves and his friend Hugh Laurie played Wooster. 'Thank you for this novel and for all the novels that have gone before and, in advance, for all the novels that are to come,' he wrote in conclusion. 'England, for all its recent descent, is a much, much better place for having you in it, loving and despairing of it as you do.'

Two years later David sent Fry an inscribed copy of *The Night Manager*. 'It really is one of the most magnificent things you've ever done,' wrote Fry after reading it. 'That a story so international manages to say more about England than any novel I have read for years is an astounding achievement in itself.' Fry was very struck by the anger in the novel, 'the anger that you make the reader find in himself as well as (I assume) the fury in which you wrote'. He commented perceptively on David's writing:

> I have always thought that a greatly overlooked quality of yours is an observation one might call Nabokovian if one was being pompous (which one is), but which I think of more often by suggesting that if you hadn't been a writer you would have made a great stand-up comic. You just *notice* things better than anyone else. Not only vocal mannerisms, tricks of speech and phrasing, but also the (often sad) psychology of [a] character's gestures and gait . . . TNM is full of such moments of supreme character observation of which any actor or comic would be proud. Corkoran* alone is worth the entrance money . . . The *meetings*, as always, you do incomparably: the horse-trading, the committee atmospheres, the heartily second-hand metaphorical dialogue of the functionary. No one ever made more drama out of a smoke-filled room or a cabinet full of files.

* Corkoran is Roper's factotum, a jealous homosexual, suspicious of Pine from the outset.

By this time they were on first-name terms. Gratefully acknowledging 'your wonderful letter', David referred to Sydney Pollack's plan to film *The Night Manager*. 'For my money, I would ask you to play Corkoran tomorrow, but we are dealing with minds, if that is the word, that operate on other planes, so they will probably give it to Dicky Attenborough.' Later that year Fry sent David a proof copy of his second novel *The Hippopotamus*, 'laid at your feet with all respect, gratitude and admiration'. He emphasised that this was '*not* a request for a "quote" as publishers call them'. Towards the end of 1994 Fry and Laurie came to David's sixty-third birthday party at the Villa Bianca. 'I do hope we meet again soon,' Fry wrote afterwards.[1]

Fry's letter about *Our Game* was sent from a hotel in Osnabrück in northern Germany. He had fled England after walking out of *Cell Mates* only three days into its run. The production of *Cell Mates* would close a few weeks later; its producers were threatening to sue him for breach of contract. Fry's disappearance was a big news story, creating headlines day after day. There was intense press speculation about where he might be, and fears for his safety. It was reported at the time that he had suffered an attack of stage fright. Later he disclosed that he had been diagnosed as bipolar. 'I am quietly riding out the storm of flight from Britain,' explained Fry. 'Not sure I'll return for much longer than it takes to "settle my affairs". Perhaps I'll live on here in N. Saxony or Münsterland – it's as good a spot as any other, and like you, and unlike most Britons, I rather love the German language and land.' In a faxed letter David responded warmly to Fry's predicament:

> I know something about acquiring huge audiences I don't want, and about being spoken for by assholes, and about being good at everything, and never hitting the mark . . . I think you're a polymath, école Coward, with the same gravitas and the same rhythms of engagement, challenge and escape . . . I completely relate to your duck dive & it fascinates me that the German muse sang to you at that moment, and I am instinctively fond & protective of you . . . I escaped from Sherborne to Bern (at 16), dived into a monastery in an effort to escape marriage, escaped to the spooks, escaped the spooks to writing, nearly at times escaped writing for the ultimate escape, and now I'm 63 and who gives a fuck anyway?. . . Cornwall is my feeble substitute for exile.

He suggested meeting in Zurich in the middle of March. The Dolder Grand, he advised, was completely discreet. But he was willing to meet Fry anywhere in Europe; 'have suitcase, will travel', he wrote. 'PS: Fuck them all.'[2]

By the time he replied Fry had found a new refuge in the south of France, where he was staying under the alias 'Colin Melmoth', a nod to Oscar Wilde.* His chum Hugh Laurie was driving down by motorbike to keep him company for a few days. 'Your letter made me laugh, bounce and cheer,' he wrote to David by fax. 'I can't tell you how much it meant to me.' He revealed that he had returned briefly to England by private plane, to see his parents and meet his lawyers. The two men planned to spend a few days together walking in the forest around Zurich, but illness forced David to cancel his trip. 'Poor David, I hope he recovers soon,' Fry wrote in a fax to Jane. 'I may in fact be returning to England at the w/end,' he continued. 'A Daily Mirror photographer bagged me in Uzès yesterday and it's only a matter of time before they track me to this little retreat. I may as well be in England and in the horrid world of "prepared statements" as be hunted to a lonely lair in France.'[3] Fry returned to England and checked into a London hospital, where he was said to be receiving treatment for depression.

Our Game was published in America in April 1995, and in Britain at the beginning of May. Reviews in both countries were generally favourable, some very much so. 'It's an extraordinary novel,' enthused Michael Ratcliffe in the *Observer*. Sean O'Brien in the *Times Literary Supplement* rated it 'far superior' to *The Night Manager*, 'an absorbing and thought-provoking piece of work, a clear return to form'. Louis Menand, writing in the *New York Review of Books*, was not the only reviewer to detect allusions to *Heart of Darkness* and *Lord Jim*: 'the Conradian undertone is hard to miss'.[4]

John Updike, on the other hand, heard echoes of Kipling, Rider Haggard and A. E. W. Mason. *Our Game* took him back 'to Victorian

* Wilde had used the alias 'Sebastian Melmoth' after his discharge from Reading Gaol. *Melmoth the Wanderer* (1820) is the title of a Gothic novel by Wilde's great-uncle Charles Maturin, in which John Melmoth sells his soul to the devil in exchange for prolonging his life for an extra 150 years.

times, when the great multicoloured globe existed as a vast playing field on which truehearted Englishmen could chase their personal rainbows while the picturesque heathen cheered'. Updike bracketed le Carré with Tom Clancy, Robert Ludlum and Frederick Forsyth, as authors of Cold War thrillers read on aeroplanes by men in business suits – 'rather, in business trousers, with their jackets nicely folded in the overhead rack and their neckties loosened away from their shirt collars an artful inch'. His review, which appeared in the *New Yorker*, was both witty and malicious. 'Le Carré's prose has an overheated expertise about it,' wrote Updike, 'as if it wished to be doing something other than spinning a thriller.'[5] David believed that Tina Brown had orchestrated a wounding review 'as a punishment for making a public fool of her'.[6]

Updike was one of several reviewers to observe that the psychological tension in the novel derives from the uneasy relations between Cranmer and Pettifer. The reader gains a vivid sense of the two men's contrasting characters, while the woman in the triangle remains a remote figure. David's depiction of women has often been criticised. 'Le Carré's women consist of physical attributes but not much else,' wrote Richard Boston, in a typical comment. Perhaps it would be more accurate to say that they are objects of desire, invariably beautiful and almost always unattainable. If many of le Carré's women are viewed from afar, that is how his men see them. If Emma is enigmatic, that is because she seems so to Cranmer, the novel's narrator – as Camilla does to Guillam, or Ann to Smiley. Such incomprehension is perhaps regrettable, but it is surely credible. The women in le Carré's novels are more complex and convincing than the 'love interest' of the James Bond novels, and more substantial than the female characters (such as they exist at all) in most of the airport fiction mocked by Updike. The character of Roper's mistress, Jed, is all too believable. She is shallow, naïve and infuriating: like Lizzie Worthington, a rich man's plaything. It may be deplorable that men should be attracted to such women – but it is surely unrealistic to deny that they are.

In a piece published in 1999, the novelist Diane Johnson would comment on the fact that le Carré's heroes seldom have satisfactory relations with women. 'Le Carré's women are faithless, restless, complicated, and kept, the men mistrustful and always forlornly adoring of some unworthy woman who has gone off with another male, like a cat.'[7]

The British edition of *Our Game* would be a milestone, as the first mainstream novel to be published in hardback outside the terms of the Net Book Agreement (NBA). For almost a century this pact between publishers and booksellers had ensured that British books were sold at fixed prices. It had been established to allow the largest possible number of dedicated booksellers to stock a wide range of titles, safe in the knowledge that they could not be undercut by predatory retailers selling only bestsellers at a discount. Its detractors argued that this was an old-fashioned, paternalistic measure that kept prices artificially high and depressed sales.

By the 1990s the NBA was coming under pressure. Several retailers had started selling paperbacks at discounted prices, under the flimsy pretence that they were damaged copies. One publishing group, Reed Books, withdrew from the Agreement in 1992; and two years later Hodder Headline did the same. 'The NBA is crumbling around the booksellers and publishers,' Tim Hely Hutchinson told the *Independent*. 'If people feel they are just performing a King Canute act they will give up.'[8] But there was strong resistance within the book trade, particularly from booksellers, who feared losing business to supermarkets and other mass retailers. Some made disdainful references to books being sold alongside tins of beans. The *Bookseller*, 'The Organ of the Book Trade', led the defence of the NBA.

Hely Hutchinson had decided to use *Our Game* as a trailblazer for his new policy. Le Carré's unusual status, as an author whose writing appealed to every segment of the market, made his novel ideal for such a trial. Hodder Headline set a target of 200,000 sales – a big increase on the 130,000 sold of *The Night Manager*, and more than double the quantity Hodder had expected to sell of a le Carré in the 1970s and 1980s. In April 1995, a month before the book's UK publication, the *Bookseller* ran a story claiming that booksellers were cutting their orders for the novel. W. H. Smith's fiction buyer announced that he would be ordering only 1,500 copies of 'the new le Carré', far fewer than his usual order of 5,000.[9] In contrast, the bookselling chain Dillons doubled their usual order for a le Carré novel, and proposed to sell the new book at £12.99, a substantial discount on the recommended retail price of £16.99. The supermarket chain Asda discounted the book further, to £8.49. 'I can't really see the point of backing a book that will be sold more cheaply by other groups,' the Smiths buyer was quoted as saying. 'As for le Carré himself, I wonder what he thinks about being treated as a mass-market author, being sold in supermarkets and service stations? Not a lot, I should think.'

'Actually,' countered Hely Hutchinson, 'the author would like as many people as possible to read his stories. He is very keen to reach beyond a literary or a committed book-buying elite in order to embrace a new readership. He is supporting everything we do.'

David was irritated to be 'dragged into this battle'. He fired off a fax to Hely Hutchinson, in which he took strong exception to the way in which he had been spoken for. 'You really did not have my authority to say that you have my blanket support, nor to represent my views.'[10] Nevertheless he would be delighted by the book's sales. Asda sold a thousand on its first day. The book rocketed straight to the top of the UK bestseller list, fuelled by aggressive marketing and widespread review coverage. Three weeks after publication David congratulated Hodder's managing director, Martin Neild, 'on a splendid sales performance'.[11]* The eventual number of sales of the Hodder hardback edition would be half as many again as for *The Night Manager*. In the US *Our Game* reached no. 2 on the bestseller list, kept from the top spot by a hugely popular piece of hokum called *The Celestine Prophecy*.

'We left the net book agreement because we wanted to expand sales across the industry and bring a greater sense of excitement to the book market,' said Hely Hutchinson. 'There is no doubt that this initiative will bring le Carré to a wider market than ever before and will set the agenda for the future expansion of books.'[12] When two more large publishing groups withdrew from the NBA in the autumn, the Agreement was effectively dead. David was invited to make a speech at the annual Booksellers' Association conference, held in the Stationers' Hall in London. It was the year of the BA's centenary, so it was a special occasion. Unfortunately the circumstances were not ideal for an after-dinner speech: listeners were

* Hodder Headline paid an advance of £550,000; by 31 March 1996 all but £40,000 of this had been earned.

distracted by the clatter of plates being cleared and the hubbub as people left the table to stretch their legs.

The brouhaha surrounding the book's publication helped make *Our Game* a success, stimulating stories on the financial as well as the literary pages. A piece in the *Observer* was accompanied by a photograph of the book nestling among groceries in an Asda supermarket trolley.[13] A bookshop in Milton Keynes issued a statement that it would continue to sell the book at full price, but offered customers a free can of beans with every copy purchased.[14]

Francis Ford Coppola showed interest in adapting *Our Game* for the big screen, and invited David to come and stay several days at his Napa Valley ranch, to discuss the matter. Back in the late 1970s Coppola had been interested in filming *The Naïve and Sentimental Lover*, but the discussions had come to nothing, as so often happens in the movie business. During his four or five days with Coppola, David was sufficiently enthused to write a screenplay. The intention was that Harrison Ford would star, but he withdrew, perhaps realising that to portray an introverted Englishman was beyond his powers. Coppola would not commit to directing it himself, though he continued to toy with the project. He wanted David to go back and rework the script with him, but David saw little point in doing so until a director was aboard. Besides, he was now deep in another novel.

In his letter to Martin Neild, David had mentioned that he had been out of the country at the time of publication, travelling in California and Panama, and thus had been able to avoid the NBA controversy. 'Mercifully a new novel has taken me over, and I barely lift my head,' he wrote.

David's visit to Panama while researching the arms industry for *The Night Manager* had made him 'determined' to set a story there.[15] Panama was effectively an American creation: a nation that had come into being solely in order to allow its powerful neighbour to implement a grand engineering project, a canal linking the Atlantic to the Pacific. By supporting the rebels who had founded Panama at the beginning of the twentieth century as a breakaway from Colombia, the United States had gained sovereignty over the so-called 'Canal Zone', despite the fact that this strip of territory had cut the new nation in two. Under the terms of a treaty made in 1977 the Zone was due to revert to full Panamanian control on 31 December 1999, though this outcome remained uncertain as the country was bedevilled by corruption, political instability, coups and uprisings. In 1989 an American invasion, Operation Just Cause, had ousted the government of President Manuel Noriega. 'They got rid of Ali Baba but they forgot the forty thieves,' ran a popular joke in Panama.

David was drawn by the prospect of a tiny, much colonised country asserting its independence. He was intrigued by Panama as 'a microcosm of the United States' colonial experience' – a colony of the great nation that was not supposed to have colonies – and was particularly fascinated by the peculiar community of 'Zonians', 'the mostly American employees of the canal company who, unable to own property in the Zone, had reverted to a kind of watered-down Christian Communism dating from the 1920s'. He was struck by the fact that Panama's contribution to the great anti-Communist crusade had died at the very moment when American colonial tenure in Panama was coming to an end. Above all, he was drawn to the canal: as a power symbol, as an item of colonial nostalgia, and as a geopolitical wild card at the end of the twentieth century. As the deadline for ending American control of the Zone approached, other powers were said to be lobbying for influence, particularly the Japanese. David envisaged that Western spies would take a close interest in such developments.[16] He imagined an agent with access to some of the most important people in Panama – a hairdresser, perhaps, whose upmarket clientele would be attracted by his proficiency and flair. He pursued the story for some months, but the character remained elusive.

Then John Calley, in London on a visit from Hollywood, insisted that the two of them should drop in on Doug Hayward, known as the 'tailor to the stars', who specialised in making suits for showbiz customers. Hayward turned out to be an amusing personality, whose effortless charm was said to have inspired Michael Caine in creating the role of Alfie. He aimed to make his customers feel comfortable. 'You've got to make them feel good before you can make them look good,' he would say. His Mount Street premises were reminiscent of a relaxed gentlemen's club, with a cosy old sofa, and a low table strewn with books and magazines. Callers could expect a chat and a glass of champagne or a cup of tea, without any pressure to buy.

It was this chance encounter which inspired David to contemplate a tailor as the protagonist of a novel. He noticed the discreet atmosphere, which encouraged customers' confidences. It occurred to him that a tailor with well-placed customers could be a valuable agent, especially in a hothouse of rumour like Panama. Though Harry Pendel, the character he created, was nothing like Hayward, he shared some of the same origins. David acknowledged that Hayward had allowed him 'his first misty glimpse of Harry Pendel the tailor'. Hayward had almost entirely shed his cockney accent, but he remained proud of his working-class roots. 'If you close your eyes one quiet summer's evening in his shop, you may just hear the distant echo of Harry Pendel's voice extolling the virtues of alpaca cloth or buttons made of tagua nut.'

He imagined Harry Pendel as half Jewish, half Irish, a former East End boy with a prison record who has found what seems to be a safe berth as a high-class tailor in Panama. Married to a beautiful Zonian and blessed with children, he is outwardly content. But, unknown to his wife, his success is illusory: he has mortgaged his business to meet the debts from the struggling rice farm on which he has squandered her inheritance. Pendel is a self-made man in the fullest sense; he has invented himself just as he invents others. His business, Pendel & Braithwaite, formerly of Savile Row, is based on a fantasy; Arthur Braithwaite never existed, nor had Harry Pendel ever worked in Savile Row. He is a fabricator, both literally and metaphorically. Pendel was already playing a part before his controller, the unscrupulous Old Etonian Andrew Osnard, walked into his shop and tempted him to dissemble further.

David saw how a tailor, like a novelist, could be a fabulist. He depicted Pendel as an impersonator, imagining himself in his customer's clothes and becoming that person. Pendel went further still, seeing himself as the creator of character, both in dressing his clients and in imagining worlds for them. He even had a neologism for it – 'fluence'.

> It was tailoring. It was improving on people. It was cutting and shaping people until they became understandable members of his internal universe. It was

> fluence. It was running ahead of events and waiting for them to catch up. It was making people bigger or smaller according to whether they enhanced or threatened his existence . . . It was a system of survival that Pendel had developed in prison and perfected in marriage, and its purpose was to provide a hostile world with whatever made it feel at ease with itself.[17]

David continued tinkering with the text until the last moment, removing a total of fifteen pages at proof stage, all in small chunks (the British edition went through four stages of proof).[18] The result was a book that he would rate as one of his best – together with *The Spy who Came in from the Cold*, *Tinker, Tailor, Soldier, Spy* and *The Constant Gardener* – though not, perhaps surprisingly, *A Perfect Spy*.[19]

Though it stands on its own, *The Tailor of Panama* is an obvious tribute to Graham Greene, the writer with whom John le Carré has most often been compared.* In the 1980s David had re-read Greene's *Our Man in Havana*, which he found even more enjoyable on the second reading. The notion of an intelligence fabricator would not let me alone,' David wrote in his acknowledgements. Like Greene's Wormold, Pendel would cook up intelligence for his controller, to feed the appetites of his greedy masters back in London. Like *Our Man in Havana*, *The Tailor of Panama* is a black comedy, a satire set in a chaotic environment where no story seems too fantastic, no conspiracy too far fetched, and where the separation between tragedy and farce is paper thin.

The Tailor of Panama was published in the UK on 14 October 1996. Three weeks after publication it had reached no. 3 in the *Sunday Times* bestseller list, and remained in the top ten into January. By this time actual sales of the British edition had overtaken those of *Our Game*, reaching over 110,000. Knopf published simultaneously, with an advertised first print run of 300,000 copies. Perhaps American readers did not share David's distaste for American meddling in their own back yard; or perhaps they were disconcerted by a comic le Carré, which was seen as something new for him – though David himself sees a comic thread running through his fiction, which he believes has gone largely unrecognised. Whatever the reason, American sales of

* In 1999 David declined a request to write a brief introduction to a reissue of Greene's *The Honorary Consul*.

The Tailor of Panama were disappointing by comparison with its predecessors; it reached no higher than no. 7 in the *New York Times* bestseller list, and by Christmas had dropped off the list altogether.

There was a bizarre postscript to the publication of *The Tailor of Panama*. A letter arrived at Hodder Headline from a man called Sior Pendle, saying that he was the son of the late George Pendle, a director of Pendle & Rivett, cloth merchants to Savile Row. It seemed that Pendle Senior had lived in Paraguay, where he had been on close terms with ministers in the Paraguayan government and other leading personalities; and further, that he had been recruited to act as an agent for SIS by an Old Etonian, Eugen Millington-Drake. His wife had been born in Argentina, where she had inherited a share in a struggling family ranch.

'This book is clearly based on part of my father's life,' wrote Sior Pendle. He wondered who had been given access to his father's Foreign Office file. He and his family felt that it was 'very unfortunate' that they had not been consulted about this book in advance, because, 'in spite of the very many exact parallels', his father had never served a term in prison. They had always sought the utmost discretion regarding his activities, he wrote, and asked for a 'full and immediate' explanation.

David's first thought was that this must be some kind of hoax. He replied to Pendle expressing his astonishment. 'I am appalled by the string of similarities you recite in your letter,' he wrote. 'Nothing so strange has happened to me for a long while.'

> I sincerely ask you to accept that . . . I never heard of your father, never knew of him or anyone like him, and that Harry Pendel (named after the German Pendel meaning pendulum) is entirely a creature of my own imagination . . . People often claim to recognise themselves (always wrongly) & some hope for money, in vain. That's par for the course if you're a well-known writer. But if matters are as you describe, I can only share your distress and offer you abject apologies for being its unwitting cause.[20]

Sior Pendle took the matter no further.

The film of *The Tailor of Panama*, released in 2001, is inexplicably poor. Co-written by the experienced TV screenwriter Andrew Davies, the director John Boorman and David himself, and filmed partly on location in Panama, it stars Geoffrey Rush as Pendel,* Jamie Lee Curtis as Pendel's wife Louisa, and Pierce Brosnan as Osnard. Harold Pinter appears in a cameo role as the ghost of Pendel's Uncle Benny, and Daniel Radcliffe makes his screen debut as one of Pendel's children. With such a strong team it is hard to explain why the result should have been so disappointing. Perhaps it just goes to show how difficult it is to hit the right note with black comedy.

John Boorman, the gentlemanly director of such films as *Point Blank*, *Deliverance* and *Hope and Glory*, had stepped into the role after Tony Scott, a more rumbustious personality, had withdrawn, but not before he had accompanied David, with several helpers, on a riotous scouting trip to Panama, funded by Columbia Pictures at colossal expense. They flew from California to Panama by private plane, equipped with a very expensive satellite phone which they were never able to work, and kept the plane with them in Panama while they reconnoitred, exploring in limos and helicopters and staying in the best hotel in town. At night, Scott went about his own explorations of Panama City's hotspots; David didn't go with him, though he enjoyed his ebullient, wayward company hugely. Scott never wore anything but frayed denim shorts, with a bottle of Tabasco in the pocket. He did not like to read, so one of his helpers either read to him or described to him passages from David's novel. Soon after they returned, Scott had apparently put in a budget that was far too high for the studio's taste, and they had engaged John Boorman instead.

Brosnan was then the incumbent James Bond. He introduces himself with 'The name's Osnard,' an echo of Bond's opening line. There is another knowing reference to the Bond persona when Pendel is measuring up Osnard for a suit, and Osnard selects a cloth. 'I thought you'd like that one, sir,' says Pendel. 'Mr Connery's choice. Matter of fact, when you came in I thought, "Who does he remind me of?" And that's it. In the build, too. Golfer's shoulders.'

In the *New York Times Book Review*, the novelist Norman Rush praised *The Tailor of Panama* as a 'tour de force', though he found the American characters 'rather sketchily delineated', which he thought might be ascribed to

* Kevin Kline was originally cast to play Pendel, but withdrew because he did not want to spend so long on location in Panama.

'Mr. le Carré's famous ambivalence towards Americanity'. For Rush, a more substantial defect lay in a troubling aspect of Pendel's character: 'here we have, however little Mr le Carré intended it, yet another literary avatar of Judas'. The detail of Pendel's background added to his unease. 'As you read, the phrase "rootless cosmopolitans" scratches at the doors of your mind.'[21]

Rush's review caused dismay at Knopf. The suggestion of anti-Semitism, in America's greatest newspaper, was extremely damaging. After several anguished telephone conversations, David went into his publishers' offices to discuss how he should respond. 'The atmosphere was of near catastrophe and collective funk,' David would write later. He was 'deeply wounded' by what he saw as a 'smear'; he wanted to react strongly by writing a letter of protest to the *New York Times*, but as he offered one text after another for collective consideration, he discovered that he was only compounding his offence: 'David, if you write that, your career in the United States will be ruined'; 'David, are you trying to tell us that this city is full of Jews?'; 'David, are you suggesting that the *New York Times* is Jewish-controlled?' A further complication was that Rush, a past winner of a National Book Award, was himself a Knopf author.

Later, David would write that he very much regretted moderating his response, to calm the 'tumult of alarm' raging within his publishers. If so, his instinct must have been to write a very strong letter indeed, because his published response was certainly robust. It was obvious that he resented 'the attempt to tar me with the anti-Semitic brush'. David made a case for Harry Pendel as 'the most lovable character I have created'. In conclusion, David wrote that 'Mr Rush has reviewed not a book but a mirage. He has attributed to me a premise that derives from his poor head, not mine.'

Rush's reply was printed below David's letter. He denied that he had either said or implied 'that Mr. le Carré is an anti-Semite, and I do not think it'. Nevertheless, he insisted, 'Pendel–Judas parallels, however inadvertent, are inescapable.'

David was unwilling to leave it at that, and another letter of his appeared in a subsequent issue of the *New York Times*. He was delighted, he wrote, to learn from Norman Rush's reply:

> that he doesn't think I'm an anti-Semite, because he could have fooled me. Not one of the whole army of literary agents, editors, publishers and friends

who commented on my novel 'The Tailor of Panama' on its way to publication expressed a whisper of discomfort about my treatment of Pendel's Jewishness. No other reviewer in Britain or America has referred to it.

As to your own wisdom in giving currency to such non-accusations, I trust your readers will form their own opinion. Mine is unprintable.[22]

In an interview with George Plimpton of the *Paris Review*, conducted in front of an audience while David was still in New York promoting *The Tailor of Panama*, he was asked about the charge of anti-Semitism. 'I have had some pretty big tomatoes thrown at me in my time, but this one missed,' he told Plimpton. 'All my life . . . I have been fascinated, enchanted, drawn to and horrified by the plight of middle European Jews . . . It is the one issue in my own life on which I may say I have a clean record.'[23] An article in the Israeli daily newspaper *Ha'aretz* dismissed the accusation of anti-Semitism in *The Tailor of Panama* as 'rubbish'.[24]

After the publication of *The Spy who Came in from the Cold* David had been been ostracised or at least mistrusted by many of his former colleagues in MI5, and especially in MI6. There was a prevalent sense that he had let the side down, disloyally depicting British intelligence as unscrupulous or, worse, incompetent. In recent years there had been signs of a change of attitude, culminating in an invitation to lunch at MI6 with the reigning 'C'.

David Spedding (Sir David Spedding since 1996) was a generation younger than David, and had not joined the Service until 1967, some years after David had left. Like David, he had been educated at Sherborne and then at Oxford; after serving mostly in the Middle East he had been appointed Chief of the Secret Intelligence Service in 1994. As an intelligence officer he had earned a reputation as dedicated, methodical and hard working. 'Chiefs of secret services are generally portrayed in books and on screen as devious, callous and calculating,' wrote one of his subordinates, thinking perhaps of Control: 'David [Spedding] was quite properly the latter in professional matters, but in person he was cheerful, decisive, gregarious and straightforward, well liked and rightly trusted.' As Chief, Spedding had overseen the Service's move to an expensive new building in Vauxhall, on the south bank of the Thames, criticised by some as ostentatious. In

1998 he would invite Dame Judi Dench to MI6's Christmas lunch, after the actress, who had played 'M' in recent Bond movies, expressed interest in learning more about her real-life counterpart.[25]

'We want to thank you for what you have done for our image,' Spedding told David when they met. Taken as a whole, David's oeuvre had portrayed British intelligence as highly effective in the Cold War – arguably, as much more effective than it had been in reality. George Smiley could scarcely have been more different from James Bond, but he had been equally successful in countering the Soviet threat. In the Cold War, perception was all, and Spedding recognised the significance of popular culture in shaping public perception of British intelligence, abroad as well as at home. Bestselling fiction was therefore an extension of 'soft power'. Spedding's predecessor Sir Colin McColl told a friend that 'the Firm likes the le Carré stuff, because it makes us look so *good*'. David's invitation to lunch with the Chief marked his welcome back in from the cold.

Spedding retired early when he was diagnosed with lung cancer, and died in 2001, at the age of only fifty-eight. After his retirement he had brought his family to Tregiffian for a day. He told David that he admired him most for escaping from Sherborne at an early age, a thing that he wished he had done himself. In a conversation about the changed realities of spying, Spedding said, 'You can't imagine how disgusting our world has become.'[26]

In 1997 David was invited to speak at the annual dinner of the Anglo-Israel Association. It was suggested, perhaps mischievously, that he might care to say something about 'the oversensitivity of the Jews of the diaspora'. David took the opportunity to examine 'the mystery of what I may call my Jewish conscience', tracing his experience of Jewish people from childhood, and the portrayal of Jews in his work. Norman Rush's review of *The Tailor of Panama* formed his starting-point. The implied charge of anti-Semitism, he said, 'hurt me more deeply than any other brickbat that has been tossed my way in forty-odd years before the literary mast'. As someone who felt himself to be 'an outsider in his own country', David claimed 'a spiritual kinship' with Jews, 'that embraces what is creative in me, and forgives what is despicable, and shares with me the dignity and solitude and anger that are born of alienation'. In his conclusion, David hit back at 'the whole oppressive weight of political correctness, a form of modern McCarthyism in reverse'. He insisted on his right, as a non-Jew but as a convinced supporter of the nation state of Israel, to condemn Israeli actions without being branded an anti-Semite. He vigorously asserted his right to depict Jewish characters in his novels with as many flaws as any other. His talk was a plea for tolerance and openness, with respect but without inhibition. His closing exhortation encapsulated his message: 'Take me back to Israel, where people are free to speak their minds!'

When an extract from this talk appeared in the *Guardian*, Salman Rushdie could not resist the opportunity to snipe at him. 'John le Carré complains that he has been branded an anti-Semite as a result of a politically correct witch-hunt and declares himself innocent of the charge,' wrote Rushdie, in a letter published in the newspaper. 'It would be easier to sympathize with him had he not been so ready to join in an earlier campaign of vilification against a fellow writer.'

Though eight years had passed since David had urged that the paperback edition of *The Satanic Verses* be postponed, it seems that Salman Rushdie was still smarting from his criticisms. His letter was the opening discharge in an increasingly vituperative exchange between the two novelists on the letters page of the *Guardian*.

David was shocked by Rushdie's charge that he had 'eagerly, and rather pompously, joined forces with my assailants', and was sufficiently upset to ask a lawyer whether this phrase was not defamatory, but was advised not to pursue the matter. Instead he retaliated with a letter of his own. 'Rushdie's way with the truth is as self-serving as ever,' he wrote, in a letter published two days later. He denied joining Rushdie's assailants. 'My position was that there is no law in life or nature that says great religions may be insulted with impunity.' He reiterated his belief that by the time of his letter anyone who wanted to read the book had been able to do so. 'When it came to the further exploitation of Rushdie's work in paperback form, I was more concerned about the girl at Penguin Books who might get her hands blown off in the mailroom than I was about Rushdie's royalties,' he continued. 'My purpose was not to justify the persecution of Rushdie, which, like any decent person, I deplore, but to sound a less arrogant, less colonialist, and less self-righteous note than we were hearing from the safety of his admirers' camp.'

The tone of the letters rapidly deteriorated. 'I'm grateful to John le Carré for refreshing all our memories about exactly how pompous an ass he can be,' Rushdie wrote in a letter published the following day. 'We have the freedoms we fight for, and we lose those we don't defend. I'd always thought George Smiley knew that. His creator appears to have forgotten.'

On the same day Christopher Hitchens leaped into the fray with a characteristically colourful contribution to the debate, comparing le Carré's conduct to 'a man who, having relieved himself in his own hat, makes haste to clamp the brimming chapeau on his head'.

This had become a slanging match, played out in public. In response, David referred to 'the cockeyed logic of these two fairly vile letters'. He expressed doubt that the friendship between his two opponents would last: 'I am amazed that Hitchens has put up with Rushdie's self-canonization for so long.'* He claimed back Smiley to his cause. 'Smiley, if he stood for anything, stood for tolerance, compassion, humility, self-doubt and respect for the beliefs of others,' he wrote. 'Above all, he was a man of compromise. Rushdie and Hitchens would do well to brush up on him.'

Yet another letter from Rushdie appeared on the *Guardian*'s letters page the next day. By now, any pretence at civility had been dropped. 'If he wants to win an argument,' began Rushdie, 'John le Carré could begin by learning how to read.' He used the same metaphor as Hitchens had done, but to less comic effect. 'It's true I did call him a pompous ass, which I thought pretty mild in the circumstances. "Ignorant" and "semi-literate" are dunces' caps he has skilfully fitted on his own head. I wouldn't dream of removing them.' He referred sneeringly to 'our Hampstead hero', and affected to welcome criticism from le Carré. 'Every time he opens his mouth, he digs himself into a deeper hole. Keep digging, John, keep digging. Me, I'm going back to work.'[27]

The press relished the dispute, giving it extensive coverage. 'Writers' Eight-Year Feud Erupts' read a headline in the *Sunday Telegraph*. 'The Insults Fly in a Poisonous War of Words,' trumpeted the *Daily Express*. The American press, less used to invective, delighted in the mudslinging.

* In fact the two had not been close friends until this point. Their friendship survived until Hitchens's death in 2011.

'All is Not Lost: Art of Insult Survives "New Britain"', read a headline in the international edition of the *New York Times*.

'I actually feel very proud,' David wrote to his son Tim, by now a journalist himself. 'I've said what everybody says in secret and nobody has the balls to say aloud.'[28] David's clash with Rushdie distanced him still further from the bien-pensants who dominated the literary landscape. 'I have never felt so right, or so lonely – or until yesterday when I heard that Willie Shawcross was going to the barricades for me,' he wrote to his editor at Hodder, Roland Philipps. 'Otherwise the only sound was the tiptoeing of one's friends out of the back door.'[29]

In 1992 David had sprung to the defence of his friend Shawcross; now Shawcross returned the favour – though it was awkward for him to do so, as he was chairman of the human rights organisation Article 19, which existed to defend freedom of expression and which had co-ordinated the campaign to defend Rushdie. In an article for the *Guardian* he made it clear that he was a friend of le Carré's, writing in a personal capacity. Rushdie's allegation that le Carré had 'eagerly . . . joined forces with my assailants' was not only untrue; it was 'outrageous'. He referred to 'a stink of triumphalist self-righteousness which one might expect from some of Mr Rushdie's followers, but not from the persecuted writer himself'.[30]

When Rushdie was telephoned by the editor of the *Guardian*, Alan Rusbridger, to ask if he wanted to respond to Shawcross, he declined. 'If le Carré wants to get his friends to do a little proxy whingeing, that's his business,' he told Rusbridger: 'I've said what I had to say.' In fact Rushdie had sent Shawcross a furious fax, copied to his colleagues, questioning his ability to remain chairman of Article 19.

David withdrew from the field of battle, though he was keeping his powder dry, as he indicated to Shawcross. 'For self preservation, having decided I would say no more pro tem, but *a lot* when I have finished my novel, I closed the door on the whole fuss & went back to scribbling.'[31]

Rainer Heumann had died suddenly in 1996, at the age of seventy-two. David was one of several speakers at the memorial gathering in Zurich. In a touching tribute he looked back over their thirty-five years of association. There was never a bad day, he told the mourners. 'We never disagreed about anything, except possibly what we wished for one another,' he said.

'He was the perfect agent, and the perfect friend.'[32] The paperback of *The Tailor of Panama* would be dedicated 'In memory of Rainer Heumann, literary agent, gentleman and friend'.

Heumann's death led to a shake-up in David's representation. A few years before he had left his longstanding American lawyer, Mort Leavy, for Michael Rudell, an entertainment lawyer who also handled the crime writer Patricia Cornwell (who of course was no relation). In 1997 he left Lynn Nesbit, his American agent for the past dozen years. Bruce Hunter of David Higham Associates took over from her, thus becoming David's representative in America, as he had been in Britain since the late 1980s. Hunter was responsible for selling the next le Carré novel, entitled *Single & Single*. In the summer of 1998 it was announced that John le Carré was leaving Knopf, his American publisher for almost thirty years; his new American publisher would be Scribner's, a long-established house with a proud history, though now no more than an imprint of Simon & Schuster, itself part of the conglomerate Viacom.

Speculation within the industry and the press suggested that his much publicised feud with Salman Rushdie had played a part in his departure. Sonny Mehta had been one of Rushdie's editors in England and was said to be a 'close friend' of his. But David denied that he had ever discussed the matter with Mehta, or with anyone else at Knopf. David's American lawyer Rudell told the trade press that 'this has nothing to do with Rushdie'. According to *Publishers Weekly*, the real reason why le Carré was leaving Knopf was the disappointing sales of his recent books. *The Tailor of Panama* had sold significantly fewer than *The Night Manager*, which itself had not earned its advance.[33] 'I felt they'd had me too long & forgotten how to sell me,' David wrote to a friend in Panama, '& never considered how to present me post Cold War.'[34]

23

The Secret Centre

In a Simon & Schuster press release announcing the novel's acquisition, *Single & Single* was described as 'the masterful story of a British merchant banking house in business with criminal elements in post Cold War Russia and Europe'. Like *A Perfect Spy*, it was also 'an extraordinarily compelling story of family betrayal'.

The comparison was apt, because a son's anguished relations with his father lie at the emotional heart of the book, as they do in *A Perfect Spy*. In this case the father is 'Tiger' Single, founder of the merchant bank that bears his name; the son is Oliver, Tiger's heir-designate. Just as Magnus Pym betrays his father in *A Perfect Spy*, so too does Oliver, by 'shopping' him to the British Customs & Excise. Afterwards Oliver goes to ground, re-emerging in a new identity as a magician and children's entertainer in Cornwall.

Though only sketchily drawn, Tiger is a recognisable version of Ronnie, like Rick in *A Perfect Spy*. In this version, David imagined how Ronnie might have become if things had worked out differently:

> What if my father, instead of being rumbled by the forces of the law, which sadly for him was regularly the case – what if, like so many of the bent businessmen around him, he had got away with his scams scot-free, and become, as he always dreamed of becoming, a respected fat cat of the West End, owner of an instant ancient pile in Buckinghamshire, president of the local football club, cricket club, giver of garden fêtes for the church roof?
>
> What if, instead of merely enrolling from time to time as a law student, he had possessed enough self-discipline to *study* law rather than just finger

it – and had thus acquired the skills that enable so many crooked lawyers to flourish in the world of finance?

David further imagined what might have become of him if, instead of sneaking off to Oxford to read modern languages, he had obediently submitted to his father's demands to study law, as his brother had done; and if, in due course, he and Tony had meekly entered his father's firm and had taken up the places prepared for them. The case of the flamboyant publishing magnate Robert Maxwell showed what might have happened. On the day when Maxwell's sons Kevin and Ian were brought to trial for their alleged complicity in their father's fraudulent dealings, David's sister telephoned him. 'It could have been you two,' she said.[1] In a further twist, David drew on aspects of his own sons in creating Oliver – particularly Nick, who was a juggler and always seemed to wear a heavy coat, as Oliver did.

Single & Single is the story of Oliver's quest for his father, threatened by his own business associates after the authorities begin to clamp down on their operations. Tiger has bolted, seeking safety in flight. Guilt-stricken, Oliver goes in search of his father, following him to Switzerland and then to Turkey; and eventually finds him in the shadow of the Caucasus mountains, a half-naked prisoner in a stable, chained hand and foot, his face blackened with bruises. The scene is a heightened version of the episode in *A Perfect Spy* when Magnus arrives at the prison to set his father free; or of the occasion when David had done the same for Ronnie. Like Rick, and Ronnie, Tiger is belittled; once rescued, he co-operates meekly with the authorities. For Oliver, this is a moment of epiphany: 'He had arrived at the last, most hidden room of his search, he had prised open the most top-secret box, and it was empty. Tiger's secret was that he had no secret.' David would later summarise *Single & Single* as 'the story of how a father-obsessed son finally sprang over his own shadow and discovered the monster who ruled his life was just another sad and empty little man'.[2]

He made two trips to the Caucasus, one while writing the book, and a second after he had finished the first draft and then rewritten it in response to comments from Roland Philipps. On both occasions he was escorted into the mountains by two brothers connected to Georgian special forces. One drove, the other interpreted.

Even after completing *Single & Single*, David was still not free of Ronnie. As so often in the past, he began planning an autobiographical book, 'one final attempt to come to terms with a mercurial, tragically driven and totally incomprehensible father'. Previous tries had made him mistrustful of his own memories; as a novelist he had quarried his own history so often that he no longer knew what was real and what was not. 'We all reinvent our pasts, but writers are in a class of their own,' he wrote later, in a passage looking back on this episode: 'even when they know the truth, it's never enough for them.' He sought collateral information, facts to corroborate his imaginative fictions. Within weeks of finishing *Single & Single*, he had commissioned a pair of private detectives – 'one thin, one fat, both recommended by a London solicitor, and both good eaters' – to investigate his father. He gave them as many leads as he could think of and sent them out into the world to gather information about Ronnie and his business ventures. David proposed that their findings should be juxtaposed and contrasted with his own memories, on facing pages; 'in that way my readers will see for themselves to what extent an old writer's memory is the whore of his imagination'. But the experiment was a failure. 'Ten thousand pounds and several excellent meals later, all they had to offer was a bunch of press clippings about old bankruptcies and the Great Yarmouth election and a pile of useless company records.'[3] After six months he abandoned the project – though he was able to retrieve something from this fiasco by writing a piece about it for the *Sunday Times*, 'Son of a Swindler'.[4]

Single & Single was published early in 1999. 'Le Carré is more than just a great storyteller,' wrote Tom Wolfe: 'he captures the Zeitgeist itself, in this case the very funk of post-Soviet Euro-fear.'* Critics commented that David had once again produced a story that felt extremely topical – of greed, exploitation and callousness, of the feeding frenzy of asset stripping which had brought Russia to its knees, of profiteering by crooks and oligarchs, and of the West's tragic indifference to the fate of its former enemy. Even so, few of them could resist the temptation to frame their reviews in terms of how successfully le Carré had adapted to the World

* So far as I have been able to ascertain, this was a quote solicited by Scribner's.

after Communism. No matter how much he wrote about the present, it seemed that he could not escape from his association with the past. For journalists, it was all too easy to depict David as a writer who had lost his subject when the Cold War had ended, though *Single & Single* was his fourth novel to appear since then. His supposed spikiness could be explained as disgruntlement, his apparent inaccessibility as pique. This was exasperating for David. 'John le Carré's silence has gone on, in England at least, for years,' wrote an interviewer from *The Times*, in an especially preposterous piece:

> The cold hung on long after the break-up of the Soviet Union. It deepened with the decade, and reports suggested that it was hardening into a permafrost. It was impossible to gauge the truth since the man himself was not talking. He was more remote than ever, shunning London and only breaking his silences for short, splenetic bursts. It was impossible to get to him through his friends, even if you knew who they were, as they were all so discreet, or dead, or overseas. And so he took on the air of Eighties Edward Heath, digging in for the long winter of the new order.

David could be forgiven for becoming irritable when confronted with such stuff. 'Ridiculous,' he snapped, when *The Times* man asked whether the end of the Cold War had 'ever looked like destroying his fiction's context and environment'. The suggestion that he had been cut off from his lifeline was 'sheer nonsense'. On the contrary, he said: the end of 'the supposed stand-off between the two great monoliths' was from his point of view 'a great relief'.[5]

One of the more interesting reviews of *Single & Single* came from D. J. Taylor, who was alive to the exuberant quality of the writing. 'Single & Single manages to make some serious points about history amid a riot of whoops and skips, genre flourishes and delighted winks to the gallery,' wrote Taylor in the *Guardian*. 'It is an axiom, of course, that the fate of the sixty-something novelist is stylisation. They go on being themselves, only more so. And the interest in reading them lies mostly in their efforts to resist this process.'[6] *Single & Single* reached no. 2 in the UK bestseller list, and spent fifteen weeks in the top ten; in the US, it reached no. 3.

A few weeks before the book appeared, David had given an address to an early-evening gathering of agent-runners at MI5's headquarters, Thames House, on the north side of Lambeth Bridge. He was there at the invitation of the Director-General, Sir Stephen Lander. This was David's second visit to Thames House; some years earlier he had read from his work at a meeting of MI5's Bernini Society, which offered a programme of guest speakers. On this occasion Sir Stephen's aide had suggested that he should speak on 'Trust and Treachery in Agent Operations': a topic of particular relevance to his listeners, most of whom were young intelligence officers, as once he had been. His insights into the process of agent-running were remarkably perceptive, not least because he was able to draw on his experiences, both as an agent-runner himself and, before that, as an agent.

David's next novel would take him still further away from the Circus. Its origins went back twenty years, to a chance encounter one summer's evening, when he was drinking in a beer hall in Basel. A black-bearded cyclist in a beret had ridden through the open double doors, parked his bike at David's table and started talking. He was a former chemist, he explained, but now he was an anarchist because he refused to take part in the poisoning of mankind. The bearded cyclist filled David's head with the wicked deeds of the 'multis', the multinational pharmaceutical companies clustered along the banks of the upper Rhine. They would poison the globe, he said, if by doing so they could bump up their share prices. David enjoyed a frisson of forewarning; one day, he thought, I'll find a way to write about you and your 'multis'. He ditched the beard, the beret and the bicycle, but stored away the cyclist's fury for future use.[7] He would often retrieve scraps like this when a suitable context arose.

About fifteen years later, David was sitting in a small London restaurant when an elegant, grey-suited man appeared with a basket of fresh-cut flowers under his arm and began bestowing bouquets on each group of diners, before accepting a kiss and a glass of wine from the proprietress. 'We call him the mad gardener,' she explained to David, once the visitor had shyly taken his leave. Together they decided that he must have suffered bereavement and that bestowing flowers gave him comfort. David was inspired to write the first page of a first chapter, under the heading 'The Mad Gardener', introducing an eccentric Englishman in a straw hat, an ageing and bereaved former diplomat who has taken himself to live in Morocco, where he tours the cafés and nightclubs in the evenings, dispensing flowers to the diners. David pinned this page on his noticeboard, where it remained for a few years, until he took it down and filed it away, apparently a lost cause; but it would prove to be the first sketch of the character at the centre of his next novel, Harry Clapham, later renamed Justin Quayle: a dignified, quietly spoken, middle-aged diplomat, a mild-mannered gardener. He too has lost someone close to him – Tessa,* an impetuous, headstrong, unswerving young woman, to whom he will remain constant, even when it appears that she has betrayed him: hence the eventual title of the novel, *The Constant Gardener*.

David planned to set the novel in Africa. Partly he was drawn by the lure of getting to know somewhere new; until then his only experience of Africa had been of safari holidays with the children, of 'lines of striped jeeps queuing up to photograph the same disconsolate lion'. He retained an uneasy memory of his schooldays, when English boys were prepared for the burdens of imperial rule in the colonies: remembering in particular the flutter caused by a well-intentioned careers adviser, who had warned that anyone who condemned a native to death jolly well ought to attend his execution. He wanted to write about the crimes of unbridled capitalism – nowhere more evident than in Africa. At first he contemplated a book set in Nigeria, which had been plundered and polluted by international oil companies, but that seemed somehow too obvious. Then Ted Younie, a former SIS man who had spent almost all his career in Africa, whispered 'pharmaceuticals' in his ear. If one was looking for a metaphor for the exploitation of Africa, beyond even oil, he suggested, it was the pharmaceutical industry. 'I'll help you in any way I can,' promised Younie: 'this book needs writing.' David spent some weeks in Basel talking in confidence to middle managers in pharmaceutical companies, who told him shocking stories of falsification of clinical trials, and humans in poor countries being used as guinea pigs. He had decided to set the novel in Kenya rather than Nigeria, and flew out to Nairobi a few weeks after the publication of *Single & Single*. He was shocked by what he found. The country had been devastated by the

* In the earliest draft she is named Prunella, then Miranda, Julia and eventually Tessa.

AIDS epidemic and by rampant corruption. 'Nobody has so far offered me the least hope for the future of Kenya,' he wrote in his notebook.[8]

In Nairobi, David met civil rights lawyers, trawled the city's hospitals and talked to local representatives of pharmaceutical companies. One location he did not visit was the British High Commission, though the novel opens in the Commission and several subsequent scenes are set there or within the tight community of British diplomats and their families. 'It is not the place I have described, for I have never been inside it,' he would write of the High Commission, in an afterword to the novel. 'It is not staffed by the people I have described, because I have never met nor spoken to them' – though he did admit to a chat with the High Commissioner over a ginger ale on the verandah of the Norfolk Hotel. The novel would convey his cynicism about Whitehall, 'the permanent government of England, on which her transient politicians spin and posture like so many table dancers'.

A young man in a suit appeared beside David as he was walking around Nairobi and engaged him in conversation. He introduced himself as the receptionist at his hotel and explained that he was on his way to buy flowers. Would David like to come with him to the flower market? David was beguiled by the young man's pleasant demeanour and agreed to accompany him. He was led down a side street, straight into the arms of two men, one of whom held a knife to his throat. They wanted only cash, not even his wristwatch. Fortunately David had a couple of hundred dollars on him.

Some of the most vivid scenes of the novel would be set in the remote north, near the banks of Lake Turkana. David engaged a pilot and a private plane to fly him up there, so that he could take a look around. Turkana borders South Sudan, a region devastated by famine, drought and a civil war that had been raging, on and off, since the mid-1950s; the government in Khartoum employed a local militia of armed horsemen, the Janjaweed, to terrorise the population and suppress the insurgency. In Nairobi David talked to fighters from one of the principal rebel groups, General Garang's Sudan People's Liberation Army. Under the auspices of one of the NGOs involved in the United Nations relief operation, Operation Lifeline Sudan, he undertook a hazardous journey across the border into South Sudan, as a passenger on one of the UN's short-take-off-and-landing Buffalo transports. He stayed several nights on the northernmost food station in South Sudan, spent time with local elders and dignitaries, watched a couple of food drops and saw the local Dinka women emerging naked from the bush to collect the food. During his stay they received a red alert that the food station was about to be attacked; he and the other aid workers were evacuated to an island, where the Janjaweed were unlikely to follow.

The more that David investigated the behaviour of drug companies in Africa, the more outraged he became. They dumped inappropriate or out-of-date medicines on the Africans, suppressed information about their contra-indications and their side-effects, and encouraged their indiscriminate use. The most effective drugs were arbitrarily over-priced, and attempts to manufacture generic substitutes blocked. Africans were encouraged to buy drugs they did not want and prevented from getting drugs they desperately needed. Increasingly, the 'multis' used them as guinea pigs in their trials. David was shocked to discover how closely the industry was tied to Western governments: all too often, it seemed, doctors and research facilities were in the pocket of pharmaceuticals. 'The pharmas, whether they know it or not, are engaged in the systematic corruption of the medical profession,' he would write.[9] No dissent was tolerated. 'There has been a steady trickle of alarming cases where inconvenient scientific findings had been suppressed or rewritten, and those responsible for them hounded off their campuses, with their professional and personal reputations systematically trashed by public relations agencies in the pay of pharmas.' David believed it possible that *in extremis* the most unscrupulous pharmaceutical companies might resort to murder in order to silence their critics. 'I am sure people have died,' he would tell interviewers.[10] His novel begins with the discovery that Tessa Quayle has been found stabbed to death in the remote northern region of Kenya, near the banks of Lake Turkana. The driver of her jeep has been decapitated. Her companion, the African doctor Arnold Blum, is missing. As the story develops, it emerges that he and Tessa have been urgently trying to draw attention to the dangerous side-effects of a new TB drug, Dypraxa. Tessa has protected her husband by keeping him ignorant of her activities. After her death he tries to reconstruct what she has been doing by accessing files on her laptop. For David, this was an expedition into unknown territory: he knew nothing of computers and relied on his youngest son Nick to advise him.

Though Tessa is dead before the action of the book starts, she is a vivid presence throughout, both in flashback and in Justin's interior dialogue with her. She becomes his conscience, and he takes up her cause. In the end he sacrifices himself, as the ultimate individual act of defiance against corporate power.

David had been in touch with Yvette Pierpaoli before leaving for Kenya. In a faxed letter he informed her that his next book would have an African setting, and told her teasingly that his heroine would be somebody as impossible as herself. As he would later acknowledge, it was Yvette's work that he wished to celebrate when he embarked on the novel. Though Tessa differs from Yvette Pierpaoli in age, occupation, nationality and birth, 'her commitment to the poor of Africa, particularly its women, her contempt for protocol, and her unswerving, often maddening determination to have her way stemmed, quite consciously so far as I was concerned, from Yvette's example'. They planned to meet on his return from Africa. 'I adore the idea of your new book,' she wrote to him before he left.[11] She was on her way to the mountains of Albania, to help refugees from Kosovo.

He had been in Kenya only a few days when Jane called to say that Yvette was dead. In bad weather the car in which she was travelling had driven over a precipice and fallen several hundred feet. The driver and two other aid workers had been killed in the same accident. David flew back from Kenya for Yvette's funeral, the most moving that he and Jane had ever attended. Her ashes were buried, with both Christian and Buddhist rites, in the garden of her farmhouse near Uzès. Friends came from America, Cambodia and Thailand to embrace one another in the afternoon sunlight. *The Constant Gardener* would be dedicated: 'For Yvette Pierpaoli / who lived and died giving a damn'.

There was a mystical side to Yvette that had always made David uneasy. After reading a draft of her autobiography he had advised her to tone down her insistence that she was a child of destiny. Now he found himself confronted with the disconcerting feeling that he had anticipated her death. It was David's practice to inhabit the character of his secret sharer, in this case the bereaved husband Justin Quayle. For months, therefore, he had been mourning Tessa. But Tessa was a version of Yvette: so he had been mourning Yvette ahead of the fact.

In May 1999 it was announced that Hodder Headline had been sold to the booksellers W. H. Smith – 'this unattractive alliance', as David described it to Tim Hely Hutchinson; he had always regarded Smiths as 'a dismal house, an ailing giant, and I have always greatly resented their influence on British publishing – which extended, in the past, as far as dictating book covers. Their banality has been a curse on the industry.' Though Hely Hutchinson was quick to reassure him that the change was a positive one, David let it be known that he did not want to be published by Hodder again.[12] By the following summer, as he put the finishing touches to *The Constant Gardener*, he had softened his position, though it remained 'far from certain' that the book would be offered to Hodder exclusively. Roland Philipps reported to Hely Hutchinson on a lunch with Bruce Hunter: David had been wondering whether his reviews might not improve if he were with a 'more literary' publishing house, among writers of similar stature. In fact, wrote Philipps, his recent British reviews had been 'superb', though, as he noted, 'David only remembers the dispraise.'[13]

In the event David decided to stay with Hodder, not least because he valued the 'sure touches of reassurance and discreet counsel' that his editor provided. The urge to move to a 'more literary' publisher was restrained by David's sense of being a literary loner. 'On the whole I've avoided the company of my fellow English writers,' he told the literary editor of the *Observer*, Robert McCrum: 'I just feel completely out of step with the English literary scene.'[14] Asked by another interviewer to comment on 'his relationship with the critical establishment', he answered pithily: 'It doesn't exist.'[15]

Relationship or no relationship, the British reviews of *The Constant Gardener* would be generally positive: in the *Times Literary Supplement*, for example, Sean O'Brien praised the novel as 'a very impressive piece of work' and rated it 'certainly one of John le Carré's best books'.[16] O'Brien observed that the book was 'fuelled by carefully controlled but immense rage' – a quality commented upon by other reviewers, such as John Sutherland in the *Sunday Times*, who wrote that 'this is old-man le Carré's angriest work of fiction'.[17] In a letter to Philipps, David acknowledged that 'a bit of rage' had helped him to write the book quickly.[18] Indeed he had at one stage thought of entitling it 'The Angry Gardener'.

Helped by the positive press, Hodder Headline worked hard to make a success of *The Constant Gardener*, which was published on both sides of the Atlantic in January 2001; it became a no. 1 bestseller in the UK, remaining thirteen weeks in the top ten. Afterwards, in a letter to the company's new managing director, Jamie Hodder-Williams, David expressed his appreciation of the whole Hodder team. 'It's a new Hodder's these days, & a far happier one to deal with, and a most impressive array of talent.'[19]

One place where *The Constant Gardener* did not sell was Kenya itself. The depiction of a nation riddled with corrupt policemen, officials and politicians was not appreciated by the authorities, who banned the book from sale; it became a joke in Nairobi that, to avoid trouble with the authorities, bookshops stocked it in the gardening section. Kenyans who travelled abroad brought back multiple copies, to circulate among friends and neighbours.

David responded stingingly to criticism from representatives of the pharmaceutical industry, and declined to debate with them.[20] 'As my journey through the pharmaceutical jungle progressed,' he wrote in his afterword to the novel, 'I came to realise that, by comparison with the reality, my story was as tame as a holiday postcard.' About six months after the book's publication he received a letter from the recently appointed director of Oxfam, Barbara Stocking, who wanted 'to make sure you know how helpful *The Constant Gardener* has been to our "Cut the Cost" campaign to make drugs more accessible to people in developing countries at prices they could afford'. She referred to the recent success in getting pharmaceutical companies to drop their court case against the South African government for manufacturing generic anti-HIV drugs. 'We are certain that public opinion was influenced by *The Constant Gardener*,' she told him. David forwarded a copy of this letter to Roland Philipps. 'For me better than 6 Bookers and 20 Soapy awards,' he scribbled in a covering note.[21]

The American edition of *The Constant Gardener* sold reasonably well, reaching no. 4 in the *New York Times* bestseller list; though this was a falling-off from the heady days when four successive le Carré novels had gone to no. 1. The book's sales reflected a cooler response from the American critics. In the *New York Review of Books*, the novelist Hilary Mantel (herself

English) characterised the novel as 'a polemic cast in the form of a thriller'. In her view the polemical form created problems:

> Reader and writer are brought up time after time against the limitations of the polemical novel. If you choose to deal with such complicated and sensitive topics in the form of fiction, you are creating great difficulties for yourself, given that dramatic tension and the recitation of facts are often incompatible, and the use of characters as the equivalent of newscasters tends to bore and worry the reader . . . The Constant Gardener, strident, repetitious, and urgent, is less a novel than a cry from the heart . . . It is a furious, hasty, and at times embarrassing book.

Mantel found Tessa 'tiresome, given to flitting against the light in flimsy dresses while Justin and the author salivate over her'.[22]

The *New York Times* reviewer, the short-story writer Rand Richards Cooper, seemed equally irritated by Tessa; and, like Mantel, he found the polemical nature of the novel problematic. '"The Constant Gardener" makes some ungainly narrative moves,' he wrote, 'using whole chapters of police interrogation to establish basic plot points, and dishing out boatloads of documents for us to sort through.'

> The effort hints at another kind of book altogether – namely, investigative journalism – and as we follow Justin's search for the truth, 'The Constant Gardener' feels ever more like an exposé, an angry diatribe against corporate malfeasance, adorned with sentimental descriptions of Tessa and her courageous actions . . . that fall far below the subtle insights of le Carré at his best.
>
> It's not that a novelist can't also enlighten and exhort. But where in Dickens the desire to improve the real world – to weigh in on the subject of debtors' prisons or child labor in factories – never interfered with creating a supremely inviting fictional world, one senses an impatience in 'The Constant Gardener', as if le Carré were chafing in his eagerness to have us admire his heroine as he does, to get us to believe. Taking sides with the angels, his novel unabashedly wears its heart on its sleeve. It's almost enough to make you long for the old cold war bleakness and ambiguity.[23]

David was annoyed by the American reviews. He told Philipps that he could 'never quite accept' the way the book had been received there, 'but

Jane says I'm unreasonable on the subject & as usual she's right. In fact, I'm becoming seriously unbalanced about America altogether. But I'm not sure that isn't the right thing to be.'[24]

If the Americans longed for le Carré to return to his past, the Europeans greeted *The Constant Gardener* as a new beginning. As his sales waned in America, they increased in Europe. The novel was a no. 1 bestseller in France, for example, selling more than 400,000 copies. His German publishers sold 50,000 copies in the first week. Spies were almost entirely absent from *The Constant Gardener*, but European publishers felt little nostalgia for the Circus; they welcomed his engagement with the present. Since the end of the Cold War his books had addressed the realities of the New World Order, tackling big themes one by one. *The Constant Gardener* represented a further step towards the polemic. Gone was the moral ambiguousness of the Smiley novels, or even of *The Little Drummer Girl*. Henceforth there would be a clear line between right and wrong. 'I can't write small any more,' David wrote to Philipps, soon after the publication of *The Constant Gardener*: 'Single & Single cd never have followed TCG – it had to be the other way round.'[25]

No doubt there were complex cultural reasons why *The Constant Gardener* should have appealed more to European readers than to Americans; but it may also have been due to the fact that it was published with extra energy and enthusiasm. In 2000 he had asked David Higham Associates to begin handling his foreign rights as well as his English-language rights. Bruce Hunter and his colleague Ania Corless instigated a systematic review of David's publishing throughout the world. They found some surprising gaps: territories where some books had been sold and not others; territories where rights had technically lapsed and been neither renewed nor terminated; and a few territories which seemed to have been forgotten altogether. In others the existing publisher had become complacent, suggesting that a change might benefit David. Corless set about tackling the territories one by one, considering which publisher might do the best job and setting up a new publishing programme, reverting rights where necessary, and often negotiating improved royalty rates. Some publishers offered to issue his collected works in a uniform edition. As a somewhat different sort of book from its predecessors, *The Constant Gardener* provided an opportunity to find new publishers for David. In at least one commercially significant territory, the existing publisher stated that it was not a novel that they could sell in large quantities, so Corless sold it instead to one who was more bullish. Among several new arrangements entered into, none was more rewarding than in Germany, the country closest to David's heart and his most lucrative market outside the English-speaking world. Corless moved him to Ullstein, one of Germany's largest publishing companies.

An advance copy of *The Constant Gardener* had found its way to Simon Channing Williams, who only months before had established an independent production company, Potboiler Productions. Best known for his longstanding collaboration with Mike Leigh, the genial and generous-spirited Channing Williams had a reputation as an unflappable, 'can do' producer. On reading the novel, he was so taken with it that he faxed an impassioned letter to David's lawyer, Michael Rudell, pleading his case for being given the chance to turn it into a film. To demonstrate his seriousness he volunteered to fly from London to New York that same evening to meet Rudell. 'It was such a heartfelt, angry book,' he said later, 'and at the root of it all, an utterly compelling love story' – told unusually from the male point of view.

Channing Williams's enthusiasm convinced David and his advisers to entrust the project to him. To write the screenplay he proposed Jeffrey Caine, a television veteran whose credits included the 1995 James Bond film *GoldenEye* – subject to David's approval, which he gave after meeting Caine for lunch. As an admirer of his novels, Caine welcomed David's input into the writing, his presence at script meetings and the notes he provided on Caine's various drafts, during the two years that the film was in development. It was obvious that changes would be needed to make the story work on the screen; in fact, David urged Caine to make more. One came at the end: the last chapter of the novel, a report of what happened after Justin's death, is dramatised in the film as a memorial service, at which the duplicitous Sir Bernard Pellegrin is unmasked.

The first choice to direct the film was Mike Newell, who had made the enormously successful *Four Weddings and a Funeral* (1994); but he withdrew when offered the opportunity to direct the fourth Harry Potter film. Channing Williams then recruited Fernando Meirelles, whose 2002 film *City of God* had won awards around the globe. Having witnessed the struggle to make generic drugs available in his native Brazil, Meirelles was strongly in sympathy with the book. The two men made a 'recce' together to the original locations in Kenya and agreed that they should film there if possible. A new government had been elected in 2003, offering the possibility that the anticipated difficulties might be overcome. The British High Commissioner, Sir Edward Clay, made no secret of the fact that he had been 'outraged' by the novel's 'hostile caricature of British diplomats'; but he overcame his resistance, in the interests of Kenya itself and of the wider causes espoused by the novel. Clay and his staff provided much practical help and advice, including introductions to Kenyan ministers that proved crucial in obtaining the necessary consents.

City of God had won worldwide acclaim for its convincing portrayal of organised crime in the slums of Rio de Janeiro; Meirelles had cast amateur actors from similar backgrounds to those of the violent young gang members they were playing, and filmed in the deprived neighbourhoods where they lived. For *The Constant Gardener*, Meirelles aimed to achieve a similar level of authenticity, by shooting as much of the film as possible in the real locations where the story was set, using local people as extras. Some of the most startling footage was shot in the shanty town of Kibera, a suburb of Nairobi, the most populous slum in Africa, where up to one million people lived in squalid huts, without access to clean water, sanitation or mains electricity. Members of the cast and crew were so affected by what they had seen that afterwards they set up a charity to improve living conditions for people in the areas where filming had taken place. Its patrons were David himself, Meirelles and the film's co-stars, Ralph Fiennes and Rachel Weisz. The Constant Gardener Trust has since supported many projects, providing freshwater tanks, shower blocks and toilets in Kibera, building a bridge there to allow easier access to the local health clinic, and funding a much needed secondary school in Loiyangalani, a small town on the banks of Lake Turkana which served as a base for the crew while they were filming in the area.

The sense of authenticity was accentuated by Meirelles's extensive use of a hand-held camera, making the drama feel like a documentary. His naturalistic directing style allowed his actors exceptional scope to improvise, so that the dialogue became theirs as much as Caine's or David's. 'There's hardly a line left, hardly a scene intact that comes from my novel,' David has said. 'Yet I don't know of a better translation from novel to film.' Even Caine found himself improvising, in his cameo role as a porter at Sir Bernard's club.

The Constant Gardener was a critical and commercial success, winning many awards, including Oscars for Jeffrey Caine and Rachel Weisz, a Golden Globe for Weisz, and a BAFTA for the editor, Claire Simpson.

In the foreword to a new edition of *The Tailor of Panama*, published in April 2001, David inveighed against 'the long, dishonourable history of United States colonialism in the region'. He took the opportunity to attack current American foreign policy, especially the failure to ratify the Kyoto protocol on climate change. 'The new American realism, which is nothing other than gross corporate power cloaked in demagogy, means one thing only: that America will put America first in everything,' he wrote. 'Quite simply and emphatically, I do not believe that the United States is fit to run the post-Cold War world, and I think the sooner Britain and Europe wake up to that fact, the better.' David expressed contempt for the newly elected President of the United States (son of the George Bush who had sent him a letter of praise for *The Night Manager*). 'I happen also to believe that George W. Bush is not fit to run America, or for that matter a single-decker bus, but that's America's business. Unfortunately, he has been given charge of the world's only superpower.'[26]

David was scarcely less contemptuous of the British Prime Minister, Tony Blair. He had been 'thrilled' by Labour's victory in the 1997 general election, which seemed to offer fresh hope after almost twenty years of Conservative rule; but by the time of the next election in June 2001, disillusion had replaced his excitement. In an interview with the playwright David Hare, he said that he would like to 'punish' Blair in the coming poll, then only three weeks away. Not only had he failed to instigate much-needed reform, he had continued the Thatcherite legacy – 'he would have privatised air if he could'. Worst of all, Blair had kowtowed to the Americans. 'We don't have a single member of the Blair administration lifting a public finger against the ecological ruin that George W is promising in the United States,' he said. He deplored 'the whimpering echo' from Blair when the American President supported the drug companies in their legal action against the South African government. 'I thought Blair was lying when he denied he was a socialist,' David told Hare. 'The worst thing I can say about him is that he was telling the truth.'

Yvette Pierpaoli had introduced David to her close friend Stéphane Hessel, a diplomat and human rights activist. He and David became friendly, to the extent that Hessel and his wife would be guests at David's seventieth-birthday celebration. Though born German, Hessel had become a naturalised Frenchman in 1939: he served in the French Resistance before being captured and interned in a concentration camp, where he had been tortured by the Gestapo. In later life he called for a new form of resistance to the injustices of the modern world; his short book *Time for Outrage!* became an international bestseller. After his death in 2013, at the age of ninety-five, David would pay tribute to him. 'I admired Hessel immensely and shared, and supported, his views on the present world situation and the need for great popular anger.'

When Hare had suggested that David's increasing engagement with politics was in the 'great tradition of writers becoming radicalised in later years', David responded by citing the German term *Alterszorn* – 'the rage of age'. He recognised the danger that he might lose readers if his books became too polemical. 'Story and character must come first,' he said. 'But I am now so angry that I have to exercise a good deal of restraint in order to produce a readable book.'[27]

After finishing *The Constant Gardener*, David had submitted to an hour-long television interview, in which he spoke more frankly about aspects of his life than he had done in the past. The programme opened with an archive recording of David denying outright that he had ever been a spy, followed by a voiceover comment that 'spies are not meant to tell the truth'. Towards the end of the programme David told the interviewer, Nigel Williams, 'I feel now, I've forgotten how to lie.'[28]

David admitted to spying on friends at Oxford, behaviour that still troubled him. He had been prompted to think afresh about the morality of his actions by Timothy Garton Ash, who had come down to Cornwall to consult him as 'an expert on all varieties of loyalty and betrayal'. He had been a postgraduate student in Berlin in the late 1970s. After the collapse of East Germany, the Germans had opened the records of the disbanded East German State Security Service (the 'Stasi'), where Garton Ash had found his own file, showing that the Stasi had set people to inform on him. He had decided to write a book* about his discoveries.

* *The File: A Personal History* (1997).

As he and David walked along the Cornish clifftops, David spoke of his own career in intelligence, 'with a mixture of nostalgia, irony and scruples'. Subsequently Garton Ash sent David a typescript of his book, and received a sixteen-page, handwritten reply. In his letter David asked Garton Ash not to present himself as a victim; according to him, 'the real victims' were 'the poor East Germans' who had informed on him – 'crabbed, intimidated, blackmailed'. There was of course a similarity between the actions of those East German informers and what David himself had done; he acknowledged that 'I betrayed, in your terms.' Yet, he argued, it was justifiable to betray the trust of people whom you have befriended in order to gain information for the British state, as it helped to defend a free society. 'For me – but I'm one of your bad guys in the end – you're *too* fine, *too* unaccepting of the realities of having to *do & act* and protect what's worth protecting.' Garton Ash thought this 'a marvellous but also a troubling letter', which led to a further round of correspondence and conversation about what David called 'a question that's haunted me these forty-five years'.[29]

The television interview with Nigel Williams sparked an outburst from David's undergraduate friend Stanley Mitchell. He and David had lost contact after leaving Oxford; Mitchell had pursued a career as a university teacher and a specialist in Russian literature, producing a much admired translation of Pushkin's *Eugene Onegin*. He had never surrendered his faith in the essential truth of Marxism, though he had become critical of Stalinist orthodoxy. Now, almost half a century later, Mitchell learned that David had been passing information about him to MI5 throughout most of the time that they had known each other.[30] Some of David's comments in the television interview only worsened the offence. 'It felt like betrayal, but it had a voluptuous quality,' he told Nigel Williams: 'this was a necessary sacrifice of morality and that is a very important component of what makes people spy, what attracts them.'[31]

Furious and upset, Mitchell sent David a strongly worded letter, denouncing him as a Judas. His old friend responded by inviting him to lunch; and, after some hesitation, Mitchell accepted. It seems to have been an emotional reunion, at which the two men were only partially reconciled. David confessed to Mitchell that he had spied on several other students at

Oxford, including Newton Garver, whose girlfriend was believed to be a Communist. Mitchell felt that David was seeking his absolution for what he had done.

Another ghost from David's past emerged a few weeks later. Vivian Green copied out for David a letter extracted from the Lincoln College files, written to the Rector almost fifty years earlier by David's housemaster at Sherborne, R. S. Thompson, advocating that David should be made to wait a year before being admitted to the college. David wrote to thank Green. 'I found his letter very sad,' he wrote, '– a sense of personal failure turning outward into a rather pitiful and petty suggestion that I be made to cool my heels for a year to teach us Cornwells that we can't always have our own way!' In the same reply David paid tribute to Jane, 'my extraordinarily loyal and ever-decent support for 30 years now'.

> And you, dear Vivian, even in the times when we barely communicated, have been one of those lifelong secret sharers to whom I owe a debt I can never repay . . .
>
> Yes, we must both keep writing, keep creating, it's the only weapon against death. When I'm writing properly I still feel 23. When I'm not, I can hardly sleep for despair: such an awful life in so many ways, and looks so terribly impressive from the outside. But the inside has been such a ferment of buried anger and lovelessness from childhood that it was sometimes almost uncontainable.[32]

Once again David began to draft a memoir. Though headed 'The Novel of My Life', it was really about Ronnie, or at least about David's relationship with him (in a later draft he would head it 'Son of the Author's Father'). Attentive readers would notice a distinctly Dickensian flavour to the subheadings, 'On being Born, and Other Adventures', 'In which I have My First Taste of Prison', 'In which I hire Detectives to Investigate the Real Me', and so on. These echo the chapter titles of *David Copperfield* – one of the greatest of all autobiographical novels, but not an autobiography, and not necessarily a reliable guide to Dickens's early life. Perhaps the memoir should be read in this light. Like Dickens, David had endured the shame of his father's bankruptcy and imprisonment, and the ruin of all his prospects. There is a further connection. One reason why Dickens chose the name David Copperfield was because the initials were an inversion of his own. And of course these are the same as David Cornwell's.

By early summer he had written about 15,000 words, which he sent to Roland Philipps. It was a fine piece of writing, ironic, self-deprecatory and humane; but it was not a book: it was much too short, and to expand it would only weaken its punch. 'I was wrong,' David wrote to Philipps after they had discussed it together.

> When I got home, I re-read (by coincidence) the S. Times stuff for tomorrow,* and then dug into A Perfect Spy a bit, then looked at the accumulated bits of short writing I've done – intros, newspaper articles. An autobiography would be a duplication/rehash of so much of it, even if the slant were neater – as it is in the stuff I sent you. In some cases it's a *triplication*, to my embarrassment, and I wd be hard-pressed to re-style it at all. So I've shoved it all aside, I hope for the last time, and I'm going to stick to the novel.

David thanked Philipps for helping him 'think straight'. Instead of continuing with the memoir, he would publish what he had already written, virtually unchanged, as an article in the *New Yorker* – no longer edited by Tina Brown – under the title 'In Ronnie's Court'.

In his letter to Philipps, he mentioned as an aside that he had withdrawn from a planned appearance on the BBC Radio programme *Desert Island Discs*, which traced the life of guests through a choice of their favourite recordings. 'No more regurgitations of the past, I hope,' he commented. It seems that he had not yet let go of the idea, however. In another letter to Philipps a couple of months later, he divulged that he had 'started a second chunk of memoir & binned it, to our shared relief'.[33]

Roland Philipps and his wife Felicity (Hilary Rubinstein's daughter) were among the guests at David's seventieth birthday celebration in October 2001, which took place in Italy. There were some thirty to thirty-five in all, mostly family, with a few close friends. David's first wife Ann came, with her husband Roger. By this time all three sons of his first marriage were

* That is, 'Son of a Swindler'.

married with young children. Simon was living in London, after a period abroad including five years working for a refugee organisation in Thailand, where he had met and married Mimi, a Thai working for the UN; Stephen had become a screenwriter living in California, after working initially as a photojournalist, and was married to Clarissa, an Englishwoman whom he had met through his youngest brother; and Timothy was a journalist based in Edinburgh, married to Alice, daughter of David Greenway. The party stayed in a hotel a few miles outside Siena, a cluster of converted medieval buildings. The birthday party itself was held in the city centre, on the *piano nobile* of a ducal palazzo overlooking the Campo. The many-roomed apartment was packed with antiques, which looked to the anxious parents as though they had been placed there deliberately for the children to break, though no damage was done. The group was entertained by a nightclub singer; when the cake arrived, she began crooning 'Happy birthday, dear John', and could not understand why everyone burst out laughing.

24

'Mr Angry'

'The time drags awfully when I'm not working,' David had written to Philipps in January 2001.[1] Far from slowing down in his seventieth year, he was impatient to accelerate. But in the aftermath of *The Constant Gardener*, he had no new novel to fill his hours. 'I'm back to empty at the moment,' he told an interviewer from the *New York Times*.[2]

The period between finishing one book and starting another was always difficult for David. Three months after his letter about the time dragging, he wrote again to Philipps, apologising for cancelling a weekend *en famille*. 'I felt it was the wrong time for a jolly because I've been trying, & continue to try, to cut free of the last book and enter the magnetic zone of the new one, & I'm not good company while I swing between half-made choices,' he explained. 'I have a feeling that the only way to find out is [to] give myself a good shake, and the pieces too, & see where they/we end up.'[3]

Soon, however, a story was forming in his mind. At its core would be a man whose radical past has caught up with him in middle age. David envisaged a naïve young Englishman isolated in Berlin at the end of the 1960s, who drifts into revolutionary anarchism; thirty years on, he is living quietly in Munich when he is contacted by his old comrade Sasha, whom he suspects of planning an act of terrorism. While writing *The Constant Gardener* David had attended meetings of anti-corporate groups: he had seen for himself the frustration of the young at what they perceived as the exploitation of the Third World, wrecking the lives of the powerless. His experiences led him to speculate that this anger might be breeding a new generation of young terrorists – rather as an earlier generation of terrorists had emerged from the radical left in the 1960s and 1970s. David himself had witnessed violent student demonstrations in Paris in the late 1960s. Investigating what had become of the 1960s firebrands, David found that many of them were now orthodox citizens: a paediatrician neighbour of his in Hampstead, for example; or Lothar Menne, once a comrade of Angela Davis and Tariq Ali, now one of the pinnacles of his German publishers, Ullstein. Some were still active, like the campaigning journalist John Pilger. Timothy Garton Ash put David in touch with Anthony Barnett, a former member of the committee of *New Left Review*, who had visited communes in Berlin and Frankfurt in the late 1960s, and who still described himself as a revolutionary in his seventies.

An accidental comment by Alfred Brendel's German-born wife Reni touched David on a sore spot. They had been talking about her brother, a radical activist in Berlin in the 1960s. 'He might not wish to think that he was providing material from his own life for a big bestseller,' she remarked, over an otherwise agreeable lunch. David was stung by this and brooded on it afterwards. He decided that he had to explain himself, to ask her 'whether you knew how clearly you had expressed the prejudice I have lived with for years':

> In the eyes of so many of my peers I have never been a novelist at all – just a maker of successful artefacts, a rich nonentity. Maybe you can imagine what it's like, therefore, to walk into a roomful of fellow writers & artists, particularly in England. Or as Roger Hilton, the artist, said to me in front of an amused group, 'Ah yes, I know who you are. The little boy who had the smash hit.'* Maybe it would have been better to sell less, but it doesn't feel like that at the time. Any more than Alfred, presumably, would enjoy playing to empty houses. I write this because you lamented, very kindly, that I was given to disappearing from society. But I have my reasons for being wary, & reckon I know more than most about envy. Certainly I'm very tired of apologising for my success.[4]

'I want terribly to bring a sensitive understanding of Germany to my large, anglophone audience,' David assured Reni Brendel: 'my intentions

* Almost certainly in the early 1970s, when both men were living in West Cornwall. Hilton died in 1975.

are entirely protective.'[5] The protest movement in Germany had been harsher than elsewhere. Young people throughout the Western world had been in revolt against the mindless materialism of their parents in the late 1960s and early 1970s, but in Germany their protests had been more urgent, because of the conviction that the Nazi past had been conveniently forgotten; until the poison was purged, democracy could never be healthy. The angriest of them had formed the Red Army Faction (better known as the Baader-Meinhof Gang), which had carried out bombings and assassinations, and made common cause with the revolutionaries of the Third World, Palestinian terrorists and others. David had known some of the BND officers charged with hunting them down.

In constructing his central character, Ted Mundy, David awarded him elements of his own past. Like David, Mundy has a loving father and an absent mother; like David, he has fallen in love with the German muse; like David, he has acted in a schoolboy production of *Snow White and the Seven Dwarfs*; like David, he has attended a boarding school in the West Country. And like David too, he has become involved in spying, so that now 'he no longer knows which parts of him are pretending'.[6] Mundy's marriage has broken down under the strain of living a double life. David felt that he knew Mundy's background, because it was so similar to his own. To remind himself of what it was like, he arrived at Sherborne one evening, heavily disguised, and strolled around the playing fields in the gloom, immersing himself in the place that had once been so familiar. But where was Mundy living now, and what was he doing? With Jane, David took a 'thinking holiday' in southern Germany in the early summer of 2001, on the lookout for models: could he be the maître d'hôtel in the restaurant where they were eating, could he be driving their cab, or carrying their luggage? For a guided tour of the Linderhof, one of the three lavish palaces built by Ludwig II in the late nineteenth century, they joined the queue with the other English-speakers, as Jane did not speak German; their guide was a tall, balding Englishman with the robust heartiness of a traditional seaside entertainer. By the end of their twenty-minute tour David had found his character. He slipped effortlessly into this new role himself; in his mind he was conducting the obedient audience round Ludwig's dream castle, entertaining them with his repertoire of feeble jokes.[7]

The novel opens at the Linderhof, with a reunion between Mundy and Sasha, whom he has known since 1969, when they had shared a squalid room in Berlin. Years later, Sasha, by this time an officer in the Stasi, offers to become a double agent. Though not a professional, Mundy becomes his case officer. Their loyalty to each other overrides their loyalty to family, or country. 'You are my absolute friend,' declares Sasha. Their friendship transcends the division between East and West, between England and Germany. It is reminiscent of the central relationship between Magnus and Axel in *A Perfect Spy*: Sasha is a version of Axel, and of his progenitor Alexander Heussler, with the same limp and the same quick wit. The contradictions involved in running a double agent allow David to explore notions of duality, as he had done in *A Perfect Spy*. 'Let's all pretend to be someone else,' Mundy reflects as he is being followed in Prague, 'and then perhaps we'll find out who we are.'[8]

By 11 September David had written the first two chapters. That day the Cornwells were in Hamburg: they had spent the morning watching archive footage of Rudi Dutschke, Daniel Cohn-Bendit and other 1960s radicals, and were back at their hotel, relaxing in the bar, when they received an urgent message from David's secretary to find a television. They rushed up to their room and switched on the set, in time to see the second plane fly into the twin towers. In the next few hours, David made impotent efforts to contact his son Stephen, who lived in California with his English wife and their eight children. Like so many other people around the world, he felt 'an enormous, inexpressible sympathy for the victims, for America' at that moment. As for his book, David's immediate reaction was that it was 'dead in the water'. Even to be contemplating a novel about a terrorist plot at such a time seemed unacceptable.[9]

David's perspective soon changed, however. After President Bush had declared a worldwide 'War on Terror', he began to feel that his book had a renewed validity. He was horrified when the American government set up a detention camp within the US naval base at Guantánamo Bay in Cuba, where prisoners could be held indefinitely without trial, outside US jurisdiction and the protection of the Geneva Convention. He deplored the use of 'extraordinary rendition' – the abduction and transfer of a person from one country to another without legal process, much used by the Americans to bring prisoners to Guantánamo. Indeed, as the months passed, his mounting outrage at what was being said and done by the leaders of the West added urgency to the novel. He had reluctantly supported the invasion of Afghanistan, and favoured attempts to eliminate the leadership of Al-Qaeda, but was bitterly opposed to the moves to take action against Iraq, and was appalled that so many Americans had been gulled into believing that Saddam Hussein was implicated in the attacks on America. 'The lies that have been distributed are so many and so persistent', he would say, 'that arguably fiction is the only way to tell the truth.'[10]

Anthony Barnett was the editor and co-founder of openDemocracy, a global website or 'commons' created to provide an alternative to the conventional, 'corporate' media and he brought David to meet its staff. In contrast, David's old friend William Shawcross was one of the loudest advocates for 'regime change' in Iraq. David was invited by the *Guardian* to debate the issue with Shawcross in its pages, but David was reluctant to clash with his chum in print and declined the opportunity.

In September 2002 the Cornwells joined an anti-war rally in central London. Days earlier Tony Blair had released a document presenting the case for going to war with Iraq. The marchers, whose numbers were estimated to be between 150,000 and 400,000, were 'kettled' (corralled) by the police. David found the whole experience 'extremely moving'. He was fascinated by the variety of people participating, young and old, white and black, radical and conservative: those with whom he spoke ranged from an enraged Muslim from Birmingham to a quietly spoken white doctor from Winchester. It seemed to David that the police were much more hostile to the peace demonstrators than they had been to the marchers from the Countryside Alliance, who had held their own rally the week before. 'Jane and I marched against the war last month,' David wrote afterwards to John and Miranda Margetson, '& hope we'll get a chance to do it again before the world ends.'[11] In fact they would do so again the following February, as part of a worldwide protest against plans to invade Iraq. Around one million people gathered in London for the demonstration, described as the largest ever held in Britain. When the marchers were brought to a halt in Whitehall, a huge roar rose from the packed crowd. David tried to imagine Tony Blair sitting in Downing Street, listening to that sound.

John Miller had died of cancer during the previous month, after a short illness, through which Michael Truscott had nursed him with loving care. David came over to see him regularly in the last few weeks of his life. He delivered a moving eulogy at Miller's funeral in a Penzance church. 'Very old, very dear friend,' he began,

> Nobody I have ever known was better prepared for death than you were. Who else would lie smiling up at me while I read these words to him? But you did. And you worried for me, that I would be too upset to read them. I had come to comfort you. But you got there ahead of me, and comforted me instead.

'We shall never know a better man than John Miller,' he said in his peroration, 'or a happier one.'

About eighteen months earlier David himself had been diagnosed with prostate cancer. The first advice was that he should submit himself to an immediate operation; a second opinion recommended that he should watch and wait. Since then he has undergone no special treatment. 'I'm fine, as far it goes,' he wrote to Kaspar and Erica von Almen in a 2003 New Year's message. 'A little woodworm, a little dry rot, some death-watch beetle, notably in the form of prostate cancer, but emphatically in good health and writing, writing, because, after marching, it's the best insurance against death.' He referred to Alec Guinness's death two years before, and complained that 'we seem to spend all our Sundays at memorial services – the cocktail round for geriatrics': 'I have become a sort of cantor for my vanished friends, which I resent. They should live longer, and sing for me.'[12]

Despite his illness, David was determined to go on writing. Declining an invitation from the Margetsons to spend Christmas with them, he apologised for being so elusive. 'I have had a very uphill struggle with the new novel, and much frustration, and at last things are beginning to look right,' he wrote.

> Endless underpainting, scraping off, and beginning again somewhere else on the canvas, standards getting ever higher, time and energy diminishing in inverse proportion – but the will, thank heaven, unbowed so far. The problem is always continuity: not stealing a few hours but getting a sustained run of weeks and months in the same place without the delightful diversions – persons from Porlock – that send one scurrying back to the beginning in order to get inside the cage again.

He had been pleased to read that Lucian Freud had recently failed to attend the opening of an exhibition of his own work in Paris because he was too busy painting – 'so I'm not the only loony in the world after all'.[13]

From an invitation to speak to the editorial team at openDemocracy came the idea that David should write an article on the ever-louder drumbeat for war in America. As a publisher of a digital newsletter, Barnett thought it quaint that David should want to publish it in *The Times*, the 'newspaper of record'. His article appeared there on 15 January 2003, under the title 'The United States of America Has Gone Mad'. By this time war was imminent: coalition armies were massing on the Iraqi border, and air strikes against Iraqi military targets had begun. 'America has entered one of its periods of historical madness, but this is the worst I can remember,' David wrote: 'worse than McCarthyism, worse than the Bay of Pigs and in the long term potentially more disastrous than the Vietnam War.'

> The reaction to 9/11 is beyond anything Osama bin Laden could have hoped for in his nastiest dreams. As in McCarthy times, the freedoms that have made America the envy of the world are being systematically eroded. The combination of compliant US media and vested corporate interests is once more ensuring that a debate that should be ringing out in every town square is confined to the loftier columns of the East Coast press . . .
>
> How Bush and his junta succeeded in deflecting America's anger from bin Laden to Saddam Hussein is one of the great public relations conjuring tricks of history. But they swung it. A recent poll tells us that one in two Americans now believe Saddam was responsible for the attack on the World

> Trade Centre. But the American public is not merely being misled. It is being browbeaten and kept in a state of ignorance and fear . . .[14]

The invasion of Iraq, which began in March 2003, seemed to feed directly into David's writing. Several of the novel's reviewers would remark on an abrupt change of tone in chapter 11, the chapter he was writing as the war began. In this chapter Mundy is reborn ('Mundy *redux*') as David's spokesman. Like David himself, Mundy marches in protest against the Iraq invasion, 'with a conviction he never felt before because convictions were essentially what he borrowed from other people':

> Suddenly he is mad as a hornet . . . The lies and hypocrisies of politicians are nothing new to him. They never were. So why now? Why leap on his soap-box and rant uselessly about the same things that have been going on since the first politician on earth lisped his first hypocrisy, lied, wrapped himself in the flag, put on God's armour and said he never did it in the first place?
>
> It is the old man's impatience coming on early. It's anger at seeing the show come round again one too many times . . .
>
> It's the discovery, in his sixth decade, that half a century after the death of empire, the dismally ill-managed country he'd done a little of this and that for is being marched off to quell the natives on the strength of a bunch of lies, in order to please a renegade hyperpower that thinks it can treat the rest of the world as its allotment.[15]

David modified his original plot, to make it so that Mundy and Sasha, though innocent, are blackened as terrorists; and, though unarmed, are gunned down by American special forces, in what the docile press misleadingly refers to as 'The Siege of Heidelberg' (his provisional title). Some reviewers would criticise this apocalyptic finale as implausible.

By early June he had finished the book in draft. After further revision he sent it out for comment to readers, with a note asking them to forgive any topographical inaccuracies; he had never been to Heidelberg and would go there to correct these, and go back to Berlin and to Munich after finishing the first draft. 'I have always preferred to work this way,' he wrote: 'first to make the story work, then to relive it on the ground.'[16] In asking Anthony

Barnett to read the second draft, David made a similar point. 'I have never found it possible to write a novel out of a mass of research,' he wrote: 'better to write to form the theatrical and human point of view first, & correct the backcloth retrospectively.'[17] Barnett provided him with detailed notes and editorial suggestions on this and subsequent drafts.

In general, David would reveal very little about any book he was writing until he felt that it was ready to be shown to his publisher. At that stage Bruce Hunter would submit a typescript to Tim Hely Hutchinson, and they would rapidly make a deal. Then Roland Philipps became involved. 'You don't suggest anything,' Hunter had advised him when he became David's editor back in the early 1990s. 'You talk about stuff.' His response to a new book would be discursive rather than prescriptive: typically he would spend a couple of days with David discussing characters and themes, often while walking on the Heath or along the Cornish clifftops. David always listened carefully, and often made changes as a result of these discussions, for example, by fleshing out a character. The books almost always grew longer as a result.

For Philipps, it was always instructive to hear David's audiobook recordings, because the characters came alive as he spoke their lines. Of course this was the wheel coming full circle, in that part of David's method of forming a character in the first place was to speak his lines as he imagined them.

In 2004 Hodder Headline would be sold again, this time to the French publishing group Hachette Livre, which already owned the publishers Orion and Octopus, and would soon acquire the Time Warner Publishing Group, which included Little, Brown. Though Hely Hutchinson became the chief executive of the Hachette Group UK, he continued to take a close personal interest in David's publishing.

David decided against the title 'The Siege of Heidelberg', perhaps because it betrayed the book's climax; he considered 'Sasha's Virtue' and 'The Stay-Behind Man' before settling on *Absolute Friends*. He had been dissatisfied with the way that Scribner's had published *The Constant Gardener* and asked Bruce Hunter to find another American publisher for the new novel, which was sold to Little, Brown for $2.1 million. Even more than usual, David tested the patience of his publishers by continuing to rewrite until the very last moment, necessitating three stages of proof before he was done. The British edition was scheduled to appear in December 2003, with the American edition following a month after. Only weeks earlier, David and Jane joined Anthony Barnett and his partner Judith Herrin and at least 100,000 others to demonstrate against a state visit by President Bush. In the run-up to publication a succession of journalists made the journey down to West Cornwall to interview him, most bringing a photographer who would invariably take a picture of a windswept David against a background of sea and cliff. One of these was the young novelist Lev Grossman, who interviewed him for *Time*. 'His anger burns cold and clear,' wrote Grossman: '*Absolute Friends* is a work of fist-shaking, Orwellian outrage.'[18] Another of those visitors to Tregiffian was the writer and broadcaster James Naughtie, who interviewed David both for *The Times* and for the BBC Radio 4 *Today* programme. 'His anger is real,' wrote Naughtie. 'To the extent that it is possible for a figure of his upbringing, bearing and voice, he rages.' David reserved his bitterest bile for Tony Blair. 'To me,' he told Naughtie in his radio interview, 'there's no bigger sin that a politician can commit than allowing his country to go to war under false pretences.' His fulminations against the Prime Minister enabled *The Times* to use the stand-first 'John le Carré: Blair Must Go' to advertise the interview on the front cover of its *Weekend Review*.[19]

The anger crackling in the novel dominated the review coverage. 'Few could fail to be thrilled by the unbridled rage that fuels his storytelling,' wrote Robert McCrum in the *Observer*. 'If he was seething when he wrote *The Constant Gardener*, he is now incandescent.'[20] Most reviewers agreed with the view expressed by Stephen Amidon in the *Sunday Times*, who wrote that 'le Carré's anger comes across as a bit too raw to work as fiction, its rhetoric more in line with a Harold Pinter column than a Graham Greene novel'.[21] T. J. Binyon, who had reviewed David's books since the 1970s, usually favourably, described the tone of the book as one of 'fierce moral indignation', which by the end has become 'wearisome'.[22] For George Walden, writing in the *Daily Telegraph*, 'a once entertaining writer is subsiding into ranting moralism'.[23] In a comment piece in the same newspaper, Daniel Johnson wrote sneeringly: 'John le Carré is Mr Angry now that Smiley's Day has gone.'[24] A. N. Wilson, on the other hand, gave his opinion that *Absolute Friends* was 'John le Carré's finest novel'.[25] In a letter to Vivian Green, David dismissed the negative coverage as 'an onslaught from the right-wing press'.[26]

One of the most thoughtful reviews came from Steven Poole in the *Guardian*. He dismissed the criticism that the book's denouement was implausible. 'Anyone betting against the deviousness of unofficial American foreign policy over the last several decades would have lost countless shirts.' But he found the novel's ending problematic, 'not because it is unlikely, but because it is both over-determined and gratuitous'.

> Over-determined, because in the scheme of this novel there is no other villain in the modern world than America. And gratuitous because it is a *deus ex machina* that merely serves to illustrate the novel's politicised ranting . . .
>
> Given his enormous and undimmed skills as a storyteller, that could have been a brilliant book. But the sophisticated analysis of moral questions, of deceit personal and political, and of shabby ends to justify honourable means, that characterised his classic cold war novels is here finally drowned out by strident editorialising, the monotonous expression of an anger imperfectly interrogated and so unhoned. Where once there was a subtle knife, here there is only a blunt stick.[27]

Most of the reviewers saw *Absolute Friends* as anti-American. The British writer Geoffrey Wheatcroft used the book as a starting-point for an article in the *New York Times* on the general topic of anti-Americanism; he referred to le Carré as 'a writer who has enjoyed much success in America despite an aversion to American power dating from his earliest books, who has no very subtle political understanding, but who all too accurately voices the bitterness of national impotence and decline'.[28] James M. Murphy, reviewing *Absolute Friends* for the *Times Literary Supplement*, speculated that the novel might be a Circus plot. 'The author's anti-Americanism is a matter of record,' remarked Murphy. 'But would this not provide an excellent level of cover to produce a work whose indictment of the United States so overshoots reasonable levels of credibility that it undermines the very political message it pretends to send?'[29]

One hazard of writing such overtly political novels was that David exposed himself to ridicule as a pundit. 'With a political statement this pungent, le Carré knows he risks alienating his sizeable American following, even of being written off as a crank – an aging, forgotten ex-spook railing at the world from his Cornish crag,' suggested Lev Grossman. The book was reviewed in the *New York Times* by Michiko Kakutani, a Pulitzer Prize-winning critic notorious for her harsh reviews; for her, *Absolute Friends* was 'a clumsy, hectoring, conspiracy-minded message-novel meant to drive home the argument that American imperialism poses a grave danger to the new world order'.

> The plot has been constructed to illustrate this message, and it not only feels hastily jerry-built but ridiculously contrived as well. Whereas Mr. le Carré's Smiley novels were famous for their nuanced depiction of the ambiguities of the cold war and their demythologizing of the grubby world of spying, this latest novel suffers from large heapings of sentimentality and naïveté.
>
> It is simplistic where his earlier novels were sophisticated; dogmatic where those books were skeptical. Paradoxically enough, it also purveys the same sort of black and white moralism that Mr. le Carré's nemesis, the Bush administration, is so fond of, and it does so not by persuasively dramatizing the author's convictions but by bashing the reader over the head with dubious assertions and even more dubious scenarios.[30]

It was hard to imagine that the novel could thrive after such a battering in the most important arena in America. On publication the book entered the *New York Times* bestseller list at no. 3, but within a month it had slipped out of the list.

David tried to remain impervious to the criticism. He demurred when Anthony Barnett urged some sort of response to the 'anguished' English critics. 'There's no sillier fellow than a writer complaining about his reviews, & I can't be another,' he replied.[31] But references to his age, and suggestions that he was out of touch, were infuriating, especially at a time when he felt that he was engaging with the modern world more directly than at any previous point in his career. 'We are in Tregiffian at last, a bit bruised but recovering,' he wrote to Vivian Green a couple of months after publication. 'I think we both got a bit weary of the clamour about the book, the bouquets as well as the brickbats. (So of course the only thing to do is to start another one.)'[32]

While writing a novel David immerses himself in the story and shuts himself off from the world, trying to avoid commitments and refusing all but the most urgent social engagements. As he began to get going with the new book David again felt the need to apologise for declining another invitation from John Margetson. 'I know it irritates you that I'm always working,' he wrote: 'I *do* want to write myself into the grave, as most writers do, and as most musicians want to play themselves into the grave and painters paint themselves etc . . .'[33]

The origins of David's next book are obscure: he can no longer recall them himself. Probably the character came first. This time his secret sharer would be an interpreter: Bruno Salvador, known to all as Salvo. As a young diplomat with fluent German, David had acted as an interpreter for German politicians visiting Britain, and for British politicians visiting Germany. The role fascinated him, not least because interpreters have to bridge the gulf that exists between all cultures, even very sophisticated ones.

Salvo is a 'zebra', the half-caste natural son of an Irish Catholic missionary and a Congolese village woman whom he never knew. He spends his boyhood living on a mission in eastern Congo, where he cultivates his aptitude for languages in the servants' hostel, curled up unnoticed on a wooden pallet as he listens to the talk of hunters, witch-doctors, spell-sellers, warriors and elders. Orphaned at ten years old, Salvo discovers to his surprise that he is British, a foundling adopted by the Holy See, whose purported father had been a Northern Irish seafarer. He is sent to England, to attend a Catholic boarding school in Sussex; after studying at the School of Oriental and African Studies he becomes an interpreter, specialising in the languages and dialects from the region of his birth. The book would be called *The Mission Song*, a reference to the place where Salvo develops his aptitude for languages, to a jingle sung by one of the characters and to the mission which drives the plot.

As usual, David put much of himself into his character, and indeed the book is told in the first person.* Notwithstanding appearances, Salvo and his creator have much in common. Both grew up without mothers and with fathers who were absent for long periods; David felt effectively orphaned even if he was not literally so. He remembers his childhood as

* Several reviewers would suggest that this was the first time that le Carré had written a novel in the first person, forgetting *Our Game* and *The Secret Pilgrim*.

populated by preachers, just as Salvo is surrounded by priests. Like Salvo, he was despatched from a chaotic home to the discipline of a boarding school. 'I remember not belonging anywhere and taking refuge in a foreign language,' David has said – like Salvo. After the novel was published David would summarise Salvo's qualities: 'a hybrid, caught between worlds, struggling to do the right thing, a bit thick about a lot of things, rash in love, wanting to serve, but serve whom? I can't pretend he isn't like someone I used to know fairly well when I was young: me.'[34] On the other hand, he and Salvo were obviously different. David could only imagine Salvo's Congolese background because he had never been there. Even if Salvo had been brought up in England, it would still have been hard for a white man in his seventies to inhabit the mind of a black man in his twenties. Salvo was young enough to be David's grandson; it was scarcely to be expected that David could share his habits and cultural references, or relate to women in the same way. One of David's readers had to point out to him that a man of Salvo's generation was unlikely to charge for his time in guineas.

David had enjoyed writing *The Constant Gardener* and was attracted by the possibility of another book with an African theme – particularly the white man's exploitation of Africa's riches. A dramatic example suggested itself within weeks of the publication of *Absolute Friends*. In March 2004 a group of mercenaries was arrested at Harare airport, where they had landed to collect a consignment of machine-guns, mortars, assault rifles, hand grenades, rocket-propelled grenade launchers and ammunition. Their leader was Simon Mann, an Old Etonian and a former officer in the Scots Guards and the SAS. It was alleged that they were en route to Equatorial Guinea, where they had planned a *coup d'état* to depose the President, a dictator who had ruled the country with an iron hand since 1979;* indeed, he had himself come to power in a coup. Not that this concerned the mercenaries: prosecutors would allege that they had agreed to install a prominent opposition leader in return for the grant of valuable rights to extract oil to corporations affiliated to the coup's financial backers. One of these was Sir Mark Thatcher, a fact that ensured worldwide publicity for

* At the time of writing he is still President, thirty-five years after seizing power.

the thwarted coup; this was only the latest in a succession of embarrassing incidents connected with the son of the former Prime Minister.

David imagined a plot to stage a similar coup, with the object of forming a breakaway state in eastern Congo. The Democratic Republic of Congo, known as Zaire until 1997, is a nation the size of Western Europe, blessed by abundant mineral resources but cursed by rampant corruption and lack of infrastructure. It had been destabilised by the incursion of Rwandan refugees after the 1994 genocide, leading to a succession of civil wars and the establishment of heavily armed militias. The country was devastated by disease and sexual violence, by indiscriminate slaughter and by the fighting itself. David had been strongly advised not to go there.

Of course it was hard to write a serious novel about the Congo without a reference to Conrad, and David paid appropriate homage to the Master, with an epigraph taken from *Heart of Darkness*:

> The conquest of the earth, which mostly means the taking it away from those who have a different complexion or slightly flatter noses than ourselves, is not a pretty thing when you look into it too much.

The action of the book is compressed into a short period of only a few days, and is confined to London and an unnamed island in the North Sea. Salvo is called upon to interpret at a secret conference between the powerbrokers in the mineral-rich region. At first he sees nothing sinister in the plan. As one of the mercenaries puts it, 'Congo's been bleeding to death for five centuries'.

> Fucked by the Arab slavers, fucked by their fellow Africans, fucked by the United Nations, the CIA, the Christians, the Belgians, the French, the Brits, the Rwandans, the diamond companies, the gold companies, the mineral companies, half the world's carpetbaggers, their own government in Kinshasa, and any minute now they're going to be fucked by the oil companies. Time they had a break, and we're the boys to give it to 'em.

But Salvo is innocent to the point of naïvety. Too late, he realises that these altruistic protestations are sham, cover for the corporate backers of the coup to secure valuable mineral deposits. When he attempts to make public what he has heard, the authorities step in to silence him: Salvo is detained without trial and his African girlfriend is deported. On one level the book is about 'old-fashioned colonial exploitation'; but it is also about political hypocrisy and the assault on civil liberties in Tony Blair's Britain.

David had read and admired the writer and journalist Michela Wrong's much praised account of her experiences as a foreign correspondent, *In the Footsteps of Mr Kurtz: Living on the Brink of Disaster in the Congo* (2000). He invited her to lunch at Wilton's, in Jermyn Street. 'I want to pick your brains, not too severely, about the Congo,' he explained in an email. Over the meal he told her that he had an idea for a 'corking' story about a translator. 'I have a beautiful little story to write, but it's missing its African heart,' he wrote to her afterwards. 'I'm looking for a champion researcher, preferably indigenous, because somehow every book I've written has thrown one up: somebody who is not daunted by my elementary ignorance, which in this case is pristine, but warms to the theme, drives me nuts, and gets me moving.'[35] He was willing to pay handsomely for such help. She replied with a list of possible researchers, as well as offering to work on the book herself. It was agreed that she would act as a second pair of eyes, reading and commenting on what he wrote.

Still furious with George W. Bush, David took part in the *Guardian*'s attempt to influence the American presidential election of 2004. Together with Antonia Fraser and Richard Dawkins, he launched the newspaper's letter-writing campaign ('Operation Clark County'). *Guardian* readers were encouraged to write to 'undeclared' voters in Clark County, a marginal district in the swing state of Ohio, to press home the international ramifications of re-electing President Bush for a second term. 'Probably no American President has been so universally hated abroad as George W. Bush,' wrote David, in an open letter to Clark County voters, published initially in the *Guardian* and subsequently republished in American newspapers and magazines.[36] In a letter to his stepmother Jean, David described the response as 'almost uniformly abusive'.[37] The campaign seemed to rile American voters, arousing resentment of foreign interference even in those who might have agreed with the message. In the election, Bush won Clark County by 1,404 votes, and took Ohio by a margin of 2.1 per cent. He was duly re-elected as President.

Six months later David would be invited by the *Guardian* to interview Tony Blair, in the run-up to another British general election in the spring.

Apparently the Prime Minister's private office had agreed to the proposal in principle. But after much consideration David declined, reckoning that it would be an unequal contest, given his opponent's experience in debate and the support that he could rely on from his formidable array of spin-doctors. He had no wish to participate in an event that would serve merely as a platform for Blair's views.

David contributed a short story to the Swiss German-language magazine *Du*, entitled 'The King Who Never Spoke'.* This was a simple, childlike tale of a monarch who failed to respond to urging from his royal advisers to make war on his enemies, and who maintained the peace by keeping his silence. It was hard not to see this as an ironic fable about the disastrous impulse of our rulers to take up arms, when they would be better advised to do nothing.

Vivian Green died in January 2005, at the age of eighty-nine. He had been a Fellow of Lincoln since 1952, and Rector of the college from 1983 to 1987, becoming a well-known Oxford figure, instantly recognisable in his green leather trousers and stridently checked jackets. For some years he had lived in a thirteenth-century house in Burford and latterly in a nursing home. David spoke at Green's memorial service in Oxford, paying warm tribute to his old friend as 'a preacher who, in the sixty years,† never preached to me, never pulled rank, never asked me why, never said "Don't do it" or "I told you so"'. Asking himself who Green had been for him, David answered, 'a good shepherd, and a proxy father certainly'. He alluded to the fact that he had drawn on Green's qualities to create George Smiley. 'No wonder then, when I was searching for a character to guide my readers – and myself – through the fiendish complexities of my fictional plots, that I should have turned once more to Vivian for my support – even if, with the deviousness of the novelist, I didn't tell him.'[38]

By this time David had grown accustomed to letters from readers around the world, but even so he was surprised to hear from a reader in space.

* An English version appeared in the volume *Fire* in a series published in support of Oxfam, 'Ox-Tales' (Profile, 2009).

† That is, since David arrived at Sherborne.

In April 2005 he received a message from NASA on behalf of Leroy Chiao, then coming to the end of a six months' tour of duty aboard the International Space Station. Apparently his favourite author was John le Carré.

Chiao, an American of Chinese descent, had a doctorate in chemical engineering. He was an experienced astronaut, who had undertaken a number of space walks during three previous missions aboard the Space Shuttle. Since the Shuttle *Columbia* had disintegrated on re-entry two years earlier, the Shuttle fleet had been grounded, so Chiao had flown to the Space Station aboard a Russian Soyuz spacecraft from a launch site in Kazakhstan.

David agreed to a request to speak to Chiao above the earth. The conversation took place only a few days before Chiao was due to return. David spoke on the landline at Tregiffian, using the kitchen extension. The call lasted twenty-two minutes, which was as long as the 'window' permitted. The two men talked about David's books, and Chiao told him about his new bride, who would be waiting for him at the landing site in Kazakhstan. Afterwards Chiao sent David several emails from the space station, with photographs taken as it passed over Cornwall.* In the summer he and his wife came to lunch with David and Jane at Tregiffian.

That spring David received a letter from the French Embassy, forwarded by David Higham Associates. The Cultural Attaché congratulated him on being nominated to the rank of Commandeur in the Ordre des Arts et des Lettres. Enclosed was a formal letter to this effect from the French Minister of Culture. 'Cette distinction veut honorer les personnalités qui se sont illustrées par leurs créations dans le domaine artistique ou littéraire, ou par la contribution qu'elles ont apportée au rayonnement de la culture en France et dans le monde.'

* While in Moscow in 1986 Graham Greene met a cosmonaut who had taken a copy of *Our Man in Havana* with him into space, as one of only three books he was allowed. He told Greene that he had read his novel three times during that mission. In a subsequent interview with Nicholas Shakespeare at his flat in Antibes, Greene produced the tatty paperback which the cosmonaut had insisted on giving him.

The nomination was completely unexpected. David had no hesitation in accepting, despite the fact that he had refused a British honour: he reasoned that the nomination had been made by a cultural committee assembled for the purpose, unlike British awards, which were the product of an obscure 'advisory' system managed by 'the faceless great and good'.

David invited around fifty guests to attend the investiture, which took place early in the evening at the Ambassador's residence in Kensington Palace Gardens. The Ambassador made an impromptu address of welcome; David responded with a short, prepared acceptance speech. He referred to his love of French literature, of Balzac in particular, and concluded with a veiled allusion to the French decision not to take part in the attack on Iraq. He spoke in English, except for his final paragraph of thanks, which was delivered in French. Michela Wrong, who was present as one of his guests, was struck by how good his French was, and how sophisticated his phraseology and grammar.

Afterwards guests were invited to a celebratory dinner at L'Escargot in Soho. David had hired a red double-decker bus to take them there.

David's discontent at his diminishing sales in America surfaced in a bruising correspondence with his agent. In September 2004 he had warned Bruce Hunter not to make any preliminary soundings about his future work, as he did not consider it settled that he would 'remain with the present constellation, either in terms of publication or representation'.

Hunter had been David's agent since 1986. Though David had stipulated at the start that he wanted a business rather than a social relationship, they had become quite close over the years. Hunter and his partner Belinda Hollyer (a writer and publisher of children's books) regularly dined with David and Jane when they were in London, and visited them in Cornwall perhaps half a dozen times; in 1997 they had been David's guests for a fortnight on board a yacht cruising along the Turkish coast, together with two other couples, the film producer 'Buzz' Berger and his wife Janet, and Hampstead neighbours Chris Robbins and his wife Mary Agnes Donoghue. They had been among the small group of friends invited to David's seventieth birthday celebrations in Siena. More recently, however, Hunter had become aware of mounting dissatisfaction from his most important client.

Six months of silence followed before David resumed contact. 'I am on my way to completing a large, commercial novel, and the time is approaching for me to decide how it should be represented,' David wrote ominously. 'Absolute Friends left me with a bad taste I can't get over,' he explained. 'I lost confidence in your commitment to my work, both at a professional & personal level, & have found it hard to recover.' His instinct was to ask his lawyer, Michael Rudell, to handle the sale of the new book in America, on a fee basis rather than a commission. Hunter protested at the 'injustice' of David's complaints. 'For the last few years you have been angry, and in that time your anger has fuelled two great novels, and some excellent journalism,' Hunter suggested. 'But recently you have turned it on your agent and that is not appropriate.' Perhaps unwisely, he tried to force the issue of the American rights at the very moment when David had announced that he wanted to 'keep my head down and get to the end of what I believe will be a big novel'. Hunter had a point: there had been clashes between David's British and American publishers over the right to sell English-language editions in Europe, and he argued that these could be most easily resolved if he were represented by the same agency in both territories. But David took his letter to be an ultimatum.

> As I understand your letter of 11th April, you have responded to my criticism of your personal performance in the American market with an ultimatum covering all your work that the agency does for me worldwide. In short: give me America, or go. You know me very little if you believe I would remain with you under such a threat . . .
>
> Let me remind you again that I have persistently praised Higham's performance. I have occasionally, but not very often, criticized it. I remain of the opinion that you did not serve me well in America in recent years, and I have said so. To most observers, that would be normal commercial discourse. To you it is, somewhat insultingly, an old man's anger and he must pay for it.
>
> What a pity. What a waste. What vanity. What folly.

In reply, Hunter restated the problems of territory and timing of publication. 'Splitting up the world English language market is not the answer,' he maintained. He suggested that they should meet face to face to discuss the issues. But David was in no mood for a meeting. 'You have been less than gracious about my age, and pretty much implied that I am an insufferable person to deal with,' he responded. 'You have managed to paint me in the colours of an ageing nuisance who must be slapped down once and for all.' He suggested terminating their professional relationship.

At this stage Jane took over the correspondence with Hunter. A compromise was speedily agreed whereby Rudell would handle American rights, while Higham's would continue to represent David's work in the rest of the world.[39]

By October 2005 the new novel was sufficiently far advanced for David to send a first draft to Michela Wrong. She responded with sixteen pages of detailed notes, and over the following months she would provide further feedback on successive drafts, informed by her knowledge of the region, by her local contacts and also by her own dual heritage (she is half Italian) – for example, she pointed out that people tend to take on the personality of the language that they are speaking, an idea that David has Salvo voice: 'An Englishman breaking into German speaks more loudly. His mouth changes shape, his vocal cords open up, he abandons self-irony in favour of dominance. An Englishwoman dropping into French will soften herself and puff out her lips for pertness, while her male counterpart will veer towards the pompous.' She was impressed by how quickly David picked up on her editorial suggestions, by his readiness to accept her recommendations, even on matters outside her areas of expertise, and by his willingness to make significant changes, right up to a very late stage in the process.* Among her many recommendations was that he should cut down the 'gooey' sex scenes between Salvo and his girlfriend Hannah. To confirm her feeling that a proposed alliance between the rival warlords in the region was not credible, she consulted her friend Jason Stearns, then a senior analyst for the International Crisis Group,† who had spent three

* When she was writing her book about a Kenyan whistleblower, *It's Our Turn to Eat* (2009), David suggested that she should show him the typescript, and in due course returned it, marked up with his suggestions and advice. She was struck by his willingness to help. 'How many writers of his stature would offer to act as editor to someone like myself?'

† The International Crisis Group describes itself as 'an independent, non-profit, non-governmental organisation committed to preventing and resolving deadly conflict'.

years in eastern Congo working for human rights groups and the UN peacekeeping mission. 'It's all about character,' David remarked in response to her qualms – 'plot doesn't really matter.' She recommended that Congo should be more present in the book, to compensate for the fact that the action never takes the reader there: the story would benefit from 'more of the sights, tastes, smells and sounds of the place', expressed in Salvo's thoughts, dreams and memories. For his part, David felt comfortable with Salvo, but he was less sure about the warlords whose conference formed the central part of the plot. To trust in the characters he had invented, he needed to meet their real equivalents, in their own environment.[40]

Even after the book was finished and in proof, David was still considering whether or not he should go to eastern Congo. He had written the book in a period when he had felt unable to leave England. Now he was tempted to make the trip, not only to connect with the subject matter of his novel, but also from a sense of intellectual honesty, and the knowledge that the book would have more credibility if he had been there himself. And he wanted to prove he could still go out into the field in his seventies. But the Foreign Office cautioned him against doing so, and his friend Al Alvarez loudly echoed this advice. David's Congolese contacts in Britain had added their own dire warnings about the risks of entering such an unstable and precarious zone; though, as Michela Wrong suggested, such exiles tended to exaggerate the danger because they did not want to be sent back. She and Jason Stearns offered to accompany him on a trip. They could make it easy for him, as they knew the kind of people he needed to meet and the locations he needed to see. Wrong tried to reassure him about security, though she would be the first to admit that it was a frightening place to visit. 'The quiet thud of fear would be there throughout my time in Zaire,' she had written on the opening page of her book. As David would remark afterwards, he had done a lot of travelling in his life, but had never before been in a country where people talked so casually about killing. Moreover it was one thing for her and for Stearns, both comparatively young, to go back to a place with which they were familiar; it was another thing for David, at his age, to disregard the warnings he had received from almost every side. Nonetheless he decided to do so.

In April 2006 the three of them flew in to the Rwandan capital of Kigali and then travelled by car into eastern Congo. En route they stopped at

Murambi, where twelve years earlier a massacre had taken place: people who had taken shelter in the local technical school had been hacked to death, their bodies dumped in trenches and covered in lime. More recently the school had been designated a genocide memorial centre: 800 mummified corpses had been exhumed and were laid out on display. The three visitors explored this grisly exhibit alone and in silence. David was understandably distressed by what he saw.

They drove on into eastern Congo, to the regional capital, Bukavu, on the shores of Lake Kivu, where David would spend five nights, staying at the Hotel Orchid, a gated, low-built lakeside colonial villa in lush gardens, dotted with discreet cabins. It was an idyllic setting – though not a place of calm. The hotel's Belgian owner had been held up at gunpoint numerous times and regaled Wrong with the story of how he had been shot in the leg during a firefight. Only two years earlier the city had been sacked by troops of a renegade general. Even while David was there, rioting broke out after unpaid soldiers had broken into a house and killed its owner in order to steal his money. If this were not enough, there was a flash flood, stranding a man in his car only a few yards away from where they stood. Never being able to relax was tiring. David felt ill much of the time, an effect perhaps of the powerful anti-malarial drugs he was taking.

They travelled around Bukavu without a bodyguard. David recorded his impressions in notebooks, using a Parker rollerball pen with refills. He seemed to Wrong remarkably observant: he noticed everything, even in such an alien situation. He was especially interested in dialogue, and relished the African habit of peppering conversation with proverbs. It struck her that David's pseudonym enabled him to travel in his real identity 'under the radar' – indeed, as the author of a recent book on Congo, her name was more often recognised than his. Even when she introduced him under his pseudonym, there was sometimes confusion: one Catholic missionary took him to be the author of *The Hunt for Red October*. On the other hand, the former Rwandan intelligence chief Patrick Karegeya knew exactly who he was when they were introduced in Kigali. 'When you said a well-known author,' Karegeya said to Wrong, 'I didn't realise that you meant *this* author.' He and David recognised each other as kindred spirits, fellow practitioners in the same game. David would be haunted by this encounter, as it was already clear that Karegeya was doomed. He was a prominent figure in the opposition to the Rwandan President, Paul Kagame. After surviving several assassination attempts, he would be found strangled in a Johannesburg hotel room on 1 January 2014.

Stearns refused to accept payment for his help on the project. When David was insistent, Stearns suggested that instead he might like to make a contribution to StandProud, a charity providing funding to help Congolese young people with disabilities, assuming that the sum would be a thousand dollars or so. He was therefore stunned to learn that David had in fact made over $25,000. Later that year David would collaborate with Stearns in writing an 'op-ed' piece for the *Boston Globe*, urging the World Bank to investigate mining deals made by the Congolese transitional government in 2005 – deals that, according to the article, signed away, on terms that will not benefit the Congolese people, 75 per cent of the country's copper and cobalt reserves for the next thirty-five years.[41]

The Mission Song was published on both sides of the Atlantic simultaneously in September. After all the kerfuffle about the American rights, the book had been sold to Little, Brown, David's existing publishers. The critics seemed to like the book more than its predecessor. The reviewer in the *San Francisco Chronicle*, for example, welcomed the more relaxed tone of the novel, which he found much less strident than in its two immediate predecessors: 'le Carré has regained his lighter touch'. He saw *The Mission Song* as 'a marvelous return to the John le Carré of old, with all the captivating characters, finely rendered landscapes and messy complexities that have always powered his best work'.[42] The journalist Philip Caputo, best known for his memoir *A Rumor of War* (1977), praised the book in the *Washington Post*. 'To categorize le Carré as a "spy" novelist is to do him a disservice,' wrote Caputo: 'he uses the world of cloak-and-dagger much as Conrad used the sea – to explore the dark places in human nature.'[43] On the other hand the *Boston Globe* reviewer found the novel disappointing, and expressed the wish that le Carré would go back to 'the good old days' of the Circus.[44]

'At 74, le Carré's eye is undimmed, his passion for his craft as strong as it ever was,' wrote Robert McCrum in the *Observer*. 'He delivers a tale that few could equal and none will surpass.'[45] For the reviewer in the *Sunday Times*, John Dugdale, this was a 'thriller without thrills'; nevertheless, he noted le Carré's 'distinctive ability to fuse social comedy with moral anger'.[46] 'Salvo is one of the most beguiling characters Le Carré has teased into life,' wrote the South African novelist Christopher Hope in the *Guardian*; 'this is very much a book shaped and fuelled by anger, but the anger has been given a perfect foil in the imperturbable, gentle, unstoppable Salvo'.[47] In contrast, William Finnegan, reviewing *The Mission Song* for the *New York Review of Books*, found Salvo 'annoying', and thought it implausible that Salvo should not have smelt a rat sooner: 'his egregious naïveté lasts far too long'. Finnegan, who specialised in writing about Southern Africa, thought it had been a mistake to place such tight constraints on the story. 'To say that staying in Europe, mostly talking, attenuates the inherent drama of this African war story would be too diplomatic,' he wrote; 'it very nearly starves it. The liveliest discussion at a conference center is still a discussion at a conference center.'[48]

'This is my last book,' David had told his travelling companions in Bukavu. 'It's time for me to stop.' He wanted to concentrate on writing shorter pieces, and perhaps to write plays, an as yet unrealised ambition. He had, for example, long contemplated a play about Nicholas Elliott and his friend Kim Philby.* Secretly, he suspected that this might be easier than writing novels. After *The Mission Song* he once again began toying with a memoir. A fragment exists from this period, describing the moment in the spring of 1961 when the half-dozen new recruits to MI6 sat aghast in a safe house in Victoria, as the head of training told them that the service had a traitor in its midst, and then broke down in tears. Its title, 'Scenes from a Secret Life', indicates that he envisaged a companion piece to the essay about his father published in the *New Yorker*. But the fragment amounts to only a few pages, suggesting a lack of commitment to proceed.[49] Besides, 'an extraordinary stroke of luck' had given him an idea.

* The subject of Ben Macintyre's *A Spy Among Friends: Kim Philby and the Great Betrayal* (2014), to which David contributed an afterword.

25

Beating the System

'I'm going for a new novel,' David wrote excitedly to Nicholas Shakespeare, only a couple of months after publication of *The Mission Song*.[1] He had that very day returned from Hamburg, a city crammed with associations for him. It had been his home during an unsettled period in the early 1960s, when he had been hopelessly in love with a married woman, while his life was being transformed by the extraordinary success of *The Spy who Came in from the Cold*. He had gone back to Hamburg in 1978 to check the locations for *Smiley's People*; this was where George Smiley had put on his German identity like a uniform and picked up the trail in his long pursuit of Karla. In the 1990s he had explored the Turkish community in Hamburg, for a novel set in the Muslim diaspora in Europe, which he had then abandoned. And it was in Hamburg that he had learned of the attack on the twin towers; he did not know then, of course, that the Al-Qaeda cell which had carried out the attacks on 11 September 2001 had been formed there.

'Today it's a pounding, thriving, beautiful, confident city,' David would write: 'the richest city in Europe.'[2] But Hamburg was also a 'guilty city', haunted by ghosts of terrorists and uneasy about the strangers in its midst. The German authorities were anxious to refute American accusations that they were 'soft' on terrorism; rival organs of the security apparatus jostled with each other in their attempts to detect those who might commit further outrages.

'An accident of life' had started David on a journey towards the new book. Some months earlier he had gone to Hamburg to do a television interview. The programme's researcher, a young journalist called Carla

Hornstein, had mentioned another story that she was working on, that of a twenty-four-year-old due to be released imminently from the detention centre in Guantánamo. This was Murat Kurnaz, a Turkish citizen living in Germany, who had been arrested on a visit to Pakistan and flown to Guantánamo Bay in shackles, clad in a muzzle, opaque goggles and sound-blocking ear muffs. During his four and a half years in detention he claimed to have been tortured by electric shocks and waterboarding, denied sleep for weeks on end and kept for periods in solitary confinement. When he had gone on hunger strike in protest at his treatment, he had been fed through the nose.

Hoping that David might write a book on the case, Hornstein arranged for him to meet Kurnaz at his home in Bremen, where he interviewed 'the poor bugger' over two days. 'My hat, there's a grown-up!' he exclaimed afterwards to Shakespeare. 'He's now conducting useless lawsuits against the Germans, US & Turks. *Nobody* suggests he was ever guilty of being anything remotely like a terrorist.' Afterwards David would refer to his feelings of guilt, protectiveness and debt towards those who have been wrongly imprisoned and maltreated: 'the tortured are a terrible aristocracy'.

The encounter with Kurnaz fired David to write a novel about a suspected terrorist on the run, a potential victim of 'extraordinary rendition'. Moreover he had stumbled across a human story to set against the theme. 'I will write a story about you, Murat and me,' he told Carla Hornstein. He imagined the sexual tension between a young Muslim man who had not been in the company of women for years and an idealistic young Western woman moved by his plight. At one point, the three of them had been together in a car: the bitter former detainee, the secular German idealist wearing a headscarf in deference to him, and the worldly older novelist. 'I thought, "Let's imagine the circles of desire here that are unfulfilled,"' David would tell an interviewer after the book was published.[3] He envisaged an aloof young man suspected of terrorist involvement and sought by the forces of the state, an attractive young woman trying to help him, and an older man besotted with her. 'It was a circle of frustrated love,' he would say in another interview: 'for me the chemistry worked.'

Though Kurnaz's lawyer was a man, Bernhard Docke, his fictional equivalent would be a woman: David drew on his perception of Carla Hornstein to create the character of Annabel Richter, the high-minded human rights lawyer from a 'good family' with a rebellious streak who represents the interests of the suspected terrorist, and who finds herself emotionally involved with him. He would describe Annabel as 'puritanical but free-thinking, anti-establishment but part of it, and decorous to a fault'. For the characters of the two men David delved into his past. He remembered a tall, emaciated boy named Issa* – Chechen for Jesus – whom he had met in Moscow in 1993, the product of the union between a colonel in the Russian army of occupation in Chechenia and a Chechen village woman, whose family had killed her, as a matter of honour, after deciding that she had acquiesced in her rape. When the colonel had been posted back to Moscow, he had taken Issa with him and tried to turn him into a good Russian; the young man had converted to Islam in memory of the mother he had never known, and taken up the cause of Chechen separatism to spite his father. In David's novel the colonel has died, but not before telling his son of a fortune awaiting him in the West, deposited in a private bank. Issa makes a clandestine journey to Hamburg to claim his birthright. Knowing that he has arrived illegally and is wanted by the Russians, he takes shelter with a family of Turkish immigrants.

Hornstein introduced David to her landlord Helmuth Landwehr, a retired private banker whom he would thank for 'initiating me into the ways of his less scrupulous erstwhile colleagues'. But for the character of the older man, David reached back to the period when he was living in Vienna in the mid-1960s: he remembered a bibulous Scottish banker who was forever trying to persuade him to open a numbered bank account. 'It wasn't my money he wanted, it was my companionship,' recalled David. 'He was just a lonely expat with a failing marriage, and money was just an excuse to attach himself to people he liked.'

These individuals inspired the characters that David created. But as he would often say, 'to turn real people into fictional characters, we have to supplement our limited understanding of them by injecting bits of ourselves'.[4] Like David, both men would have troubled relations with their late fathers: Issa Karpov chooses to repudiate his inheritance; Tommy Brue, sole surviving partner in the private, family-owned bank that bears his name, struggles to understand how his father could have allowed Russians

* Not to be confused with Issa Kostoyev, the Ingush policeman-turned-politician.

to launder money through the bank. Though jaded and cautious, he longs to make things right again.

Hunting Issa is Günther Bachmann, a middle-aged, burned-out spook with a turbulent past, a maverick in the European 'espiocracy', a German equivalent of Alec Leamas, an honest and decent man made weary by failure and compromise. 'I've known several Bachmanns in my time,' David said in an interview. Bachmann tries to keep Issa out of the clutches of his Russian and American counterparts. It seems everyone is looking for him: hence the title, *A Most Wanted Man*.

David was grateful when Anthony Barnett reacted enthusiastically on reading a typescript of the novel. 'As all we scribblers know, this is the time when encouragement most helps,' he wrote.

> I think I am pleased with the book, which isn't always by any means the case . . . Sometimes the journey doesn't quite take me to the expected destination, but this time it seems to have done. I had such luck with my researches: everywhere I looked, I seemed to hear the right things at the right time. As if, like Bachmann, I was making the weather . . . When an ex-Guantanamo inmate casually remarked that it was a rule among the prisoners always to let a man sleep after he had been tortured, I knew I was blessed.[5]

David befriended Murat Kurnaz, and provided a quote for his memoir, *Five Years of My Life: An Innocent Man in Guantánamo* (2007).* He invited Kurnaz to lunch when he came to London for the launch of the British edition. Some years earlier, in his local pub, David had met Philippe Sands, a professor of international law who lived near by, and had begun a series of discussions about the Iraq War, on which they were largely in agreement. Sands had written books arguing that the war had been illegal and condemning the use of torture in the interrogation of terrorist suspects. 'Come over and meet Murat,' David said to Sands, who took his children with him to David's house in Gainsborough Gardens. A few days later the former Guantánamo detainee, accompanied by

* 'The most compassionate, truthful and dignified account of the disgrace of Guantánamo that you are ever likely to read'.

David, came to speak at the north London school attended by Sands's son. 'Children, it turns out, are willing to ask the questions that adults are too polite to ask,' wrote Sands afterwards: 'seeking details about the food and toilet facilities, and asking him to re-enact various acts of torture.'[6]

David's youngest son Nick and his wife Clare Algar had been present at the lunch with Murat Kurnaz. Clare was another source for the character of Annabel Richter; indeed traces of his daughter-in-law can be detected in characters in David's novels from *Single & Single* onwards. After leaving university in 1997 she had gone to New Orleans to work for Clive Stafford Smith, then running a non-profit law office representing poor people in death-penalty cases. In 1999 he had founded Reprieve, an international human rights organisation that supported prisoners accused of the most extreme crimes, such as acts of murder or terrorism. Nine years later Algar became Reprieve's executive director.

Stafford Smith was deeply involved with the prisoners detained at Guantánamo: he had been one of the first lawyers to sue for access to the prison camp and had acted for far more of them than any other lawyer. David, who had met him at Nick and Clare's wedding in 2006, sought his advice while writing *A Most Wanted Man* and would acknowledge his help in the book.

Nick's first novel, *The Gone-Away World*, was published in June 2008. To avoid any suggestion that he might be trading on his father's success he wrote under a pseudonym, Nick Harkaway – like his father.

Kaspar von Almen died towards the end of 2007. David travelled out to Lauterbrunnen for the funeral. Despite von Almen's occasional explosions of temper, he and David had remained friends for sixty years. Though largely self-taught, von Almen had been a cultivated man and a superb athlete, who had been a fine skier and had scaled some extraordinary peaks into old age. He always loathed leaving the valley, so it was very satisfying to David and Jane when they were able to lure Kaspar and his wife Erica to Tregiffian for a short stay. Von Almen had been president of the council in the community of Lauterbrunnen, and his funeral was attended by an array of Swiss bankers and other bigwigs who had been guests at his hotel. It was very much a 'valley' funeral in dialect, with many local references.

He was buried in style in the Lauterbrunnen churchyard, in the valley that he loved.

'Just back from burying a friend in Switzerland,' David wrote to Roland Philipps on his return. 'Knew him sixty years. O Mother. But at least he won't be around to make a speech at my funeral, which cheers me.'[7]

By late 2007 *A Most Wanted Man* was ready to be shown to publishers. Bruce Hunter negotiated a deal with Tim Hely Hutchinson in the usual way; as had happened in the past, the initial offer from Hodder was rejected as insufficient, but a subsequent, higher one proved acceptable. David and his agent were back on cordial terms after their sharp exchanges in the first few months of 2005. In September 2007 Hunter gave a dinner to celebrate the millionth-copy sale of *The Constant Gardener*. Afterwards David wrote thanking him for 'a memorable, magnificent evening'. Jane wrote a separate letter of thanks. 'Apart from the huge effort Hodder's sales people have evidently made for the book, there was in my mind the fact that you and Ania (and everybody at Higham's) have contributed enormously to the general expansion and awareness of David's books around the world,' she wrote. 'We thank you for that, and look forward to enhancing our collaboration wherever we can in the years to come.'[8]

David had indicated that he was willing in principle for Hunter to resume handling the American rights, as he had done until *The Mission Song*. By the end of the year Hunter had done a considerable amount of preparatory work towards the sale of the book in the USA and Canada. It became clear, however, that David and his agent had different perceptions of the book's potential. David wanted Hunter to 'play a long game', letting publishers pursue them for the book rather than actively trying to sell it. Hunter thought this unrealistic: sales of *The Mission Song* had been disappointing, and le Carré was no longer the hot property in New York that he once had been. Moreover there was a timing problem. If the American sale was delayed, enabling Hodder to publish the book a season or more ahead of the Americans, and thus scooping the open market, American publishers were likely to offer substantially less. Nor would they like it if the book were sold first in Canada. After an exchange of views, David asked Hunter to handle the

American sale on a reduced commission. This Hunter declined to do, so David entrusted the task to his lawyer Michael Rudell, who sold *A Most Wanted Man* to Scribner's, the publishers of *Single & Single* and *The Constant Gardener*.

At a point when the discussions had become fraught, Hunter had mentioned that he had it in mind to retire soon, and suggested that a younger agent in the firm might take over from him, while he was still around to supervise and ease him in. David was not receptive to this suggestion. Instead he chose to move to a new agency, Curtis Brown, where he would be represented by a dynamic agent of a younger generation, Jonny Geller. This brought to an end a working relationship that had lasted twenty-two years. 'I shall never forget all the wonderful work you did, and the splendid deals you brought off, & the loyalty you showed, throughout nearly all our years together,' David wrote to Hunter; 'and I hope that our recent disagreements will never overshadow that memory, or dim my appreciation.'[9] Hunter wrote David an equally gracious letter in return.

An 'exclusive interview', given to the *Sunday Times* journalist Rod Liddle in the run-up to the publication of *A Most Wanted Man*, stoked a blaze of perhaps unwelcome publicity. During their conversation David appeared to tell Liddle that while working for MI6 he had considered defecting to the Soviet Union. In the 'gentle crepuscular gloom' of dusk at Tregiffian, as he sipped his calvados, Liddle probed further.

> 'You were genuinely tempted?' I ask him, in some surprise.
>
> 'Yes, there was a time when I was, yes,' he says.
>
> 'For ideological reasons, like the rest of them – Blunt, Philby, Maclean?'
>
> 'God, no, no, no. Never for ideological reasons, of course not . . .'
>
> 'Then why?' Not money, surely, I think to myself.
>
> 'Well, I wasn't tempted ideologically,' he reasserts, in case there should be any doubt, 'but when you spy intensively and you get closer and closer to the border . . . it seems such a small step to jump . . . and, you know, find out the rest.'[10]

The revelation was the subject of a separate news story in the *Sunday Times* and was subsequently picked up by Associated Press and reported across the world.[11]

In a letter published on *The Times*'s website, David claimed that he had been misrepresented, stating that Liddle had made 'no visible use of a tape recorder, preferring, he assured me, to take written notes'.

> He must be forgiven therefore if, while he too was sipping post-prandial Calvados in the evening darkness he describes, he failed to encompass or indeed record the general point I was making about the temptations of defection . . .
>
> I painted for Mr Liddle the plight of professional eavesdroppers who identify so closely with the people they are listening to that they start to share their lives.
>
> It was in this context that I made the point that, in common with other intelligence officers who lived at close quarters with their adversaries, I had from time to time placed myself intellectually in the shoes of those on one side of the Curtain who took the short walk to the other; and that rationally and imaginatively I had understood the magnetic pull of such a step, and empathised with it.[12]

A Most Wanted Man was published simultaneously around the world on 2 October 2008. Most reviewers welcomed it as a return to form by le Carré. Alan Furst, himself a highly praised author of historical spy thrillers set in and around the Second World War period, lauded the book in the Sunday edition of the *New York Times* as 'one of the best novels he's ever written'.[13] Another spy writer, the young Scot Charles Cumming, praised *A Most Wanted Man* in the *Daily Telegraph* as 'a first-class novel about the most pressing moral and political concerns of our time, not least the scandal of extraordinary rendition'.[14] The novelist Hari Kunzru, reviewing the book for the *Guardian*, rated it 'one of the most sophisticated fictional responses to the war on terror yet published, a humane novel which takes on the world's latest binarism and exposes troubling shades of grey', though he found it 'uneven'.[15] For the critic and writer Andrew O'Hagan, writing in the *New York Review of Books*, 'le Carré continues to be the world's most reliable witness to the vicissitudes of international paranoia; his books conceive of a Western world that has a costly obsession with its possible enemies; he shows you this world's secret missions; its botched jobs, its manifold attempts to thwart the corrupting and sometimes terrifying idealism of others, while keeping the reader close to the exact lineaments of the way we live now'.[16]

A Most Wanted Man came in for special praise in Germany. *Die Zeit* hailed it as 'a literary masterpiece'. A contributor to *Süddeutsche Zeitung* argued that 'no other writer' had captured Germany's 'blend of idiosyncratic provincialism and world stage, of marginalization and centrality' like le Carré: during the Cold War he had captured like no one else 'the pathos and introspective nature of the political situation of the two Germanys'.

The main review in the *New York Times* came once again from Michiko Kakutani, and once again she wielded her stiletto . . .

> the novel is flawed, like his 2004 book, 'Absolute Friends', by an overly schematic narrative devised to drive home the author's contempt for the take-no-prisoners methods employed by the United States in the war on terror. As a result, the moral chiaroscuro and nuanced ambiguities that distinguished his cold war novels give way, in these pages, to a blunter, more predictable story line that lurches, at times, into sentimentality and contrivance . . .
>
> For that matter, Mr. le Carré's contempt for the United States' post-9/11 approach to the war on terror not only makes for a story told in blacks and whites – with none of the grays that distinguished his famous Smiley novels – but also results in an ending that the reader can see looming a mile off.[17]

In the UK and Germany *A Most Wanted Man* was a no. 1 bestseller. It was four weeks on the *New York Times* bestseller list, rising to no. 4.

David received a letter commenting on the issues raised by *A Most Wanted Man* from the German intelligence chief August Hanning, who had served as head of the BND from 1998 until 2005. It had been during Hanning's term of office that testimony provided to the BND by an Iraqi agent had been used by the American administration to bolster their case for the

2003 invasion, despite warnings from his German handlers that the agent, codenamed 'Curveball', could not be trusted.*

David had met Hanning at a dinner in Bonn almost twenty years earlier, given by the British Ambassador to mark the closing of the Embassy before the move to Berlin. The Ambassador had taken it into his head to invite the equivalents of every German official who had been featured in *A Small Town in Germany*; Hanning took the role of Ludwig Siebkron, head of the German Ministry of the Interior. Guests had to read the book in advance, and during dinner identify themselves in a short speech. David and Hanning warmed to each other and had meetings thereafter: Hanning brought his wife and daughter to Tregiffian for a couple of weeks, and David visited Hanning's headquarters in Pullach (Martin Bormann's old country house) and received a 'breakfast briefing' from his staff, largely about the Middle East. David resisted attempts by Hanning's head of training to persuade him that he should address the BND spy school in Munich.

In February 2008 Hanning had been invited by his friend the Prince of Oettingen to speak to a select audience of mainly aristocratic Bavarians and Austrians, and David had been invited to reply. The subject of Hanning's talk was the population problems arising from immigration: and most notably the effect of three million, mostly non-integrated Turks living in Germany. David advocated sympathy for and understanding of 'the Muslims that live among us'. He spoke of their sense of collective humiliation, of the radicalising effect of Western foreign policy on young Muslims.

Hanning had been one of the most prominent of those resisting the return of Murat Kurnaz from Guantánamo, arguing that he should be deported to Turkey rather than to Germany. Thus he and David found themselves on opposite sides on this issue. 'It is my fortune and misfortune to live in an imaginary parallel universe to the realities of your profession,' David wrote to him, 'to twist it and shape it until it does the work of the wider world in which the reader can find himself. In consequence, I take my criticism and compliments from two fronts; from those who know the

* Curveball had testified to his BND handlers to the existence of a programme of weapons of mass destruction in Iraq.

real world, and are incensed that I have misrepresented it; and those who take my parallel universe at face value.'[18]

Some months after the publication of *A Most Wanted Man*, David was again invited to speak at Thames House, as part of a programme of events to commemorate MI5's centenary. His host was the Director-General, Jonathan Evans. David spoke in the atrium of the central courtyard, standing beside the statue of MI5's founding Director-General, Sir Vernon Kell. He reminisced about his own career within the Service. 'If I'd known as much about myself then as I know now,' he told his audience, 'I wouldn't have cleared myself for secret work.'

His next book could be seen as a state-of-the-nation novel, showing the corruption of British society by greed. A Russian wheeler-dealer, under threat from his confederates, wishes to defect: in return for protection and resettlement in Britain with his family, he offers details of a vast money-laundering operation involving a prominent politician* and other influential individuals in British society. At one point in the book, intelligence officers examine amateur film footage showing the politician and his associates enjoying a party on board an oligarch's luxury yacht moored off the Dalmatian coast – a scene reminiscent of a party that actually took place off the coast of Corfu in 2008, aboard a yacht belonging to the Russian oligarch Oleg Deripaska, attended by both the Conservative shadow Chancellor, George Osborne, and the EU Trade Commissioner and architect of New Labour, Peter Mandelson. For David, the pernicious effect of laundered money went far beyond the venal instincts of a few individuals; it penetrated deep into the institutions of government, the civil service and indeed the intelligence services. He was appalled by the alacrity with which the City of London accommodated the rewards of crime; and by how little, if anything, the supposed regulators did to stop the practice.

For the character of the Russian gangster at the centre of the story, David retrieved a figure from his past: Dima, the huge bald man whom he

* Aubrey Longrigg MP. Johnnie Longrigg (1923–2007) served in SIS for thirty years, including a spell in Bonn in the mid-1950s; his brother, the prolific novelist Roger Longrigg (1929–2000), had been a close friend of James Kennaway.

had interviewed in his nightclub on his visit to Russia in 1993. The book opens in Antigua, where 'Perry' Makepiece and Gail Perkins, a young Oxford don and his solicitor girlfriend, are enjoying a treat, a holiday in the Caribbean. After an impromptu but fiercely competitive game of tennis with Perry, Dima asks him to act as an intermediary with the British authorities. The young couple become part of the operation to bring Dima and his family to Britain. Dima has few requests of the British: only that his daughter be allowed to attend Roedean.

While the character of Dima was taken straight from life, Perry and Gail were composites. Superficially they resembled David's son Nick and his wife Clare, but in creating these characters he drew on other young people he had met among their thirty-something circle, and on Federico Varese, the young Professor of Criminology at Oxford, whose 'creative and ever-patient counsel' he would acknowledge in the book.

Like *Absolute Friends*, the novel ends in an apocalypse, leaving the reader shocked and pessimistic. David would entitle it *Our Kind of Traitor*, an ironic reference to the very English phrase 'our kind of person' or 'our kind of man', meaning someone who will not necessarily stick closely to the rules, but whose heart is in the right place, wherever that place may be. The book would be dedicated in memory of Simon Channing Williams, who died of cancer in April 2009.

Ann died in June, after a long illness. 'She continued to be her robust, unbiddable & amazingly courageous self to the end,' wrote David, in reply to a letter of commiseration from Philipps.[19] She had lived in Coxley for forty-four years, serving as a parish councillor and governor of the village school. As she had wished, the funeral took place in the local church. The parish priest, a woman, led the simple ceremony. Afterwards Ann's body was buried in the churchyard, next to her mother's grave. Mourners went back to Coxley Manor, where a marquee had been erected on the lawn. David and Jane both came to the funeral. There was a brief and somewhat testy exchange between David and his former close friend Robin Cooke, though Jane, Charlotte and David's eldest son Simon all spent time trying gently to engineer a rapprochement: sadly, none was forthcoming. More than a year afterwards, in a letter to John Margetson, David complained that he had been 'airbrushed' out of the funeral, 'which really hurt me – I seem to have mourned Ann for much longer, & more deeply, than I expected, which says something'.[20]

It became increasingly clear that David's next book would not be published by Hodder. 'I haven't been in touch because, as you will have surmised, a lot is in the air, most notably the question of my backlist, which seems to occupy many of Jonny's working hours,' David wrote to Philipps in April. A month or so later Geller held a meeting with Hodder to discuss David's future; he suggested that 'when it comes to securing an author's posterity, Hodder cannot, & does not pretend to, match the attractions of a long-established paperback house with a world reputation & a classic list'. It was obvious which long-established paperback house was meant. The programme of making contracts with limited licences initiated by Bruce Hunter enabled David to move to a new publisher even if the old one kept the books in print. Hodder produced a 'Le Carré Legacy Plan', but this was just going through the motions; the decision had already been taken.

In mid-October David wrote to tell Philipps that he had decided, 'with profound sadness', to take his new novel, and by degrees his backlist, to Penguin, which would become his English-language publishers worldwide. The book, then as yet untitled, would be issued in hardback under Penguin's Viking imprint; his backlist would be reissued in Penguin Modern Classics over the next nine years, as the licences expired. 'My reasons are primarily to do with my posterity, such as it may be, and the prospect of seeing my work included on a classic & enduring list,' he explained to Philipps. 'In the end we must do what we believe is right for ourselves, and – in my case – for my heirs and assigns.' In a letter to Jamie Hodder-Williams, David hinted at another reason why he was leaving Hodder after thirty-eight years. 'Increasingly I have felt over the last few years that I was not a natural feature of the house, & that my standards were becoming egregious by comparison with those of other authors.'[21]

In a statement issued to the press, David paid tribute to his former publishers. He said that he was saddened to be leaving Hodder, and applauded the 'inimitable' team's 'good fellowship, unfailing support and sales energy'. However, he added: 'The opportunity to see my life's work presented by a classic paperback house with a unique backlist is at this stage in my career unmissable.'

Tom Weldon, deputy chief executive of Penguin UK, said he was 'thrilled' by the move, describing it as 'an honour' to have been entrusted with le Carré's front and backlist. 'There are very few novelists writing today who combine such terrific narrative, unforgettable characters and urgent engagement with our own times,' Weldon said. 'He is one of the most enthralling and important chroniclers of our age, and his books are, in the truest sense of the phrase, modern classics.' David's new editor would be Mary Mount, daughter of his former pupil at Eton, Ferdinand Mount.

It was hard for Tim Hely Hutchinson and his colleagues not to feel bitter, after putting so much effort into meeting David's wishes. Nevertheless Hely Hutchinson reacted graciously. 'Hodder & Stoughton is very proud to have been John le Carre's publisher and we are sorry that this relationship, which was based on mutual admiration and affection, is come to an end,' he said.[22]

Though he had left Hodder, David remained in touch with Roland Philipps, and continued to see him socially. After he had finished *Our Kind of Traitor* he wrote him a long letter of news. Yet again he was contemplating an autobiography, 'but the prospect is so sad, and potentially disquieting for my children, & the truth of it so hard to get at, that I'm already looking beyond it to another novel, which mercifully is beginning to form on the skyline'. But he would be unable to start writing the new book until after *Our Kind of Traitor* was published in the autumn. 'Writing is waiting,' he added – an adaptation of the last sentence of *The Russia House*, 'Spying is waiting,' and perhaps a further indication that David saw writing and spying as comparable activities.[23]

One reason why he had been thinking about an autobiography was that he had been invited to lecture at the annual Oxford Literary Festival, and had chosen the subject. In March he spoke to a packed audience in the Sheldonian Theatre, the official ceremonial hall of the University of Oxford, designed by Sir Christopher Wren. 'A life of writing has been extraordinarily kind to me,' he said.

> And since it began, give or take, fifty years ago, I thought it appropriate that tonight I should offer some account – heavily redacted – of the implausible route that got me from there to here, one I confess I still marvel at.

Now, I do know the pitfalls.

We all, as we grow old, meddle with the storyline of our lives, edit stuff out, re-cast the darker passages in a kindlier light.

And old novelists are the worst at this by a mile. All their lives they've been reshaping the truth to the point where imagined and real experience are indistinguishable.

Our Kind of Traitor was published in September 2010. Not for the first time, critics remarked on the anger propelling the story. For James Naughtie, who reviewed the novel in the *Sunday Telegraph*, its denouement was 'stamped with the outrage and near-despair of late le Carré'.[24] The anonymous reviewer in the *Scotsman* noted 'le Carré's familiar rage at corporate greed and amorality', but judged that it was here kept in close check: 'like so much of what he writes, the violence, cruelty and real horror are off-stage, while the less obvious violence is front and centre, in the amoral and treacherous world of money-broking, money-laundering, influence-selling, and unprincipled politics'.[25] The *Guardian* gave the book to Christopher Tayler, an admiring critic of le Carré's vintage period. 'It's possible to find some of his later novels a bit preachy without denying that they're classily assembled or failing to appreciate the leftish indignation behind them,' wrote Tayler, who felt that 'his younger characters don't always ring true' now that le Carré was nearing eighty:

> Somerset Maugham, another writer of dark spy stories, once had a character say of an aspiring grand old man of letters: 'It is no good his thinking that it is enough to write one or two masterpieces; he must provide a pedestal for them of forty or fifty works of no particular consequence.' *Our Kind of Traitor* may fall into the second category, but it's good to see Le Carré having fun as he reinforces the pedestal under his classic productions.[26]

Once again, the review in the *New York Times* came from Michiko Kakutani. This time she seemed to have got out of bed on the right side: she praised *Our Kind of Traitor* as 'the author's most thrilling thriller in years', and rated it as 'part vintage John le Carré and part Alfred Hitchcock':

> Though set in the present, the novel's plot involving British intelligence officers and Russian operatives is reminiscent of the many cold war face-offs – with defections or purported defections propelling the story – that animated the author's most keenly observed earlier work. And its depiction of two unsuspecting civilians who find themselves caught up in a dangerous, high-stakes espionage game summons memories of those classic Hitchcock movies starring the likes of Cary Grant or Jimmy Stewart as innocents who abruptly stumble into exotic, life-threatening situations on the international stage . . .[27]

One evening David received a telephone call from John Makinson, chairman and CEO of Penguin. Makinson had been asked to sound him out about whether he might accept a knighthood. There was a reluctance to make him a formal offer, given that he had turned down a CBE in the 1980s, and since then had often expressed his unwillingness to accept an honour in public. 'I will never be Sir David, Lord David or King David,' he had told an American interviewer back in 2004.[28] More recently, however, he had accepted a French honour, which suggested that his attitude might be softening.

In fact David did not hesitate to decline, saying that he did not want his name to go forward for consideration for a knighthood. He explained that while working in Bonn he had been privy to the disputes about which German dignitaries should be offered British honours, and on what grounds, and thought the whole process corrupt. 'Titles do disagreeable things to people,' he said; he had observed several instances of this among former Foreign Office friends and preferred not to expose himself to that risk. The British, unlike the French or the Germans, threw all their titles into one hat, lumping artists together with party-political donors, arms dealers, and so on, 'which seems to me to devalue the coinage'. Moreover he did not want to be welcomed by the establishment: 'I prefer to stay outside the tent.' A cynic might say that the tent was bulging with angry old men such as Sir David Hare, Sir Salman Rushdie, and Harold Pinter,

Commander of the British Empire,* all fierce critics of New Labour as they had been of Thatcherism.

Afterwards David wrote to his old friend John Margetson, who had been knighted in 1986, towards the end of a distinguished career in the Diplomatic Service. 'Did I tell you I passed on a K? All right for public servants, not good for artists, writers & the like.' Margetson disagreed.[29]

Some months later David caused a stir by asking for his name to be taken off the shortlist for the 2011 Man Booker International prize.

The £60,000 prize is awarded every two years to a living novelist, in recognition of his or her lifetime contribution to fiction. It is connected to, but separate from, the better-known Man Booker prize for fiction, which is awarded annually to a specific book. A panel of three judges chooses writers to be considered for the award, then selects a shortlist and finally a winner – unlike the annual Man Booker prize, which is judged on submissions from publishers. In this case there was a shortlist of thirteen.

'I am enormously flattered to be named as a finalist of the 2011 Man Booker International prize,' David said, in a statement issued through his publishers. 'However, I do not compete for literary prizes and have therefore asked for my name to be withdrawn.'

Rick Gekoski, the chairman of the judging panel, respectfully declined the request. 'John le Carré's name will, of course, remain on the list,' he said. 'We are disappointed that he wants to withdraw from further consideration because we are great admirers of his work.'

The prize was awarded to Philip Roth.

A feature film of *Tinker, Tailor, Soldier, Spy* was released in 2011. The project had been initiated by the screenwriter Peter Morgan, known for his fact-based films, including *The Queen* (2006), *Frost/Nixon* (2008) and *The Damned United* (2009). Morgan developed a script in collaboration with David. Back in 2008, he had told a reporter about a conversation between the two of them. 'When you return to earlier work,' David said, 'you feel

* Pinter had accepted his CBE in 1966. In the 1990s he declined the offer of a knighthood.

two rather unpleasant emotions. One is God, this is awful; and the other is, how can I ever write something as good ever again?'[30]

Morgan wrote a draft of the screenplay and took it to the production company Working Title, but withdrew after his mother became seriously ill; the task was completed by the husband-and-wife team of Peter Straughan and Bridget O'Connor, with input from David. This was the first English-language film directed by the Swede Tomas Alfredson, who had made the cult horror movie *Let the Right One In* (2008).* It starred Gary Oldman, the sixth actor to play the part of George Smiley;† other members of the cast included Benedict Cumberbatch as Guillam, John Hurt as Control, Colin Firth as Haydon, Kathy Burke as Connie and Mark Strong as Prideaux. David played another cameo, as an unnamed figure seen joining in an ironic rendition of the Red Flag at a Circus Christmas party.

Tinker, Tailor, Soldier, Spy was a critical and commercial success, becoming the highest-grossing film at the British box office for three consecutive weeks. It was nominated for eleven BAFTAs, but faced strong competition from *The Artist*, and picked up only two: Outstanding British Film and Best Adapted Screenplay. It would also receive three Academy Award nominations: Best Actor for Gary Oldman, Best Adapted Screenplay and Best Original Score.

The film attracted much attention and comment. Many viewers said that they found the plot difficult to follow. Inevitably it drew comparisons, some unfavourable, with the beloved television series adapted from the same novel, which viewers had found equally incomprehensible, if not more so. Perhaps such comparisons were unfair. The film is just over two hours long, the television series more than five hours. Inevitably the longer version provides greater suspense and more opportunity for the audience to become involved with the characters.

Much was made of Alfredson's evocation of London in the 1970s, which he remembered from a visit at the time as brown and grey, a city of shadows and uncovered light bulbs, and dirty streets. In a witty piece the *New Yorker* reviewer Anthony Lane warned cinemagoers to 'brace themselves for an explosion of brown':

* *Tinker, Tailor, Soldier, Spy* was jokingly referred to as 'Get the Wrong One Out'.

† At an earlier stage Jim Broadbent had been considered for the part.

> Welcome to the fashionable nineteen-seventies, where your walls matched your sideburns. The sealed, podlike chamber in which the high priests of intelligence convene is a nightmare of muddy orange, and Guillam, the resident cavalier of the Circus, drives not a sporty MG, as he did on TV, but a Citroen DS the color of light manure.[31]

In June 2011 it was announced that David was to receive the Goethe Medal, in honour of his life's work. The Goethe-Institut, founded in 1952 to promote German culture and language abroad, awarded a handful of medals each year to those 'who have performed outstanding service for the German language and international cultural relations'. Also being honoured with David that year were the French filmmaker Ariane Mnouchkine and the Polish journalist and human rights activist Adam Michnik. Among British citizens who had received the Medal in the past were Karl Popper and Ernst Gombrich.

The announcement cited David as 'Great Britain's most famous German-speaker'. It referred to the keynote speech he had given at the national 'Think German' conference the previous year. 'Le Carré has always been convinced that language learning is the key to understanding foreign cultures.'

The Medal was awarded later that summer at an event in Weimar, where Goethe had spent much of his adult life; in fact the ceremony took place in a room dedicated to his memory within the Stadtschloss Weimar, which had been rebuilt under the supervision of a commission directed by Goethe himself after it had been destroyed by fire in 1774. The event lasted over a weekend, and included banquets and group discussions. In the ceremony itself, which took place on Goethe's birthday, the Goethe-Institut's president, Klaus-Dieter Lehmann, described David as an author of great humanistic literature, a critical and astute observer of current affairs with a 'feel for global shifts and turbulences' and a 'great interest in other cultures'. He outlined David's writing career. 'Now 80 years old,* le Carré continues to write about current political issues, including terrorism, corruption, and the Mafia,' concluded Lehmann. 'He'll never run out of material.'

* In fact David was some months short of his eightieth birthday.

In his speech of acceptance David spoke of his lifelong love of German language and literature. He traced his experience of Germany, beginning with the moment when, as an eight-year-old boy, he had heard Neville Chamberlain announce that Britain was at war and had looked out nervously at his grandparents' tennis court. David speculated on what the giants of German literature would make of the state of Europe today. 'Europe is in a frightful muddle,' he stated. 'There has never been a time when members of the European family needed one another more – or needed the new Germany more.'

Later that year, on the eve of the Frankfurt Book Fair, David was guest of honour at a grand party in Berlin given by his German publishers, Ullstein. This was a belated celebration of Ullstein's centenary (in 2003), and commemorated the publication of a history of the company through the troubled twentieth century. David was invited to give the keynote speech by Ullstein's publisher and CEO, Siv Bublitz: this was an extraordinary honour for a foreign author, a mark of his significance in Germany. His speech, delivered in impeccable German, attracted loud laughter from an appreciative audience. 'The motor of every writer's life has three essential, working parts: childhood, education, experience,' he said, 'and when I came to look closely at those parts of my life, I noticed that each one had "Made in Germany" stamped on it.'

David contrasted the book business in Germany with its equivalent in his own country. 'British publishing remains the last outpost of the enlightened amateur,' he suggested. 'People seem to enter publishing by the same mysterious route that we used to enter the secret service.' German publishing, on the other hand, was much more professional:

> Here suddenly is a publisher who has not merely bought the book, but read it. Here are editors and translators who are as obsessive as we authors are. I am thinking of those infuriating editorial questions, as unexpected as they are challenging, that start flowing in almost before the ink is dry on my contract with the German publisher. Why didn't my British publisher pick this up? Or my American publishers?. . . And so it happens, far too often, that at the eleventh hour before going to press, the British publisher receives a salvo of last minute corrections, which must be passed to the American,

> the Canadian, Australian, and then all the other foreign language publishers. Everyone has a nervous breakdown, everyone blames the Germans.

'To be published in Germany is to have our work taken seriously,' he argued. 'In Germany a writer is socially admissible, even respectable. His words have weight. His peccadilloes are forgiven in the name of art . . .'

David's eightieth birthday in October 2011 was celebrated with a lunch at Tregiffian. The day was planned with military precision – except the weather, which was cold. Around a hundred people came, including fifteen or so children, who were entertained by a magician and then given hamburgers. Most of those attending were members of the family, but there were about twenty other adults, including Nicholas Shakespeare and his wife Gillian Johnson, John and Miranda Margetson, James Naughtie and his wife Eleanor Updale, William Shawcross and Olga Polizzi, Eric Abraham, and Roland Philipps. Tony and his wife Nettie were invited, but he was too ill to come.

Guests were asked to leave their cars in a field, from which they were transported to the site by taxi-van. In the gardens at Tregiffian, two long white tents flapped in a stiff sea-breeze: one for champagne, the other for the meal, provided by Rick Stein's caterers. Plenty of staff dressed in black were in attendance, including a detail from St John Ambulance. The rumour spread that Gary Oldman was invited, to account for the presence of security men, but in fact their function was to prevent walkers on the coastal footpath from straying into the party.

Speeches followed the meal. David's four sons all spoke, each emphasising that David was still in the present, still living life to the full, still teaching them so much. His half-brother Rupert generously compared David's portrait of their father to a Rembrandt, against which any version he might offer would be a caricature of the type displayed against the railings at Hyde Park. William Shawcross sprang to his feet and delivered a spontaneous tribute to his old friend. The occasion finished with fireworks, before guests departed at about 6.30 in the evening.

It had been announced earlier in the year that David had offered his literary archive to Oxford's Bodleian Library. 'I am delighted to be able to do this,' he wrote. 'Oxford was Smiley's spiritual home, as it is mine. And while I have the greatest respect for American universities, the Bodleian is where I shall most happily rest.' The first batch of archival material arrived in February; previously it had been stored in a barn at Tregiffian. By 2012 the Library had taken possession of 498 boxes, containing manuscripts of books from *The Looking-Glass War* to *Absolute Friends*. In these it was possible to trace the progress of David's novels through successive drafts, and to observe the painstaking care he took with his prose.

On 20 June 2012 David dressed in black velvet bonnet and scarlet academic gown to accept an honorary doctorate of letters from Oxford University, at a ceremony in the Sheldonian Theatre. The event was dominated by the presence of the Burmese pro-democracy campaigner Aung San Suu Kyi, who had been awarded a doctorate in civil law back in 1993, but had been prevented by the Burmese regime from collecting it. 'When I was under house arrest I was also helped by the books of John le Carré,' she recalled in her acceptance speech. 'They were a journey into the wider world, not just to other countries, but to thoughts and ideas.'

Another of those receiving an honorary degree at the same ceremony was the former head of MI5, Baroness Manningham-Buller. In so far as they communicated at all at the ceremony, she and David were amiable, though he might have been forgiven for treating her with some reserve, after reading disparaging remarks she had reportedly made to Salman Rushdie. Not long after his spat with David in 1997, Rushdie had been invited to 'Spy Central' to address 'a bunch of British intelligence station chiefs' – or so he said, though of course MI5 does not have station chiefs. Manningham-Buller was apparently furious about David's letters to the *Guardian*. 'What does he think he's doing?' she demanded. 'Does he understand nothing? Is he a complete fool?' According to Rushdie, she had snorted 'hah!' when asked whether David hadn't been 'one of your lot' in the distant past. 'I suppose he did work for us in some sort of minor capacity for about five minutes, but he never, my dear, reached the levels you've been talking to tonight, and let me tell you, after this business, he never will.'* So Rushdie relates, though this seems an odd comment to make about a bestselling author past retirement age.

* 'She must have known pretty well', commented David, 'that when I was in MI5 I ran one of its most prolific and successful agents for the better part of two years without mishap.' He would not be drawn on who this was.

This conversation was recounted in Rushdie's memoir, *Joseph Anton*, published in the autumn of 2012. The title referred to a pseudonym he had used while living in hiding. Unusually he wrote in the third person, as if he were writing about somebody else. In the book Rushdie presented a detailed account of his quarrel with David, described by the *Guardian* as 'one of the most gloriously vituperative literary feuds of recent times'.[32] At its end, wrote Rushdie, he had been 'suddenly overcome with sadness about what had happened. The le Carré of *Tinker, Tailor, Soldier, Spy* and *The Spy who Came in from the Cold* was a writer he had long admired.'[33] He quoted from the interview David had given to Rod Liddle in 2008, in which he conceded that perhaps he had been wrong; though if so, 'I was wrong for the right reasons.' Despite what he had said to Shawcross back in 1997, David had kept silent on the issue since then.

Publicising his book at the Cheltenham Literature Festival, Rushdie expressed his regret at their quarrel fifteen years earlier. 'I wish we hadn't done it,' he said. 'He's a writer I really admire.' He stated his opinion that 'le Carré's novels transcended the spy genre and should be considered literary' – a considerable modification of the position he had taken when reviewing *The Russia House*, the piece that was generally believed to have provoked the feud. 'I think of *Tinker, Tailor, Soldier, Spy* as one of the great novels of postwar Britain.'

Earlier in the year David had granted permission for Rushdie to reproduce his side of their exchange in his memoir. Now he took up *The Times*'s invitation to respond to Rushdie's peace offering. 'I too regret the dispute,' he said in a statement.

> I admire Salman for his work and his courage, and I respect his stand. Does that answer the larger debate which continues to this day?
>
> My position was that there is no law in life or nature that says great religions may be insulted with impunity. Should we be free to burn Korans, mock the passionately held religions of others? Maybe we should – but should we also be surprised when the believers we have offended respond in fury? I couldn't answer that question at the time and, with all good will, I still can't. But I am a little proud, in retrospect, that I spoke against the easy trend, reckoning with the wrath of outraged Western intellectuals, and suffering it in all its righteous glory.

And if I met Salman tomorrow?* I would warmly shake the hand of a brilliant fellow writer.[34]

'I've become more radical in old age than I've ever been,' David told an interviewer from the *Telegraph*. Even so, he voted Liberal Democrat in the general election of May 2010 – the first time he had ever voted for a party other than Labour. He was disgusted by New Labour's willingness to suspend civil liberties, its supine foreign policy and its 'relaxed' attitude to the rich. 'Why did I desert Labour? Total bloody disillusionment,' he told the *Telegraph* interviewer. 'The party was a corpse. It had no ideology, it became detached, old, spineless and needed to go.'[35] In 2015 he would vote Labour again.

The theme of David's next book would be the outsourcing of intelligence requirements to commercial contractors, which he saw as part of a larger picture of the 'corporatisation' of Britain. In 2005 David had suggested that Britain might be sliding towards fascism. 'Mussolini's definition of fascism was that when you can't distinguish corporate power from governmental power, you are on the way to a fascist state. If you throw in God power and media power, that's where we are now,' he told an interviewer from the *Guardian*. When asked if he was saying that Britain had become a fascist state, he replied, 'Does it strike you as democratic?'[36]

By the summer of 2012 David had finished a first draft of his new novel, provisionally entitled 'Secret and Beyond'.

It begins with 'Operation Wildlife', in which American private defence contractors try to snatch a suspected terrorist mastermind as he comes ashore on the Rock of Gibraltar one dark night. The operation has been authorised by a bullish New Labour minister, who asks Christopher 'Kit' Probyn, a low-flying diplomat nearing the end of his career, to be his eyes and ears on the spot. Three years later Probyn, who has been unexpectedly knighted in recognition of his services, is enjoying his retirement in a Cornish manor house when a figure materialises from his past: Jeb, a

* Some reports suggested that the two had spoken since their argument, and that David had voiced regret; in fact there had been no direct contact between them.

Welsh special forces man also present that night on the Rock. Probyn is shocked to learn that the operation was botched, and that an innocent young woman and her infant child were killed.

In a parallel strand of the story, Toby Bell, the minister's young private secretary, has become suspicious of his secretive master and makes a tape recording of a meeting with the private defence contractor. The two strands come together when Bell calls on Probyn and becomes involved with his daughter, a doctor.

'I seem to have written two versions of myself into it – or better, two ages,' wrote David, in his introduction to a special Waterstone's edition of the novel. 'In Toby Bell, thirty-something rising star of Her Majesty's Foreign Service, I see the striving ambitious fellow I fancy myself to have been at much the same age, until I went and messed everything up by writing *The Spy Who Came in from the Cold* in my spare time.' Bell, 'a decent, diligent, tousled, intelligent-looking fellow' (who incidentally is also writing a novel), does his duty 'until the day comes when his tolerance of himself snaps, and Toby the good soldier transmogrifies into Toby the scheming felon, planning a criminal act against the very Foreign Office minister he is pledged to serve and advise'. As Jon Stock, who reviewed the novel in the *Daily Telegraph*, would point out, 'it's almost as if le Carré has dropped his younger self into the modern mix, to see what he would do'.[37]

David's other secret sharer is of course Probyn, who is closer to him in age and, like him, lives in rural Cornwall.

> I'm a sucker for Kit's humanity, his love of people, his parade-horse but genuine rectitude, and yes, his good manners. I like it that, when he goes to visit his Old Shop, as he might call the Foreign Office, he is disconcerted by the unfamiliar managerial style as it strives to emulate the jargon and manners of the private sector . . .
>
> But I like best his secret honesty with himself when, out of the blue, he is confronted with the accusing ghost of his past . . . And that's how he discovers in himself wells of fury that are deeper and greater than anything he has felt in his sixty-three years till now: a fury directed not just at the Service he has so long honoured and obeyed, but at himself, at his own shaming complicity in his deception.

> And for some reason, which I have yet to discover, that seems to be the nature of the bond between us: an owning-up of some kind, a coming to terms with ourselves.

David adopted a revised title for the novel, *A Delicate Truth*. In his day, the term 'delicate' was used in the civil service as a form of security classification, if only conversationally. Here *A Delicate Truth* refers to an ultra-sensitive matter which should be swept under the carpet.

Most of the critics welcomed *A Delicate Truth* – except Frederic Raphael, who wrote a mocking review in the *Times Literary Supplement*. But he was very much the exception: most agreed with Robert McCrum that the novel represented a 'remarkable return to mid-season form'.[38] Edward Snowden's revelations of the extent of the National Security Agency's wire-tapping activities were published in the press only weeks after the book was published, enhancing David's reputation for prescience. 'He's always had his finger on the pulse of the times,' observed the reviewer in the *Berliner Zeitung*, 'but with his new novel John le Carré has surpassed himself.'[39]

A Delicate Truth reached the top of the UK bestseller list, almost half a century after *The Spy who Came in from the Cold* had dominated the US bestseller list. To have written two no. 1 bestsellers fifty years apart was a remarkable, possibly a unique achievement; it is difficult to think of any other writer who has stayed at the top so long.

Penguin marked the fiftieth anniversary of the first publication of *The Spy who Came in from the Cold* in August 2013 with a special edition, featuring a retro cover design, archival images and a new afterword from David. The occasion prompted a number of pieces recalling the novel's original publication in 1963 and reflecting on its achievement. 'It's a fabulous book and all spy fiction today is written in its deeply sinister shadow,' wrote Robert Gore-Langton in the *Sunday Express*.[40] 'What is most satisfying about John le Carré's first great success – first of many, as it turned out – is how well it holds up on this, its 50th anniversary,' wrote Jonathan Yardley in the *Washington Post*.[41] As the novelist William Boyd remarked in a piece about re-reading *The Spy who Came in from the Cold*, 'its cynicism is resolutely *de nos jours*'.

> One forgets just how unsparing the book is, how the picture it paints of human motivations, human duplicities, human frailty seems presciently

> aware of all that we have learned and unlearned in the intervening decades. The world was, on the surface, a more innocent, more straightforward place in the early 1960s: there were good guys and bad guys and they were easy to spot. One of the shock effects of reading *The Spy* when it was published must have been the near-nihilism of its message. It is unremittingly dark – or almost so – and this fact, I believe, lies at the root of its greatness . . .

Boyd commented on the skill with which the book is constructed and written. It came after two other 'highly creditable' novels. 'But there is a clear sense in *The Spy* of a writer hitting his stride with resolute confidence . . . Technically, on a purely writerly analysis, le Carré seems to me to be operating at the highest levels . . .'

> I think what I relish about it – and this is maybe how le Carré transformed the genre – is the implicit respect that he gives the reader. It is a very exciting read but it's also highly complicated. There is a lot of challenging subtext, a lot is implicit, a lot seems initially confusing. In other words, it's very sophisticated and one of the appeals of sophistication in art is the understanding that such precision, such tastes, such values, such understatements are shared. Le Carré's novel says, as it were, I know this appears unduly complex and obfuscated but you, the reader, are an intelligent person: you will follow this – you will understand what is going on, I don't need to spell it out or join the dots. The sheer aesthetic pleasure of reading is massively enhanced, thereby . . .[42]

A film adapted from *A Most Wanted Man* was released in the summer of 2014, to generally positive reviews. Directed by Dutch photographer-director Anton Corbijn, it is a moody, melancholic movie, which conveys a vivid sense of contemporary Hamburg. The Australian screenwriter and playwright Andrew Bovell, whose previous credits include *Lantana* (2001), simplified the complex plot, omitting the role played by British intelligence in the novel. Philip Seymour Hoffman dominates the screen almost throughout, in a commanding performance as Günther Bachmann. It was the actor's last leading role; he died only a fortnight after the film's premiere at the Sundance Film Festival. Other members of the cast include Rachel

McAdams as Annabel Richter and Willem Dafoe as Tommy Brue, and some excellent German actors in lesser roles, including Daniel Brühl and Nina Hoss. Once again, David plays a cameo, with a beard specially grown for the part, though he is glimpsed only fleetingly in a booth of a café, next to the one where Hoffman is sitting.

A Most Wanted Man, which was developed with Film4, was a co-production between Potboiler Productions, the company that produced *The Constant Gardener*, and the Ink Factory, founded in 2010 by David's two eldest sons, Simon and Stephen. Their skills complement each other: Simon has been a London-based venture capitalist specialising in technology and the internet, while Stephen is a Hollywood screenwriter. 'We didn't set off with the intention of getting involved in my father's stuff, but he found out about it when he was writing his last book, and he suggested we take it on,' Simon told *Variety* soon after their start-up. 'Financially we're all in it together,' he said. Of his father's involvement, Simon commented, 'He likes to be available as a resource to the scriptwriters, but he also hands people the flexibility to do it their way. He says don't make a film of the book, make a film of the film.'

The success of Tomas Alfredson's film of *Tinker, Tailor, Soldier, Spy* proved encouraging in the Ink Factory's early days. *A Most Wanted Man* was the company's first production, and it will be followed by their adaptation of *Our Kind of Traitor*, scheduled for release in 2016. A film of *A Delicate Truth* is in development. The Ink Factory is also producing a six-part dramatisation of *The Night Manager* for the BBC Television, and developing *Absolute Friends* as a three-part television series.

Although David is closely associated with the company, it is developing a number of projects unrelated to his work. 'We would like to grow to become one of the larger players in the European independent media sector,' Simon told *Variety*.[43]

In his eighty-fourth year, David shows little sign of slowing down. Though he no longer starts work quite so early in the morning, he still drives himself harder than most men half his age. He cannot walk so far as he used to, but he still tries to walk for an hour every day. For him, writing is 'the whole of life'. When he is not working on a book, he is restless and uncomfortable; and when he is working on a book, he is absorbed in it. He and Jane 'talk book' all the time. This involves the sacrifice of leisure and social life, not just for himself, but for Jane also. 'It may be senile delusion, but I seem to be writing well just now, and long after my sell-by date,' David wrote recently, in a letter of apology for declining two invitations from his old friend August Hanning. 'The writing days have become so precious, and necessarily so short, that I have to hoard every one of them.'[44]

Why does David persevere, at an age when most men are mowing the lawn or relaxing in a deckchair? His near-contemporary Len Deighton, for example, published his last novel in 1996. It cannot be for the financial rewards, because he has earned more money than he could ever spend; nor for the acclamation, because even a droplet of criticism sours a mouthful of praise.

A glib answer might be that writing has become a form of addiction for him. Perhaps there is some truth in this, though he has often said that he will stop writing if told (who would tell him?) that his books are not as good as they used to be. In 2015 he abandoned the novel that he had been working on since finishing *A Delicate Truth*. It is obvious from even a superficial examination that his books are intensely personal; indeed, one reason why they are so compelling is that he puts so much of himself into them. David himself has suggested that, if he had not become a writer, he might have become a criminal, like his father. One could conclude that writing was David's version of the psychoanalyst's couch. Perhaps his books are his way of ordering an untidy life.

Asked how it felt to be eighty, David replied that it seemed premature:

> It was always in the contract, I just didn't know they would deliver so soon. But it's okay. I feel ready to die. I've had an incredibly good life, an exciting one. I've got 13 grandchildren and fantastic wives for my sons. I was the bridge they had to cross to get from my father to life . . . I find it very difficult to read my own stuff, but I look at it with satisfaction. So if it were over very soon, I would not feel anything except gratitude. To have had my life and be ungrateful for it would be a sin.[45]

Notes

Where the name of the author is not given, it is John le Carré. All quotations from his books are from the first British editions, unless otherwise stated.

Abbreviations: DC David Cornwell
AC Ann Cornwell
JC Jane Cornwell

Introduction

1 'Espionage is an accident' (interview with Olga Craig), *Seven* (*Sunday Telegraph* magazine), 29 August 2010; John C. Q. Roberts, *Speak Clearly into the Chandelier: Cultural Politics between Britain and Russia, 1973–2000* (Curzon, 2000), p. 168.
2 Blake Morrison, 'Love and betrayal in the mist', *Times Literary Supplement*, 11 April 1986; William Boyd, 'Rereading: The Spy who Came in from the Cold', *Guardian*, 24 July 2010; Carlos Ruiz Zafón, 'My Hero', *Guardian*, 2 April 2011.
3 Ian McEwan, 'John le Carré deserves Booker' (interview with Jon Stock), *Daily Telegraph*, 3 May 2013.
4 David Mamet, 'The Humble Genre Novel, Sometimes Full of Genius', *New York Times*, 17 January 2000.

1: Millionaire paupers

1 Clyde Binfield, 'Sir Makepeace Watermaster and the March of Christian People: An Interaction of Fiction, Fact and Politics', in J. P. Parry and Stephen Taylor (eds), *Parliament and the Church, 1529–1960* (Edinburgh University Press, 2000); James Johnson, *A Hundred Commoners* (Herbert Joseph, 1931); *A Perfect Spy* (Hodder & Stoughton, 1986), and 'In Ronnie's Court', *New Yorker*, 18 and 25 February 2002.
2 'A Serious Outlook: Future of Poole Cricket Club', 'Changing Political Situation', 'Preparing for a Sale' and 'Poole Cricketer Injured', *Poole and East Dorset Herald*, 13 March, 3 and 24 July 1924.
3 This was in a tape-recorded message to her sons, in which she recalled her early life, her marriage and her subsequent relations with Ronnie.
4 Ed Perkins, 'Why le Carré's Father went to Jail' and 'Le Carré's Other People', *Daily Echo* (Bournemouth), 15 August and 20 September 2011.
5 Margaret Chatterjee to DC, 12 April 2001.

6 'Carré on Spying', *Daily Echo* (Bournemouth), 24 April 1999; Patricia Wilnecker to DC, 27 April 1999.
7 '"The Ninth" at Poole' and 'Admiral Cornwell', *Poole and East Dorset Herald*, 15 and 22 November 1928.
8 'In Ronnie's Court', p. 135.
9 Ibid., p. 134.
10 Anthony Cornwell, 'My Brother's Father and Mine' (unpublished, 1986).
11 Ibid.
12 'In Ronnie's Court', p. 150.
13 'Spying on my Father', *Sunday Times Review*, 16 March 1986.
14 'In Ronnie's Court', p. 144.
15 Anthony Cornwell, 'My Brother's Father and Mine'.
16 *Poole and East Dorset Herald*, 29 November 1928.
17 *History of the Poole Round Table No. 12 (1929–2008)* (privately published).
18 'Brothers in Business', *Poole and East Dorset Herald*, 22 January 1931.
19 *Western Gazette*, 29 August 1930.
20 *Poole and East Dorset Herald*, 15 October 1931; *Western Gazette*, 23 October 1931.
21 These and subsequent details of Ronnie's business activities are taken from the account of his cross-examination by the Official Receiver in the *Poole and East Dorset Herald*, 11 June 1936.
22 *A Perfect Spy*, p. 81.
23 'In Ronnie's Court', p. 136.
24 Ibid., p. 143.

2: 'We seek higher things'

1 Ronnie's words quoted in this paragraph derive from 'In Ronnie's Court'.
2 DC to Tony Cornwell, 15 May 2007.
3 *A Perfect Spy*, pp. 320–1.
4 Ibid., p. 181.
5 Clive Powell-Williams, *With All Thy Might: The History of St Martin's School, 1922 to 1992* (privately published, 1992), p. 194.
6 'In Ronnie's Court', p. 149.
7 'Carré on Spying', *Daily Echo* (Bournemouth), 24 April 1999.
8 Ibid.
9 'In Ronnie's Court', p. 142.
10 I am indebted for this and many other details to the current headmaster of St Andrew's, Dr David Livingstone. His article about David's career at the school appears in the *Chronicle* (the school magazine) for 2012.
11 'In England Now', *New York Times Magazine*, 23 October 1977, p. 34.
12 Ibid.
13 Ibid.
14 Gordon Ross, *Playfair Cricket Monthly*, c. 1965, extracted on the Cricinfo website.
15 'In England Now', pp. 34–5.
16 Ibid., p. 34.
17 Unpublished autobiographical fragment.
18 Melvyn Bragg, 'A Talk with John le Carré', *New York Times*, 13 March 1983.
19 'In Ronnie's Court', p. 149.
20 William Douglas Home, *Half-Term Report: An Autobiography* (Longman, 1954), pp. 151–62.
21 'Earl's son, now in jail, wants to be an M.P.', *Sunday Express*, 27 May 1945.
22 'In Ronnie's Court', p. 134.
23 Peggy Duff, quoted in the *Chelmsford Chronicle*, 16 March 1945.

24 JC to Alec Howe and Alison Whyte, undated 1987.
25 DC to R. S. Thompson, 24 June 1945, Sherborne School Archives.

3: God and Mammon

1 Huw Ridgeway, 'A Short History of Sherborne School', from the school website. Some of the subsequent details are derived from this source.
2 Afterword to the Penguin Classics edition of *A Murder of Quality* (2010).
3 A. B. Gourlay and D. F. Gibbs, *Chief: A Biography of Alexander Ross Wallace, 1891–1982* (privately published, 1983). See also Gourlay, *A History of Sherborne School* (privately published, 1971).
4 Alec Waugh: *The Loom of Youth* (Methuen, 1917), pp. 12 and 21.
5 'In England Now', p. 35.
6 *A Perfect Spy*, pp. 138–9.
7 'Violent Image' (interview with Alan Watson), *Sunday Times*, 30 March 1969.
8 Ronnie Cornwell to R. S. Thompson, 3 June 1946; Jean Cornwell to R. S. Thompson, 22 November 1945.
9 'In Ronnie's Court', p. 150.
10 *Shirburnian*, Summer 1948.
11 *Shirburnian*, Summer 1951.
12 Contribution to the Arvon Fundraising Crisis Appeal, April 1988.
13 *Shirburnian*, Summer 1948.
14 Keynote address by John le Carré at the opening of the 'Think German' Conference at Archbishop Whitgift School, Croydon, 25 June 2010.
15 Ibid.
16 'In Ronnie's Court', p. 142.
17 'John le Carré at the NFT' (interview with Adrian Wootton), *Guardian*, 5 October 2002.
18 'Spying on my Father'.
19 Wodehouse, John, 4th Earl of Kimberley, *The Whim of the Wheel: The Memoirs of the Earl of Kimberley* (privately published, 2001), p. 51.
20 'Spying on my Father'; 'In Ronnie's Court', p. 147.
21 'In Ronnie's Court', p. 151.
22 *The Whim of the Wheel*, p. 61.
23 Gourlay and Gibbs, *Chief*, p. 62.
24 'Spying on my Father'; 'In Ronnie's Court', p. 147.
25 Ronnie Cornwell to Canon Wallace, 3 May 1948, Sherborne School Archives.
26 Ronnie Cornwell to R. S. Thompson, 12, 15 and 19 January 1948, Sherborne School Archives.
27 Jean Cornwell to R. S. Thompson, 2 March 1948, Sherborne School Archives.
28 Ronnie Cornwell to R. S. Thompson, 8 April 1948, Sherborne School Archives.
29 R. S. Thompson to Keith Murray, 2 May 1952, Lincoln College Archive.
30 'In Ronnie's Court', p. 147. After this story appeared in the *New Yorker*, Tony told David that he had 'stolen' it from him. He argues that he had been sent to see the Ansorges alone and that David had learned about this from him. David sticks to his account that both boys were present. Whatever the truth of the matter, it seems clear that David was distressed by the fact that he and his brother were being made complicit in his father's dealings.
31 DC to R. S. Thompson, 5 May 1952, Sherborne School Archives.
32 Ronnie Cornwell to R. S. Thompson, 21 September 1948, Sherborne School Archives.
33 Canon Wallace's note to Thompson on the above letter, undated, Sherborne School Archives.
34 R. S. Thompson to Keith Murray, 2 May 1952, Lincoln College Archive.
35 R. S. Thompson to Frank Fisher, 9 February 1956, ibid.
36 Keynote address by John le Carré at the opening of the 'Think German' Conference at Archbishop Whitgift School.

37 'In Ronnie's Court', p. 149.
38 Interview with Hunter Davies in the *Mail on Sunday*, 17 February 1991. This interview was mocked in *The Times* diary ('In from the cold', 21 February 1991).
39 Canon Julian Eagle and Bill Blackshaw to R. S. Thompson, 18 and 23 February 1991, Sherborne School Archives.
40 DC to R. S. Thompson, undated but probably written on 16 September 1948, Sherborne School Archives.
41 'In Ronnie's Court', p. 150.
42 DC to R. S. Thompson, 5 May 1952, Sherborne School Archives.

4: Wandering in the fog

1 This paragraph and much of the detail that follows is taken from the text of a speech given by David Cornwell on the occasion of the 175th anniversary of the University of Bern on 6 June 2009.
2 I am grateful to Professor John E. Jackson of the University of Bern for information on David's professors.
3 DC to Jon Meccarello (in a letter to Andrew Ross, 30 October 1996).
4 For an interesting article on this subject, see Martin Swales, 'Manichean Realism? Reflections on John le Carré's Indebtedness to German Literature', *Angermion VI* (Berlin, 2013).
5 DC to Ann Sharp, 4 December 1950.
6 'At the Edge of the Real World', *Sunday Telegraph Review*, 14 November 1999.
7 'In Ronnie's Court'; Foreword to the Lamplighter edition of *Single & Single* (2001).
8 DC to Ann Sharp, 3 January 1951.
9 'Spying on my Father'.
10 'Standing for Yarmouth', *Eastern Daily Press*, 20 January 1950.
11 'Notes by the Way', *Yarmouth Mercury*, 13 and 20 January 1950.
12 'Liberal Candidate Attacks Conscription', *Yarmouth Mercury*, 3 February 1950.
13 'Hitch Waggon to This Star', *Eastern Daily Press*, 2 February 1950.
14 'Fair Crack of the Whip', *Eastern Daily Press*, 4 February 1950.
15 'To the Electors of the Yarmouth Division of Norfolk', 11 February 1950.
16 'Constantine at Brains Trust', *Eastern Daily Press*, 18 February 1950.
17 'Through the Storm a Message', *Eastern Daily Press*, 21 February 1950.
18 'Secrets and Lies' (interview with Alan Franks), *The Times*, 13 February 1999.
19 'Statement by Mr Cornwell', *Eastern Daily Press*, 22 February 1950.
20 'John le Carré: The Secret Centre' (interview with Nigel Williams), BBC 2, 2000.
21 'Not Death of Liberalism' and 'Liberals Prepare for Next Fight', *Yarmouth Mercury*, 3 and 10 February 1950.

5: Serving your country

1 *A Perfect Spy*, pp. 430–1.
2 For background information on National Service I am indebted to Trevor Royle's *The Best Years of Their Lives: The National Service Experience, 1945–63* (Michael Joseph, 1986).
3 DC to Ann Sharp, 11 October and 4 November 1950.
4 Christopher Andrew, *The Defence of the Realm: The Authorized History of MI5* (Allen Lane, 2009), p. 390.
5 DC to Ann Sharp, 26 May 1951.
6 DC to Ann Sharp, 19, 20, 22, 24 and 30 November 1950.
7 DC to Ann Sharp, 7 December 1950 and undated.

8 David Cornwell, 'Pretty Blue Pullovers', *Downhill Only Club Journal*, vol. 2, no. 9 (November 1951).
9 Foreword to the Lamplighter edition of *Call for the Dead* (1992).
10 DC to Ann Sharp, 3 and 15 January, 11 February 1951.
11 DC to Ann Sharp, 18 February 1951 and undated.
12 DC to Ann Sharp, 1 January 1951.
13 DC to Ann Sharp, undated and 13 March 1951.
14 DC to Ann Sharp, 24, 26 and 27 March 1951.
15 DC to Ann Sharp, 30 March and 13 April 1951. The letters are dated '1954', but this must be a slip.
16 DC to Ann Sharp, 3 and 9 May 1951.
17 Andrew, *Defence of the Realm*, pp. 385–96.
18 DC to Ann Sharp, 28 June 1951.
19 *A Perfect Spy*, pp. 339–40.
20 DC to Ann Sharp, 1 September, 11, 18, 24 and 27 October and 13 November 1951.
21 DC to Ann Sharp, 18 October 1951.
22 'The Madness of Spies', *New Yorker*, 29 September 2008.
23 DC to Ann Sharp, 30 November and [illegible] December 1951.
24 'D.H.O. Team Report, Season 1951–52', *Downhill Only Club Journal*, vol. 2, no. 10 (November 1952).
25 DC to Ann Sharp, 16, 22 and 27 January 1952.
26 'In Ronnie's Court', pp. 144–6.
27 DC to Ann Sharp, [illegible] February 1952.
28 DC to Ann Sharp, 12 and 17 February 1952.
29 DC to Ann Sharp, 22 February and 8 March 1952.
30 'BBA Law Day Dinner Remarks', *Boston Bar Journal*, July/August 1993.
31 DC to Ann Sharp, 17 March 1952.
32 'In Ronnie's Court', pp. 134–5.
33 DC to Ann Sharp, 24 March 1952.
34 R. S. Thompson to Keith Murray, 2 May 1952, Lincoln College Archive.
35 DC to Ann Sharp, 26 May 1952.
36 DC to Ann Sharp, 6 May and 25 June 1952.
37 DC to Ann Sharp, 20 August 1952.
38 DC to Ann Sharp, 8 September 1952.
39 DC to Ann Sharp, 15, 18 and 29 September 1952.
40 DC to Ann Sharp, 25 September 1952.
41 'In Ronnie's Court', p. 144.
42 DC to Ann Sharp, 6, 7 and 8 October 1952.

6: 'That little college in Turl'

1 Vivian H. H. Green, *The Commonwealth of Lincoln College 1427–1977* (Oxford University Press, 1979), p. 586.
2 DC to Ann Sharp, 7 and 8 October 1952.
3 Ann Sharp's diary, 28 August 1952; Tim Cornwell private archive.
4 'Behind an Iron Curtain' (interview with Zoë Heller), *Independent on Sunday*, 1 August 1993.
5 DC to Ann Sharp, 15 February 1953.
6 DC to Ann Sharp, 8 September 1952.
7 DC to Ann Sharp, 24 October 1952.
8 DC to Ann Sharp, 22 July 1953.
9 DC to Ann Sharp, 24 November and 4 December 1952.

10 DC to Ann Sharp, 27 April 1953.
11 DC to Ann Sharp, 4 February 1953.
12 DC to Ann Sharp, 22 July 1953.
13 DC to Ann Sharp, 13 April 1953.
14 'At the Edge of the Real World'.
15 DC to Ann Sharp, 18 May 1953 [mistakenly dated 1955].
16 Richie Benaud, *Anything But: An Autobiography* (Hodder & Stoughton, 1998), p. 79.
17 Ibid.
18 DC to Ann Sharp, 6 June 1953.
19 DC to Ann Sharp, 8 June 1953.
20 DC to Ann Sharp, 8 and 14 June 1953.
21 DC to Ann Sharp, 13 and 22 July, 11 August 1953.
22 DC to Ann Sharp, 16 and 11 May 1953. As with the letter of 18 May cited above, the second of these two letters is dated 1955, but it seems clear from the context that this must date from two years before.
23 'Le Carré draws a veil over a lost chapter', 'New Grub Street', *Sunday Times*, 5 January 1992.
24 Eric Homberger, 'Knight, (Charles Henry) Maxwell (1900–1968), intelligence officer and naturalist', *Oxford Dictionary of National Biography*.
25 DC to Newton Garver, 1 April 1999.
26 DC to Newton Garver, 29 October 2007.
27 Martin Kettle, 'What MI5's records on my father tell us about the uses of surveillance', *Guardian*, 28 July 2011.
28 *Lincoln Imp*, Michaelmas Term 1953 (no. 6).
29 DC to Ann Sharp, 26 May 1954.
30 DC to Ann Sharp, 1 and 26 May 1954.
31 DC to Ann Sharp, 27 April 1954.
32 'Secrets and Lies' (interview with Alan Franks), *The Times*, 13 February 1999.
33 'New Grub Street', *Sunday Times*, 12 January 1992.
34 DC to Barbara, Carla and Dan (Mitchell's family), 25 October 2011.

7: 'This really is the end'

1 DC to Ann Sharp, 8 June 1953.
2 Unheaded document marked 'confidential', 14 November 1953.
3 DC to Ann Sharp, 5 May 1954.
4 DC to Ann Sharp, 9 October 1953.
5 DC to Ann Sharp, 24 November 1953.
6 DC to Ann Sharp, 18 January, 1 and 3 February, 5 April and 9 March 1954.
7 DC to the Bursar, Lincoln College, 11 February 1954, Lincoln College Archive.
8 National Archives, Kew, BT 22 15692.
9 'A Good Deed in a Naughty World' (Victim Support, 2000).
10 DC to Vivian Green, 7 April 1954.
11 DC to Ann Sharp, 5 and 10 April 1954.
12 'At the Edge of the Real World'.
13 'Sarratt and the Draper of Watford', in *Sarratt and the Draper of Watford, and other unlikely stories about Sarratt* (privately published, 1999), pp. 18–19.
14 DC to Ann Sharp, 6 and 16 May 1954.
15 Walter Oakeshott to D. E. Cooke, 11 and 12 June 1954.
16 DC to Ann Sharp, 26 June 1954.
17 'A guide through the complexities of my plots', *Guardian*, 5 March 2005, originally, "Vivian H. H. Green', a eulogy given at his memorial service in Oxford in 2005.

18 See, for example, the eulogies by Susan Brigden and Paul Langford, published in the *Lincoln College Record 2004–2005*.
19 'John le Carré: The Secret Centre' (interview with Nigel Williams), BBC 2, 2000.
20 'A guide through the complexities of my plots'.
21 DC to Ann Sharp, 28 June 1954.
22 *Daily Express*, 1 July 1954.
23 'In Ronnie's Court', p. 150.
24 Foreword to the Lamplighter edition of *Single & Single* (2001).
25 'At the Edge of the Real World'.
26 DC to Ann Sharp, 29 September and undated [October?] 1954.
27 DC to Vivian Green, undated [September 1954].
28 DC to Kaspar von Almen, 3 October 1954.
29 DC to Kaspar von Almen, 13 October 1954.
30 DC to Vivian Green, 29 October 1954.
31 DC to Ann Sharp, 17 November 1954.
32 DC to Vivian Green, 13 December 1954.
33 Ibid.

8: Poor but happy

1 Christopher Martin (ed.), *Millfield: A School for All Seasons* (privately published, 2007).
2 DC to Vivian Green, undated (late 1954/early 1955).
3 'Violent Image' (interview with Alan Watson), *Sunday Times*, 30 March 1969; Michael Dean, 'John le Carré: The Writer who Came in from the Cold', broadcast on BBC 2, published in the *Listener*, 92 (5 September 1974); 'John le Carré: The Art of Fiction No. 149' (interview with George Plimpton), *Paris Review*, 143 (Summer 1997).
4 Foreword to the Lamplighter edition of *Tinker, Tailor, Soldier, Spy* (1991).
5 'Mum's boy – man with a mission', article in *Daily Echo* (Bournemouth)(date not found).
6 DC to Robin Cooke, undated (late 1954/early 1955).
7 DC to Walter Oakeshott, 2 May 1955, Lincoln College Archive.
8 DC to Vivian Green, 14 June 1955, ibid.
9 Walter Oakeshott to D. E. Cooke, 14 May 1955, ibid.
10 DC to Vivian Green, 29 April 1955.
11 'A guide through the complexities of my plots'.
12 J. R. Thring to Walter Oakeshott, 25 October 1955; Oakeshott to Thring, 26 October 1955, Lincoln College Archive.
13 DC to Vivian Green, 9 September 1955, ibid.
14 Vivian Green, 'A Perfect Spy: A Personal Reminiscence' (unpublished paper), pp. 12–13.
15 DC to Robin Cooke, undated (late 1955/early 1956).
16 DC to Robin Cooke, 7 October 1955.
17 DC to Vivian Green, undated (early 1955), Lincoln College Archive.
18 DC to Vivian Green, 31 December 1955.
19 Jean Cornwell to Vivian Green, 8 February and 15 March 1956.
20 Andrew, *Defence of the Realm*, p. 331.
21 Walter Oakeshott to the Warden, St Edward's School, 1 February 1956, Lincoln College Archive.
22 R. S. Thompson to the Warden, St Edward's School, 9 February 1956, ibid.
23 Robert Birley to Walter Oakeshott, 1 and 6 March 1956; Oakeshott to Birley, 5 March 1956, ibid.
24 'Making ends meet on £70 a week', *Poole and East Dorset Herald*, 20 July 1955.
25 AC to Lynn Sharp, 2 May 1956.
26 'Secrets and Lies' (interview with Alan Franks), *The Times*, 13 February 1999.
27 DC to Alison Shacklock, 26 June 1956.

28 Ibid.
29 DC to Vivian Green, 26 June 1956, Lincoln College Archive.

9: 'Milk in first and then Indian'

1 'For the Record' (interview with Alan Watson), London Weekend Television, 1968.
2 DC to Vivian Green, 24 October 1956, Lincoln College Archive.
3 Tim Card, *Eton Renewed: A History from 1860 to the Present Day* (John Murray, 1994), p. 242.
4 'For the Record' (interview with Alan Watson).
5 DC to Vivian Green, undated [probably February 1957], Lincoln College Archive.
6 P. S. H. Lawrence (ed.), *Grizel: Grizel Hartley Remembered* (Michael Russell Publishing, Wilton, 1991), pp. 167 and 198.
7 DC to Vivian Green, 24 October 1956, Lincoln College Archive.
8 Ferdinand Mount, *Cold Cream: My Early Life and Other Mistakes* (Bloomsbury, 2008), p. 88.
9 DC to Vivian Green, 24 October 1956, Lincoln College Archive.
10 DC to Vivian Green, undated (March 1956), Lincoln College Archive.
11 Mount, *Cold Cream*, pp. 57–8.
12 DC to Vivian Green, 24 October 1956.
13 'For the Record' (interview with Alan Watson).
14 DC to Vivian Green, undated [probably February 1957].
15 Boyle papers, MS 660, correspondence on Suez, 3499–948, Brotherton Library, University of Leeds.
16 'The betrayal of Smiley's people' (interview with James Naughtie), *The Times*, 29 November 2003.
17 Mount, *Cold Cream*, p. 80.
18 DC to Hugh Cecil, 12 March 2009.
19 Mount, *Cold Cream*, p. 58.
20 DC to Vivian Green, undated [probably February 1957].
21 AC to Vivian Green, undated [August 1957].
22 DC to AC, dated Monday, Monday night, Wednesday and Thursday [probably August 1957].
23 DC to AC, undated [August 1957].
24 Colin Clark, *Younger Brother, Younger Son: A Memoir* (HarperCollins, 1997).
25 DC to Vivian Green, 29 November 1957.
26 'The Secret Life of John le Carré' (interview with Stephen Schiff), *Vanity Fair*, 52 (June 1989).
27 'Obituary: John Wells', *Independent*, 12 January 1998.
28 DC to Vivian Green, 29 November 1957.
29 D. R. Thorpe, *Supermac: The Life of Harold Macmillan* (Chatto & Windus, 2010), p. 660, n. 40.
30 Foreword to the Lamplighter edition of *A Murder of Quality* (1990).
31 *A Murder of Quality* (Lamplighter edition), pp. 48 and 51.
32 Foreword to the Lamplighter edition of *Call for the Dead* (1992).
33 'John le Carré: The Secret Centre' (interview with Nigel Williams), BBC 2, 2000.
34 Speech in the Sheldonian Theatre to the Oxford Literary Festival, 24 March 2010.
35 'Don't be Beastly to your Secret Service', *Sunday Times Review*, 23 March 1986.
36 DC to AC, undated.
37 DC to AC, 16 March 1958 and undated [spring 1958].

10: 'A dead-end sort of place'

1 Andrew, *Defence of the Realm*, p. 327.
2 Peter Wright, *Spycatcher: The Candid Autobiography of a Senior Intelligence Officer* (Viking Penguin, 1987), p. 35.

3 Ibid., pp. 37 and 39.
4 Andrew, *Defence of the Realm*, p. 338.
5 'Now You See It, Now You Don't', *The Times Magazine*, 7 August 1993.
6 Wright, *Spycatcher*, p. 39.
7 DC to AC, undated.
8 'Now You See It, Now You Don't'.
9 Wright, *Spycatcher*, p. 54.
10 Foreword to the Lamplighter edition of *Call for the Dead* (1992).
11 'Now You See It, Now You Don't'.
12 Stella Rimington, *Open Secret: The Autobiography of the Former Director-General of MI5* (Hutchinson, 2001), p. 101.
13 Andrew, *Defence of the Realm*, p. 332.
14 Ibid., pp. 332 and 333.
15 Rimington, *Open Secret*, p. 102.
16 Andrew, *Defence of the Realm*, p. 331.
17 Rimington, *Open Secret*, pp. 90, 98 and 101–2.
18 Ibid., p. 100.
19 'Now You See It, Now You Don't'.
20 Foreword to the Lamplighter edition of *Call for the Dead* (1992).
21 Andrew, *Defence of the Realm*, p. 325.
22 Ben Macintyre, *A Spy among Friends: Kim Philby and the Great Betrayal* (Bloomsbury, 2014), p. 159.
23 'Now You See It, Now You Don't'.
24 'In my day, MI6 – which I called the Circus in the books – stank of wartime nostalgia' (interview with Pip Ayers), *Daily Mail*, 15 July 2011.
25 Wright, *Spycatcher*, pp. 71ff.
26 Rimington, *Open Secret*, p. 94.
27 Andrew, *Defence of the Realm*, p. 393.
28 Foreword to the Lamplighter edition of *Call for the Dead* (1992).
29 Andrew, *Defence of the Realm*, p. 395.
30 DC to AC, 20 July 1959.
31 From Madeleine Bingham's unpublished autobiography 'Smiley's Wife'. I am indebted to Michael Jago for sending me copies of the relevant passages from the typescript.
32 Foreword to the Lamplighter edition of *Call for the Dead* (1992).
33 *Call for the Dead*, p. 46. The *Oxford English Dictionary* entry for 'tradecraft' is muddled, citing the passage in *Call for the Dead* to illustrate an alternative meaning of the term: 'the craft or art of trading or dealing'.
34 'Don't be Beastly to your Secret Service'.
35 Introduction to the paperback reissue of John Bingham's *My Name is Michael Sibley* (Simon & Schuster, 2000).
36 DC to Lord Clanmorris, 10 August 2010.
37 Andrew, *Defence of the Realm*, pp. 410 and 406.
38 'Julia Pirie: MI5 agent who for two decades worked at the heart of the British Communist Party', *Daily Telegraph* obituary, 28 October 2008.
39 DC to Lord Clanmorris, 10 August 2010.
40 'The Spy who Stayed out in the Cold', *Guardian*, 27 November 1999.
41 Andrew, *Defence of the Realm*, pp. 431–2.
42 DC to AC, both undated [early 1959?].
43 DC to AC, undated [1959?].
44 DC to Kaspar von Almen, 29 May 1960.
45 Michael Jago, *The Man Who Was George Smiley: The Life of John Bingham* (Biteback, 2013), pp. 251–2.

46 Foreword to the Lamplighter edition of *Call for the Dead* (1992).
47 DC to Horace Hale Crosse, 7 August 1963.

11: A small town in Germany

1 Keith Jeffery, *MI6: The History of the Secret Intelligence Service 1909–1949* (Bloomsbury, 2010), p. 225.
2 'In my day, MI6 – which I called the Circus in the books – stank of wartime nostalgia' (interview with Pip Ayers), *Daily Mail*, 15 July 2011.
3 Wright, *Spycatcher*, pp. 28–9.
4 'White, Sir Dick Goldsmith (1906–1993), intelligence officer', *Oxford Dictionary of National Biography*, 2004.
5 For the account that follows of the new entrants' training course I gratefully acknowledge as a principal source the unpublished memoir by Sir John Margetson.
6 Peter Watt to Hilary Rubinstein, 20 October 1960, Gollancz Archive.
7 Leonard Downie Jr, 'Le Carré: Author Cloaked in Mystery', *Washington Post*, 29 September 1980.
8 Gollancz Archive.
9 John Bingham to Hilary Rubinstein, 22 November 1960, Gollancz Archive.
10 'Fifty Years Later', the afterword to the fiftieth-anniversary edition of *The Spy who Came in from the Cold* (Viking Penguin, 2013).
11 DC to Roger Hermiston, 12 April 2012, Gollancz Archive.
12 DC to Hilary Rubinstein, 21 January 1961, Gollancz Archive.
13 DC to John Margetson, 5 July 1961.
14 DC to AC, 6 June 1961.
15 *A Small Town in Germany* (Pan edition, 1969), pp. 18–19.
16 Ibid., p. 106.
17 Foreword to the Lamplighter edition of *A Small Town in Germany* (1991).
18 'John le Carré in Conversation' (interview with Anne McElvoy), broadcast on BBC Radio 3, 29 July 2013.
19 Foreword to the Lamplighter edition of *A Small Town in Germany* (1991).
20 Michael Marten (ed.), *Tim Marten: Memories* (privately published, 2009).
21 DC to AC, undated [June 1961].
22 Foreword to the Lamplighter edition of *A Small Town in Germany* (1991).
23 *A Small Town in Germany* (Pan edition, 1969), p. 142.
24 AC to John Margetson, 2 August 1961.
25 *A Small Town in Germany* (Pan edition, 1969), pp. 36–7.
26 Foreword to the Lamplighter edition of *The Spy who Came in from the Cold* (1990).
27 DC to Miranda Coldstream, undated [June 1961].
28 Foreword to the Lamplighter edition of *A Murder of Quality* (1990).
29 Sheila Hodges to Victor Gollancz, 1 February 1962, Gollancz Archive.
30 DC to AC, undated [March 1962?].
31 Godfrey Smith, introduction to the reissued edition of James Kennaway's *Tunes of Glory* (Mainstream, 1980).
32 DC to AC, 11 March 1962.
33 *The Spy who Came in from the Cold* (Gollancz, 1963), p. 20.
34 Foreword to the Lamplighter edition of *The Spy who Came in from the Cold* (1990).
35 DC to AC, 30 June 1962.
36 Foreword to the Lamplighter edition of *The Spy who Came in from the Cold* (1990).
37 Dan Neil, 'The 50 Worst Cars of All Time', *Time*, 4 September 2007.

38 *The Lively Arts*, BBC TV interview, transmitted 25 September 1977.
39 DC to AC, 30 June 1962.
40 DC to Horace Hale Crosse, 7 August 1963. In this letter David says that he 'decided to begin the task of giving final shape' to *The Spy who Came in from the Cold* in August 1961, while he was still engaged on *A Murder of Quality*, but I have assumed that this is an exaggeration.
41 'John le Carré: The Secret Centre' (interview with Nigel Williams), BBC 2, 2000.

12: Becoming John le Carré

1 Peter Watt to Victor Gollancz, 26 November 1962, Gollancz Archive.
2 *The Spy who Came in from the Cold*, p. 20; William Boyd, 'Rereading: The Spy Who Came in from the Cold by John le Carré', *Guardian*, 24 July 2010.
3 Victor Gollancz to Peter Watt, 8 February 1963; Watt to Gollancz, 27 February 1963, Gollancz Archive.
4 DC to AC, 30 January 1963.
5 DC to Vivian Green, 6 February 1963.
6 Richard Davenport-Hines, *An English Affair: Sex, Class and Power in the Age of Profumo* (HarperCollins, 2013), p. 262.
7 Jack Geoghegan, 'Discovering "The Spy" – 25 years later', a new introduction to *The Spy who Came in from the Cold* (Book of the Month Club, 1988).
8 Eleanor Doemstag, 'Behind the Lines: A Literary Casebook: How the home office got *The Spy* home', *Book Week*, 27 May 1964.
9 DC to Vivian Green, 7 July 1963.
10 'The spy who liked me: On the set with Richard Burton and Martin Ritt', *New Yorker*, 15 April 2013.
11 Tom Carver, 'Philby in Beirut', *London Review of Books*, 11 October 2012.
12 Julian Maclaren-Ross, 'Cloak without Dagger', *Times Literary Supplement*, 8 February 1963.
13 Victor Gollancz to DC, 17 February 1964.
14 Horace Hale Crosse to DC, 6 September 1963.
15 'Son of the Author's Father' (unpublished).
16 DC to Vivian Green, 14 November 1963.
17 Horace Hale Crosse to DC, 11 October 1963.
18 DC to AC, 23 November 1963.
19 Victor Gollancz to Peter Watt, 20 November 1963.
20 Graham Watson, *Book Society* (André Deutsch, 1980), pp. 104–5.
21 *The Looking-Glass War* (Lamplighter edition, 1991), pp. 18 and 155.
22 James MacGibbon to DC, 10 February 1964.
23 Peter Watt to James MacGibbon, 15 March 1964; MacGibbon to Watt, 10 and 16 March 1964, A. P. Watt Archive.
24 Hamish MacGibbon, 'Diary', *London Review of Books*, 16 June 2011.
25 Graham Greene to Victor Gollancz, 26 September 1963; Gollancz to Greene, 30 September 1963, Gollancz Archive.
26 'The author who came in from obscurity', *Sunday Times*, 12 January 1964.
27 Tom Bower, *The Perfect English Spy: Sir Dick White and the Secret War 1935–90* (Heinemann, 1995), p. 270.
28 Peter Watt to Victor Gollancz, 20 January 1964, and Watt to DC, 21 January 1964, A. P. Watt Archive.
29 Horace Hale Crosse to DC, 13 February 1964.
30 Doemstag, 'Behind the Lines: A Literary Casebook: How the home office got *The Spy* home'.
31 Anthony Boucher, 'Temptations of a Man Isolated in Deceit', *New York Times*, 12 January 1964.

32 Doemstag, 'Behind the Lines: A Literary Casebook: How the home office got *The Spy* home'.
33 'Wrong Man on Crete', *Holiday*, December 1965.
34 Ibid.
35 'Fifty Years Later', the afterword to the fiftieth-anniversary edition of *The Spy who Came in from the Cold* (Viking Penguin, 2013).
36 CBS, *To Tell the Truth*, aired on 27 April 1964.
37 'The spy who liked me: On the set with Richard Burton and Martin Ritt'.
38 C. P. Snow to DC, 15 April 1964; DC to Snow, 19 April 1964, Harry Ransom Center, University of Texas.
39 Doemstag, 'Behind the Lines: A Literary Casebook: How the home office got *The Spy* home'.

13: Naïve and sentimental love

1 James and Susan Kennaway, *The Kennaway Papers* (Jonathan Cape, 1981), p. 22.
2 James Kennaway to his mother, September 1961, quoted in ibid., pp. 70–2; Trevor Royle, *James and Jim: A Biography of James Kennaway* (Mainstream, 1983), p. 126.
3 Royle, *James and Jim*, pp. 51–2, 153–4, 188–9; Kennaway and Kennaway, *The Kennaway Papers*, p. 9.
4 Royle, *James and Jim*, pp. 51–2, 153–4, 188–9; Kennaway and Kennaway, *The Kennaway Papers*, p. 151.
5 'Violent Image' (interview with Alan Watson), *Sunday Times*, 30 March 1969.
6 DC to James Kennaway, undated [June?] 1964.
7 'Early success', essay first published in *American Cavalcade* (1937).
8 DC to Victor Gollancz, 30 May 1964; Peter Watt to Victor Gollancz, 11 June 1964 and to Livia Gollancz, 17 June 1964.
9 Foreword to the Lamplighter edition of *The Looking-Glass War* (1991).
10 Victor Gollancz to DC, 22 July 1964; Peter Watt to Victor Gollancz (two letters), 17 August 1964; DC to Victor Gollancz, 28 August 1964, Gollancz Archive.
11 Undated letters [late August 1964] from James Kennaway to Susan Kennaway, Kennaway papers, National Library of Scotland 12760: 58.
12 Undated letter from DC to Charles Pick, late August/early September 1964.
13 Kennaway papers, National Library of Scotland 12760: 44.
14 DC to James Kennaway, 28 August 1964.
15 Kennaway and Kennaway, *The Kennaway Papers*, pp. 17 and 19–20.
16 Horace Hale Crosse to DC, 22 May, 27 July and 3 September 1964.
17 Undated letter from DC to James Kennaway, probably September 1964.
18 The account that follows is based largely on the one given by Susan Kennaway in *The Kennaway Papers*. David left an account of the same events, which differs in several details.
19 Kennaway and Kennaway, *The Kennaway Papers*, p. 31.
20 Ibid., pp. 30–2.
21 DC to James Kennaway, 22 November 1964.
22 DC to Susan Kennaway, undated [March 1965?].
23 Ibid.
24 This passage draws extensively on le Carré's 'The spy who liked me: On the set with Richard Burton and Martin Ritt'.
25 Kennaway and Kennaway, *The Kennaway Papers*, pp. 53–4.
26 Frank Delaney, introduction to the reissued edition of Kennaway's *The Bells of Shoreditch* (Mainstream, 1981), p. x; Frederic Raphael, introduction to the reissued edition of Kennaway's *The Cost of Living like This* (Mainstream, 1980), p. viii.
27 Kennaway and Kennaway, *The Kennaway Papers*, p. 100.
28 Ibid., p. 58.

29 James Kennaway to Susan Kennaway, 1 September 1967, in ibid., p. 142.
30 DC to Susan Kennaway, undated but probably March 1965, National Library of Scotland 12760: 64.
31 Several undated letters to Susan Kennaway, probably March–April 1965, National Library of Scotland 12760: 64.
32 Undated letter from AC to DC, undated [early 1965?].
33 Kennaway and Kennaway, *The Kennaway Papers*, p. 24.
34 James Kennaway to Susan Kennaway, 1 March 1965, National Library of Scotland 12760.

14: Caught in the machine

1 DC to AC, undated [April 1965?].
2 DC to Graham Greene, 4 August 1964. I am indebted to Richard Greene for supplying me with copies of Graham Greene's letters.
3 DC to AC, 21 April 1965.
4 Carol Smith at A. P. Watt to Shaun MacLoughlin, script editor, *The Wednesday Play*, 17 July 1969, T 48/368/1, BBC Written Archives Centre, Caversham.
5 Kingsley Amis, 'Slow Boat to Haiti', *Observer*, 30 January 1966.
6 DC to Graham Greene, undated [February 1966?].
7 'Le Carré comes in from the cold' (interview with Anthony Haden-Guest), *Town*, date unknown [July 1965?].
8 James Kennaway to Susan Kennaway, 1 March 1965 [misdated 1964], in *The Kennaway Papers*, p. 91.
9 'Vienna: In search of a lost spy story', *Weekend Telegraph*, June 1966.
10 DC to AC, 21 April 1965.
11 AC to DC, undated [summer 1965].
12 'Spy Writer Finds Success is Cold', *New York Times*, 5 June 1965.
13 Maurice Richardson, 'Le Carré tries too hard', *Observer*, 20 June 1965.
14 Anthony Curtis, 'Work Out for a Keen Spy', *Sunday Telegraph*, 20 June 1965.
15 I owe this phrase to Toby Manning.
16 'Twenty Years After', *Times Literary Supplement*, 24 July 1965.
17 Foreword to the Lamplighter edition of *The Looking-Glass War* (1991).
18 See, for example, Julian Symons, 'A Spy Goes Out', *Sunday Times*, 20 June 1965.
19 Orville Prescott, 'Books of the Times', *New York Times*, 25 and 23 July 1965.
20 Stephen Marcus, 'Grand Illusions', *New York Review of Books*, 5 August 1965.
21 Eric Ambler, 'John Le Carré escapes the follow-up jinx', *Life*, 30 July 1965.
22 Hilde Spiel, 'Weder Gott noch Marx', *Frankfurter Allgemeine Zeitung*, 15 March 1966.
23 Foreword to the Lamplighter edition of *The Looking-Glass War* (1991).
24 John Bingham to Victor Gollancz, 13 August 1965. I am grateful to Michael Jago for supplying me with a copy of this letter.
25 Jago, *The Man Who Was George Smiley*, p. 193.
26 DC to Horace Hale Crosse, 14 July 1965.
27 John Bingham to Victor Gollancz, 13 August 1965.
28 Ibid.
29 DC to AC, 23 September 1965 and undated [probably the next day].
30 DC to John Margetson, 29 September 1969.
31 Ronnie Cornwell to Victor Gollancz, 3 April 1965.
32 DC to AC, undated, postmarked 28 October 1965.
33 DC to John and Miranda Margetson, 17 December 1965.
34 DC to Ronnie Cornwell, 28 December 1965, quoted in Fred Hauptfuhrer, 'The Complex Man who Writes as John Le Carré', *People*, 19 August 1974.

35 'Playbill', *Playboy*, December 1965, p. 5.
36 DC to AC, undated [1966?].
37 Foreword to the Lamplighter edition of *A Small Town in Germany* (1991).
38 Charles Pick to H. G. Vevers (Hon. Sec., Savile Club), 5 May 1966, 'Le Carré author file', Random House Archive.
39 These and subsequent quotations in this passage are taken from an interview David Cornwell gave to Alan Clark's biographer, Ion Trewin.
40 DC to Charles Pick, 21 August 1967.
41 'The Maharajah's Elephant' [unpublished].

15: Rich but restless

1 DC to Charles Pick, 1 January 1968.
2 'The Enemy Within', *Sunday Times*, 18 February 1968.
3 Frank Keating, 'André Deutsch', *Guardian*, 12 April 2000.
4 Norman Sherry, *The Life of Graham Greene*, vol. 3: *1955–1991* (Jonathan Cape, 2004), pp. 751–2.
5 'The Writers Engage in Battle,' *The Times*, 4 September 1967.
6 'Our Man in Moscow', *Observer*, 18 February 1968.
7 'Britain: The Old School Spy', *Time*, 1 March 1968.
8 'The Night of the March', *Weekend Telegraph*, 5 July 1968.
9 Charles Pick to Arthur Cohen, *Reader's Digest*, 4 January 1967.
10 DC to Charles Pick, 19 May and 26 July 1967 and 1 January 1968.
11 DC to Horace Hale Crosse, 13 February and 1 March 1967.
12 DC to AC, 28 May 1968.
13 DC to AC, 13 June 1968.
14 DC to AC, undated [summer 1968].
15 DC to John Margetson, 11 July 1968.
16 'Behind an Iron Curtain' (interview with Zoë Heller) Independent on Sunday 1 August 1993.
17 George Greenfield, *A Smattering of Monsters: A Kind of Memoir* (Little, Brown, 1995), p. 276.
18 DC to R. S. Thompson, 8 October 1968.
19 Roland Gant to Malcolm Muggeridge, 21 October 1968.
20 Christa Rotzoll, 'Hunnen heraus!', *Frankfurter Allgemeine Zeitung*, 26 November 1968.
21 DC to Vivian Green, 24 August 1968.
22 Telegram from DC to Charles Pick, 26 April 1968. I am indebted to Martin Pick for access to his father's papers.
23 'Labyrinthine Ways', *Times Literary Supplement*, 31 October 1968.
24 H. R. F. Keating, 'From Bonn, a literary bundle', *The Times*, 2 November 1968.
25 Neal Ascherson, 'Looking Forward in Anger', *Observer*, 27 October 1968.
26 C. P. Snow, introducing *A Small Town in Germany* to members of the Book of the Month Club, 9 July 1968.
27 T. G. Rosenthal, 'Thrillers into Novels', *New Statesman*, 8 November 1968.
28 Richard Boston, 'What Became of Harting?', *New York Times Book Review*, 27 October 1968.
29 DC to Charles Pick, 2 November 1968.
30 'Poole Tablers' 40th Milestone', *Poole and East Dorset Herald*, 6 March 1969; Bryan E. Keeping to Ed Perkins (deputy editor, *Daily Echo*), 27 April 1999.
31 DC to John Margetson, 15 June 1969.
32 Jason Lewis and Kim Willsher, 'The KGB's Spy at the Palace', *Mail on Sunday*, 20 February 2000.
33 'Strange Magic I Could Never Quite Deny', *Weekend Telegraph*, 9 November 1996.

34 'Karl', a tribute given at the memorial service for Karl Weschke in Newlyn Art Gallery, 15 March 2005.
35 From David's notes for the eulogy cited in ibid.
36 DC to AC, 4 February 1969.
37 Sydney Pollack to DC, dated '13 April' [1993?].
38 DC to AC, undated but postmarked 13 June 1968.
39 DC to Susan Kennaway, 18 February 1969.
40 DC to Susan Kennaway, undated [February/March 1969?].
41 DC to Susan Kennaway, dated '8 May' [1969].
42 DC to Susan Kennaway, undated [June 1969?].
43 DC to AC, 24 October and 14 November 1969; AC to DC, undated [October/November 1969].
44 DC to AC, 18 January and 27 May 1970; AC to DC, undated [1970].
45 DC to Vivian Green, 5 June 1970.
46 DC to John Margetson, 15 June 1969.
47 DC to Charles Pick, undated [June 1970].
48 Foreword to the Lamplighter edition of *The Naïve and Sentimental Lover* (2000).
49 Ibid.
50 *The Naïve and Sentimental Lover* (Penguin, 2011), pp. 58–9.
51 DC to James Kennaway, undated [1965].
52 DC to Horace Hale Crosse, 4 and 6 March 1968.
53 This paragraph draws on Sabine Ibach's address at the memorial gathering for Rainer Heumann on 26 March 1996.
54 DC to Andreas Heumann, 7 March 1996.
55 'Obituary', *Publishing News*, 5 May 2000.
56 Greenfield, *A Smattering of Monsters*, pp. 276–8.
57 DC to Charles Pick, 14 April 1970.
58 DC to Charles Pick, undated [June 1970].
59 Charles Pick to DC, 24 June 1970, Random House Archive.
60 DC to Charles Pick, 7 November 1970.
61 Original draft of a passage from John St John's *William Heinemann: A Century of Publishing, 1890–1990* (William Heinemann, 1990), p. 498. In the printed version the word 'embittered' is replaced by 'let down'.
62 Greenfield, *A Smattering of Monsters*, pp. 201–2.
63 'Whitefriar', *Bookseller*, 13 March 1971.
64 DC to Charles Pick, 15 March 1971.
65 Susan Kennaway to DC, 16 May, year not given [1971?].
66 DC to Susan Kennaway, undated [May 1971?].
67 Foreword to the Lamplighter edition of *The Naïve and Sentimental Lover* (2000).
68 'Wishful Thinking', *Times Literary Supplement*, 24 September 1971.
69 D. Jones, 'The New Le Carré', *Listener*, 23 September 1971.
70 Claire Tomalin, 'Liberated Englishman', *Observer*, 19 September 1971.
71 Auberon Waugh, 'Piers Paul Read and Other Novelists', *Spectator*, 25 September 1971.
72 H. R. F. Keating, 'The Prime Gift of Story-Telling', *The Times*, 30 September 1971.
73 Graham Lord, 'Now John Le Carré Turns his Back on Spies', *Sunday Express*, 19 September 1971.
74 Frederic Raphael, 'Looking-Glass Hero', *Sunday Times*, 26 September 1971.
75 Jochen Schmidt, 'Der wachsame Träumer', *Frankfurter Allgemeine Zeitung*, 29 July 1972.
76 Georg Hensel, 'In Ermangelung eines Spions', *Süddeutsche Zeitung*, 6 May 1972.
77 Geoffrey Wolff, 'All Naked into the World of Art', *New York Times Book Review*, 9 January 1972.
78 Christopher Lehmann-Haupt, 'Falling in love with love . . .', 'Books of The Times', *New York Times*, 9 January 1972.

79 'Le Carré's Circus' (interview with Paul Vaughan), *Listener*, 13 September 1979.
80 DC to Buzz and Janet Berger, 8 January 1972.
81 'Well Played, Wodehouse', *Sunday Times*, 10 October 1971.
82 DC to J. W. Lambert, 28 September 1971, Bodleian Library Ms Eng c. 2296.

16: Keeping the bitterness at bay

1 DC to Nicholas Shakespeare, 19 April 1991. Shakespeare had then just given up work as a literary journalist to concentrate on writing full-time.
2 DC to Dmitri Khrebtukov (in a letter to Andrew Ross), 30 October 1996.
3 'The Things a Spy Can Do' (interview with Melvyn Bragg), *Listener*, 22 January 1976.
4 'Who Watches the Watchmen?', *Waterstone's Books Quarterly*, Issue 30 (2008).
5 'John le Carré: The Art of Fiction No. 149' (interview with George Plimpton), *Paris Review*, 143 (Summer 1997).
6 Robert Gottlieb, 'The Art of Editing' (interview with Larissa MacFarquhar), *Paris Review*, 132 (Fall 1994).
7 JC to Tim Hely Hutchinson, 27 October 1993.
8 Introduction to the Lamplighter edition of *Smiley's People* (2000).
9 Eric Homberger, *John le Carré* (Methuen, 1986), p. 88.
10 Foreword to the Lamplighter edition of *Tinker, Tailor, Soldier, Spy* (1991).
11 DC to Vivian Green, 9 December 1973.
12 'Le Carré's Circus' (interview with Paul Vaughan), *Listener*, 13 September 1979.
13 'John le Carré: The Art of Fiction No. 149' (interview with George Plimpton).
14 Foreword to the Lamplighter edition of *Tinker, Tailor, Soldier, Spy* (1991).
15 Paula Span, 'Tinker, Tailor, Soldier . . . Tourist', *Washington Post Magazine*, 11 October 1982.
16 Robert Burchfield to John le Carré, 18 March 1981.
17 Michael Straight, *After Long Silence* (Collins, 1983), p. 62.
18 Frank Steele to DC, 27 June 1989; 'Mole-catchers', letter to the *Sunday Times*, 2 July 1989.
19 Phillip Knightley, *Philby: The Life and Views of the K.G.B. Masterspy* (André Deutsch, 1988), pp. 136–9.
20 DC to John ?, 27 July 1973, Hodder & Stoughton Archive; DC to Vivian Green, 9 December 1973.
21 DC to Vivian Green, 28 March 1974.
22 Robert Gottlieb, 'The Art of Editing'.
23 'The Constant Muse', *New Yorker*, 25 December 2000.
24 H. D. S. Greenway, 'Travels with le Carré', *Newsweek*, 10 November 1977. The account that follows is based largely on this source.
25 Richard Hughes, 'I Spy', *Sun*, 11 November 1977.
26 H. D. S. Greenway, 'A Life at the Empire's End', *Boston Globe*, 6 December 2002.
27 Introduction to the Lamplighter edition of *The Little Drummer Girl* (1993).
28 H. D. S. Greenway, *Foreign Correspondent: A Memoir* (Simon & Schuster, 2014), pp. 110–11.
29 Derek Davies, 'Memories of John le Carré' (written for the *Sunday Correspondent* c. 1989 but unpublished).
30 DC to Vivian Green, 28 March 1974.
31 DC to Horace Hale Crosse, 2 October 1975.
32 Yvette Pierpaoli to JC and DC, 8 September 1997.
33 'The Constant Muse'.
34 Ibid.
35 Greenway, 'Travels with le Carré'.
36 Michael Dean, 'The Writer who Came in from the Cold', broadcast on BBC 2, published in the *Listener*, 92 (5 September 1974).

37 Karl Miller, 'Gothic Guesswork', *New York Review of Books*, 18 July 1974.
38 Richard Locke, 'The Spy who Spied on Spies', *New York Times*, 30 June 1974.
39 Pearl K. Bell, 'Coming in from the Cold War', *New Leader*, 24 June 1974; DC to Bell, 3 July 1974.
40 'Hunt the Sleeper', *Times Literary Supplement*, 19 July 1974.
41 H. R. F. Keating, 'Life without Roots', *The Times*, 4 July 1974.
42 [Unsigned], 'Crime Compendium', *Spectator*, 6 July 1974.
43 Timothy Mo, 'Human Spy', *New Statesman*, 12 July 1974.
44 Maurice Richardson, 'The Spy Circus', *Observer*, 30 June 1974.
45 Derek Mahon, 'Dolls within Dolls', *Listener*, 4 July 1974.
46 Edmund Crispin, 'Moling Away', *Sunday Times*, 30 June 1974.
47 Matthew Coady, 'Our Sort', *Guardian*, 4 July 1974.

17: 'You treated your father very badly'

1 DC to Graham Greene, 7 and 12 November 1974; Greene to DC, 11 November 1974.
2 DC to Tony Cornwell, 15 May 2000.
3 Joseph Lelyveld, 'Le Carré's Toughest Case', *New York Times Magazine*, 16 March 1986.
4 *Smiley's People*, p. 275.
5 *Tinker, Tailor, Soldier, Spy* (Penguin Canada, 1991), p. 365.
6 'The Things a Spy Can Do' (interview with Melvyn Bragg), *Listener*, 22 January 1976.
7 DC to Vivian Green, 28 September 1976.
8 I owe this point to Toby Manning, and I wish to acknowledge his help in finding these reviews.
9 H. R. F. Keating, 'With Sweep and Vision', *The Times*, 8 September 1977.
10 T. J. Binyon, 'A Gentleman among Players', *Times Literary Supplement*, 9 September 1977.
11 Thomas Hinde, 'Spy Story Plus', *Sunday Telegraph*, 18 September 1977.
12 Maurice Richardson, 'Our Man in a Maze', *Observer*, 11 September 1977.
13 Louis Finger, 'The Manly One', *New Statesman*, 23 September 1977.
14 Clancy Sigal, 'Smiley's Villains', *Guardian*, 8 September 1977.
15 Anthony Burgess, 'Moscow Drugs, Peking Gold', *New York Times Book Review*, 25 September 1977.
16 Rudolf Walter Leonhardt, 'Das Leben – eine Verschwörung', *Die Zeit*, 23 September 1977.
17 Jürgen Busche, 'Der Betrüger wird betrogen, Held und Feigling zerbrechen unterschiedslos', *Frankfurter Allgemeine Zeitung*, 11 October 1977.
18 Clive James, 'Go Back to the Cold!', *New York Review of Books*, 27 October 1977.
19 Alex Hamilton, 'Top of the Pops', *Guardian*, 6 October 1979.
20 DC to George Greenfield, 17 October 1977.
21 Knightley, *Philby*, pp. 11–12.
22 'In England Now', *New York Times Magazine*, 23 October 1977.
23 Philip Oakes, 'Hard Cash and Le Carré', *Sunday Times*, 11 September 1977.
24 H. D. S. Greenway, 'Travels with le Carré', *Newsweek*, 10 October 1977.
25 'The Little Drummer Girl' (interview with Melvyn Bragg), *South Bank Show*, 27 March 1983; reprinted in Matthew J. Bruccoli and Judith S. Baughman (eds), *Conversations with John le Carré* (University Press of Mississippi, 2004).
26 Catalogue introduction to John Miller's 'New Horizons' exhibition, 1982.
27 DC to John Margetson, 17 December 1978.
28 Karel Reisz to Norman Trewin, 6 September 1974, Reisz papers KRE 1/7/2, British Film Institute.
29 'Master of the Spy Story: John le Carré Strikes Again', *Time*, 3 October 1977. The inside story was headed 'The Spy Who Came In for the Gold'.
30 'John le Carré at the NFT' (interview with Adrian Wootton), *Guardian*, 5 October 2002.

31 DC to John Margetson, 5 January 1975.
32 Assistant Head of Copyright to HBCTel, 6 July 1977, R CONT 20, BBC Written Archives Centre, Caversham.

18: 'Does anyone know what's going on?'

1 Jean Seaton, *Pinkoes and Traitors: The BBC and the Nation, 1974–1987* (Profile, 2015), p. 300. I am indebted to Professor Seaton for allowing me to read her draft of this episode.
2 In the transcript of a 2002 conversation with Piers Paul Read, who was researching the authorised biography of Alec Guinness (Simon & Schuster, 2003).
3 DC to Alec Guinness, 27 February 1978, British Library Add MS 89015/2/7/5.
4 Alec Guinness to DC, 2 March 1978.
5 DC to Alec Guinness, 3 March 1978, British Library Add MS 89015/2/7/5.
6 Seaton, *Pinkoes and Traitors*, p. 301.
7 DC to Alec Guinness, 8 March 1978, British Library Add MS 89015/2/7/5.
8 Preface to Alec Guinness, *My Name Escapes Me: The Diary of a Retiring Actor* (Hamish Hamilton, 1996).
9 Ibid.
10 'The Secret Life of John le Carré' (interview with Stephen Schiff), *Vanity Fair*, 52 (June 1989).
11 Memo by Clyde Logan, 9 January 1978, R CONT 16, BBC Written Archives Centre, Caversham.
12 DC to Jonathan Powell, 28 June 1978.
13 Seaton, *Pinkoes and Traitors*, p. 302.
14 DC to David Goodall, 27 August 1979.
15 'A Secret Surface' (interview with Tom Sutcliffe), *Guardian*, 8 September 1979.
16 Alec Guinness to DC, 29 September 1978.
17 DC to Alec Guinness, 28 April, 27 June and 31 August 1979, British Library Add MS 89015/2/7/5.
18 DC to Arthur Hopcraft, 31 July 1979.
19 Richard Ingrams, 'Tinkering', *Spectator*, 22 September 1979.
20 Philip Attenborough to Eric Major and others, 28 September 1979; Michael Attenborough to Philip Attenborough, 5 October 1979. I am indebted to Michael Attenborough for allowing me to see his personal records.
21 DC to Alec Guinness, undated [c. 22 October 1979], British Library Add MS 89015/2/7/5.
22 Bill Grundy, 'Memo to the Circus: First Class Mission', *Evening Standard* (after series had finished).
23 'Television: Selections', *Time Out*, 19–25 October 1979.
24 David Smiley to DC, 19 November 1979 and 3 December 1980; DC to David Smiley, 14 December 1979. I am indebted to David Smiley's son Xan for supplying me with a copy of this letter.
25 Tom Shales, 'The spies have it', *Washington Post*, 29 September 1980.
26 Michael Attenborough to Eric Major and others (reporting on a telephone conversation with DC), 7 October 1980.
27 'Birthmarks, Chess Games & Policemen', *New Statesman*, 17 March 1978.
28 T. J. Binyon, 'In the Direction of Moscow', *Times Literary Supplement*, 17 March 1978.
29 'Plonking Purgatory', 'West Wins Through' and 'Marginally Better', *Observer*, 16 and 30 September, 7 October 1979.
30 'Tinker, Tailor, and the Mole who Never was', *Guardian*, 7 November 1979.
31 DC to Mary-Kay Wilmers, 27 November 1979.
32 Alec Guinness to DC, 3 March 1979.
33 DC to Alec Guinness, undated [c. 22 October 1979], British Library Add MS 89015/2/7/5.
34 DC to Buzz Berger, 29 November 1979.

35 DC to Vivian Green, 12 February 1980.
36 Michael Wood, 'Spy Fiction, Spy Fact', *New York Times Book Review*, 6 January 1980.
37 Matthew Coady, 'Spy Story', *Guardian*, 7 February 1980.
38 S. S. Prawer, 'The Circus and its Conscience', *Times Literary Supplement*, 8 February 1980.
39 C. P. Snow, 'Estonian Connection', *Financial Times*, 2 February 1980.
40 Michael Ratcliffe, 'George's Black Grail', *The Times*, 7 February 1980; John Coleman, 'A Crafty le Carré', *Sunday Times*, 3 February 1980.
41 Rudolf Walter Leonhardt, 'Die geheime Welt des John Le Carré', *Die Zeit*, 4 April 1980.
42 DC to Al Alvarez, 15 December 1979, British Library Add MS 88602.
43 'Half-angels versus half-devils', *Observer*, 3 February 1980.
44 Len Deighton to Al Alvarez, 11 December 1979, British Library Add MS 88602.
45 DC to Vivian Green, 12 February 1980.
46 'Le Carré's Circus' (interview with Paul Vaughan), *Listener*, 13 September 1979.
47 Anonymous to DC, 14 September 1979; DC to John Bingham, 27 September 1979; Bingham to DC, 2 October 1979. I am grateful to Michael Jago for supplying me with copies of these letters.
48 Introduction to the paperback reissue of John Bingham's *My Name is Michael Sibley* (Simon & Schuster, 2000).
49 'Don't be Beastly to your Secret Service'.
50 Jago, *The Man Who Was George Smiley*, p. 250.
51 'Don't be Beastly to your Secret Service'.
52 Susan Kennaway to Adam Sisman, 18 February 2014.
53 Peter Grosvenor, 'The Lover who Stayed out in the Cold', *Daily Express*, January 1981.
54 DC to Susan Kennaway, 8 and 24 September 1979; Susan Kennaway to DC, 20 September 1979.
55 James Campbell, 'The Novelist as Character', *Times Literary Supplement*, 27 February 1981.
56 Allan Massie, 'A History', *London Review of Books*, 19 February 1981.
57 Philip Oakes, 'Three for the Road', *Sunday Times*, 25 January 1981.
58 Paul Bailey, 'An Affair to Forget', *Observer*, 25 January 1981.
59 Philippa Toomey, 'Three Sides', *The Times*, 29 January 1981.
60 *Sunday Times*, 26 October 1980.
61 Valerie Grove, 'The Wife who Came in from the Cold', *Evening Standard*, 27 January 1981.
62 DC to Alec Guinness, Alec Guinness to DC, both dated 29 January 1982, British Library Add MS 89015/2/7/5.
63 Nicholas Wapshott, 'Tinker, Tailor, Soldier, Novelist', *The Times*, 6 September 1982.
64 'Le Carré interview' (letter to the editor), *The Times*, 10 September 1982.
65 DC to Graham Greene, 6 September 1982; Greene to DC, 12 September 1982.
66 DC to Max Reinhardt, 26 September 1982.
67 Kim Philby to Graham Greene, 23 November 1982.

19: 'The Love Thief'

1 DC to Vivian Green, 25 October 1982.
2 'The Secret Life of John le Carré' (interview with Stephen Schiff), *Vanity Fair*, 52 (June 1989).
3 'The Little Drummer Girl' (interview with Melvyn Bragg), *South Bank Show*, 27 March 1983; reprinted in Bruccoli and Baughman (eds), *Conversations with John le Carré*.
4 This passage is based on David's unpublished account. A fictionalised version of this episode appeared in chapter 8 of *The Secret Pilgrim*.
5 Introduction to the Lamplighter edition of *The Little Drummer Girl* (1993).
6 'Memories of a Vanished Land', *Observer*, 13 June 1982.
7 DC to David Goodall, 29 August 1982.

8 George Will, 'Little Drummer Girl', *Free Lance-Star* (and elsewhere), 12 May 1983.
9 Lewis Chester, 'What Makes a Book Sell 400 Thousand before it's Published', *Sunday Times*, 20 March 1983.
10 William F. Buckley Jr, 'Terror and a Woman', *New York Times*, 13 March 1983.
11 Walter Laqueur, 'Le Carré's Fantasies', *Commentary*, June 1983.
12 David Pryce-Jones, 'A Demonological Fiction', *New Republic*, 18 April 1983.
13 Introduction to the Lamplighter edition of *The Little Drummer Girl* (1993).
14 John Gross, 'Shadow of a Terrorist', *Observer*, 27 March 1983.
15 Julian Symons, 'A Book to be Buried With', *Sunday Times*, 27 March 1983.
16 Robert Nye, 'Night Flight to Berlin', *Guardian*, 31 March 1983.
17 'Keine spielt besser als Charlie', *Die Welt*, 3 September 1983.
18 Peter Laemmle, 'Verratene Menschlichkeit', *Süddeutsche Zeitung*, 17 September 1983.
19 'The Spymaster Returns', *Newsweek*, 7 March 1983.
20 Hugh McIlvanney, 'The Secret Life of John le Carré', *Observer Magazine*, 6 March 1983.
21 'The Clandestine Muse', originally written as the James Tait Black Memorial Prize Lecture in 1978, and published privately as the G. Harry Pouder Memorial Lecture, delivered at Johns Hopkins University on 20 May 1986.
22 David Pryce-Jones, 'Drumming up Hatred', *Spectator*, 16 April 1983.
23 Letter quoted on the website of the Thatcher Foundation.
24 'TV Actress is Awarded £10,000 Libel Damages', *Glasgow Herald*, 19 December 1985.
25 'Spying on my Father', draft notes for the Book of the Month Club edition of *A Perfect Spy*. The passage that follows draws extensively on these sources.
26 *A Perfect Spy*, pp. 461–2 and 169–70.
27 Ibid., p. 421.
28 Ibid., p. 270.
29 Ibid., pp. 121–2.
30 Ibid., p. 246.
31 'The Secret Life of John le Carré' (interview with Stephen Schiff).
32 Michael Attenborough to George Greenfield, 24 May 1985.
33 Greenfield, *A Smattering of Monsters*, p. 79.
34 DC to Michael Attenborough, 27 May 1985.
35 Robert Gottlieb, 'The Art of Editing' (interview with Larissa MacFarquhar), *Paris Review*, 132 (Fall 1994).
36 Anthony Clare, 'Exorcizing Father's Ghost', *Sunday Times*, 30 March 1986.
37 Anthony Burgess, 'Defector as Hero', *Observer*, 16 March 1986.
38 Blake Morrison, 'Love and betrayal in the mist', *Times Literary Supplement*, 11April 1986.
39 Jochen Schmidt, 'Ein teuflischer Pakt oder Verraten, was man liebt', *Frankfurter Allgemeine Zeitung*, 29 January 1988.
40 Eberhard Falcke, 'Ein Agent wird Autobiograph', *Süddeutsche Zeitung*, 7 January 1987.
41 Frank Conroy, 'Sins of the Father', *New York Times Book Review*, 13 April 1986.
42 Morton Kamins, 'A Perfect Spy', *Los Angeles Times*, 20 April 1986.
43 Noel Annan, 'Underground Men', *New York Review of Books*, 29 May 1986.
44 *A Perfect Spy*, p. 15.
45 'The Secret Life of John le Carré' (interview with Stephen Schiff).
46 'Books of the Year', *Observer*, 30 November 1986.
47 Joseph Lelyveld, 'Le Carré's Toughest Case', *New York Times Magazine*, 16 March 1986.
48 'Spying on My Father' and 'Don't be Beastly to your Secret Service'.
49 DC to 'Auntie Ella', 3 May 1986.
50 'Spymaster holds the mirror up to his own secrets', *Sunday Times*, 1 November 1987.
51 DC to Alec Guinness, 6 March 1989, British Library Add MS 89015/2/7/5.

20: Moscow Rules

1 'The Secret Life of John le Carré' (interview with Stephen Schiff), *Vanity Fair*, 52 (June 1989).
2 Roberts, *Speak Clearly into the Chandelier*, p. 169.
3 Foreword to the Lamplighter edition of *The Russia House* (2001).
4 Alvin Sanoff, 'The Thawing of the Old Spymaster', *US News & World Report*, 19 June 1989.
5 DC to John Margetson, 24 September 1987.
6 Tom Mathews, 'In from the Cold', *Newsweek*, 5 June 1989.
7 *The Russia House*, pp. 160, 78 and 89.
8 Ibid., pp. 337 and 281.
9 Christopher Andrew and Oleg Gordievsky, *KGB: The Inside Story of its Foreign Operations from Lenin to Gorbachev* (Hodder & Stoughton, 1990), pp. 389–90.
10 'Wardrobe of Disguises', *Sunday Times*, 10 September 1967.
11 Craig R. Whitney, 'Russians Warm to le Carré', *New York Times*, 22 May 1989.
12 DC to Alec Guinness, 8 October 1987.
13 Lev Loseff, *Joseph Brodsky: A Literary Life* (Yale University Press, 2011), pp. 233–4.
14 Charles Pick to DC, 11 October 1988.
15 DC to Charles Pick, 18 October 1988.
16 Charles Pick to DC, 26 October 1988; DC to Charles Pick, 28 October 1988.
17 John St John to DC, 3 November 1988; DC to John St John, 5 November 1988.
18 Charles Pick to DC, 10 November 1988.
19 St John, *William Heinemann: A Century of Publishing*, pp. 497–8.
20 DC to Ion Trewin, 5 January 1989.
21 Tom Mathews, 'In from the Cold'.
22 Christopher Lehmann-Haupt, 'Le Carré Takes Espionage into the Age of Perestroika', *New York Times*, 18 March 1989.
23 Conor Cruise O'Brien, 'Bad News for Spies', *New York Times*, 21 May 1989.
24 T. J. Binyon, 'The Honourable, Naïve and Sentimental Publisher', *Times Literary Supplement*, 4 August 1989.
25 Salman Rushdie, 'From Russia without Love', *Observer*, 2 July 1989.
26 'A book not worth the bloodshed', *Guardian*, 15 January 1990.
27 Salman Rushdie, 'In Good Faith', *Newsweek*, 12 February 1990.
28 Salman Rushdie, *Joseph Anton* (Random House, 2012), p. 527.
29 Jimmy Carter, 'Rushdie's Book is an Insult', *New York Times*, 5 March 1989; John Berger, 'Two Books and Two Notions of the Sacred', *Guardian*, 29 February 1989; Hugo Young, 'Weighing the Price of a Paperback', *Guardian*, 11 January 1990; 'Pulp book to save lives, says Dahl', *The Times*, 17 February 1989.
30 Tim Rayment, 'Rushdie's wife says he is self-obsessed and vain', *Sunday Times*, 31 March 1991.
31 Mark Lawson, 'The Row which Came in from the Cold', *Guardian*, 22 November 1997. Lawson mistakenly wrote that Rushdie's review of *The Russia House* had been published in the *Independent on Sunday*.
32 Craig R. Whitney, 'Russians warm to Le Carré'.
33 DC to Alec Guinness, 7 December 1989, British Library Add MS 89015/2/7/5.
34 Michael Attenborough to Eric Major and others, 10 January 1990.
35 DC to Sir Antony Duff, 7 December 1992.
36 *The Secret Pilgrim*, p. 332.
37 Ibid., p. 347.
38 Alec Guinness to DC, 5 November 1982; DC to Guinness, 23 March 1983 and 7 June 1990; British Library Add MS 89015/2/7/5.
39 William Boyd, 'Oh what a lovely Cold War', *New York Times*, 6 January 1991.
40 Ian Buruma, 'After the Fall', *New York Review of Books*, 28 March 1991.

41 'The Unbearable Peace', *Granta*, 35 (Spring 1991).
42 DC to Alec Guinness, 4 May 1989; Guinness to DC, 9 May and 30 October 1989.
43 Steve Clark, 'Smiley defects from le Carré television film', *Sunday Times*, 18 November 1990.
44 Kay Gardella, 'A Smiley who Winks', *Daily News*, 13 October 1991.

21: 'Whatever are you going to write now?'

1 Terry Coleman, 'Carré on Writing', *Guardian*, 17 July 1993.
2 'Smiley's People are Alive and Well', *Guardian Review*, 16 November 1989.
3 Address to Exeter University, 13 July 1990.
4 DC to Stephen Fry, 4 March 1995.
5 DC to Nicholas Shakespeare, 14 January 1989 and 19 April 1991.
6 DC to Cyrus Ghani, 20 September 1996.
7 DC to Nicholas Shakespeare, 29 March 1995.
8 DC to Nicholas Shakespeare, 19 April 1991.
9 DC to John Margetson, 24 October 1991.
10 DC to Vivian Green, 24 October 1991.
11 *The Night Manager* (Coronet, 1994), pp. 404–5.
12 Ibid., p. 389.
13 Ibid., pp. 164 and 121.
14 Ibid., p. 161.
15 Foreword to the Lamplighter edition of *The Night Manager* (2001).
16 DC to John Calley, 30 August 1991.
17 Foreword to the Lamplighter edition of *The Night Manager* (2001).
18 'When Harry Met Willie', *Newsweek*, 26 October 1992.
19 Rupert Murdoch to DC, 1 November 1991; DC to Rupert Murdoch, 10 November 1991; Philippe Sands, 'Conversations with John le Carré', *FT Magazine*, 6 September 2013. In this interview David suggests that he demanded lunch from Murdoch, but the surviving correspondence suggests otherwise.
20 Ed Vulliamy, 'William the Conqueror', *Observer*, 13 July 2003.
21 Robert Harris to DC, 12 and 22 January 1991; DC to Harris, 20 January 1991 (misdated 1990).
22 'Grovel', *Private Eye*, 26 February 1993.
23 'Competing quests for le Carré', *Bookseller*, 22 January 1993.
24 David Sexton, 'The personal cold war of le Carré', *Evening Standard*, 16 February 1993, quoting a story that had appeared some weeks earlier in the same newspaper's 'Londoner's Diary'.
25 Tim Walker, 'Fatherland author Robert Harris has John Le Carré in his sights', *Daily Telegraph*, 24 March 2011.
26 DC to Susan Vereker, 16 February [dated 1992, but it must be 1993].
27 'Le Carré sues Graham Lord', *Bookseller*, 29 January 1993.
28 *Private Eye*, 15 January 1993.
29 'In confidence?', *Bookseller*, 23 April 1993.
30 David Sexton, 'The personal cold war of le Carré'.
31 'Delia holds battling titans at bay', *Bookseller*, 23 July 1993.
32 DC to Tim Hely Hutchinson, 10 September and 23 July 1993.
33 Tim Hely Hutchinson to JC, 29 October 1993.
34 'A Rushdie to Judgment on le Carré defection?', *Publishers Weekly*, 22 June 1998.
35 Michael Ratcliffe, 'Good Hearts, Angry Men', *Observer*, 27 June 1993.
36 Julian Symons, 'Our Man in Zurich', *New York Times*, 27 June 1993.
37 Penny Perrick, 'Battle of the Big Guns', *Sunday Times*, 27 June 1993.

38 George H. W. Bush to John le Carré, 26 September 1993 and 2 March 1995.
39 David Remnick, 'Le Carré's New War', *New York Review of Books*, 12 August 1993.
40 DC to Alec Guinness, 16 July 1996.
41 Stanley Kubrick to DC, 8 November 1992.
42 Michael Herr, *Kubrick* (Grove Atlantic, New York, 2000), pp. 8 and 19.
43 'Behind an Iron Curtain' (interview with Zoë Heller), *Independent on Sunday*, 1 August 1993.
44 'Profile: Running Away from the Circus', *Sunday Times*, 27 October 1996.
45 Martin Neild, 'John le Carré', 30 October, published in the *Sunday Times* on 17 November 1996.
46 Foreword to the Lamplighter edition of *Our Game* (2001), and 'My Friends in the New Russia: In Search of a Few Good Crooks, Cops and Former Agents', *New York Times*, 19 February 1995. Much of what follows in the next few paragraphs draws on these two sources.
47 Foreword to the Franklin Library edition of *Our Game* (1995).
48 'Demons Dance as the West Watches', *Observer*, 18 December 1994.
49 'We Distorted our own Minds' (interview with Walter Isaacson and James Kelly), *Time*, 5 July 1993.
50 DC to Sydney Pollack, 27 May 1994.
51 Piers Paul Read, *Alec Guinness: The Authorised Biography* (Simon & Schuster, 2003), pp. 553–4.
52 'Smiley's supper with Karla', *The Times*, 1 March 1977.
53 Strobe Talbott, *The Russia Hand: A Memoir of Presidential Diplomacy* (Random House, New York, 2002), pp. 138 and 244–5.

22: 'He makes us look so *good*'

1 Stephen Fry to DC, 22 February 1995, 25 January 1991, 18 August and 1 December 1993 and 3 November 1994; DC to Stephen Fry, 13 September 1993.
2 DC to Stephen Fry, 4 March 1995.
3 'Colin Melmoth' (Stephen Fry) to DC, 12 and 16 March; DC to 'Mellers', 12 March 1995.
4 Michael Ratcliffe, 'The Joe's Revenge', *Observer*, 30 April 1995; Sean O'Brien, 'Exercising Tradecraft', *Times Literary Supplement*, 12 May 1995; Louis Menand, 'Under Western Eyes', *New York Review of Books*, 20 April 1995.
5 John Updike, 'Le Carré's Game', *New Yorker*, 20 March 1995.
6 DC to 'Hils and J & J' [unidentified], 31 March 1995.
7 Diane Johnson, 'Missionary', *New York Review of Books*, 20 May 1999.
8 Marianne Macdonald, 'Collapse of Net Book Agreement "within months"', *Independent*, 26 December 1994.
9 'Shops Go Cold on le Carré', *Bookseller*, 7 April 1995.
10 DC to Tim Hely Hutchinson, 7 April 1995.
11 DC to Martin Neild, 25 May 1995.
12 Annette McCann, 'Cut-price le Carré opens book war', *Scotsman*, 1 May 1995.
13 Roger Tredre, 'Check out the value of cut-price literature', *Observer*, 7 May 1995.
14 'Cranfield plays their game', *Daily Telegraph*, 16 May 1995.
15 Foreword to the Lamplighter edition of *The Night Manager* (2001).
16 'Quel Panama!', *New York Times Magazine*, 20 October 1996.
17 *The Tailor of Panama* (Coronet edition, 1997), p. 78.
18 DC to Richard Koster, 7 August 1998.
19 Interview with Mark Lawson broadcast on BBC 4, 5 October 2008.
20 Sior Pendel to Martin Neild, 2 December; DC to Sior Pendel, 4 December 1996.
21 Norman Rush, 'Spying and Lying', *New York Times Book Review*, 20 October 1996.
22 'The Tailor of Panama', *New York Times Book Review*, 3 and 17 November 1996.

23 'John le Carré: The Art of Fiction No. 149' (interview with George Plimpton), *Paris Review*, 143 (Summer 1997).
24 Teddy Preuss, *Ha'aretz*, 14 March 1977; Preuss to DC, 23 March 1977.
25 Richard Norton-Taylor, 'Sir David Spedding' (obituary), *Guardian*; Alan Judd, afterword to the anonymous obituary 'Sir David Spedding', *Daily Telegraph*; both 14 June 2001.
26 Sarah Lyall, 'Cloak, Dagger and Abuses of a New Era', *New York Times*, 3 October 2008.
27 John le Carré, 'Dark Side of the Star', *Guardian*, 15 November, letters to the editor, 19 and 21 November 1997; Salman Rushdie, letters to the editor, 18, 20 and 22 November; Christopher Hitchens, letter to the editor, 20 November 1997.
28 DC to Tim Cornwell, 25 November 1997.
29 DC to Roland Philipps, 25 November 1997.
30 William Shawcross, 'Stinking Satanic Self-Righteousness', *Guardian*, 25 November 1997.
31 DC to William Shawcross, 29 November 1997.
32 *Rainer Heumann 26.9.1923–5.3.1996* (privately published, Zurich).
33 'A Rushdie to Judgment on le Carré defection?', *Publishers Weekly*, 22 June 1998.
34 DC to Richard Koster, 28 June 1998.

23: The Secret Centre

1 Foreword to the Lamplighter edition of *Single & Single* (2001).
2 Ibid.
3 'In Ronnie's Court'.
4 'Son of a Swindler', *Sunday Times*, 1 July 2001.
5 'Secrets and Lies' (interview with Alan Franks), *The Times*, 13 February 1999.
6 D. J. Taylor, 'Agents of Evil', *Guardian*, 20 February 1999.
7 'The Constant Muse'. Much of what follows in the next few paragraphs is drawn from this source.
8 Box 410, John le Carré Archive, Bodleian Library.
9 'The Biggest Pushers of All', *Spectator*, 16 December 2000.
10 Ann Treneman, 'Le Carré comes in from the cold', *The Times*, 9 December 2000.
11 Yvette Pierpaoli to DC, 14 April 1999.
12 DC to Roland Philipps and Tim Hely Hutchinson; Hely Hutchinson to DC, 24 May 1999.
13 Roland Philipps to Tim Hely Hutchinson, 30 June 2000.
14 'I don't miss Smiley' (interview with Robert McCrum), *Observer*, 17 December 2000.
15 'Secrets and Lies' (interview with Alan Franks).
16 Sean O'Brien, 'A Fate Far Worse than Death', *Times Literary Supplement*, 5 January 2001.
17 John Sutherland, 'This Time it's Personal', *Sunday Times*, 17 December 2000.
18 DC to Roland Philipps, 19 January 2001.
19 DC to Jamie Hodder-Williams, 30 September 2001.
20 DC to Andreas Setter and Katharina Amacker, Novartis AG, 11 April 2001.
21 Barbara Stocking to John le Carré, 29 June 2001; DC to Roland Philipps, 6 July 2001.
22 Hilary Mantel, 'The Devil's Playground', *New York Review of Books*, 19 July 2001.
23 Rand Richards Cooper, 'Company Man', *New York Times*, 7 January 2001.
24 DC to Roland Philipps, 8 April 2001.
25 DC to Roland Philipps, 19 January 2001.
26 Foreword to the new edition of *The Tailor of Panama*, April 2001.
27 'My vote? I would like to punish Blair' (interview with David Hare), *Daily Telegraph*, 17 May 2001.
28 'John le Carré: The Secret Centre' (interview with Nigel Williams), BBC 2, broadcast on Boxing Day, 2000.

29 Timothy Garton Ash, 'The Real Le Carré', *New Yorker*, 15 March 1999.
30 The journalist Matt Born was researching a story based on revelations in le Carré's forthcoming BBC 2 interview, published as 'Le Carré to reveal his secret past as a spy', *Daily Telegraph*, 9 December 2000.
31 Peter Barnard and Dominic Kennedy, 'Le Carré confesses: I spied at Oxford', *The Times*, 26 December 2000.
32 DC to Vivian Green, 25 January 2001.
33 DC to Roland Philipps, 27 and 30 June and 14 August 2001.

24: 'Mr Angry'

1 DC to Roland Philipps, 19 January 2001.
2 'In a Plot far from the Cold, le Carré Sums up the Past' (interview with Mel Gussow), *New York Times*, 19 December 2000.
3 DC to Roland Philipps, 8 April 2001.
4 DC to Irene Brendel, 28 June 2001.
5 Ibid.
6 *Absolute Friends*, p. 198.
7 DC to Andrea Daschner, 9 March 2004.
8 *Absolute Friends*, p. 199.
9 'The Spy World is "My Playpen": 40 Years of Making a Point in Novels, and Rising Activism at 72' (interview with Mel Gussow), *New York Times*, 7 January 2004.
10 Ibid.
11 DC to Miranda and John Margetson, 17 November 2002.
12 DC to Kaspar and Erica von Almen, 11 January 2003.
13 DC to Miranda and John Margetson, 17 November 2002.
14 'The United States of America Has Gone Mad', *The Times*, 15 January 2003.
15 *Absolute Friends*, pp. 255–7.
16 Box 480, John le Carré Archive, Bodleian Library.
17 DC to Anthony Barnett, 30 June 2003.
18 Lev Grossman, 'The Spy in Winter', *Time*, 12 January 2004.
19 'The betrayal of Smiley's people' (interview with James Naughtie), *The Times*, 29 November 2003.
20 Robert McCrum, 'A Master's Voice', *Observer*, 7 December 2003.
21 Stephen Amidon, 'Dispatches from an angry old man', *Sunday Times*, 14 December 2003.
22 T. J. Binyon, 'Too Furious for Fiction; Moral Outage Overwhelms le Carré's Latest offering', *Evening Standard*.
23 George Walden, 'Tinker tailor soldier propagandist', *Daily Telegraph*, 15 December 2003.
24 Daniel Johnson, 'John le Carré is Mr Angry now', *Daily Telegraph*, 2 December 2003.
25 A. N. Wilson, 'Le Carré: Old Wars on New Fronts', *Daily Mail*, 26 December 2003.
26 DC to Vivian Green, 13 December 2003.
27 Steven Poole, 'Spies and Lies', *Guardian*, 20 December 2003.
28 Geoffrey Wheatcroft, 'Smiley's (Anti-American) People', *New York Times*, 11 January 2004.
29 James M. Murphy, 'Friends of the Friends', *Times Literary Supplement*, 2 January 2004.
30 Michiko Kakutani, 'Adding Reality's Worries to a Thriller', *New York Times*, 7 January 2004.
31 DC to Anthony Barnett, 1 January 2004.
32 DC to Vivian Green, 16 February 2004.
33 DC to John Margetson, 30 July 2004.
34 Vicki Phillips to Karen Geary, 6 August 2007 (for *The Times* Book Group).
35 DC to Michela Wrong (by email), 21 November 2004.
36 'Dear Clark County Voter', *Guardian*, 13 October 2004.

37 DC to Jean Cornwell, 21 October 2004.
38 'A guide through the complexities of my plots'.
39 DC to Bruce Hunter, 16 September 2004, 7 and 14 March, 13 April and 1 May 2005; Hunter to DC, 8 March, 11 and 26 April, 9 May 2005; Hunter to JC, 1 June 2005; JC to Hunter, 11 May and 15 June 2005.
40 'My Date with the Warlords', *Seven* (*Sunday Telegraph* magazine), 10 September 2006.
41 'Getting Congo's Wealth to its People', *Boston Globe*, 22 December 2006.
42 Dan Zigmond, 'Back to moral ambiguity', *San Francisco Chronicle*, 10 September 2006.
43 Philip Caputo, 'The Interpreter', *Washington Post*, 17 September 2006.
44 Sam Allis, 'Fall from Grace: Blunt passion trumps ambiguity in a disappointing novel from John le Carré', *Boston Globe*, 17 September 2006.
45 Robert McCrum, 'Back into the Heart of Darkness', *Observer*, 24 September 2006.
46 John Dugdale, 'Carnage in Congo', *Sunday Times*, 17 September 2006.
47 Christopher Hope, 'Candide in Africa', *Guardian*, 23 September 2006.
48 William Finnegan, 'Double-Cross in the Congo', *New York Review of Books*, 12 April 2007.
49 'Scenes from a Secret Life', dated 11 December 2006.

25: Beating the System

1 DC to Nicholas Shakespeare, 14 November 2006.
2 'Who Watches the Watchmen?'. Much of what follows is taken from this source.
3 Elizabeth Renzetti, 'Slinkers, Jailers, Soldiers, Lies', *Globe and Mail* (Toronto), 4 October 2008.
4 'Who Watches the Watchmen?'.
5 DC to Anthony Barnett (by email), 23 March 2008.
6 Philippe Sands, 'Conversations with John le Carré', *FT Magazine*, 6 September 2013.
7 DC to Roland Philipps, 13 December 2007.
8 DC and JC to Bruce Hunter, 5 September 2007.
9 DC to Bruce Hunter, 31 March 2008.
10 Rod Liddle, 'John le Carré has a surprising new story to tell', *Sunday Times News Review*, 14 September 2008.
11 Maurice Chittenden, 'Tinker, tailor, soldier, defector – John le Carré: I nearly left the West', *Sunday Times*, 14 September 2008.
12 John le Carré, *Times Online*, 20 September 2008.
13 Alan Furst, 'Out in the Cold', *New York Times*, 11 October 2008.
14 Charles Cumming, 'A Most Wanted Man', *Daily Telegraph*, 20 September 2008.
15 Hari Kunzru, 'Trapdoor to the secret world', *Guardian*, 27 September 2008.
16 Andrew O'Hagan, 'The Weather Makers', *New York Review of Books*, 28 May 2009.
17 Michiko Kakutani, 'Terrorists and Spies, Weaving their Webs', *New York Times*, 6 October 2008.
18 DC to August Hanning, 24 December 2008.
19 DC to Roland Philipps, 17 April and 16 October 2009; DC to Jamie Hodder-Williams, 16 October 2009.
20 DC to John Margetson, 3 August 2010.
21 DC to Roland Philipps, 16 June 2009.
22 *Bookseller*, 26 October 2009.
23 DC to Roland Philipps, 7 February 2010.
24 James Naughtie, 'Our Kind of Traitor', *Sunday Telegraph*, 12 September 2010.
25 [Unsigned], 'Our Kind of Traitor', *Scotsman*, 10 September 2010.
26 Christopher Tayler, 'Our Kind of Traitor', *Guardian*, 10 September 2010.
27 Michiko Kakutani, 'Innocents Caught in a Web of Intrigue', *New York Times*, 11 October 2010.

28 Lev Grossman, 'The Spy in Winter', *Time*, 12 January 2004.
29 DC to John Margetson, 3 August; Margetson to DC (by email), 6 August 2010.
30 Peter Morgan, interview with Christina Radish, collider.com, 14 October 2010; Francesca Martin, 'Tinker, Tailor, Soldier, Film Star', *Guardian*, 4 June 2008.
31 Anthony Lane, 'I Spy: John le Carré and the rise of George Smiley', *New Yorker*, 12 December 2011.
32 Alison Flood, 'Salman Rushdie and John le Carré end fatwa face-off', *Guardian*, 12 November 2012.
33 Salman Rushdie, *Joseph Anton* (Jonathan Cape, 2012), pp. 530–1.
34 Jack Malvern, 'My feud with Salman Rushdie is all in the past, says John le Carré', *The Times*, 12 November 2012.
35 'Espionage is an accident' (interview with Olga Craig), *Seven* (*Sunday Telegraph* magazine), 29 August 2010.
36 'I do give a damn' (interview with Stuart Jeffries), *Guardian*, 6 October 2005.
37 Jon Stock, 'A Delicate Truth', *Daily Telegraph*, 3 May 2013.
38 Robert McCrum, 'A Delicate Truth', *Observer*, 20 April 2013.
39 Günther Grosser, 'Als hätte er von Snowden gewusst', *Berliner Zeitung*, 17 November 2013.
40 Robert Gore-Langton, 'The novel that made spies angry', *Sunday Express*, 8 August 2013.
41 Jonathan Yardley, 'The book that changed spy fiction', *Washington Post*, 6 September 2013.
42 William Boyd, 'Rereading: The Spy who Came in from the Cold', *Guardian*, 24 July 2010.
43 Adam Dawtrey, 'Le Carré's Sons Spy Opportunity', *Variety*, 24 September 2011.
44 DC to August Hanning, 18 April 2011.
45 Interview with Andrej Sokolow from 'Monsters and Critics' website, 18 October 2011.

Select Bibliography

1. Manuscript Sources

David Cornwell's private archive is currently kept at his home in Cornwall. Unless otherwise stated, all letters and documents cited derive from this source, or have been supplied privately by other owners. David's son Timothy has an archive of material relating to his mother. The majority of John le Carré's surviving manuscripts are in the Bodleian Library, Oxford (see below).

BBC Written Archives Centre, Caversham

British Film Institute

British Library

Papers and Correspondence of Al Alvarez

Papers and Correspondence of Sir Alec Guinness

Eton College Archives

Gollancz Archive

Harry Ransom Center, Austin, Texas

Papers and Correspondence of C. P. Snow

Papers and Correspondence of Tom Stoppard

Papers and Manuscripts of John le Carré relating to *The Little Drummer Girl*

Hodder & Stoughton Archive

Leeds University, Brotherton Library

Papers and Correspondence of Lord Boyle

National Archives, Kew

Official Receiver's file on R. T. A. Cornwell

National Library of Scotland

Papers and Correspondence of James Kennaway

Oxford University

Bodleian Library

John le Carré Archive

Lincoln College Archive

Papers and Correspondence of Vivian Green

Papers and Correspondence of Keith Murray

Papers and Correspondence of Walter Oakeshott

Poole Local History Centre

Random House Archive

Heinemann Papers

University of Salford Library

Papers and Correspondence of Arthur Hopcraft

Sherborne School Archives

A. P. Watt Archive

2. Books

Andrew, Christopher, *The Defence of the Realm: The Authorized History of MI5* (Allen Lane, 2009)
Bower, Tom, *The Perfect English Spy: Sir Dick White and the Secret War 1935–90* (Heinemann, 1995)
Bruccoli, Matthew J. and Judith S. Baughman (eds), *Conversations with John le Carré* (University Press of Mississippi, 2004)
le Carré, John, *Call for the Dead* (Gollancz, 1961)
— *A Murder of Quality* (Gollancz, 1962)
— *The Spy who Came in from the Cold* (Gollancz, 1963)
— *The Looking-Glass War* (Heinemann, 1965)
— *A Small Town in Germany* (Heinemann, 1968)
— *The Naïve and Sentimental Lover* (Hodder & Stoughton, 1971)
— *Tinker, Tailor, Soldier, Spy* (Hodder & Stoughton, 1974)
— *The Honourable Schoolboy* (Hodder & Stoughton, 1977)
— *Smiley's People* (Hodder & Stoughton, 1980)
— *The Little Drummer Girl* (Hodder & Stoughton, 1983)
— *A Perfect Spy* (Hodder & Stoughton, 1986)
— *The Russia House* (Hodder & Stoughton, 1989)
— *The Secret Pilgrim* (Hodder & Stoughton, 1991)
— *The Night Manager* (Hodder & Stoughton, 1993)
— *Our Game* (Hodder & Stoughton, 1995)
— *The Tailor of Panama* (Hodder & Stoughton, 1996)
— *Single & Single* (Hodder & Stoughton, 1999)
— *The Constant Gardener* (Hodder & Stoughton, 2001)
— *Absolute Friends* (Hodder & Stoughton, 2004)
— *The Mission Song* (Hodder & Stoughton, 2006)
— *A Most Wanted Man* (Hodder & Stoughton, 2008)
— *Our Kind of Traitor* (Viking Penguin, 2010)
— *A Delicate Truth* (Viking Penguin, 2013)
le Carré, John et al., 'The Unbearable Peace', *Granta* 35 (1991)— 'Sarratt and the Draper of Watford', in *Sarratt and the Draper of Watford, and other unlikely stories about Sarratt* (privately published, 1999)
Clark, Colin, *Younger Brother, Younger Son: A Memoir* (HarperCollins, 1997)
Davenport-Hines, Richard, *An English Affair: Sex, Class and Power in the Age of Profumo* (HarperCollins, 2013)
Douglas Home, William, *Half-Term Report: An Autobiography* (Longman, 1954)
Gourlay, A. B., *A History of Sherborne School* (privately published, 1971)

Gourlay, A. B. and D. F. Gibbs, *Chief: A Biography of Alexander Ross Wallace, 1891–1982* (privately published, 1983).
Green, Vivian H. H., *The Commonwealth of Lincoln College 1427–1977* (Oxford University Press, 1979)
Greenfield, George, *A Smattering of Monsters: A Kind of Memoir* (Little, Brown, 1995)
Greenway, H. D. S., *Foreign Correspondent: A Memoir* (Simon & Schuster, 2014)
Guinness, Alec, *My Name Escapes Me: The Diary of a Retiring Actor* (Hamish Hamilton, 1996)
Rainer Heumann 26.9.1923–5.3.1996 (privately published, Zurich)
Jago, Michael, *The Man Who Was George Smiley: The Life of John Bingham* (Biteback, 2013)
Jeffery, Keith, *MI6: The History of the Secret Intelligence Service 1909–1949* (Bloomsbury, 2010)
Kennaway, James and Susan, *The Kennaway Papers* (Jonathan Cape, 1981)
Knightley, Phillip, *Philby: The Life and Views of the K.G.B. Masterspy* (André Deutsch, 1988)
Macintyre, Ben, *A Spy among Friends: Kim Philby and the Great Betrayal* (Bloomsbury, 2014)
Marten, Michael (ed.), *Tim Marten – Memories* (privately published, 2009)
Martin, Christopher (ed.), *Millfield: A School for All Seasons* (privately published, 2007)
Mount, Ferdinand, *Cold Cream: My Early Life and Other Mistakes* (Bloomsbury, 2008)
Oxford Dictionary of National Biography
Powell-Williams, Clive, *With All Thy Might: The History of St Martin's School, 1922 to 1992* (privately published, 1992)
Read, Piers Paul, *Alec Guinness: The Authorised Biography* (Simon & Schuster, 2003)
Rimington, Stella, *Open Secret: The Autobiography of the Former Director-General of MI5* (Hutchinson, 2001)
Roberts, John C. Q., *Speak Clearly into the Chandelier: Cultural Politics between Britain and Russia, 1973–2000* (Curzon, 2000)
Royle, Trevor, *James and Jim: A Biography of James Kennaway* (Mainstream, 1983)
— *The Best Years of Their Lives: The National Service Experience, 1945–63* (Michael Joseph, 1986)
Rushdie, Salman, *Joseph Anton: A Memoir* (Random House, 2012)
St John, John, *William Heinemann: A Century of Publishing, 1890–1990* (Heinemann, 1990)
Seaton, Jean, *Pinkoes and Traitors: The BBC and the Nation, 1974–1987* (Profile, 2015)
Sherry, Norman, *The Life of Graham Greene*, vol. 3: *1955–1991* (Jonathan Cape, 2004)
Talbott, Strobe, *The Russia Hand: A Memoir of Presidential Diplomacy* (Random House, New York, 2002)
Thorpe, D. R., *Supermac: The Life of Harold Macmillan* (Chatto & Windus, 2010)
Waugh, Alec, *The Loom of Youth* (Methuen, 1917)
Wodehouse, John, 4th Earl of Kimberley, *The Whim of the Wheel: The Memoirs of the Earl of Kimberley* (privately published, 2001)
Wright, Peter, *Spycatcher: The Candid Autobiography of a Senior Intelligence Officer* (Viking Penguin, 1987)

3. Articles by John le Carré

'Vienna: In search of a lost spy story', *Weekend Telegraph*, 24 June 1966
'Well Played, Wodehouse', *Sunday Times*, 10 October 1971
'In England Now', *New York Times Magazine*, 23 October 1977
'Spying on my Father', *Sunday Times Review*, 16 March 1986
'Don't be Beastly to your Secret Service', *Sunday Times Review*, 23 March 1986
'The Clandestine Muse', originally written as the James Tait Black Memorial Prize Lecture in 1978, and published privately as the G. Harry Pouder Memorial Lecture, delivered at Johns Hopkins University on 20 May 1986
'Smiley's People are Alive and Well', *Guardian Review*, 16 November 1989
'Now You See It, Now You Don't', *The Times Magazine*, 7 August 1993
'Quel Panama!', *New York Times Magazine*, 20 October 1996

'At the Edge of the Real World', *Sunday Telegraph Review*, 14 November 1999
'The Constant Muse', *New Yorker*, 25 December 2000
'A Good Deed in a Naughty World', Victim Support, 2000
'Son of a Swindler', *Sunday Times*, 1 July 2001
'In Ronnie's Court', *New Yorker*, 18 and 25 February 2002
'The United States of America Has Gone Mad', *The Times*, 15 January 2003
'Dear Clark County Voter', *Guardian*, 13 October 2004
'A guide through the complexities of my plots', *Guardian*, 5 March 2005, originally 'Vivian H. H. Green', a eulogy given at his memorial service in Oxford in 2005
'My Date with the Warlords', *Seven* (*Sunday Telegraph* magazine), 10 September 2006
'The Madness of Spies', *New Yorker*, 29 September 2008
'Who Watches the Watchmen?' *Waterstone's Books Quarterly*, Issue 30, 2008
'The Spy Who Liked Me: On the set with Richard Burton and Martin Ritt', *New Yorker*, 15 April 2013

Index